Dedication

To Ann who shared fifty years with me.

Catholic Sioux of St. Francis Industrial School
Left to Right, Top Row: Isaac Iron Shell, John White Horse, Cecil Two Teeth
Lower Row: Arthur Jackson, Robert Little Hawk and Thomas Garsia

Photo Credit: Marquette University Archives

South Dakota Warriors in Khaki

Native American Doughboys from South Dakota

by

Michael J. and Ann Knudson

Plus

"More Than Names"

by

JoLavae Gunville

A special section on WWI warriors from the Cheyenne River Lakota

South Dakota Warriors in Khaki

Copyright © 2025 Michael J. Knudson

ISBN: 978-1-61170-329-0

All rights reserved. No part of this publication may be reproduced, stored in a retrieval system or transmitted in any form or by any means, electronic, mechanical, photocopies, recording or otherwise, without the prior written consent of the author.

Although the authors have made every to ensure the accuracy and completeness of information contained in this book, we assume no responsibility for errors, inaccuracies, omissions, or any inconsistency herein. Any slights of people, places or organizations are unintentional.

Corrections or additions are welcome, especially photos of veterans, in or out of uniform. All photos used will receive proper credit. Contact the authors at mikeannknudson@outlook.com.

Front cover, photo of Private Paul Widow, courtesy of Mathers Museum of World Cultures, Bloomington, IN. We wish to thank Ed Widow for his approval of our use of his father's photo.

Published by:

Robertson Publishing™
www.RobertsonPublishing.com

Printed in the USA and UK on acid-free paper.

Table of Contents

Introduction 1

Roster 3

Appendix A: 1930 Census listing some "WW" veterans 262

Appendis B: *Word Carrier* article about Arther Frazier......................263

Appendix C: Letter to Mrs. Helen Little 264

Appendix D: **More Than Names**, By JoLavae Gunville 265

Sources and Acknowledgements 272

South Dakota Soldiers

INTRODUCTION

Since the U.S. Army began making forays into the Northern Plains, the native residents of South Dakota have volunteered to serve in the military. In the 1870s, many men enlisted to serve as Scouts and Interpreters. Again, in the 1890s, more men enlisted to serve with the Army. In 1891, the Army began recruiting Lakota men to serve in the both infantry and cavalry regiments. Troop L, 3rd Cavalry at Fort Meade, SD, was composed of 55 Native soldiers. Many of them were recruited from the Cheyenne River Reservation. Chauncey Eagle Horn first enlisted as a young man in 1892 and served with the 16th Infantry. In a society that honors its warriors, young men were interested in the challenge of combat and military service, even though they were not citizens. War was a means of training men to defend and protect their families, their homeland. Many families have members of each generation who have served. The men did not volunteer only during wartime. By the time the First World War began in Europe, another generation of young men was reaching military age. In the summer of 1916, the 4th South Dakota Infantry began accepting recruits. Among these early volunteers were Joseph Crazy Thunder from Manderson on the Pine Ridge Reservation and Job High Elk from Thunder Butte on the Cheyenne River Reservation. They took part in the campaign against Poncho Villa along the Mexican Border. Both these men served more than three years in the Army.

Meanwhile, the war was heating up in Europe. In February of 1917, President Wilson cut off diplomatic service with the German government. That spring, even before the U.S. officially declared war on Germany, young men attending boarding schools in South Dakota began to enlist in the South Dakota National Guard. Students in Rapid City skipped school to join Company I, 4th SD Infantry. At the same time, many students at the Riggs Institute in Flandreau enlisted in Troop D, 1st SD Cavalry. Francis Janis was one of these students. He remembered that a flatbed truck came onto the school grounds and the driver yelled out to the students, "Do you want to fight the Kaiser?" Francis was one of close to 60 students and staff who joined the military. These students were from Wisconsin, Minnesota, North and South Dakota, Nebraska, and Montana. After the war, the school raised a bronze monument listing the names of these men.

On the nine reservations in South Dakota, many men enlisted while others were drafted, though they were not yet citizens. A few women also enlisted to serve as nurses. Joining the native men and women were many of their neighbors, men of European descent who had made their homes in Indian Country. These men married into local families and became part of the community. On the Standing Rock Reservation, James Makes Trouble was one of these young soldiers. Shortly before he was inducted into the Army, his sister, Lulu, married a neighbor, Mike Frank. Mike was born in Transylvania in Central Europe and brought to Corson County as a child by his parents. Mike also joined the Army and was sent to Camp Funston, KS. After his discharge, James Makes Trouble married Lillie Clown, whose brother, Moses, was killed in action on Nov. 1, 1918. Another of James' sisters, Emma, married Martin Frank, the brother of Mike. The sons of Mike and Lulu also served in the military.

After the Armistice was signed on November 11, 1918, men continued to enlist to serve in the Army and Navy. Among these was James Clown, a brother to Moses, who enlisted in 1920. Some of these men were assigned as replacements to troops still on occupational duty in Europe. Others served with some Cavalry regiments stationed near the Mexican border. Once the fighting was over, the U.S, Military officials and some private organizations were interested in how the Native servicemen had performed. Officers and NCOs were asked to identify and evaluate the Native men who served under them. Almost all the Native veterans were rated as good soldiers by their white officers. Men on the battlefield were generally color blind once the heat of battle revealed who they could trust their lives with. Joseph K. Dixon, who had traveled around Indian Country as a photographer before the war, was also interested in recording how the war affected the veterans. Working with Rodman Wanamaker, Dixon developed his own questionnaire that he sent to men on the reservations to complete. When the 1930 U.S. Census was collected, the enumerator asked the men if they had served in the military, and if so, what war. Many of the native veterans were first identified by this census information. Many of the men who had enlisted in peacetime in the 1920's were also shown as World War (WW) veterans.

After the war, most of the veterans who returned to their reservations fell on hard times. Some men had lost title to their land. Other men had sold their livestock before entering the training camps. In the questionnaires sent out by Joseph Dixon, many men indicated that they had lost livestock and crops while they were in France. For example, Casper LeCompte wrote that he'd "lost 20% of stock. My land went to ruin hay crop + fences. No rental on land." Though some of them were now citizens, conditions had not improved and jobs were few. Many of the returned soldiers had severe health problems due to war injury and exposure to gas in France. Health care clinics were non-existent. When the Depression and the drought of the 1930s hit South Dakota, the people on most of the reservations suffered severely. In the mid-1930s, the state created the South Dakota Emergency Relief Administration (SDERA). South Dakota State employees, accompanied by interpreters, visited families on the reservations. People described what type of work they were doing, as well as their housing situation. Many of the families lived in tents near the job site while working on emergency conservation projects such as dams and roads. Many of the men mentioned their time in the military, both during the war and in peacetime.

ROSTER

Ackerman, Wesley G. Wesley was an enrolled member at Fort Peck, MT. He was born near Poplar, MT, on April 8, 1900. In the 1911 Census Roll for Fort Peck, Wesley and his brother, Charles, are listed as the adopted sons of Spotted Bull. Shortly after this, Wesley was sent to the boarding school at Flandreau, SD. In April 1917, he enlisted in Troop D, 1st South Dakota Cavalry (ASN 1427428). Around this time, his brother, Charles, was working for Jacob Jordan in Fort Yates. Pvt. Ackerman traveled in September of 1917 to Camp Cody in Deming, NM, with the rest of his South Dakota National Guard unit. He was assigned to Co. 14, Camp Cody June Automatic Draft Replacement, which sailed from the U.S. aboard the S.S. *Tereisias* on June 28, 1918. After arriving in France, he was transferred to Battery F, 19th Field Artillery (5th Division). The 19th F.A. Regiment served in the Sectors at St. Die, Villers-en-Haye, St. Mihiel, Limey, and Puvenelle. After the Armistice, his commanding officer reported that he "made good soldier." The 5th Division formed part of the Army of Occupation. The 19th FA was billeted for a short time in Roeser, Luxembourg. Pvt. Ackerman sailed with his unit from Brest, France, aboard the *America* on July 13, 1919, arriving in Hoboken on July 22. His brother also served in France, with the 9th Infantry Regiment, 2nd Division. Wesley's name was engraved on a monument honoring soldiers at the Flandreau School around 1920.

After the war, Wesley married Katie Little Thunder and lived in Todd County for a number of years. Around 1940 they moved back to Montana. His second wife was Bertha. In the 1950's, he moved to Browning, MT. Wesley entered the spirit world on Sept. 15, 1966, at the PHS hospital in Harlem, MT. Military graveside rites were accorded him by the local American Legion Post in the Browning Cemetery where he is buried.[1]

Aloysius Adams
Oglala Lakota College

Adams, Aloysius. Navy, photo in Oglala Lakota College library, Kyle, SD. Aloysius was born on Dec. 6, 1905, on the Pine Ridge Reservation. In the 1910 U.S. Census, he was living with his step father, Edward White Crow, and his mother, Julia, on the Pine Ridge Reservation. He likely enlisted in the Navy in the 1920s, as he would not have been old enough to serve during the World War. He married Bernice Neiss in 1929. In the 1930 U.S. Census, he is listed as being a military veteran, and working as a carpenter. In the 1940 U.S. Census, he was working as a carpenter at the Holy Rosary Mission School. His children, Aloysius and Laurine were living with him, though he was divorced. VA records show that he served in World War II from Aug. 6, 1942 to Sept. 1, 1945, as well as during the Korean Conflict from Aug. 18, 1952, to Feb. 15, 1954. He likely was in the Seabees, as his final Navy rating was BULC, which is "builder (light construction), Chief Petty Officer. Aloysius entered the spirit world in Boston on Feb. 1, 1985. He is buried in the Black Hills National Cemetery, Section F, Site 1606.

Adams, John. John was born on March 10, 1900, in Ponsford, MN, on the White Earth Reservation. His mother was Sophia Hanks. In 1912, John came to the Flandreau boarding school. While a student he went down to Sioux Falls to enlist in the Army, on May 1, 1918. He was assigned to Battery B, 39th Artillery, Coast Artillery Corps

(ASN 476386). Pvt. Adams was discharged at Camp Dodge, IA, on Dec. 19, 1918. After the war, his name was engraved on a plaque erected at the Flandreau boarding school to honor the veterans.

John moved back to his home in the Pine Point Community, where he married Mary Gravelle. In the 1940 U.S. Census, John and Mary were living with their children, Sullivan, Mary Jane and Darlene. John was working as a laborer on road construction. He entered the spirit world in St. Mary's Hospital in Detroit Lakes on Sept. 18, 1962. The Jess-Omundson VFW Post conducted military rites and burial was in Breck Episcopal Cemetery, Ponsford, MN.[2]

Afraid of Bear, Paul. Paul Moses Afraid of Bear was born in the month of May in the mid-1890s near Okreek on the Rosebud Reservation. In the 1900 U.S. Census, he is listed with his parents, Paul and Rose (Yellow Hawk) as well as a brother, Isaac. When he registered for the draft, his date of birth was May 28, 1896. Paul entered the Army on June 24, 1918, and served in the 2nd Development Battalion, 6th Co., 5th Regiment of the 164th Depot Brigade at Camp Funston, Kansas (ASN 3315833). He received an honorable discharge as a Private on Nov. 25, 1918. He married Cora Milk. In the 1920 U.S. Census, they had a daughter, Lida. He later married Agnes LaPointe. In 1935, the family was interviewed by a worker with the SDERA program. They were living in a tent near his sister's house in Okreek. Moses was a member of the American Legion. In the 1940 U.S. Census, Moses and Agnes are listed with their son, Amos, as well as their step children, Harry, Evelyn, Stella and Les LaPointe. Paul Moses entered the spirit world on Feb. 28, 1951. He is buried in St Peter's Catholic Cemetery at Okreek.[3]

Agard, James. James was born near Bullhead in November 1893. His parents were Louis Catka [Left] and Monica Agard. James entered the U.S. Army at Camp Funston on June 24, 1918. He served as a Private in the 46th Company, 164th Depot Brigade (ASN 3309370). He received an honorable discharge on Dec. 4, 1918. After the war, he wrote that his "time was spent at Camp Furnston [sic] till was discharged. Done orderly work most of my time." In the 1930 U.S. Census, he was living near Bullhead with his wife, Isabel Shoe String, and their children, Jennie, Willie, Henry, Dixie, Aljoe and Seraphina. Isabel's older brother, James, also served in the Army. James entered the spirit world on May 26, 1931 and is buried in the Catholic Cemetery in Bullhead. James' son, Al Joseph, served in the Army in the Korean Conflict. He also served as tribal chairman.[4]

Ahrens, Philip C. Philip was born on Dec. 1, 1895, at Geddes. His father, Carl, was born in Germany. His mother, Maggie Vollin, was an enrolled Yanktonai Dakota. In the 1900 Census Roll, Maggie is listed with her three oldest children, Philip, Mabel and Helen. When Philip registered for the draft on June 5, 1917, he was farming near Geddes. He joined the Army on Aug. 29, 1918. He was discharged as a Private 1st Class on Jan. 31, 1919. After returning home, he married Albia Vraspir. In 1924, he married Fae Myers. They farmed near Armour. In the 1934 Yanktonai Census Roll, Philip is listed with his daughter, Ruby. Philip entered the spirit world on Nov. 3, 1982, and is buried in Pleasant Ridge Cemetery, Armour.

Alexis, Amos. Amos was born in Peever, SD, on the Sisseton-Wahpeton Reservation on April 25, 1894. In the 1911 Census Roll, Amos was listed with his mother, Mary, and a sister. He was living in Peever when he registered for the draft on June 21, 1917. On Sept. 19, 1917, he left Sisseton with a group of recruits headed to Camp Funston, KS. After the war, he returned home. In 1925, he married Della Greeley. In the 1930 U.S. Census, he was living with his mother and his sister, Lucy, who was married to Silas Greeley. Amos suffered from paralysis and malnutrition when he entered the spirit world on Nov. 2, 1933.

All Around, Joseph B. Joseph was born on the Crow Creek Reservation around Dec. 10, 1879. He married Lucy Pretty Day and had a son, Robert. Joseph enlisted in the Army on Aug. 14, 1918, and served in Co. I, 2nd Infantry, 19th Division (ASN 3776554). The 19th Division trained at Camp Dodge but did not go overseas. Pvt. All Around was discharged on Feb. 27, 1919. His son also served in the 19th Division. In the 1930 U.S. Census, Joseph was living with his family at the Immaculate Conception Mission in Hyde County. Joseph suffered from tuberculosis and entered the spirit world in Fort Thompson on June 22, 1941. He is buried in St. Joseph's Catholic Cemetery in Fort Thompson.

All Around, Robert H. Robert was born on the Crow Creek Reservation on July 31, 1899. His parents were Joseph and Lucy (Pretty Day). Robert enlisted in the Army. While serving with the 19th Division, he contracted Tuberculosis. In the 1919 Census Roll, he is also listed as Robert Shoots Wood. He entered the spirit world at the Crow Creek Agency on May 4, 1921, and is buried in St. Joseph's Cemetery, Fort Thompson, SD.[5]

Amiotte, Albert. Albert was born on the Pine Ridge Reservation on March 13, 1893, the son of Steve and Zoe (Leboeuf). Albert enlisted in the US Marine Corps on April 19, 1917. He was first stationed at the Marine Barracks at Mare Island, CA. He served in the 18th Company, 2nd Battalion, 5th Marine Regiment (SN 117071). In the fighting at Belleau Wood on June 11, 1918, he received gunshot wounds to both legs. He spent time in a number of hospitals, including the Naval Hospital at Brooklyn, NY. He was discharged on Feb. 27, 1919. On Nov. 18, 1924, Albert married Mary Matilda Metz in Denver. They had two children, Loraine and Delbert, who served with the Air Force. In the 1937 Census Roll, Albert was living on the Pine Ridge Reservation. In 1948, the family was living in San Francisco. In the 1950s, they were living in Pueblo, CO. He entered the spirit world on Nov. 27, 1959, and is buried in Imperial Memorial Gardens in Pueblo, CO.

Andersen, Jacob P. Jacob was born on March 17, 1891, in Holt County, NE, to Christ Andersen and Theresa Herman. He was enrolled on the Rosebud Reservation. His mother entered the spirit world in 1910. He enlisted in the Marine Corps on July 25, 1911, serving till July 24, 1915. He re-enlisted on April 18, 1917. He was discharged as a Corporal on March 18, 1919. In the 1920 U.S. Census, he was living on his dad's farm in Bristow Township, NE. In the 1930 U.S. Census, he was working as a truck mechanic in Portland, OR. He entered the spirit world in Oakland, CA, on April 26, 1939. He is buried in Bristow, NE.

Ankle, Henry. Henry was born in North Dakota on the Standing Rock Reservation on April 5, 1893. His parents belonged to the Flying By band of Hunkpapa. His father, Daniel, had enlisted in the Army and served with the 22nd Infantry at Fort Yates. Sgt. Daniel Ankle passed away at Fort Yates on June 3, 1894. After Fort Yates was closed as a military base, Daniel's grave was moved to Keokuk National Cemetery in Keokuk, IA. After Daniel died, Henry's mother took the family to the Flying By Band near the Grand River. Later she worked as a housekeeper for a priest at the Cheyenne Agency. In the Standing Rock Census Roll for 1894, Henry is listed with his mother, Marcella, a brother, George, and an uncle, Matthew, who also served in WWI. In the 1900 U.S. Census, Henry lived with an uncle in Morton County. In the 1910 U.S. Census, he is listed as a student at the Bismarck boarding school. Before the war, he moved to Keldon, SD.

He was inducted in South Dakota and sent to Camp Funston (Fort Riley, KS) on April 26, 1918. He served with Co. H, 355th Infantry Regiment (89th Division) (ASN 2845212). After the fighting ended, his commanding officer, Captain Oscar B. Abel, was interviewed. Capt. Abel stated that Corporal

Ankle "proved himself very good at night work and on maps and buzzers." Ankle told Joseph Dixon that he was in no man's land eleven times, volunteering each time. Corporal Ankle added that "in the Battle of Argonne our supply wagons couldn't reach us for several days—and some of the boys got weak and faint. I showed the boys how they could keep their strength up by eating elm tree buds and bark. While marching into the forest I observed that some of the trees were slippery elm trees, which acted as food to all those that eat it." On Dec. 17, 1918, Ankle sent a letter home that was published in the *Sioux County Pioneer*. He wrote: "We are here in a town called Cordel, having been here for a week. We don't know how much longer we will be here. I hope our next move will be towards the U.S., as I think I have seen as much of this country as I want to, although it is a beautiful country in its summer scenery, but now the leaves have fallen and it is rainy and cold but not as cold as South Dakota."

However, Corporal Ankle's regiment became part of the Occupational Army in Germany. The 355th was quartered in the Saarburg District and remained there for the rest of the winter and most of the spring months. In early May of 1919, the regiment began its move towards the French sea coast, arriving on May 12. After being fed some chow, the soldiers were asked to exchange their French money for American greenbacks. One of the soldiers noted that "this money made the boys homesick as it was such a contrast to the foreign money which resembled cigarette coupons rather than money." The 355th Infantry Regiment sailed from Brest, France, on May 15, 1919, aboard the *Leviathan*. Corporal Ankle received his honorable discharge on May 31, 1919.

After the war, Henry married Ethel Many Deeds. Ethel's brother, Edmund, had served with a Balloon Company in the Air Service. Henry and Ethel raised their family in Little Eagle, SD. In 1935, Henry was serving as a policeman in Little Eagle. In the Standing Rock Census Roll for 1939, Henry and Ethel were listed with their children, Jesse, Elaine, Thomas and Amelia. Henry died in a vehicle accident near Little Eagle in rural Corson County on July 27, 1954. He was riding with several friends who were hurrying to avoid a severe storm coming across the prairie. His wife, two sons, Ted and Jesse, as well as two daughters survived Henry. His was buried in Messiah Congregational Cemetery in Little Eagle. Henry's family received a Code Talker's medal at a ceremony in Wakpala on March 17, 2017.[6]

Ankle, Matthew. Matthew's name is engraved on a WWI Memorial in Little Eagle, SD. He was also known as Matthew Ishkahula [Ankle]. He was born in Dakota Territory in the mid-1870s. Military records list his place of birth as Miles City, MT. His parents were reported to have been killed in a battle at Lame Deer, MT. At the age of 12, he became a friend and protégé of James McLaughlin, who enrolled him at the boarding school in Hampton, VA. Matthew was a student there from August 1890 to 1898, when he received a carpentry certificate. One of Matthew's teachers was Annie Beecher Scoville, who corresponded extensively with him. Matthew traveled often on the East Coast and mailed his lessons to Miss Scoville for correction. In one letter he mentions ice skating in Central Park. His Hampton uniform intrigued some of the other ice skaters. On July 16, 1896, he sent her a letter from Fort Yates describing his efforts to interview some of the men who had fought at Little Big Horn. Around this time, Miss Scoville visited the Standing Rock Reservation and received an assignment as a special agent of the Commissioner of Indian Affairs. In the 1900 U.S. Census, Matthew was working as a carpenter in Stamford, CT. After leaving Hampton in 1898, he studied for a while at Union Academy in Meridien, NH. In 1901, he returned to Hampton Institute for their post-graduate business course. He worked as a clerk and general laborer until WWI began. In the 1898 Census Roll taken at Standing Rock, Matthew is listed with his nephew, Henry. In his later years, Matthew did not visit Standing Rock very often.

In the 1905 New York State Census, Matthew Ishkahula is listed as a carpenter in New York City. In the 1915 Census, he was still working as a carpenter. While living in New York City, Matthew Ishkahula enlisted in the 19th Company, 9th Coast Defense Command on May 2, 1917. When he was reassigned to the U.S. Army, he served in Battery B, 57th Artillery, Coast Artillery Corps (CAC) (ASN 626240). He was promoted to Private 1st Class. The 57th Artillery sailed aboard the USS *Rijndam* out of New York harbor on May 10, 1918. They arrived in France on May 25, 1918, and were stationed in St. Denis de Piles, near Bordeaux for training. Each battery received four 155 mm Grande Porte Filloux guns and two machine guns for defense against planes. In September of 1918, they moved to the town of Void in the St. Mihiel region. The 57th Artillery played an active role in the Meuse-Argonne Offensive. Records indicate that the First Battalion, to which Battery B belonged, fired 8000 rounds of 155 mm shells against the German Army. Following the Armistice, the 57th moved back to a staging area near Brest, France, to await the availability of home ward bound shipping. The 57th sailed from Brest, France, on Jan. 2, 1919, aboard the USS *Huntington*.

When Matthew returned to the U.S., he was still suffering from the effects of being exposed to gas in France. He had spent some time in French hospitals as well as hospitals in the U.S. After leaving the hospital, he enrolled in the Law School of the National University in Washington, D.C. While a student, Matthew did some modeling and also some acting in movies. He was associated with William S. Hart, who was a silent film actor. Matthew practiced law in Washington, D.C. He entered the spirit world in his home in Washington, D.C., on March 2, 1930, and is buried in Arlington Cemetery, Section 18 Site 4889. His headstone reads "Matthew Iskahula."[7]

Apple, Frank – listed on WWI veterans memorial plaque at Oglala Lakota College, Kyle, SD. Frank was born on the Pine Ridge Reservation on July 5, 1895. In the 1898 Census Roll for Pine Ridge, he is listed with his father, Taspan [Apple], and his mother, Caje Wancia [This person has no name], as well as his other brothers and sisters. When Frank registered for the draft on June 5, 1917, he was living in Martin with his wife, Theresa Quigley, and oldest son, Stephen. He joined the Army on May 25, 1918. He likely was sent to Camp Lewis, WA, as he served with Battery A, 347th Field Artillery (FA), which was part of the 91st Division (ASN 3130117). The Division sailed from New York aboard the *Adriatic* on July 14, 1918. Other men in Battery A were Moses Marshall, Elbridge Gerry and Peter Rouillard. The *Adriatic* first landed at Liverpool, England. When the 91st Division arrived in Cherbourg, France in July 1918, the artillery regiments were sent to a separate training area in the Garonne valley near Bordeaux. In September, the regiment was equipped with ten-ton tractors and 4.7-inch guns. When the 91st Division took part in the Meuse-Argonne Campaign, the artillery units were not with them. After the Armistice, the 347th FA was likely billeted in private homes in four towns along the Moselle River in Germany. Pvt. Apple sailed from Marseille aboard the *Patria* on March 1, 1919. He was traveling with St. Aignan Casual Company No. 1914, so it is likely he had been sick and did not return with his unit. He arrived in Brooklyn on March 17, 1919. Pvt. Apple received his honorable discharge on March 30, 1919. The rest of the 347th FA sailed from Brest on March 23, 1919. Pvt. Apple's name was not included in the published unit roster.

In the 1932 Census Roll for Pine Ridge, Frank was living with his wife, Grace (No Neck), and his children, Stephen, Victoria and Leroy. In 1935, he was driving the school bus in Kyle. Frank entered the spirit world on May 15, 1955, and is buried in Mediator Cemetery near Kyle, SD.

Archambeau, David R. David was born at Greenwood, SD, on June 12, 1891. In the 1903 Census Roll for the Yanktonai Sioux, he is listed with his parents, Baptiste and Amelia, as well as his brothers and sisters. After his father died in 1906, the family moved to Fort Peck, where his mother remarried. David attended the Fort Shaw boarding school. He married Jeanette Eagle. When he registered for the draft on June 5, 1917, he was farming near Poplar, MT, with his wife and three children, Dave Jr., Martha and Edward. He enlisted on Sept. 18, 1917, and served as a Cook in the Coast Guard. He was discharged on March 19, 1919. David's sister, Susan, married Frank Ferris, a fellow veteran from Charles Mix County, SD. In 1919, David received a Seaman's Certificate, with his occupation listed as Baker/Cook. On Aug. 16, 1920, David sailed from Trieste to the Army Base at Brooklyn, traveling on U.S.A.T. America. In 1929, David worked as a baker on the merchant ship, *William* Rockefeller, which sailed from Columbia to New York City. In the 1930 U.S. Census, David was living in Astoria, OR, and working as a cook on merchant ships, for the Columbia River Packers Assn. In the 1940 U.S. Census, he was working as a cook in a logging camp near West Chiloquin, OR. His sons, Dave and Edward, were living with him. In 1942, he registered with the Selective Service while working for the NP Railway, out of Tacoma, WA. David entered the spirit world in Hays Springs, NE, on Oct. 6, 1972, and is buried in the Black Hills National Cemetery, Section C, site 1261.[8]

Arcoren, Charles. Charles was an enrolled member on the Rosebud Reservation, but was born near Valentine, NE, on Feb. 20, 1892. His parents were John and Josephine (Fast Dog) Arcoren. In the 1900 U.S. Census, Charles was living on the Pine Ridge Reservation with his parents and two brothers, Frank and Edward. He attended the St. Francis Mission School until October 1907, when he was enrolled at the Carlisle Boarding school. Charles was trained as a shoemaker and was rated as a good student. He returned home in June 1910. In 1912, he wrote to staff at Carlisle that the family had 2,080 acres, with 30 head of horses and 40 head of cattle. When Charles registered for the draft on June 5, 1917, he was living in Okreek. He joined the Army on June 24, 1918, and was assigned to Battery D, 338th Field Artillery, 88th Division (ASN 3315643). He sailed from Brooklyn aboard the *Tres Os Montes* on Aug. 18, 1918. The 338th Field Artillery trained near Bordeaux but did not serve on the Front. Not long after the Armistice, this unit began to prepare to return to the United States. The 338th began to return home on Dec. 24, 1918. Pvt. Arcoren was discharged on Jan., 17, 1919. Charles was married to Minnie Olive Farmer (1904-1962). Minnie's brother, Lee, also served with the Army in France. Charles and Minnie had three boys, Claude, Henry and John. Henry served with the Army during WWII. Charles entered the spirit world in Rosebud on Sept. 11, 1973 and is buried in Saint Charles Catholic Cemetery in St. Francis.

Antoine Arpan
Delbert Arpan

Arcoren, Frank. Frank was an older brother to Charles. He was born around October 1890 near Valentine, NE. He served as a Private with the 88th Infantry, 19th Division, which was organized at Camp Dodge, IA, in September of 1918. Units were demobilized on Jan. 29, 1919. Frank entered the spirit world on June 19, 1920, and is buried in Saint Charles Catholic Cemetery, in St. Francis.

Arpan, Antoine. Antoine was born on the Cheyenne River Reservation on May 2, 1895. His parents were Albert and Sarah (Bowker). Antoine entered the military on June 23, 1918, likely at Camp Funston, Kansas. Pvt. Arpan sailed from Hoboken aboard the *America* on Sept. 17, 1918. He was listed as "unassigned" and was traveling with Overseas Casual Co. No. 400. When he reached France, he was transferred to Company B, 60th Infantry Regiment (ASN 3309071), which was part of the 5th Division.

After the Armistice was signed, the Red Diamond formed part of the Army of Occupation. The 60th Infantry was stationed near Esch, Luxembourg. Pvt. Arpan's commanding officer wrote "this man has proven to be above the average type of man in the enlisted ranks. He has all the qualities of a good infantryman. He has exceptional courage and physical endurance, well liked, keen, observing, more than average intelligence." Pvt. Arpan sailed from Brest aboard the *Aquitania* on July 20, 1919, and was discharged on July 28, 1919.

Antoine married Lema Nezena on Dec. 16, 1921. They had a son, Robert, who served in World War II. In the 1930 U.S. Census, Antoine was working as a ranch hand on the Crow Indian Reservation, Big Horn County, Montana. Antoine's wife died of TB in 1932. He then married Amy LeBeau. In 1935, the family was living in a house south of Timber Lake, in the White Horse Precinct. Antoine owned 4 mules and used them to haul rock for local (ICEW) conservation projects. It was hard work and Antoine injured his hip while lifting rocks. He was a member of the local American Legion Post. He was interested in watching the local baseball teams. In the 1940 U.S. Census, Antoine and Amy were listed with their children, Albert, Wesley, and Lenora. Another son, Alvin was born to them in 1942. Alvin served in the Army from 1965-68. Antoine entered the spirit world west of Faith on Nov. 16, 1950 and is buried in Emanuel Episcopal Cemetery in White Horse, Dewey County.[9]

Arrow, Arthur T. Arthur Thomas was born in Flandreau on Dec. 8, 1896. In the 1909 Census Roll for the Yanktonai, Yankton Agency, Arthur was listed with his mother, Annie, and his brothers and a sister. Arthur graduated from the Rapid City Boarding School. When Arthur registered for the draft on May 31, 1917, he listed his home as Greenwood, SD. He was employed as a student stenographer at the Haskell Institute in Lawrence, KS. He also wrote that he had served as 1st Sergeant of the cadets at the boarding school. Arthur enlisted on May 2, 1918, and served as a Sergeant with General Hospital # 43, Medical Department (ASN 976098). The 43rd Base Hospital was in Blois, France. Sgt. Arrow was discharged on July 22, 1919. In 1921, Arthur was a member of the Chauncey Eagle Horn Legion Post No. 125, Rosebud, SD.

After returning home from military service, Arthur married Nancy Schmidt, whose brother, Fred, served in the Army during the war. Nancy was one of the first women from the Rosebud Reservation to attend college at the Normal School in Aberdeen. Nancy passed away from tuberculosis in 1929. In the 1930 U.S. Census, Arthur was living in Chandler, AZ, with his wife, Aletha, and children, Irene, Glenn, Lois. Arthur was working as a bookkeeper. In the 1940 U.S. Census, Arthur was widowed and living in the Black Hills and working on a tree planting crew. On Nov. 16, 1940, he married Violet Hough in Broadus, MT. They moved to Butte, MT, where Arthur worked as a miner in the copper mines. Violet passed away in May 1952. Arthur passed away at the county hospital on April 1, 1953. A daughter and a step-daughter survived him. He is buried in Mountain View Cemetery in Butte.[10]

Arrow, Luther F. Luther was born in Flandreau around 1899 to Thomas Arrow and Annie Lyman. In the 1910 U.S. Census, the family was living in Wahehe Township, Charles Mix County. Thomas was a hotel keeper. When Luther joined the Army, he was assigned to Battery D, 50th Artillery, Coast Artillery Corps (ASN 598745). The 50th Artillery was formed at Camp Eustis, VA, and was scheduled to sail from Newport News, VA, for Europe aboard the *America* on Oct. 7, 1918. Bugler Arrow's name was included on the ship's manifest, but was crossed off, possibly due to being sick. The 50th arrived in France shortly before the Armistice, so it did not fight in the war. Bugler Arrow was discharged on Dec. 26, 1918. In the 1920 U.S. Census, Louis was living with his parents and working as a clerk in a grocery store. Shortly after this, he married Julia Necklace. In the 1934 Yankton Reservation Census Roll, Louis is listed with his three sons, Irvin, Herbert and Leo, and his step daughter, Pauline Necklace. In the 1940 U.S. Census, Louis was working on a C.C.C. project planting trees in the Black Hills. He entered the spirit world on May 6, 1976.

Titus Arrow
Ancestry.com

Arrow, Titus. Titus was born on the Lower Brule Reservation around 1894. His father was Silas and his mother, Julia Pte luta win (Red Buffalo Woman). Around 1897 they moved to the Rosebud Reservation. When Titus registered for the draft on June 5, 1917, he was farming near Hamill. He likely joined the Army in 1918. On Sept. 14, 1918, Pvt. Arrow sailed from New York aboard the NY298, with Overseas Casual Co. 396 (ASN 3129664). Upon arriving in France, he was assigned to Co. K, 49th Infantry, which was stationed in Le Mans, France. Pvt. Arrow likely became sick shortly before his regiment sailed for the U.S. in January of 1919. He entered the spirit world on Feb. 23, 1919. His body was brought back aboard the *Pocohontas* from Nazaire, France, on Oct. 10, 1920. Pvt. Arrow is buried in Red Hill Cemetery in Hamill, SD.[11]

Artichoker, John. John was born in Tomah, WI, on Jan. 8, 1893, as an enrolled member of the Ho Chunk Nation. He attended boarding schools in Tomah, Toledo, IA, and Haskell Institute. He had served as captain of infantry while at Haskell. When he registered for the draft on June 5, 1917, he was working as a general ranch hand for a rancher near Porcupine, SD. Not long after this, he took a position as coach and adviser at the Flandreau Boarding School. He enlisted in the Army on Jan. 2, 1918. He served as a Sergeant in Co. D, 529th Engineers (ASN 2201975), which worked on various engineering projects near the port of Brest, France. Their unit had sailed from Hoboken aboard the *Von Steuben* on June 30, 1918. Most of the enlisted men in that unit were black. They returned home from Brest aboard the S.S. *Mobile* on June 17, 1919. Sgt. Artichoker was discharged on July 5, 1919.

John married Emily Agnes Lessert on Nov. 16, 1919. After the wedding, John worked for many years with youth at a number of boarding schools, both as an advisor and an athletic coach. From 1943-46, he coached football at Martin. It was at that time that the boys' sports teams at Martin became known as the Warriors. From 1946 to 1963, he was headmaster at Bishop Hare Home for Boys in Mission. John retired in 1963. John was a lineal chief of the Ah-who-ghoe-ga (Blue Wing) band of the Ho Chunk Nation. He entered the spirit world in the Rosebud Indian Hospital on April 10, 1979. His wife, Emily, and three sons and a daughter survived him. He is buried in the Black Hills National Cemetery, Section E, Site 2166. Emily, who passed away in 1989, is buried with him.[12]

Ashes, Henry. Henry was born near Wagner, SD, on May 20, 1891. His parents, Adam Cahota [Ashes] and Eliza Ashes were Yanktonai. In 1913, he married Sarah Bago. When he registered for the draft in Wagner on June 5, 1917, he was supporting his wife and son, Benedict. He was a tall man of slender build. Henry joined the Army on Aug. 26, 1918. He served as a Private in the 7th Company, 5th Regiment, 164th Depot Brigade, at Camp Funston, KS (ASN 4265976). Pvt. Ashes was discharged on Dec. 2, 1918. In 1923, his first wife died. He married Julia Charging Hawk in 1924. Julia passed away in 1935. In the 1937 Census Roll, Henry is listed with his three children, Benedict, Cyphus and Henrietta. Henry came down with influenza and entered the spirit world in the Indian

Hospital in Wagner on May 7, 1939, and is buried in the Presbyterian Cemetery in Greenwood, SD.[13]

Atkinson, Adolph. Adolph was born on April 8, 1900, the son of John and Annie Atkinson. He was an enrolled member on the Rosebud Reservation. He was a student at the Flandreau boarding school. He enlisted in the Army in World War I and served with the Medical Department (ASN 484575). His unit returned to the U. S. from Brest aboard the S.S. *Mobile* on June 10, 1919. His name was engraved on a plaque honoring veterans that was erected at the Flandreau School in 1920. After the war he married Jeanette Fallis. After Jeanette passed away in 1929, he married Mayme Larson (1915-1994). In the 1930 U.S. Census, he was working as a house painter. In the 1940 U.S. Census, Adolph was living in Wood, SD, with Mayme and her parents, Mr. and Mrs. Lars Larson, along with three children, Darlene, Duane and Loretta. Other children born to Adolph and Mayme were Janice, Janet, Jane and June. Adolph was working as a truck driver on a dam construction project. Adolph served in WWII as a TSgt, from Aug. 26, 1942 to April 2, 1943. He later worked as a barber. Adolph passed away at the VA hospital in Hot Springs on April 9, 1978. He was survived by his wife and eight daughters, Geraldine, Darlene, Loretta, Janice, June, Janet, Jane and Debbie, as well as two sons, Duane and Danny. Adolph is buried in Evergreen Cemetery in Hot Springs. Mayme is buried next to him.[14]

Augustine, Paul Alex. Alex was born on Oct. 6, 1895, in Minnesota. He was enrolled as Pembina Ojibwe on the White Earth Reservation. In the 1911 White Earth Census Roll, Paul is listed with his sister, Margaret. In his early years, he used the name Alex Alex, or Alex Alix. In the 1905 SD State Census, he was listed as a student at the boarding school in Pierre, SD. He likely joined the Co. A, 4th South Dakota Infantry when he enlisted on April 29, 1917, using the name Alex Alex. Once the SD National Guard arrived in Camp Greene, NC, they were informed they were now an artillery regiment. Pvt. Alex served in Co. C, 147th Field Artillery (ASN 139435). His unit sailed for France aboard the *Olympic* on Jan. 11, 1918. For most of the war, they were attached to the 32nd Division. However, the 147th FA was supporting the 3rd Division in early October of 1918. Pvt. Alex was severely wounded on Oct 1, 1918, near Nantillois, north of Montfaucon. Alex later received a Purple Heart. He sailed from St. Nazaire aboard the *Princess Motoika* on Dec. 1, 1918. The manifest read: "sick & wounded, Ambulatory Surgical BH #69." Pvt. Alex was discharged on July 22, 1919. He spent more time in a hospital, as most of his fellow soldiers were discharged in the spring of 1919. Around 1930, he married Melda Johnson. In the 1930 U.S. Census, they were living in LaPlant. In the 1940 U.S. Census, Alex and Melda were living in Pierre with their children, Irma, Alton, Rita and Velma. Alex passed away on May 14, 1956, at the VA Hospital in Hot Springs. He is buried in Riverside Cemetery in Pierre.[15]

Aungie, Henry N. Henry was born on the Yankton Reservation on May 18, 1900. In the 1901 Census Roll, he is listed with his father, Thomas, and his brothers, Silas and Howard. Henry joined the Army on Aug. 6, 1918, and served in the 4th Company, 164th Depot Brigade (ASN 3913990) at Camp Funston, KS. He was discharged on Dec. 24, 1918, as a Private. Henry's first wife was Winnie Frazier, with who he had two children, Mabel and Henry Jr. In 1922, he married Olwin St. Pierre. Henry worked in the packing plant in Sioux City, IA. In 1935, the family was interviewed by a worker with the SDERA program. The family was living in a two-room frame house, three miles from Greenwood. They had two children, Erwin and Velma. Henry had been working on road construction projects. In the 1940 U.S. Census, they lived in Wagner, where Henry was working as a laborer on the construction of the hospital. Henry entered the spirit world on Jan. 19, 1969, and is buried in Greenwood Presbyterian Cemetery.

Azure, James J. James was born near Dunseith, ND, on Sept. 26, 1888, and grew up on the Turtle Mountain Reservation. His parents were James and Eliza (Delorme). When James registered for the draft on June 5, 1917, he was farming near McLaughlin, SD. On April 26, 1918, he traveled to Camp Funston, KS, with a group of men from Corson County. James served with Co. B, 340th Machine Gun Battalion, as part of the 89th Division (ASN 2845218). On June 4, 1918, Pvt. Azure sailed from New York aboard the *Khyber*, which arrived in England on June 16, 1918. The 340th MG Battalion fought in the St. Mihiel and Meuse-Argonne Campaign and served in the Lorraine Defensive Sector, at Euvezin and Lucey. On Dec. 5, 1918, the 89th Division entered Germany as part of the Army of Occupation. The 340th MG Bn. Was stationed near Erdorf. On May 15, 1919, the 340th MG Bn. boarded the U.S.S. *Leviathan* to return to the U.S.A. Pfc. Azure was discharged on June 2, 1919.

James returned to McLaughlin after the war. On Oct. 19, 1920, he married Emma Norquay in McIntosh, SD. In the 1920s, James returned to Dunseith. In the 1930 U.S. Census he was farming near Dunseith and was now married to Madeline Decoteau. In the 1940 U.S. Census, their children listed were Rose, Cecelia and Richard. James entered the spirit world in the Bottineau Hospital on Nov. 3, 1950. He is buried in St Anthony's Cemetery in Rolette County.[16]

B

Bad Cob, Thomas – listed on WWI veteran's memorial plaque at Oglala Lakota College, Kyle, SD. Thomas was born on the Pine Ridge Reservation on Feb. 14, 1900. His parents were Ellis Bad Cob [Wahuwapi Sica] and Annie Cold Water. Thomas joined the Army on May 19, 1918. He served as a Private, and was discharged on June 19, 1919. In the 1920 U.S. Census, he was living with his parents. Shortly after this, he married Louisa Jumping Bull. In the 1927 Census Roll, they are listed with two children, Sylvester and Christina. Louisa died later that year. Thomas married Victoria Red Elk. The family lived near Wanblee in 1935, when they were interviewed by a worker with the SDERA program. They had a two-room log home, near a creek from which they drew their drinking water. Around 1940 he married Annie Rose Moves Camp (1914-1995). In the 1940 Census, they lived in Wanblee with their children, Sylvester, Agatha, Sarah, and Iona. He also had a son, Rede. In 1943, a daughter, Renabelle, was born. Thomas' son, Sylvester, served in the Navy in WWII and the Korean Conflict. Thomas worked as a construction laborer. He entered the spirit world near Faith, SD, on Nov. 16, 1975. Thomas is buried in the Black Hills National Cemetery, Section D, Site 525. Annie Rose is buried with him.[1]

Bad Hair, John. John is listed on WWI veteran's memorial plaque at Oglala Lakota College, Kyle, SD. John was born on the Pine Ridge Reservation on June 12, 1891. In the 1904 Census Roll, he is listed with his step father, Alex Yellow Wolf, and his mother, Mary (Walks with Pipe). John joined the Army on April 10, 1918, and was sent to Camp Funston, KS. He was assigned to Company B, 355th Infantry Regiment (ASN 2195602) as part of the 89th Division. Pvt. Bad Hair sailed with his regiment from New York aboard the *Adriatic* on June 4, 1918. The first combat element of the 89th Division to enter the Front Line was the 1st Battalion, 355th Infantry, which included Company B. Other soldiers who served in Company B with Bad Hair were Vincent Bad Wound of Wanblee and Peter Shephard of Waubay. The 89th Division spent 28 days in Active Sectors and suffered 7,291 casualties. After the Armistice was signed, the 355th Infantry was stationed in Saarburg, Germany, as part of the Army of Occupation. In an evaluation written by his commanding officer, Capt. John

C. Moora, Pfc. Bad Hair "was a willing worker, but was handicapped by being hard-of-hearing." Pfc. Bad Hair embarked on the *Leviathan* at Brest on May 15, 1919 and arrived back in New York on May 22, 1919. Pfc. Bad Hair was discharged on May 31, 1919. In the 1920 Census Roll, John was living with Mary Mousseau. He later married Lucy Gertrude Lee of Greenwood. He worked for ranchers. As an elder, John lived in Kyle. He entered the spirit world at the VA Hospital in Hot Springs on Dec. 26, 1975. He is buried in the Kyle Cemetery.[2]

Bad Horse, Ernest. Ernest was born on January 11, 1894, on the Lower Brule Reservation. In the 1902 Census Roll for the Lower Brule, Ernest is listed with his parents, Bad Horse and Red Woman, as well as three sisters. When Ernest registered for the draft on June 5, 1917, he was farming. Shortly after this, he married Emma High Elk (1894-1978). Emma had two brothers, Job and Joseph, who served in the Army during the war. Ernest joined the Army on June 24, 1918. He was assigned to Company E, 351st Infantry Regiment (ASN 3309975). Other local men who served with him in Co. E included Joseph Otterman, Paul Eagle Deer, Frank Black Horse, Joseph Beads, William Shooter and David Turning Bear. As part of the 88th Division, the 351st Regiment sailed for Europe aboard the *Scotian* on Aug. 15, 1918. The 351st served in "quiet" sectors in France, though two of the men listed died of the flu. They were Joseph Otterman and David Turning Bear. After the fighting was over, Pfc. Bad Horse's commanding officer wrote an evaluation, saying that he "demonstrated fitness for automatic rifleman. Regarded by whites as an unusually good man." As part of the Army of Occupation, the 351st Regiment remained overseas in Houdelainecourt, France, until May 1919. On May 20, 1919, Pfc. Bad Horse sailed from St. Nazaire, France, for the United States aboard the U.S.S. *Mercury*. After docking in Newport News, Pfc. Bad Horse was discharged on June 6, 1919.

In the 1930 U.S. Census, Ernest is listed as a stockman. He and Emma had five children, Harry, Cora, James, and the twins, Mary and Melvin. In 1935, they were living in the Iron Nation District. They had a two-room home with a porch. Other farm buildings included a barn, chicken coop and a tool shed. Their water was hauled from a creek about 2 miles away. The family owned 3 horses, 2 cows, and was farming about 20 acres. In the 1940 U.S. Census, two sons, Ernest and Daniel were added to the family. Ernest was working on one of the nearby emergency conservation projects. Ernest entered the spirit world in his home in Lyman County on April 15, 1978. He is buried in St. Mary's Cemetery, Lower Brule. Emma had entered the spirit world in January of that year.[3]

Bad Wound, Daniel. Daniel was born on the Pine Ridge Reservation on Dec. 25, 1898. His parents were Robert and Day Bad Wound. Daniel married Julia Monroe in 1925. In 1935, a worker with SDERA interviewed the family at their home. Daniel told the interviewer that he had served in the Army but did not indicate when. Daniel and his family were living in a one room home located five miles south of Allen, close to his parent's home. The family hauled water from a nearby creek. Daniel had worked on some relief projects. He owned a saddle horse, a team, and seven mares. They obtained some food from his parents. In the 1940 U.S. Census, Daniel was listed as a rancher. His family included his wife and children, Robert, James, Vera, Wesley, Gary, as well as his widowed mother, Day, and a niece, Stella. Daniel passed away in July 1976.[4]

Bad Wound, Vincent– listed on WWI veterans memorial at Oglala Lakota College, Kyle, SD. Vincent was born on the Pine Ridge Reservation on Feb. 9, 1895. His parents were Noah and Mary Bad Wound. In the 1930s, Noah was a tribal judge in Hisle. When Vincent registered for the draft on June 5, 1917, he was farming near Greenwood, SD. He likely joined the Army in the spring of 1918 and went to training camp at Camp Funston, KS. He was assigned to Co. B, 355th Regiment,

89th Division (ASN 2202975). Pvt. Bad Wound sailed with his regiment from New York aboard the *Adriatic* on June 4, 1918. The 355th Regiment was billeted initially in the towns of Grand, Brechainville and Aillianville, in the Haute Marne District. Also serving with Pvt. Bad Wound were Pfc. John Bad Hair and Pfc. Peter Shepherd of Waubay. After the Armistice was signed, the 355th Regiment was billeted in Saarburg, Germany. Pvt. Bad Wound's commanding officer wrote an evaluation stating Bad Wound "is a good scout. Men have confidence in this Indian as a good soldier and is respected by them." Pfc. Bad Wound sailed from Brest, France, on May 15, 1919, aboard the *Leviathan*. After the war, Vincent wrote that he had served in the Lucie Sector from Aug. 8 to Sept. 11, St. Mihiel Offensive from Sept. 12 to Sept. 16, Euvezine Sector from Sept. 17 to Oct. 7, and the Meuse-Argonne Offensive from Oct. 19 to Nov. 11.

In 1922, Vincent married Rosa Brown (1895-1972). In the 1930 U.S. Census, the family was living in Wanblee, where Vincent was working for the tribal police. In 1935, the family was interviewed by a worker from SDERA. They were living in a two-room stucco home in Wanblee. Vincent had built this home, starting with logs he had cut from his allotment. The yard was fenced in, while water was obtained from a nearby well. In the 1940 U.S. Census, Vincent was working on a WPA project. They had six children, Eloise, Lavina, Leroy, Evelyn, Rose, and Pearl. Vincent retired as a munition's handler at the Ordnance Depot. Vincent entered the spirit world at Felix Cohen Memorial Home on June 7, 1968. He is buried in Red Cloud Cemetery.[5]

Bagola, Johnson. Johnson was born on the Cheyenne River Reservation on Oct. 2, 1892. In the 1895 Census Roll for the Cheyenne River Reservation, Johnson is listed with his parents, George and Laura Bagola. When he registered for the draft on June 5, 1917, he was living on his wife's allotment near White Horse, in Dewey County. Johnson was inducted on March 15, 1918, at Timber Lake, and sent to Fort Logan, and later to San Francisco. He served as a Private with Battery D, 57th Artillery, Coast Artillery Corps (CAC) (ASN 503099). Pvt. Bagola sailed from Hoboken, NJ, aboard the *Mongolia* on Oct. 28, 1918. He traveled with the 3rd Company, October Automatic Replacement Draft (CAC). The 57th CAC had fought with French-made, tractor drawn, 155 mm. guns. The unit left France aboard the U.S.S. *Huntington* on Jan. 2, 1919. Pvt. Bagola landed in New York on Jan. 19, 1919, and was discharged on Feb. 1, 1919, at Camp Dodge, IA. After returning home, he lived about a mile south of Fort Yates. He told the *Sioux County Pioneer* that he did not like France or the other European countries, but preferred to be home. After the war, Johnson married Sophia Fearless Hawk, who had been married to Robert Philbrick, a fellow veteran. In the 1930 U.S. Census, Johnson was listed with Sophia, and children, Reuben, Delma, Evelyn and Silas. In 1935, the family was living northwest of Fort Thompson on the Crow Creek Reservation when they were interviewed by a social worker with the SDERA program. Their son, Silas, told the social worker that Johnson and Sophie had gone to Standing Rock to celebrate the Fourth of July. He also said that he and Johnson liked working on cars. In the 1940 U.S. Census, the family lived in Pierre and Johnson was a laborer in the CCC program. Johnson later lived with his wife, Lucy, in Bullhead, SD. Their son, Silas, served in the Army during WWII. Johnson entered the spirit world at the VA Hospital in Hot Springs on Jan. 18, 1966. He is buried in Bullhead, SD.[6]

Bailly, Alexis A. Alexis was born at the Sisseton Agency on Aug. 2, 1893. His parents were Alexis and Lilly Bailly. In the 1897 Census Roll for the Sisseton-Wahpeton Reservation, Alexis is listed with his father and two sisters, Abbey and Blanche. When he registered for the draft on June 5, 1917, he was living in Peever. On Sept. 19, 1917, he traveled with a group of recruits to Fort Riley, KS, and later transferred to Camp Cody, NM. Pvt. Bailly was assigned to Co. 18, Camp Cody June Automatic Replacement Draft, which sailed from New York aboard the *Honorata* on June 28,

1918. After arriving in France, he served with Co. I, 305th Infantry, 77th Division (ASN 1429434). The 305th Infantry served in the Sectors at Baccarat, Vesle, Oise-Aisne, Fôret d'Argonne, and Meuse-Argonne. Pvt. Bailly was likely wounded or gassed. On Dec. 25, 1918, he sailed from Bordeaux aboard the *Koningin der Nederlanden.* He was attached to Bordeaux Casual Co. No. 9. The manifest for the ship bore the statement, "I certify that Casual Co. No. 9 has this date been examined and found free from any contagious or veneral disease or vermin." The ship arrived in Newport News on Jan. 8, 1919. Pvt. Bailly was discharged on Feb. 15, 1919. In the 1920 U.S. Census, Alexis was living with his parents and working as a carpenter. In the 1920s, he married Emma Foell. In the 1930 U.S. Census, the family was living in Scranton, ND, where Alexis ran a billiard parlor. In the late 1930s, they moved to Whitman, WA. Alexis worked for the Columbia Paper Mill. He later lived in Vancouver, WA. He entered the spirit world in Vancouver Memorial Hospital on March 28, 1971, and is buried there in Evergreen Memorial Gardens, Vancouver, WA.[7]

The artist, Lt. P.L. Crosby, served with Pvt. Alexis Bailly in the 305th Inf.

Capt. P.L. Crosby

Bailly, Arthur. Arthur (Art) was born at Sisseton on April 26, 1895, the son of Charles and Inez Bailly. In the 1901 Census Roll, he was listed with his father, Charles, and his other brothers, Frank, Charles Jr., Edward, Harry, Daniel, and Louis. After his father passed away in 1903, the family moved to Alberta, where his mother remarried and established a homestead. Art had an older brother, Edward, who had served three years with the SD National Guard before the war. Art was inducted into the Canadian Army on May 31, 1918. He served with the 1st Depot Battalion, Alberta Regiment (Military Service No. 3210374). Art loved horses and was a jockey for many years. He met his wife, Florence, while riding in the race circuit. They had two children who died as infants. They adopted a little girl, Rosella. Sometime after the war, he moved to Washington State. In the 1930 U.S. Census, Arthur lived with his wife, Florence, in Neilton, WA, where he worked as a logger. Art was an expert at handling dynamite. In the 1940 U.S. Census, he was still working in a logging camp in western Washington. When he registered for the draft in 1942, he was employed by the Polson Logging Co. After he retired from the logging business, he and his wife ran a convenience store. Art passed away in Hoquiam, WA, on Dec. 27, 1965. He is buried in Sunset Memorial Park in Hoquiam.

Bailly, Hayden Clyde. Hayden was born at Sisseton on May 5, 1890, the son of George Bailly and Phoebe Eastman. In the 1899 Census Roll, he is listed with his father and his three sisters, Millie, Christina and Edith, as well as a brother, Joseph. When Hayden registered for the draft on June 5, 1917, he was farming with his father. He joined the Army on June 24, 1918, and served with the Quartermaster Corps (ASN 3308426). Pvt. Bailly sailed from Newport News, VA, aboard the *Zeelandia* on Sept. 8, 1918. He was serving with the 25th Squad, 4th Detachment Labor Foremen, QMC. After a year in France, Sgt. Bailly sailed from Brest aboard the *Orizaba* on Sept. 27, 1919. He was serving with the Headquarters Detachment at Gievres. Sailing with Brest Casual Co. No. 5201, he arrived in the U.S. on Oct. 6, 1919, and was discharged on Dec. 12, 1919, as a Sergeant. On Nov. 16, 1922, he married Cecilia Krosch. They moved to Shields, ND. In 1929, they moved to Selfridge, ND, and started ranching. Hayden was a life member of the American Legion. Hayden entered the spirit world at the VA Hospital in Fargo on Oct. 4, 1973. His wife (1901-1977) survived him. Hayden is buried in Selfridge Community Cemetery.

Bailly, Louis. Louis was born at Sisseton on Sept. 2, 1893, the son of Charles E. and Inez Bailly. After Charles passed away in 1903, Inez moved to Alberta in 1906 with some of her children. The family homesteaded near Wardlow, Alberta. Louis, who was known as "Toots," was inducted into the Canadian Army at Calgary on May 16, 1918. He was assigned to the 1st Depot Battalion, Alberta Regiment, Reg. No. 3210372. He was discharged as a Private. Louis married Hester Thrun in Patricia, Alberta, on Nov. 18, 1924. Toots was an excellent horseman and hunter, and was skilled at rawhiding, braiding ropes and hackamores. He and his brothers enjoyed hunting coyotes with their dogs and fine horses. Louis was hired to annually plow a firebreak for the Canadian Pacific Railway from Patricia to Empress, using a three-bottomed plow and 18 head of horses. In the 1936 Lake Traverse Census Roll, Louis is listed with two children, Leslie and Doris. Louis became ill while traveling with his family through the Crow's Nest Pass area. He passed away in a Blairmore hospital on Jan. 19, 1960, and is buried in Brooks, Alberta.[8]

Baine, Walter William. William was born on the Sisseton Reservation on Jan. 28, 1894 to William and Jennie Baine. When he registered for the draft in Lake City on June 1, 1917, he was already serving with the SD National Guard. At Camp Cody, he was assigned to Co. I, 136th Infantry, 34th Division (ASN 1428606). Corporal Baine sailed from Brooklyn, NY, aboard the *Lycaon* on Oct. 13, 1918. He later served in Co. K, 59th Infantry, 4th Division. He sailed with his unit from Brest, France aboard the *Texan* on July 24, 1919. He married Edna Lock in 1922. In the 1930 U.S. Census, he was farming in Marshall County. When he registered for the "Old man's Draft" in 1942, he was living in Hoquiam, WA, and working for Anderson-Middleton Lumber Co. in Aberdeen. His son, Leonard, served as a naval pilot in WWII. William entered the spirit world on June 9, 1969, and is buried in Hoquiam, WA.

Baker, Charles Baptis. Charles was born in Gladstone, Manitoba on Jan. 22, 1894. He was likely Anishinabe. As a child, his family moved to the Turtle Mountains, in North Dakota. He married Lena Demery around 1915. When he registered for the draft in 1917, Charles was living in Fort Yates and working for Jim Demery, who was his wife's brother. The Demery family, (sometimes spelled Demarais), were also Metis from Canada. Jim Demery and his brother, Robert, served in the military during the war. Charles was inducted at Fort Yates on March 29, 1918. He was first sent to Camp Dodge, IA, where he served as a Private in Company A, 163rd Depot Brigade (ASN 2559187). He later was transferred to Camp Bowie, TX, where he received an honorable discharge on March 27, 1919. While at Camp Bowie, he served in the 48th Company, Demobilization Center.

After the war he returned to McLaughlin, SD. In the 1920s, Charles started working as a section hand for the railroad, but always was laid off in the fall and rehired in the spring. In the 1930 U.S. Census, Charles and Lena were living in McLaughlin with their children, Robert, Melvin, Joseph, Roger, Sydney and Frank. Charles worked as a section hand. He was a member of the local American Legion Post. In November 1935, the family was interviewed by a social worker for the South Dakota Emergency Relief Administration (SDERA). Charles and Lena now had two more boys. They were living in railroad property in an old boxcar with a lean-to made of grocery boxes. Because of the drought, they had no production from their garden. The day of the visit, the only food they had was some frosted potatoes and a jack rabbit that Charles had just shot. Because they were not enrolled members, they were not eligible to receive help from the Agency. The social worker suggested they should contact the county commissioners to obtain relief. In the 1945 South Dakota Census, the family was living in Wakpala. Charles passed away at the VA Hospital in Hot Springs, SD, on March 8, 1954, and is buried in Riverside Cemetery in Dunseith, ND.[9]

Baker, Francis. Francis was born in Gladstone, Manitoba on March 17, 1897. He was a brother to Charles. His parents were Fritz and Mary Jane Baker. When Francis registered for the draft in June 1918, he was working for William Mullally in Kenel, SD. Francis was sent to Camp Fremont, CA, on Aug. 6, 1918. He was discharged on Oct. 1, 1919. He may have stayed in the Army for several years, possibly stationed at Fort Lee, VA. In 1925, he married Eliza Dejarlais in Rolla. The family lived in Dunseith until the late 1960s. Around 1967, Francis moved to Belcourt to live with one of his daughters. His wife, Eliza, had passed away in 1944. Francis entered the spirit world in Bottineau on July 2, 1970. Military rites were performed at St. Louis Cemetery in Dunseith by the Archie Jardine American Legion Post No. 185. Francis and Charles Baker had another brother, Alfred, who likely joined the Army while living in South Dakota. Alfred had attended the boarding school in Pierre, and registered for the draft while living in McLaughlin, SD. In the 1920 U.S. Census, Alfred was living with Robert Demery in McLaughlin, SD.[10]

Baldwin, Thomas F. Thomas was born in Vale, Butte County, SD, on Dec. 10, 1898. His parents were Thomas and Edith Baldwin. Thomas enlisted in the Army on Jan. 8, 1918, and was assigned to the Flying School Detachment at Souther Field, Georgia. He was discharged as a Pfc. on March 31, 1919. After returning home, he married Blanche Collins, a sister to Henry Collins who also served. Thomas and Blanche had a son, Fay Thomas. In the 1930 U.S. Census, Thomas was working for the Indian Service at the Cheyenne Agency. His wife was an enrolled member. Thomas entered the spirit world in Homestake Hospital in Lead on June 9, 1937, and is buried in Bear Butte Cemetery at Sturgis.[11]

Banks, Philip Sheridan. Philip was born on April 7, 1899, on the Crow Creek Reservation and is listed as Lower Yanktonai. His parents were George Banks and Annie Red Thunder. Philip joined the Army on Aug. 14, 1918. He served in the 88th Infantry, 19th Division at Camp Dodge, IA (ASN 3776583). He was discharged as a Corporal on Jan. 24, 1919. He married Elizabeth LaRoche at Chamberlain on Feb. 23, 1921. In 1930 they lived in Lyman County, where Philip worked as a farm laborer. In the 1940 U.S. Census, he was working as a laborer for the Indian Service. Philip and Elizabeth had seven children, Josephine, Philip, Melvin, Clyde, Mary, Sylvia, and Amelia. Their oldest sons, Philip Jr. and Melvin served in the Army during WWII. On March 3, 1943, Philip Sr. enlisted in the Navy. His rating was Painter 1/C (NSN 6488537). He was discharged on June 16, 1945. Philip entered the spirit world at the VA Hospital in Hot Springs on Feb. 26, 1947. He is buried in St. Mary's Mission Cemetery in Lower Brule.[12]

Barker, Charles. Charles was born on the Santee Reservation in Nebraska on Sept. 3, 1887. His parents were Jacob Natuhpi [The enemy charged him] and Mary Topawanyakewin [Who sees Four] Barker. In the 1910 U.S. Census, Charles was living with his parents in Easter Township, Roberts County, SD. Soon after, he married his wife, Annie Wacehinkoyakewin [Who wears an eagle plume], who was from Spirit Lake. When Charles registered for the draft on June 5, 1917, he was farming near Peever, SD, with his wife and three children. Charles enlisted in the Army on Sept. 21, 1917. He served as a Private in Co. D, 114th Machine Gun Battalion, 30th Division (ASN 2192897). Pvt. Barker sailed from New York aboard the *Elpenor* on May 11, 1918. The 30th Division served under the command of the 4th British Army, including the Sectors at Canal, Ypres-Lys and Somme. After the Armistice, Pvt. Barker sailed from St. Nazaire aboard the *Rijndam* on March 7, 1919, and was discharged on March 29, 1919. He returned to Roberts County. In the 1930 U.S. Census, he and Annie were living near the Goodwill Mission with their children, Victoria and Joseph. Charles had been a member of the American Legion, but dropped his membership due to lack of funds to pay the dues. During the 1930s, he worked on the gopher eradication project. Charles entered the spirit world at the PHS hospital in Sisseton on April 23, 1958, and is buried in St. John's Episcopal Cemetery, Roberts County, SD.[13]

Barse, Horace C. Horace was born at Waubay on Feb. 1, 1896. His father, Albert Barse, had served in the Civil War with a regiment from New York. His mother was Mary Horpionajinwin. In the 1900 U.S. Census, Horace was a student at the boarding school in Genoa, NE. When he registered for the draft on June 5, 1917, he was farming at the boarding school in Genoa. After he joined the Army, he was initially assigned to Co. F, 158th Infantry Regiment, 40th Division (ASN 2787812). The 158th Infantry sailed from Brooklyn aboard the *Vauban* on Aug. 11, 1918. Upon arrival, he was re-assigned to Co. I, 306th Regiment, 77th Division. The 306th Infantry took part in the opening of the Meuse-Argonne Offensive on Sept. 26, 1918. On Oct. 14-15, the regiment was fighting near the town of St. Juvin. Pfc. Barse was one of the soldiers killed on Oct. 15, 1918. The regiment lost a total of 7 officers and 37 men killed, along with 4 officers and 213 men wounded in the fighting at St. Juvin. The body of Pvt. Barse was brought back aboard the *Wheaton*, which sailed from Antwerp, Belgium, on Sept. 20, 1921. Horace is now buried in St. James Episcopal Cemetery next to Enemy Swim Lake.[14]

Bartlett, Edward. Edward was born at Peever, SD, on Aug. 3, 1896. In the 1897 Sisseton-Wahpeton Census Roll, he was listed with his parents, Anthony (Ho Wa Kana) and Mary, as well as three sisters, Agnes, Libby and Ida. When Edward registered for the draft on June 5, 1917, he was working for Robert Iron Lightning in Tokio, ND. Edward joined the Army on June 24, 1918, and was assigned to Co. G, 20th Infantry, 10th Division (ASN 3308680). The 10th Division was formed in August 1918 at Camp Funston, KS. Pfc. Bartlett was discharged on June 16, 1919. After the war, he married Martha Hayes. They lived in Easter Township, Roberts County. In the 1940 U.S. Census, Edward and Martha were living with their step daughter, Josephine, and her child, Ramona. Edward was working on a CCC Reforestation Project. Edward entered the spirit world on Sept. 7, 1956, and is buried in St. James Episcopal Cemetery by Enemy Swim Lake.

Beads, Joseph. Joseph was born on the Rosebud Reservation on Oct. 28, 1889. He was the son of George Beads and Eagle Woman. In the 1890s, George was a Private in the Indian Police on the Rosebud Reservation. Joseph joined the Army on June 24, 1918. He was assigned to Co. E, 351st Infantry (ASN 3315866), one of the four infantry regiments of the 88th Division. Other local men who served in Co. E were Joseph Otterman, Ernest Bad Horse, Paul Eagle Deer, Frank Black Horse, William Shooter and David Turning Bear. Joseph likely started his training at Camp Funston, but was transferred to Camp Dodge, IA, to help make up the 88th Division. The 351st Infantry sailed for Europe aboard the ships, *Saxon* and *Scotian,* on August 15, 1918. The unit stayed in quiet sectors until the war's end. After the Armistice, the 351st was part of the Army of Occupation, with Co. E being billeted in the French town of Liffol-le-Grand. Pvt. Beads received an evaluation from his commanding officer, saying he was "always attentive to duty under all conditions." On May 20, 1919, the regiment sailed from France aboard the ship *Mercury*. After arrival at Hampton Roads, VA, the regiment returned to Camp Dodge, IA, where most of the men were discharged on June 6, 1919. Pvt. Beads was detailed to Casual Detachment 693, Demobilization Group. He was discharged on June 10, 1919, at Camp Dodge.

Joseph returned to Saint Francis, SD, and married Lillian Thunderhawk. In the 1930 U.S. Census, Joseph and Lillian were living with their children, Evelyn, Alice, Grover, Philip, Golda and Joseph, Jr. In the 1940 U.S. Census, Joseph was farming. Those living with him included his wife and daughters, Goldie, Grace and Evelyn, who was now married to Walter Bad Hand, who also lived with the family. Joseph's mother, Eagle Woman was living with them, as well as Paul Good Breast, an adopted son. Their son, Philip, served with the 101st Airborne and was killed June 6, 1944. Joseph entered the spirit world on Oct. 29, 1969, and is buried in Saint Charles Catholic Cemetery in Saint Francis.[15]

Bear, Andrew. Andrew was born in Peever, SD, on Oct. 3, 1895, the son of John Bear and Mary Marlow. In the 1909 Sisseton-Wahpeton Census Roll, Andrew Matoitewakan [A bear whose face looks sacred] was listed with his brother, Jonah. When Andrew registered for the draft on June 5, 1917, he was farming near Peever. He joined the Army and was sent to Camp Funston where he served as a Private in the 3rd Company, 164th Depot Brigade. After his discharge, he returned home and married Ida Irene Robertson. In the 1930 Census Roll, Andrew and Irene were living at Fort Totten with their children, Gladys, Jonah and Levi. In the 1940 U.S. Census, the family was living in Long Hollow Township, where Andrew was working at wrecking cars (salvaging parts?) for a garage. His son, Jonah, served in the Army in Korea and Levi served in the military at the end of WWII. Andrew entered the spirit world in Sisseton on Feb. 13, 1964. His sons, Levi, Jonah and Raymond, and daughters, Marie, Yvonne and Gladys, survived him. Fellow veteran, Aaron Bernard, was the organist at his funeral service at Gethsemane Episcopal Church. Andrew is buried in the Veterans plot at the Sisseton Cemetery.[16]

Bear, Sampson Mato. Sampson was born in Waubay on the Sisseton-Wahpeton Reservation on April 27, 1884. He married Sara Hoffman. When he registered for the draft on June 5, 1917, he lived with his family and worked as a stock raiser in Santee, NE. He served in the military and was discharged on Jan. 6, 1919. His sister, Julia, married Moses Trudell, a fellow veteran. In the 1930 U.S. Census, Sampson lived In Santee Township. In the 1937 Santee Census Roll, he is listed with his children, Norman, John and Sarah. Sampson entered the spirit world on Feb. 16, 1971, and is buried in the congregational cemetery in Santee, NE.

Bear Horse, John. John was born on the Rosebud Reservation on Nov. 5, 1892. His parents were Frank and Mary Bear Horse. He attended the Carlisle Boarding School. John joined the Army on July 22, 1918, and was initially assigned to Co. D, 333rd Infantry, 84th Division ASN 3955917). Pvt. Bear Horse sailed with his unit from New York on the *Baltic* on Sept. 1, 1918. After arriving in France, he was reassigned to Co. A, 140th Infantry Regiment, 35th Division. The 35th Division suffered heavy casualties in the opening days of the Meuse-Argonne Offensive in late September. The total casualties for the 35th Division were 7,283 killed and wounded. After the Armistice was signed, the 140th was billeted in the town of Boncourt. Pvt. Bear Horse received an evaluation from his commanding officer, 1st Lieutenant John Robertson, saying that he was an "excellent soldier." The 140th Regiment sailed from France aboard the *Nansemond* on April 15, 1919, and arrived in Newport News, VA, on April 28, 1919. Pvt. Bear Horse received his honorable discharge on May 7, 1919. In the 1930 U.S. Census, John was living in Curlew Township, Tripp County with his wife, Lena, and their children, Philomine and Calvin. John entered the spirit world on Oct. 19, 1939, at the Rosebud Indian Hospital. He is buried in St. Catherine's Cemetery in Wood, SD.[17]

Bear Looks Running, Frank. Frank was born around 1892 near Cherry Creek on the Cheyenne River Reservation. His parents were Bear Looks Running and Eagle Body. On April 6, 1917, Frank enlisted in the Army and was assigned to Co. A, 4th South Dakota Infantry. For about five months, the 4th Infantry trained in South Dakota, before entraining for Camp Greene, NC. Private Bear Looks Running received his discharge after that five-month period. This likely was a medical discharge. Once the National Guard units arrived at Camp Greene, the Regular Army medical staff rigorously screened the recruits. He wrote to Joseph Dixon saying, "serve five months and I was turned down in the final Exmanimation" [sic].

After returning home, Frank married Phoebe Little Crow in 1922. In the 1930 U.S. Census, they were living with their children, Norah, Ramona and Franklin. Frank was well known as a bronc rider. In 1933, Frank married Edith Little Shield. In his later years, Frank used the name, Waloke. He entered the spirit world in Eagle Butte on April 24, 1994, at the age of 102. Survivors include two sons, Franklin and Sylvester, and three daughters, Clementine, Arlene and Irene. Burial with military honors was conducted by the Cheyenne River Vietnam Veterans and American Legion Post No. 308 at the Congregational Cemetery in Cherry Creek.[18]

Bear Shield, Julius. Julius was born at Fort Yates, ND, on Dec. 24, 1895. In the Standing Rock Census Roll taken in 1908, Julius is listed with his father, Martin Matowahacanka [Bear shield] and his mother, Oyatelutawin [Scarlet Nation]. They belonged to the Teal Duck Band of the Yanktonai. In the 1915 Standing Rock Census Roll, Julius was living with his wife, Lena, an enrolled member from Crow Creek. Julius was inducted in the Army at Fort Yates on March 4, 1918, and sent to Camp Dodge, IA. Initially, Private Bear Shield was assigned to Co. A, 351st Infantry (ASN 2558366). On March 25, 1918, he was reassigned to Headquarters, 43rd Engineers, and then on March 29, 1918, assigned to Co. D, 42nd Engineers. On May 10, 1918, the Engineers sailed for Europe on the transport *Abraham Lincoln*. When they arrived in France, part of Co. D, 42nd Engineers was sent to the forested region of Les Landes in southwest France, while the rest of Co. D went to the Vosges in eastern France. The duty of these men was to cut trees and produce lumber in sawmills for the Army to use in construction, probably both buildings and coffins. After Nov. 1, 1918, Pvt. Bear Shield's unit was re-designated as the 45th Company, 20th Engineers, Forestry. Much work remained to be done after the Armistice was signed. The unit sailed from France in late May 1919, and arrived in Hoboken, NJ, on June 1, 1919. Once the unit left the ship, there was an eight-mile hike on a warm, sunny day with full equipment to Camp Merritt, NJ. The last vivid memory for the unit was that of a Major, leading the march in an auto, and wildly condemning his subordinates for letting their men fill their canteens. Pvt. Bear Shield was discharged at Camp Dodge, IA, on June 9, 1919.

Julius arrived back in Fort Yates on June 11, 1919. Julius enjoyed playing baseball. The local newspaper noted that he played third base in a game against Selfridge. In the Standing Rock Census Roll for 1926, Julius was listed with his son, Joseph. In 1927, Julius re-enlisted in the Army. He was stationed with Troop A, 4th Cavalry at Fort Meade, SD. The Army had sent him to their School for Bakers and Cooks at Fort Riley, KS. An article in the *Sioux County Pioneer* stated that the task of the cooks was to "take the regulation army ration and day after day convert the materials into dozens of palatable dishes, both appetizing and wholesome." Julius served three years with the 4th Cavalry. He had also served in the Infantry at Fort Lincoln. In 1934, he married Pearl Grindstone. Julius and Pearl had a son, Reynolds. In the summer of 1935, Julius was paid to camp out with his family in the Black Hills to attract tourists to a store near Rapid City. Julius entered the spirit world on June 19, 1936, in Little Eagle. He is buried in Little Eagle.[19]

Bear Stops, James. James was born in Bridger on the Cheyenne River Reservation about Aug. 4, 1894. His parents were Peter and Agnes Bear Stops. When James registered for the draft on May 31, 1917, he was farming near Zeal, SD. James married Fannie Fish (1900-1982) on Aug. 1, 1917. The *Dupree Leader* reported that James was one of a group of men sent to Fort Riley, KS, for military training in September of 1917. Others traveling with him to camp were John Slow, Luke Black Eagle and Thomas Hawk Eagle. James was likely discharged for medical reasons. John Slow was discharged on Nov. 24, 1917. James farmed near Red Scaffold. In the 1940 U.S. Census, James and Fannie were living with their sons, Peter and Romanus, as well as their daughter, Lena, who was married to Gilbert Black Moon. James entered the spirit world at Red Scaffold on Sept. 26, 1951. He is buried in Sacred Heart Cemetery at Red Scaffold.

Bear Thunder, James. James was born May 8, 1887, at Ring Thunder on the Rosebud Reservation. When he registered for the draft on Dec. 20, 1917, he was working as a laborer for the Boss Farmer at White River. He wrote that he was separated from his wife. In 1918, he joined the Army at Camp Funston, KS. He was assigned to Battery D, 28th Field Artillery, which was part of the 10th Division. The unit was organized in August 1918 and demobilized in February 1919. Bear Thunder was discharged as a Pfc. In the 1930 U.S. Census, he was farming in Todd County with his wife, Alice. James passed away on Jan. 15, 1948, at the Sioux Sanatorium in Rapid City. He is buried in St. James' Cemetery in White River.[20]

Bellecourte, George. George was born on the White Earth Reservation in Minnesota on Aug. 2, 1898. In the 1900 U.S. Census, he is listed with his grandparents, Frank and Olive Bellecourt. As a youth, he was enrolled at the boarding school in Flandreau, SD. On April 4, 1917, he enlisted in Co. D, 1st South Dakota Cavalry. A large group of students from the boarding school enlisted shortly after President Wilson declared war on Germany. Unfortunately, this National Guard regiment spent its time performing infantry drills, as neither, horses nor cavalry equipment was provided. On Sept. 15, 1917, the unit received orders to report to Camp Cody, NM. Private Bellecourte received his honorable discharge on Oct. 16, 1917. This likely was for medical reasons. George returned to the White Earth Reservation. On Sept. 7, 1918, he was required to register for the draft. At that time, he was working on a threshing crew near Page, ND. Sometime after this he moved to the Bad River Reservation near Ashland, WI. In the 1940 U.S. Census, he was living near Ashland with his wife, Sarah, and daughter, Marcella. George was working as a carpenter on a

WPA project. George passed away on Feb. 26, 1978, in Milwaukee, and is buried in the Bad River Cemetery near Odanah, WI.

Benoist, Douglas. Douglas was born on the Cheyenne River Reservation on Dec. 16, 1903. His parents were Felix Benoist and Cora Poor Bear. He joined the Army on Feb. 14, 1927, and was discharged as a Private on June 12, 1928. In 1930, he married Ellen Ward. In the 1940 U.S. Census, Douglas was working as a wood chopper at Cherry Creek. He and Ellen had two children, Donivan and Mildred. Donivan served in the military during the Korean Conflict and in Vietnam. After World War II, Douglas worked for the C & NW Railroad. He entered the spirit world on May 18, 1986, and is buried in Cherry Creek.

Benoist, Louis. Louis was born at Fort Bennett, SD, on May 9, 1891. In the 1892 Cheyenne River Census Roll, he is listed with his parents, Narcisse and Millie, and a sister, Nellie. After his father died around 1902, his mother married Charles DuCharme. When Louis registered for the draft, he was living in Mobridge and working for Louis LeCompte. Louis joined the Army on April 28, 1918, and served with Co. M, 69th Infantry, 10th Division at Camp Funston, KS. He was discharged on Jan. 31, 1919. Louis's sister, Elsie, married William Mern, a fellow veteran. His brother, Martin Ducharme, had served in the Navy. Louis worked as a mechanic and blacksmith is various locations after the war. He owned a small mining claim in the Black Hills, west of Lead. He was familiar with some of the bootlegging being done. He told a state employee that "for him, the Depression began when prohibition was repealed." In 1935, he was living with his brother, Melvin Ducharme, in the old family home in the Swift Bird Precinct. When Louis registered for the Selective Service in 1942, he was working for Charley Bartel in a saw mill along the Moreau River. Louis lived in Mobridge and entered the spirit world on July 24, 1972.[21]

Bernard, Aaron. Aaron was born near Owl Lake on July 18, 1899, and was an enrolled member of the Sisseton-Wahpeton Oyate. His parents were William and Elizabeth Bernard. In the 1900 U.S. Census, he is listed as Eldred. When his father died, his mother married Edwin Bluedog. While Aaron was a student at the Flandreau boarding school, he enlisted in the Army on May 1, 1918. He was discharged as a Corporal on May 14, 1919. Aaron's name is included on a plaque at the Flandreau Boarding School listing students who served in the military. In 1922, he married Lavina Blackstone at the Enemy Swim Church. In the 1930 U.S. Census, Aaron and Lavina are listed with their children, Estelline, Delvina and Maynard. In the 1940 U.S. Census, Aaron was working as a gravel shoveler on a road construction project. By then, they had three more children, Orson, Delano and Olivia. Aaron served as a lay reader and senior catechist in the Episcopal Church. He was a member of the Otto-Quande-Renville American Legion Post and the Native American Veterans Association. Aaron passed away in his home near Sisseton on March 29, 1979. His wife and three sons, Maynard, Orsen and Eddy, as well as two daughters, Estelline and Delvinia, survived him. He is buried in the Veterans Section of the Sisseton Cemetery. Military honors were provided by the Native American Veterans Association.[22]

Bernie, Oscar. Oscar was born on March 25, 1890. In the 1893 Yanktonai Census Roll, he is listed with his parents, Jesse and Jennette Bernie. He first married in 1909 to Grace Shunk. They had two daughters, Helen and Juana. He later married Emma LeClaire. When he registered for the draft on June 5, 1917, he was farming with his family near Greenwood, SD. He may have enlisted in 1917. He served with the Machine Gun Company of the 30th Infantry Regiment, 3rd Division (ASN 2193002). Others who served with him were Pvt. Jasper Blaine, Jesse Picotte, and Napoleon Ducheneaux. They sailed from New York aboard the *Aquitania* on April 2, 1918. In mid-July of 1918, the 30th

Regiment was in the front line along the Marne River. The unit suffered heavy casualties, including 25 officers and 1400 men. After the Armistice, Pfc. Bernie was evaluated by his Commanding Officer, Capt. Samuel Marshall. He wrote that Pfc. Bernie was a "Good Machine Gunner; courage is of the best; and his endurance is better than the average white man's. When suffering hardships there never was a complaint and if given an order I heard no complaint no matter how trying the circumstances. His senses are very keen." As part of the Army of Occupation, the Machine Gun Company was billeted at Metternich, Germany. Pfc. Bernie sailed from Brest, France, for home aboard the *America* on Aug. 12, 1919, and was discharged on Aug. 26, 1919.

After Oscar returned to South Dakota, he married Isabelle Zephier, whose brother, Wallace, had served in the Army. In the 1940 U.S. Census, they are listed with their children, Clifford, Bernard, Joseph, Thelma, Peter, Dorothy. Isabelle passed away in 1942. When Oscar registered for the Selective Service in 1942, he was living in Greenwood. Oscar hauled barrels of water from the river and sold them in town. He had a small boat that he used to harvest wild fruit from the Nebraska side of the Missouri River. He traded this fruit for eggs, milk, home-made bread and other produce. He also kept several horses in a pasture. In the late 1940s, Russell Means lived with his grandmother, who was Oscar's neighbor. Oscar let Russell and his brother ride his horses. Oscar entered the spirit world on Feb. 6, 1958.[23]

Big Mane, David. David was born near Bullhead on April 17, 1896. In the 1903 Census Roll, David is listed with his parents Adolph Big Mane and Tunkaskawin, who were Hunkpapa. David was inducted into the Army on June 24, 1918, but reported on Aug. 2, 1918, at Camp Funston, KS. He served as a Private in the 44th Company, 164th Depot Brigade (ASN 4262198). He was discharged on Dec. 3, 1918. In the 1920s, he married Mary Grant in Montana and lived on the Fort Peck Reservation for a number of years. In the 1940 U.S. Census, he was living in Dewey County with his wife, Rose Gabe, and their daughter, Doris. David passed away on March 12, 1945 and was buried in St John's Cemetery. After the dam construction, he was reinterred at the Episcopal Cemetery in LaPlant.

Big Owl, George. George was born on the Rosebud Reservation on March 22, 1889. His parents were Hinhan Tanka [Big Owl] and Lucy. His first wife was Ellen Bordeaux. When he registered for the draft on June 5, 1917, he was farming with his wife and son, William, at their home near White River. George enlisted in the Army on Oct. 6, 1917. He served with the Machine Gun Company of the 4th Infantry Regiment, 3rd Division (ASN 2214328). Pvt. Big Owl sailed from Newport News, VA, aboard the *Great Northern* on April 6, 1918. The 4th Infantry Regiment served in the Sectors at Aisne, Chateau-Thierry, Champagne-Marne, Aisne-Marne, St. Mihiel and Meuse-Argonne. Once the Armistice was signed, the 3rd Division marched into Germany for occupational duty. Pfc. Big Owl was evaluated by his commanding officer, stating that he "demonstrated special fitness for sniping and as a scout and MGs. As a scout he has shown keenness of senses, cool headedness, endurance and courage." Pfc. Big Owl sailed from St. Nazaire aboard the *Antigone* on May 17, 1919. He was traveling in St. Aignan Casual Co. #4487, Special Discharge. He was discharged on June 3, 1919. After he returned to South Dakota, he married Nettie Jumping Elk. George passed away on July 6, 1943, and is buried in Holy Family Cemetery, south of White River.[24]

Bingham, Leon. Leon was born in Hot Springs on July 31, 1889. In the 1893 Pine Ridge Census Roll, he was listed with his mother, Ettie. His father was Thomas Bingham. On June 26, 1912, he married Jennie Williams in Wagner. Leon lived in Ravinia. When he registered for the draft in 1917, he was living in Lake Andes. He joined the Army on June 27, 1918, and was assigned to Battery D,

337th Field Artillery, 88th Division (ASN 3315376). On Aug. 17, 1918, he left New York aboard the *Bohemian* with Battery D. The artillery units of the 88th Division did not serve at the Front. Pvt. Bingham sailed to the U.S. from Bordeaux on Jan. 7, 1919, aboard the *Sierra.* He was discharged on Jan. 31, 1919. His sister, Alice, married Louis Iron Shell, a fellow veteran. In the 1920 U.S. Census, Leon was living in the Winnebago Precinct, NE, and working as a janitor in the Agency Hospital. Later he was listed with the Santee Sioux at Yankton. In the 1942 draft, he was living in Harrington, in Todd County. He entered the spirit world in Hot Springs on Sept. 8, 1948. He is buried in Hot Springs.

Bird, Adam Feather. Adam, a Yanktonai, was born around 1894 on the Yankton Reservation. In the 1902 Census Roll, he was listed with his parents, Joseph Zitkana [Bird] and Mary Feather. He joined the SD National Guard on June 2, 1917. When the 4th SD Infantry arrived in Camp Greene, they were converted over to the 147th Field Artillery. Pvt. Bird served in Battery C. He was scheduled to leave for France with his regiment on Jan. 11, 1918, but was dropped from the rolls on Jan. 3, 1918. He received a medical discharge. He married Sarah Bago, with whom he had a daughter, Viola. On March 28, 1925, he married Jessie Crow at Tyndall. In the 1930 U.S. Census, they were farming in Rouse Township, Charles Mix County. Adam became ill with pneumonia and entered the spirit world on May 11, 1937, and is buried in the Presbyterian Cemetery near Greenwood.[25]

Bird, Nathan Porter. Nathan was born on the Sisseton Reservation to Alvin Bird and Angelique Crawford on July 25, 1899. When he registered for the draft on Sept. 12, 1918, he was living in Wilmot. He served in the Army from March 30, 1922 until March 29, 1925. In the 1930 U.S. Census, he was farming near Watertown. He married Hazel Simmons in 1934. When he registered for the "Old man's draft" in 1942, he was living in Denver. He later moved to Dupree. He entered the spirit world at Fort Meade Hospital on Sept. 1, 1979, and is buried in the Black Hills National Cemetery.

Birdhead, Otto Joseph. Otto was born in Niobrara, NE, on Sept. 1, 1895, the son of Peter and Bertha Birdhead. When he registered for the draft on June 5, 1917, he was working as a farm hand in Niobrara. He joined the Army on May 1, 1918, and was discharged as a Saddler on Feb. 18, 1919. In the Ponca Census Rolls for the 1920s, he is listed with the Yankton Agency in South Dakota. On June 10, 1925, he married Lulu Rose Leroy in Burke, SD. They had four children, Otto Jr., Dean, Leroy and Maxine. In the 1954 City Directory for Norfolk, NE, Otto was working as a roofer. Otto entered the spirit world on Dec. 17, 1976, and is buried in Ponca Indian Cemetery in Niobrara.

Black, James. James was born in North Dakota on the Standing Rock Reservation about June 5, 1893. In the 1913 Census Roll for Standing Rock, he is listed with his father, Black Prairie Dog, and his mother, Wamblipewin [Whose head is shaped like an eagle], as well as his other siblings. In some of the Census Rolls, he is listed as James Joseph Black Prairie Dog. A few years later he married Rose Alice Yellow Bird. When James registered for the draft on Sept. 11, 1918, he was working as a farm hand for the government at Fort Yates. Not long after this he enlisted in the Army. He reported that he had spent 3 days at Aberdeen, just before the Armistice was signed. In the 1930 Census, he was still living in Sioux County. In 1933, he married Olive One Skunk at Cherry Creek, on the Cheyenne River Reservation. In 1935, they were interviewed by a worker with the SDERA program. The family was living with their children in a tent about ¼ mile from the Cherry Creek School and store. In the 1940 U.S. Census, James was working as a laborer on a reservoir construction project. In 1946, James began working for the C & NW Railroad.

Blackbird, Thomas L. Thomas was born in the spring of 1898. In the Census Roll taken at Pine Ridge in 1898, Thomas, at age 2 months, is listed with his father, Zintkala Sapa [Blackbird], and his mother, Glinapa [Comes Out], and two older brothers, Isaac and Richard. Thomas likely attended the Haskell boarding school at Lawrence, KS. Thomas enlisted in the U.S. Army on March 2, 1917 (ASN 1466222). He first served with Battery B, First Regiment, Kansas Field Artillery, stationed in Lawrence, KS. During WWI he served in France as a Bugler in Battery B, 130th Field Artillery, 35th Division. He sailed from New York aboard the *Ceramic* on May 19, 1918. The 35th Division suffered heavy casualties in the opening fighting in the Meuse-Argonne Offensive. He sailed home from Brest, France, aboard the *Mobile* on April 13, 1919. He was discharged on May 10, 1919. After the war, he served in the Army for another 16 years. In the 1920 U.S. Census, he was stationed at Fort D.A. Russell in Cheyenne, WY. In the 1920s he transferred to Kansas, where he married Loretta Marie Day. In the 1930 U.S. Census, he was stationed at Fort Riley, KS, as a Corporal. After this he transferred to western New York, likely Fort Niagara. In the 1937 Census Roll for Pine Ridge, Thomas was listed as living in Niagara Falls, NY. He and his wife had a daughter, Mary Ann. In the 1940 U.S. Census, Thomas was working as a farm laborer. He later got a job with Harrison Radiator Division of General Motors Corp., and lived in Barker, NY. He last worked at the Lockport factory as a welder and solderer on Feb. 22, 1957. His body was found on April 28, 1957, near the shore of Lake Ontario, near the mouth of the Niagara River. His hands were tied behind his back. Thomas is buried in Riverdale Cemetery near Lewiston, NY.27

Black Cat, John. He is listed on WWI veteran's memorial at Oglala Lakota College, Kyle, SD. John was born on the Pine Ridge Reservation on Sept. 21, 1887. In the 1898 Census Roll for Pine Ridge, he is listed with his uncle, Itunkasan Gleska [Spotted Weasel] and his wives, Cedar and Wicincala. When John registered for the draft on June 5, 1917, he was working as a herder for Edgar Firethunder. When John joined the Army, he was assigned to Co. B, 157th Infantry Regiment, 40th Division (ASN 3135034). The 40th Division had trained at Camp Kearny, CA. Pvt Black Cat left Philadelphia with his unit aboard the *City of Bombay* on Aug. 7, 1918. In France, he was re-assigned to Co. K, 322nd Infantry, 81st Division as a Bugler. The 322nd Infantry served in the Sectors at St. Die and Meuse-Argonne. The 81st Division suffered 1224 casualties. The 322nd Infantry returned home aboard the *Matsonia*, which sailed from St. Nazaire on June 7, 1919. In the 1930 U.S. Census, John was farming in Bennett County with his wife, Bessie, and children, Joseph and Chris. John's aunt, Cedar, was also living with them. John entered the spirit world on Feb. 22, 1966, and is buried in the Inestimable Gift Cemetery in Allen, SD.

Joseph Francis Black Cloud

Ron Black Cloud

Black Cloud, Joseph Francis. Joseph was born in Wakpala, SD on April 4, 1891. In the 1894 Census Roll for Standing Rock, he is listed with his father, Black Cloud, and his mother, Appearing (Hinapewin). He entered the military service on July 21, 1918, at Camp Dodge, IA. Joseph was transferred to Fort Lee, VA, where he was in the 2nd Company, Veterinary Training School (ASN 3954585). On Nov. 4, 1918, Detachment #5, Veterinary Hospital # 18 sailed from Brooklyn aboard the *Manchurian Prince*. Private First-Class Black Cloud served with Veterinary Hospital #18 at

Sougy, France. Pfc. Black Cloud returned to the U.S. aboard the U.S.S. *Pretoria* on July 12, 1919. He was discharged on July 19, 1919. Joseph returned to Wakpala and married Elizabeth Houle. In 1935, they were living with their son, Ivan, in a log home about nine miles north of Wakpala. At that time, they owned four horses, but a number of years before, they owned 30 head of horses. In 1934, they had camped out near a dam construction site. However, someone had broken into their home and stole some carpenter's tools, a log chain and harness. People were uncomfortable leaving their home to go camp near one of the emergency conservation projects. The family later moved to Cannonball, ND, where Joseph died on July 3, 1941. He is buried in St. Elizabeth's Cemetery, Cannonball, ND.[28]

Black Eagle, Luke. Luke was born on the Cheyenne River Reservation on March 30. 1896. His parents were Justin Black Eagle and Louise Short Bear. When he registered for the draft on June 5, 1917, he was farming near Dupree. In September of 1917, the *Dupree Leader* reported that Luke was one of a group of men traveling to Fort Riley, KS, for military training. Among the group were John Slow, Thomas Hawk Eagle and James Bear Stops. Luke was likely discharged for medical reasons. John Slow was discharged on Nov. 24, 1917, and Luke may have returned home with him. Luke continued to farm near Dupree. Around 1926, he married Elizabeth Loves the War (1903-1965) from Standing Rock. Luke entered the spirit world at the PHS Indian Hospital in Eagle Butte on July 20, 1967. He is buried in St. Peter's Episcopal Cemetery in Thunder Butte.

Blackhorse, Frank. Frank was born on the Rosebud Reservation on Dec. 18, 1891. In the 1896 Census Roll, he is listed with his father, Louis Black Horse, and his mother, Nellie (Her Holy Hand). Louis had served as a Private in the 6th Cavalry from 1891-1894. As a young boy, Frank was known as Red Fish. Frank joined the Army on June 23, 1918, and was assigned to Co. E, 351st Infantry Regiment (ASN 3310028). Other local men who served in Co. E were Joseph Otterman, Ernest Bad Horse, Paul Eagle Deer, Joseph Beads, William Shooter and David Turning Bear. As part of the 88th Division, they arrived in England on Aug. 27, 1918. On Sept. 5, 1918, they crossed the Channel to France. Though the Division was not involved in the combat at the front, a number of soldiers did die from the flu. Two men from the Rosebud Reservation, Pfc. Joseph Otterman and Pvt. David Turning Bear died of the Spanish Influenza in France. After the Armistice, Pfc. Black Horse received an evaluation from his commanding officer stating that he was "quick and active. Very attentive to duty. Excellent man with automatic rifle." The 351st Infantry Regiment left France aboard the *Mercury* on May 20, 1919, and arrived Newport News, VA, on June 1. Pfc. Black Horse was discharged on June 6, 1919.

In the 1930 U.S. Census, Frank and his wife, Ellen, lived at Rosebud with their children, Harry, Faith and Charley White Pipe, a step son. In the late 1930s, Frank married Alice High Eagle. In the 1940 U.S. Census, Frank was living in Parmelee and making Indian relics. After 1945, Frank and Alice moved to Denver. Frank entered the spirit world on Sept. 14, 1967. He is buried in Fort Logan National Cemetery, Section R, Site 653. Alice (1902-1972) is buried with him. Frank had a younger brother, **Francis**, who also served in the military. Francis was born on May 11, 1898. He enlisted in the Army and served as a Private in the 4th Cavalry from Dec. 16, 1926, to Jan. 3, 1931. In the 1930 U.S. Census, he was stationed at Fort Meade, SD. Francis entered the spirit world on June 6, 1932, and is buried in a cemetery near Bad Nation.[29]

Blacksmith, Raymond A. Raymond was born on Nov. 21, 1895, in Santee, NE. His parents were Stephen and Elizabeth Blacksmith. When he registered for the draft, he was living in Wagner, SD, and worked for John Omaha at Greenwood. Raymond joined the Army at Lake Andes, SD, on

June 27, 1918, and was assigned to Co. D, 313th Supply Train, 88th Division (ASN 3315339). Pvt. Blacksmith sailed with his unit from New York aboard the *Empress of Britian* on Aug. 24, 1918. After providing occupational duty, the 313th Supply Train returned to the U.S. from St. Nazaire aboard the *Canonicus* on May 21, 1919. Pfc. Blacksmith was discharged on June 15, 1919. Raymond had married Winnie Hedges before the war. In the 1930 U.S. Census, they were living in Greenwood with their children, Edward and Mildred. In 1938, Raymond married Mabel Frazier. In 1940, they lived in Huron, where Raymond worked as a truck driver in a CCC camp. A fellow veteran from the Greenwood community, Peter Frederick, also worked in that camp. In 1948, Raymond was working as a laborer for Armour and Co. His wife, Mable, worked at reupholstering sofas and chairs. Her grandson, Russell Means, and his parents were staying with the family in Huron. Raymond entered the spirit world on Oct. 15, 1969, and is buried in the Protestant Cemetery in Marty, SD.[30]

Blacksmith, Thomas. Thomas was born in July 1899, on the Cheyenne River Reservation. In the 1900 Census Roll for Cheyenne River, he is listed with his parents, John Blacksmith and Laura Lazy White Bull. In the 1910 U.S. Census, he is listed with his grandparents, Moses and Jannie. Thomas enlisted in the Army at Jefferson Barracks, MO, on March 24, 1918. He was assigned to Troop D, 7th Cavalry (ASN 472672). He was discharged as a Private on April 19, 1919, at Ft. Bliss, TX. He re-enlisted. In the 1920 U.S. Census, he was a Corporal at Ft. Bliss. In the 1930 U.S. Census, he was living on the Cheyenne River Reservation with his wife, Ida Black Elk, and their two children, Laura and Bernard. They had another son, Hugh. Thomas suffered from tuberculosis and was admitted to Battle Mountain Sanitarium on Nov. 3, 1935. He entered the spirit world in Hot Springs on Jan. 14, 1936. He is buried in St. Peter's Cemetery in Oglala, SD.

Black Spotted Horse, Paul. Paul was born on the Rosebud Reservation around Aug. 16, 1896. His parents were Black Spotted Horse and Her Blanket. Paul attended a day school from 1902-1905 and the Mission School at St. Francis from 1905-1909. He attended Carlisle from 1909-1912. In the 1910 U.S. Census, he was working as a hired man for a farmer in West Amwell, NJ. When Paul registered for the draft on June 5, 1917, he was doing construction work for Bro. Andrew Hartman at St. Francis. Paul enlisted at Rosebud on July 22 1918 and was assigned to the Air Service. He was discharged in Garden City, Long Island, NY, as a Private on Dec. 13, 1918, probably for medical reasons. After his discharge he lived in Rosebud with his wife, Lena. Paul was admitted to the Battle Mountain Sanatorium on Sept. 9, 1927. He entered the spirit world on Sept. 30, 1927, at the veteran's hospital in Hot Springs. The hospital sent a flag with his casket to Lena. He is buried in Saint Charles Cemetery in St. Francis, SD.

Black Tomahawk, Joseph. Joseph was born on the Rosebud Reservation on Nov. 25, 1893. In the 1900 U.S. Census, he was a student at the Mission School in St. Francis. When he registered for the draft on June 5, 1917, he was farming near St. Francis. Joseph likely joined the Army in the spring of 1918. He was assigned to Co. C, 350th Infantry Regiment (ASN 3315763). As part of the 88th Division, they sailed from New York on August 11, 1918. Pfc. Black Tomahawk was a passenger on the H.M.S. *Delta*, along with Pvt. Louis Big Horn Elk from Fort Yates, ND. Company C was assigned to Decks "B" and "F." Upon arriving in England, they disembarked at Tillbury-on-Thames. Three days later they marched to the port city of Southampton. They sailed for Cherbourg, France aboard the S.S. *Maid of Orleans*. They were then billeted in Torcy. As part of the Intelligence Platoons for the 350th Regiment, Pfc. Black Tomahawk was one of the scouts for the First Battalion. After the Armistice, his commanding officer evaluated him, saying of Pfc. Black Tomahawk, "excellent character, excellent soldier." The 350th Infantry was stationed near Gondrecourt, France until early May of 1919. On May 19, 1919, the 350th Regiment sailed from St. Nazaire, France, aboard the

U.S.S. *Aeolus*. Around the first week of June, the men were discharged at Camp Dodge, IA. Pfc. Black Tomahawk was included in a group photo that was published in the regimental history. In 1921, Joseph was a member of the Chauncey Eagle Horn Legion Post in Rosebud. In the 1940 U.S. Census, Joseph was living in St. Francis with his wife, Mary, and son, James. He was working as a laborer on a road construction project. Joseph entered the spirit world on Sept. 29, 1967, and is buried in Saint Charles Cemetery in St. Francis.[31]

Black Tongue, John. John was born on the Cheyenne River Reservation on Oct. 30, 1900. In the 1902 Census Roll for the Cheyenne River, he is listed with his parents, William Black Tongue and Carrie Blue Beaver. William had served as a scout in the Army from 1876-77. When John registered for the draft on Sept. 12, 1918, he was living in Promise. Sometime after this he enlisted in the Army. When he was interviewed in 1935 by a worker for the SDERA program, he said he had served two years in military training at Fort Snelling, MN. He also told the interviewer that he had worked for five years on the tent crew for Barnum and Bailey Circus. In 1929, he married Helen Pratt. In 1930 John had a stroke, after which he had trouble walking. In 1935, the family was living in the White Horse District. Their home was located on a winding trail four miles from a main road. Their water was obtained from the Moreau River, about ¼ mile away. The school at Promise was eight miles away. They had three children, Thelma, Carolyn and Melvina. John entered the spirit world on Dec. 23, 1936, and was buried near Promise.[32]

Blaine, Albert. Albert was born around Oct. 30 1893, in Greenwood, SD. His father, James, was Yanktonai and his mother, Josephine, was Santee. In the 1911 Census Roll, Albert is listed with his wife, Mary Sitting Crow. When he registered for the draft on June 4, 1917, he was working for his father. Albert enlisted on June 27, 1918, and was assigned to Battery E, 30th Field Artillery (ASN 3315340). The 30th Field Artillery was part of the 10th Division, which remained in the U.S, and was demobilized at Camp Funston. Charles Picotte also served with Albert in Battery E. Pfc. Blaine was discharged on Jan. 26, 1919. Shortly after, he married Ruth Hare. In the 1930 U.S. Census, their oldest son, Albert Jr. was a patient at the hospital in Canton, SD. In the 1934 Census Roll, Albert is listed with his children, Albert Jr. and Melissa. Albert accidently drowned on July 28, 1936. He is buried in the Presbyterian Cemetery in Greenwood, SD.

Blaine, George. George was the younger brother of Albert. George was born on August 12, 1895. George likely enlisted in the 4th Infantry, SD National Guard in the summer of 1917. When his regiment arrived at Camp Greene, NC, in September of 1917, he was reassigned to Battery C, 147th Field Artillery (ASN 139472). Pvt. Blaine sailed with his unit from New York aboard the *Olympic* on Jan. 11, 1918. For much of the war, the 147th FA was attached to the 32nd Division and served in the Sectors at Toul-Boucq, Center, Aisne-Marne, Fismes, Oise-Aisne, Avocourt, and Meuse-Argonne. After the Armistice, his commanding officer, 1st Lt. A.M. Knudtson, wrote an evaluation saying that Pvt. Blaine was "a very good horseman." The 147th Field Artillery sailed from Brest, France on May 1, 1919, aboard the U.S.S. *Kansas,* one of the Navy's battleships. After the war, George married Josephine James. In the 1930 U.S. Census, George and his brother, Albert, lived with their uncle near Greenwood. In the 1937 Census Roll, George is listed with Josephine and their daughter, Rosie. George entered the spirit world at his home in Greenwood on Oct. 4, 1980. He is buried in the Presbyterian Cemetery near Greenwood.[33]

Blaine, Jasper. Jasper was born May 23, 1893, near Greenwood, SD. His parents were Steven and Sarah Blaine. Around 1915, Jasper married Jennie Comes Out Bear. When Jasper registered for the draft in 1917, he was farming with his wife near St. Charles in Gregory County. He enlisted in the Army on Sept. 22, 1917. He was assigned to the Machine Gun (MG) Company, 30th Infantry Regiment (ASN 2193289). As part of the Third Division, they sailed for France aboard the Aquitania on April 2, 1918. The 30th Infantry took part in the fighting along the Marne River in June. In the fighting in June and July, the regiment suffered casualties of 25 officers and 1400 men. In the Meuse-Argonne Offensive in September-November, their casualties were 48 officers and 1438 men. After the Armistice, Pvt. Blaine's commanding officer, Samuel Marshall, wrote an evaluation stating that Blaine displayed "courage and endurance exceptional, his senses are very keen. He has done good work in bringing up rations at night." When the roads were impassable, donkeys were used to haul the rations. As part of the occupational forces in Germany, the MG Company was billeted in Metternich. Pvt. Blaine sailed from Brest aboard the *America* on Aug. 12, 1919. After Pvt. Blaine returned to the U.S. he was assigned to Casual Detachment 1311 to help in the demobilization process for the returning soldiers. Pvt. Blaine received his honorable discharge on Aug. 26, 1919.

After the war, he married Cordelia Black Eagle. Jasper and Cordelia lived with Jasper's parents and farmed near Greenwood. In the mid-1930s, Japer lived with his family in a farm house located 10 miles north of Wagner. Due to the drought, their well went dry, so they hauled water from the river. At that time, Jasper worked at hauling coal to the Crow Creek Agency. In the 1940 U.S. Census, they are listed with their children, Florence, Arthur, Oliver and Earlwin. Jasper entered the spirit world in Wagner on Nov. 24, 1944 and is buried in the Presbyterian Cemetery in Greenwood.[34]

Blue Bird, John. John was born on July 6, 1895, in St. Charles, SD. His parents were Joseph and Susan Bluebird. After his father died, his mother married Felix Buckman. They were enrolled on the Rosebud Reservation. John's sister, Lizzie, was married to Silas LeClaire, who also served in the war. When John registered for the draft on June 5, 1917, he was married and living in Gregory County. When he enlisted in the Army, he was initially assigned to Co. A, 333rd Infantry, 84th Division (ASN 3954873). This unit sailed from New York aboard the *Baltic* on Sept. 1, 1918. The 84th Division was used to supply replacements for divisions who had heavy casualties. Pvt. Bluebird was reassigned to Co. H, 312th Infantry Regiment, 78th Division. The 312th Infantry served in the Sectors at Limey and Meuse-Argonne. The 78th Division suffered 7,245 casualties. After the fighting had ended, Pfc. Bluebird was evaluated by his commanding officer, Capt. J.A.W. Simson, who wrote that Pfc. Bluebird was "an excellent all-around soldier." Pfc. Bluebird sailed home from Bassens, France, with his unit aboard the U.S.S. *Montpelier* on May 11, 1919. After his discharge, he returned to the St. Charles area. He married Bertha Knudson, with whom he had a son, Orlo. He later married Olive Archambeau. They had a daughter, Lucille. In the 1937 Rosebud Census Roll, John is listed with Orlo and Lucille. In the 1945 South Dakota Census, John was living in Ellston, SD. He later lived near Naper, NE. When he registered for the Selective Service in 1942, he was working in Naper. John last lived just north of the Nebraska State Line, north of Naper. He entered the spirit world in the Indian Hospital in Wagner on June 14, 1962. He is buried in the Congregational Cemetery, six miles SW of St. Charles. Military rites were conducted by the Allen Louden American Legion Post No. 220 of Herrick.[35]

Blue Coat, Robert. Robert was born on the Cheyenne River Reservation on Nov. 19, 1894. His parents were Philip and Carrie Blue Coat. Robert enlisted in the Army on Jan. 26, 1918. He was assigned to Co. F, 314th Ammo Train, 89th Division (ASN 2195232), which trained at Camp Funston, KS. He served with Louis Brings Three White Horses and Fred Fast Horse. Pvt. Blue Coat sailed from New York aboard the *Cretic* on June 28, 1918. The 314th Ammo Train was billeted near Bordeaux with the Field Artillery Regiments, before moving to the Euvezin Sector in the Lorraine.

The 89th Division suffered 7,291 casualties in the war. After the Armistice, Pvt. Blue Coat received an evaluation from his commanding officer, 1st Lt. Frank Brannigan, stating that he was "a reliable soldier. Prefers Cavalry. Good night worker, runner and observer. He did not have an opportunity for scouting." The final billeting for the 314th Ammunition Train was at Bitburg, Germany. The 314th sailed from France aboard the ship *Agamemnon*, which arrived in New York on May 24, 1919. Pvt. Blue Bird was discharged at Camp Dodge, IA, on June 4, 1919. In Nov. 1919, Robert married Lillian Horse with Horns. In the 1930 U.S. Census, their family was living with Lillian's parents. In the 1937 Cheyenne River Census Roll, they are listed with their children, Robert Jr., Cora, Alberta, Jerry Ruby, Rose. Robert entered the spirit world on Sept. 10, 1968, at the VA hospital in Hot Springs. He is buried in On The Tree Cemetery near Eagle Butte, SD.[36]

Blue Coat, Thomas. Thomas was born on the Cheyenne River Reservation on Sept. 15, 1891. He was Robert's older brother. He married Lilly Mann on May 23, 1913. Their first daughter, Linda, was born in 1914. When Thomas registered for the draft on June 4, 1917, he was supporting his wife and daughter, as well as his father and younger brother. Thomas joined the Army at Timber Lake on Aug. 28, 1918. He spent about three months in training after being assigned to 3rd Company, 3rd Battalion, 164th Depot Brigade. He was discharged as a Private at Camp Funston on Dec. 5, 1918. After returning home, he continued to farm. The dry years in the 1930s made it hard to raise a crop and put up feed for livestock. In 1935, the family was living in a log home in the Green Grass Precinct. Their drinking water was hauled four miles from a dam. The family was interviewed by a worker with the SDERA program. Thomas indicated he was making plans to buy 600 head of cattle. Their children were Samuel, Homer, Joseph, Severt and Norman. Homer served in the Army during WWII, and Norman served in the Korean Conflict with the Army. Thomas entered the spirit world in the Indian Hospital in Eagle Butte on Jan. 5, 1979 and is buried in St. Thomas Episcopal Cemetery near Eagle Butte.[37]

Blue Horse, William J. William was born on the Rosebud Reservation on Feb. 9, 1900. In the 1910 U.S. Census, he was listed with his parents Blue Horse and Anna. William likely enlisted in the 4th SD Infantry in the spring of 1917, before being sent to Camp Greene in North Carolina in September of 1917. He was then reassigned to Co. B, 148th Machine Gun (MG) Battalion (41st Division) (ASN 112170). On Jan. 11, 1918, the 148th MG Battalion sailed from Hoboken, NJ, for France with Transport No. 527. Upon arrival in France, many of these soldiers were reassigned to the 42nd Division. Pvt. Blue Horse served with Company C, 151st Machine Gun (MG) Battalion. The 151st MG Battalion served in the Sectors at Luneville, Baccarat, Esperance-Souain, Champagne-Marne, Aisne-Marne, St. Mihiel, Essey-Pannes, Meuse-Argonne. He likely was wounded or gassed. He sailed home from Brest, France, on April 1, 1919, on the *Mauretania*. He was traveling with Camp Dodge Detachment 12A, 337th Infantry, 85th Division. He was discharged as a Private 1st Class. In the 1920 U.S. Census, he was living with his father and his sister, Irene, who was married to Dick Fool Bull. In the 1930 U.S. Census, he was ranching with Dick Fool Bull and Irene. In the 1940 U.S. Census, he was living with his wife, Kate, and their children, Irene and Marie. William entered the spirit world at his home near St. Francis on Dec. 15, 1964 and is buried in St. Charles Cemetery in St. Francis.[38]

Bonnin, Barnabe Conger. Conger was born May 28, 1896, near Wagner, SD. His parents, Henry and Mercy Bonnin were Yanktonai. When Conger registered for the draft on June 5, 1917, he was handling "Indian curios" for a traveling carnival. At that time, he was in Dixon, IL, with the Ed Evans Carnival Co. In the fall of 1917, he married his first wife, Rosalie. In the summer of 1918, he joined the Army and was stationed at Camp Funston, KS. He served in a machine gun company, 69th

Infantry, 10th Division. While at Camp Funston, he was captain of the Camp Funston football team. He was discharged as a Private 1st Class on Jan. 26, 1919. In the 1920 U.S. Census, he and Rosalie were living in Wagner with his parents. His father was Postmaster, while Conger was a postal employee. In the 1930 U.S. Census, Conger was living with his children and second wife, Mae, on a farm near Wagner. In the early 1930s, they moved to a ranch near Sweetwater, WY, where Conger was the manager. He last lived at Rock Springs, but passed away while visiting in El Cajon, CA, on Feb. 8, 1976. He and his wife, Mae (1905-1962), are buried in Riverview Cemetery in Green River, WY. His oldest son, Edwin, served in the Army in WWII. His second son, Cassius, served 10 years in the U.S. Navy.[39]

Bonnin, Raymond T. Raymond was born near Wagner, SD, on June 17, 1880. His parents were Joseph and Emily Bonnin. Raymond was a brother to Henry, the father of Conger. He married Gertrude Simmons on May 10, 1902. Gertrude was a writer who often used the name, Zitkala-Sa, or Redbird. In 1921 she published her book, *American Indian Stories.* In 1903, Raymond and Zitkala-Sa moved to Utah, where Raymond had a job as an issue clerk with the Indian Service. While in Utah, their son, Ohiya, was born. They lived in Utah until Raymond enlisted in the Army on Aug. 14, 1917. He served as a Captain with the Quartermaster Corps in Washington, D.C. One of his jobs was obtaining food for the Army. He also represented the Army on the price determining board for foods. Capt. Bonnin was discharged on Aug. 18, 1919. In the 1920 U.S. Census, Raymond was in the real estate business. Zitkala-Sa's occupation was listed as "Lecturer on Indians." During the war, she had served as the secretary of the Society of American Indians. In the 1930 U.S. Census, Raymond was a clerk in a law office, while Zitkala-Sa was writing about Indian Welfare. She passed away on Jan. 26, 1938. Raymond passed away on Sept. 24, 1942. They are buried in Arlington National Cemetery.[40]

Bonser, Delmar F. Delmar was born on the Rosebud Reservation to William and Mattie Bonser on Oct. 12, 1890. When he registered for the draft on May 31, 1917, he was working as a traveling salesman in Duluth, MN. He joined the Army and was assigned to Truck Co. C, Army Artillery Park, Coast Artillery Corps (ASN 821583). Sgt. Bonser sailed with his unit from New York aboard the *Chicago* on June 29, 1918. After the Armistice, 1st Sgt. Bonser sailed from Pauillac, France, aboard the *Canonicus* on April 19, 1919. In 1925, he was working as a traveling salesman in Sioux Falls, SD. Later that year, he married Lela Mae Wilson in North Carolina. During the 1930s, he lived in Brookings, SD. At the start of WWII, he re-enlisted in the Army. When he registered with the Selective Service in 1942, known as the "old man's draft," he indicated that he had just been released from the Army. In 1954, he was living in Los Angeles. Delmar entered the spirit world in San Bernadino on April 4, 1966. He is buried in Ft. Rosecrans National Cemetery. His headstone lists his WWI and WWII service as a 1st Sgt. with the 320th Sta. Hospital.

Harry H. Bonser
Carlisle Website

Bonser, Harry H. Harry was born on Dec. 16, 1892, to William and Mattie Bonser on the Rosebud Reservation. He was a brother to Jack Bonser. As a student, he attended school at Pipestone and Rapid City before going to the Carlisle boarding school. He was a classmate and friend of Jim Thorpe. In 1914, Harry married Cecelia DuCharme, a Kootenai who had also attended Carlisle. Around 1916, Harry took a job in Knoxville, TN, while trying to obtain title to some land on the Rosebud Reservation. The Agent at Rosebud did not approve his Patent, so he returned to farm his wife's land on the Flathead Reservation. When Harry registered for the draft on June 16, 1917, He and Cecile were ranching near Polson with their two oldest children.

Harry enlisted in the U.S. Marine Corps on Oct. 21, 1918, and was discharged as a Private on Feb. 10, 1919. He served in Co. C, Recruit Depot at Mare Island, CA. Cecelia entered the spirit world in 1928. In the 1930 U.S. Census, Harry was living with his children and his mother, Mattie, in Missoula, MT. His children were Theresa, Ethel, Emerald, Dorothy, Gretchen, Rachel and Mildred. Harry was working as a custodian in the federal building. In the 1940 U.S. Census, Harry was teaching music in Ronan Lake. When he registered for the Selective Service in 1942, he was working for the Post Office in Sacramento, CA. He had also joined the USMC Reserves on March 25, 1942, and was discharged on Oct. 14, 1943, likely as a Corporal. He served as a guard at the Naval Yard at Bremerton, WA. After the war he continued to work at the Sacramento Post Office. In 1954, he received a twenty-year pin for government service. He was a member of the Disabled American Veterans. Harry entered the spirit world at his home in Sacramento on Aug. 13, 1960. His daughters, Mrs. Fred Montgomery, Mrs. Emerald French, Mrs. Dorothy Dolan, Gretchen Scalese, Mrs. Paul Tomljanovich, and Mrs. Fred Gerber, survived him. He is buried in the veteran's section of the Sacramento City Cemetery.[41]

Laverne Jack Bonser
Ancestry.com

Bonser, Laverne Jack. Laverne Jack was born on the Rosebud Reservation on April 12, 1896. His parents were William and Mattie Bonser. He attended the Pipestone boarding school from 1907-1913. After that he attended the Carlisle boarding school from October 1913 to August 1915. Laverne joined the Army on June 24, 1918, most likely at Camp Funston, KS. Men were sent from Camp Funston to Camp Dodge, IA, where the various regiments of the 88th Division were preparing to go overseas. Private Bonser was assigned to Battery E, 338th Field Artillery (ASN 3315606). The 338th sailed from Hoboken, NJ, on the *Tras Os Montes* on Aug. 18, 1918. Upon arrival in France, the regiment was billeted at Camp de Souge near Bordeaux, where they received extensive training. The 338th did not go to the Front when the rest of the 88th Division was moved forward. After the Armistice was signed on November 11th, the unit was ordered to begin turning in their equipment. The 338th sailed from France on Dec. 24, 1918, aboard the *Pocohontas*. He was traveling with the Camp Funston Casual Co., Artillery unassigned, 338th FA. Pvt. Bonser was discharged at Camp Dodge, IA, on Jan. 17, 1919.

Jack married Anna Desersa (1897-1942) in 1919. In 1921, he was a member of the Chauncey Eagle Horn Legion Post No. 125. In the 1930 U.S. Census, Laverne was working for a truck driver in Crookston, NE. In the 1937 Census Roll for Rosebud, they are listed with their children, Roy, William, Virginia, Robert, Alverna, Ruby, Audrey and Shirley. In the 1940 U.S. Census, the family was living in Rosebud where Laverne was working as an auto mechanic in the government garage. The family later moved to Aurora, CO. Laverne entered the spirit world on July 26, 1972, and is buried in St. Charles Cemetery in St. Francis, SD. His sons, Francis and William served in WWII.[42]

Bordeaux, Francis. Francis was born on June 17, 1895, on the Rosebud Reservation. In the 1895 Census Roll, he is listed with his parents, Charles and Agatha Bordeaux. When he registered for the draft on June 5, 1917, he was farming with his father near White River. Francis joined the Army on June 23, 1918, and was assigned to Battery A, 337th Field Artillery (FA), 88th Division (ASN 3310019). Pvt. Bordeaux sailed from New York aboard the *Bohemian* on Aug. 17, 1918, and first landed in Liverpool, England on Aug. 31. Once in France, the 337th FA was trained with 155 mm guns at Clermont-Ferrand, east of Bordeaux. This training was completed shortly before the Armistice, so the 337th FA did not serve at the Front. On Nov. 30, they received orders to report to Bordeaux, France. Everybody was deloused and issued new uniforms. Pfc. Bordeaux sailed with his unit from Bordeaux aboard the *Sierra* on Jan. 7, 1919 and was discharged on Jan. 31, 1919. Francis told his family that the locals in Bordeaux were fascinated by his last name. They accepted him as a relative. "I was treated like royalty." He also spoke about the food being so good. He also spoke about the place he stayed in Bordeaux; the bed coverings were a puffy, feather tick that was warm and comfortable.

Francis Bordeaux
Ron Bordeaux family

Francis married Caroline (Carrie) Roubideaux (1896-1990) on Feb. 8, 1920. They lived in the White River community. In the 1940 U.S. Census, Francis was a catechist for the St. Ignatius Catholic Church. Francis and Carrie were listed with their children, Laurine, Pansy, Francis, Arline, Joyce, Jackson, Narcisse, and the twins, Christopher and Chester. Christopher served in the Air Force, while Chester and Narcisse served in the Army. Francis entered the spirit world in the hospital at Rosebud on July 20, 1979 and is buried in St Ignatius Cemetery in White River. His sons, Chester and Narcisse served in the Army.[43]

Bowker, William C. William was born on Oct. 13, 1891, at Ft. Pierre, SD. His mother, Anna, was from the Cheyenne River Reservation, but she died when he was about two years old. William's father, Matthew Bowker was from England. After Anna died, he married Nancy Quits Him. Matthew had served as a scout with the 2nd U.S. Infantry at Fort Sully. When William registered for the draft on 1917, he was living in LaPlant. When asked to list his employer, he wrote, "no one in particular." William enlisted on Sept. 22, 1917. He took the train to Camp Funston, accompanied by Armstrong Four Bear, Napoleon Ducheneaux, Kiutus Jim, and Basil Flanagan. Pvt. Bowker was assigned to the Machine Gun (MG) Company of the 38th Infantry Regiment, 3rd Division (ASN 2193003). His unit sailed from Halifax, N.S., aboard the British steamship *Corsican* on March 25, 1918. The *Corsican* docked at Glasgow, Scotland. The 38th Infantry took a train to southern England and sailed to France aboard the *Austrilind*. On April 11, the MG Company arrived at their assigned billet in Arc-en-Barrois. By early June, they were on the Front at Chateau-Thierry. They helped hold off a drive by the Germans. The 38th earned its nickname, "Rock of the Marne" in the fighting in June and July. The total casualties of the enlisted men from the 38th Regiment in the war was 500 killed, 2092 wounded and 307 missing. After the Armistice, the Machine Gun Company was billeted in Obermendig, Germany, as part of the Army of Occupation. Pfc. Bowker sailed from Brest aboard the *Agamemnon* on Aug. 11, 1919 and was discharged on Aug. 24, 1919.

William married Cecelia Chasing Crow on Jan. 15, 1922, at Timber Lake. In the 1930 U.S. Census, William and Cecelia were living with their children, Melda and Emily, in the Agency Precinct. In 1935, they were interviewed by a social worker for the SDERA program. The family was living in an 18' x 21' cabin. They carried their water from the river in buckets, up to ¾ mile away. William said he had been a member of the American Legion when it had been active. He also said that at one time he had owned 150 head of horses. He spoke of health problems and had checked into the hospital at Hot Springs, where they told him nothing was wrong. William entered the spirit world at the Hot Springs hospital from tuberculosis on May 27, 1939. He was buried at St. John's Episcopal Cemetery, but later re-interred in St. Pauls Cemetery, LaPlant, SD.[44]

Boyer, James. James was born in 1902 in Porcupine, SD. In the 1904 Census Roll for Pine Ridge, he is listed with his parents, John and Lucy Boyer. His father had served as a scout in the Army. James enlisted at the age of 15, to serve as a Bugler with 6th Nebraska Infantry at Chadron. He trained at Camp Cody, NM, where the 34th Division was formed. He was assigned to Headquarters Co., 109th Engineers, 34th Division (ASN 1438199). Bugler Boyer sailed from New York aboard the *Cretic* on Sept. 17, 1918. After the war, he headed home from St. Nazaire aboard the *Pastores* on June 17, 1919. After he was discharged, he filled out a questionnaire for Joseph Dixon. He described his experiences.

> The only experience I had in the war is I found out that Army life is a tough life for a kid for I was only 15 years of age when I enlisted. Was very glad to see the European Country. Especially the time I was in Paris.
>
> I would like to ask you why they don't give us our patents & our rights. After serving with the U.S. Army through the World War. A lot of our boys would like to become citizens. I would like to get my citizenship papers & also my rights, so would like to have you help one to get it.

In the 1920 U.S. Census, James was farming with his father on the Pine Ridge Reservation. James entered the spirit world on March 20, 1922, and is buried in St. Paul Cemetery in Porcupine. His father, John, entered the spirit world in 1940.[45]

Brave Bird, Elmer. Elmer was born on the Rosebud Reservation around 1900 to Edward and Rosa Brave Bird. During the war, he served as a Seaman 1st Class in the Navy. In the 1920 U.S, Census, he was stationed at Fort Mills, The Philippines. In the 1937 Rosebud Census Roll, he was listed with his wife, Elizabeth, and their children, Gladys, Lenabelle, Noah, Sterling, Cleveland and Roman. In the 1940 U.S. Census, he was working on a road construction project. He entered the spirit world in 1977, and is buried St. Charles Cemetery in St. Francis.

Brave Boy, Alexander. Alexander was born on the Rosebud Reservation about July 2, 1899. His parents were George and Millie Brave Boy. In the 1900 U.S. Census, he is listed with his parents and brother, Joseph, and sisters, Nellie and Emma. Alex joined the Army on Feb. 1, 1918, and was assigned to the 499th Aero Squadron, Air Service (ASN 1335485). Pvt. Brave Boy sailed with his unit from Newport News, VA, aboard the *M. Washington* on Oct. 21, 1918. The 499th Aero Squadron did construction work in France. He served with Pfc. Jacob Douglas, from the Standing Rock Reservation. After the Armistice, Cpl. Brave Boy sailed from St. Nazaire aboard the *Mexican* on Feb. 20, 1919, and was discharged on March 22, 1919. After returning home, he married Nellie Andrews (1907-1988). In the 1937 Census Roll, they are listed with two daughters, Mary and Glorietta. They farmed near Bad Nation, Mellette County. Alex entered the spirit world on Nov. 21, 1948, and is buried in Bad Nation Cemetery.

Brave Crow, Samuel. Samuel Louis was born near Bullhead, SD, on December 7, 1890. In the 1906 Census Roll, Louis is listed with his parents, Kangiohitika [Brave Crow] and Hocokainyanke

[Running Center], and his brother, Walter Steven. Samuel entered the military on June 24, 1918. He was sent to Camp Funston, KS, and was assigned to the 38th Company, 164th Depot Brigade (ASN 3309357). He later served as a Pfc. with Co. E, 2nd Battalion, Chemical Warfare Service (CWS). Private Brave Crow received an honorable discharge on March 8, 1919. Sam married Julia Hawk on June 1, 1920. They had a daughter, Mildred. Sam served as the Vice-Commander of the American Legion Post in 1928. They were interviewed by a state worker with the SDERA program. In 1935, the family was living in a tent in the Bullhead Precinct. Their home site was about ¾ mile from the school, where their daughter could attend. Sam did carpentry work and planned on finishing the home he had started. He was an active member of the American Legion, while Julia was a member of the Auxiliary. Sam owned a Model-T Ford. He suffered from Leukemia and entered the spirit world on June 27, 1938, and is buried in St. Aloysius Cemetery in Bullhead.[46]

Brave Crow, Steven W. Walter Steven was born near Bullhead, SD, on March 23, 1896. He was the younger brother of Samuel. Steven served as a Private First Class in the 69th Infantry Regiment with Eugene Young Hawk. He became a member of the American Legion. After the war, he married Mary Cedar. In 1935, the family was living in a home they rented from the Episcopal Church. He worked as a truck driver for the Indian Emergency Conservation Work. In the 1937 Census Roll, they are listed with their children, Amelia, Albert and Richard. In 1960, he married Marie Brave Crow. They had three children, Dale, Gale and Etta. Steven worked as a heavy equipment operator, and served as the Commander of Legion Post 82. Marie was also very active in local veteran's auxiliary groups. In 1991 she received an Award from the National American Legion Auxiliary President. Steven entered the spirit world in his home in Bullhead on April 3, 1974. He is buried in St. John's Episcopal Cemetery, Bullhead. Marie entered the spirit world on July 4, 2011.[47]

Brave Thunder, John. John was born around 1883 near Little Eagle, on the Standing Rock Reservation. In 1910, he married Medith Dog Eagle at Fort Yates, ND. They ranched in the Bear Creek on the Cheyenne River Reservation, where Medith was enrolled. In 1935, the couple was interviewed by a worker for the SDERA program. At that time, they were living in a tent near the Bear Creek Dam Site. John indicated that he had served in the Army during WWI. That summer, they managed to grow some vegetables in their garden, near Bear Creek. They owned eight horses, a cow and calf, and a rooster. John said that in better years he usually planted up to 27 acres of corn and oats for feed. John entered the spirit world on April 11, 1955, in the Indian Hospital in Fort Yates. He is buried in the Elk Horn Church cemetery in Little Eagle.[48]

Brings Plenty, Daniel. Daniel was also known as Daniel Iron Bull. He was born on the Pine Ridge Reservation around June 5, 1901. As a child, he moved with his family to Cherry Creek on the Cheyenne River Reservation. When he registered for the draft on Sept. 12, 1918, he was living with his step father, Charles Little Crow. Daniel joined the Army on Feb. 14, 1927, and served as a Private in Troop B, 4th Cavalry at Fort Meade. He was discharged on April 1, 1930. After this he lived with his brother, Hobson. In the 1937 Census Roll, he was living with his wife, Amy Lee. He entered the spirit world on May 11, 1972.

Brings Three White Horses, Louis. Louis was born in November 1890, near White River, SD. In the 1909 Census Roll for the Rosebud Reservation, he is listed with his parents, Levi and Lizzie. When Louis registered for the draft on June 5, 1917, he was married and farming near Wood, SD. The 1917 Census Roll for Rosebud lists him with his wife, Lucy Stands and Looks Back. After he was drafted in October 1917, his wife became ill. He was very unhappy when the Army would not let him go home to be with her. Louis eventually served with Co. F, 314th Ammunition Train, 89th

Division (ASN 2195337). He served with Robert Blue Coat and Fred Fast Horse. The 314th Ammo Train sailed from New York aboard the *Cretic* on June 28, 1918. Upon arrival in France, they were billeted with the Field Artillery regiments near Bordeaux. After the Armistice, his commanding officer, 1st Lt. Frank Brannigan, wrote an evaluation, saying that Pvt. White Horse was "a good horseman. Good night worker, verbal reporter and observer. No opportunity for scouting. Prefers cavalry." As part of the Army of Occupation, Pvt. White Horse was billeted in Bitburg, Germany. The 314th Ammo Train left France aboard the *Agamemnon* on May 16, 1919 and arrived in New York on May 24. The unit was discharged at Camp Dodge, IA. His wife, Lucy, had died while he was overseas. After he returned, he married Lucy's sister, Agnes, who died in 1923. In the late 1920s, Louis lived in Kansas. He entered the spirit world in the home of his mother-in-law, Millie, in Wood, SD, on May 10, 1930, and is buried in Evergreen Cemetery in Wood, SD. He was survived by a daughter Rebecca, who was living with her grandmother in 1940.[49]

Louis Brings Three White Horses
National Archives

Brother of All, Joseph. Joseph was born on the Crow Creek Reservation on Feb. 22, 1895. His parents were Thomas and Annie Brother of All. Joseph married Hanna Shield from Lake Andes. When Joseph registered for the draft on June 5, 1917, he was farming with Hanna's father, Ezekiel, near Lake Andes, SD. He joined the Army on June 27, 1918. He completed his basic training at Camp Dodge, IA, and was assigned to Company F, 351st Regiment, which was part of the 88th Division (ASN 3315331). Five other men from the Lake Andes area were in the same company. They were Samuel Dion, Peter Hopkins, Jesse Kezena, Roy Cook and Daniel Jandreau. The 351st Regiment sailed from New York aboard the *Scotian* on Aug. 16, 1918. Upon arrival in France, the 88th Division spent 28 days in quiet sectors. After Armistice was signed, Pfc. Brother of All received an evaluation from his commanding officer, stating that he was "amenable to discipline and Army life. Showed excellent qualities during scout work. Exceptionally good bomber. Well-liked by men and regarded as a good man." During occupation duty, the men in Co. F were billeted in Liffol-le-Grand. On May 20, 1919, the 351st Regiment sailed aboard the *Mercury* from St. Nazaire, France, bound for Hampton Roads, VA. Pfc. Brother of All was discharged at Camp Dodge, IA, on June 7, 1919. His wife's brother, Amos, also served in the Army. After the war, Joseph and Hanna were separated. Joseph passed away at McKennan Hospital from appendicitis in Sioux Falls, SD, on Sept. 26, 1935, and is buried in Christ Episcopal Cemetery in Fort Thompson.[50]

Brought, Barney. Barney was born in July 1892 near Bullhead, SD. In the 1903 Census Roll, he is listed with his parents, Aglila (Pius) and Tipi, as well as two sisters. Barney enlisted on August 29, 1918, and served as a Private in Company C, 30th Machine Gun Battalion, 10th Division (ASN 4502191). He died on Oct. 12, 1918, while serving in the line of duty. The 10th Division was training at Camp Funston, KS, so that is likely where Pvt. Brought entered the spirit world. He is buried in the Catholic Cemetery in Bullhead. The Barney Brought American Legion Post No. 82 is named in his honor. Barney's sister, Mary, was married first to Ben Short Baldhead, and later to Joe Leaf. They were both veterans. In 1935, a worker with the SDERA program interviewed Pius, who said he was receiving a $57.50 payment on Barney's pension. He also told the state employee that he had once been jailed for six days for leaving the reservation without permission.[51]

Brought Plenty, August. August was born at Fort Yates, ND, on May 9, 1900. His parents were Charles Brought Plenty and Annie Left Hand Bull. August and his brother, John, were later adopted by Tom Frosted. Around 1915, August became a student at the boarding school at Flandreau, SD.

On April 4, 1917, he enlisted in Troop D, 1st Cavalry, South Dakota National Guard (ASN 1427432). This was 2 days after President Wilson declared war on Germany. A large group of students at Flandreau also enlisted on that day. The National Guard unit was sent to Camp Cody, NM, where it became part of the 136th Infantry, 34th Division, on October 22, 1917. While in training at Camp Cody, Pvt. Brought Plenty sent a letter to the *Sioux County* Pioneer, thanking them for his subscription. He wrote that reading "the *Pioneer* is just like a letter written to me from my folks back home." He added that "I am certainly in a good Company and the officers are all good to us, as we have an Indian Lieutenant and Sergeant." Pvt. Brought Plenty traveled overseas with the 34th Division. He sailed aboard the S.S. *Tereisias* on June 28, 1918. He was attached to Co. 14, Camp Cody June Automatic Replacement Draft. Upon arrival, he was briefly assigned to Company A, 162nd Infantry, 41st Division. On July 31, 1918, he was transferred to Company A, 28th Infantry, which was part of the 1st Division. The 28th Infantry and the 26th Infantry formed the Second Brigade of the 1st Division.

On September 30, 1918, the 1st Division was ordered to replace the 35th Division, which had suffered many casualties in the opening days of the Meuse-Argonne Campaign. After a sixteen-kilometer forced march in a rainstorm, the 1st Division moved into position to the southeast of Exermont. On October 1, the day that Pvt. Brought Plenty was wounded, an officer with the 26th Infantry reported that the Germans "pounded the area with high explosives and drenched the ravines and woods with gas, and machine guns and snipers harassed constantly whenever movement was observed." After the Armistice, Joseph Dixon interviewed Pvt. Brought Plenty, when he stated that "it was hell over there. Wounded in the left hip by a machine gun bullet. In the Hospital two months. All right now." He received the French Fourragère and the Purple Heart and was promoted to Private First Class on Feb. 19, 1919. Pfc. Brought Plenty returned to the U.S. on Aug. 30, 1919, and was discharged at Camp Dodge, IA, on Sept. 24, 1919. Brought Plenty was one of the charter members of the Albert Grass American Legion Post at Fort Yates.

In the 1920 U.S. Census, August was living with Thomas and Susie Frosted. In the 1920s he married Lulu End of Horn. In the 1930 U.S. Census, August and Lulu were living in Corson County with their daughter, Genevieve, as well as Lulu's father, William. Lulu died in 1934. August married Christine Red Horn in Selby, SD, on July 3, 1936. Christine was the widow of George Red Horn, a fellow veteran who died in 1935. August's stepson, William, died at the age of 17 while serving in Korea in 1951. William Red Horn is buried at Arlington. August entered the spirit world in the VA Hospital in Minot on Dec. 8, 1956. His son, Cyril, and daughters, Genevieve, Irene, and Rose, survived him. He is buried in St. Peters Cemetery in Fort Yates.[52]

Brown, Carl – listed on WWI veterans memorial at Oglala Lakota College, Kyle, SD. Carl was born on the Pine Ridge Reservation on May 27, 1894. He was one of four sons of Joseph and Alice Pourier Brown who served in WWI. When Carl registered for the draft on June 5, 1917, he was ranching with his father near LaCreek. When he Joined the Army, he was assigned to Co. D, 145th Machine Gun Battalion, 40th Division (ASN 3129710). He sailed from New York aboard the *Metagama* on Aug. 7, 1918. After arriving in France, he was reassigned to Co. D, 130th Machine Gun Battalion, 35th Division. After the Armistice, Pvt. Brown sailed for home from St. Nazaire aboard *Antigone* on April 14, 1919, arriving in Newport News, VA, on April 27. He was discharged on May 3, 1919. After arriving home, Carl wrote to Joseph Dixon that he had lost cattle and horses while overseas. On Dec. 9, 1923, Carl married Jennie Williams in Martin, SD. Jennie's brother, Morris, had also served in the Army. In the 1940 U.S. Census, Carl and Jennie are listed with their children, Erma, William,

Shirley, Charlotte, and Joseph Carl. Carl entered the spirit world at the VA Hospital in Hot Springs on March 12, 1958, and is buried in the Martin Community Cemetery.[53]

Brown, Donald B. Donald was born in Sisseton on April 19, 1898. His parents were Joseph and Kate Brown. His father was an enrolled member of the Sisseton-Wahpeton Oyate and his mother was of Irish descent. Donald was a student at the boarding school at Carlisle from 1913-16. For a while, he worked full time in their print shop. He enlisted in Minneapolis, MN, on Dec. 15, 1917. He served as a Private in the MG Company, 4th Infantry. He was discharged at Camp Dodge, IA, on Aug. 28, 1918, likely for medical reasons. Donald's sister, Irene, married Robert Renville, a fellow veteran. In the 1930 U.S. Census, Donald was living in Sisseton with his parents, along with Kenneth Renville, the six-year-old son of Irene and Robert. Donald worked as a plumber and a mechanic. He later worked as a printer for a publishing company. He entered the spirit world in the Tekakwitha Nursing Home in Sisseton on Dec. 22, 1974, and is buried in the Veterans Circle of the Sisseton Cemetery.[54]

Brown, James A. James is listed on WWI veteran's memorial at Oglala Lakota College, Kyle, SD. James was born on the Pine Ridge Reservation on April 17, 1891. When James registered for the draft on June 5, 1917, he was ranching with his parents, Joseph and Alice (Pourier). James joined the Army on Aug. 9, 1918, and was sent to Camp Fremont, CA. He was assigned to serve as a sharpshooter in Headquarters Company, 13th Regiment, 8th Division. The Division left Camp Fremont on Oct. 10, 1918, bound for Camp Merritt, NJ. Headed overseas, they had been sailing for four days when they heard the Armistice had been signed. James was discharged as a Private. In the 1930 U.S. Census, James was living with his parents in Chadron. He married Alma Lamoreaux, the mother of Paul Lamoreaux. James and Alma had a son, also named Paul Peter Brown. In the 1940 U.S. Census, Alma was working as a book binder in the Martin Public Library, and her son was doing carpentry work. When James registered with the Selective Service in 1942, he was working for a rancher near Martin. James entered the spirit world on Nov. 20, 1963.[55]

Brown, James E. James' name is engraved on a monument honoring veterans in Little Eagle. He was born on the Standing Rock Reservation around June 1878. His father was Lawrence Brown, and his mother is listed as Medicine Rock. He had an older sister, Ellen. In the Census Rolls from the late 1880s, he is listed as an orphan. Around 1900, he married Bessie Otaagliwin [Brings home a lot]. On May 31, 1918, he enlisted in the Army at Ft. Douglas, Utah. His home town was listed as Thunder Hawk, which is where his sister, Ellen Duncan, was living. Ellen had a son, Jefferson, who served overseas. James was assigned to Co. E, 27th Engineers (ASN 891731). On Sept. 1, 1918, his unit sailed from New York for Europe aboard the *Nevasa*, and arrived in Le Havre on Oct. 16. These engineers worked on road construction, filling shell holes, widening some stretches and rebuilding destroyed sections. In November, they switched over to bridge construction. On Dec. 7, they went into quarters at Le Chatelier. On March 6, 1919, they boarded the S.S. *Dakotan* to return to the U.S. Pvt. Brown was discharged at Ft. Russell, WY, on April 5, 1919. Sometime after his discharge, he moved to Butte, MT, where he worked as a miner. In the 1930 U.S. Census, James was living in the Montana State soldier's home at Columbia Falls. He suffered from miner's lung and tuberculosis and entered the spirit world on April 4, 1934, at the VA Hospital in Fort Harrison, MT. He is buried in Wakpala, SD.[56]

Brown, Lewis Francis. Lewis was born on the Sisseton Reservation to Joseph Renshaw and Kate Brown on Sept. 13, 1895. Donald was his younger brother. When Lewis registered for the draft on June 5, 1917, he was working on a farm in Wisconsin. At that time, he had already enlisted in the

National Guard. He was assigned to Battery E, 149th Field Artillery, 42nd Division (ASN 142718). He sailed with his unit from Hoboken, NJ, aboard the *President Lincoln* on Oct. 18, 1917. The 149th FA served in the Sectors at Luneville, Baccarat, Esperance-Souain, Champagne-Marne, Aisne-Marne, Vesle, St. Mihiel, Essey-Pannes, and Meuse-Argonne. Pvt. Brown returned home with his unit, sailing from Brest aboard the Leviathan on April 18, 1919. He was discharged on May 10, 1919. After returning home, he married Ercell Mensinger in Chicago in 1919. In the 1920 U.S. Census, Louis was working as a clerk on the Shoshone Reservation in Wyoming. In 1930, he was working as a bookkeeper for a plumber in Phoenix. When he registered for the "Old man's draft" in 1942, he was working for BIA in Muscogee, OK. Louis entered the spirit world on Feb. 20, 1978, and is buried in the Santa Fee National Cemetery.

Brown, Louis. Louis was born on the Pine Ridge Reservation on July 19, 1896. Some records list his date of birth as Nov. 22, 1896. His parents were Joseph and Alice Pourier Brown. When Louis registered for the draft on June 5, 1918, he was ranching with his father. He likely enlisted shortly after this. He was discharged on Dec. 14, 1918. After the war, his mother wrote a letter to Joseph Dixon about her four sons who served, including Willie, who died overseas. In the 1920 U.S. Census, Louis was working as a mechanic. On Jan. 10, 1925, he married Frances Usher. They had a daughter, Frances. In the 1930 U.S. Census, Louis was driving a truck for the Indian Service. He worked for the Indian Service for many years. After he retired from there, he worked at Mount Rushmore. Louis passed away in St. John's Hospital in Rapid City on May 25, 1971. His wife and daughter survived him. He is buried in Mt. Calvary Cemetery in Rapid City.[57]

Brown, Ora. He is listed on WWI veteran's memorial at Oglala Lakota College, Kyle, SD. He was born on Oct. 16, 1898, in Pierre, SD. His parents were Alonzo and Caroline Brown. They were not enrolled. Ora enlisted in the Army on July 5, 1918, at Fort Logan, CO. He served with the Ordnance Detachment, 9th Engineers (mtd) and was discharged as a Private at El Paso, TX, on April 23, 1919. In the 1920 U.S. Census, he was farming in Bennett County. Sometime later he moved to Rapid City and worked as a switchman for the railroad. He entered the spirit world on July 1, 1978, in San Bernadino, CA. He is buried in Desert Lawn Memorial Park, Calimesa, CA.

Brown, William Denver. He is listed on WWI veteran's memorial at Oglala Lakota College, Kyle, SD. William Denver was born on the Pine Ridge Reservation on Oct. 11, 1892. His parents were Joseph and Alice Pourier Brown. He likely joined the Army in the spring 1918, and was sent to Camp Funston. He was in Company G, 355th Infantry, 89th Division (ASN 2846770). His regiment sailed from New York aboard the *Baltic* on June 4, 1918. When the 89th Division moved to the Front in early August 1918, Corporal Brown was wounded while scouting. On Oct. 21, 1918, he received the French Croix de Guerre. After the Armistice, the 89th Division occupied a section of Germany. Part of the 355th Regiment was billeted in Saarburg. Corporal Brown became ill and died there on Feb. 7, 1919. On Sept. 10, 1920, his body was brought back to the U.S. aboard the U.S.A.T. *Antigone*, which sailed from Antwerp, Belgium. He is buried in the Red Cloud Cemetery, Pine Ridge, SD.

Browning, Roger. Roger was born near Fort Peck, MT around 1900. In the 1908 Census Roll for the Yanktonai Sioux at Fort Peck, he was listed with his parents, Otto (Wi-ya-ka-ska) and Ada (Ta-sun-ka-o-ta-win), as well as two sisters. Sometime after this, Roger became a student at the Flandreau Boarding School. Roger's name is included on a plaque in front of the school listing the students who entered the military. In the 1920 U.S. Census, Roger was stationed at Camp Furlong, Columbus, NM. In 1920, the 24th Infantry Regiment was stationed at Camp Furlong. He was discharged on Aug. 10, 1921. After his discharge he moved back to Fort Peck, where he married Elizabeth Harrison. Around 1947, the family moved to Tacoma, WA. Roger worked as a chauffeur for the U.S. Indian Agency. Roger entered the spirit world in a Tacoma hospital on June 1, 1955, and is buried in Poplar, MT. He was survived by his wife and two children, Trivian and Asa.

Bullhead, Francis. Francis was born on Standing Rock Reservation on Nov. 15, 1888. His parents were Henry and Mary Bullhead. His father, Lt. Henry Bullhead, was killed in the Sitting Bull fight on Dec. 15, 1890. In the 1894 Standing Rock Census Roll, Francis is listed with his mother, Mary Wakanglimaza [Iron lightning]. When he registered for the draft on June 5, 1917, he was supporting his mother, his wife, and three children. Francis likely was drafted, entering the service on June 24, 1918. He served as a Private in the 164th Depot Brigade at Camp Funston, KS. He was discharged on Jan. 6, 1919. Francis and Julia lived in their 28' x 16' log house located 5 miles SW of Bullhead. Francis's mother passed away in 1925. In 1935, the family was interviewed by a state worker with SDERA program. They owned a 1932 Plymouth. Francis had once owned 50 head of cattle and horses, as well as 50 hogs, but in 1935, he only had three cattle, three head of horses and 20 chickens. In recent years, the grasslands around them had been heavily grazed by sheep, so forage was in short supply. Their oldest daughter, Evelyn, had graduated from high school in Wakpala, and had plans to attend college in Brookings. In 1935, she was serving as the president of the American Legion Auxiliary. Francis was a member of the American Legion. He had served as the Post's Adjutant. His other children were Xavier and Christine. Francis entered the spirit world at Hot Springs on May 7, 1938 and is buried in the Bullhead Catholic Cemetery. Julia passed away in 1939. In 1943, their daughter, Evelyn, enlisted in the Women's Army Corps.[58]

Burnette, Grover C. Grover was born on the Rosebud Reservation on Oct. 17, 1893. His parents were John and Amelia Burnette. In 1910, Grover married Clemantine Richards. When he registered for the draft on June 5, 1917, he was farming. On Oct. 6, 1917, Grover joined the Army at Camp Funston, KS. He was assigned to Company B, 342nd Machine Gun Battalion, 89th Division. Sgt. Burnette was discharged on Jan. 21, 1918. The rest of 342nd MG Bn. sailed from New York aboard the *Caronia* in June 1918. In 1921, Grover was a member of the Chauncey Eagle Horn Legion Post No. 125. That same year, he married Winnie Rogers. Winnie's brother, Gilbert, also served in the Army. In the 1937 Census Roll, they are listed with their children, Grover Jr., Elnora, Robert Philip, Marjorie, John, Martha, Gilbert and Viola. The family ranched along the White River. Grover served as a tribal judge, tribal councilman, and as treasurer for the Rosebud Tribe. His son, Robert, also served as president of the Rosebud Tribe. Robert is the author of *The Tortured Americans*. Grover entered the spirit world at Hot Springs on April 21, 1970. His wife and nine children survived him. He is buried in Spotted Tail Cemetery. Grover's daughter, Viola, wrote *Confessions of an Iyeska*, a story of her life while growing up in Todd County. She described how her parents raised money by going to powwows and setting up a hamburger stand. Her dad liked to read, and subscribed to detective magazines. After her dad's funeral, the line of cars stretched for more than a mile. He was a pillar of the community.

Butte, Lott Forked. Lott was born on the Lower Brule Reservation on Jan. 7, 1891. His father was Charles Forked Butte and his mother was Very Handsome. When Lott registered for the draft on June 5, 1917, he was ranching on the Lower Brule Reservation. When Lott joined the Army, he was first assigned to Co. A, 158th Infantry, 40th Division (ASN 3127703). Pvt. Butte sailed from New York aboard the *Laomedon* on Aug. 11, 1918. Upon arriving in France, he was reassigned to Co. L, 111th Infantry Regiment, 28th Division. The 111th Infantry served in the Sectors at Oise-Aisne, Clermont, Meuse-Argonne and Thiaucourt. Pfc. Butte sailed for home with his unit from St. Nazaire aboard the *Kroonland* on April 18, 1919. After arriving home, he married Tena Scott. Tena's brother, Daniel, had also served in the Army during the war. Lott had contracted tuberculosis while in the Army and entered the spirit world on Feb. 21, 1932. He is buried in Red Hill Cemetery, Hamill, SD. Tena, his widow, moved back home to support her parents. They lived in a four-room house northwest of Hamill, in Lone Star Township. She and Lott had two daughters, Eva and Daisy. Tena did some sewing for which she received some money and received a small pension.[59]

C

Cadotte, Gilbert C. Gilbert was born in Wakpala on the Standing Rock Reservation on Jan. 7, 1897. His parents were Nicholas and Elizabeth. When Gilbert registered for the draft on June 5, 1918, he was working for James Fitzpatrick in Kansas City, MO. Shortly after this he enlisted in the U.S. Navy (SN1200213). In the 1920 U.S. Census, he was living with his sister and her husband, Robert Hoehner, in Wakpala. He is listed as a sailor. In the 1931 Census Roll for Standing Rock, his address is USN, New York City. In 1935, his brother said that Gilbert was with the Navy in China. He likely had been living in California for a number of years. His official service dates are listed as Feb. 15, 1918 to Oct. 11, 1919, and from Nov. 12, 1936 to May 12, 1938. He passed away on March 30, 1959, in the VA Hospital in Livermore, CA. He is buried in Los Angeles National Cemetery, plot 75, B21.[1]

Campbell, George M. George was born on the Sisseton-Wahpeton Reservation on Feb. 9, 1896. His parents were Joseph and Ann Campbell. When George registered for the draft on June 9, 1917, he was farming near Peever. He joined the Army on Aug. 28, 1918 and was discharged as a Private on Dec. 10, 1918. He married Mable Amos, who entered the spirit world in 1924. In the 1930 Census Roll, George was listed as widowed. His children, Catherine and Meredith, were living with their grandmother. In the 1931 Census Roll, George is listed as living on Pine Ridge. In 1933, he married Jennie Hawk (1893-1976) in Gann Valley. In the 1940 U.S. Census, they were living in Buffalo County. He entered the spirit world in the Public Health Hospital in Sisseton on Oct. 7, 1986. He is buried in the Sisseton Cemetery.

Campbell, James J. James was born on the Sisseton-Wahpeton Reservation on June 8, 1891. His parents were John and Lydia Campbell. In the 1910 U.S. Census, James was a student at the Carlisle Boarding School, Carlisle, PA. He was first enrolled in October 1908 and received some training in the printing trade. When he registered for the draft on June 2, 1917, he was living in Peever, SD. After joining the Army, he was assigned to the 6th Company, Infantry Replacement and Training Troop, as a Private. He was discharged on Jan. 6, 1919. In the 1920 U.S. Census, James was living with his mother and step father, Charley Duggan. James passed away on Sept. 15, 1927. He is buried in St. Mary's Episcopal Cemetery, at the Agency.

Carlow, Abraham. Abraham (Abe) was born on the Pine Ridge Reservation on May 13, 1898, the son of Theodore and Mary Carlow. He was the younger brother of Frank and Robert, who both served in the military. Abe enlisted in the U.S. Navy. On Aug. 24, 1918, he registered for the draft in Los Angeles, CA. After the question about his occupation, he wrote, "just out of Navy." In the 1920 U.S. Census, he was farming in Bennett County. On July 6, 1925, he married Vera Oval Scott (1901-1986). Around this time' they moved to Lead. Abraham worked as a miner in the local gold mine. In 1940, they were still living in Lead with their sons, Bard and Jack. Bard enlisted in the Army in WWII. Abe retired in 1963 from the Homestake Mining Co. He was a member of the Homestake Veterans Association. Abe entered the spirit world in a Deadwood Hospital on May 16, 1980. Vera and two sons, Bard and John, survived him. He is buried in Mountain Lawn Cemetery, Englewood, SD.[2]

Carlow, Frank. He is listed on WWI veteran's memorial at Oglala Lakota College, Kyle, SD. Frank was born on the Pine Ridge Reservation on Nov. 15, 1891. When Frank registered for the draft on June 5, 1917, he was living at the Crow Agency in Montana and working as a laborer for the U.S. Biological Survey. He was inducted into the Army in Big Horn County on Nov. 19, 1917. He received his basic training in the 166th Depot Brigade in Camp Lewis, WA. On Jan. 31, 1918, he was transferred to Company D, 115th Engineers, 40th Division (ASN 1623902). Pvt. Carlow sailed to Europe aboard the *Balmoral Castle* on Aug. 8, 1918. One of the first tasks for the 115th Engineers was the construction of a Classification Camp for 8000 casuals, at La Guerche, France. Before the engineers completed the Camp, they were transferred to the Front. After the Armistice, they were part of the Army of Occupation. Carlow was promoted to Wagoner on May 1, 1919. He sailed from St. Nazaire aboard the U.S.S. *Minnesotan* on June 19, 1919 and arrived on June 29, 1919. Wagoner Carlow was discharged on July 10, 1919. He married Elva Little Chief on Nov. 24, 1919, in Billings. In the 1930 U.S. Census, they were living near the Crow Agency. In 1942, Frank was working on a construction project at the airport in Havre, MT. While installing a manhole, he was caught in a cave-in, and entered the spirit world Aug. 5, 1942. His wife and daughter, Irene Bad Horse, survived him. Frank is buried at the Custer National Cemetery, Section C, #18.[3]

Carlow, Robert. He is listed on WWI veteran's memorial at Oglala Lakota College, Kyle, SD. Robert was born on Aug. 17, 1897 on the Pine Ridge Reservation. He was a brother of Abraham and Frank Carlow. Robert joined the Army on June 26, 1918 and was discharged on Feb. 18, 1919. He also served in World War II. He married Elizabeth Allen (1886-1954). Robert and Lizzie had a son, Robert Jr., who served in the 17th Airborne Division. He died during the Battle of the Bulge. Robert worked for the Indian Service at Pine Ridge. He later married Arta Irving. He entered the spirit world in a Pine Ridge Hospital on Jan. 15, 1977 and is buried in Holy Cross Cemetery in Pine Ridge. His widow, five daughters, Elleen, Phoebe, Wynema, Joyce and Ella, as well as three sons, Pat, Mike and Darwin, plus three step-children survived him.[4]

Carlow, Theodore H. Theodore was born on the Pine Ridge Reservation to Theodore and Mary Carlow on March 29, 1884. He married Alma Wilson in the early 1900s. In the 1910 U.S. Census, they were living in Washington D.C. Sometime after this, the family moved to Bremerton, WA. Theodore enlisted in the Navy and served during the war. He was discharged in December of 1918. In the 1920 U.S. Census, he was working as an ordnance man at the Naval Yard in Bremerton. He and Alma had four children, Theodore Jr., Alma, Ruth and Randolph. When Theodore registered with the Selective Service in 1942, he was still working Naval Ammunition Depot in Bremerton. After the war, the family moved to Port Hueneme, CA. Theodore worked as a laborer for the Pacific Maritime Association. He entered the spirit world in Bellinda Hospital in Port Hueneme on Aug. 3, 1965. He is buried in Forest Lawn Cemetery in Bremerton.

Carpenter, Ansel. Ansel was born on the Crow Creek Reservation (Lower Yanktonai) on Aug. 14, 1896. In the Census Roll for 1903, he is listed with his parents, Jay and Martha Carpenter, as well as two sisters. Ansel joined the Army on Oct. 15, 1918 and was assigned to the Student Army Training Corps (SATC) (ASN 5293585). Pvt. Carpenter was stationed at the State University of Iowa in Iowa City, IA, and was discharged on Dec. 15, 1918. In the 1930 U.S. Census, he was living with his mother. A few years later he married Shirley Onihan. In the 1937 Census Roll, they are listed with their children, Ansel and Adrienne. In the late 1930s, Ansel became a patient at the Yankton State Hospital. Ansel entered the spirit world on Jan. 29, 1953 and is buried in a cemetery in Fort Thompson.[5]

Carter, Thomas. Thomas was born on March 28, 1888, at LeBeau on the Cheyenne River Reservation, to Thomas and Esther Takes Him Standing. In the 1892 Census Roll, he is listed with his mother and his brothers and sisters. In the 1900 U.S. Census, he was a student at the Standing Rock boarding school. When he registered for the draft on June 4, 1917, he was ranching and supporting his mother. They had about 75 head of cattle. Thomas enlisted in the Army on May 24, 1918. He was sent to Camp Lewis, WA, for training and assigned to Company B, 13th Train Headquarters and MP, 13th Division (ASN 2787191). He was discharged on Jan. 24, 1919 as a Wagoner. In the 1920 U.S. Census, Thomas was living with his sister, Sallie Wright. Around 1929, he married Magdalen Bagola, a sister to Johnson Bagola, who also was a veteran. In 1935, they were interviewed by a worker for the SDERA program. Thomas and his wife were living in an 18' x18' log home two miles west of the agency. They hauled water several times a week from the river. They owned three horses, two cows and two calves, plus a 1928 Nash. Thomas had been doing relief work but wanted a job with the highway department. He was a member of the American Legion and said he liked to read detective novels. The Cheyenne Agency had equipped a truck with a traveling library. Marguerite worked as a cleaning lady at the Agency. Thomas later ranched. He entered the spirit world in the Cheyenne River Indian Hospital on Aug. 21, 1957 and is buried in Mossman Cemetery.[6]

Cash, Anderson W. Anderson was born on Feb. 24, 1894, on the Santee Reservation in Nebraska. His parents were Joseph Cash and Clara Graham. In the 1910 U.S. Census, Anderson was living with his parents and sister in Springfield, SD, where his father was working as a laborer in a pool hall. When Anderson registered for the draft on June 5, 1917, he was living in St. Cloud, MN. When Anderson joined the Army, he was sent to Camp Dodge, IA. He served as a Private in the 32nd Company, 163rd Depot Brigade (ASN 3962209). He was discharged on Dec. 9, 1918. After the war, Anderson was one of the returned soldiers who helped start the veteran's organization, American Indians of the World War, which was headquartered in Minneapolis. Henry Flood was one of the other founders. In the 1933 Santee Census Roll, Anderson is shown as living in Chicago. Shortly after this, he moved to New York City where he worked as a printer. He entered the spirit world at his home in New York City on March 30, 1939, and is buried in Holy Fellowship Cemetery in Greenwood, SD.[7]

Cavender, William R. William was born at Flandreau around Feb. 20, 1886. His parents were Ray Cavender and Julia Goodteacher. Around 1911, he married Eliza Roberts (1894-1969). When William registered for the draft on June 5, 1917, he was farming near Granite Falls, MN. He and Eliza had three children. William also worked as a gardener. William joined the Army at Granite Falls on July 26, 1918. He was assigned to Co. M, 54th Pioneer Infantry (ASN 4065784). He was sent to Camp Wadsworth, SC. On Aug. 29, 1918, his unit sailed from Newport News, VA, aboard the liner *Caserta*. After arriving in France, they made a night march to Clermont. From there, Co. M was ordered on Sept. 26, 1918, to assist two units of engineers in extending the light rail line towards the advanced zone. Pvt. Cavender took part in the Meuse-Argonne Offensive. On Dec. 2, 1918, Co. M was ordered to Longwy, near the Belgian border to guard the old fort surrounding Longwy, and to guard the old German Supply Depot at Rehon. In December, Co. M was sent to Germany to guard various places along the Rhine. Pvt. Cavender sailed from Marseilles, France, aboard the *Italia* on May 10, 1919. He was traveling with St. Aignan Casual Co. No. 4449, labeled as "Special

Discharges." On May 29, 1919, Pvt. Cavender arrived back in New York and was discharged at Mitchel Field, NY, on June 3, 1919. After the war, the family continued to live near Granite Falls. In the 1940 U.S. Census, their children still living with them were Mary, John, William Jr., Carolyn, Lawrence and Gary. Their son, John served in WWII. William entered the spirit world in Granite Falls Manor on March 24, 1972. He is buried in Hillcrest Cemetery.[8]

Charging Crow, Samuel. He is listed on WWI veteran's memorial at Oglala Lakota College, Kyle, SD. Samuel was born on the Pine Ridge Reservation on May 16, 1896. His parents were Jacob and Jennie Iron Road Charging Crow. Samuel joined the Army on May 25, 1918. Pvt. Charging Crow (ASN 3129692) sailed from New York aboard the *Ortega* on Aug. 31, 1918, traveling with Mixed Overseas Casual Co. No. 361. He likely was wounded or gassed. He sailed home from Le Havre aboard the S.S. *Touraine* on June 14, 1919. He was traveling with St. Aignan Casual Co. 5947. St. Aignan was a large military hospital. His unit was listed as ASC, Ser. Co. 3, CPS. School, APO 786. Pvt. Charging Crow was discharged on July 5, 1919. Shortly after he returned home, he married Lizzie Strikes Enemy. In the 1930 U.S. Census, they were farming in Bennett County. Samuel was a member of the Bennett County American Legion Post No. 240. Lizzie passed away in 1940. In 1943 he married Daisy Gay. Samuel entered the spirit world at the VA Hospital in Hot Springs on July 2, 1976. He is buried in Mediator Cemetery near Kyle. His widow and five sons, James, Everett, Joseph, Ray and Carl, as well as two daughters, Ruth and Charlotte survived him.[9]

Charging Whirlwind, Wallace. Wallace was born on July 4, 1896, in Wood, SD. In the 1906 Census Roll for the Rosebud Reservation, he is listed with his father, Charging Whirlwind, and his mother, Alice (Red Blanket). Wallace registered for the draft on June 5, 1918. He entered the Army on Aug. 27, 1918, and was discharged on Nov. 13, 1918, two days after the Armistice. After the war he married Emma Bear Looks Behind. In the 1930 Census Roll, he and Emma are listed with their children, Andrew, Harriet, Winnie, Cecelia, Alice, as well as Wallace's father, Charging Whirlwind. Wallace entered the spirit world on June 14, 1988.

Chasing Hawk, Paul. Paul was born on Feb. 27, 1891, on the Cheyenne River Reservation. According to the Ziebach County History published in 1982, Paul served in the military, and was discharged on April 19, 1918. He was one of the men who filed their discharge papers at the Ziebach County Courthouse. His parents were James Chasing Hawk and Hannah Black Eagle. In the 1940 U.S. Census, he and his wife, Esther were farming in Ziebach County with their children, Mary, Evelyn, Philomene, Allan, Wilma, Cecile, and Josephine. Paul entered the spirit world in the PHS hospital in Rapid City on Dec. 14, 1959.[10]

Chasing Horse, Titus. Titus was born on the Rosebud Reservation on July 7, 1897. His parents were Silas and Hattie Chasing his Horse. In the early 1900s, Silas was a Private in the Indian Police. Titus registered for the draft on June 5, 1918. On Aug. 24, 1918, he joined the Army. He served as a Private in the Headquarters Troop, 19th Division at Camp Dodge, IA, (ASN 4821716). Titus served with Cpl. James Holy Eagle. Pvt. Chasing Horse was discharged on Jan. 28, 1919. The 19th Division did not go overseas. In 1924, Titus married Millie First in Trouble (1902-1990). In the 1930 U.S. Census, Titus was farming his heir allotment. In 1935, the family was interviewed by a worker with the SDERA program. They were living in a two-room log house, six miles north of Norris, with their children, Affie and Curtis. Titus was working on a dam construction project. He entered the spirit world on Sept. 17, 1959, and is buried in the Black Hills National Cemetery, Section C, site 407. Millie is buried next to him.[11]

Cheyenne, Albert. Albert was born March 14, 1893, on the Standing Rock Reservation. According to the 1900 U.S. Census, Albert was living with his parents, Sahiyela [Cheyenne] and Si [Foot] on the Pine Ridge Reservation. In 1910, they were back on Standing Rock, in Corson County. When Albert registered for the draft on June 5, 1917, he was living in Bullhead and working as a ranch laborer on his father's ranch. Albert joined the Army on July 21, 1918, and was sent to Camp Dodge, IA. He served as a Private in Co. B, 1st Development Battalion (ASN 3954588). He was discharged on Dec. 24, 1918. In 1919, he married Annie Red Fox in Timber Lake, SD. In the 1937 Census Roll for Standing Rock, Albert and Annie were living with their daughter, Mary. Annie passed away in 1939. Albert lived in Glen Cross, before entering the hospital. He entered the spirit world in the VA Hospital in Hot Springs on Sept. 17, 1954. He is buried in Good Shepard Cemetery in Little Eagle, SD.

Chief, Albert. Albert (Ah-Be-Dah-Cumig) was born in January 1898 in Sawyer, MN, on the Leech Lake Reservation. His father was Shah-ga-cumig-gub and his mother was Mah-ge-o-say-quay. In the 1915 SD State Census, Albert was a student at Flandreau. On April 4, 1917, he enlisted in the 1st SD cavalry, Troop D. On Sept. 15, 1917, the 1st Cavalry was sent to Camp Cody in Deming, NM. Pfc. Chief was assigned to the 59th Depot Brigade. He was discharged on Oct. 16, 1917. He likely received a medical discharge. On June 5, 1918, Albert was required to register for the draft, even though he had received a medical discharge. At that time, Albert was working at the boarding school in Flandreau. Around 1920, he married Louise Johnson. In the 1940 U.S. Census, Albert and Louise were living near Leech Lake with their children, Florence, Albert Jr., Phyllis, Stanley, Gladys. Albert entered the spirit world at the Cass Lake Indian Hospital on July 23, 1942. He is buried at Onigum, MN.[12]

Chief Eagle, Albert. Albert was born around 1893 on the Pine Ridge Reservation. In the 1899 Census Roll for Pine Ridge, he is listed as David Two Sticks, living with his father Chief Eagle and his mother, Her Good Road. Albert attended the Rapid City Boarding School. Pvt. Chief Eagle enlisted in Rapid City on June 21, 1916, and served with Co. I, 4th SD Infantry along the Mexican Border near San Benito, TX, from 1916-1917. He re-enlisted in the SD National Guard in March or April of 1917. When the 4th SD Infantry arrived at Camp Greene, NC, the soldiers were all reassigned. Pvt. Chief Eagle became part of the 148th Machine Gun Battalion, 41st Division. This unit sailed from Hoboken aboard the *Olympic* on Jan. 11, 1918. Upon arriving in France, Pvt. Chief Eagle was assigned to Company M, 167th Infantry, 42nd Division. He was wounded in the right leg in the fighting near Chateau Thierry. He sailed home from Brest aboard the U.S.S. *Plattsburg* on Sept. 23, 1918. His fellow passengers were labeled as "surgical patients." He was discharged on June 28, 1919. He received disability compensation, but his wound continued to bother him for many years. In the 1920 U.S. Census, he was living with his parents in Chadron. He was first married to Julia High Bear. In 1927, he married Eva Night Pipe. They moved to Okreek on the Rosebud Reservation. In 1935, he visited with a state worker with the SDERA program about their living conditions. Their permanent home was a three-room frame house located four miles west of Okreek. When he worked on conservation construction projects, he sometimes lived in a tent. However, a 10' x 12' tent cost $24, but it only lasted about a year. In 1935, he was assigned to a work project that was 12 miles from home. He left home at 4:30 A.M. with his team to get to the jobsite. In 1940, Albert and Eva lived with their children, Juliana, Dallas, Gloria, Manfred, Thomas, Omar and Joseph. Eva entered the spirit world in 1940. Albert entered the spirit world on March 8, 1942. Dallas served in the Marine Corps in WWII, while Manfred served with the Coast Artillery Corps. Manfred died while serving in Japan after the war. Thomas served with the Army in Korea, where he was wounded and captured. He later escaped from the North Koreans. Dallas wrote a book about the Lakota in 1967 called *Winter Count*.[13]

Christenson, Joe. Joakim Marinius, also known as Joe, was born in Tømmernes, Balsfjord, Troms, Norway on May 20, 1897. His parents were Johannes Oluf and Magna Sørensdatter Christenson. He was almost 2 years old when his parents brought him to South Dakota. His father died around 1911. Joe was the oldest son. He completed 4th grade. He likely started working to help support the family upon his father's death. Joe registered for the draft on June 5, 1918. He married Florence Blue Dog at the Episcopal Church near Enemy Swim Lake on June 9, 1918. Shortly after, they built a home at Blue Dog Lake. It was a three-room home located by the lake on 33 acres that belonged to Florence. Joe joined the Army on Sept. 4, 1918. While stationed at Camp Grant, IL, he was naturalized as a citizen on Nov. 2, 1918. While in the service, he came down with the flu. He was discharged on Dec. 23, 1918.

After returning from the Service, Joe farmed. In September 1935, the family was interviewed by a case worker for the South Dakota Emergency Relief Administration (SDERA). Joe and Florence had 3 children, Floyd, Geraldine and Charlotte. At that time, they had 9 cows, 2 calves, a team of horses, 17 sheep, 1 brood sow, 5 pigs, 17 chickens, as well as a 1929 Chrysler car. Joe had been a member of the American Legion but dropped his membership when he could not afford the dues. They had tried to grow a garden in 1935, but the hot winds dried up everything. The family supported themselves by selling cream. Joe later worked as a carpenter and lived in Aberdeen for a number of years. The family liked to attend Powwows. Joe entered the spirit world on Dec. 23, 1972, at his home in Waubay. He is buried in the cemetery at St. James Episcopal Church at Enemy Swim. His widow, Florence, adopted son, Jerome Hopkins, and daughters, Geraldine and Charlotte, survived him. Florence entered the spirit world on Jan. 15, 1999, at the age of 100.[14]

Clairmont, Philip Judson. Philip was born around Jan. 4, 1892, to Joseph Clairmont and Twin Woman. On the Census Rolls for the Rosebud Reservation, he is also listed as Judson Claymore. In the 1910 U.S. Census, he was shown as a student at the Carlisle Boarding School. He first was enrolled at the school in Carlisle in 1908. He re-enlisted several times. When he registered for the draft on June 5, 1917, he was a student with Ford Motor Co. in Highland Park, MI. He joined the Army on July 22, 1918. He served with Co. 43, 11th Battalion, 163rd Depot Brigade at Camp Dodge, IA. He was discharged as a Corporal on Jan. 28, 1919. After the war, he married Susan Bordeaux (1903-1973). Susan's brother, Francis, also served in the Army. In the 1930 U.S. Census, he was working in Rosebud as an engineer in the light plant. In the 1940 U.S. Census, he worked as an assistant engineer with the Indian Service. They are listed with their children, Jesse and William, Roscoe, Roberta, Robert, Lucille and Mervill. Philip entered the spirit world at the hospital in Rosebud on Feb. 7, 1981. He is buried in Saint Charles Cemetery in Saint Francis.

Clairmont, Richard T. Richard was born on the Rosebud Reservation on May 17, 1886. His parents were John and Maggie Clairmont. He married Emma Iron Shooter at Rosebud in 1907. When he registered for the draft on June 5, 1917, he was farming in Mellette County. He joined the Army on July 13, 1917, and was assigned to Bakery Company No. 345, (ASN 1443440). His unit sailed for France aboard the *Anchises* with the 34th Division. After the war, Pfc. Clairmont sailed from Brest aboard the *Orizaba* on June 3, 1919, bound for Newport News, VA. He was discharged as a Private First Class on June 21, 1919. In the 1930 U.S. Census, he was farming with his wife and their children, Lucy, Martin, Julia, Virginia, and Cleveland. In the 1940 U.S. Census, he was working for the CCC program as a laborer in Todd County. Later that year they moved to the Belle Fourche area. He was a member of the VFW and American Legion He entered the spirit world on Nov. 9, 1968. A son, John, and a daughter, Margaret, survived him. He is buried in the Black Hills National Cemetery, Section C, site 1086.[15]

Claymore, John M. John was born on the Cheyenne River Reservation on June 2, 1896. His parents were Peter and Emma Claymore. He had a twin sister, Marguerite. When John registered for the draft in 1917, he was ranching. He joined the Army on April 25, 1918, and was sent to Camp Funston, KS. He was assigned to Company K, 355th Infantry Regiment, 89th Division (ASN 2845247). Pvt. Joseph Obago from Crow Creek also served in Co. K, 355th Regiment. Pvt. Claymore sailed from New York aboard the *Baltic* on June 4, 1918. Upon arrival in France, the 355th Regiment was stationed in the town of Grand. A number of men from the Cheyenne River area were serving in the 355th Regiment, including Pvt. Ben Young, who had worked with John Claymore for the Diamond A Cattle Company. In the St Mihiel Offensive, the 355th Regiment was in the Front. On Sept. 12, 1918, the regiment was scheduled to attack through Bois de Mont Mare, with the 3rd Battalion (Companies I, K, L, and M) designated to be the assault battalion. Among the casualties suffered was Pvt. Isaac Looking Back, of Little Eagle, who died of his wounds, and Pvt. John Claymore. According to an account written by Pvt. Ben Young, John, who served as a company runner, was wounded in the stomach and leg. It was thought initially that he had been killed, after his dog tags were found. A telegram was sent back to his family in South Dakota. A fellow soldier in Co. K, Pvt. H.G. Pierce, reported that John was a good soldier and a fast sprinter. He was later made Sergeant. He returned to the U.S., leaving Bordeaux aboard the *Matsonia* on Feb. 3, 1919. He was attached to Blois Casual Company No. 364. He was discharged on March 3, 1919.

John returned home to ranch with his father. On Dec. 8, 1930, he married Bernice Darling. In 1935, they were interviewed by a worker for the SDERA program. John had been doing some relief work, as a foreman on a gravel crew. He indicated that because of his leg wound, he could not do a job that required him to stand all day. At that time, he owned six saddle horses, but at one time he had owned 200 head of cattle and 100 head of horses. In the 1940 U.S. Census, John and Bernice was living in Belle Fourche with their daughters, Darleen, Betty, and Beverly, as well as a son, Elva. In 1942, Ben Young married John's twin sister, the widow of Hans Mortenson. Around 1950, the family moved to Sturgis, where John worked as a livestock buyer. John entered the spirit world in St. Joseph Hospital in Deadwood on Oct. 30, 1966. and is buried in the Black Hills National Cemetery, Section E, site 1842. Bernice (1910-1999) is buried with him.[16]

Cloud, George S. George was born about July 1, 1889, near Browns Valley, on the Sisseton-Wahpeton Reservation. He was listed in some of the Census Rolls as George Sevenbrothers. In the 1917 Census Roll, he is listed with his wife, Elizabeth Driver, and a son, Elijah. When George registered for the draft on June 1, 1917, he was living in Sisseton with his family. When he enlisted in the Army, he trained at Camp Funston, KS (ASN 2192916). He sailed from New York aboard the *Espagne* on April 3, 1918. He was traveling with Camp Funston April Replacement Draft, 2nd Co. Upon arrival in France, he was assigned to Co. B, 121st Machine Gun Battalion, 32nd Division. This unit served in the Sectors at Center, Aisne-Marne, Fismes, Oise-Aisne and Meuse-Argonne. Pvt. Cloud was wounded in the ankle and later received a Purple Heart medal. Pvt. Cloud sailed for the States from Brest, France, aboard the *Mongolia* on Nov. 13, 1918. The soldiers he was traveling with were labeled as "walking surgical or medical." They arrived in Hoboken on Nov. 23, 1918. He was discharged on March 21, 1919. In the 1930 U.S. Census, George was living in Easter Township, near Brown's Valley, with his brother, Bert. In the 1931 Census Roll, George was listed as widowed. In 1935, Bert and his dependents, including George, were interviewed by a worker with the SDERA program. They lived in a four-room frame house located about six miles east of Sisseton. George was receiving a disability payment of $17 per month and was otherwise unemployed. His son, Chris, entered the spirit world in 1937. George entered the spirit world at the PHS hospital in Sisseton on Jan. 1, 1949 and is buried in St. John's Episcopal Cemetery in Roberts County.[17]

Clown, James. James was born on the Cheyenne River Reservation on March 4, 1900. His parents were Amos Clown (Old Eagle) and Julia Iron Cedar Woman. Julia was a sister to Crazy Horse. The Clown family lived in the Thunder Butte Precinct. James' older brother, Moses, was killed in France on Nov. 1, 1918. Their sister, Lillie, was married to James Makes Trouble, who also served in the Army. James Clown enlisted in the Army in 1920, and served with the 6th Division at Camp Grant, IL. He was discharged in 1921. In the late 1920s he married Anna Red Bird. In 1935, the family was living in a 12' x 14' home at the Thunder Butte Station so their children would be close to a school. They traveled four miles to obtain water for their home. James was a member of the American Legion. In the 1940 U.S. Census, James and Anna were ranching with their children, True, Alma, Betty, Mary, and Carlin. Matthew Red Bird also lived with them. James entered the spirit world in the PHS Indian Hospital in Eagle Butte on April 20, 1969. He is buried in St. Peter's Episcopal Cemetery in Thunder Butte.[18]

Moses Clown
Delmar & Bev Clown

Clown, Moses. Moses was born on the Cheyenne River Reservation, Thunder Butte Precinct in May 1890. As a student, he attended Haskell Boarding School. When Moses registered for the draft on June 5, 1917, he was working as a cowboy on the Cheyenne River Reservation. He likely joined the Army in the summer or Fall of 1917, and was assigned to Co. B, 314th MP Battalion, 89th Division (ASN 2194424). This unit sailed from New York aboard the *Saxon* on June 28, 1918. The 314th was later designated as the 89th MP Company. A number of other men from South Dakota served with Moses. They included George Jewett, Thomas Hawk Eagle, Ambrose Gabe and Joseph Takes the Shield. On Nov. 1, 1918, the 89th Division was prepared to take the Heights of Barricourt. Pvt. Clown and three other men from his unit were helping to swing an artillery piece into place when a German shell hit them. Pvt. Moses Clown and Pvt. Joseph Takes the Shield were killed, and Pvt. Ambrose Gabe was severely wounded. Military records from Camp Funston indicate that Pvt. Clown was buried near the dressing station for the 354th Ambulance Company. His body was brought back to the U.S. by the *Cantigny*, which sailed from Antwerp, Belgium, on July 21, 1921. After the war, a monument was raised in Eagle Butte to honor Pvt. Clown. The monument is near the HVJ Cultural Center.

Coffey, Roy George. Roy was sometimes listed as Louis Ray Coffee in the Rosebud Census Rolls. He was born on the Rosebud Reservation around May 23, 1901. His parents were Lawrence and Mary (Tall Woman) Coffee. Roy served as a Private in the Army, but his date of enlistment is not known. In the 1920 U.S. Census, he was serving as a Private in the Army at Camp Jackson, SC. When he returned home, he married Clara Points at Him. They had two children, Ray Jr. and Zoe Fannie. Clara entered the spirit world in 1925. In the 1930 U.S. Census, Ray was listed as a veteran of the World War, living with his mother and brothers in Todd County. He still was living with his mother in 1940. He entered the spirit world on Jan. 21, 1971, and is buried in St. Charles Cemetery, St. Francis. His headstone shows he served in the U.S. Army in World War I.

Collins, Henry H. Henry was born in Whitewood, SD, on March 4, 1895. In the 1900 U.S. Census, he was living with his parents, Douglas and Lillie Collins, in Butte County. In the 1914 Cheyenne River Census Roll, Lillie is listed with her children, Weaver, Henry, Orpha, John, Milton and Blanche. When he registered for the draft on June 5, 1917, Henry was ranching at Eagle Butte. He joined the Army on June 23, 1918. He was assigned to Co. K, 69th Infantry, which was part of the 10th Division (ASN 3309150). He did not go overseas. Pfc. Collins received his honorable discharge on Feb. 5, 1919. After returning to Eagle Butte, he married Caroline Garreaux. Henry's sister, Blanche, married Thomas Baldwin, also a returned veteran. In the 1924 Census Roll for the Cheyenne River, Henry is listed with Caroline and their son, Kenneth. In the 1930 U.S. Census, he was working for a blacksmith at the Cheyenne Agency. In the 1931 Census Roll for the Cheyenne River Res., Henry and Caroline were listed with their three children, Kenneth, Isabel and William. In the 1930s, Henry and Caroline separated. On Aug. 2, 1940, Henry married Mary Hord. Henry entered the spirit world on Nov. 2, 1960, and is buried in Gettysburg Cemetery. His son, Kenneth, served in the Army in WWII.

Comes Flying, Henry. Henry was born around March 1901, on the Crow Creek Reservation. In the 1912 Census Roll, he is listed with his father, Comes Flying. Later he is listed as an orphan. Henry enlisted in the Army on July 12, 1920, and was discharged on July 11, 1921. On March 4, 1925, he married Philomena Round Head. In the 1940 U.S. Census, he lived in Fort Thompson and worked as a janitor at the Indian School. He and Philomena had four children, Bertha, George, Nathaniel and Elvera. Henry entered the spirit world on April 13, 1978, in Community Bailey Hospital in Chamberlain. He is buried in St. Joseph's Cemetery in Fort Thompson. His headstone shows him as a Private with WWI service.

Benjamin Comes From Scout

Ancestry.com

Comes From Scout, Benjamin. Benjamin was born on Feb. 29, 1896, on the Rosebud Reservation. When he registered for the draft on June 13, 1917, he was farming his father's allotment. He joined the Army and was sent to Camp Funston, KS, for training. He was assigned to Co. G, 355th Infantry, 89th Division (ASN 2846906). Pvt. Comes From Scout sailed with his unit from New York to Europe aboard the *Baltic* on June 4, 1918. Pvt. Comes From Scout was killed in action on Oct. 21, 1918, while the 355th Infantry was fighting near the Bois de Bantheville. He is now buried in Ring Thunder, Sacred Heart Cemetery.[19]

Comes from War, Frank. Frank was born on April 18, 1894, near Wososo on the Rosebud Reservation. In the 1899 Census Roll, he is listed with his mother, Move Woman, and his brother, Daniel. In the 1910 Census Roll, he is shown as the stepson of Black Thunder. Frank married Julia Good Shield on Sept. 17, 1917, in White River. On May 28, 1918, he enlisted in the military. Pvt. Comes from War was initially assigned to Co. B, 160th Infantry, 40th Division (ASN 3129634). The 40th Division had trained at Camp Kearny, CA. Pvt. Comes from War sailed with his unit from Brooklyn aboard the *Mentor* on Aug. 8, 1918. Upon arrival in France, he was reassigned to Company H, 306th Infantry, 77th Division, as a replacement. Pvt. James Crowe and Pvt. Narcisse McKenzie served with

Pvt. Comes from War in Co. H. After the Armistice, Captain E. A. Depe wrote that Pvt. Comes from War "responded readily when called upon for any kind of duty. Considered as a good man and the men of the Company think highly of him. Has great fitness as a scout. Displayed courage when he was wounded and had to be commanded by the Captain before he would allow himself to be evacuated." The 306th Infantry sailed from France on April 17, 1919, aboard the *Mt. Vernon*. Pvt. Comes from War was discharged on May 18, 1919. In the 1940 U.S. Census, Frank was farming in Todd County. He entered the spirit world on Nov. 23, 1978, and is buried in the Black Hills National Cemetery, Section E, Site 2049.[20]

Comes Out Bear, Benjamin. Benjamin was born on the Rosebud Reservation on May 7, 1893. In the 1902 Census Roll, he is listed with his mother, Louise, and his step-father, James Thompson. When he registered for the draft, he was farming at the Rosebud Agency. He joined the Army on April 26, 1918, and was assigned to Co. G, 355th Infantry, 89th Division (ASN 2846655). Pvt. Comes Out Bear sailed with his unit from New York aboard the *Baltic* on June 4, 1918. After the Armistice, his commanding officer, Capt. Ira Barlow, wrote in an evaluation that Pvt. Comes Out Bear's "courage and endurance were good." The 355th Infantry had occupation duty near Saarburg, Germany. The 355th sailed from France on the ship *Leviathan* on May 15, 1919. He was discharged on May 31, 1919. After returning home he married Pearl Iva Sackett. They had a daughter, Ellen. In the 1940 U.S. Census, Benjamin was working in the CCC program. Pearl's occupation was listed as restaurant proprietor in Parmelee. Benjamin entered the spirit world on Feb. 28, 1959. Both he and Pearl (1883-1975) are buried in Holy Innocents Cemetery in Parmelee, SD.[21]

Conroy, Harry – He is listed on WWI veteran's memorial at Oglala Lakota College, Kyle, SD. He was born on the Pine Ridge Reservation on Nov. 28, 1893. His parents were Frank Conroy and Victoria Standing Bear. When he registered for the draft on June 5, 1917, he was farming and also doing accounting. He joined the Army at Martin on July 22, 1918. He served as a Corporal in the camp headquarters, in personnel. He was discharged at Camp Dodge, IA, on Feb. 8, 1919. After the war he lived in Martin. He married Bertha Fire Thunder in 1930, but she passed away in 1939. He later married Hazel Bear Killer. Harry served as President of the Oglala Tribe from 1950-52. Harry entered the spirit world on Dec. 13, 1974, while visiting his daughters in San Francisco. His four daughters, Jean, Marie, Virginia and Colleen, survived him. He is buried in the Inestimable Gift Cemetery in Allen.[22]

Cook, Roy. Roy was born on Jan. 24, 1896, at Greenwood, SD. In the 1904 Census Roll for the Yanktonai Tribe, Roy is listed with his father, John Cook, his mother, Onipewakanwin, as well as three sisters, Fannie, Jane and Mable. When Roy registered for the draft on June 5, 1917, he was working for Thomas Sherman at Greenwood. Roy likely joined the Army in 1918. He was assigned to Co. F, 351st Infantry, 88th Division (ASN 3315365). The 2nd Battalion of the 351st Infantry sailed from New York aboard the *Scotian* on Aug. 15, 1918. Pvt. Cook was one of six Yanktonai in Company F. The others were Joseph Brother of All, Samuel Dion, Peter Hopkins, Jesse Kezena and Daniel Jandreau. Their commanding officer, Capt. H.P. Corey, stated that he would not trade these men for an equal number of white men because of their special qualifications. In October, most of the 88th Division moved into the defensive zone of Haute-Alsace. After the Armistice, Pvt. Cook's commanding officer wrote an evaluation, stating that Pvt. Cook was a "good runner, worker, observer, and scout. Exceptionally good bomber. Well regarded by whites and has extra amount of courage and endurance." After the Armistice, the 351st Infantry served with Occupation Forces near Houdelainecourt, France. The Regiment sailed from St. Nazaire, France, on May 20, 1919, aboard the U.S.S. *Mercury*. Upon arrival, they docked at Newport News, VA. Pvt. Cook was discharged on June 7, 1919. Roy returned to the Greenwood area. In the 1940 U.S. Census, he was working as a laborer for the Indian Service. He lived with his wife, Josephine, and their stepdaughter, Sophia Dog Soldier. He entered the spirit world on Nov. 15, 1968. He is buried in Cedar Presbyterian Cemetery, near the Fort Randall Casino.[23]

Cooper, Arbee C. Arby, or Arley, was born in Iowa on Sept. 21, 1894. His parents, Alexander and Annie moved to Potter County, SD before 1900. When Arbee registered for the draft on June 5, 1917, he was farming with Charley Swift along the Missouri River near Forest City. Arbee enlisted in the Army on Sept. 21, 1917, and was assigned to Co. D, 114th MG Battalion, 30th Division (ASN 2192920). Pvt. Charles Barker from the Sisseton Reservation served with Arbee in Co. D. Pvt. Cooper sailed from New York aboard the *Elpenor* on May 11, 1918. The 30th Division suffered 8,415 casualties during the war. Cpl. Cooper sailed from St.Nazaire aboard the *Rijndam* on March 7, 1919, and was discharged on March 29, 1919. In the 1920 U.S. Census, Arbee was once again living with Charley Swift in Forest City and listed as a "servant." By 1930, Arbee had moved to a farm near White Horse with his mother and brother, Harry. He was farming near the Jewett family. On April 23, 1938, he married Mollie Rousseau, whose husband had passed away in 1934. In the 1940 U.S. Census, Arbee and Mollie are listed with their step children, Virginia, Margaret and Pauline, as well as Arbee's brother, Harry. Arbee entered the spirit world in Rapid City on Dec. 30, 1943. He is buried in a corner of the Emanuel Episcopal Cemetery near White Horse with several other veterans.[24]

Roderick Cornelius
Mathers Museum

Cornelius, Roderick. Roderick was born on the Oneida Reservation near Green Bay, WI, on Nov. 9, 1895. His parents were Nelson and Mary Cornelius. In 1917, Roderick was a student at the boarding school in Flandreau, SD. He enlisted in the South Dakota National Guard on April 4, 1917, which was two days after President Wilson declared war on Germany. He trained in South Dakota with Troop D, 1st SD Cavalry (ASN 1427435). This cavalry unit, without horses, was sent to Camp Cody, NM, on Sept. 15, 1917. It shortly became part of the 136th Infantry, 34th Division. Pvt. Cornelius left the U.S. aboard the S.S. *Tereisias* on June 28, 1918. He was part of Co. 14, Camp Cody June Automatic Replacement Draft. Arriving in France, he became a replacement in Co. B, 28th Infantry, 1st Division. He took part in the fighting at St. Mihiel, Meuse-Argonne, Sedan, and the Lorraine Front. Pvt. Cornelius sailed from Brest, France, aboard the *Orizaba* on Aug. 22, 1919, and arrived in the U.S. on Aug. 30. He also served with Casual Detachment 1460, Demobilization Group, and was discharged at Camp Dodge, IA, on Sept. 24, 1919. Roderick's name was engraved on a plaque erected in 1920 at the Flandreau School to honor the war veterans. After the war, he lived near Newald, WI, for a while. He later returned to the Oneida Reservation. On Sept. 2, 1942, he re-enlisted in the Army, "for the duration." After WWII, he worked as a section hand for the railroad. He married a widow, Jenny John. He entered the spirit world on April 9, 1974, at San Luis Manor Nursing Home in Ashwaubenon, WI. He was survived by four stepsons, Jasper, Emerson, Ervin and Hyson John, as well as three stepdaughters, Rena, Helena and Reka. He is buried in Holy Apostles Cemetery in Oneida, WI.[25]

Cornelius, William. William was born Jan. 2, 1899, on the Oneida Reservation near Green Bay, WI. His parents were Chauncy Cornelius and Margaret Metoxen. In 1917, William was a student at the boarding school in Flandreau, SD. He enlisted in Troop D, 1st Cavalry, South Dakota Nation Guard in the spring of 1917. His regular military service dates from June 15, 1917. The 1st SD Cavalry was sent to Camp Cody, NM, on Sept. 15, 1917. After training at Camp Cody, he sailed for Europe aboard the S.S. *Tereisias* on June 28, 1918. He was part of Co. 14, Camp Cody June Automatic Replacement Draft (ASN 1427532). He was assigned to Co. E, 101st Engineers, 26th Division. The 101st Engineers served in the Sectors at Pas Fini, Champagne-Marne, Aisne-Marne, Rupt, St. Mihiel, Troyon, and Meuse-Argonne. Pvt. Cornelius sailed home from Brest aboard the U.S.S. *Mount Vernon* on March 27, 1919. He was discharged as a Private on April 17, 1919. William's name was engraved on a plaque erected at the Flandreau School in 1920 to honor the war veterans. After the war, he returned home to Oneida and married Elizabeth Peterson in 1921. Sometime later the family moved to Milwaukee. In 1930, he worked as a straightener in an auto factory. In 1936, he worked as a machinist. He also worked as a grinder for a machine manufacturer. He retired from Falk Corporation. He was a life member of the VFW of Lac du Flambeau. After his first wife died in 1965, he married Lucy Cornelius. The family moved back to Oneida. William entered the spirit world at his home in Depere, WI, on June 17, 1984. His wife and a son, Russell, and a daughter, Gloria, survived him. He is buried at Memorial Cemetery on the Lac du Flambeau Reservation. Graveside services were conducted by the VFW.[26]

Cottier, Edward. He is listed on WWI veteran's memorial at Oglala Lakota College, Kyle, SD. Eddie was born on April 15, 1895, on the Pine Ridge Reservation. In the 1899 Census Roll, he is listed with his parents, John and Susie Cottier. When Eddie registered for the draft on June 5, 1917, he was farming with his father. Eddie enlisted on May 10, 1918, and was sent to Camp Funston and assigned to the 164 Depot Brigade (ASN 2848658). On May 23, 1918, he was transferred to Co. I, 353rd Infantry, 89th Division. In June 1918, the 89th Division sailed for Europe. On Oct. 23, 1918, Pvt. Cottier was wounded in the leg by shell fire. At that point, the 353rd Infantry had driven the German Forces from the Bois de Bantheville. Pvt. Cottier spent time in hospitals in France. He returned to the U.S. on Feb. 12, 1919, sailing from St. Nazaire aboard the *Manchuria*. He was traveling with other "sick and wounded" passengers. His leg was amputated. He was discharged on April 3, 1919. After the war, he married Helena Geraldine Morrison. They had a daughter, Carmen. In the 1930 U.S. Census, Eddie was working as an advisory assistant for the Indian Service. He entered the spirit world on Aug. 6, 1958. He and Helena (1904-2001) are buried in the Black Hills National Cemetery, Section D, site 175.[27]

Cottier, Samuel. Samuel was born on the Pine Ridge Reservation on Nov. 30, 1890. His parents were David and Mary Cottier. When he registered for the draft on June 5, 1917, he was farming near Martin, SD. Samuel joined the Army on May 25, 1918. He served in Co. B, 160th Infantry, 40th Division (ASN 3130148), which was a replacement division. Pvt. Cottier sailed from New York for France aboard the *Ortega* on Aug. 31, 1918, traveling with Overseas Casual Co. No. 361. Other soldiers with him were Samuel Charging Crow, Joseph Dion, Eugene DuBray and Robert Dubray. Pvt. Cottier wrote to Dixon that he was "not engaged in any Battles." After the Armistice, Pvt. Cottier sailed home from Bordeaux aboard the *Walter A. Luckenbach* on March 6, 1919. He was traveling with the Camp Dodge Detachment No. 4, 160th Inf. Pfc. Cottier was discharged on April 8, 1919. He returned to the Pine Ridge Reservation where he farmed. He first married in 1944. He also lived in Gordon, NE. Around 1977, he moved into the Hot Springs VA Center. He entered the spirit world there on July 27, 1980. His son, Sylvan Lee, survived him. Samuel is buried in the Black Hills National Cemetery, Section F, site 601.[28]

Joseph A. Cournoyer
Ancestry.com

Cournoyer, Joseph A. Joseph was born at Wheeler on the Yankton Reservation on Feb. 18, 1893. His parents were Joseph Cournoyer and Annie Wheeler. When he registered for the draft, he was farming near Ravinia. He joined the Army on June 27, 1918, and was assigned to the Chemical Warfare Service (ASN 3315248) at Edgewood Arsenal, Maryland. This was a White Phosphorus processing plant. Pvt. Cournoyer was discharged on March 1, 1919. After returning home, he married Dorothy Kopke (1900-1989) in Ravinia on June 9, 1919. In the 1930s, the family lived in Royal Oak, MI, where Joseph worked for Dodge Motor Co. In the 1937 Census Roll, Joseph and Dorothy had two children, Florine and Joan. In the 1940 U.S. Census, Joseph was working as a truck driver. Joseph entered the spirit world in Detroit on March 22, 1945. He is buried in Greenlawn Cemetery in Detroit.

Courtis, William C. Jr. William was born on the Rosebud Reservation on Oct. 19, 1894, to William and Emma Courtis. His father, William Sr., was from England and had served in the U.S Army. William Jr. served in the military during WWI and became a member of the Chauncey Eagle Horn American Legion Post at Rosebud. He entered the spirit world on Sept. 29, 1921, in Rosebud. He is buried in St. Charles' Cemetery in Rosebud and has a headstone engraved with the American Legion emblem.[29]

Craven, George. He is listed on WWI veteran's memorial at Oglala Lakota College, Kyle, SD. George was born on June 27, 1879. His parents were Cornelius and Jesse Craven. George married Alice Sechler. In the Pine Ridge Census Roll for 1904, he was living with his wife and daughter, Minnie. George may have had prior service. He joined the Army at Rushville, NE, on June 20, 1918, and served as a Sergeant with Battery A, 21st Battalion Field Artillery Replacement Draft (ASN 515743). He was discharged on Dec. 13, 1918, at Camp Zachary Taylor, KY. In 1921, George was a member of the Chauncey Eagle Horn Legion Post at Rosebud. In the 1930 U.S. Census, he was living in Pringle, SD, and working in a saw mill. In the 1937 Census Roll, George is listed with Alice. George entered the spirit world on Sept. 23, 1946, and is buried in Mountain View Cemetery, Rapid City, SD.

Crawford, Edward. Edward was born at Flandreau on May 25, 1891. His parents were Charles Renshaw Crawford and Emma Ortley. Charles was a clergyman. Edward's brother, Samuel, also served in the military. When Edward registered for the draft on June 1, 1917, he was farming near Sisseton. Edward enlisted in the Army on June 24, 1918, and served in Co. G, 2nd Battalion, Chemical Warfare Service (ASN 3308425) as a Private. He was discharged on Jan. 11, 1919. On March 12, 1930, he married Jeanette Kitto in Flandreau. In the 1940 U.S. Census, Edward and Jeanette were farming in Roberts County with their children, James, Iva, Bernita, Edward, Herbert and Samuel. Edward entered the spirit world on Aug. 30, 1968, and is buried in the Goodwill Presbyterian Cemetery.

Crawford, Samuel J. Samuel was born on the Sisseton Reservation on Oct. 1, 1894, the son of Charles and Emma. He was the younger brother to Edward. When Samuel registered for the draft on June 4, 1917, he was a student at the School of Applied Arts at Battle Creek, MI. Samuel enlisted on Aug. 28, 1918, and served in the 3rd Co., 2nd Batt., 164th Depot Brigade at Camp Funston (ASN 4500210). Pvt. Crawford was discharged on Dec. 10, 1918. After the war, he married Evelyn DuMarce. Evelyn's brothers, Harry and Herman served in the Army. Samuel farmed in Bossko Township. In the 1936 Census Roll, they are listed with their children, Lillian, Mae, Blossom, Vera, Franklin and Cyrus. In the 1940 U.S. Census, they had another child, Evelyn. Samuel entered the spirit world on Nov. 23, 1966, at the VA Hospital in Fargo, ND. He is buried in Mayason Cemetery, Veblen, SD.[30]

Crazy Thunder, Jacob – listed on WWI veteran's memorial at Oglala Lakota College, Kyle, SD

Crazy Thunder, Joseph. Joseph was born Nov. 7, 1895, on the Pine Ridge Reservation. In the 1905 Census Roll for Pine Ridge, he is listed with his parents, Wakinyan Witke [Crazy Thunder] and Julia, as well as a brother Robert and a sister, Millie. Following some disturbances on the Mexican border, South Dakota's Governor, Frank Byrne, mobilized South Dakota's National Guard, the 4th South Dakota Infantry on June 21, 1916. Joseph enlisted in Co. I on that day, and served with a number of other men, including Job High Elk, James Kills Small and Albert Chief Eagle. On July 31, the Guard members departed by train for the Mexican border. The soldiers returned home to Fort Crook, NE, on Feb. 22, 1917. Joseph remained in the National Guard until the 4th Infantry was sent to Camp Greene, NC. Corp. Crazy Thunder was assigned to Co. B, 148th Machine Gun Battalion, 41st Division (ASN 156068). This unit sailed from Hoboken aboard the *Olympic* on Jan. 11, 1918. Upon arrival in France, most of the soldiers in this unit were assigned to other units in the 42nd Division. Corp. Crazy Thunder was likely wounded or gassed. He last served with Co. A, Headquarters Battalion GHQ. He sailed for home from Marseilles aboard the *Regina De Italia* on June 23, 1919. He was traveling with St. Aignan Casual Co. 5974. Corp. Crazy Thunder was discharged on July 17, 1919. After the war, he married Rose Janis. Rose passed away in 1934. In the 1940 U.S. Census, Joseph was supporting his children, Nicholas, Clement, David, Irene, Emma, Helen and Frank, as well as his mother and his brother, Louis. Other children in their family were Mary, Carl, William, Harold, and Narcisse. Joseph's oldest sons, Nicholas, Clement and David served in WWII. Clement died at Iwo Jima. Joseph later married Agnes Kills Enemy. Joseph worked as a clerk-typist. He entered the spirit world on Jan. 26, 1975, at the VA Hospital in Hot Springs. He is buried in St. Peter's Cemetery, Manderson, SD.[31]

Crooked Foot, Samson. Samson was born on the Lower Brule around Dec. 31, 1896. His family had moved from the Lower Brule to the Rosebud Reservation in 1896. Samson grew up on the Rosebud Reservation with his parents, Herman Crooked Foot and Josephine Greenwood Win Ya Ska Win [Who is White]. Samson enlisted in the 4th SD Infantry on March 28, 1917. When these National Guardsmen arrived in Camp Greene, NC, they were assigned to Co. B, 148th Machine Gun Battalion, 41st Division (ASN 98579). This unit sailed from Hoboken aboard the *Olympic* on Jan. 11, 1918. Upon arriving in France, many of the SD soldiers were reassigned to Co. M, 167th Infantry, 42nd Division. This had been an Alabama National Guard Regiment. Pvt. Crooked Foot served as a Private in Co. M, 167th Infantry, 42nd Division. The 167th Infantry served in the Sectors at Luneville, Baccarat, Esperance-Souain, Champagne-Marne, Aisne-Marne, St. Mihiel, Essey-Pannes, and Meuse-Argonne. Pvt. Crooked Foot sailed from Brest aboard the U.S.S. *Minnesota* on April 15, 1919. The 42nd Division suffered 13,919 casualties in the war. Pvt. Crooked Foot was discharged on May 9, 1919. He was awarded a Purple Heart. After returning home, Samson married Jennie Red Leaf (1881-1980). They lived eight miles south of Hamill. In 1935, Samson was interviewed by a worker with the SDERA program about their home. He indicated he did not like farming but had no other plans. He stated that he supposed the reservation officials would not let him die so he wasn't worrying about the future. He later moved to Winner. Samson was caught in a snow storm and entered the spirit world in Winner, SD, on March 5, 1965, and is buried in Bull Creek Miniska Cemetery, in Tripp County.[32]

Cross, Lawrence. He is listed on WWI veteran's memorial at Oglala Lakota College, Kyle, SD. Lawrence was born on the Pine Ridge Reservation on Dec. 6, 1900. In the 1905 Census Roll, he is listed with his parents, Frank and Rosa, as well as a sister, Sarah, and a brother, Thomas. He likely joined the 6th Nebraska Infantry at Chadron in the summer of 1917. While in training at Camp Cody, NM, he was transferred to Co. F, 109th Engineers, 34th Division (ASN 1438209). Pvt. Cross sailed from New York aboard the *Cretic* on Sept. 17, 1918. After the war, he described his service. "My War Work as a Kitchen Police at the Hospital Center Mesves France. The Company in which I belong were Building Barracks for the Wounded Soldiers. Then We Moved to Nevers, France. To where the Enginners Camp... Thirty of us men left in the Camp to Do Guard Duty Over the Camp. Then Our Officer in charge appoint me as a cook's helper." Pvt. Cross served in Co. F with Pfc. Charles White Wolf, Corp., George Red Boy, and Pvt. Ralph Red Bear. He sailed for home from Brest, France, with Brest Casual Co. No. 2284 aboard the U.S.S. *Imperator* on July 7, 1919.

After Lawrence returned home, he married Emma Red Bear. In the 1937 Census Roll, Lawrence and Emma are listed with three sons, Lawrence, Jr., James and Robert. Lawrence re-enlisted in 1942 during WWII. After the war, he worked for the C & NW Railroad in Crawford, NE. He entered the spirit world on Dec. 10, 1977.[33]

Cross Bear, Wallace. Wallace was born on the Standing Rock Reservation around February 1897. In the 1904 Census Roll, he is listed with his parents, Jacob and Hail, as well as a sister, Helen, and a brother, Frank. When he registered for the draft on June 5, 1918, he was living in Little Eagle. He was listed as a tall man of medium build. On Aug. 5, 1918, he was sent with a group of men from Corson County to Camp Fremont, CA. The others from the reservation who traveled with him were William Marshall, Benedict Red Legs, and Francis Baker. Wallace was assigned to Co. M, 62nd Infantry Regiment, 8th Division (ASN 2571729). Pvt. Cross Bear was discharged on April 9, 1919. In 1921, Wallace and Annie Catch Bear had a son, Michael. He later had children with Mary Red Bear, including Phoebe. He then married Helen Weasel Iron, and lived with her parents. In 1935, he was a patient in a sanitarium. He entered the spirit world on Aug. 5, 1938, and is buried in Messiah Congregational Cemetery in Little Eagle. On March 17, 2017, at Wakpala, SD, the Cross Bear family received a Code Talker's medal to honor Pvt. Cross Bear's service.[34]

Crow, Sam W. Sam Willie was born on the Crow Creek Reservation on June 19, 1900. His parents were Alfred Kangi [Crow] and Mary Agard. Sam joined the Army at the age of 16 on April 29, 1917. He likely enlisted in Co. M, 4th South Dakota Infantry, whose headquarters was in Yankton, SD. A number of other tribal members also enlisted in the spring of 1917. On Sept. 28, 1917, the regiment traveled to Camp Greene, NC. Upon arrival, their officers were informed that they were now 147th Field Artillery Regiment. Pvt. Crow was assigned to Battery C (ASN 139487). Other tribal members in Battery C were George Blaine, Jesse St. Pierre, Peter Frederick, Charles Little Owl and Buckley Pomani. As part of the 41st Division, they sailed to Europe aboard the ship *Olympic* on Jan. 11, 1918. On March 25, 1918, the 147th Field Artillery was attached to the 32nd (Red Arrow) Division. They supported the 32nd Division until the Armistice. Pvt. Crow's commanding officer, 1st Lt. A.M. Knudtson, wrote an evaluation stating that he was "a very good horseman and driver, fearless and willing. Very good runner and scout." Following the Armistice, the regiment was attached temporarily to the 40th Division, until Dec. 23, 1918. The 147th remained with the 88th Division until April 8, 1919. At that time, the unit rejoined the 32nd Division, which was preparing to sail back to the United States. Pvt. Crow sailed from Brest aboard the *Kansas* on May 1, 1919, and was discharged on May 23, 1919. In 1920, Sam married Viola Black Bird. In 1924, he married Amelia Jandreau. In 1935, the family was interviewed by a worker with the SDERA program. At that time, they were living in a three-room house located 2.5 miles southeast of Grace Mission. Sam was not working then as he was recovering from appendicitis. In the 1940 U.S. Census, Sam was working on a dam construction project. Sam and Amelia had three children, Contance, Dewey, and Samuel Jr. Sam entered the spirit world after receiving an accidental gunshot wound on Nov. 3, 1945. He is buried at Crow Creek Presbyterian Cemetery.[35]

Crow Eagle, William. William was born on the Rosebud Reservation on Dec. 20, 1890. In the 1905 Census Roll for the reservation, he was listed with his parents, Crow Eagle and Drop Fat Meat, as well as two brothers, George and Alvin. He was first married to Emma Black Crow around 1914. When he registered for the draft on June 5, 1917, he and his wife had a daughter, Millie. When William joined the Army, he was assigned to Co. E, 20th Infantry, 10th Division. Pvt. Crow Eagle was trained at Camp Funston, KS, but did not go overseas. He was discharged on March 10, 1919. In 1921, he was a member of the Chauncey Eagle Horn Legion Post at Rosebud. After the war he married Susan Kills Plenty (1892-1974). In the 1930 U.S. Census, William was working as a salesman in a general merchandise store on the Rosebud Reservation. In 1935, the family was interviewed by a worker with the SDERA program. They were living in a two-room cabin at the Rosebud Agency. They hauled water from a nearby creek. William had worked for one of the post traders at the agency for a few years. He had also worked as a foreman on some road construction projects. He owned three horses and 11 chickens. The family attended the Episcopal Church and liked to go to the basket socials and dinners. He was hoping to get a permanent job as a clerk with the post trader. In the 1940 U.S. Census, he was working as a janitor at the school. He and Susan had four children, Iver, Gilbert, Madeline and Dorothy. Gilbert served in the Army during WWII. William entered the spirit world on Sept. 1, 1966, and is buried in Grace Chapel Cemetery.[36]

Crow Necklace, Thomas. Thomas was born at Fort Yates, ND, on the Standing Rock Reservation on May 5, 1894. In the 1896 Census Roll for Standing Rock Reservation, Thomas, also known as Opijataska, lived with his parents, Frank Crow Necklace and Meets, as well as a brother, Louis. Thomas attended school at Flandreau, SD, and Carlisle, PA, where he played left halfback on the school's football team from 1911-13. He was a team mate of Jim Thorpe.

Thomas joined the Army at Fort Yates on April 20, 1918. He was sent to Camp Dodge, IA, where he served in Headquarters Detachment, 175th Infantry, 88th Division (ASN 2858763). He left for Europe from New York aboard the *Empress of Russia* on Aug. 7, 1918. On Sept. 12, 1918, he was transferred to Co. B, 338th Machine Gun Battalion, 88th Division. He served with that unit in eastern France. His commanding officer noted that Pvt. Crow Necklace "demonstrated fitness for machine gun." While the soldiers waited to return back to the U.S., they took part in sports activities, as well as drill exercises. Crow Necklace played football for the 88th Division's team, which was known as the Hunhuskers. According to the *Camp Dodger*, the in-country division newsletter, the football team for the 88th played some close games against other units. For uniforms, the men wore aviation caps for head guards, Red Cross sweaters for jerseys, padded blue denim fatigue trousers for pants, stockings bought in Paris and Nancy, and garrison cleats for shoes. The 88th Division had special medals designed by a Paris jeweler. The medals, shaped like the unit insignia, were presented to winners in the various athletic contests held for the soldiers. Pvt. Crow Necklace sailed for the US. from St. Nazaire, France, aboard the *Koningen der Nederlanden* on May 21, 1919. He was discharged at Camp Dodge, IA, on June 15, 1919.

Thomas was one of the many young men who played baseball for the Fort Yates team after the war. Thomas had married Alice Has Horns in 1916. In the 1930 U.S. Census, Thomas and Alice were living in Corson County with their children, Thamar, Thomas Jr., Christina, Viola, Andrew and Serena. They had a two-room frame house located ½ mile south of Bullhead. Their son, Thomas Jr., served in WWII, and died of his wounds in France in 1945. The family later moved to Lemmon, SD. Thomas entered the spirit world in Lemmon on March 1, 1962, and is buried in the Episcopal Cemetery in Bullhead, SD.[37]

Crowskin, Louis. Louis, a Hunkpapa, was born on the Standing Rock Reservation on June 7, 1894. In the 1896 Census Roll, he is listed with his father, Andrew Kangihola, and his mother, Sophia (Appearing Day). Louis was inducted into the Army in South Dakota and sent to Camp Funston, KS, on June 24, 1918. Less than a month later, he was sent to Camp Dodge, IA, where the 88th Division was completing its training. Louis was assigned to Co. I, 352nd Infantry (ASN 3309354). Pvt. Crowskin sailed from Brooklyn aboard the *Ulysses* on Aug. 16, 1918. After the Armistice, the 88th Division was billeted near Gondrecourt, France. Pvt. Crowskin returned home from St. Nazaire aboard the U.S.S. *Pocohontas* on May 21, 1919. The ship docked in Newport News, VA. Pvt. Crowskin was discharged at Camp Dodge on June 14, 1919. A photo of Louis in his uniform was published in *Memoirs of France and the Eighty-eighth Division*.

After the war, Louis returned to Kenel. He had a reputation as a "speedy baseball pitcher." He served several terms as Commander of the Martin Yellowfat American Legion Post of Kenel. For a number of years, he had a herd of around 35 cows, but drought conditions halted forage production, so he had to sell his herd. During the 1930s he worked as a laborer on emergency conservation projects. On Feb. 8, 1934, he married Philomine Sack. In the 1939 Census Roll, they are listed with their three children, Henry, Ursula and Agatha. Philomine entered the spirit world on Dec. 12, 1941. Louis later moved to Fort Yates. He entered the spirit world in the hospital in Fort Yates on July 2, 1965, and is buried in the Catholic Cemetery in Kenel.[38]

Crowe, James. James was born in Porcupine on the Pine Ridge Reservation on Nov. 14, 1890. His parents were Thomas and Alice Crow. He was a student in Carlisle, PA, from 1906-11, training as a tailor. Upon returning to Allen, SD, he started farming. He first married around 1915. When he registered for the draft on June 5, 1917, he was supporting his wife and two children. He joined the Army in Martin, SD, on May 25, 1918. He was initially assigned to Co. B, 160th Infantry, 40th Division (ASN 3129657). This division had trained at Camp Kearny, CA. Pvt. Crowe sailed from Brooklyn aboard the *Mentor* on Aug. 8, 1918. Upon arrival in France, he was reassigned to Co. H, 306th Infantry, 77th Division. Pvt. Crowe's unit was involved in heavy fighting in the Argonne Forest. On Oct. 14, 1918, H Company led an attack near the town of St. Juvin. "Some idea of the desperate fighting at St. Juvin is given by the casualty list for the period from the morning of the 14th to the evening of the 15th. The Regiment lost 7 officers and 37 men killed, 4 officers and 213 men wounded." Pvt. Crowe was wounded in the left side of his chest. He spent five months in the hospital. After the Armistice, his commanding officer wrote an evaluation for Pvt. Crowe, saying that he "acted as a scout for his platoon all through the Argonne Offensive. Popular with his comrades. Proved reliable as an observer, and his verbal reports could be depended upon." After the war, Crowe wrote a report of his experiences for Joseph Dixon.

> I have taking some good chances why I was in Aronnge Woods and I belivie that the Aronnge Woods is about the worst front of all the others front. The Germans have Machine Guns about a few yards apart. It is impossible to hold the line. But we held our line and drove them out from their nest. Capture their guns and few huns. This was Sept. 27, 1918. The day I remember pretty well.
>
> When I face a big tall hun. Made him throw up his hand. I intended to shoot him down and scalp him but my friends said let him go. So I let him go free. We sent them back to our lines.

Two other soldiers from the Rosebud Reservation in Co. H were Pvt. Narcisse McKenzie and Pvt. Frank Comes From War. They sailed home from Brest aboard the *Mt. Vernon* on April 17, 1919, and arrived on April 25. Pvt. Crowe was discharged on May 27, 1919. In 1925, he married Susie Strikes Enemy. He later married Louise Thunderhawk. James worked for the tribal police and also served five years as a tribal councilman in Pine Ridge. He entered the spirit world at the VA Hospital in Hot Springs on Oct. 23, 1972. His daughters, Mrs. John White Crane, Mrs. Albert Whiting and Mrs. Racheal Janis, as well as a son, Wilson, survived him. He is buried in Greenwood Cemetery in Alliance, NE.[39]

Cummings, Earl E. Earl Elmer was born on Oct. 4, 1895, in Bonesteel, SD. His parents were George Cummings and Louisa DuCharme. In the 1911 Census Roll for the Cheyenne River Tribe, Earl and his brother, Henry, are listed with their mother and their other brothers and sisters. When Earl registered for the draft on June 5, 1917, he was the Assistant Disciplinarian at the Indian Boarding School at Genoa, NE. Earl joined the Army on Oct. 3, 1917. He served as a Wagoner with the 314th Ammo Train, 89th Division (ASN 2194734). He sailed from New York aboard the *Cretic* on June 28, 1918. He also drove an ambulance with the YMCA. He broke his wrist and spent three weeks in the hospital. Twenty years later, his wrist still bothered him. He was discharged on June 2, 1919. After the war, he married Marie Ducheneaux. Marie was a sister to Napoleon, who also served in the Army. In the 1920s, the family moved to Charles Mix County, west of Lake Andes. Earl farmed and drove a truck for a local creamery. Around 1934, the family returned to White Horse. Earl worked as a foreman on a prairie dog eradication project. In 1940, he was still working as a foreman in the CCC Program. Earl and Marie had a number of children, including Charles, Elmer, Donna, Earl, Jimmie and Dawn. Earl entered the spirit world on Feb. 21, 1968, and is buried in the Black Hills National Cemetery, Section E, site 1444. Earl's brother, Henry, also served in the Army. Their sister, Eleanor, married another veteran, Fred Hill.[40]

Cummings, Henry. Henry was born in Charles Mix County on April 29, 1888. His parents were George Cummings and Louisa DuCharme. When Henry registered for the draft on June 4, 1917, he was ranching in Dewey County and serving as Assistant Assessor. He likely joined the Army in 1917. He served as a Saddler with the 314th Engineers, 89th Division (ASN 2202823). Pvt. Cummings sailed from New York aboard the *Carpathia* on June 12, 1918. After the war, he sailed for home from Brest aboard *Prinz Friedrich Wilhelm* on May 18, 1919. He was discharged on June 27, 1919. After returning home, he married Carrie Alice LaPlant, who had two brothers who served in WWI. Henry and Carrie had three children, Charlotte, Henry and Adelaide. Henry did some work as a harness maker. In the 1940 U.S. Census, he was living with his children in Timber Lake, SD, and operating a shoe repair business. Henry entered the spirit world at the VA Hospital in Hot Springs on May 13, 1941. He is buried in Hot Springs National Cemetery.

Cummings, Peter M. He is listed on WWI veteran's memorial at Oglala Lakota College, Kyle, SD. He was born at Rushville, NE, on June 15, 1894. His parents were Milton and Maggie Cummings. He grew up in Martin, SD, and attended school at Pine Ridge, Rapid City and Haskell Institute at Lawrence, KS. When he registered for the draft on May 31, 1917, he was a student musician at Haskell. He indicated that he had served as a 1st Lieutenant with the Cadets in the Indian School System. Peter joined the Army on May 15, 1918. He served in the band with Co. O, 22nd Engineer Regiment (ASN 3437299), which operated the narrow-gauge railroads in France. He sailed from Hoboken aboard the *Calamares* on April 16, 1918. After the war, the regiment sailed home from St. Nazaire aboard the U.S.S. *Princess Matoika* on June 12, 1919. He was discharged as a Private First Class on July 3, 1919. Peter married Olive Graham in 1918 in Minneapolis. He worked 20 years for the BIA. In the 1930 U.S. Census, he was listed as a dairyman. In the mid-1930s, he was the Agency Farmer. He later took a job as a land appraiser with the Oglala Tribe, and ranched. When his wife passed away in 1948, he married Clara Pourier, who passed away in 1978. In 1979, Peter married Margaret Gresh, the widow of his brother, Alfred. Margaret passed away in May 1987, while Peter entered the spirit world on July 9, 1987, at the VA Hospital in Hot Springs. His daughter, Virginia, as well as five stepdaughters, Edna, Anita, Joan, Betty, Marion and three stepsons, John, Newton and Doyle, survived him. He was buried in Pine Lawn Cemetery in Rapid City with military honors by the Martin American Legion Post.[41]

D

Dakota, Louis. Louis was born on the White Earth Reservation in Minnesota on August 22, 1899. His parents were Isaac Dakota and Sarah Shambow. In 1914, Louis was enrolled at the Flandreau Boarding School. While a student he enlisted in the Army on April 13, 1918, and served with Battery B, 74th Artillery, Coast Artillery Corps (ASN 465364). Pvt. Dakota served with Pfc. Luke Speaks Walking, from Standing Rock. He was stationed at Fort Wadsworth, NY, until June 7, 1918, when he was transferred to Camp Upton, NY. On Sept. 4, 1918, he sailed from Hoboken, NJ, aboard the transport USS *President Grant*. He arrived at St. Nazaire, France on Sept. 23, 1918. The 74th Artillery was Railway Artillery unit. After the war ended, he sailed aboard the USS *Mongolia* and arrived back in Hoboken, NJ, on Dec. 22, 1918. He was discharged as a Private at Camp Dodge, IA, on Jan. 9, 1919. His name is included on a plaque that was erected at the Flandreau School after the war. After the war he moved back to White Earth and married Grace Anywaush. In the 1930 U.S. Census, Louis was working as a care taker at a mink farm. In the 1940 U.S. Census, he lived with his sons, James, Donal and Leonard, and was working on a road construction project near White Earth. He re-enlisted in the Army during WWII and served as a Private in the Service Battery of the 384th Field Artillery. Louis entered the spirit world on Dec. 5, 1968, after being hit by a car just east of Ogema, MN. He is buried at Calvary Cemetery, White Earth, MN.[1]

Danforth, John A. John was born around June 4, 1900, on the Oneida Reservation in Oneida, WI. His parents were John and Ophelia Danforth. In the 1910 U.S. Census, John was a student at the Tomah Boarding School. Around 1914, John was enrolled in the Flandreau Boarding School. In April 1917, at the age of 16, he enlisted in Troop D, 1st SD Cavalry. Initially, this National Guard troop trained as an infantry unit because they were not issued saddles or horses. On Sept. 15, 1917, the soldiers were sent to Camp Cody, NM. After being in camp for ten days, the SD Cavalry Regiment was assigned to the 59th Depot Brigade, 34th Division. Cpl. Danforth sailed with Co. D, 136th Infantry, 34th Division (ASN 1427363) from New York aboard the *Melita* on Oct. 13, 1918.

Once in France, he was reassigned to Co. L, 49th Infantry. Cpl. Danforth sailed from Brest aboard the *George Washington* on Jan. 12, 1919, and arrived in Hoboken on Jan. 21. Cpl. Danforth was discharged on March 19, 1919. His name was included on a plaque erected at the Flandreau School after the war to honor students and staff who had served. John returned to Wisconsin and worked as a diesel mechanic in Delafield, WI. In the 1940 U.S. Census, he and his wife, Nancy, are listed with their children, John, Hugh, Arthur and Allen. When he registered with the "Old Man's Draft" in 1942, he was living in Clinton and working for Fairbanks Morse. John entered the spirit world at the VA Hospital in Milwaukee on Feb. 10, 1965. He is buried in Highland Memorial Park, Milwaukee, WI.[2]

Day, James Chaska. James was born at Veblen on the Sisseton-Wahpeton Reservation around June 16, 1891. In the 1902 Census Roll, he is listed with his father, William Wapaha [War Bonnet], his mother, Augusta, and his brothers and sisters, Ellen, John, Eliza and Simon. In the 1917 Census Roll, he is listed with his wife, Mary White. When he registered for the draft on June 1, 1917, he lived in Sisseton. He joined the Army on Aug. 28, 1918, and was assigned to Co. H, 41st Infantry, 10th Division (ASN 4499987). The 10th Division trained at Camp Funston, KS, but did not go overseas. Pvt. Day was discharged on June 2, 1919. In the 1930s, James married Julia Frenier. In 1935, the family was interviewed by a worker with the SDERA program. Their home was about 2.5 miles NE of Sisseton, but for the summer they were camping NW of Sisseton. James owned a team of horses which he was using on a threshing job. They also owned a cow and 15 chickens. James' mother and his sisters and their families were also living with them. They told the interviewer that they liked attending Indian celebrations. In the 1940 U.S. Census, James and Julia lived with their daughter, Hilda, in McKinley Township, Marshall County. When James registered for the Selective Service in 1942, he was living in Veblen. He entered the spirit world on Aug. 31, 1942, and is buried in Mayasan Cemetery in Veblen.[3]

DeChon, Alfred. Alfred was born near Cayuga, ND, on the Sisseton-Wahpeton Reservation on Jan. 8, 1900, the son of Albert and Mary DeChon. Alfred enlisted in Regina, Saskatchewan, as Frederick DeChon in the Canadian Army. He served as a Private in the Canadian Machine Gun Depot (ASN 2398328). He died of Jaundice in England on Oct. 31, 1918. He is buried in Seaford Cemetery, Seaford, Sussex.

Decoteau, Napolean. Napoleon was born at Belcourt, ND, on the Turtle Mountain Reservation on April 13, 1899. In the Turtle Mountain Census Roll for 1899, he lived with his mother and father, LaRose and Norbert Decoteau, as well as several brothers and sisters. He was a student at the Flandreau Boarding School when he enlisted in the Army on April 13, 1918. He was sent to Jefferson Barracks, MO, where he was assigned to Co. L, 48th Infantry Regiment (ASN 465355). During the war, the mission of the 48th Infantry was to perform guard duty at the port of Newport News, VA. Some notes from the National Archives show that Pvt. Decoteau helped guard German prisoners at Brest, France. Napolean's name was included on a plaque erected at the Flandreau Indian School to honor students and staff. After the war, Napoleon married Emma Vallie. They had two daughters, Ann and Ruth. Napoleon worked as a farm laborer. He entered the spirit world on the reservation on Dec. 11, 1922, and is buried in St. Michael's Cemetery in Belcourt.[4]

Decoteau, Winfred Louis. Winfred was born on Nov. 24, 1892, in Wilmot on the Sisseton-Wahpeton Reservation. In the 1898 Census Roll, he is listed with his parents, Louis and Virginia, as well as his siblings, William, Clarissa, Lillian and Lien. Winfred joined the Army on Aug. 28, 1918. He served as a Private First Class with the 8th Co., 164th Depot Brigade (ASN 4500091). He was discharged on Dec 3, 1918. He married Esther Mireau. In the 1930 U.S. Census, Winfred and Esther were living with Esther father. Esther passed away in December 1933. Winfred married Ella Mae Deer. In the 1937 Census Roll, they were living with their children, Clarice, Edith and Delphine. Winfred entered the spirit world in Wilmot on Sept. 4, 1954, and is buried in Ascension Presbyterian Cemetery in Spring Grove Township.[5]

Defender, Ben. Ben was born on the Standing Rock Reservation in Kenel, SD, on May 26, 1894. His parents were George Defender and Mary Packineau. Ben married Rebecca Black Fox. When Ben registered for the draft on June 5, 1917, he and Rebecca had a son, Ben Jr. Ben joined the Army on Oct. 6, 1917, and was sent to Camp Funston, KS. Pvt. Defender was assigned to the 314th Military Police, but was not given a service number. On Nov. 22, 1917, he was discharged because of physical disability, for which he received compensation. After he returned home from Kansas, his wife, Rebecca, passed away. He married Jane Waters, who later passed away, in 1927. In 1927, Ben was serving as Sergeant at Arms for the American Legion Post at Kenel. Ben then married Sadie Gilland in 1928. Sadie's brother, Robert, had also served in the Army. In the mid-1930s, the Defender family raised livestock, and had 13 cattle, 13 horses and some chickens. In the 1940 U.S. Census, the family was ranching with their three children, Nancy, Michael and Marian. Their son, Michael, enlisted in the Marine Corps and was wounded three times in WWII. Ben entered the spirit world on April 23, 1968, in the Mobridge Community Hospital. He is buried in Church of Assumption Cemetery in Kenel.[6]

Defond, Baptiste. Baptiste was born on Nov. 18, 1894, on the Yankton Reservation. In the 1895 Census Roll for the Yanktonai Tribe, Baptiste is listed with his parents, Samuel De Fond and Sophie Covell. As a boy, he attended the boarding school at Greenwood, SD. Baptiste enlisted on May 3, 1917, at Columbus Barracks, OH, and was assigned to the 2nd Cavalry at Fort Ethan Allen, VT. On Nov. 6, 1917, he was discharged to accept an appointment as an Army Clerk, Adjutant General's office. On Nov. 14, 1917, he was appointed Army field clerk in the Returns Section of the Adjutant General's office at Hq. N. E. Dept. Boston, MA. He remained in that position until his discharge on June 30, 1922. After his discharge, he served as a clerk for the Department of Agriculture in Washington, D.C., in 1925. In 1930, he was working as a clerk for the Indian Agency in Tuba City, AZ. In 1940, he was a clerk with the Indian Agency in Tulalip, WA. Sometime after this, he married his wife, Carrie (1913-1995), and moved to southern California. Baptiste entered the spirit world on Dec. 14, 1963, and is buried in Ft. Rosencrans National Cemetery. Carrie is buried with him in Section X, site 2036.[7]

Demarsche, Joseph J. Joseph was born on the Rosebud Reservation on May 1, 1895. His parents were Joseph and Emily DeMarsche. When Joseph registered for the draft on June 5, 1917, he was working as a laborer in a pool hall in White River, SD. He joined the Army on Sept. 3, 1917, and served as a Cook in the Medical Department, Camp Hospital #34, at East Norfolk, MA, (ASN15620). He was discharged on May 27, 1919. He married Jennie Brown. In the 1930 U.S. Census, the family lived in Lead, where Joseph worked as a miner in the Homestake gold mine. In the 1937 Rosebud Reservation Census Roll, Joseph and Jennie lived in Lead with their children, James, Marlin, Loretta, Alma and Ronald. Their son, James, enlisted in the Marine Corps in WWII, and died on Nov. 21, 1943, of the wounds he received at Tarawa. Ronald served in the Air Force during the Korean War. Joseph entered the spirit world on March 28, 1945, and is buried in the Black Hills National Cemetery, Section D, Site 381.

Demery, James. James was born July 27, 1887, in Westburn, Manitoba, near Lake Manitoba. His parents, Robert Charles and Harriet Demarais, were Ojibwe. They moved to Dunseith, ND, in the 1890s. The spelling of their name was changed to Demery. In the 1900 U.S. Census, James was a student at the Fort Totten Boarding School. Sometime after this, the family moved to McLaughlin, SD. When James registered for the draft on June 5, 1917, he was farming with his brothers and sisters near McLaughlin. He joined the Army on June 21, 1918, and was sent to Camp Dodge, IA. Pvt. Demery was assigned to Co. B, 333rd Infantry, 84th Division (ASN 3954654). He sailed from New York aboard the *Baltic* on Sept. 1, 1918. Upon arrival in France, he was transferred to Co. D, 140th Infantry, 35th Division. The 35th Division suffered heavy casualties in the opening days of the Meuse-Argonne Offensive. Pvt. Demery sailed for home from St. Nazaire aboard the *Nansemond* on April 1, 1919, and was discharged as a Private on May 7, 1919. After returning home, he married Alice Vermillion (1894-1959). Alice's brother, Arthur had served in the war. James' sister, Lena, married Charles Baker, also a returned veteran. James farmed near McLaughlin. In the 1940 U.S. Census, James and Alice had five children, Chester, Myrtle, Ernest, Florence and Matilda. James was working on road construction and his son, Chester, was driving a truck in the CCC program. Chester served in the military. Sometime after this, the family moved to Snoqualmie, WA. James became a wheat farmer near Snoqualmie. He entered the spirit world in Nelems Memorial Hospital in Snoqualmie on Oct. 7, 1974, and is buried in Sunset Hills Memorial Park, Bellevue, WA.

Demery, Robert. Robert was born Manitoba, Canada, on Aug. 6, 1892. His parents, Francis James and Angelique Demarais were Ojibwe. When the family moved to the U.S. their name was changed to Demery. When Robert registered for the draft on June 5, 1917, he was farming with the Demery family at McLaughlin, SD. Robert enlisted in the Navy on June 8, 1918 (NSN 1309063). He was discharged on Sept. 30, 1921, as a Fireman 3rd Class. After returning home, he married Mary Vermillion. In 1940, they were farming with their children, Edwin, Robert Jr., Loretta, Dorothy, and Leslie. Their son, Robert Jr., served with the Navy in the Pacific during WWII. Edwin was wounded while serving in Europe. Robert Sr. entered the spirit world in the hospital in Fort Yates on Nov. 17, 1945. His wife and three sons, Edwin, Bobby and Leslie, as well as two daughters, Loretta and Dorothy, survived him. He is buried in St. Benedict Cemetery, Kenel, SD.[8]

Denney, John. John was born on the Oneida Reservation in Oneida, WI, on Oct. 27, 1899. His parents were Aaron and Electra Denny. Around 1914, he became a student at the Flandreau Boarding School. In the spring of 1917, he enlisted in Troop D, 1st South Dakota Cavalry. At least 25 students enlisted in that National Guard unit. The Troop drilled as infantry, as no horses were ever provided. On Sept. 15, 1917, they transferred to Camp Cody, NM. Pvt. Denney was assigned to the 34th Division (ASN 1427338). Pvt. Denney sailed from New York aboard the S.S. *Tereisias* on June 28, 1918. He was part of Co. 14, Camp Cody June Automatic Replacement Draft. Upon arrival in France, Pvt. Denny was transferred to the 19th Field Artillery (FA), along with five other Flandreau students. Pvt. Denny served in Battery F, 19th FA, 5th Division. The 19th FA served in the Sectors at St. Die, Villers-en-Haye, St. Mihiel, Limey, and Puvenelle. After the Armistice, the 19th F.A. was billeted in four small towns in southern Luxembourg. The unit sailed for home from Brest aboard the *America* on July 13, 1919. John's name was included on a plaque erected at the Flandreau Indian School to honor students and staff who served.

After his discharge, John returned to his home in Wisconsin. He became a member of the Robert Cornelius Oneida VFW Post #7784. His wife, Florence, preceded him in death. John entered the spirit world in Oneida, WI, on July 21, 1998. At that time, he was the oldest member of the Oneida Nation. He is buried in the Holy Apostles Church Cemetery.[9]

Denney, William. William was born on the Oneida Reservation on Feb. 22, 1900. His parents were Daniel and Cassie Denny. Around 1913, he became a student at the Flandreau Boarding School. In the spring of 1917, William enlisted in Troop D, 1st South Dakota Cavalry. The Troop drilled as an infantry unit, as they never were issued horses. On Sept. 15, 1917, they traveled to Camp Cody, NM. The 1st SD cavalry was split up and the men were transferred to other units. Pvt. Denny sailed to France aboard the S.S. *Tereisias* on June 28, 1918. He was traveling with Co. 14, Camp Cody June Automatic Replacement Draft (ASN 1427387). Upon arrival in France, Pvt. Denny was assigned to Battery A, 19th Field Artillery (FA), 5th Division. After the Armistice, he was billeted in southern Luxembourg. Pfc. Denney sailed for home aboard the U.S.S. *America* on July 13, 1919, and arrived on July 22. William's name was included on a plaque erected at the Flandreau Indian School to honor the students and staff who had served. After his discharge, William returned to Wisconsin. He lived in Hobart, WI, with his wife, Marie, and children, Isabel and Leroy. Around 1945, he started a job at the Badger Ordnance Works, at Baraboo, WI. William died in an explosion at the Ordnance Works on July 19, 1945. He is buried in Kingston Cemetery.[10]

Denoyer, Silas H. Silas was born on April 22, 1900. His parents, Charles and Laura Denoyer were enrolled members of the Rosebud Reservation. As a young man, Silas was enrolled at the Flandreau Boarding School, when he enlisted in the Army in 1917. School records indicate that he was sent home, after being discharged on Oct. 16, 1917, most likely due to eye troubles. When Silas registered for the draft on Sept. 12, 1918, he was a student at the Rapid City Boarding School. In the 1920 U.S. Census, he was living with his parents. In 1921, he was a member of the Chauncey Eagle Horn Legion Post in Rosebud. Sometime after this, he married a widow, Angeline Decory. In 1930, he was working at odd jobs. By the 1940 U.S. Census, he was working as a truck driver for the Indian Service in Todd County. He and Angeline had four children then, Carl, Alberta, Martha and Edna. Silas entered the spirit world on May 18, 1967, and is buried in Trinity Cemetery, Mission, SD.

Deon, Harold Wilbur. Harold was born on the Pine Ridge Reservation on June 5, 1897, to Sam and Susie Deon. He had a younger brother, Ross, who also served in the military. Harold enlisted in the U.S. Navy and served as a baker during the war. He was discharged on March 22, 1921. He became ill with tuberculosis and entered the spirit world at the Pine Ridge Agency on Feb. 8, 1922, and is buried in Holy Cross Cemetery, Shannon County.[11]

Deon, Louis A. Louis was born on the Pine Ridge Reservation around 1897, the son of Louis and Mary Deon. Louis attended the boarding school at Carlisle from 1911-1914. Louis enlisted in the Army on July 26, 1916. He likely served with the SD National Guard on the Mexican border. Mus. 2nd Cl. Deon sailed from Hoboken, NJ, aboard the *Great Northern* on May 2, 1918. While serving in France, he was a Musician 1st Class in the Headquarters Detachment of the 110th Engineers, 35th Division (ASN 1469029). The 35th Division was involved in very heavy combat at the opening of the Meuse-Argonne Campaign. After the Armistice, Deon's commanding officer evaluated him, saying the he "served as a litter bearer in Meuse-Argonne, showing coolness and courage when in action." The 35th Division suffered 7,283 casualties in the war. Mus. 1st Cl. Deon sailed from Brest, France, aboard the *Von Steuben* on April 11, 1919, and arrived in Hoboken on April 19. The 110th Engineers arrived in Camp Funston, KS, on April 30, 1919. Musician Deon was discharged on May 3, 1919. Louis started working for the Chicago and Northwestern Railroad on July 13, 1919. He married his wife, Florence (1903-1958), around 1922. In the 1930 U.S. Census, the family was living in Chadron, NE, where Louis was working as a brakeman for the railroad. He died in a car accident on Feb. 10, 1935, and is buried in Holy Rosary Cemetery on the Pine Ridge Reservation. His wife, Florence, and a daughter, Nancy, survived him.[12]

Deon, Ross. Ross was born on the Pine Ridge Reservation on July 5, 1899. In the 1905 Pine Ridge Census Roll, he is listed with his parents, Sam and Susie Deon, plus a brother, Harold. After joining the Army, Pvt. Ross served with the 31st Infantry Regiment in Manila, Philippines and in Vladivostok, Russia, during the war. He was discharged on Oct. 8, 1919. In the 1935 Census Roll, Ross is listed with his wife, Lucille Williams. Around 1955, he moved to Ogden, Utah, where he married Frances Mae Hymas. He worked for the highway department. Ross entered the spirit world on Dec. 8, 1970, following a vehicle accident in Ogden. He was survived by his widow, two step sons and two step daughters. He is buried in Washington Heights Memorial Park, Ogden, UT. Military honors were accorded by World War I Veterans, Barracks 1011.

DeRockbraine, Andrew. Andrew was born about August 8, 1899, on the Standing Rock Reservation, near Bullhead, SD. His parents were Charles and Josephine DeRockbraine. Andrew was a student at the Flandreau Boarding School. Andrew enlisted in the Army on April 13, 1918. In the 1920 U.S. Census, he was stationed at Fort Bayard, NM. He was discharged on Jan. 20, 1920. Andrew's name was included on a plaque erected at the Flandreau Indian School. In the late 1920s, he had a minor role in the film, "They Died with Their Boots On." Andrew made almost $1000 and met a number of famous actors. Errol Flynn played the role of Custer. In the 1937 Standing Rock Census roll, Andrew was listed as single. In the 1940 U.S. Census, he was working as a laborer in the CCC program. Andrew entered the spirit world on May 7, 1973, at the Public Health Service hospital in Fort Yates. He is buried in St. Aloysius Cemetery in Bullhead, SD.[13]

DeRockbraine, Antoine. Antoine was born about June 2, 1895, on the Standing Rock Reservation. He was the son of Charles and Josephine DeRockbraine. He was a brother to Andrew. Their sister, Mary Ann, married John Garter, who also served in the military. When Antoine registered for the draft on June 5, 1917, he was working as a farm laborer near Bullhead, SD. Antoine enlisted in the Army on June 24, 1918, and was sent to Camp Funston, KS. He was assigned to the Quartermaster Corps, Utilities Detachment, Construction Division (ASN 3309590). He was discharged as a Private on April 4, 1919. After returning home to Bullhead, he married Emma Black Fox, but they were divorced in 1928. In 1935, Antoine was renting a house from his brother-in-law, John Garter. He owned four horses and did some work as an employee of the emergency conservation program. Antoine entered the spirit world in McIntosh on Jan. 22, 1960 and is buried in Bullhead Cemetery.[14]

DeRockbraine, Thomas. Thomas was born about Oct. 27, 1895, on the Standing Rock Reservation. His parents were Antone and Domitilla DeRockbraine. Two of Thomas' sisters were married to WWI veterans. Josephine married Luke Speaks Walking and Margaret married Allen Little Eagle. Thomas attended school in Rapid City. When he registered for the draft on June 5, 1917, he was farming with his father. Thomas enlisted in the Army on Sept. 21, 1917. He was assigned to the Machine Gun Company, 38th Infantry, 3rd Division (ASN 2193005). Pvt. DeRockbraine sailed from Halifax, Nova Scotia, aboard the *Corsican* on March 25, 1918. The *Corsican* first docked at Glasgow, Scotland. From there, the 38th Infantry took the Caledonian Railroad south to Camp Woodsley, England. After a 12-mile hike to Southhampton, they sailed aboard an old cattle boat, the *Austrilind,* to France. Pvt. DeRockbraine served 17 months overseas, in the same unit as Charles Howard, Martin Medicine and James Eagle Horn. The 38th Infantry served in the Sectors at Aisne, Chateau-Thierry, Champagne-Marne, Aisne-Marne, Vesle, St. Mihiel and Meuse-Argonne. After the war, the 38th Infantry was known as "The Rock of the Marne." Pvt. DeRockbraine sailed home from Brest aboard the *Agamemnon* on Aug. 10, 1919, and arrived in Hoboken on Aug. 18. Thomas was discharged on Aug. 24, 1919, as a Private. About a week later he married Josephine Hawk in McIntosh. They farmed near Bullhead. In 1935, the family was interviewed by a worker with the SDERA program. They were living in a one room log house near Bullhead and used a kerosene lamp for light. Their home was 3.5 miles from a graded road. The family owned a scraper, a plow and two wagons. Thomas rented horses from Thomas Yellow Earring to use on local conservation projects. Before the war, he had owned 50 head of cattle and 15 horses. He was a member of the VFW and the American Legion. In the 1940 U.S. Census, Thomas and Josephine had six daughters, Marie, Margaret, Dorothy, Bertha, Theresa, and Matilda. Thomas entered the spirit world on Nov. 28, 1970, at a Bismarck hospital. He is buried in St. Aloysius Cemetery in Bullhead.[15]

Desersa, Alex. Alex was born on the Rosebud Reservation on Dec. 17, 1898, to Mitchell and Josephine Desersa. Mitchell had served with the 6th Cavalry, U.S. Army, from 1892-1894. Alex's older sister, Josephine was married to Thomas New, who had served in the Army during WWI. His sister, Anna, married Jack Bonser, who served in the Army during the war. Alex first married Gertrude Stover, whose brother, John, served in the Navy during the war. After Gertrude entered the spirit world in 1925, Alex enlisted in the Army and served from 1925-1928 at Camp Meade. He later married Angelique Turning Holy, whose father, Frank, had served in the Army during the war. In 1935, the family was interviewed by a worker with the SDERA program. The family was living near Rapid City in a wood framed structure covered with a tent. Alex had done some relief work, working on a bridge construction site. In the 1940 U.S. Census, he and Angelique are listed with their children, Eli, Clara, Maymie, Bernice and Claudine. Alex entered the spirit world in his home in Pine Ridge on Oct. 23, 1968. He is buried in Martin Cemetery.[16]

Desersa, Charles. Charles was born on March 4, 1893, on the Rosebud Reservation. His parents were Alex and Susie Desersa. When Charles registered for the draft on June 5, 1917, he was working for the government as an apprentice plumber at Rosebud. When Charles enlisted in the Army, he was sent to Camp Lewis, WA. He was assigned to Co. 38, 166th Depot Brigade. He suffered from pneumonia and entered the spirit world in the Base Hospital at Camp Lewis on June 13, 1918. He is buried in St. Francis, SD. His younger brother, Felix, also served in the Army.[17]

Desersa, Edward. Edward was born around 1888 on the Rosebud Reservation to Alex and Susie Desersa. In 1912, he married Laura Stover from Pine Ridge. When he registered for the draft on June 5, 1917, he was working for the U.S. Government in Martin. When he joined the Army, he was assigned to the Veterinary Corps (ASN 3176554). He was scheduled to travel with the 9th Vet. Hospital on July 26, 1918. However, he was held back, possibly due to illness. He finally sailed from Brooklyn aboard the *Federal* on Nov. 27, 1918, with "Casuals of Replacement Units, Vet Corps." He was stationed at Vet. Hospital No. 9, in St. Nazaire, France. After the war, he returned home to his family. His wife had a brother, George, who died in France due to the flu. Edward's brother, Charles, also died due to illness while with the Army in Camp Lewis, WA. Edward later married Lavina Bissonette. Edward was shot by a policeman in Rapid City on Jan. 17, 1925. He is buried in Mountain View Cemetery.

Desersa, Felix. Felix was born around 1909 on the Rosebud Reservation to Alex and Susie Desersa. He was a brother to Charles. Felix enlisted in the Army at Camp Meade, SD, on Jan. 31, 1927. He served in Co. B, 4th Cavalry (ASN 6769993). He was discharged in Denver on June 9, 1930. He entered the spirit world at Battle Mountain Sanatorium on June 1, 1932, and is buried in Hot Springs National Cemetery, plot 9, 6R4.

Dewitt, Ben. Ben Ash Dewitt was born about June 23, 1899, on the Lower Brule Reservation. He likely was named after Ben Ash, the Agent in charge of the Agency at that time. Ben's parents were Louis and Julia (Arconge) Dewitt. They farmed near the old Fort George site by the Missouri River. In the 1910 U.S. Census, Ben was a student at the Pierre Boarding School. He enlisted in the Army on March 9, 1918, and may have served with the 19th Infantry at Camp Travis, Texas. He was discharged on Feb. 1, 1919. In the 1920 U.S. Census, he was once again attending the Pierre Boarding School, and lived with Oliver Russell, a fellow veteran. Shortly after this, he married his first wife, Dollie. They had three children. Dollie entered the spirit world in 1925. In 1933, Ben married Celestine Blackbird Goodlow (1908-1990). In the 1940 U.S. Census, Ben was working as a tribal judge. Ben and Celestine raised seven children, Ben Jr., Charles, Grace, Marvin, Truman, Mary, and Carol. Ben's son, Ben Jr. was killed in WWII in Europe in 1944. Ben Sr. entered the spirit world in the community hospital in Chamberlain, SD, on March 29, 1979. He is buried in Messiah Episcopal Cemetery, Iron Nation, SD.[18]

Dickerson, Harry Byron. Harry was born in Wakonda, SD, on Jan. 17, 1893. His parents were Martin and Ella Dickerson. When he registered for the draft on June 5, 1917, he was farming in Brule County. Shortly after this, he married Beulah Bailly of Sisseton. Harry joined the Army on May 24, 1918, and was first assigned to Co. E, 159th Infantry, 40th Division (ASN 2788942). He sailed from New York aboard the *Otranta* on Aug. 8, 1918. Upon arrival in France, he was reassigned to Co. C, 126th Infantry, 32nd Division. The 126th Infantry served in the Sectors at Oise-Aisne, and the Meuse-Argonne. Pfc. Dickerson sailed from Brest aboard the *F.J. Luckenbach* on April 28, 1919, and arrived in Boston on May 14. He was discharged on May 22, 1919. In the 1932 Sisseton-Wahpeton Census Roll, Harry is listed with Beulah, but he was not enrolled. In the 1940 U.S. Census, Harry was working for the Sisseton street department. Harry and Beulah lived with their five children, Rosale, Elaine, Amelia, Myrton and Betty. Their son, Myrton, served in WWII. Harry entered the spirit world on July 30, 1972.

Did Not Butcher, Isaac. Isaac was born around March 1892 on the Standing Rock Reservation. In the 1910 U.S. Census, he is listed with his parents, Paul and Harriet Did Not Butcher, as well as two sisters. Isaac enlisted in the Army on Sept. 18, 1917, and was sent to Camp Funston, KS. He was served as a Private in Co. C, 340th Machine Gun Battalion. He passed away at Camp Funston on Jan. 2, 1918. He is buried in the Congregational Cemetery at Wakpala. His name is engraved on a monument in that cemetery.

Didier, Reason O. Reason was born on the Rosebud Reservation to Henry Didier and Ellen Walker on Dec. 31, 1891. Reason was farming when he registered for the draft on June 5, 1917. He joined the Army on Oct. 2, 1917, and was assigned to Co. B, 342nd Machine Gun BN, 89th Division (ASN 2185783). He trained at Camp Funston, KS. The 342nd MG BN served in the Sectors at Lucey, St. Mihiel, Euvezin, and Meuse-Argonne. Wagoner Didier sailed from Brest aboard the *Prinz Friedrich Wilhelm* on May 18, 1919. He was discharged on June 9, 1919. He married Fern Jenks and ranched with his family near Wewela, SD. They had two children, Carol and Merle. Merle served with the Army in Korea. Reason entered the spirit world on Nov. 10, 1960, and is buried in Mount Hope Cemetery in Springview, NE.

Dillon, Rienzol. He is listed on the WWI veteran's memorial at Oglala Lakota College, Kyle, SD. Reinzie was born on the Pine Ridge Reservation on March 8, 1899. In the 1904 Census Roll, he is listed with his father, Peter. In 1915, Reinzie was a student at the Rapid City boarding school. While enrolled there, he enlisted in the Army on March 28, 1917. This most likely was the 4th South

Dakota Infantry. When Pvt. Dillon arrived at Camp Greene, NC, in September of 1917, he was assigned to Co. B, 148th Machine Gun (MG) Battalion, 41st Division (ASN 98584). He sailed with his unit from Hoboken aboard the *Olympic* on Jan. 11, 1918. On arrival in France, he was one of the many SD soldiers who were transferred to Co. M, 167th Infantry, 42nd Division. The 167th Infantry served in the Sectors at Luneville, Baccarat, Esperance-Souain, Champagne-Marne, Aisne-Marne, St. Mihiel, Essey-Pannes, and Meuse-Argonne. Pvt. Dillon sailed for home from Brest aboard the U.S.S. *Minnesota* on April 15, 1919, and was discharged on May 9, 1919. Shortly after returning home, he married Susie Larvie. They lived in Norris for 13 years. Reinzie served as a policeman for several years. In 1935, they moved to some land northeast of Wanblee. The family was interviewed by a worker with the SDERA program. They owned three horses and four head of cattle. Reinzie told the state worker that he was not interested in farming. Their land was more suited to raising cattle. In 1935, he was in charge of organizing the rodeo scheduled for September. In the 1940 U.S. Census, Reinzie and Susie were living with their children, Rowland, Irene Elsie, Rose Evelyn, Elaine and Evans. In 1957, Reinzie was working as a painter in Rapid City. He later moved to the State Veterans Home in Hot Springs, where he passed away on May 8, 1964, and is buried in the Black Hills National Cemetery, Section D, site 362.[19]

Dion, Alfred. Alfred was born on Nov. 16, 1886, in White Swan Township, Charles Mix County. His parents were Isaac and Hattie Dion. In his first marriage, he had two children, including a son, Ward, who served in World War II. When Alfred registered for the draft on June 5, 1917, he was ranching in Buffalo County. Alfred enlisted on Sept. 20, 1917. After Alfred joined the Army, he was promoted to Corporal and served in Company B, 340th Machine Gun Battalion, 89th Division (ASN 2193114). After the fighting was over, his commanding officer wrote that Corporal Dion was "above average in courage, endurance and good humor." The 340th MG Bn. sailed from France on May 15, 1919, aboard the ship *Leviathan*. Corporal Dion was discharged on June 2, 1919. Alfred returned to White Swan. In the 1920 U.S. Census, he and his children were living with his father. In 1934, he married Lillian Fine Voice Crow. In the 1940 U.S. Census, Alfred and Lillian were living in White Swan Township with Lillian's mother, Susie Fine Voice Crow. Alfred entered the spirit world on Nov. 22, 1964, at the VA Hospital in Sioux Falls. He is buried in Cedar Presbyterian Cemetery, across from the Fort Randall Casino.[20]

Dion, George James. George was born in Burke, SD, on Sept. 13, 1898. In the 1905 Census Roll for the Rosebud Reservation, George is listed with his parents, Oliver and Susan Dion, along with his older brother, Joseph. Family records indicate that George served in the military. He married Johanna Flynn in 1918. George entered the spirit world on April 19, 1926, and is buried in St Joseph's Cemetery in Gregory, SD. Earl, the son of George and Johanna, was killed in Action in Europe during WWII.

Dion, Joseph M. Joseph was born on March 10, 1896, in Wetstone, SD. He was the son of Oliver and Susan (Langdeau) Dion. When Joseph registered for the draft on June 5, 1917, he was farming with his brother, John. Joseph enlisted in the Army on May 26, 1918, at Bonesteel, SD. He likely trained at Camp Funston, KS. Pvt. Dion sailed from New York aboard the *Ortega* on Aug. 31, 1918. He was traveling with Overseas Casual Co. No. 361 (ASN 3130118), listed as unassigned. After arriving in France, he was assigned to Co. K, 357th Infantry, 90th Division. The 357th Infantry served in the Sectors at Villers-en-Haye, St. Mihiel, Puvenelle and Meuse-Argonne. The 90th Division suffered 7,277 casualties in the war. After the Armistice, the 357th Infantry was billeted at Hillesheim, Germany. Pvt. Dion left St. Nazaire, France, aboard the U.S.S. *Huron* on May 16, 1919. Pvt. Dion was discharged on June 16, 1919, at Camp Dodge, IA.

After Joseph arrived home, he married Zeta Foley (1896-1979). In the 1930 U.S. Census, they were living in Gregory, SD, with their daughters, Marjorie and Dorothy. Joseph was working as a salesman, selling clothing and paint. He was a member of the VFW. In the 1940 U.S. Census, he was working as a laborer on a highway construction project. He later worked as a truck driver, and moved to Las Vegas, Nevada. He passed away in Las Vegas on Sept. 24, 1990, and is buried in Palm Valley View Memorial Park.[21]

Dion, Samuel. Samuel was born on Aug. 9, 1894, in Greenwood, SD. In the 1906 Yanktonai Census Roll, he is listed with his parents, Isaac and Hattie. His older brother, Alfred, served in the Army. Samuel married Bessie Fine Voice Crow in 1916. He joined the Army on June 27, 1918. He was assigned Co. F, 351st Infantry Regiment, 88th Division (ASN 3315370), which was trained at Camp Dodge, IA. Other local men who served with Pfc. Dion were Roy Cook, Daniel Jandreau, Jesse Kezena, Joseph Brother of All and Peter Hopkins. The 351st Infantry sailed from New York aboard the *Scotian* on Aug. 15, 1918, and arrived in France around Sept. 1, 1918. They did not serve in the front trenches before the Armistice, but they were assigned to be part of the Army of Occupation along the French- German border. Pfc. Dion received an evaluation from his commander stating that he "has shown a marked amount of good humor, initiative, courage and dexterity. Exceptionally good bomber. Efficient as a night worker, runner and observer." The 351st Infantry was billeted near Houdelainecourt until May 1919. On May 20, 1919, the 351st Infantry sailed for America aboard the U.S.S. *Mercury* and docked at Newport News, VA. Pfc. Dion was discharged on June 7, 1919. Samuel returned to his home in White Swan Township. In the 1940 U.S. Census, he and Bessie were farming with their younger children, Neuland, Dwight and Vernida. Samuel entered the spirit world on Sept. 2, 1977, and is buried in Cedar Presbyterian Cemetery, across from Fort Randall Casino.[22]

Dixon, John York. He is listed on WWI veteran's memorial at Oglala Lakota College, Kyle, SD. John was born April 20, 1895, on the Pine Ridge Reservation. His parents were John Dixon and Elizabeth Sechler. When John registered for the draft on June 5, 1917, he was working as a ranch laborer. He joined the Army on July 23, 1918, and was first assigned to Co. C, 333rd Infantry, 84th Division (ASN 3955223). Pvt. Dixon sailed from New York aboard the *Baltic* on Sept. 1, 1918. After arriving in France, he was assigned to Co. F, 138th Infantry, 35th Division. The 35th Division suffered heavy casualties in the opening days of the Meuse-Argonne Offensive. Pvt. Dixon sailed from St. Nazaire aboard the *Aeolus* on April 16, 1919. He was discharged as a Private on May 12, 1919. After returning home, he married Clara Twiss. In the 1940 U.S. Census, he and Clara were living on the reservation with their children, Kathryn, Mildred, Raymond and Frederick. Their son, Frederick, served in the military during the Korean Conflict. John entered the spirit world at the VA Hospital in Hot Springs on Jan. 16, 1974. He is buried in the Black Hills National Cemetery, Section C, site 788.[23]

Dog, Joseph Lawrence. Joseph was born about July 9, 1894, on the Standing Rock Reservation. His parents were Louis Dog and Win Yan Waste. He had a younger brother, Louis, who served with the Army in France. In Sept. 1911, Joseph was sent to the boarding school at Carlisle, PA, where he was enrolled in the carpentry trade. In 1914, he was sent to the Fort Lapwai Sanatorium in Idaho to be treated for a mild case of tuberculosis. When he registered for the draft, he was ranching near Bullhead, SD. Joseph enlisted in the Army on Oct. 5, 1917. He was assigned to Co. B, 314th Train HQ. and MP, 89th Division (ASN 2194431). He was discharged on March 12, 1919, as a Private First Class. After returning home, he married Mary Shot At. In the 1932 Census Roll for the Standing Rock Reservation, Joseph and Mary are listed with their children, Genevieve and

Helen. In 1932, Joseph changed his name to Joel Farrell. On Jan. 15, 1939, he married Mae Viola Chapman (1918-1999) in Rapid City. He worked as a laborer and gardener. When he registered for the Selective Service in 1942, he was working at the Cement Plant in Rapid City. He entered the spirit world in St. John's Hospital in Rapid City on Aug. 2, 1955, and is buried in the Black Hills National Cemetery, section A, site 637. His widow, Mae, requested that his name be inscribed as Joel Farrell. Mae is also buried in the Black Hills.[24]

Dog, Louis. Louis, a younger brother of Joseph, was born on the Standing Rock Reservation about May 4, 1899. He was the son of Louis Dogg and Win Yan Waste. Louis was enrolled in the boarding school at Flandreau, SD. On April 4, 1917, he enlisted in Troop D, 1st South Dakota Cavalry at Flandreau. This National Guard unit trained in South Dakota until they received orders to report to Camp Cody, NM, on Sept. 15, 1917. Upon arrival at Deming, NM, they were transferred to the 34th Division. Pvt. Dog sailed to France aboard the S.S. *Tereisias* on June 28, 1918. He was assigned to Co. 14, Camp Cody June Automatic Replacement Draft (ASN 1427439). After arriving in France, Pvt. Dog was assigned to Battery A, 19th Field Artillery, 5th Division. He served as a Private in Battery A, along with Pvt. Francis Janis and Pvt. Willie Mountain. After completing training at La Valdahon, France, the Artillery Brigade took a position in the St. Die area and was provided with 75 mm guns. After the Armistice, Pvt. Dog received an evaluation from his commanding officer, who wrote that Pvt. Dog "can be counted upon to perform his duties well." The 19th Field Artillery performed occupational duty in Luxembourg, until returning home on July 13, 1919. Pvt. Dog sailed with his unit from Brest, France, aboard the *America*. Pvt. Dog was discharged July 29, 1919, at Camp Dodge. Louis's name is included on a plaque erected at the Flandreau Indian School to honor the war veterans. After returning home, Louis lived near Little Eagle with his wife, Rachel. He was a member of the American Legion Post at Kenel. Louis developed Peritonitis and was admitted to the VA Hospital on Jan. 8, 1932. He entered the spirit world on Jan. 29, 1932, at the VA hospital in Hot Springs. Initially he was buried at Kenel, but his grave has been moved to the Black Hills National Cemetery.[25]

Dog Eyes, Charles. Charles was born about Sept. 15, 1883, on the Rosebud Reservation. His parents were Matthew Dog Eyes and Ellen Good Woman. When Charles registered for the draft on June 5, 1917, he was working as a policeman in Norris. Charles enlisted in the Army on Sept. 21, 1917. He was assigned to the 2nd Cavalry Training Troop (ASN 2192743). Pvt. Dog Eyes was assigned to the 340th Machine Gun (MG) Battalion, which sailed from Hoboken aboard the *Kroonland* on April 30, 1918. He was traveling with Casual Detachment, 3rd Division. Charles Walking Bull and Napoleon Ducheneaux were on the ship with him. Pvt. Dog Eyes was assigned to the 9th MG Battalion. He likely was wounded or gassed while serving with the 3rd Division. He was discharged on Dec. 14, 1918, as a Private. In the 1930 U.S. Census, he was living in Corn Creek Township, Mellette County. In the mid-1930s, he married his wife, Ella. When Charles registered for the Selective Service in 1942, he was living in Norris. Charles entered the spirit world in rural Norris on March 10, 1948, and is buried in St. Thomas Cemetery, Norris, SD.

Doxtator, Mark E. Mark was born around April 7, 1900, on the Oneida Reservation near Green Bay, WI. In 1913, he was enrolled in the boarding school in Flandreau, SD. On April 4, 1917, Mark enlisted in Troop D, 1st SD Cavalry. This National Guard unit trained initially as an infantry unit, as they were not issued any horses or tack equipment. On Sept. 15, 1917, they were sent to Camp Cody, NM. Once there, they became part of the 34th Division. Pvt. Doxtator sailed to France aboard the S.S. *Tereisias* on June 28, 1918, as one of the soldiers in Co. 14, Camp Cody June Automatic Replacement Draft (ASN 1427441). Upon arrival in France, Pvt. Doxtator was assigned to Headquarters Company, 19th Field Artillery (FA), which was part of the 5th Division. The 19th FA served in the Sectors at St. Die, Villers-en-Haye, St. Mihiel, Limey and Puvenelle. After the Armistice, the 19th Field Artillery was billeted in several small towns in Luxembourg as part of the Army of Occupation. Pvt. Doxtator sailed for home from Brest, France, aboard the *America* on July 13, 1919. He arrived in Hoboken, NJ, on July 22, and was discharged on July 30, 1919. Mark's name is included on a plaque erected at the Flandreau Indian School honoring the students and staff who served. After his return, he married his wife, Martha. On Sept. 15, 1920, he enlisted in the US Navy. He was discharged as a Fireman 2nd Class on Sept. 14, 1922. In the 1930 U.S. Census, the Doxtator family was living in Milwaukee, where Mark was working as a die molder. In 1937, he was working for Stroh Die Molding Co. In 1940, they were living with their children, Vernon, Gloria, Kenneth, Shirley and Phyllis. In 1953, Mark was still working for Stroh. Mark entered the spirit world on May 12, 1977, in the VA hospital in Milwaukee. He is buried in Wood National Cemetery. [26]

Dozark, Frank John. Frank Dozark's name is included on the Oglala Tribe's list of veterans. Frank was born in Plankinton, SD, on Jan. 1, 1888, the son of Joseph and Julia Dozark. When he registered for the draft on June 5, 1917, he was farming near Pukwana, SD. When Frank joined the Army, he was assigned to the 104th Mobile, Ordnance Repair Shop (ASN 1161543), 29th Division. This was a unit which traveled to different regiments and inspected and made repairs on individual soldiers' rifles. Pvt. Dozark sailed from New York aboard the *Medic* on June 29, 1918. After the Armistice, he returned home from St. Nazaire, France, aboard the *Manchuria* on May 11, 1919, and docked at Hoboken. Pfc. Dozark also served with the 621st Casual Detachment, Demobilization Group. Returning home, he had a blacksmith shop in Pukwana. In the 1930 U.S. Census, he had a shop in Washington County, likely at Kyle. On March 29, 1932, he married Agnes Clifford. In the 1937 Pine Ridge Census Roll, Frank is listed with Agnes and their daughter, Violet, though Frank was non-enrolled. Frank and Agnes ranched on her family's land near Three Mile Creek. Agnes loved horses and had a herd of Palominos. She and Frank had four daughters, Violet, Annette, Connie and Norma. Frank entered the spirit world on Jan. 23, 1965.

Drapeau, Benjamin. Benjamin was born on Feb. 15, 1889, as an enrolled member of the Rosebud Reservation. His parents were Leon and Emma Drapeau. In the 1900 U.S. Census, he was a student at the Chamberlain boarding school. When Benjamin registered for the draft on June 5, 1917, he was living in Gregory, SD. He joined the Army on Sept. 22, 1917, in Bonesteel. He was assigned to Co. A (Second Squad), 114th Machine Gun (MG) Battalion, 30th Division (ASN 2193211). Pvt. Drapeau sailed from New York aboard the *Elpener* on May 11, 1918. The 114th MG Battalion served in the Sectors at Canal, Ypres-Lys and Somme. Pfc. Drapeau was discharged on Jan. 15, 1919. He likely had been wounded or gassed, as the rest of his unit did not leave France until March of 1919. In the 1940 U.S. Census, he was single and living with his parents in Gregory. He moved to Rapid City in 1953. He was a member of VFW Post 1273. He entered the spirit world on Feb. 22, 1968, in a Rapid City hospital. He is buried in the Black Hills National Cemetery, section D, site 628. [27]

Drapeau, David W. David was born in Platte, SD, on Sept. 9, 1891. In the 1895 Yanktonai Sioux Census Roll, he is listed with his parents, Louis and Julia, and two sisters, Emma and Minnie. When David registered for the draft on June 5, 1917, he was working as a clerk for the Indian Service at Rosebud. He enlisted on April 26, 1918, and was assigned to Co. E, 355th Infantry, 89th Division (ASN 2186841). Pvt. Frank Ferris, also from Platte, served in Co. E. On June 4, 1918, the men in Co. E sailed for Europe aboard the ship *Baltic*. Company E suffered light casualties during the fighting,

Eugene Rouillard, Phillip Frazier, David W. Drapeau
Ancestry.com

though the 89th Division did have 7,291 casualties. After the Armistice, Captain Charles A. Wright prepared an evaluation for Pfc. Drapeau. He wrote,

> This man is an excellent soldier. He displayed no nervousness under fire and handles men well. Associates readily with white men and is considered by everyone to be an unusually good man. He is good at scouting, has plenty of courage, endurance, and good humor. Knows what is going on all the time and uses good judgement. He is good on maps, as a runner, observer and reporter.

Company E was billeted in Saarburg, Germany, as part of the Army of Occupation. They returned to the U.S. on May 15, 1919, aboard the *Leviathan*. Pfc. Drapeau was discharged on May 31, 1919 and returned home. In 1919, a photo of Pfc. Drapeau was published in a unit history of Company E, 355th Infantry. In the 1920 U.S. Census, he was living in Lakes Andes and working as a book keeper in the auditor's office. He married Ethel Bowe. In the 1934 Census Roll, David was working on the Crow Creek Reservation. Sometime around then, he joined the Officers Reserve Corps. He made 2nd Lieutenant in the Reserves. When he registered for the Selective Service in 1942, he was working for the Carson Indian Agency at Stewart, Nevada. He later moved to Portland. David entered the spirit world in Portland, OR, on Oct. 22, 1956. His widow, Ethel, and children, Anna May, Paul, and Patty survived him. He is buried at Willamette National Cemetery. Ethel (1898-1971) is buried with him.[28]

Drapeau, George Dewey. George was born on March 21, 1899, in Charles Mix County. In the 1902 Census Roll for the Yanktonai Sioux, George is listed with his parents, Frank and Maggie, as well as two sisters and a brother, Raymond, who served in the Navy during the war. George joined the Army on Aug. 6, 1918 and was discharged as a Private on Dec. 31, 1918. After returning home, he married Hermine Cournoyer. They had a son, William. Hermine passed away in January 1940. In March, George married Alice McBride. George was working as a bus driver for the St. Paul's Indian Mission, Marty, SD. William Drapeau served in the U.S. Navy from 1946-49. George entered the spirit world on Sept. 7, 1978, in Alameda County, California. He is buried in Lone Tree Cemetery, Hayward, CA.

Drapeau, Philip. Philip was born at Platte, SD, on Jan. 3, 1889. His parents were Narcisse Drapeau and Elizabeth Keeler. He married Viola Highrock on March 12, 1917. When he registered for the draft on June 5, 1917, he was working as a blacksmith in Ravinia. He served in the military, and was discharged on Dec. 31, 1918. In the 1922 Census Roll, he and Viola had a daughter, Carrie. In the 1930 U.S. Census, Philip worked as a carpenter in Thurston County, NE. He entered the spirit world on Oct. 31, 1957, in the Yankton Indian Hospital in Wagner. He is buried at St. Paul's Mission.[29]

Drapeau, Ray E. Ray was born on Jan. 11, 1896, In Charles Mix County. He was a brother to George. Their parents were Frank and Maggie Drapeau. Ray enlisted in the U.S. Navy on May 15, 1917. He received his honorable discharge on Sept. 22, 1919. After the war he wrote to Joseph Dixon, saying, "I played with the largest Band in the world led by John Philip Sousa, for eighteen months. I made all the Liberty Loans all over the U.S." After the war, he married Rose Hopkins, who was a sister to Peter Hopkins, a fellow veteran. In the late 1930s, Ray moved to Petaluma, CA, where he farmed. He suffered from heart problems and entered the spirit world at the VA Hospital in San Francisco on Jan. 12, 1940. He is buried in San Francisco National Cemetery, Section DS, site 1174-B.[30]

Driver, Moses Heyoka. Moses Heyoka [Clown] was born in Sisseton on July 3, 1896. In the 1910 U.S. Census, he is listed with his parents, Elias and Nancy, and a sister, Elizabeth. Moses joined the Army on Sept. 21, 1917, and was sent to Camp Funston, KS. He was assigned to Co. B, 341st Machine Gun (MG) Battalion, 89th Division (ASN 2192926). He sailed from Brooklyn aboard the *Tennyson* on June 4, 1918. Pfc. Driver was gassed on Oct. 22, 1918, when the 89th Division was fighting near the Bois de Bantheville. He sailed from St. Nazaire aboard the *Manchuria* on Jan. 10, 1919, and arrived at Hoboken on Jan. 22. He traveled with St. Nazaire Casual Co. No. 127. Pfc. Driver was discharged on Feb. 8, 1919. He married Mary Jones on March 29, 1919. In the 1930 U. S. Census, he was farming in Long Hollow Township, Roberts County. In the 1930s, he married Lena Max. In the 1937 Census Roll, they were living with their children, Doris and Caroline. Moses lived in Sisseton until November 1970. Moses entered the spirit world in Oakland, CA, on Aug. 19, 1972. A son, Vernie, and a daughter, Doris, survived him. He is buried in the Veterans Circle, Sisseton Cemetery.[31]

Drops at a Distance, David. David was born on the Cheyenne River Reservation around August 12, 1894. In the 1897 Census Roll, David was listed with his parents, James Drops at a Distance and Jessie High Horse. James had served in the Indian Police. David first married Nancy Shoulder, but she passed away in 1917 from tuberculosis. When he registered for the draft on June 5, 1917, he was farming near White Horse. David joined the Army on May 24, 1918. He likely was sent to Camp Funston, KS, for training. He was first assigned to Co. K, 157th Infantry, 40th Division (ASN 3126947). Pvt. Drops At A Distance sailed with his unit from Boston aboard the *Berrina* on Aug. 9, 1918. Many soldiers from the 40th Division were reassigned a few days before the start of the Meuse-Argonne Offensive. On Sept. 23, 1918, Pfc. Drops at a Distance joined Co. K, 305th Infantry, 77th Division, along with Pfc. Joseph Jewett, also from White Horse, SD. After the Armistice, the 305th Infantry was billeted in several French towns, including St. Martin and Bouere. Pfc. Drops At A Distance sailed from Brest, France, aboard the H.M.T. *Aquitania* with Pfc. Jewett on April 19, 1919. Pfc. Drops at a Distance was discharged on May 18, 1919. After the war, he sent to Joseph Dixon his reason for serving, "I wanted to go and fight, even though I was not a citizen."

Around 1921, David married Emma Horn. He was also known as David Goodbear. In October of 1935, the family was interviewed by a worker as part of the SDERA program. They were living in a one room log home along the Moreau River, 3 miles SW of White Horse. David had had a heart attack in January and then had a leg amputated after gangrene set in. It was difficult for him to get around. He was a member of the American Legion and was active in community affairs of the White Horse District. By his good talks and advice, he helped many people to settle their problems. He also was a faithful member of the St. Thomas Episcopal Church. He was lover of music and gave his talent to the church where he was organist for many years. In the 1940 U.S. Census, David and Emma were listed with their children, Henry, Earlwin, Anne and Evelyn. Earlwin served in the Army after WWII. David entered the spirit world at his home in White Horse on Sept. 29, 1941. An escort of honor was provided by Gene Gelino Post of the American Legion of Timber Lake, as a token of respect to a man who had been their comrade. His pallbearers included Joseph, George and Sullivan Jewett, Clayton Many Deeds, Arbee Cooper and William LaPlant, whose wife was a sister to Joseph and George. David is buried with a number of other veterans in a corner of the Emmanuel Episcopal Cemetery, White Horse.[32]

Dubray, Eugene. He is listed on WWI veteran's memorial at Oglala Lakota College, Kyle, SD. Eugene was born on the Pine Ridge Reservation on Nov. 23, 1895. In the 1899 Census Roll, he is listed with his parents, Charles and Elizabeth, and a sister, Sallie. When Eugene registered for the draft on June 5, 1917, he was farming near Martin with his father. He joined the Army on May 25, 1918. Pvt. Dubray sailed from New York aboard the *Ortega* on Aug. 31, 1918. He was traveling in Overseas Casual Co. No. 361 (unassigned), along with Robert Dubray, Joseph Dion and Samuel Charging Crow. Upon arriving in France, he was assigned to Co. I, 357th Infantry, 90th Division (ASN 3129661). The 357th Infantry served in the Sectors at St. Mihiel, Puvenelle and Meuse-Argonne. The 90th Division suffered 7,277 casualties. After the Armistice, the 357th Infantry was part of the Army of Occupation. The 357th Infantry was billeted in Hillesheim, Germany. Pvt. Dubray sailed from St. Nazaire, France, aboard the U.S.S. *Huron* May 16, 1919, and docked at Newport News, VA. Pvt. Dubray was assigned to Casual Detachment #797, Demobilization Group. He was discharged on June 16, 1919. After he returned home, he married Eva Hawkins. In the 1940 U.S. Census, the family was ranching with their children, James, Dave, Everett, Amelia, Ora Jane, Vivian, Jefferson, Leroy, Pershing and Permelia. Eugene entered the spirit world on Sept. 2, 1948, and is buried in the Inestimable Gift Cemetery, Allen, SD.

Dubray, Everett Edward. Everett was born in Greenwood, SD, on July 21, 1901. His parents were Joseph and Mary Dubray. Joseph had served in the Army during the Spanish American War. He later served as a minister on a number of reservations. Everett registered for the draft on Sept. 12, 1918, while attending the Rapid City Boarding School. At this time, his father was living in Peever, on the Sisseton Reservation. Shortly after this, he transferred to the boarding school in Hampton, VA. Sometime in 1919, Everett skipped school and joined the Navy. In the 1920 U.S. Census, he was stationed at Norfolk, VA. VA records show that he re-enlisted in 1924. Everett's younger brother, Louis, served in the Navy in the 1930s. The 1934 Yanktonai Census Roll lists Everett as living on the Rosebud Reservation with his wife, Floreine Frederick. In the 1940 U.S. Census, they were living on the Pine Ridge Reservation with three children, Roberta, Rochelle and Everett, Jr. Everett Sr. was working as an assistant engineer for the Indian Service. Everett later married Anna Marie Montova (1916-1996). Everett passed away in New Mexico on Dec. 20, 1988. He and Marie are buried in Santa Fe National Cemetery.

Dubray, Robert. Robert was born in Wood, SD, on May 21, 1894, to Antoine Dubray and Jennie Bissonette. Robert joined the Army in Winner, SD, on May 26, 1918. He served with his cousin, Eugene Dubray. They sailed from New York aboard the *Ortega* on Aug. 31, 1918. They were traveling with Overseas Casual Co. 361, unassigned. Upon arriving in France, they were assigned to Co. I, 357th Infantry, 90th Division (ASN 3130133). The 357th Infantry served in the Sectors at St. Mihiel, Puvenelle, and Meuse-Argonne. After duty with the Army of Occupation, Pvt. Dubray sailed from St. Nazaire, France, aboard the U.S.S. *Huron* on May 16, 1919. Pvt. Dubray also was assigned to Casual Detachment 957, Demobilization Group. He was discharged at Camp Dodge, IA, on June 16, 1919. In the 1927 Rosebud Census Roll, Robert was listed with his wife, Olive Anderson, and step-son, Alfred. In the mid1930s, the family was interviewed by a worker with the SDERA program. In 1935, they were living 11 miles north of Witten, and owned eight horses, five milk cows and 75 chickens. Robert later married Camilla Winsell. After ranching near Wood, Robert moved to Hot Springs in 1966. He was a member of VFW Post 1640 at Hot Springs. Robert entered the spirit world at the SD State Veterans Home in Hot Springs on Nov. 17, 1988. A son, Robert, and two grandchildren survived him. He is buried in the State Veterans Home Cemetery.[33]

DuCharme, Martin. Martin was born on the Cheyenne River Reservation on Sept. 26, 1898. His parents were Charles Ducharme and Mary L. Landreaux. In the 1900 U.S. Census, Martin lived with his grandparents. When his mother died in the early 1900s, his father married Millie Benoist, the mother of Louis Benoist. On Dec. 14, 1917, Martin enlisted in the U.S. Navy in Omaha. He was discharged in Minneapolis on Aug. 12, 1919. On Feb. 25, 1921, Martin married Alice Rouse, whose brother, Jesse, served in the Army during the war. In the 1927 Cheyenne River Census Roll, Martin his listed with his children, Margaret and Martin Jr. In the 1930 U.S. Census, the family was living in Missoula. In 1931, Martin was admitted to Battle Mountain Sanitarium at Hot Springs. He was discharged on Oct. 5, 1931, and entered the spirit world on Oct. 27, 1931. His son, Martin Jr. served in the Navy in WWII.

Ducheneaux, Napoleon. Napoleon "Curley" was born on Dec. 16, 1895, on the Cheyenne River Reservation. His parents were Willie Ducheneaux and Jennie Rivers. When he registered for the draft on June 5, 1917, he was raising cattle near Promise, SD. He enlisted in the Army at Timber Lake on Sept. 22, 1917. He was in the second group of men from Dewey County who left for Camp Funston. Others with him included Kiutus Jim, Basil Flanagan, Armstrong Four Bear and William Bowker. Napoleon served as a Saddler with the Machine Gun Co., 30th Infantry, 3rd Division (ASN 2193006). The 30th Infantry served in the Sectors at Aisne, Chateau-Thierry, Aisne-Marne, Vesle, St. Mihiel, and Meuse Argonne. Saddler Ducheneaux sailed for Europe aboard the *Kroonland* on April 30, 1918. After the Armistice, Ducheneaux received an evaluation from his commanding officer, stating that he was a "first class saddler and a good man with horses." During the Occupation period, the Machine Gun Co. was billeted at Metternich, Germany. Saddler Ducheneaux returned home from Brest aboard the U.S.S. *America* on Aug. 12, 1919, and was discharged at Camp Dodge, IA, on Aug. 26, 1919. Napoleon married Ruth Janis (1900-1960) at Ideal, SD, on June 12, 1926. In the 1940 U.S. Census, Napoleon was working as a clerk in a department store in Winner. He and Ruth had six children, Duane, Lois, Wayne, Clinton, Bernard and Yvonne. Their son, Wayne, served in the Navy during the Korean War. Napoleon's younger brother, Fred, served in the Navy during WWII. Another brother, Moses, served in the military from 1923-27. Napoleon entered the spirit world on June 22, 1963, at Hot Springs. He is buried in Hot Springs National Cemetery.[34]

Dugan, Amos. Amos was born around 1887 on the Sisseton-Wahpeton Reservation. In the 1890 Census Roll, he is listed with his grandmother, Julia Grey Cloud, his mother, Louisa Dugan, and two brothers, Charles and Jacob, and a sister, Helen. He married an Ojibway woman named Margaret, with whom he had a daughter, Winona. Amos enlisted in the Army at Ft. Logan, CO, on Aug. 1, 1916, and served in the Medical Dept. He was discharged as a Private on Sept. 24, 1917, because of foot deformity. In the 1920 U.S Census, Amos was living in L'Anse, MI, with his wife and his brother, Jacob. In the 1920s, he was a patient at a number of VA hospitals. He entered the spirit world in Roberts County on March 1, 1928. He is buried in Ascension Presbyterian Cemetery in Spring Grove.[35]

Dull Knife, Guy. Guy was born at Yellow Bear Camp, Pine Ridge Reservation on Feb. 17, 1899. His parents were George Dull Knife and Mary Red Rabbit. His grandparents were Cheyenne. As a young boy, his parents sometimes traveled to Montana to visit their Northern Cheyenne relatives. Guy served with the Army in Europe, possibly with the 42nd Division. While overseas, he made friends with Henry Medicine Blanket from the Rosebud Reservation. Guy returned to Pine Ridge after his service. In the 1920 U.S. Census, he was working as a laborer for the city of Pine Ridge. He married Rose Bull Bear on Jan. 21, 1928. In the 1930 U.S. Census, Guy and Rose were living with rose's father, Peter Bull Bear. In the 1940 U.S. Census, Guy was working in the CCC program in Bennett County. In the 1950's Guy helped build the Saint Timothy Episcopal Church at Potato Creek. Guy served on the tribal council representing the Eagle Nest District from 1980-82. Guy entered the spirit world on Aug. 17, 1995, at Rapid City Regional Hospital. His son, Guy Jr., adopted son, Michael Murphy Dull Knife and a daughter, Doris Fleming survived him. His son, Guy Jr., served in Vietnam. Guy is buried in Trinity Episcopal Cemetery, Yellow Bear.[36]

DuMarce, Harry. Harry was born on June 12, 1889, on the Sisseton-Wahpeton Reservation. His parents were John Baptiste Dumarce and Lydia Frenier. In the 1890 Census Roll, he is listed with his parents and a brother, Haman. When Harry registered for the draft on June 1, 1917, he was farming near Veblen. Harry enlisted in the Army, and served as a Private in the Medical Department. After his discharge on Jan. 25, 1919, he married Mary Red Thunder on July 27, 1919, at Veblen. Harry's sister, Evelyn, married Samuel Crawford, a fellow veteran. In the 1930 U.S. Census, Harry was farming in Bossko Township, Roberts Co. In 1935, the family was interviewed by a worker with the SDERA program. They were living in a one-story frame house about 10 miles east of Sisseton. Harry had worked as an investigator at the county relief office. They also mentioned that Harry's brother, Herman, had served with the Army for many years in Alaska. In the 1937 Census Roll, Harry and Mary were listed with their children, Malcolm, Audrey, Muriel, Maxine, and Margaret. Harry entered the spirit world on Nov. 28, 1967, and is buried Lake Traverse Presbyterian Cemetery.[37]

DuMarce, Herman. Herman was born in the early 1890s and was a younger brother to Harry. In the early census rolls, he was listed as Haman, or Hayman. According to the 1930 U.S. Census, Herman had served in the Army during the world war. In the 1920 U.S. Census, Herman was living in Copper Center, 3rd Judicial District, Alaska Territory. In the 1930 U.S. Census, he was now employed as a telegrapher with the U.S. Army at Seward on Resurrection Bay. His wife, Helen (1884-1936) lived with him. A few years later they moved to Seattle. Helen had passed away in 1936. In the 1940 U.S. Census, Herman was stationed at Fort Sam Houston, Texas. He and his wife, Duane, had two children, Annette and James. After the war, he worked for Boeing Aircraft. Herman entered the spirit world in Gardner's Sanitarium in Seattle on Dec. 23, 1955. He is buried in Holyrood Catholic Cemetery, Shoreline, WA.[38]

Jefferson L. Duncan
Ancestry.com

Duncan, Jefferson L. Jefferson was born on the Standing Rock Reservation in South Dakota on May 1, 1895. His parents were Charles Duncan and Ellen Brown. Jefferson attended school at Standing Rock and Kenel. In September 1911, he was sent to school in Carlisle, PA. Jefferson was over six feet tall and played football on the Carlisle team. However, after less than two years, he ran from the school, in June 1913, on his way home he passed through Chicago. He managed to land a job as a cook on the passenger train, *Olympian,* operated by the Milwaukee Road between Chicago and Seattle. He was soon promoted to second chef. His mother wrote a letter to the staff at Carlisle saying that Jefferson was paid $70 a month, which was a lot more than a farm worker made. When Jefferson registered for the draft on June 5, 1917, he was working as a cook for the D.Z. Cattle Co. in Timber Lake. He enlisted in the Army on June 24, 1918, and was assigned to Co. F, 349th Infantry, 88th Division (ASN 3309082). Pvt. Duncan left New York for France aboard the *Olympic* on Aug. 9, 1918. After the Armistice, Pvt. Duncan received an evaluation from his commanding officer stating that he was a "very careful and reliable man. Good humor at all times. Good initiative." Pvt. Duncan left France on May 19, 1919, aboard the U.S.S. *Rijndam*. He was discharged on June 11, 1919. After the war, he married Myrtle Cummings, whose brothers, Henry and Earl served in the Army. In the 1920s, they moved to California. In the 1930 U.S. Census, the family lived in Gridley, CA, while Jefferson was working as a laborer for the railroad. Later he worked as a carpenter on tunnel construction in mines, near Pasadena. In the 1940 U.S. Census, "Jeff" and Myrtle lived there with their children, Earl, Ken, Velda and Peggy. Jefferson entered the spirit world at the VA Hospital in Los Angeles on Oct. 9, 1957. He is buried in Los Angeles National Cemetery, Section 238, row A, site 18.[39]

DuPris, Joseph. Joseph was born on the Cheyenne River Reservation around March 1897. His parents were Annie and David Xavier Dupris. David died around 1900. Joseph likely joined the 4th Infantry of the South Dakota National Guard in 1917. When these soldiers arrived at Camp Greene, NC, they were converted over to the 147th Field Artillery (FA) Regiment. He was assigned to Battery C, 147th FA (ASN 139439). Pvt. Dupris sailed from New York aboard the transport ship *Olympic* on Jan. 11, 1918. The 147th FA was attached to the 32nd Division for most of the war. They served in the Sectors at Toul-Boucq, Center, Aisne-Marne, Fismes, and Oise-Aisne. Pfc. Dupris was wounded lightly on Aug. 31, 1918, near Valpriez, France. Pfc. Dupris was killed in action near Juvigny on Sept. 6, 1918. His body was returned to the U.S. and buried in the Dupris Cemetery in Ziebach County.

E

Eagle, Jonas. Jonas was born on the Cheyenne River Reservation on Jan. 6, 1894. His parents were George and Madaline Eagle. George had served as a scout for the Army in the 1890s. When Jonas registered for the draft, he was working for the Agency. He enlisted in the Army at Timber Lake on May 24, 1918. He served as a Private with 3rd Co., 166th Depot Brigade, training with the 13th Division. He had some eye troubles. He was discharged from Camp Lewis, WA, on Nov. 20, 1918. He lived with his parents near the Missouri River after his discharge. In the 1930 U.S. Census, he was a patient at the Battle Mountain Sanatorium. He married Mable Jones at Gettysburg on Nov. 6, 1937. In the 1940 U.S. Census, he was listed as Jonas Crow Eagle. He and Mable and their daughter, Georgia, lived with Mable's father. Jonas was working on road construction. They later ranched. Jonas passed away at the home of his daughter in Great Falls, MT, on April 17, 1986. He is buried in Black Hills National Cemetery.[1]

Eagle Deer, Paul. Paul was born at Cut Meat on the Rosebud Reservation on Jan. 3, 1891. In the 1900 U.S. Census, he is listed with his parents, Eagle Deer and Holy Owl, as well as two sisters, Katie and Clara. When Paul registered with the draft on June 6, 1917, he was farming with his father. Paul enlisted in the Army on June 24, 1918, and was assigned to Co. E, 351st Infantry, 88th Division (ASN 3315623). Pvt. Eagle Deer sailed with his regiment from New York aboard the *Scotian* on Aug. 15, 1918. Other men in Co. E were Joseph Otterman, Ernest Bad Horse, Frank Black Horse, Joseph Beads, William Shooter and David Turning Bear. Otterman and Turning Bear died while the regiment was serving in France. After the Armistice, Pfc. Eagle Deer received an evaluation from his commanding officer, saying he was a "very good soldier." The 351st Infantry was billeted in Houdelainecourt, France, as part of the Army of Occupation. On May 20, 1919, the regiment boarded the ship *Mercury*. Pfc. Eagle Deer was discharged on June 7, 1919. After the war, Paul married Martha White Lance. Her younger brother, John, had served in France with the 147th Field Artillery. In the 1930 U.S. Census, the family was ranching. In the 1940 U.S. Census, the family included their children, Rufus, Herman, Noah, Dorothy and Leonard. Rufus served in the military in WWII. Paul entered the spirit world in the Pine Ridge Hospital on July 24, 1955, and is buried in St. Charles Cemetery, St. Francis, SD.[2]

Eagle Elk, George. George was born on the Rosebud Reservation on Oct. 31, 1901, the son of Jesse Eagle Elk. He joined the Army on May 13, 1918 and was discharged on June 30, 1919. In the 1940 U.S. Census, George and his wife, Amy, lived with their son, Joseph. In 1943, George began working as a section laborer for the Chicago & Northwestern Railway in Gordon, NE. In 1958, he married Hilda Winters. George entered the spirit world on May 29, 1978, at Parmelee.

Eagle Feather, Thomas Lawrence. Thomas was born around May 23, 1902, according to military records. The Rosebud Census Rolls shows his year of birth as 1905. In the 1906 Census Roll, he is listed with his parents, Ralph and Julia Eagle Feather, as well as two brothers, Felix and Isadore. It is likely that Felix joined the Army in 1918, but failed the camp physical, according to a letter from Richard Fool Bull. Felix likely entered the spirit world in December of 1918. Thomas joined the Navy on Oct. 25, 1920, at Omaha (SN 3159061). He served as a Fireman 3rd Class on the U.S.S. *Charleston*, and the U.S.S. *Arkansas*. He was discharged at the U.S. Naval Hospital in San Diego on Dec. 23, 1921, with an 80% disability. He entered the spirit world on May 28, 1922, and is buried in Sacred Heart Cemetery, Parmelee, SD.[3]

Eagle Feather, Lynn. Lynn was born on the Rosebud Reservation on June 19, 1898. In the 1901 Census Roll, he is listed with his parents, Oliver and Bessie. Lynn likely enlisted in the 4th SD Infantry in the summer of 1917. This National Guard unit was transferred to Camp Greene, NC, where some of the men were assigned to Co. B, 148th Machine Gun Battalion, 41st Division (ASN 98585). This unit sailed from Hoboken, NJ, aboard the *Olympic* on Jan. 11, 1918. When they arrived in France, Pvt. Eagle Feather was reassigned to Co. M, 167th Infantry, 42nd Division. The 42nd Division suffered 13,919 casualties. Pvt. Eagle Feather likely was wounded. He sailed from France aboard the S.S. *Leviathan* on Feb. 3, 1919. The manifest for his unit read: "Sick and Wounded (C)." He arrived in Hoboken on Feb. 11, 1919. After his discharge on May 10, 1919, he married Rebecca Crow. In the 1930 U.S. Census, Lynn was working as a truck driver for a general store. In the 1940 U.S. Census, Lynn was farming with his family in Todd County. Their family included four children, Mercy, Oliver, Loraine, Charity, as well as Rebecca's father, John. Lynn entered the spirit world in the Rosebud hospital on July 22, 1956, and is buried in an Episcopal cemetery in Parmelee.[4]

Eagle Hawk, William. William was born on the Lower Brule Reservation around May 4, 1886. His parents were Amos Eagle Hawk and Yellow Woman. Around 1897, Yellow Woman moved her family to the Rosebud Reservation, where they became enrolled. William was listed in the Rosebud records as Tasunka Nopa [Owns Two Horses]. In the 1899 Census Roll, William is listed with his mother and step-father, Edward Charging Horse, as well as his brother, John. William enlisted in the Army at Winner, SD, on March 5, 1918. He served in the Sanitary Detachment, 117th Field Signal Battalion, 42nd Division (ASN 937616). The 42nd Division served in France. Pvt. Eagle hawk sailed from Brest, France, aboard the *South Carolina* on April 15, 1919, and was discharged at Camp Dodge on May 7, 1919. In the 1920 Census Roll, he was listed with his wife, Slow. He entered the spirit world in the VA Hospital in Sioux Falls on June 29, 1958, and is buried in Messiah Episcopal Cemetery, Lyman County.[5]

Eagle Heart, Jackson. Jackson was born on Sept. 28, 1898, on the Pine Ridge Reservation. In the 1901 Oglala Census Roll, he is listed with his father, Wanbli Cante [Eagle Heart], and his mother, Jennie Eagle Heart. When Jackson registered for the draft on Sept. 12, 1918, he was living at Kyle. He joined the Army shortly after this. He was discharged as a Private First Class. Jackson passed away on March 31, 1925, and is buried in Mediator Cemetery, Kyle, SD.

Eagle Horn, Chauncey. Chauncey was born around 1874 on the Rosebud Reservation. He lived at Okreek, SD. In 1892, he enlisted in the Army and served two years in the 16th Infantry. He likely re-enlisted. In the 1910 U.S. Census, he was listed with his wife, Molly, and two children, Nicholas and Agnes. In 1915, their daughter, Annie, was born. On May 4, 1917, Chauncey enlisted at Fort Meade, SD, in Co. I, 4th South Dakota Infantry (ASN 98586). He arrived in Camp Greene, SC, in September 1917, and was transferred to the 148th Machine Gun Battalion, 41st Division. This unit was first transferred to Camp Mills, NY, and then to Camp Merritt, NJ, before sailing for France aboard the *Olympic* on Jan. 11, 1918. Pvt. Eagle Horn was eventually assigned to Company M, 167th Infantry, 42nd Division. The 167th Infantry had started out as a National Guard unit from Alabama. Quite a few men who had enlisted in the SD National Guard were transferred to Co. M of the 167th after they arrived in France. In March 1918, the 167th went into the trenches at Luneville about the time the German Army opened a big drive in the Champagne Sector. In late July of 1918, the 167th was attacking the German Army near La Croix Rouge Farm in the Ourcq River valley. According to a unit history, in the afternoon of July 26, "the left of Company F was joined by the right of Company M, 167th and together, these two companies, which bore the brunt of the fighting, advanced on the farm. The platoon of Lt. Fisher of Company F had been hard hit. He turned to the Lieutenant on his left and said, 'Lt., my men are about all gone, we will join you.' No sooner had this been done than a bursting shell made a casualty of the Lieutenant from Alabama. Then Fisher assumed command of all the men of both platoons and they advanced on the farm.

"Chaplain Robb, the day afterwards, in conjunction with the burying party from the Alabama Regiment (167th), found 100 bodies near the farm….But we did know how bravely the men had advanced under such a heavy fire and that every report that came in told of the greatness and of the terrible loss that we had suffered."

One of the casualties who survived was Pvt. Herbert Omaha Boy. He said Chauncey had been hit by shrapnel in the left leg and had died on the battlefield about a half hour after being hit. Herbert had been hit multiple times himself and was unable to provide assistance to Chauncey.

According to Jennings Wise, Chauncey Eagle Horn was the first soldier from South Dakota to receive a decoration in France. He received a Croix de Guerre.

On Dec. 2, 1919, American Legion Post 125 received their charter. The Post was named for Pfc. Chauncey Eagle Horn. On June 19, 1921, the body of Pvt. Eagle Horn, was brought back home by the transport ship *Wheaton*, which sailed from Antwerp, Belgium. Eagle Horn was reburied in Calvary Cemetery, Okreek, SD, on Sept. 8, 1921.[6]

Eagle Horn, James. James was born on the Standing Rock Reservation on Feb. 4, 1894. His parents, Allen Eagle Horn and Ozanwastewin, were Hunkpapa. Allen belonged to the Chief Gall Band. James joined the Army at McIntosh, SD, on Sept. 21, 1917. He was assigned initially to Co. C, 340th Machine Gun Battalion, 89th Division (ASN 2193008). After being transferred to the Machine Gun Company, 38th Infantry, 3rd Division as replacements, Pvt. Eagle Horn sailed from Halifax, Nova

Scotia, aboard the British steamship *Corsican* on March 25, 1918. The *Corsican* docked at Glasgow, Scotland. From there the 38th Infantry took a train to Camp Woodsley, England, before crossing the Channel on the cattle boat *Austrilind*. Other soldiers from Standing Rock serving with Pvt. Eagle Horn were Charles Howard, Martin Medicine and Thomas DeRockbraine. The 3rd Division suffered 16,117 casualties in the war. Pvt. Eagle Horn sailed from Bordeaux aboard the *South Bend* on June 5, 1919, arriving on June 19. He was traveling with Bordeaux Casual Co. No. 1515. Pvt. Eagle Horn was discharged at Camp Dodge, IA, on Aug. 28, 1919. In the 1920 U.S. Census, James was living with his parents. In 1923, James married Rose Take the Hat. In the 1930s, the family was living in a two-room home near Mahto and hauled water from a spring some distance away. The family was interviewed in 1935 by a worker with the SDERA program. A few years earlier, the family had owned 40-50 head of cattle and 40-50 head of horses, but as the drought worsened, they could not support that many animals. They had tried planting a garden in 1935, but they got no crop. James and Rose had a daughter, Annabelle. James' father, Allen, was also living with them. James was a member of the American Legion. James worked as a rancher and section hand for the Milwaukee Road. He entered the spirit world near Mahto on March 7, 1972 and is buried in St. Bede's Cemetery at Wakpala.[7]

Eagle Shield, Samuel. Samuel was born at Little Eagle on the Standing Rock Reservation around September 1894. His parents were Thomas Eagle Shield and White Buffalo. Thomas, a brother to Mary Crawler, had served in the 22nd Infantry in the early 1890s. Samuel graduated from the Rapid City boarding school in 1913. After taking a non-competitive Civil Service exam, he started working at the land office on the Standing Rock Reservation. When Samuel registered for the draft, he was farming at Little Eagle. Samuel joined the Army and was sent to Ft. Riley, KS, but was discharged due to illness on April 22, 1918. He entered the spirit world on Nov. 15, 1918. He had been married to Alice Vermillion, who later married James Demery, a fellow vet.

Eagle Thunder, Thomas. Thomas was born on the Lower Brule Reservation on May 5, 1896. In the 1909 Census Roll, he is listed as an orphan. When he registered for the draft on June 5, 1917, he was working as a stable man for the Indian Service in Lower Brule. Thomas joined the Army on Oct. 6, 1917, and was assigned to the Machine Gun (MG) Company, 4th Infantry, 3rd Division (ASN 2214419). He served with George Big Owl. Pvt. Eagle Thunder sailed from Newport News, VA, aboard the *Great Northern* on April 6, 1918. The 4th Infantry served in the Sectors at Aisne, Chateau-Thierry, Champagne-Marne, Aisne-Marne, St. Mihiel and Meuse-Argonne. Pvt. Eagle Thunder likely was wounded. The 3rd Division suffered 16,117 casualties. Pvt. Eagle Thunder sailed from St. Nazaire aboard the *Antigone* on Dec. 18, 1918. His fellow passengers were identified as "sick and wounded." Pvt. Eagle Thunder was discharged on June 27, 1919, so he must have spent time in a hospital. Most of the 3rd Division did not return stateside until August of 1919. Thomas married Madeline Tompkins (1903-1982) on Sept. 15, 1925. Their children were William, Doris, Katherine, Florence and Arthur, who served in the Army. Thomas worked as a laborer in the Lower Brule area. He entered the spirit world on March 4, 1963, following a vehicle accident near Lower Brule. He is buried in the Episcopal Cemetery at Lower Brule.[8]

Earring, Harvey. Harvey was known as Harvey Left Handed Bear in many of the Census Rolls. In the 1896 Cheyenne River Census Roll, Harvey was listed with his parents, Mattias and Sophia Left Handed Bear. He was born around 1877. Around 1900, he married Anna Horn. They had several children, including Ella, Phillip and Lena. Around 1916, he was living in Bullhead, SD, when he married Regina Low Dog. Harvey enlisted in the Army on July 26, 1918, at Jefferson Barracks, MO. He served with the 3rd Regiment Field Artillery Replacement Draft (ASN 3770204). He was discharged at Louisville, KY, on Dec. 13, 1918. After his discharge from Camp Taylor, Harvey purchased two horses in Kentucky which he had shipped to his home in Bullhead. After the war, he wrote to Joseph Dixon: "I was held at Camp as an instructor and training new recruits and was told that my service was more needed at home. So I spent my time at Camp and did not have any chance going over and at times I beg my officer to get me a chance to go over. But was turn down every time. I enlisted and claim that I am the only Indian that enlisted over draft age."

In the 1930 U.S. Census, Harvey was living in Rapid City, where he worked as a janitor in a hotel. Harvey developed tuberculosis and entered the spirit world on Jan. 12, 1937, at the VA hospital in Hot Springs. He is buried with some other veterans in a corner of the Episcopal Cemetery near White Horse, SD.[9]

Eastman, Andrew. Andrew was born at Okreek on the Rosebud Reservation about April 23, 1887. In the 1891 Census Roll, he is listed with his father, Alexander Iyesni [Deaf and Dumb], his mother, Mary White Buffalo, and a brother, David, and two sisters, Hope and Ida. On Aug. 9, 1915, Andrew married Martha Stranger Horse (1891-1977), who had first married Moses Stranger Horse. When Andrew registered for the draft on June 5, 1917, he and Martha were raising two children. At that time, Andrew owned a billiard hall in Wood. He joined the Army on Aug. 29, 1918. He was assigned to the 4th Co., 1st Battalion, 163rd Depot Brigade at Camp Dodge, IA (ASN 4821667). He was discharged as a Private on Dec. 12, 1918. In the 1930s, he was farming in Mellette County. In 1935, the family was interviewed by a worker with the SDERA program. They were living near Wood in a two-room house covered with tin on the roof and sides. Andrew had been working on a dam construction project. He had also worked as a police officer for a while. However, he had some health problems and had applied to the Veteran's Bureau to receive help with medical care. In the 1940 U.S. Census, he and Martha are listed with three sons, Andrew Jr., Everett and Devere. Everett served in the Army from 1944-1966. Devere served in the Army from 1946-1949. Andrew entered the spirit world on April 2, 1947, and is buried in Riverside Cemetery, Wood, SD.[10]

Charles Ohiyesa Eastman
Ancestry.com

Eastman, Charles Ohiyesa. Ohiyesa [Wins Always] was born on Sept. 18, 1898, in Fairfield, Connecticut. His parents were Dr. Charles Eastman and Elaine Goodale. He is listed on the Census Roll for the Flandreau Sioux Tribe. In the 1900 U.S. Census, the family was living at Carlisle, PA. Ohiyesa was living in Baltimore, MD, when he enlisted in the Navy in February of 1918. On March 23, 1918, he was stationed at the Naval Training Station, Newport R.I. He was stationed at the Naval Torpedo Station, Newport, R.I., on June 30, 1918, and went on inactive duty on Aug. 15, 1919. He was awarded the Order of St. Sava (Serbian). On Ancestry.com, a photo of Charles in a sailor's uniform has been published. In the 1920 U.S. Census, Charles was living with his parents and working as a book keeper for a sign Company in Northampton, MA. In the 1930 U.S. Census, he was working as an advertising manager with Kelvinator Corporation in Detroit, MI. The 1936 Flandreau Census Roll lists him as still living in Detroit. He married Marion Nutting (1895-1971). His father sometimes lived with him in the winter. Ohiyesa developed pneumonia and entered the spirit world in Mt. Carmel Hospital in Detroit on Jan. 16, 1940. He is buried in Evergreen Cemetery in Detroit.

Eckman, Leo Francis. Leo was born in Flensburg, MN, on Jan. 19, 1899, the son of Paul and Francis Eckman. Leo enlisted in the Navy in Minneapolis on April 7, 1918. He was an Apprentice Seaman (NSN 1403074) and did not serve overseas. He was discharged on Jan. 28, 1919, at Baltimore. After returning to Minnesota, he married Elizabeth McLean, whose brother, James, served in the Army. In the 1920 U.S Census, they were living in Minneapolis, where Leo was working as an electrician for the telephone company. In the 1921 Standing Rock Census Roll, Leo is listed but not enrolled. The family moved back to Wakpala in 1924. The family lived in a three-room house on the NE edge of town. In the 1940 U.S. Census, Leo and Elizabeth had six children, Adele, Leo Jr., Paul, Loraine, Marie and Herold. Paul served in the Army in WWII. Leo was working on a WPA project pouring concrete. He was a member of the American Legion and Elizabeth was in the Legion Auxiliary. Leo entered the spirit world in Wakpala on Feb. 7, 1942, and is buried St. Bede's Cemetery in Wakpala.[11]

Elbridge, Gerry – listed on WWI veteran's memorial at Oglala Lakota College, Kyle, SD. See **Gerry, Elbridge S**.

Emery, Albert. Albert was born on Oct. 5, 1891, in Gregory County on the Rosebud Reservation. His parents were Robert H. Emery and Rose Dion. Albert had a younger brother, Robert. In the 1900 U.S. Census, Albert was a student at the Rosebud boarding school. When he registered for the draft on June 5, 1917, he was living in Winner and working as a horse buyer. He joined the Army on June 27, 1918, and served as a Corporal with the Headquarters Troop, 10th Division. He was discharged on Feb. 1, 1919. On March 22, 1923, he married Julia Moles at Sioux Falls. They were living in Sioux Falls at the time of the 1930 U.S. Census. Albert was working as a laborer for a paving company. He and Julia had a daughter, Mary Ann. Albert entered the spirit world on Dec. 24, 1969, in Sioux Falls. He and Julia (1897-1973) are buried in Hill of Rest Memorial Park, Sioux Falls.

Emery, Robert. Robert was born on the Rosebud Reservation on April 1, 1896. His parents were Robert H. Emery and Rose Dion. Robert attended the Rapid City Indian School and Rapid City High School from 1914-1917. He was captain of the football team and class valedictorian. When he registered for the draft on July 10, 1917, he was farming with Alex Whipple near Wososo. He joined the Army on May 25, 1918, and served as a Private in Co. C, 213th Engineers at Camp Lewis, WA. He was discharged at Camp Lewis on March 7, 1919. After returning home, he ranched near Parmelee. On Jan. 19, 1927, he married Mable Whipple (1904-1989), the daughter of Alex. Robert was a member of the American Legion. He entered the spirit world in a hospital in Valentine, NE, on Dec. 12, 1971. His widow and a daughter, Lois, survived him. He is buried in Trinity Cemetery, Mission, SD.[12]

English, Peter. Peter English was a student at the Flandreau boarding school who served in the Army during WWI. He likely enlisted in the early part of 1918. In the summer of 1919, he re-enlisted, and was stationed at Fort Snelling, MN. His name is engraved on a plaque to honor veterans that was erected at the school in Flandreau in 1920. Peter English was born on the Red Lake Indian Reservation on Feb. 2, 1900. In the 1910 Red Lake Census Roll, he is listed with his mother, Be Dway Way Sush Eke. In the 1930 U.S. Census Roll, Peter was living on the Red Lake Reservation and working as a laborer in a lumber mill. He was married to Maud Weaver. Peter later moved to Eureka, California, where he worked as a machine operator in a saw mill owned by Arcata Redwood. Peter entered the spirit world on Aug. 19, 1968, in the VA Hospital in Livermore, CA. He is buried in Red Lake Cemetery in Minnesota.[13]

Enos, Louie Heyoke. Louie was born on the Sisseton Reservation around April 14, 1892. In the 1905 Minnesota Census, he was attending school in Pipestone, MN. In the 1910 U.S. Census, he was a student at Haskell, KS. In the 1917 Sisseton Census Roll, he was listed with his wife, Marger. He served as a Private with Co. B, 341st Machine Gun Battalion, 89th Division. He likely entered the spirit world in Camp Funston, KS, on March 20, 1918. He is buried in Long Hollow Cemetery on the Sisseton Reservation.

Evans, Benjamin. Ben was born in Hanover, IL, on Dec. 6, 1893, the son of John and Mary Evans. The Evans family moved to western South Dakota in the early 1900s. When Ben registered for the draft on June 5, 1917, he was working as a bronco buster near Edgemont, SD. When he joined the Army, he was assigned as a cook to Battery B, 71st Artillery, Coast Artillery Corps (CAC) (ASN 503430). He served with Pvt. George Red Fox, from Standing Rock. The 71st sailed from Boston aboard the *Margha* on July 31, 1918. Upon arrival in France, the unit was trained to use eight-inch howitzers. The First Battalion was billeted at St. Sylvain. The unit returned to the U.S. on Feb. 12, 1919, aboard the U.S. Transport *Manchuria*. The men were discharged at Camp Dodge, IA, in early March 1919. On April 26, 1923, Ben married Ruby Sickler. They ranched near Interior, SD. In the 1937 Pine Ridge Census Roll, Ben is listed with Ruby and their children, but was non-enrolled. Their children were Mildred, Myrtle, Norman and Ralph. Ben was a member of the American Legion in Kadoka. He entered the spirit world on Aug. 25, 1968. His widow, son, Norman, and daughter, Mildred, survived him. Ruby (1902-1973) is buried with Ben in the Black Hills National Cemetery, Section D, Site 672.[14]

Evans, James W. James was born in Greenwood, SD, around Aug. 26, 1896. His parents were Thomas Evans and Emily Ladeaux. His mother was first married to Charles Picotte Sr. In the 1906 Census Roll for the Yanktonai Sioux, James is listed with his mother and brother, Charles Picotte, and his step father, Samuel Wangina. James enlisted in the Army at Sioux City, IA, on May 8, 1917. He first served as a Private with Troop K, 1st Cavalry, Fort Apache, AZ. He re-upped as a Saddler, Quartermaster Detachment, Fort Apache (R1001450). He was discharged as a Pfc. on June 13, 1920. In the summer of 1919, he had married Jessie Pond, who was enrolled at the Bad River Reservation in northern Wisconsin. In the 1920 U.S. Census, he was working as a shoemaker at Fort Apache. In the late 1920s, he married a woman named Olga. In the 1930 U.S. Census, they were living in St. Cloud, MN, where James worked as a truck driver. In 1940, they lived in Sauk Rapids, MN, with their daughters, Dorothy, Shirley and Darlene. In 1947, he was still living in Sauk Rapids. James entered the spirit world in Fergus Falls, MN, on June 17, 1958, and is buried in Oak Grove Cemetery, Fergus Falls.[15]

F

Face, John. John was born in December 1899 on the Rosebud Reservation, to Charles Hehaka Witko [Foolish Elk] and Mary Face. John was a student at the Rapid City Indian School when he first enlisted in the Army on Jan. 24, 1918 and was discharged on May 7, 1919. He volunteered to go to Russia to help the Tsar fight the Red Army. After he re-enlisted, he sailed from Hoboken, NJ, aboard the *Sierra* on July 28, 1919. He was assigned to the 44th Co., Camp Meade Replacement Unit #11 (ASN R-2341784). In the 1920 U.S. Census, Pvt. Face was stationed in Bendorf, Germany, with the 13th Company, Provisional Guard Battalion. When he returned home, he sailed from Antwerp, Belgium, aboard the *Cantigny* on Sept. 1, 1921. He was traveling with Overseas Casual

John Face
Francis Whitebird

Detachment #34, and served with Co. K, 5th Infantry. In the 1930 U.S. Census, John was farming in Todd County with his wife, Minnie (1901-1972), and son, Frederick. John also enlisted in World War II on May 5, 1942. He was discharged on Aug. 26, 1942, as a Pfc. After his discharge, he was recruited by the Office of Strategic Services and was stationed in San Francisco. After the war, he started a 2300-acre ranch and was very successful. John and Minnie adopted two of Minnie's nephews, Noah Jr. and Francis Whitebird. John entered the spirit world on Dec. 2, 1980 and is buried next to Minnie in the Black Hills National Cemetery, Section C, Site 1381.

Fallis, Antoine. Antoine was born on the Rosebud Reservation on Feb. 22, 1893, the son of Joe and Maggie Fallis. Around 1917, Antoine married Susie Bear Doctor. Antoine served as a Private with Co. D, 8th Ammo Train, 8th Division. Part of this division was shipped to France late in the war but did not see any combat. He was discharged on Dec. 9, 1918. After returning home, Antoine farmed. In the 1920 U.S. Census, he was living with his wife and son, Joseph, near Greenwood, SD. In 1935, the family was interviewed by a social worker with the SDERA program. Antoine told the worker that he had carried his marriage license for three years before getting married. In 1935, he raised 45 acres of corn and 1.5 acres of potatoes. They owned seven goats, six hens, 1 rooster and four horses. Antoine indicated that he wanted his oldest sons to become farmers. In the 1940 U.S. Census, Antoine and Susie were farming in Mellette County with their children, Joseph, Stephen, Leona, Claire and Orson Dale. Joseph served in the Army in WWII. Susie entered the spirit world on Jan. 11, 1946. Claire and Orson served in Korea. Orson died in a North Korean Prison Camp in 1951. Antoine entered the spirit world in a Hot Springs hospital on July 11, 1971. He is buried in a cemetery in Wood, SD. His brother, Charles, served in WWII.[1]

Fallis, Edward C. Edward was born on June 24, 1897, on the Lower Brule Reservation. His parents were Felician (Phil) and Bessie Fallis. Edward first enlisted in the Army on July 22, 1918, and was discharged as a Private on May 18, 1919 (ASN 3769563). He may have served with the 33rd Infantry in the Canal Zone. Edward re-enlisted during WWII on Sept. 30, 1942. He served with the 9th Armored Infantry Regiment and was discharged on April 10, 1943. He married Mabel Whiting in 1936 at Winner, SD. In 1944, he married Gladys. Edward entered the spirit world on March 20, 1948, and is buried in Ft. George Catholic Cemetery, Lyman County.

Faribault, Ethelbert. Ethelbert was born around 1902 on the Sisseton Reservation. He was listed on the tribal census rolls with his parents, Albert Faribault and Esther Greeley. In the U.S. govt. census rolls, his name was listed as Albert Babe Faribault. In the 1920 U.S. Census, the family was living with Smiley Finley. In 1925, Albert Babe was listed as a Private with the USMC (33rd MG Co., 4th Regiment). In the 1930 and 1931 Sisseton-Wahpeton Census Roll, he was listed as serving with the U.S. Navy. In the 1937 Census Roll, he was listed as living in Minneapolis. When he registered with the Selective Service in 1942, he was living in Wilmot, SD.

Farmer, Lee L. Lee was born on the Rosebud Reservation around April 16, 1896. In the 1898 Rosebud Census Roll, he is listed with his mother, Clara, and two brothers, Peter and Joseph. His mother later married George Pawnee Leggings. Lee joined the Army on May 24, 1918, and was first assigned to Co. C, 158th Infantry, 40th Division (ASN 3127678). Pvt. Farmer sailed with his unit from New York aboard the *Laomedon* on Aug. 11, 1918. When he arrived in France, he was reassigned to the Railhead Detachment (QMC). After the Armistice, Pfc. Farmer sailed for home from Brest aboard the *Artemis* on July 21, 1919. He was traveling with Brest Casual Co. No. 2771, and was discharged as a Pfc. on Aug. 11, 1919. He married Lizzie Bear Old Woman. His sister, Olive, married Charles Arcoren, a fellow veteran. In the 1940 U.S. Census, Lee and his children were living with his brother, Peter, in Todd County. Lizzie had passed away in 1938 from Tuberculosis. Their children included Viola, Harvey, Ada, Effie, Monica and Velma. Later that year, Lee married Martha Janis. Lee's son, Harvey served in WWII. Lee entered the spirit world in the Winner Baptist Hospital on May 19, 1991, and is buried in St. Thomas Catholic Cemetery, Antelope, Todd County.[2]

Farrell, Joseph Earl. Joseph was born on July 24, 1894, possibly on the Rosebud Reservation. In the 1901 Census Roll, he was listed with his mother, Minnie George, also known as Minnie Sky Arrow Bonser. When he registered for the draft on June 4, 1917, it was written that he was enrolled at the Rosebud Agency. Joseph was farming in Todd County. When he arrived at Camp Funston, he was assigned to a Utilities Det., Construction Div., QMC (ASN 3315496). Pvt Farrell served from June 24, 1918 until Dec. 31, 1918. After the war, he married Agnes Drohan in 1919. She died of the flu in 1923. In 1929, Joseph married Josephine Holechek in Kennebec. When he registered for the draft in 1942, he was living in Lincoln, NE. In 1945, he was living in Rosebud. He entered the spirit world on April 13, 1961, and is buried in Mankato, KS.

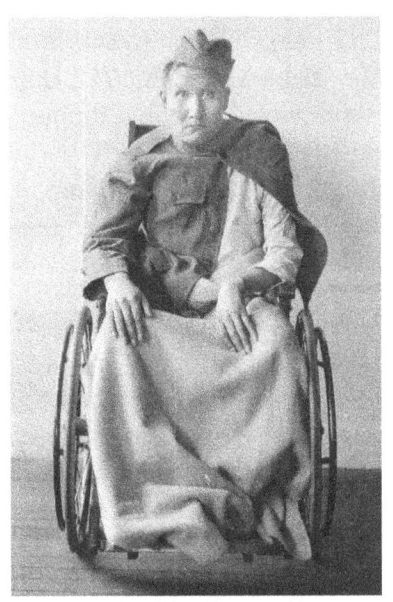

Fred Fast Horse
Mathers Museum

Fast Horse, Fred. Fred was born around September of 1888 on the Rosebud Reservation. His parents were Fast Horse and Hail. He married Lucy Six Shooter. They had two children, Elizabeth and Moses. When Fred registered for the draft on June 2, 1917, he was farming near White River, SD. Fred was drafted and assigned to Co. F, Ammunition Train, 89th Division (ASN 2195260). Pvt. Fast Horse sailed from New York aboard the *Cretic* on June 28, 1918. He served with Robert Blue Coat and Louis Brings Three White Horses. Pfc. Fast Horse was wounded during the Meuse-Argonne Offensive. He sailed from Brest aboard the steamship *Great Northern* on March 20, 1919, and arrived on March 27 at Greenhut Debarkation Hospital, NY. He visited with Joseph Dixon in the hospital about his service. He stated that "when they drafted me, I wanted to go because my people were fighters. My father was a chief and fought Custer, and I wanted to go and fight the Germans because they would come over here and destroy our free Government. I felt every time I could get a load of shells up to the guns that I was hitting the Germans, whom I despise. One very dark night, while we were getting shells up, a big shell struck our train and killed 12 mules and gassed the men." Pfc. Fast Horse was left paralyzed on the left side. He was discharged on June 21, 1919. Fast Horse entered the spirit world in White River on Dec. 28, 1919, and is buried in St. James Cemetery, White River.[3]

Fenelon, Vincent. Vincent was born in Ripon, WI, on April 18, 1896. His parents were Eugene and Mary Ann Fenelon. In the 1910 U.S. Census, Vincent and his parents lived in Devils Lake, ND. When Vincent registered for the draft on June 5, 1917, he was farming near McLaughlin, SD. Vincent joined the Army on Oct. 10, 1917, and was sent to Camp Funston. He was assigned to Troop B,

314th MP Co., 89th Division (ASN 2194376). Sgt. Fenelon sailed for France from New York aboard the *Saxon* on June 28, 1918. The MP Co. served in the Sectors at Lucey, Euvezin, St. Mihiel and Meuse-Argonne. He sent a letter to the *McIntosh Globe-Chief* describing being hit by mustard gas. He also mentioned that some of the men he served with wanted to bring back some live Germans to put in a cage in Central Park in New York City. Sgt. Fenelon sailed for home from Brest aboard the *Prinz Friedrich Wilhelm* on May 18, 1919, and was discharged on June 9, 1919. In 1921 he married Etta McLaughlin (1902-1994). Vincent was listed with her on the Standing Rock Census Rolls, but was non-enrolled. In the 1931 Census Roll, they are listed with their children, James, William and Eugene. In the 1940 U.S. Census, the family was living in Devils Lake, where Vincent worked as the manager in a Potato Seed Warehouse. By then, Vincent and Etta had a daughter, Mary Ann. Their son, James, served with the 164th ND Infantry at Guadalcanal in the Pacific during WWII. Vincent later was the Executive Director of the ND Beverage Dealers Association. Vincent entered the spirit world in the Missouri Slope Lutheran Care Center in Bismarck on March 6, 1992. He is buried in McLaughlin City Cemetery.[4]

Ferris, Frank. Frank was born on Feb. 24, 1894, in Charles Mix County, SD. His parents were Edward and Julia Ferris. In the 1897 Yanktonai Census Roll, he is listed with his mother and brothers, William and Harry. His brother, William, served in the Army. Frank married Susan Archambeau (1890-1960) in 1912. Susan's brother, David, served in the military during the war. When Frank registered for the draft, he was living in Platte with Susan and their three children. Frank joined the Army on April 26, 1918, and served in Co. E, 355th Infantry Regiment, 89th Division (ASN 2186488). Pvt. Ferris completed his training at Camp Funston and traveled to France from Boston aboard the *Persic* on June 30, 1918. When the fighting ended, Pvt. Ferris's unit hiked over to Saarburg, Germany, in time to celebrate Christmas. Each soldier received a bar of chocolate, two cookies, a package of cigarettes and a cigar. On May 15, 1919, the 355th Infantry boarded the transport *Leviathan,* which formerly had been the German ship *Fatherland.* Pvt. Ferris was discharged on May 31, 1919. A photo of Pvt. Ferris was published in a unit history in 1919. In the 1940 U.S. Census, Frank and Susan were living in Greenwood with their children, Darlene, David and Frank, Jr. Frank Sr. was working as a blacksmith in the C.C.C. camp. Frank entered the spirit world on April 21, 1950, and is buried in the Platte City Cemetery.[5]

Ferris, Harry A. Harry was a brother to Frank and William. Harry was born on Dec. 6, 1894, in Geddes, SD, on the Yankton Reservation to Edward Ferris and Julia Archambeau. He was a brother to Frank and William. When Harry registered for the draft on June 5, 1917, he was working as a blacksmith. Around this time, he married Marie Analla, with who he had a son, Lyle. In tribal records, he is listed as a veteran of the World War, and was discharged on Jan. 24, 1919. After the war, he married Dorothy Smith. They had a daughter, Norma. In the 1930 U.S. Census, they were living in Huron where Harry was working as a meat cutter in a packing plant. In the 1930s, Harry moved to California. When he registered for the Selective Service in 1942, he was working in a shipyard in San Pedro, CA. He entered the spirit world on Oct. 7, 1959.

Ferris, William. William, the older brother of Frank, was born on March 9, 1892. When William registered for the draft on June 5, 1917, he was working with his dad as a blacksmith in Platte. On June 23, 1917, he married Meadie Rabe. He joined the Army on June 27, 1918, at Lake Andes. He served as a Private with the 322nd Auxiliary Remount Depot (ASN 3315322). He was discharged at Camp Dodge on March 4, 1919. He was a member of the American Legion. In the 1920 U.S. Census, he was working as a truck driver for a dray line in Platte. In the 1930 Yanktonai Census Roll, he is listed with his children, Maxine, Dorothy, Kenneth and Beverly. William developed pneumonia and entered the spirit world on June 26, 1935, and is buried in Pleasant Lawn Cemetery, Geddes, SD. His son, Kenneth, served in the Navy in WWII.

Fielder, Francis Folsom. Francis was born on June 14, 1902, on the Cheyenne River Reservation. His parents were Henry and Clara Fielder. Francis joined the Army and was assigned to Battery A, 49th Field Artillery, CAC, (ASN 505071). He sailed with his unit from Newport News, VA, aboard the *Lutetia* on Oct. 5, 1918. After the war, Pvt. Fielder sailed for home from Pauillac aboard the *Martha Washington* on Feb. 22, 1919, arriving in Newport News on March 8. He was discharged on March 19, 1919. He married Julia LeBeau on July 27, 1921. In the 1930 U.S. Census, he was working as an Assistant Farmer on the Pine Ridge Reservation. In the 1937 Cheyenne River Census Roll, he lived on the Pine Ridge Reservation with his wife and children, Clara, Fay, Elsie, Roland, Ramona and Juanita. Francis entered the spirit world in the clinic in Eagle Butte on Feb. 2, 1966, and is buried in the LaPlant Cemetery.[6]

Finley, Smiley Lucas. Smiley was born in Peever on the Sisseton-Wahpeton Reservation on June 14, 1892, to Charles and Agnes Finley. As a child, he was known as Sampson. In the 1910 Census Roll, he was listed as an orphan. When he registered for the draft on June 5, 1917, he was living in Peever. He joined the Army on June 24, 1918, and was assigned to Co. G, 41st Infantry, 10th Division. The 10th Division was formed at Camp Funston, KS, after the 89th Division left for Europe. Pvt. Finley was discharged on Jan. 29, 1919. In the 1920 U.S. Census, Smiley was living with his wife, Ellen Renville, and her children, Herbert, Ruby, Harold, Leonard and Thelma. They were later divorced. In the 1930 U.S. Census, Smiley was a patient in the VA Hospital in Minneapolis. When Smiley registered for the Selective Service in 1942, he was working in Seattle for the U.S. Government at the Port of Embarkation. He later married Vera LaPointe. Smiley entered the spirit world on Oct. 23, 1973, following a car accident north of Pine Ridge. He and Vera (1896-1979) are buried together in the Black Hills National Cemetery, Section C, Site 905.

Fire Cloud, Silas. Silas was born in 1896 on the Standing Rock Reservation, the son of Alfred and Mary (Turn Holy) Fire Cloud. He registered for the draft on June 7, 1918. Shortly after this, he joined the Army at Camp Funston and was assigned to Co. 5, 164th Depot Brigade. After his discharge on Nov. 26, 1918, he returned to his home in Little Eagle. He lived with his parents until marrying Ella Bearshield in 1938. Ella had been married to Julius Bearshield, a veteran who passed away in 1936. In the 1940 U.S. Census, Silas was working in the C.C.C. program in Corson County. Silas entered the spirit world in Little Eagle on Sept. 16, 1949, and is buried in Little Eagle. His widow married Noah Shoots Walking, a fellow veteran.[7]

Fire Place, Dallas. Dallas was born in October 1896, on the Pine Ridge Reservation. His parents were William and Mille Fire Place. He registered for the draft on June 5, 1918. He likely enlisted shortly after this. Around 1920, he married Emma Horn Chips, with whom he had a daughter, Pansy. In 1930, Dallas married Christine Two Lances. In 1935 they were living seven miles east of Allen. When they were visited by a worker with the State Emergency Relief Program (SDERA), Dallas stated that he had trained at Camp Dodge, IA. He later ranched near Batesland. Dallas passed away on Jan. 23, 1984, in the Rapid City Regional Hospital. His wife and two daughters, Dorothy and Vicki survived him. He is buried in Messiah Cemetery at Wounded Knee.[8]

Fire Thunder, William. William was born on June 27, 1894, on the Pine Ridge Reservation. In the 1896 Census Roll, William is listed with his parents, Edgar and Susie Wakinyan Peta [Fire Thunder], as well as two sisters, Julia and Lydia. His father had served as a Corporal with the Indian Scouts worked for the Indian Service, so William lived with his grandmother, Mary Weasel Bear. At the age of 14, William enrolled at Haskell Institute, Lawrence, KS. A fellow student was Henry Standing Bear. William married Maud Humphrey in Hardin, MT, on Jan. 3, 1916. When William registered for the draft on June 5, 1917, he was living in Allen, SD, and raising livestock. He joined the Army on June 26, 1918, and was sent to Camp Cody, NM. He served as a Corporal in Co. 4, 2nd Development Battalion (ASN 3315463). He was discharged on Dec. 10, 1918. In 1920, he worked for International Harvester in Montana. In the late 1920s, he moved back to the Pine Ridge Reservation. Around 1937, he married Stella Pulliam. They had two children, Edgar and Suzanne. William worked for the Indian Service as Assistant Farmer. In 1944, he was elected president of the Oglala Tribal Council and served two years. He was outspoken in his support for equal rights for his fellow tribal members, especially veterans. For a number of years, his wife worked as a cook at the day school in Allen. William later worked in Rapid City. He entered the spirit world on May 14, 1959, and is buried in Inestimable Gift Cemetery in Allen, SD.[9]

Fisher, Frank. Frank Fisher was a student at the Flandreau boarding school who served in the military during WWI. His name is engraved on a plaque erected at the school around 1920. He likely was from the Fort Belknap Reservation in Montana. Frank was born on July 3, 1897, the son of Ignatius and Jennie Fisher. He joined the Army on April 22, 1918, and was assigned to Battery F, 48th Artillery (Coast Artillery Corps) (ASN 474696). Bugler Harry Jones of Flandreau also served in the 48th Artillery. The 48th Artillery sailed from Newport News, VA, in October 1918 and arrived in France on Oct. 26, 1918. Pfc. Fisher sailed for the U.S. aboard the *Kroonland* on March 12, 1919, and was discharged on April 8, 1919. Upon returning to Fort Belknap, he married Mamie Shortman. In the 1940 U.S. Census, he was working in the C.C.C. program. He entered the spirit world on April 30, 1954, and is buried in Saint Paul Mission, Hays, MT.[10]

Flammond, Louis Parris. Louis was born in Rolla, ND, on March 29, 1891. His parents, Peter and Elsie Flammond, were Ojibwe. Louis attended school at Fort Totten from 1904-1913. In 1913, Louis started school at Carlisle, PA. At this time his parents were living in Medicine Lake, MT. However, Louis did not like the academic side of the school, preferring to learn a trade. In 1915, he left Carlisle to go to Winner on the Rosebud Reservation. He married Corrinne Janis around 1915. When Louis registered for the draft on June 5, 1917, he lived at Winner with his wife and son, George. Louis joined the Army on June 27, 1918, and was assigned to Co. B, 352nd Infantry, 88th Division (ASN 3316005). On Aug. 15, 1918, Pvt. Flammond sailed for Europe aboard the S.S. *Ascanius*. After occupational duty in France, the 352nd returned home aboard the ship *Canonicus* on May 21, 1919. Pvt. Flammond was discharged on June 14, 1919. In the 1930 U.S. Census, Louis was the Postmaster at St. Francis. In the 1936 Rosebud Census Roll, Louis and Corrinne had four children, George, Rita, Lloyd and Mary Ann. Louis passed away from typhoid fever at the Rosebud Hospital on Sept. 20, 1936, and is buried in St. Charles Cemetery in St. Francis. Louis's son, George, served in the Army in WWII. Lloyd served with the Navy. Louis's widow married George Kills in Sight, a WWI vet. In the 1940 U.S. Census, Corrinne was the Postmistress at St. Francis.[11]

Flanagan, Basil C. Basil was born on the Cheyenne River Reservation on Oct 27, 1895. His parents were John J. Flanagan and Louise Claymore. In the 1900 U.S. Census, Basil was living with his grandfather in Dewey County. When Basil registered for the draft on June 5, 1917, he was farming near LaPlant with his step-father. Basil joined the Army on Sept. 22, 1917. Basil was in the 2nd group of men to leave Dewey County for Camp Funston. Other soldiers with him were Armstrong Four Bear, Napoleon Ducheneaux, William Bowker and Kiutus Jim. He was assigned to Co. B, 340th Machine Gun Battalion, 89th Division (ASN 2193071). Pfc. Flanagan sailed from New York

Basil C. Flanagan
Mike Flanagan

aboard the *Khyber* on June 4, 1918. After the Armistice, Bugler Flanagan returned home from Brest, France aboard the *Leviathan* on May 15, 1919. He arrived in Hoboken, NJ, on May 22, 1919. He was discharged as a Pfc. on June 2, 1919. Basil married Alta Alexander in Pierre in December 1923. In the 1940 U.S. Census, they lived with their children, Alma and Rockne at the Cheyenne Agency, where he worked as a property clerk in the C.C.C. program. Basil entered the spirit world in California on Aug. 21, 1974. He is buried in Riverside Cemetery in Pierre, SD.

Flanagan, Daniel E. Daniel was born on the Cheyenne River Reservation on Sept. 15, 1897. His parents were John J Flanagan and Louise Claymore. In the early 1900s, his mother married Joseph Hiett. In the 1910 U.S. Census, Daniel and his brother, Basil, were attending the Pierre boarding school. When Daniel registered for the draft on Sept. 12, 1918, he was a student at the University of Minnesota, St. Paul. He was living with his father. He enlisted on Oct. 10, 1918, and was sent to Officer Training School at Camp Pike, Arkansas. He was discharged as a Private on Dec. 6, 1918. In the 1920 U.S. Census, he was living in St. Paul, MN. In the 1940 U.S. Census, he was working for the Post Office in Chicago. His last position was as personnel officer. He married Winifred Winsor. After retirement he moved to Palm Coast, Fl. He entered the spirit world in Coastal Communities Hospital in Bunnell, Fl, on Apr. 1, 1988. He is buried in Mid-Florida Crematory in Deland, FL.[12]

Fleury, George P. George was born on April 27, 1897, on the Crow Creek Reservation. His parents were Samuel and Ella Fleury. George joined the SD National Guard on May 8, 1917. The 1st SD Cavalry was sent to Camp Cody, NM, in September of 1917. Pvt. Fleury was first assigned to Co. 18, Camp Cody June Automatic Replacement Draft. Pvt. Fleury sailed with this unit from New York aboard the *Honorata* on June 28, 1918. After arriving in France, he was assigned to Co. I, 306th Infantry, 77th Division (ASN 1429213). The 306th Infantry served in the Sectors at Baccarat, Vesle, Oise-Aisne, Fôret-d'Argonne and Meuse-Argonne. Pvt. Fleury served with Pvt. Horace Barse, who was killed in the Meuse-Argonne Offensive on Oct. 15, 1918. The 306th Infantry sailed from Brest aboard the *Mt. Vernon* on April 19, 1919. Pvt. Fleury later served in Casual Company 481. He was discharged on May 18, 1919. In 1921, he married Bessie St. Pierre. In the 1930 U.S. Census, George was working for the Indian Service. In the 1940 U.S. Census, George was working on a dam construction project. He and Bessie had three daughters, Sophie, Thelma and Irma and five sons, Samuel, Lorenzo "Buddy", Wilmer, Sidney and Roger. Lorenzo served in the Navy in WWII. Wilmer was killed while serving with the Army in Korea in 1951. Sidney also enlisted in the Army during peace time in the 1950s. George was working as the light plant operator when he entered the spirit world at Wessington Springs Memorial Hospital on Aug. 18, 1954, and is buried in the Presbyterian Cemetery in Fort Thompson.[13]

Flood, Bernard. Bernard was born around Christmas in 1900 on the Rosebud Reservation. His parents were Thomas and Nanette (Desersa) Flood. Around the time of World War I, Bernard enlisted in the Navy. In the 1920 U.S. Census, Bernard was an apprentice seaman at Great Lakes Naval Station. He served three years in the Navy. He was a Musician 1st Class and played the trombone in the Navy Band. When he returned home, he married Ada Little Money, whose brother, Charles, served in the Army. In the 1930 Rosebud Census Roll, Bernard and Ada are listed with their children, John, Jeanette and Bernard Jr. John served in the Army in WWII. Bernard Jr. served with the Army in Korea. In 1935, the family was interviewed by a worker as part of the SDERA program. At that time, they were living in a two-room house located ¾ mile east of Okreek. Bernard mentioned that he had once worked as a lineman for a phone company in Chicago. This likely was just after his service with the Navy. Ada passed away in 1984. Bernard passed away at Rosebud Hospital on Dec. 28, 1994. His children, Jeanette, Maybelle, Bernard Jr., Lavern, John and Collins survived him. He is buried in Calvary Cemetery at Okreek.[14]

Flood, Henry. See **Standing Bear, Henry.**

Flood, John. John was born near Okreek on the Rosebud Reservation on Dec. 15, 1894, to Thomas and Goldie (Desersa) Flood. Bernard was his younger brother. When John registered for the draft on June 5, 1917, he was working as an apprentice painter at the boarding school in Genoa, NE. He joined the Army on Aug. 3, 1917, and likely was sent to Camp Cody, NM, where the 34th Division was training. Pvt. Flood was assigned to Co. F, 109th Supply Train, 34th Division (ASN 1441580). He sailed for France aboard the *Olympic* on Sept. 2, 1918. After the war, Pfc. Flood returned home from St. Nazaire aboard the *Dekalb* on June 12, 1919, and was discharged as a Private First Class on June 28, 1919. In 1921, John was a member of the Chauncey Eagle Horn Legion Post at Rosebud. In the 1937 Census Roll, he is listed as single. He entered the spirit world at the VA Hospital in Hot Springs on Nov. 1, 1983. He is buried in St. Charles Cemetery, St. Francis, SD.

Fly, Felix. Felix was born near McIntosh on the Standing Rock Reservation on March 21, 1895. His parents were Thomas and Alma Fly. His father passed away when Felix was a child. His mother then married Edwin Shooter. In 1910, Felix attended the Bismarck boarding school. In October 1912, he started school at Carlisle, PA, but did not like it. He had become more interested in playing baseball than studying. In February 1915, he returned home to Corson County to play baseball. When he registered for the draft on June 5, 1917, he was working for his step father, Edward Shooter. On June 24, 1918, Felix joined the Army and was sent to Camp Funston, KS. He was assigned to Co. F, 352nd Infantry, 88th Division (ASN 3309452). The 352nd Infantry, Second Battalion, left for France aboard the S.S. *Ulysses* on Aug. 16, 1918. They did not take part in active fighting at the Front, but they were part of the Army of Occupation after the Armistice. The 2nd Battalion was billeted at Ribeaucourt. They returned to the U.S. from St. Nazaire on May 21, 1919, sailing on the U.S.S. *Pocahontas*. Pvt. Fly was discharged on June 14, 1919. After the war, Felix played baseball for a number of years. He and Joseph Grey Day played for the Plano Indians. Felix was known as "Home Run King of the Northwest." Around 1925, he married Irene Echo Sherman. He later married Nellie Good Weasel. He lived in the Black Hills for many years and worked as a sheet metal and iron worker. On Oct. 16, 1954, he married Marie Parks. Felix entered the spirit world on Sept. 4, 1974, in a Rapid City Hospital. His widow, Marie, a daughter, Regina, and two sons, Tommy and Felix survived him. Felix and Marie (1907-1996) are buried together in the Black Hills National Cemetery, Section D, Site 1202.[15]

Fogg, Louis J. Louis was born on the Pine Ridge Reservation around 1900 to Frank Snow Dust Fogg and Evelyn Merivel. Louis served in the Army during WWI. Louis' sister, Frances, married Peter Hopkins, a fellow veteran. Louis married Edna Ross in Gann Valley on Sept. 22, 1923. In the 1930 U.S. Census, Louis lived with his family in Huron, where he was working as a plasterer. In the 1937 Census Roll, Louis and Edna are listed with their children, Rosalia, Louis Jr., Bertha, Emma, Henry, Joyce, and Alexis. Edna entered the spirit world in 1938. On March 8, 1944, Louis re-enlisted in the Army at Ft. Snelling. His son, Louis Jr., was killed at Normandy in June of 1944. Louis was discharged on Nov. 17, 1944. After the war, he worked as a carpenter. He entered the spirit world in Sioux Valley Hospital in Sioux Falls on Nov. 7, 1967. He is buried in St. Joseph's Cemetery in Fort Thompson. His headstone indicates he served as a Private in WWI and WWII.

Folson, Frank. Frank was born on the Pine Ridge Reservation on June 28, 1892. His parents were Edward Two Two and Helen Garcia. On the Pine Ridge Census Rolls, he is listed as Richard Two Two. Frank joined the Army on May 7, 1918, and was assigned to Co. C, 342nd Machine Gun (MG) Battalion, 89th Division (ASN 2848530). Pvt. Folson sailed from New York to France aboard the *Caronia* on June 4, 1918. The 342nd MG Bn. was assigned to a training area at Vesaignes. After the Armistice, the 342nd MG Bn. was billeted at Pfalzal, Germany, near Trier. Pvt. Folson sailed from Brest, France, aboard the *Prinz Friedrich Wilhelm* on May 18, 1919, and arrived in Hoboken on May 27. Pfc. Folson was discharged on June 14, 1919. In the 1930 U.S. Census, Frank and his wife, Evangeline, were farming in Mellette County with their children, Lorean, Earl and Leonard. Frank's wife was from Crow Creek. Their son, Earl, served in the Army in WWII. Frank entered the spirit world at the VA Hospital in Hot Springs on July 7, 1959, and is buried in Wounded Knee Cemetery.[16]

Fool Bull, Richard. Richard was born around 1887 on the Rosebud Reservation. His father was Fool Bull. When he registered for the draft on June 5, 1917, he was working as a laborer for the Government at Rosebud. He joined the Army and was sent to Camp Funston, KS. After receiving his training, he wrote home that he was "getting to be quite a soldier learning right along…I got a dandy rifle and bayonet and am anxious to make use of them on some German. When the war is over I'll bring a German scalp with me back to Rosebud." He was discharged in August 1918. After the war, he married Irene Blue Horse, whose brother, William, had also served in the Army. Richard and Irene had two sons, Benjamin and Leslie. Benjamin served in the Marine Corps in Korea. Richard was known for the fine flutes he made. He is buried in St. Charles Cemetery in St. Francis.[17]

Foote, Jesse. Jesse was born in Cutmeat on the Rosebud Reservation on April 6, 1892. His parents were Foot and Oglala. Jesse attended the Carlisle Boarding School for several years. When Jesse registered for the draft on June 5, 1917, he was living in Cutmeat and farming with his father. He joined the Army on July 22, 1918 at White River. He was assigned to Co. C, 333rd Infantry, 84th Division (ASN 3955925). Pvt. Foote sailed from New York aboard the *Baltic* on Sept. 1, 1918. He likely was reassigned to another unit upon arrival in France. Pvt. Foote left Brest on the S.S. *F. J. Luckenbach* on July 18, 1919. He was serving with an ASC Headquarters Detachment, and temporarily assigned to Le Mans Casual Co. No. 1815. He was discharged on Aug. 5, 1919, at Camp Dodge, IA. He married Alice White Feather Tail. In the 1930 U.S. Census, Jesse and Alice lived in Mellette County with Jesse's mother. He had been a patient at the Battle Mountain Sanatorium in August of 1929. He entered the spirit world on Feb. 7, 1934, and is buried in Holy Family Cemetery in Todd County.

Foote, Stephen. Stephen likely was born about Sept. 11, 1895, on the Lower Brule Reservation. His parents, Frank and Mary Foot, were one of the families who moved to the Rosebud from the Lower Brule around 1896. Stephen was a student at Carlisle, PA, for several years and also worked in the trainee program at Ford Motor Co. in Detroit. Stephen was living in Tripp County when he registered for the draft on June 5, 1917. He joined the Army on June 7, 1918, and was assigned to Co. I, 164th Infantry, 41st Division (ASN 3315981). Cpl. Foote sailed from New York aboard the *Ortega* on Aug. 31, 1918. He traveled with Overseas Casual Co #362. The 164th Infantry did not serve at the Front. After the war, Cpl. Foote headed home from Brest aboard the S.S. *President Grant* on Feb. 8, 1919 and was discharged on March 12, 1919. After returning home, he married Martha King. In the 1937 Rosebud Census Roll, they were listed with their children, William and Caroline. William served in the Army in Korea. Stephen entered the spirit world on Jan. 12, 1955 and is buried in Holy Spirit Cemetery in Tripp County.

Foster, Samuel. Samuel was born about June 19, 1897, near Little Eagle, SD, on the Standing Rock Reservation. His parents were John and Amelia Foster. When Samuel registered for the draft on June 5, 1917, he was ranching near Little Eagle. The clerk indicated that Samuel had "bad eyes." When Samuel joined the Army, he was assigned to Co. D, 136th Infantry. He was discharged on Dec. 29, 1917, on account of physical disability. He had suffered from Trachoma. He received a disability pension of $25 per month. In 1919, he married Louise No Heart in Timber Lake. In the 1920 U.S. Census, Samuel and Louisa were living with Samuel's parents. Samuel was a member of the American Legion. Louise entered the spirit world in 1934. In the 1937 Census Roll, Samuel was listed with their children, Edna, Collins, Selina, May and Hattie. Samuel entered the spirit world at the VA Hospital in Hot Springs on May 1, 1938. He is buried in Little Eagle.[18]

Chester Armstrong Four Bear
Marcella LeBeau

Four Bear, Chester Armstrong. Armstrong was born on June 20, 1889, on the Cheyenne River Reservation. His parents were Chester Four Bear and Louise Bear Face. When Armstrong registered for the draft on June 5, 1917, he lived at Promise and listed his occupation as "bronco buster," looking after his own stock. He was well-known for his bronc riding and rope spinning skills.

He entered the Army in September 1917, leaving from Timber Lake to Camp Funston, KS. Armstrong was in the second group of men to leave Dewey County. Other local men with him were Basil Flanagan, William Bowker, Napoleon Ducheneaux and Kiutus Jim. He received additional training at Camp Sevier, SC, until March 1918. He was assigned to a Machine Gun Company, 118th Infantry Regiment, 30th Division (ASN 2192998). Upon arrival at Camp Mills, NY, he sailed from New York on May 11, 1918 aboard the *Elpenor*. Pfc. Four Bear was selected as a sniper and received further training in marksmanship, use of bayonet, carrying messages, prismatic map reading, and minor camouflage. He returned to his company and was ordered to Belgium in July 1918. They relieved an English unit and occupied a canal sector at Ypres. After being on an active front for a month, the 30th Division retired to rest at St. Pol, France, for ten days. Then they moved to the Somme Sector, relieving a British unit in the front-line trenches. Pfc. Four Bear acted as a runner, carrying messages to Regimental Headquarters, thru terrific gun barrage, on the evening of the major offensive on the Hindenberg Line. He was gassed, but delivered the message, at times it was necessary for him to crawl. The officer to whom he gave the message sent him to a hospital. He refused to go, returning to his Company thru the same barrage on the front line. He encountered a French runner who was wounded by a high explosive shell. After receiving first aid from Pfc. Four Bear, the French soldier took his Croix de Guerre medal and pinned it on Four Bear. The Somme Offensive lasted three weeks, during which he did messenger work constantly, through all sorts of shell fire and barrages. Pfc. was cited for bravery in action.

He remained in heavy action until Oct. 20, when he was sent to a rest camp, where he still was on Nov. 11. Pvt. Four Bear sailed from St. Nazaire, France, aboard the *Madawaska* on March 17, 1919. He was traveling with "Headquarters Troop, 30th Division." He was discharged on May 8, 1919.

After returning home, he married Jennie Meeter. They ranched and Armstrong traveled to take part in rodeos. He performed for the King and Queen of England. In the 1940 U.S. Census, they had four children, Joseph, Arthur, Julia and Chet. Jennie passed away in 1942. Armstrong was living in Moreau at that time. He entered the spirit world in the Mobridge Community Hospital on May 19, 1970, and is buried in St. Elizabeth Cemetery, Wakpala.[19]

Frank, Michael. Michael (Mike) was born on Feb. 11, 1896, in Hermanstadt, Austria, now known as Sibiu, Rumania. It was part of the Austro-Hungarian Empire. His parents, Martin and Catherine, brought him to the U.S. in 1904. They lived in Cedar Rapids, IA, before moving to South Dakota. They settled in McIntosh, SD. When he registered for the draft on June 5, 1917, he was farming with his father. On March 3, 1918, he married Lulu Makes Trouble (1896-1979), whose brother, James, also served in the Army. Mike joined the Army on June 24, 1918. As a Private, he was assigned to 9th Company, 3rd Bn., 164th Depot Brigade at Camp Funston. He was discharged on Nov. 23, 1918. After the war, he joined the American Legion and worked for the Milwaukee Road. Around 1924, the family moved to Lulu's allotment near Firesteel. Mike was included in the Standing Rock Census Rolls, but was non-enrolled. Mike worked for a while in the Firesteel coal mine. Their home was a single-room, 18' x 14' located 12 miles from Firesteel. In the 1930s, Mike worked in an Indian Emergency Conservation Work (ICEW) camp that was 22 miles from their home. Mike owned a 1926 Chevrolet. They had four children then, Flora, Sophia and Mike Jr., and Kenneth. Their school was five miles away. The family later moved into Firesteel where Mike worked as the school custodian from 1953 to 1968 and Lulu worked as a cook. When the school closed in 1968, the family moved to Isabel, SD. Mike passed away at the VA hospital at Fort Meade on Oct. 23, 1973, and is buried in the Black Hills National Cemetery, section C, site 907. Lulu is buried with him. Their son, Mike Jr. served in the Korean War. Kenneth served during the Vietnam conflict.[20]

Arthur Frazier
Nebraska Historical Society

Frazier, Arthur. Arthur was born around 1898 on the Santee Reservation in Nebraska. His parents were Charles and Hannah (Howe) Frazier. His father was a minister on the Rosebud Reservation for around 20 years. Arthur and his brother, Charles, were students at the Flandreau boarding school. They both enlisted in the South Dakota National Guard on April 4, 1917. They were assigned to Troop D, 1st SD Cavalry. That unit trained in South Dakota but was not issued saddles or horses until they arrived at Camp Cody, New Mexico in September 1917. Sometime after that, the men were transferred to other units undergoing training at Camp Cody. Pvt. Frazier was assigned to Co. 14, Camp Cody June Automatic Replacement Draft (ASN 1427445). He sailed for France with his unit aboard the S.S. *Tereisias* on June 28, 1918. After arriving in France, he was reassigned to Co. B, 28th Infantry, 1st Division. During the Meuse-Argonne Offensive, Pvt. Frazier was wounded and affected by shell shock. He may have suffered from amnesia. His parents were told that their son had been killed. In 1921, a body marked as Pvt. Arthur Frazier, killed in France, was shipped to the Rev. and Mrs. Charles Frazier at Niobrara, NE. Two years later, Mrs. Frazier saw a young man who she believed was her son. Because she believed her son was still alive, she refused to accept any compensation from the government on her son's life insurance policy. Arthur lived with his parents for a few years before moving to the state hospital in Hastings. In the 1930 and 1940 U.S. Censuses, Arthur was listed as a patient at a state hospital in Hastings, NE. Arthur entered the spirit world in 1958 and is buried in the Santee Cemetery. Arthur's name is included on a plaque honoring the war veterans that was erected at the Flandreau School.[21]

Frazier, Charles B. Charles Ben was born on Dec. 9, 1895 on the Santee Reservation near Niobrara, NE. His parents were the Rev. Charles and Hannah Frazier. After his father was called to a congregation in South Dakota, Charles was enrolled at the Flandreau boarding school and took up carpentry. Charles enlisted in the SD National Guard on April 4, 1917, and served as a Private 1st Class with Troop D, 1st Cavalry. The 1st Cavalry trained in South Dakota until being transferred to Camp Cody, NM, where they became part of the 34th Division. Cpl. Frazier left for France with Co. D, 136th Infantry (ASN 1427360) from New York aboard the *Melita* on Oct. 13, 1918. He later was assigned to Co. L, 49th Infantry. Cpl. Frazier sailed from Brest, France, on Jan. 12, 1919, and was discharged on Feb. 15, 1919. After the war, his name was engraved on a monument honoring the war veterans that was erected at the Flandreau boarding school. Ben first married Josephine Little House, with whom he had a son, Calvin. In 1933, Ben married Mable Arconge, who was a seamstress. In 1935, the family was interviewed by a worker with the SDERA program. They were renting a room in a house in Martin and obtained their water from the court house pump. Ben was looking for work as a carpenter. Mable later married Ray Blacksmith. Ben entered the spirit world near Mission, SD, on March 14, 1940, and is buried at Inestimable Gift Cemetery near Allen, SD. His son, Calvin, served in the Navy during WWII.[22]

Frazier, Chester. – listed on WWI veteran's memorial at Oglala Lakota College, Kyle, SD

Frazier, Francis Philip. Philip was born in the parsonage of the Ponca Creek Congregational Church near St. Charles, SD, on June 2, 1892. He is listed on the 1894 Santee Census Roll with his parents, Francis and Maggie Frazier. His father was a minister. In the 1910 U.S. Census, they were living on the Santee Reservation in Nebraska. Philip likely joined the Army in the spring of 1918 and was sent to Camp Funston, KS. Private Frazier was assigned to Headquarters Company, 355th Infantry (ASN 2847151), which was part of the 89th Division. Pvt. Frazier sailed from New York aboard the *Baltic* on June 4, 1918. Early in August of 1918, the Division was moved to a frontline sector near Toul. The 89th Division spent 28 days in the Front and suffered 7,291 casualties. When the fighting ended, Pvt. Frazier received an excellent rating from his commanding officer, Capt. Dan H. Hughes.

> Pvt. Frazier is an excellent soldier. Stands nervous strain very well. He has an excellent ability as a leader. Was on duty in the signal platoon of the Co. and was considered an excellent soldier in all respects. Very well educated and is good or better than average in the use of buzzers, maps, etc.

The 355th Regiment left Brest, France, aboard the *Leviathan* on May 15, 1919. He was discharged on June 2, 1919. A few years after returning, Philip married Susie Meek (1895-1976), who was enrolled in the Sauk and Fox Nation. In the 1930 U.S. Census, Philip and Susie were clergy members for the Quaker Faith on the Shawnee Agency in Oklahoma. In the 1930s, they moved up to Ft. Pierre, SD. In the 1940 U.S. Census, they were missionaries in Santee, NE. They had three children, Wilbur, Winona and Thomas. They later had another son. Wilbur and Thomas served in the Armed Forces in WWII. During WWII, Philip worked in a defense plant in Los Angeles. After WWII, he served as a minister for a number of churches on the Standing Rock Reservation. Philip entered the spirit world on Sept. 29, 1964 and is buried in the Santee Cemetery.[23]

Frazier, William C. William was born on the Cheyenne River Reservation on July 3, 1895, to John Frazier and Edna Traversie. After his father died in the early 1900s, his mother married George Swift Horse. When William registered for the draft on June 5, 1917, he was ranching on his allotment near White Horse. He joined the Army on Oct. 5, 1917. Pvt. Frazier sailed from New York aboard the *Scandinavian* on June 20, 1918. He was traveling with Co. 4, Camp Pike June Replacement Draft Detachment-Artillery. After arriving in France, he was assigned to Battery F. 6th Field Artillery, 1st Division (ASN 2114088). Pvt. Frazier sailed home from Marseilles, France, aboard the *Guiseppe Verdi* on June 22, 1919. He traveled with St. Aignan Special Casual Co. No. 6425. St. Aignan was a large military hospital in France. He was discharged as a Pfc. on July 15, 1919. After the war, he returned home and lived with his parents. He remained single. In the 1940 U.S. Census, he was working on a dam construction project. William entered the spirit world on Dec. 23, 1947, after his house near White Horse caught fire. He is buried Emanuel Episcopal Cemetery near White Horse.[24]

Margaret Frazier Frederick
Columbia University

Frederick, Margaret Frazier. Margaret was born near Niobrara, NE, on the Santee Reservation around 1889. Her parents were Albert Frazier and Lizzie Howe. She was baptized on Jan. 13, 1889. She attended school on the Santee Reservation and in St. Johnsbury, VT. In 1915, Margaret was a student at the Brightlook Nurses Training School in St. Johnsbury. On Easter of that year, she was visited by her brother, David, and her cousin, Philip, who were going to school in Northfield, Mass. Margaret enlisted in the Army Nurse Corps on Aug. 27, 1918, at Niobrara. She served as a Registered Nurse until her discharge at Camp Bowie, TX, on July 24, 1919. On Feb. 18, 1920, she married Peter C. Frederick, who was a returned veteran. She was member of the American Legion Auxiliary. They lived in Greenwood, SD. After an extended illness, Margaret entered the spirit world on Jan. 21, 1935, and is buried in Greenwood Presbyterian Cemetery.[25]

Frederick, Peter C. Peter was born near Wagner, SD, on Sept. 1, 1895, the son of Henry and Agnes Frederick. Peter likely enlisted in the 4th Infantry, SD National Guard (ASN 139419) in 1917. When this regiment arrived at Camp Greene, NC, many of the soldiers were reassigned to Battery C, 147th Field Artillery (FA). Horseshoer Frederick left with this unit for France on Jan. 11, 1918, aboard the ship *Olympic*. Initially the 147th FA was part of the 41st Division, but in March 1918, it was attached to the 32nd Division and provided artillery support for the Red Arrow Division. After the Armistice, the 147th was assigned to the 88th Division. Pvt. Frederick received his evaluation from 1st Lt. A.M. Knudtson, who wrote: "Excellent night worker, runner, verbal reporter and observer. Has demonstrated fitness for mounted arms of the service." The 147th FA served in the Sectors at Toul-Boucq, Center, Aisne-Marne, Fismes, Oise-Aisne, Avocourt and Meuse-Argonne. Pvt. Frederick sailed for home with his unit from Brest aboard the U.S.S. *Kansas* on May 1, 1919. After his discharge on May 23, 1919, Peter returned home and married Margaret Frazier, who had served with the Army Nurse Corps at Camp Bowie, TX. Margaret entered the spirit world in 1935. In the 1940 U.S. Census, Peter worked as a tractor operator in a C.C.C. camp near Huron, SD. On May 25, 1959, Peter married Velma Loretta Pettett in Cheyenne, WY. Peter entered the spirit world in the VA Hospital in Cheyenne on March 1, 1966. Velma and her children, Lorene, Donald and Earl, survived Peter. Peter is buried in Greenwood Cemetery in Sidney, NE.[26]

Frog, Felix. He is listed on WWI veteran's memorial at Oglala Lakota College, Kyle, SD. Felix was born on Sept. 28. 1899, on the Pine Ridge Reservation. In the 1904 Census Roll, Felix is listed with his parents, Alfred Knaska [Frog], Julia White Rabbit, and two brothers, Luke and Oliver. Felix first enlisted in the Army on Jan. 24, 1918, and served in Co. H, 63rd Infantry, 11th Division. He was discharged on April 5, 1919. He re-enlisted on April 7, 1919, and was assigned to the 34th Company, Camp Meade Replacement (ASN R-2340928). He sailed with this unit from Hoboken aboard the *Cap Finisterre* on June 21, 1919. He served with Co. F, 8th Infantry. He returned from Antwerp. Belgium, aboard the *Buford* on Feb. 5, 1920. He was discharged on May 5, 1922. He wrote to Joseph Dixon: "There is quite a few of us Indian boys who we did our part in the Worlds War. There is a few of us boys got over there and saw the whole thing through which we think that we ought to be entitled to a State Bonus. I am still willing to fight for the Old Glory, any minute when I am call for the service I am a soldier in the American Army and I am proud of it."

In the 1920s, Felix married Mattie Martin. In the 1930 U.S. Census, they were farming. Felix entered the spirit world on May 21, 1992, at the VA Hospital in Hot Springs, SD. His daughters, Minnie, Bernice and Joy, survived him. He is buried in Our Lady of Lourdes Cemetery in Slim Buttes, SD.[27]

Frog, Luke. Luke is the younger brother of Felix. He was born on the Pine Ridge Reservation on April 1, 1901. Luke enlisted in the Army on May 13, 1918, and served in Co. I, 48th Infantry Regiment, 20th Division. He was discharged as a Private on July 9, 1919. After returning home, he married Nellie Little Soldier in the mid-1920s. In the 1940 U.S. Census, Luke was working on a dam construction project. In 1943, he worked for the C & NW Railroad out of Chadron, NE. The children of Luke and Nellie were Edith, Ephraim, Cecil and Florence. Luke entered the spirit world on Nov. 14, 1975.

From Above, Pierre. Pierre was born on the Lower Brule Reservation around April 12, 1896. His parents were Amos From Above and Cetan Hotyiwin [Sounding Hawk Woman]. The family moved to the Rosebud Reservation in 1896. In the early 1900s, Amos was a Private in the Indian Police. As a child, Pierre was known as Wawapila kiya [Benevolent]. When Pierre registered for the draft on June 5, 1917, he was farming near Hamill, SD. Pierre likely was drafted. After he arrived at Camp Funston, he wrote back to the Rosebud Agency, that he wanted to be granted citizenship before going to fight. After being transferred to Camp Cody, NM, he was assigned to Co. 15, Camp Cody June Automatic Replacement Draft (ASN 1427447). He sailed for France aboard the S.S. *Tereisias* on June 28, 1918. Corp. From Above was reassigned to Battery F, 124th Field Artillery, 33rd Division. The 124th FA was part of the 58th Field Artillery Brigade, which underwent training at Ornans and Valdehon. In August 1918, the 58th FA Brigade became artillery support for the 89th Division, and later supported the 1st Division. In late October, the Brigade once again supported the 89th Division. There were 39 men from the 124th FA who were killed. Nine men in the regiment were awarded the Distinguished Service Cross. From November 1 to November 5, the 58th FA Brigade advanced 32 kilometers by continuous fighting. In an evaluation from his commanding officer, Cpl. From Above had a talent "especially for any branch of the service where care of horses is part of the routine." He sailed for home from Brest aboard the *America* on May 16, 1919, and was discharged on June 8, 1919.

After the war, Pierre married Ruth Long Crow at Winner. He later married Sophia Lever. In the 1930 U.S. Census, Pierre and Sophia were farming. In the 1940 U.S. Census, Pierre served as a missionary for the Presbyterian Church in Tripp County. Pierre entered the spirit world at Reliance, SD, on May 23, 1963, and is buried in Holy Spirit Cemetery, Tripp County.[28]

G

Gabe, Ambrose. Ambrose was born in Promise, SD, on Jan. 11, 1893. In the 1894 Standing Rock Census Roll, he is listed with his parents, Baptiste and Maggie Gabe. When Ambrose registered for the draft on June 5, 1917, he was working with his father near Wakpala. Ambrose joined the Army on Oct. 5, 1917, and was sent to Camp Funston, KS. He was assigned to Troop B, 314th MP Battalion (ASN 2194439), which became part of the 89th Division. A number of other men from SD's Indian Country served with Pvt. Gabe. They were Joseph Takes the Shield, Moses Clown, Thomas Hawk Eagle, George Jewett, James Wind, Vincent Fenelon and Cyril LeCompte. These soldiers sailed from New York aboard the *Saxon* on June 28, 1918. On Nov. 1, 1918, Pvt. Gabe was seriously wounded by artillery shrapnel. Pvt. Moses Clown and Pvt. Joseph Takes the Shield were killed in that same explosion. For Ambrose, the war was over. He sailed back to the States from Bordeaux aboard the S.S. *Antigone* on March 12, 1919. He was suffering from a gunshot wound to the left knee and traveled with Convalescent Detachment #142. His destination was Greenhut Hospital in New York. He was discharged on April 29, 1919.

In the late 1920s, Ambrose married Eva Yellow. They had two children, Carl and Madeline. Ambrose entered the spirit world on April 13, 1932 and is buried in Wakpala. Eva later married Walter Strong Heart. On March 17, 2017, the Gabe family received a Code Talker's medal in honor of Pvt. Gabe's service.

Gabe, Charles. Charles was the younger brother of Ambrose. He was born Feb. 9, 1898. When he registered for the draft on Sept. 12, 1918, he was working for Joe Claymore. Charles first joined the Army in 1926, serving with the Fourth Cavalry at Fort Meade, SD. He was a member of the Presidential Honor Guard when President Calvin Coolidge visited the Black Hills. Most of the Guard members were from Troop C. A local newspaper reported, "quite a change in half a century when white soldiers were sent into this country to protect the whites from the Indians. Now the Indians are sent to protect the President of the United States from the whites." Soldiers who served as guards received copies of a letter of recommendation that Coolidge had sent to the regiment. They also received special medallions.

Charles married Olive Larrabee from Cheyenne River. In 1935, the family was visited by a worker with the SDERA program. They were living in the Wakpala District in an old two room log house owned by Charles' father, Baptiste. They hauled their water from the Missouri River, about ¼ miles away. They owned a milk cow, three horses and some chickens. Olive was a member of the Legion Auxiliary. Charles tried to find odd jobs to support his family. In the 1937 Census Roll, they were listed with three children, Jeraldine, Lucille and Rudolph. During World War II, Charles served as a Private 1st Class in Co. C, 611th Tank Destroyer Battalion. He was discharged on March 12, 1943. After the war he ranched near Mobridge. Charles entered the spirit world in the Mobridge Community Hospital on Feb. 9, 1968. He is buried in St. Elizabeth's Episcopal Cemetery near Wakpala.[1]

Garcia, Thomas. Thomas was born on the Pine Ridge Reservation around Sept. 9, 1887. His parents were Telesforo Garcia and Helena Galligo. In the 1894 Pine Ridge Census Roll, he is listed with his brothers and sisters. Thomas joined the Army on Aug. 27, 1918, and was assigned to Battery A, 28th Field Artillery, 10th Division (ASN 4265913). He was discharged as a Private on Jan. 24, 1919. After returning home, he married Vienna Janis. In the 1930 U.S. Census, Thomas was working as a laborer in the Indian Hospital. In the 1937 Pine Ridge Census Roll, Thomas and Vienna were listed with their children, Helena and Leo. In the 1940 U.S. Census, Thomas was working as a carpenter. Thomas entered the spirit world on Nov. 30, 1960, and is buried in Red Cloud Cemetery near Pine Ridge.

Garter, John. John was born around 1886. In the 1892 Cheyenne River Census Roll, he is listed with his parents, Thomas and Lucy, and a brother, Daniel. In 1908, he married Mary Ann DeRockbraine (1884-1961) in Bullhead. Mary Ann's brothers, Andrew and Antoine, served in the Army during the war. In the 1910 U.S. Census, John and Mary Ann were living on the Standing Rock Reservation. John is listed as Oglala, while Mary Ann's father was Yanktonai. When John registered for the draft on Sept. 12, 1918, he was working as a police officer in Bullhead. In 1935, John was interviewed by a worker with the SDERA program. He stated that he was drafted two weeks before the Armistice. He had to sell his livestock at that time. He then owned 50 head of horses and 50 head of cattle. He likely was discharged in the fall of 1918. In 1935, the family had ten horses and a calf. They lived in the Bullhead District in a small, one-room log house, which was three miles from a graded road. Their school was nine miles away. They had two children living, Florence and Soloman. John worked as a janitor at the school. He entered the spirit world in Bullhead on Jan. 22, 1942 and is buried in Bullhead.[2]

Gary, Emmett H. Emmett was born on the Rosebud Reservation on Oct. 9, 1900. His parents were Henry and Ida Gary. Emmett enlisted in the Army on Feb. 27, 1918. In the 1920 U.S. Census, collected on Jan. 20, Pfc. Gary was serving in the 7th Cavalry at Ft. Bliss, El Paso, TX. Later that year he re-enlisted. Upon returning home, he married Adelia Afraid of Bear (1900-1996) on Dec. 9, 1931. They lived at Okreek. Emmett entered the spirit world on March 20, 1994, at the Winner Regional Healthcare Center. A number of grandchildren survived him. He is buried in the Black Hills National Cemetery, Section G, site 5831.[3]

Gary, George. George was born on the Rosebud Reservation on Dec. 10, 1898, the son of Henry and Ida Gary. George was the older brother of Emmett, who also served in the Army. George joined the South Dakota National Guard (ASN 98587) on March 28, 1917. When his unit arrived in Camp Greene, NC, it was converted to the 148th Machine Gun (MG) Battalion, 41st Division. Pvt. Gary sailed with the Co. B, 148th MG Battalion aboard the *Olympic* on Jan. 11, 1918. Upon arrival in France, many of the South Dakota soldiers were transferred to Co. M, 167th Infantry, 42th Division. The 42nd Division suffered 13,919 casualties. Pvt. Gary was one of the many wounded men. He sailed from Bordeaux aboard the *Pastores* on Dec. 25, 1918. He was attached to Beau Desert Casual Co. No. 20, patients requiring dressing. Pfc. Gary was discharged on June 11, 1919. After the war, he married Emma Grace Gassman. In the 1930 U.S. Census, George was farming and had three children, Verna, John and Vero. His wife, Emma, entered the spirit world in 1938. On Sept. 6, 1940, he married Eva Titus. George entered the spirit world on Jan. 25, 1969 in a Hot Springs hospital. Eva and a daughter, Arlene, survived him. George is buried in the Black Hills National Cemetery, Section E, site 1334.[4]

Gassman, Louis. Louis was born near Lake Andes on Aug. 3, 1890. In the 1895 Yanktonai Census Roll, he is listed with his parents, Wakinyangi [Brown Thunder Cloud] and Akicitawin, as well as two older brothers, Samuel and Joseph. In the 1911 Census Roll, Louis was listed as Louis Yellow Thunder. Louis married his wife, Lillian around 1913. When he registered for the draft on June 5, 1917, he was farming with his wife and daughter in White Swan Township. He joined the Army on May 24, 1918, and was first assigned to Co. C, 159th Infantry, 40th Division (ASN 2788616). Pvt. Gassman sailed from New York aboard the *Otranta* on Aug. 8, 1918. In September of 1918, many

Louis Gassman and Family
Frieda Garreau-Hunter

men from the 40th Division were assigned to the 77th Division as replacements. After arriving in France, Pvt. Gassman was assigned to Co. D, 307th Infantry, 77th Division. During the war, the 77th Division received 12,728 replacements. After the Armistice, Pvt. Gassman was evaluated by his commanding officer, Capt. H.D. Palmore, who wrote of Louis: "Great night worker, runner, observer and verbal reporter." At this time, the 307th Infantry was billeted west of Chaumont, along the Aube River. Pfc. Gassman sailed for home from Brest, France, aboard the *America*, on April 19, 1919. The ship had several canteens where the soldiers could buy ice cream and candy. Magazines were provided and many soldiers spent time reading. The *America* traveled at about 400 miles per day and arrived in Hoboken on April 28. Pfc. Gassman was discharged at Camp Dodge, IA, on May 18, 1919. He had been gassed in France and received a small pension for the remainder of his life. He returned to Lake Andes, SD. In the 1930 U.S. Census, Louis and Lillian lived in Lake Andes with their children, Gertrude, Raymond and Lavina. In the 1940 U.S. Census, he was farming with his wife near Lake Andes. Living with them was their daughter, Lavina, and a granddaughter, Frieda. Louis entered the spirit world on Feb. 22, 1970, and is buried in St. Philip Deacon Cemetery, Lake Andes.[5]

Gasto, Thomas. His name is engraved on a plaque in Bullhead, SD, honoring WWI veterans. Though Thomas was born in Canada, he had relatives in South Dakota. Some of his family now lives on the Cheyenne River Reservation. In Canada, the family name is spelled Kasto. Thomas was born around May 1, 1892, in the Turtle Mountains near Pipestone, Manitoba. His mother was Maggie Kasto. They lived on the Oak Lake Dakota Reserve. Thomas enlisted in the Canadian Army at Brandon on April 13, 1916. He was first assigned to the 203rd Battalion and trained at Camp Hughes near Carberry, Man. This camp had an extensive trench system built to train soldiers in trench warfare. Pte. Kasto (Reg. No. 234732) was later assigned to the 27th Battalion. He sailed with his unit from Halifax aboard the S.S. *Grampian* on Oct. 26, 1916, and arrived in Liverpool on Nov. 5, 1916. Pte. Kasto was killed in the Battle of Passchendaele, Belgium, on Aug. 21, 1917. He was initially listed as missing in action. His name is inscribed on the Vimy Memorial in Pas de Calais, France. An author in Belgium named Geert Noppe has written a book about the war which mentions Pte. Kasto.

Gerry, Elbridge S. Elbridge was born May 25, 1893, on the Pine Ridge Reservation at Martin. His parents were Seth and Mary Gerry. Elbridge likely is a descendent of Elbridge Gerry who was a signer of the Declaration of Independence. Elbridge was living in Martin when he registered for the draft on June 5, 1917. In November 1917, he married Magdalene Boyer. He joined the Army on May 25, 1918, and was assigned to Battery A, 347th Field Artillery (FA), 91st Division (ASN 3129682). Pvt. Gerry sailed from New York aboard the *Adriatic* on July 14, 1918. After arriving in Cherbourg, France, the 347th FA traveled to the artillery training area at Camp de Souge along the Garonne River near Bordeaux. Their unit was equipped with ten-ton tractors and 4.7-inch guns. The 347th FA did not serve at the Front. On Christmas Day, they were billeted in private homes in several small towns along the Moselle River near Trier, Germany. On March 13, 1919, the 347th FA enjoyed the distinction of acting as guard of honor to President Woodrow Wilson, who was attending the Paris Peace Conference. Pvt. Gerry left Brest aboard the *Aquitania* on March 23, 1919. Other soldiers serving with him in Battery A were Moses Marshall, and Peter Rouillard. Pvt. Gerry traveled with Camp Dodge Detachment No. 1, of 347th FA, and was discharged on April 17, 1919. In the 1940 U.S. Census, he and Magdalene lived with their children, Seth, Melvina and Mervin, as well as two grandchildren, Pearl and Verna. Elbridge worked in construction. His two sons served in the Army during the WWII era. In his later years, he lived with his daughter in Alliance, Nebraska. He entered the spirit world on Dec. 20, 1973, at a Hot Springs hospital. His daughter, Bonnie, survived him. Elbridge is buried in the Black Hills National Cemetery Section C, site 780.[6]

Gilbert, William Andrew. William was born in 1887 in Texas. In the 1930 U.S. Census, he is listed as a veteran of the World War (USN). William first came to South Dakota as a range rider. He found a job as a foreman on a stock ranch in Armstrong County, near White Horse. In 1933, he married Ethel Emily Thompson (1911-1998). In the 1934 Cheyenne River Census Roll, he is listed, though non-enrolled, with Ethel and their son, William "Scotch" Jr. William and Ethel had two more children, Mary and Horace. In 1935, Willie and his family were interviewed by workers with the SDERA program. They ranched near Promise. They had a frame home next to the Moreau River. Their farmstead included a barn, root cellar, chicken house and a garage. They owned a 1929 Ford Roadster. For livestock, they had 25 head of horses and a milk cow. Willie was interested in raising horses. He used one of his teams to work on conservation projects. William entered the spirit world on June 3, 1949. He is buried in Blackfoot Ascension Cemetery. His son, William "Scotch," served in the Army during the Korean Conflict.[7]

Gilland, Robert. Robert was born around January 1888 on the Standing Rock Reservation, the son of Benjamin and Elizabeth Gilland. Benjamin had been a soldier in the 17th Infantry. Robert was also known as Red Eagle and as Bob. In the 1890 Census Roll, Robert is listed with his mother and a brother, Benjamin as well as two sisters, Annie and Sarah. Robert attended school in Mandan until 8th grade. He then ranched, raising horses and cattle, and traveled around a lot taking jobs in a 3-4 state area. At that time everybody carried a gun and kept it handy. Rustlers and other law breakers were dealt with quickly. It could be rough out there. Some cowboys got in scrapes with the law. It was not always clear who was at fault. Bob was involved in an altercation with some friends while driving cattle from Fort Yates to the Gilland's land near Thunder Hawk. Bob joined the Army in 1918 and was first sent to Ft. Riley, KS, on March 5. He eventually ended up in France. He served as a Private in the Medical Department. He was discharged on Feb. 21, 1919. On July 25, 1927, he married Elizabeth Williamson (1904-1979). About that same time, his sister, Sarah, married Ben Defender, a fellow veteran. Bob and Elizabeth ranched near Shields until 1946. After that they ranched along the Grand River southeast of Thunder Hawk. He was a member of the American Legion. Bob passed away on Dec. 5, 1965, when a car he was working on slipped off the jack. His wife and four sons, Robert, Jim, Abe and George, as well as four daughters, Betty, Annie, Gladyce and Sadie, survived him. He is buried in Greenhill Cemetery in Lemmon, SD. Robert's son, George, has written *Along the Trail to Thunder Hawk*, which describes early life for the Gilland family.[8]

Giroux, Claude C. Claude, sometimes known as Clyde, was born on the Rosebud Reservation around March 1899. His parents were George Giroux and Emily Crazy Bear. When Claude registered for the draft on Sept. 12, 1918, he was working as a laborer at St. Francis. Around this time, he married Eva Roan Bear. He enlisted in the Army on June 26, 1920. He was discharged as a Pfc. on June 25, 1921. In the 1930 U.S. Census, he was living with his wife and four children, Melissa, Evelyn, Mildred and Mary Lou, in Mission. He was working in a printing office. In 1935 the family was interviewed by a worker with the SDERA program. They had a three-room frame house in Mission. Claude was working on emergency conservation projects and earned $5 per month. In 1938, he married Agnes Fox. In the 1940 U.S. Census, he was working on a landscaping project in Mission. In the 1945 Rapid City Directory, he was working as a mechanic. He entered the spirit world on Jan. 12, 1986, and is buried in St. Charles Cemetery in St. Francis.

Giroux, Ralph Samuel. Ralph was born on the Rosebud Reservation on April 6, 1896, the son of Louis and Emily Giroux. When he registered for the draft on June 5, 1917, he was living with his parents near White River. Family information shows he served in the military, possibly with the 340th MD Bn., 89th Division. He was discharged on Jan. 14, 1918. In the 1930 U.S. Census, he and his wife, Irene, were farming in Mellette County. Ralph entered the spirit world in the Indian Hospital at Pine Ridge on Sept 8, 1934.

Giroux, Roy F. Roy was born on the Rosebud Reservation on Sept. 6, 1900. His parents were Louis and Emily Giroux. When he joined the Army, he was assigned to Co. D, 53rd Coast Artillery Corps (ASN 514160). Pvt. Giroux sailed from Hoboken aboard the *Mongolia* on Oct. 28, 1918. He was traveling with the October Automatic Replacement Draft (CAC). He was stationed at the Operation and Training Center at Mailly and Houssimont. They fired large caliber railroad artillery. Pvt. Giroux sailed for home from Brest, France, aboard the *Pueblo* on Jan. 20, 1919. He had served with Co. D, 53rd Ammo Train, CAC. He was discharged as a Private on Feb. 5, 1919. On May 13, 1919, he married Julia Presho, whose brother, Joe, also had served in the Army. In 1921, Roy was a member of the Chauncey Eagle Horn Legion Post in Rosebud. In the 1930 U.S. Census, Roy and Julie lived in Crookston, Nebraska, with their children, Violet and Roy Jr. Roy was a mail carrier. In the 1940 U.S. Census, the family lived in Todd County where Roy drove a truck for the road department. In 1958, he married Olivia Valandra. Roy entered the spirit world in Albany, OR, while visiting on Dec. 31, 1970. He is buried in Trinity Cemetery, Rosebud.

Giroux, William G. William was born on Feb. 22, 1892, the son of George Giroux and Emily Crazy Bear. He was enrolled on the Rosebud Reservation. He married Marjorie Courtis. When he registered on June 5, 1917, he and his wife lived at Carter. He joined the Army on June 24, 1918, and was assigned to Co. E, 20th Infantry, 10th Division (ASN 3315702). The 10th Division did not go overseas. Pfc. Giroux was discharged on March 10, 1919. In 1921, he was a member of the Chauncey Eagle Horn Legion Post at Rosebud. In the 1930 U.S. Census, the family lived in Todd County with their son, Walter. William entered the spirit world in the Rosebud Hospital on Feb. 20, 1940. He is buried in St. Francis.[9]

Goings, Earl. See **Kelly, Fred**

Good Bear, David. See **Drops at a Distance, David**

Good Breast, Joseph Baptist. Joseph was born on the Rosebud Reservation around March 22, 1892. When he registered for the draft on June 5, 1917, he was farming near St. Francis. He entered the Army on Aug. 6, 1918, and was discharged on March 30, 1919. In the 1940 U.S. Census, he was living with his wife, Barbara, and daughter, Viola. In 1944, he worked as a laborer for the C & NW RR. He entered the spirit world on Dec. 1, 1973, and is buried in St. Charles Cemetery.

Good Eagle, Alfred. Alfred was born on the Lower Brule Reservation on Dec. 5, 1888. In 1896, his parents, Joshua Wanbli Waste [Good Eagle] and Mary, moved their home to the Rosebud Reservation. When Alfred registered for the draft on June 5, 1917, he was farming near Dixon

Alfred Good Eagle
Mathers Museum

with his parents. On May 17, 1918, he married Rosie LaPointe (1898-1979), whose family had also moved to Rosebud from the Lower Brule in 1896. Rosie's older brother, Samuel, also served in the Army during the war. Alfred joined the Army on May 26, 1918. He was first assigned to the Co. K, 333rd Infantry, 84th Division (ASN 3129666). Pvt. Good Eagle sailed from New York aboard the *Aquitania* on Sept. 2, 1918. Many soldiers from the 84th Division were used as replacements in Divisions which had suffered casualties. Pvt. Good Eagle was reassigned to the Headquarters Company, 363rd Infantry, in the 91st Division. The 91st Division suffered 5,778 casualties. After the fighting had ended, Pvt. Good Eagle received an evaluation from his commanding officer, Capt. John Richards, describing him as "an excellent soldier in every respect. Cool under fire. Endurance and good humor excellent." He sailed for home from St. Nazaire aboard the U.S.S. *Kentuckian* on March 20, 1919. After he returned to the U.S., Joseph Dixon took a photo of Pvt. Good Eagle in uniform. He was discharged on April 22, 1919. Alfred and Rosie had a daughter, Vera. In the 1930 U.S. Census, Alfred was farming, and his father was living with them. In 1935, the family was interviewed by a worker with the SDERA program. They were living in a well-furnished farm home near Hamill. They had a good well, which he used to keep his garden alive. They owned a Star auto, three horses and five chickens. Alfred was working on a dam construction project, but had also done some farming. They leased out some of their land. Alfred entered the spirit world on April 12, 1972, and is buried at Bull Creek Mniska Cemetery in Tripp County.[10]

Goodman, Daniel V. Daniel was born on April 23, 1894, at Ponsford, MN, on the White Earth Reservation. In 1911, he was enrolled at the Flandreau boarding school. In April of 1917, he was serving as Duty Sergeant with Troop D, 1st SD Cavalry. This National Guard Regiment trained in South Dakota until September of 1917, though they were never issued horses or saddles. After the regiment arrived at Camp Cody, NM, they became part of the 34th Division. Sgt. Goodman was assigned to the Mail Detachment, 34th Division (ASN 1427331). He sailed from New York aboard the *Cretic* on Sept. 17, 1918. The 34th Division did not serve at the Front. Sgt. Goodman sailed for home from St. Nazaire, France, aboard the U.S.S. *Manchuria* on July 8, 1919. He was traveling with Le Mans Casual Co. #1284. He was discharged on July 25, 1919 as a Sergeant. His name is engraved on plaque erected at the Flandreau School in 1920. Daniel returned to Flandreau where he held the position of Assistant Disciplinarian. In the 1930 U.S. Census, he was working for the Standing Rock Tribe at Fort Yates. He likely lived in Wakpala. In the 1930s, he married Sophia Long Bull (1905-1985), whose brother, Baptiste, had served in the Army. Daniel and Sophia had four sons, Vincent, Daniel Jr., Herb and Cedric. Daniel entered the spirit world in the VA Hospital in Hot Springs on Dec. 27, 1982. He is buried with Sophia in the Black Hills National Cemetery, section F, site 1373. Their son, Daniel Jr., served in the Army from 1958 to 1964.[11]

Good Shield, Philip. Philip is listed on WWI veteran's memorial at Oglala Lakota College, Kyle, SD. He was born on the Pine Ridge Reservation in the spring of 1900. His parents were Oliver Good Shield and Mary White Wolf. Philip joined the Army on May 13, 1918. He was assigned to the Headquarters Company, 48th Infantry, 20th Division (ASN R-488527). He was honorably discharged on April 28, 1919, and re-enlisted on April 29, 1919. He was discharged on May 28, 1920. After returning home, he married Helen Eagle Bear. They farmed in Shannon County, north of Porcupine. Their children were Caroline, Matthew, Alphonso and Cordelia. Matthew was killed on June 6, 1944, while serving with the Army in New Guinea. The American Legion Post No. 294 in Porcupine is named in his honor. Philip entered the spirit world at his home on Nov. 30, 1959 and is buried in Our Lady of Lourdes Cemetery at Porcupine.[12]

Goodteacher, Levi. Levi was born on March 22, 1899, on the Santee Reservation. In the 1900 U.S. Census, he is listed with his parents, Joseph and Mary, and his brother Oscar. Joseph was a clergyman, in Charles Mix County. Around 1913, Levi was enrolled at the Flandreau Boarding School. On April 4, 1917, he enlisted in Troop D, 1st SD Cavalry at Flandreau. This unit performed infantry exercises, as they were not issued horses or saddles. When they arrived at Camp Cody, NM, on Sept. 15, 1917, they received cavalry equipment but no horses. A few days later they were told they were being re-assigned. All soldiers who passed the rigorous physical were re-assigned and trained as part of the 34th Division. Pvt. Goodteacher sailed for France aboard the S.S. *Tereisias* on June 28, 1918, as part of Co. 15, Camp Cody June Automatic Replacement Draft (ASN 1427448). After arriving in France, he was attached to the 122nd Field Artillery, 33rd Division. This unit took part in the offensives at St. Mihiel and Meuse Argonne. The 33rd Division suffered 7,255 casualties. Pvt. Goodteacher received an evaluation from his commanding officer stating he "was well qualified to care for and drive horses." Pvt. Goodteacher sailed for home from Breast aboard the U.S.S. *America* on May 16, 1919, and was discharged at Camp Dodge, IA, on June 8, 1919. Levi's name is engraved on a plaque erected at the Flandreau School around 1920 to honor the war veterans. In the 1927 Santee Census Roll, Levi and his wife, Theresa Wolf, had two children, Wilford and Levi Jr. In the 1930 U.S. Census, Levi and Theresa were living with Levi's grandmother near Lake Andes. Theresa entered the spirit world in August 1930. Levi was admitted to the VA Hospital on Dec. 6, 1932. He entered the spirit world on Dec. 30, 1932, at the Battle Mountain Sanatorium at Hot Springs. He is buried in Howe Creek Cemetery in Knox County, NE.[13]

Goodteacher, Oscar. Oscar was born on the Santee Reservation on March 20, 1896. In 1900, he was living with his parents, Joseph and Mary, and his brother, Levi, near Lake Andes, where his father was a clergyman. Around 1918, Oscar married Elvina Johnson. Oscar served in the Army during the war and was discharged as a Private on Sept. 25, 1918. His brother, Levi, also served. In the 1937 Census Roll, Oscar and Elvina were listed with their children, Emil, Joseph, Stephanie and Thomas. Joseph served in WWII. Oscar entered the spirit world on April 18, 1971, and is buried in Howe Creek Cemetery, Knox County, NE.

Good Thunder, Leopold. Leopold was born on May 5, 1896, on the Rosebud Reservation. In the 1898 Rosebud Census Roll, Leopold is listed with his parents, Andrew Good Thunder and Good Cow, and a brother and sister, Benjamin and Myra. When Leopold registered for the draft, he was farming near Norris. When he enlisted, he was assigned to Co. A, 158th Infantry, 40th Division (ASN 3127679), which trained at Camp Kearny, California. Pvt. Good Thunder sailed with his unit from New York on the *Laomedon* on Aug. 11, 1918. Upon arrival in France, he was reassigned to Co. D, 128th Infantry of the 32nd (Red Arrow) Division. Leopold died of wounds on Oct. 14, 1918. His body was brought from Cherbourg, France, aboard the *Wheaton* on May 1, 1921. He is buried in St. Paul Episcopal Cemetery, Norris, SD.

Good Voice Elk, Frank. Frank is listed on WWI veteran's memorial at Oglala Lakota College, Kyle, SD. He was born on the Pine Ridge Reservation on Sept. 25, 1895. In the 1910 U.S. Census, his is listed with his mother, Annie, and his step father William Gerton. When he registered for the draft on June 5, 1917, he lived in Allen and farmed with his mother. He joined the Army on July 15, 1918 (ASN 3784979), and was discharged on Feb. 26, 1919. In the early 1920s, he and his wife, Minnie, had two children, May and Ulysses. Minnie entered the spirit word in 1927. In the 1937 Census Roll, Frank was listed with his wife, Eva Fox Belly, and daughter, May. When he registered for the Selective Service in 1942, he lived in Wanblee. He later moved to Pine Ridge. On February 15, 1964, he fell on the icy steps of his home and banged his head. Frank entered the spirit world on Feb. 15, 1964, and is buried in St. Timothy's Episcopal Cemetery in Potato Creek.

Grabbing Bear, Leo. Leo was born in Pine Ridge on Jan. 15, 1900. In the 1915 Rosebud Census Roll, he was listed with his father, Grabbing Bear. When Leo registered for the draft on Sept. 12, 1918, he was farming for the Pine Ridge Agency. He likely enlisted shortly after this. He was assigned to the 22nd Co., Camp Meade Replacement Unit (ASN 6411365). Pvt. Grabbing Bear sailed for Europe from Hoboken, NJ, aboard the *Great Northern* on June 4, 1919. He later was assigned to the Training, Hdq. and MP Battalion, 4th Division. Pvt. Grabbing Bear developed eye trouble, known as Keratitis, and returned to the U.S. He sailed with other convalescent soldiers from Brest, France, aboard the *Orizaba* on July 28, 1919. After returning to the States, he was sent to Fort Lyon, CO. This military camp had been set aside for soldiers with Tuberculosis. Pfc. Grabbing Bear entered the spirit world on March 6, 1922, and is buried at Fort Lyon, CO.

Graham, Alexander M. Alex was born on the Santee Reservation in Niobrara on May 17, 1898, the son of Daniel Graham. He enlisted in the U.S. Navy during the war. After the war, he summarized his experiences, saying he "had mostly convoy duties; distroying [sic] Sea mines and subs all along the English Channel." At that time, he listed his home as Fort Thompson, SD. He was discharged as a Gun Pointer Second Class Sept. 9, 1919. After he returned home, he married Cora Frazier (1906-1956). In 1926, they moved to Sioux City, IA, where he worked for Swift & Co. Alex entered the spirit world in a Sioux City hospital on July 19, 1961. His sons, Charles, Donald and Robert survived him. He and Cora are buried in the Congregational Cemetery in Santee, NE.[14]

John Grass
Mathers Museum

Grass, John. John was born about April 16, 1896, on the Pine Ridge Reservation near Porcupine. His parents were Thomas Grass and Julia Little Commander. As a student, John was enrolled at the Flandreau boarding school. On April 4, 1917, he enlisted in Troop D, 1st SD Cavalry. Upon arriving at Camp Cody, NM, he was assigned to the Headquarters Co., 136th Infantry. He sailed from New York aboard the *Melita* on Oct 13, 1918. He was a Bugler and was re-assigned to the Headquarters Co., 4th Infantry, 3rd Division (ASN 1426622). For his outstanding service, he was later transferred to a composite 3rd Army Corps Regiment, known as "Pershing's Own." Bugler Grass was rated by his commander as "a man of excellent character and a very good musician." He sailed for home from Brest aboard the *Leviathan* on Sept. 1, 1919 and arrived at Hoboken on Sept. 8. After returning to the U.S., he was photographed by Joseph Dixon. John was discharged on Sept. 24, 1919. His name was engraved on a plaque erected at the Flandreau School around 1920. John loved music and regularly performed with other musicians at American Legion annual conventions. Upon returning home, he married Etta Weston (1907-1976). In the 1930 U.S.

Census, John was working as an auto mechanic. His children were Christine, Kenneth and Velma. Their youngest daughter was Alvina. John also served as a clergyman at various churches around South Dakota. John was on the tribal council representing Porcupine District from 1960-62. On Sunday, April 21, 1963, relatives and friends of John were waiting for him at a local church, but he never made it to the church service. John entered the spirit world on that day near Porcupine. He had stopped to change a tire, when the jack slipped. He is buried in St. Luke's Episcopal Cemetery in Porcupine.[15]

Gray, Reuben. Reuben is included on the list of Yankton veterans. He was born in Chamberlain on Nov. 5, 1895, to Sherman and Harriet Gray. When he registered for the draft on June 5, 1917, he was farming near Platte. When he joined the Army, he was assigned to Evac Hospital No. 1, Medical Dept. (ASN 16044). Pfc. Gray sailed with his unit from Portland, ME, aboard the S.S. *Canada* on Dec. 24, 1917. He sailed for home from St. Nazaire aboard the *Princess Motoika* on April 14, 1919. After the war, he married Elsie Stargardt. They farmed near Platte. Reuben entered the spirit world on June 25, 1964, and is buried in the Platte City Cemetery.

Green, James Oliver. James was born on the Rosebud Reservation on March 12, 1892, to Charles Green and Emma Walking Holy Woman. On Aug. 20, 1916, he married Mary Schmidt. When he registered for the draft on June 5, 1917, he was farming near Mission. When he joined the Army on June 24, 1918, he was assigned to Co. E, 20th Infantry (ASN 3315588), which trained at Camp Funston, KS, after the 89th Division went to France. He was discharged on March 10, 1919. He later married Ida Frost on April 9, 1938. Their children were Faith and Wanda. James entered the spirit world on Jan. 1, 1969, and is buried in Calvary Cemetery in Alliance, NE.

Greenwood, James. James was born on the Rosebud Reservation around April 1884. In the 1896 Census Roll, his parents are listed as Paul and Mary Greenwood. When James registered for the draft, he was working as a cowboy near Witten, SD. James joined the Army on May 26, 1918, and was first assigned to Co. F, 33rd Infantry, 84th Division (ASN 3129683). Pvt. Greenwood sailed from New York aboard *Carmania* Sept. 1, 1918. After arriving in France, he was reassigned to the 348th MG Battalion. Silas Kills Plenty served in the same battalion with Greenwood. The 348th MG Bn. fought in the campaigns at Meuse-Argonne and Ypres-Lys as well the Defensive Sector at Lorraine. The 91st Division began leaving France in March of 1919. Pvt. Greenwood sailed from St. Nazaire, France with Pvt. Kills Plenty aboard the *Orizaba* on March 25, 1919. After returning back to the States, Pvt. Greenwood served in Casual Detachment 312, 163rd Depot Brigade at Camp Dodge and was discharged on April 22, 1919. After returning home, he married Julia Stone, whose brother, Paul, had served overseas also. In the 1930 U.S. Census, James and Julia had three girls, Elsie, Esther and Phoebe. By 1940, they had three more children, Paul, Fanny and Effie. James entered the spirit world on Aug. 13, 1960, and is buried in Mediator Cemetery, Wood, SD.

Gresh, John. John was born on the Pine Ridge Reservation on April 25, 1896, the son of John and Mary Gresh. His father was born in Pennsylvania. In the 1896 Pine Ridge Census Roll, John is listed with his mother and siblings, Millie, Lizzie, Susie and Todd. John enlisted in the U.S. Navy during the war and was discharged as a Seaman 2nd Class on Feb. 21, 1919. In 1928 he married Myrtle Clifford. In 1935 they lived in Port Orchard, WA. In the 1940 U.S. Census, John was working as a carpenter on the Pine Ridge Reservation. His son, John Jr., was attending a boarding school on the reservation. John Jr. served in the Army during the Korean Conflict. The family moved to the Seattle area. John Sr. passed away on March 12, 1968, and is buried at the Williamette National Cemetery, section S, site 740.

Grey Buffalo, John. John was born in January of 1898, on the Sisseton-Wahpeton Reservation. His parents were Tatankarota and Sarah Uncagetopawin. While he was enrolled at the Flandreau boarding school, he enlisted in the Army on April 13, 1918. He served with the Medical Department at General Hospital #5, at Ft. Ontario, NY (ASN 465356). He was discharged as a Pfc. on Aug. 22, 1919. His name was engraved on a plaque honoring veterans at the Flandreau School around 1920. On May 15, 1926, he married Goldie Varns (1913-1968) in the Danish Evangelical Lutheran Church. They lived near White Stone Lake. John and Goldie had five children, Duane, Henry, Elwood, Lorraine and Betty Lou. Henry died in a vehicle accident while serving with the Army in Korea. John was a member of the American Legion. John entered the spirit world on Oct. 30, 1944. The local Legion Post provided military honors at the Sisseton Cemetery.[16]

Greyhound, John. John was born on Jan. 10, 1893, at St Charles, Gregory County. In the 1893 Yanktonai Sioux Census Roll, he is listed with his parents, Sunkapagiwanica and Unpanhotewin [Gray Elk Woman]. As a child, John was known as Dapi. When he registered for the draft on June 5, 1917, he was married and farming near Greenwood. He joined the Army and was first assigned to Co. C, 159th Infantry, 40th Division (ASN 2788625). Pvt. Greyhound sailed from New York aboard the *Otranta* on Aug. 8, 1918. After arriving in France, he was reassigned to Co. A, 111th Infantry, 28th Division. The 111th Regiment served in the various theaters of Champagne-Marne, Aisne-Marne, Oise-Aisne, Meuse Argonne, Chateau-Thierry, Fismes, Clermont and Thiaucourt. Pvt. Greyhound sailed for home from St. Nazaire aboard the U.S.S. *Minnesota* on April 16, 1919. He was discharged as a Pvt. On May 12, 1919. Around 1922, he married Ruth Long Crow. In the 1930 U.S. Census, he and his wife were farming in Tripp County. On June 21, 1960, he married Winnie Thompson. John entered the spirit world on Feb. 11, 1964, in the hospital at Wagner. He is buried in All Saints Cemetery, St. Charles, SD.

Grindstone, Dwight. Dwight was born on the Standing Rock Reservation on May 10, 1901. His parents were Stanton Grindstone and Towanka waste. Dwight was a student at the Flandreau boarding school. School records indicate that Dwight enlisted in the Army but was given a discharge for medical reasons, possibly eye troubles. In the 1930 U.S. Census, Dwight was living with his wife, Alice, and daughters, Irene and Adell, in Little Eagle. Dwight entered the spirit world on Nov. 20, 1934, in a vehicle accident. He is buried in Little Eagle. His widow obtained a job as cook for the Little Eagle Day School.[17]

Growler, John. John was born in Little Eagle on the Standing Rock Reservation around July 1896. In the 1898 Census Roll, he is listed with his parents, Henry and Angela, as well as two sisters, Kind and Susan. When John registered for the draft on June 5, 1917, he was working as a cattle man for Charlie Brown. He was described as short and slender, with a bad eye. John joined the Army on July 22, 1918, and was sent to Camp Dodge, IA. He was assigned to the 9th Labor Battalion (ASN 3954591). Pvt. Growler was scheduled to sail with his unit from Hoboken aboard the *Kroonland*. Before the ship sailed, Pvt. Growler became ill and entered the spirit world at Embarkation Hospital No.1 in Hoboken, NJ, on Oct. 10, 1918. Most of the U.S. transport ships headed for Europe sailed from Hoboken. John is buried in Messiah Cemetery in Little Eagle, SD.[18]

Guerue, Stephen. Stephan was born on the Rosebud Reservation on Sept. 4, 1902, the son of James Guerue and Elizabeth Bridgeman. He enlisted in the Army but dates are not known. He was discharged as a Private. He married Lucy LaPlante, the widow of Whitney LaPlante who had served during the war. In the 1940 U.S. Census, Stephan and Lucy were living with her children, Irene, Louis and Marjorie. Stephen worked as a foreman with the CCC program. His step son,

Louis, served in the Army in WWII. Stephan entered the spirit world on Sept. 7, 1964, and is buried at Spring Creek.

Gullickson, George J. George is included on the list of Yankton veterans. He was born in Sioux City, IA, on Sept. 30, 1894, to George and Gena Gullickson. When George registered for the draft on June 5, 1917, he was farming near Greenwood, SD. He joined the Army on May 2, 1918, and was assigned to Co. I, Development Battalion (ASN 507322). He was later reassigned as a Mechanic with Co. B, 24th Machine Gun Battalion at Camp Fremont, CA. He did not serve overseas. He was discharged on Nov. 18, 1918. He married Rena Lovejoy (1896-1963) in Greenwood on Dec. 19, 1918. In the 1930 U.S. Census, George was working as a nursery salesman in Wagner. He and Rena had three children, Warren, Ralph, and Lillian. They later moved to Flandreau, where George farmed. In the 1937 Census Roll, George is listed as non-enrolled. He and Rena had seven children, Warren, Ralph, Lillian, Goldie, Floyd, Ethel and George Jr. Warren and Ralph served with the Army during WWII. George entered the spirit world in Flandreau on Dec. 13, 1946, and is buried in Union Cemetery.

Gunhammer, Harry. Harry was born on the Rosebud Reservation around June 1895. His parents were Isadore Gunhammer and Rosa White Cow. When Harry registered for the draft, he was living in Okreek. He joined the Army in 1918, and was assigned to Co. L, 351st Infantry, 88th Division (ASN 3315608). Pfc. Jesse Taken Alive and Pfc. David Thief from Standing Rock and Pvt. Paul Three Stars were in Co. L with Pfc. Gunhammer. They sailed from Brooklyn aboard the *Ulysses* on Aug. 16, 1918. The 88th Division was primarily stationed in quiet sectors during the war. His commanding officer wrote that Pfc. Gunhammer had a "special fitness for sniping and scouting." After the Armistice, the 88th Division was in occupational duty around Houdelaincourt, France until May 1919. The 351st Infantry sailed from St. Nazaire on May 20 to the States aboard the U.S.S. *Mercury*. Pfc. Gunhammer was discharged on June 7, 1919. After returning home, Harry married Victoria Bear Doctor. Harry entered the spirit world at his home north of Mission on April 10, 1964. He is buried in Trinity Cemetery in Mission. Harry's younger brother, Abraham, also served in the Army. **Abraham Gunhammer** was born on July 3, 1908. In the 1930 U.S. Census, he was stationed with the Army at Fort Meade, SD. He married Lucinda Hare, and was working in the C.C.C. program in Charles Mix County in the 1940 U.S. Census. In 1956, the family moved from Mission to Custer. Abraham entered the spirit world in the Custer Hospital on Jan. 22, 1969, and is buried in Custer Cemetery, Custer, SD. His widow and son, Sterling, as well as ten daughters, Normanda, Charlene, Audrey, Joyce, Joann, Loretta, Galba, Mary, Betty, and Violet, survived him.[19]

Gunhammer, Philip Dillon. Philip was born on the Rosebud Reservation around Christmas of 1893. In the 1903 Census Roll, he was living with his uncle, George McCloskey. Philip joined the Army on Aug. 26, 1918, and was sent to Camp Funston, KS. He was assigned to 4th Co., 2nd Battalion, 164th Depot Brigade (ASN 4265918). He was discharged as a Private on Dec. 10, 1918. Upon returning home, he married Mabel Six Shooter. In the 1937 Census Roll, they are listed with their children, Winona, Oliver, Frank, Vincent, and Renzie Bert. Oliver enlisted in the Army in 1946. Philip entered the spirit world on Oct. 4, 1961, and is buried in Trinity Cemetery, Mission.

H

Half, Isaac. Isaac's name is engraved on a plaque honoring military veterans from the war at Flandreau. See **Skunk, Isaac**.

Halfred, Isaac. Isaac was born on the Cheyenne River Reservation about Dec. 5, 1900, to Oscar Halfred and Maggie Worn Out Horn. His date of enlistment is not known. In the 1937 Census Roll, he is listed as single. He worked as a telephone yard man for the phone company. He later was married to Josephine. They had a son, William, who served two tours in Vietnam. Isaac entered the spirit world in the Mobridge Community Hospital on Sept. 5, 1968. His grave, with a military headstone, is in United Church of Christ Cemetery, Cherry Creek, SD.[1]

Hanneman, Wilhelm F. Wilhelm Hanneman's name is included on the Oglala Tribe's veterans list. Wilhelm was born near White Lake, SD, on Jan. 10, 1894. His parents, Heinrich and Dora Hanneman, were born in Germany. Heinrich, a minister, passed away in 1904 when Wilhelm was 10 years old. In 1910, he was working as a herdsman for another farmer. When Wilhelm registered for the draft on June 5, 1917, he was farming near Wittenberg, SD. He joined the Army on June 24, 1918 and was discharged as a Private 1st Class on June 16, 1919. After the war he farmed in Shannon County. On Feb. 20, 1939, he married Sophia Conroy (1915-1984). Their children were, William Jr., Terry, Gerald, and Judy. William served in the Army during the Vietnam Conflict. Wilhelm entered the spirit world on Nov. 9, 1981 and is buried in Knight Cemetery, Batesland.

Harris, Andrew J. Andrew was born around Jan. 6, 1892, on the Sisseton-Wahpeton Reservation. In the 1906 Census Roll, he is listed as the adopted son of Frank and Jennie Harris. In the 1909 Census Roll, he is listed as the brother of George Harris, who also served in the Army. Andrew enlisted in the Army at Sisseton on Sept. 22, 1917. He was assigned to Co. D, 341st Machine Gun Battalion, 89th Division (ASN 2192938). Pvt. Harris also served with Pvt. Felix Renville. They sailed with their unit from Brooklyn aboard the *Tennyson* on June 4, 1918. Pvt. Harris was shot in the hand on Nov. 3, 1918. His medical records show he had some fingers amputated. The 89th Division suffered 7,291 casualties in the war. Pvt. Harris sailed from Brest, France, aboard the hospital ship, U.S.S. *Mercy*, on Nov. 26, 1918. The soldiers he was traveling with were labeled as "walking cases requiring dressing." Pvt. Harris was discharged at Ft. Snelling on May 22, 1919. After returning home, he married Elizabeth Goodboy. In the 1922 Census Roll, they had two children, Mildred and Clifford. In the 1940 U.S. Census, Andrew was living with the John King family in Red Iron Township in Marshall County. Andrew entered the spirit world on Feb. 1, 1954, after being hit by a car in Veblen. He is buried in Long Hollow Cemetery.[2]

Harris, George S. George was born on March 17, 1890, on the Sisseton-Wahpeton Reservation. His parents were Stanley Harris and Mary Kampeska. When George registered for the draft on June 5, 1917, he was in the auto livery business in Peever, SD. George likely enlisted in the SD National Guard in the summer of 1917, and was sent to Camp Cody, NM. He was assigned to Co. 18, Camp Cody June Automatic Replacement Draft. Pvt. Harris sailed with this unit from New York aboard the *Honorata* on June 28, 1918. After arriving in France, he was assigned to Co. D, 307th Infantry, 77th Division (ASN 1429466). The 307th Infantry served in the Sectors at Baccarat, Vesle, Oise-Aisna, Forêt-d'Argonne, Meuse-Argonne. Cpl. Louis Gassman from Lake Andes served with George. After the Armistice, Corporal Harris received an evaluation from Capt. H.D. Palmore, his commanding officer, stating that Cpl. Harris was "excellent as a night scout. Very dexterious [sic]." The 77th Division suffered 10,497 casualties in the war. Cpl. Harris sailed from Brest, France, aboard the *America* on April 19, 1919. The *America* had several canteens which sold ice cream and candy to the soldiers. The men were also entertained with band concerts and boxing tournaments. The ship traveled about 400 miles per day, arriving in Hoboken on April 28. George returned home to Peever. In the 1920 U.S. Census, he was living in Peever with the Lyman Clott family. George entered the spirit world on July 20, 1922. He was helping dig a well 70' deep when he was overcome by carbon monoxide gas. George is buried in Peever, SD.[3]

Has Horns, Charles. Charles was born at Little Eagle on the Standing Rock Reservation around March of 1896. In the 1903 Census Roll, he is listed with his parents, Frank Has Horns and Sees. When Charles registered for the draft on June 5, 1917, he was working as a cowboy on his land near Little Eagle. Shortly before joining the service, he married Elizabeth Dogman. Charles enlisted on June 24, 1918, at McIntosh and was sent to Camp Funston, KS. He was assigned to Co. L, 69th Infantry, but did not go overseas. He was discharged at Camp Funston on Feb. 5, 1919. In the 1928 Standing Rock Census Roll, he is listed as Charles Henry, née Has Horns. In the 1930 U.S. Census, Leona Many Wounds was living with Charles and Elizabeth. In 1932, Charles became a patient at Battle Mountain Sanatorium at Hot Springs, suffering from tuberculosis. He entered the spirit world on Oct. 6, 1933. On March 17, 2017, the Has Horns family received a Code Talker's medal in honor of Pvt. Has Horns' service.

Hates Him, Owen. Owen was born around January of 1898, on the Cheyenne River Reservation. In the 1899 Census Roll, he is listed with his parents, Ronald and Bess Hates Him, as well as a sister, Nellie. Owen enlisted in the Army on April 21, 1917. He likely enlisted in the 4th SD Infantry. When this National Guard regiment arrived at Camp Greene, NC, it was converted to a Field Artillery Regiment. Bugler Hates Him was assigned to Battery C, 147th Field Artillery (ASN 139500). He sailed for Europe aboard the *Olympic* on Jan. 11, 1918. In March they were attached to the 32nd (Red Arrow) Division. After the Armistice, the 147th was attached to the 88th Division, but returned home with the 32nd Division in May 1919. He was discharged on June 21, 1919. Owen summarized his experience, writing to Joseph Dixon

> "while taking active part in the battle of Chateau Thierry latter part of July 1918 I was gassed and just barely escaped. This world war in which I took part is something that will be in my memory forever. I know I might get killed yet I know that I ought to do something for my country as we Indians are the real Americans. So I enlisted, and seen some hard times yet I am glad I have done my duty and I got back safely home. I can not relate my whole experience there but do hope this is sufficient."

In the 1920 U.S. Census, he was living with his parents. His father was a night watchman at the school at the Cheyenne Agency. Owen entered the spirit world on July 18, 1921, and is buried in Ascension Cemetery in Promise.[4]

Hawk, James. He is listed on WWI veteran's memorial at Oglala Lakota College, Kyle, SD. See **Running Hawk, James**.

Hawk Eagle, Thomas. Thomas was born on the Cheyenne River Reservation on April 14, 1893. His parents were John and Ellen Hawk Eagle. In 1912, he requested to be allowed to attend the boarding school at Carlisle. He indicated that his parents had both passed away. Thomas played football for Carlisle. He also played on an Army team formed at Camp Funston, KS. After attending Carlisle for three years, he accepted a job as a mechanic with Ford Motor Co. in Detroit. When he registered for the draft on June 5, 1917, he was working for Dodge Bros. Thomas joined the Army on Oct. 2, 1917. He was assigned to the Troop B, 314th MP, 89th Division (ASN 2194386). Pvt. Moses Clown and George Jewett served with Cpl. Hawk Eagle in the Company. They sailed from New York aboard the *Saxon* on June 28, 1918. The 89th Division served in the St. Mihiel and Meuse-Argonne Offensives. During the Meuse-Argonne Campaign, Pvt. Clown and Pvt. Takes the Shield from the MP unit were killed in action on Nov. 1. While in occupational duty in Germany after the Armistice, Thomas played football for the team which won the AEF Championship. He was "proud of being the only Indian on the team." On April 23, 1919, Cpl. Hawk Eagle was photographed with his unit next to the Gasthaus von Mathias Lorig in Kyllburg, Germany. Cpl. Hawk Eagle sailed from Brest, France, aboard the U.S.S. *Prinz Friedrich Wilhelm* on May 18, 1919. He was discharged on June 9, 1919.

After he returned home, he married Nellie Wolf. In 1935, the family was interviewed by a worker with the SDERA program. The family was living in a one room home about a mile from the Green Grass School. Thomas had served as a judge for three years and also helped the teachers at the school. He was known as a good mechanic. The state worker indicated that Thomas may have had some health problems relating to his exposure to gas while fighting in France. In the 1940 U.S. Census, Thomas and Nellie had five children, Claude, Sylvester, Benjamin, Irene and Ansel. Thomas entered the spirit world at the VA Hospital at Fort Meade on Nov. 11, 1964. He is buried in Green Grass Cemetery near Eagle Butte.[5]

Hawk Ghost, John (Jack). Jack was born Wososo on the Rosebud Reservation about June 20, 1891. His parents were Hawk Ghost and Spotted Horse. When he registered for the draft on June 5, 1917, he was farming near Wososo. He joined the Army on July 22, 1918, and was discharged as a Private on Dec. 10, 1918. After the war, he lived in Todd County. In the 1940 U.S. Census, he was living with his wife, Pearl (Tuttle), as well as his sister and her children. Jack entered the spirit world in the Indian Health Service Hospital in Rosebud on Sept. 24, 1972, and is buried in Salt Camp Cemetery, Todd County.[6]

Hawk Wing, James. James was born on the Pine Ridge Reservation around 1886. His father was George Hawk Wing and his mother was Leader. James registered for the draft in Martin on Sept. 12, 1918. He enlisted shortly after that, but the Armistice was signed before he left for training. He had also enlisted for service in the Mexican Border Conflict. James was first married to Lisa Plenty Harange, who died of TB in1912. He then married Daisy Short Bull, who died around 1918. Later in the 1930s he married Eva Richard. In the 1940 U.S. Census, they were living with their children, Garfield, Florence, Levi, Joseph, and Peter. When James registered for the Selective Service in 1942, he was living in Wanamaker, SD. His son, Garfield, served in the Navy in WWII, while Joseph served in the Korean Conflict.[7]

Hayes, Edward. Edward was born in Waubay on the Sisseton-Wahpeton Reservation on April 29, 1892. His parents were Joseph Hayes and Julia Red Earth. When he registered for the draft on June 1, 1917, he was living in Waubay. He joined the Army on June 24, 1918. He was assigned to Co. A, 2nd Battalion, Edgewood Arsenal (ASN 3308395), Camp Meade, MD. This was the center for chemical warfare research. He later served with Casual Detachment #95. He was discharged on March 9, 1919, as a Corporal. After the war, Edward's sister, Martha, married Ed Bartlett, a fellow veteran. In the 1937 Census Roll, Edward was still listed as single. On Nov. 12, 1945, he married Elizabeth Keeble. Edward entered the spirit world on Feb. 11, 1963 and is buried in St. James Episcopal Cemetery next to Enemy Swim Lake.

Head, Noble. Noble was born on the Rosebud Reservation around January 1887 to Emil and Julia Head. When he registered for the draft on June 5, 1917, he was farming near St. Francis. He joined the Army on Aug. 6, 1918, and was assigned to Co. I, 62nd Infantry, 8th Division (ASN 2571829). He was discharged as a Private at Camp Dodge, IA, on March 21, 1919. The 8th Division did not serve overseas. He married Lucy Bird Necklace. Noble, also known as Joseph Pius, entered the spirit world on Jan. 22, 1940, and is buried in St. Charles Cemetery, St. Francis, SD.[8]

Hears the Wind, James. James was born on the Crow Creek Reservation on June 29, 1890. His parents were Amos Hears the Wind and Grey Elk. In March of 1904, he was enrolled as a student at Carlisle. He played in the Carlisle Band and in 1908, traveled with the band to Philadelphia. James returned home to Grosse in June 1909. He later wrote back to school staff that he owned ten head of horses and 32 head of cattle. He owned 320 acres of land and was the band leader in his home town. In 1910, he married Lillie Bobtail Goose. When he registered for the draft on June 5, 1917, he was farming in Charles Mix County. Shortly after this, he married Mary Lariat in Highmore. He joined the Army and was initially assigned to Troop B, 314th MP Battalion (ASN 2185915). This unit sailed from New York aboard the *Saxon* on June 28, 1918. In France he was reassigned to Co. K, 356th Infantry, 89th Division. The 356th Infantry served in the Sectors at Lucey, Euvazin, St. Mihiel and Meuse-Argonne. Pvt. Wind sailed home from Brest aboard the U.S.S. *Agamemnon* on May 16, 1919. He was discharged as a Sergeant. James entered the spirit world on Feb. 17, 1923, and is buried in St. John the Baptist Cemetery, Gann Valley.

Heduta, Abraham Grant. Abraham was born around May 2, 1887, on the Sisseton-Wahpeton Reservation to Jacob Heduta [Red Horn] and Emma Parr. On Aug. 13, 1911, he married Annie Abel. When he registered for the draft on June 1, 1917, he and his wife had one child. He enlisted in the Army on Aug. 28, 1918, and served in 3rd Co., 2nd Batt., 164th Depot Brigade at Camp Funston (ASN 4500008). Pvt. Heduta was discharged on Dec. 10, 1918. In the 1945 S.D. Census, Abraham was living in Long Hollow. He entered the spirit world in Sisseton on Dec. 31, 1957 and was buried in St. Benedict's Cemetery in Sisseton.[9]

Heminger, Dwight. Dwight was born on the Sisseton-Wahpeton Reservation on March 18, 1893, to Anthony Heminger and Lucy (Taphinbdayewin). He married Julia Montileau in 1910. When Dwight registered for the draft on June 1, 1917, he and Julia were farming near Wilmot. Dwight joined the Army on May 25, 1918, and was assigned to Casual Detachment #281, 163rd Depot Brigade at Camp Dodge, IA (ASN 2788084). He was transferred to Battery D, 347th Field Artillery (FA), 91st Division. Pvt. Heminger sailed for France from New York aboard the *Adriatic* on July 14, 1918, with Gideon Williams of Sisseton. After their ship arrived at Cherbourg, the unit was transferred to the artillery training facility at Camp de Souge near Bordeaux. The 347th FA was equipped with ten-ton tractors and 4.7-inch guns. The 347th FA did not serve on the Front. The unit spent Christmas Day along the Moselle River in Germany. They were likely billeted in private homes in four towns north of Trier. On March 13, 1919, the 347th enjoyed the distinction of acting as guard of honor for President Woodrow Wilson, who was attending the Paris Peace Conference. Pvt. Heminger sailed from Brest aboard the *Aquitania* on March 23, 1919. Other soldiers with him were Moses Marshall, Elbridge Gerry, Gideon Williams, and Peter Rouillard. Pvt. Heminger was discharged on April 17, 1919. After returning home, he married Laura Murray (1894-1988) in August 1919 at Wilmot. Laura's brother, Aaron, served with the U.S. Marine Corps. In 1930, Dwight and Laura were living in Spring Grove Township. Sometime in the 1930s, Dwight took a job as a Presbyterian Minister on the Reservation at Fort Peck, MT. He entered the spirit world there, suffering from Tuberculosis on Aug. 30, 1935. He is buried in Ascension Cemetery in Wilmot, SD.

In the 1940 U.S. Census, his widow, Laura, was living on the Rosebud Reservation with their three children, Gloria, Glenford and Dwight Jr. Glenford served with the USMC in WWII, while their son, Dwight Jr., served with the Navy from 1943-1947.[10]

Henry, Charles. See **Has Horns, Charles.**

Henry, James. James was born on the Rosebud Reservation on Dec. 8, 1886, the son of John and Lucy Henry. When he registered for the draft on June 5, 1917, he lived at White River and was raising cattle. He joined the Army and was assigned to Co. E, 314th Ammo Train, 89th Division (ASN 2195031). Cpl. Henry sailed for Europe from New York aboard the *Cretic* on June 28, 1918. Another soldier traveling with him was Paul Tallmandan. After the Armistice, the 314th Ammo Train was billeted in Bitburg, Germany. Pvt. Henry sailed from Brest, France, aboard the *Agamemnon* on May 16, 1919, and arrived in Hoboken on May 24. Henry was discharged as a Private on June 18, 1919. On Sept. 9, 1920, he married Effie West at Center, NE. In the 1930 U.S. Census, they lived in Mellette County. He was a member of the White River American Legion Post. In 1940, James moved to Rapid City, where he worked for Warren Lamb Lumber Co. He retired in 1951. James entered the spirit world in Rosebud Public Health Service Hospital on May 23, 1975. Two daughters, Erma and Vivian, survived him. He is buried in St. James Cemetery in White River.[11]

Henry, Mark. Mark was an enrolled member of the Flandreau Santee Sioux Tribe who was born in Nebraska on April 18, 1896. In the 1900 U.S. Census, he lived in Flandreau Township, Moody County with his parents, Pat Chaska [First Born] and Fannie (Wicayahdatewin). When he registered for the draft on June 16, 1917, he was a student at the Genoa Industrial School in Nebraska. He joined the Army on March 29, 1918. He served as a Pfc. in Company B, 355th Infantry Regiment (ASN 2202463). The 355th was part of the 89th Division. Pvt. Henry sailed from New York aboard the *Adriatic* on June 4, 1918. After the war, he wrote to Joseph Dixon that he'd fought in the St. Mihiel and Meuse-Argonne Offensives without receiving a scratch. In an evaluation of Pfc. Henry, his commanding officer, Capt. John C. Moora, wrote, "good scout, excellent with pistol." Pfc. Henry sailed for home from Brest, France, aboard the *Leviathan* on May 15, 1919, and arrived May 22. Pfc. Henry was discharged on June 20, 1919. He reenlisted on June 21, 1919. He likely served with the 135th Observation Squadron, Air Corps, which had been transferred to Henry Post Airfield, near Ft. Sill, OK. In the 1920 U.S. Census, Pvt. Henry was stationed at Ft. Sill. He was discharged on July 12, 1920.

Mark married Bertha York (1912-1980) in 1928. In the 1930 U.S. Census, they were living in Sioux City, IA, where Mark worked as a laborer in a packing house. In the 1940 U.S. Census, his occupation is listed as beef cooler laborer for the U.S. meat packing industry. Mark worked for Swift & Co. for 25 years. Their children include Mark Jr., Ralph, George, Norman and Philip. Mark entered the spirit world while seated in a Sioux City theater on Oct. 8, 1955. Military rites were conducted by Monahan Post No. 64, American Legion, at Floyd Cemetery in Sioux City.[12]

Herman, Thomas F. Thomas was born on the Rosebud Reservation on Oct. 29, 1895, the son of Frank and Mary Herman. Thomas joined the Navy on May 19, 1917, and was discharged as a Seaman on Feb. 20, 1919. He married Louise Alley, an Oto from Oklahoma. In the 1920 U.S. Census, they were living in Red Rock, OK. In 1939, Thomas married Alice Primeaux in Bonesteel. In the 1940 U.S. Census, Thomas was farming near St. Charles, SD. In the 1954 Rapid City Directory, Thomas was working in security at the Rapid City Air Force Base. He was a member of the Chauncey Eagle Horn American Legion Post at Rosebud. He entered the spirit world on Dec. 15, 1978, in a

Rapid City hospital. His daughter, Mary, and son, Thomas Jr., survived him. He is buried in Trinity Cemetery, Mission, SD.

Hero, Jasper. Jasper was born at Lake Andes on June 24, 1897. In the 1902 Yanktonai Census Roll, Jasper is listed with his parents, Adam Ptesanwicasa [Who is like a white buffalo] and Ellen Oyewakanwin [Sacred Tracks], and a sister, Rebecca. When Jasper registered for the draft on June 5, 1917, he was farming near Lake Andes. On April 25, 1918, he married Lizzie Rockboy. The next day he joined the Army and was sent to Camp Funston, where he was assigned to 164th Depot Brigade (ASN 2186637). He was transferred to Co. E, 355th Infantry, until August 21, 1918. He then was transferred to Co. B, 70th Infantry, 10th Division until his discharge as a Private on Feb. 13, 1919. In the 1920s, he married Hermine Flying Hawk, with whom he had a son, Leo. Leo joined the Army right after the end of WWII. In 1936, Jasper married Stella Marushka. Jasper became ill from tuberculosis and entered the spirit world in Lincoln, NE, on March 19, 1937. He is buried in Lakeview Cemetery in Lake Andes.[13]

Heron, Oliver. He is listed on WWI veteran's memorial at Oglala Lakota College, Kyle, SD. See **Left Heron**, Oliver.

Hicks, William. He is listed on WWI veteran's memorial at Oglala Lakota College, Kyle, SD. Will was born on Jan. 17, 1889, in Eustis, NE. When he registered for the draft on June 5, 1917, he was farming near Allen, SD. He likely had just enlisted in the SD National Guard. His military records date his enlistment to June 1, 1917. He was discharged on Feb. 3, 1919. In the 1930 U.S. Census, he lived with his brother in Bennett County. In 1931, he married Phoebe Sherman. In 1940 they were farming. Will was a member of American Legion Post No. 240. Will entered the spirit world in a Hot Springs hospital on Dec. 5, 1973. A foster daughter, Betty Barnes, survived him. He and Phoebe are buried in the Martin Cemetery.

Job High Elk
June High Elk

High Elk, Job. Job was born about June 21, 1893, in the High Elk hill area on the Cheyenne River Reservation. In the 1900 U.S. Census, he was listed with his parents, Moses and Jennie, as well as his brother, Joseph, and sisters, Emma and Mary. His sister, Emma, married Ernest Bad Horse, who also served with the Army in France. Job enlisted in the South Dakota National Guard on June 21, 1916. He likely was attending the Rapid City boarding school. During his service years, he listed Jesse House as a contact person. Pvt. High Elk served with Co. I, 4th SD Infantry Regiment. These National Guard soldiers were recruited to serve along the Mexican Border. They were mustered out on March 3, 1917. Pfc. High Elk may have stayed in the Guard until called up for active duty in the summer of 1917. On Sept. 28, 1917, the 4th Infantry took a train to Camp Greene, NC. Once they arrived there, these SD Guardsmen were reassigned to regiments making up the 41st Division. Pfc. High Elk became a soldier in the 148th Machine Gun (MG) Battalion (ASN 112142). Most of his fellow soldiers assigned to the 148th MG Battalion sailed for France in January of 1918. It is likely that Pfc. High Elk was sick at that time, as he did not sail for Europe until April 10, 1918, when he left from Newport News, VA, on the *El Sol*. After arriving in France, he was assigned to Co. C, 8th Machine Gun Battalion, 3rd Division. The 8th MG Bn. participated in campaigns at Aisne,

Champagne-Marne, Aisne-Marne, St. Mihiel, Meuse-Argonne, and Champagne. The 3rd Division suffered 16,117 casualties in the war. After the Armistice, Pfc. High Elk was evaluated by his commanding officer, who stated:

> Pfc. High Elk "rendered efficient service. Especially at the front where he showed great courage while under fire. His ability as a message carrier is most worthy of note, finding his way at all times through dense woods and underbrush, always delivering any message that was entrusted to him for delivery. He showed at all times great courage and endurance.

The 8th MG Bn. was billeted in Nickenich, Germany during the Army of Occupation. Pvt. High Elk sailed from Brest aboard the *Pretoria* on Aug. 12, 1919, and arrived in Brooklyn on Aug. 25, 1919. He was discharged on August 31. He last was assigned to Casual Detachment 1350. After the war, Job wrote about his experiences in a report to Joseph Dixon.

> In the Battle at Chateau Thierry July 14, 1918 I was a gunner and took active part and also the battle at Argonne Forest in Sept. 1918 and also St. Mihiel the latter part of Sept. I have seen some hard times and could not tell the whole story here, but it is something I shall never forget, I am an Indian and never had any experience in a war before, but I realize that I was doing my duty as a patriot and was fighting to save Democracy, and do hope that in the future we Indians may enjoy freedom which we Indians are always denied.

In 1924, Job married Estella Slides Off. In the 1930 U.S. Census, they were farming north of Thunder Butte in Ziebach County. In 1935, the family was interviewed by a worker as part of the SDERA program. The family was living ½ mile west of Thunder Butte substation to be close to a school. Their home was a 12' x 16' log building with a dirt roof. Their water came from a spring 150 yards away. They had a more permanent home that was five miles west of Thunder Butte, but it was accessible only by trails in poor condition. In 1935, the family had planted corn, oats, and a one-acre garden, but they were destroyed by hoppers and beetles. In the 1940 U.S. Census, they were listed with their children, Arthur, Wesley, Paul, Maxine, Corrine, Medrick, Theodore and Floyd. Many of Job's descendants served in the military, including six sons, two grandsons, three great-granddaughters and two great grandsons. Wesley served in the Army from 1945 to 1954. Arthur served during the Korean War, and Theodore served in Vietnam. Estella passed away in 1963. Job entered the spirit world at the VA hospital at Fort Meade on Jan. 30, 1970. He is buried in St. Peter's Episcopal Cemetery, Thunder Butte, SD. On Sept. 3, 2016, Job's son, Floyd, accepted a Code Talkers medal at a ceremony in Eagle Butte, honoring his father's service during the war.[14]

High Elk, Joseph. Joseph, the older brother of Job, was born about 1891. He belonged to the Two Kettles Band. His parents were Moses High Elk and Jennie Brings White. Around 1910, he married Bessie Flags the Bull. When Joseph registered for the draft on June 5, 1917, he and Bessie had two children. When Joseph joined the Army, he was assigned to Supply Co., 28th Field Artillery, 10th Division. He did not go overseas, but after nine months, was discharged as a Private. While he was in the service, he lost 12 head of cattle and seven horses. After the war, he divorced Bessie. In 1927, he married Lucy Landreaux, who had been married to Henry Swimmer. Joseph and Lucy had a daughter, Kate. They mostly lived in Eagle Butte, except from 1931-34, when he worked at a school in Pierre. They had had a nice home near Eagle Butte, but it had accidently caught fire in 1931 when some neighbor boys tried to smoke out a rabbit. In 1935, the family was living in an old school house on the edge of Eagle Butte. They owned 25 head of wild horses, a team and two saddle horses, as well as two sets of harness and a 1933 Model A Ford. In the 1940 U.S. Census,

Joseph and Lucy were farming in Armstrong County. They had a girl, Alice. After Lucy passed away in 1957, Joseph married Sophie Garter. Joseph entered the spirit world at the VA Hospital in Fort Meade on Nov. 5, 1969. He is buried in the Mobridge Cemetery.[15]

Hill, Fred E. Fred was born around July 2, 1897, on the Cheyenne River Reservation. His parents were Thomas Hill and Julia Ducheneaux. In the 1906 Cheyenne River Census Roll, Fred is listed as an orphan. Fred married Mabel Cummings on Dec. 5, 1917. When Fred registered for the draft on June 5, 1918, he was farming near Promise. He joined the Army on Aug. 28, 1918, and was discharged on Jan. 10, 1919. He may have served with the 20th Infantry. Not long after, he divorced Mabel. They had a son, Henry. Mabel had two brothers, Earl and Henry, who served in the World War. Fred married Mabel's sister, Eleanor (1897-1986), and moved to the Twin Cities. Fred and Eleanor had two sons, Fred Jr., and Harold. In the 1929 St. Paul City Directory, Fred was driving a cab for Diamond Cab. In the 1940 U.S. Census, Fred was working as a contractor. All three of Fred's sons served in the military during WWII. Fred entered the spirit world on June 14, 1962, and is buried in Ft. Snelling National Cemetery, Section I, site 2628. Eleanor is buried next to him. His sons, Fred Jr. and Harold are also buried in Ft. Snelling.

Honor Guard for Funeral of Isaac His Horse Is Fast

His Horse Is Fast, Isaac. Isaac was born in 1889, according to the Census Rolls for the Cheyenne River Sioux Reservation. In the 1895 Census Roll, he is listed with his father, His Horse is Fast, his mother, Alice, and his brother and sister, Robert and Lilly. In the 1910 U.S. Census, he is listed with his mother and his step father, Daniel Charging Hawk. When he registered for the draft on June 5, 1917, he stated that he was farming his step father's allotment. Isaac enlisted in the Army on Oct. 5, 1917, and was sent to Camp Funston for training. He sailed from New York aboard the *Espagne* on April 3, 1918, with the 3rd Company, Camp Funston April Replacement Draft. After arriving in France, he was assigned to Co. C, 128th Regiment, 32nd Division (ASN 2185495). On August 1, 1918, the 128th Infantry was in position near Cierges. According to a unit history, "the attack started with much promise of success, but reports from every section of the front indicated that the Germans opposed to us were not of the fleeing kind. They resisted desperately, and dozens of groups died at their posts rather than 'kamerad' before the American waves which surged forward. The German Command was under no misapprehension as to the importance of the position, and had put in fresh troops to attempt to hold the Ourcq against further American attacks. These troops were amply provided with machine guns, strongly supported by artillery, and they put up a game fight." Pvt. His Horse is Fast died in that fight on August 1. His body was brought back from Europe on the *Wheaton* on July 2, 1921. Following a military funeral, he was buried in the Episcopal Cemetery at White Horse, Dewey County.[16]

Hodgkiss, Elmo. Elmo was born on June 25, 1890, most likely, on the Cheyenne River Reservation. In the 1892 Cheyenne River Census Roll, he is listed with his parents, William and Nannie, as well as a brother, Daniel, and a sister, Marie. Elmo enlisted in the Navy in Minneapolis on Sept. 23,

1914, and served as a Ship's Cook on a receiving ship in Boston, MA. He re-enlisted on Sept. 24, 1918, and was discharged on Oct. 13, 1919. In 1931, he was a patient at the VA Hospital in Dayton, OH. He entered the spirit world at the VA Hospital in Legion, TX, on March 18, 1934. He is buried in Hodgkiss Family Cemetery in Wyandotte, OK.

William Hollow Breast
Mathers Museum

Hollow Breast, William. William was born Jan. 1, 1901, on the Northern Cheyenne Reservation in Busby, Montana. He was the son of Hubert Hollowbreast and the grandson of Wolf Name. In the 1910 U.S. Census, he was living with his grandparents. Shortly after this, he was enrolled as a student at the Flandreau Boarding School. At the age of 16, he enlisted in Co. D, 1st South Dakota Cavalry on June 11, 1917. When this SD National Guard unit went to Camp Cody, NM, in September of 1917, Pvt. Hollow Breast was assigned to training with the 34th Division. Pfc. Hollow Breast sailed for France aboard the S.S. *Tereisias* on June 28, 1918. He was traveling with Co. 15, Camp Cody June Automatic Replacement Draft (ASN 1427458). After arriving in France, he was transferred to Battery B, 122nd Field Artillery, 33rd Division. After the Armistice, Pfc. Hollow Breast received an evaluation from his commanding officer, stating: "this soldier's health is good and is regarded by the whites as a very good man. Has courage and possesses keenness of senses." Pfc. Hollow Breast finally served with 272nd MP Co., 33rd Division. He sailed from Brest aboard the U.S.S. *President Grant* on May 28, 1919, arriving in Boston on June 9, 1919. He was discharged on June 20, 1919. Before his discharge, he was photographed in uniform by Joseph Dixon at Camp Devens, MA, on June 12, 1919. He told Dixon, "I fought with them all through the war as a battery runner. I was sent out often to the front lines, and every trip was a D.S.C. [Distinguished Service Cross] trip. Lots of times I had to go over cross roads where shells [were] constantly bursting. I had to go just the same. Several times my messages were delivered as shells tore the battery to pieces, and arms and legs of the men were falling at my feet." Hollow Breast's name was engraved on a plaque honoring the war veterans, erected at the Flandreau School around 1920.

In the 1920 U.S. Census, William was living with his uncle on Tongue River District. William was married several times. He was active with the Native American Church and was one of the earliest Northern Cheyenne to convert to peyote. In the 1940 U.S. Census, William was serving as the Secretary-Treasurer for the tribal office. He lived in Busby for many years and worked for the Busby School power house. He was a member of the American Legion and the Chiefs Society of the Northern Cheyenne Tribe. He entered the spirit world on Feb. 22, 1981, at St. Vincent's Hospital in Billings, and is buried in Busby.[17]

Hollow Horn, Charles. Charles was born near Cherry Creek on the Cheyenne River Reservation around May 1890. His parents were John Hollow Horn and Susie Lays Down. In 1916, Charles married Helen Widow, whose brother, Paul, served in the Army in France. When Charles registered for the draft on July 20, 1918, he was married with one child. He enlisted shortly after that, and was discharged on Dec. 13, 1918. In the 1930 U.S. Census, he is listed as a veteran of the World War. His children were Emmett, Alice, Lydia and Sadie. Emmett served in the Army in WWII. The family was interviewed in 1935 by a worker with the SDERA program. Charles was working on a Public Works project building the Rattle Snake Dam. They lived in a tent near the worksite. Their permanent home was near Red Scaffold. They had tried to raise a garden that summer, but the hot, dry weather wiped it out. Charles entered the spirit world in Cherry Creek on May 10, 1937. Helen entered the spirit world the following November. Charles is buried in St. Marks Cemetery, Cherry Creek.[18]

Holy Eagle, James. He is listed on WWI veteran's memorial at Oglala Lakota College, Kyle, SD. James was born on the Pine Ridge Reservation on April 4, 1889. His parents were Holy Eagle and Alice. James attended the boarding school at Carlisle, where he excelled in sports. When he registered for the draft on May 29, 1917, he was working as a printer at Carlisle. He worked as a coach at Riverside Indian School, Riverside, CA. James joined the Army on July 22, 1918. He served as a Musician with the Headquarters Troop, 19th Division at Camp Dodge, IA. Pvt. Titus Chasing Horse was in the same unit. Cpl. Holy Eagle was discharged on Jan. 28, 1919. In 1922, he married Elizabeth Turning Holy, whose brother, Frank, had also served in the 19th Division. James was an accomplished musician who could play eight instruments. During the summer President Coolidge's stay in the Black Hills, James was the band director for numerous local ceremonies honoring the President. James and Eliza had a ranch near Allen. In the 1940 U.S. Census, James and Eliza are listed with their sons, Gus, Roy and William. Around 1940 the family moved to Rapid City, where James worked for Ford Motor Company. Their sons, Gus and William served in the military. After James retired in 1958, he moved back to his ranch near Allen. In 1969, he moved to Rapid City, where his home was destroyed in the 1972 flash flood. Gov. Mickelson declared April 4, 1989, as James Holy Eagle Day in honor of his 100th birthday. James entered the spirit world on Aug. 30, 1991. Four granddaughters and one grandson survived him. He is buried in the Black Hills National Cemetery, section G, site 6402.[19]

Hopkins, Abel. Abel was born on the Sisseton-Wahpeton Reservation on June 15, 1891, to Samuel and Mary Hopkins. In the 1900 U.S. Census, they lived in LaBelle Township, Marshall County. Abel attended school at Haskell. He married Agnes Bear (1889-1986). When he registered for the draft on June 2, 1917, the family was living in Peever. Abel joined the Army on Aug. 28, 1918, and was sent Camp Funston, KS. He was assigned to 3rd Co., 2nd Battalion, 164th Depot Brigade (ASN 4500096). He was discharged as a Private on Dec. 10, 1918. In the 1930 U.S. Census, Abel was farming. In 1935, the family was interviewed by a worker with the SDERA program. Their home was 12 miles SW of Sisseton. They had previously lived in the Big Coulee District, but they had trouble finding enough wood. Abel was a member of the American Legion. They owned three horses, a colt, three cows, two calves and a car. At the time, Abel was not working because he had eye trouble which made it hard for him to see. He had been received some pension money, but that had been stopped. In the 1940 U.S. Census, both Abel and his son, Solon, were working on road construction projects. Abel suffered from tuberculosis and entered the spirit world in his home on Nov. 16, 1950. He is buried in Ascension Presbyterian Cemetery, Spring Grove.[20]

Hopkins, Peter. Peter was born about March 18, 1892, in White Swan Township, Charles Mix County. In the 1893 Yanktonai Census Roll, he was listed with his parents, John and Theresa, and his brother, Alfred, and sister, Effie. When Peter registered for the draft on June 5, 1917, he was farming near Lake Andes. When he joined the Army, he was assigned to Co. F, 351st Infantry, 88th Division (ASN 3315283). Pvt. Hopkins sailed from New York aboard the *Scotian* on Aug. 15, 1918. Most of the Division was stationed in quiet sectors. After the Armistice, Pfc. Hopkins received an evaluation from his commanding officer, stating the he was "efficient as night worker, scout, runner, and observer. Associates readily with men and regarded as an unusually good man." As part of the Army of Occupation, Co. F was billeted at Liffol-le-Grand, where they did convoy duty on ration trains going into Germany. Five other Yanktonai were in Co. F with Pfc. Hopkins. 2nd Lt. Joseph Neely wrote that these six men were "well educated, one being a college man, splendid scouts and good soldiers. Their Captain, H.H. Corey, would not trade these Indians for an equal number of white men because of their special qualifications." Pvt. Ulysses Reed had also been on Co. F, but he passed away in October of 1918. On May 20, 1919, the 351st Regiment left St. Nazaire, France, aboard the ship *Mercury*, docking in Newport News, VA. Pfc. Hopkins was discharged on June 7, 1919.

In 1926, Peter married Frances Fogg, who was from Pine Ridge. In 1935, the family was interviewed by a worker with the SDERA program. The family was renting a farm in White Swan District. They lived in a four-room frame house for which they paid $60 per year plus a third of the crop. The family owned a Model T Ford, as well as six horses, one colt, six cows and some chickens. They mentioned they like to go to movies in Lake Andes about once a month. Peter had received a head injury in the war, for which he was receiving a pension. Some of his wife's relatives lived at Crow Creek. In the 1940 U.S. Census, the family was now living in Buffalo County, where Peter was working on road repair. Their son, Benedict, served in the Army during the Korean Conflict. Peter entered the spirit world in the Lauritsen Nursing Home in Mitchell, SD, on April 14, 1966, and is buried in St. Joseph's Cemetery in Ft. Thompson.[21]

Hopkins, William. William was born around 1890 on the Sisseton-Wahpeton Reservation, the son of James and Sarah. When William registered for the draft on June 7, 1917, he was living in Peever and working for Aleck Renville. In a report to Joseph Dixon, William wrote that he was drafted on July 8, 1918, but was discharged at Camp Dodge, IA, on Aug. 24, 1918. He had been assigned to Co. 15, 4th Battalion, 163rd Depot Brigade (ASN 2142358). He was very upset. He wrote to Dixon that when he was drafted, they said he was a citizen. After his discharge, he was told he was still a ward of the government. William married Emma Takes the Shield. In the 1930 U.S. Census, they were living in Fort Yates with their son, Daniel. William and Emma also had a son, Sidney, who served in the Army in the Korean Conflict. Emma passed away in 1935. William entered the spirit world in the Standing Rock Hospital on March 17, 1942.[22]

Horse Thief, Jasper. See **Strongheart, Walter.**

Hourigan, Lawrence A. Lawrence was born on the Standing Rock Reservation on Aug. 13, 1894, the son of James Hourigan and Emma Archambault. In 1915, Lawrence married Grace Flora, with whom he had two children, Delsia and Henrietta. When Lawrence registered for the draft on June 5, 1917, he was farming near Thunder Hawk. He indicated he had served three years as a Private in the SD National Guard. Records from Standing Rock Tribe list Lawrence as a veteran. In the 1930 U.S. Census, Lawrence was living in Mobridge and working for the Milwaukee Road. Grace entered the spirit world in 1932. In 1939, Lawrence married Anne Marie Schroeder. In the 1940 U.S. Census, Lawrence was working as a baggage man for the railroad in Mobridge. He later moved to Riverside, CA. His last job was yard clerk for the Milwaukee Road. Lawrence entered the spirit world in Kaiser Foundation Hospital in Fontana, CA, on Sept. 9, 1964. His widow, Anna Marie, survived him. He is buried in Crestlawn Memorial Park, Riverside, CA.[23]

Howard, Amos. Amos was born on the Standing Rock Reservation on Nov. 15, 1899. His parents were Samuel Howard and Agnes Skawin [White Woman]. As a young man, Amos was enrolled at the Flandreau boarding school. He joined the Army on April 13, 1918, and was assigned to Co. E, 47th Infantry (ASN 465-363). He broke his arm while serving at Fort Snelling. Pfc. Howard was discharged on April 29, 1919. After his discharge, his injured arm continued to bother him. His name was engraved on a plaque honoring war veterans from the Flandreau School. He returned home and lived with his parents in a two-room log house in Wakpala. They hauled water from the river. In 1935, the family was interviewed by a worker with the SDERA program. Samuel liked carving diamond willow canes. They took him about three days. In earlier years he kept busy when he could sell them for $5. In the 1930s, people only wanted to pay $2, so it didn't pay for him to spend time on carving. On Feb. 10, 1939, Amos married Agatha Holy Bull. Their children were Ruby, Beverly, Teddi, Marie, Cecil, Casey and Lee. Amos re-enlisted in the Army on Aug. 10, 1942. He served with the Headquarters Battery, 243 Field Artillery Battalion (ASN 37299317). He was discharged as a Private on Feb. 24, 1943. Amos entered the spirit world on June 2, 1945, and is buried in St. Elizabeth Cemetery, Wakpala, SD.[24]

Howard, Charles A. Charles was born at Fort Snelling, MN, on Aug. 30, 1887. His father, John Howard, was a Musician with the 25th Infantry Regiment. His mother was Marion DeRockbraine. In the 1903 Standing Rock Census Roll, Charles is listed with his mother, his sister, Daisy, and two brothers, John and James. In the 1910 U.S. Census, Charles is listed with his wife, Clara. He and Clara had two children, Luella and Charles Jr. When Charles registered for the draft, his family was living in McLaughlin while he was working at Mobridge. Charles joined the Army on Sept. 21, 1917. When he arrived at Camp Funston, KS, he was initially assigned to Co. C, 340th Machine Gun Battalion (ASN 2192999). He was transferred to Machine Gun Company, 38th Infantry Regiment, 3rd Division. Pvt. Howard sailed with this unit from Halifax, Nova Scotia, aboard the British steamship *Corsican* on March 25, 1918. The *Corsican* sailed across the north Atlantic and docked in Glasgow, Scotland. The unit traveled by train to southern England, before crossing the English Channel on the *Austrilind*. Other soldiers from Standing Rock who served with Pvt. Howard were James Eaglehorn, Martin Medicine and Thomas DeRockbraine. The 38th Infantry fought against the German Army along the Marne River in July 1918. The 38th became known as "The Rock of the Marne." Pfc. Howard likely was wounded in that battle. He later was awarded a Purple Heart. In April of 1919, Pfc. Howard wrote to the *Sioux County Pioneer* that he had a chance to attend the A.E.F University. During the Occupation period, educational courses were offered to American soldiers in Beaune, France. At the end of his letter, Pfc. Howard wrote "if you want to join a good outfit, boys, step out. Come across, it's nor dangerous, this is our last invitation. Give us a chance for one of those silver stripes. The war is over, you will be perfectly safe, so come across." Pfc. Howard sailed for home from Brest, France, aboard the *Agamemnon* on Aug. 10, 1919. Pfc. Howard was honorably discharged on Aug. 24, 1919. The 3rd Division suffered 16,117 casualties in the war. After divorcing Clara (1877-1977), he married Ester White Light in 1926. In the 1930 U.S. Census, Charles was living at the SD Sanatorium for TB in Custer County. In 1933, he married Dolly Ross. In the 1940 U.S. Census, he and Dolly were living with their daughter, Luella, in Ft. Yates, where he worked as a night fireman in the heating plant. He later lived at Ft. Thompson. He entered the spirit world on June 5, 1953, and is buried in Christ Church Cemetery, Ft. Thompson.[25]

Howard, Robert E. Robert was born on the Yankton Reservation on Feb. 10, 1895. His parents were Michael Howard and Anna Desera. His father had served in the Army as a Bugler at Fort Randall. Robert enlisted in the Army on Oct. 4, 1917, and was assigned to Co. C, 342nd Machine Gun Battalion, 89th Division (ASN 2185983). Pvt. Howard sailed from New York aboard the *Caronia* on June 4, 1918, and arrived in France on June 16. He was wounded on Nov. 1, 1918, when the 89th Division was attacking German positions on the Heights of Barricourt. Pvt. Howard spent many months in French hospitals. He never fully recovered from his wound. He sailed from Brest,

France, aboard the Leviathan on April 15, 1919. His fellow soldiers were labeled as "walking cases requiring dressing." After arriving in the U.S., he received a furlough to come home and marry Daisy I. Goodness on May 19, 1919. He was officially discharged from the Army on Nov. 5, 1919. The family lived in Armour for nine years, before moving to Lake Andes. Robert entered the spirit world on Jan. 5, 1941. His widow and sons, Wayne and Gerald, as well as his daughters, Dorothea, Donna, Jean and Yvonne, survived him. His sons served in the military during WWII. Robert is buried in Pleasant Ridge Cemetery, Armour, SD.

Hudson, Joseph H. Joseph was born in Bonesteel, SD, on June 6, 1890. In the 1891 Rosebud Census Roll, he is listed with his parents, Henry Hudson and Julia Douville, as well as a sister, Minnie, and three brothers, Leo, Claude and John. Around 1915, Joseph first married Pearl Remis. Later he married Bessie Mulvin, with whom he had two children, Lucille and Joseph Basil. When Joseph registered for the draft on June 5, 1917, he was farming near Winner. He enlisted in the Army at Winner on Sept. 22, 1917, and traveled to Camp Funston and to Camp Cody for training. On June 28, 1918, he sailed for France aboard the S.S. Tereisias, traveling with Co. 14, Camp Cody June Automatic Replacement Draft. He was later transferred to Battery A, 19th Field Artillery, 5th Division (ASN 1427460). A number of other SD soldiers were transferred with him, including Louis Dog and Francis Janis. After the Armistice, Pfc. Hudson received an evaluation from his commanding officer, which stated that he was "a very good soldier; one who can be depended upon to care for animals and handle them." As part of the Army of Occupation, the 19th FA was billeted near Hesperange, Luxembourg. Pfc. Hudson sailed from Breast aboard the U.S.S. *America* on July 13, 1919, and arrived on July 22. Pfc. Hudson was discharged at Camp Dodge, IA, on July 29, 1919. On Dec. 5, 1921, Joseph married Flora Strong. They had a daughter, Muriel. In the 1930 U.S. Census, Joe was working as an oiler on a gas shovel in Ovid, CO. In the 1940 U.S. Census, the family was farming south of Denver. They later moved to California, where Joseph entered the spirit world on June 8, 1964. He and Flora are buried in Inyo County, CA. Their son, Joseph Basil, served in the Air Force in WWII, Korea and Vietnam.[26]

Huntsman, Frank P. Frank was born on the Lower Brule Reservation on April 28, 1891. His parents were Wesley Huntsman and Carrie Johnson, who was born in Norway. In 1897, Wesley worked as an assistant carpenter for the Lower Brule Agency. In the 1902 Census Roll, Frank is listed with his parents, two sisters, Winona and Ruth, and his younger brother, Herbert [sic]. The family lived near Reliance. Frank and his brother, Hobart, both joined the Army and served together. Pvt. Frank Huntsman was assigned to Co. D, 350th Infantry, 88th Division (ASN 3309958). He sailed for Europe from Brooklyn aboard the *Delta* on Aug. 11, 1918. After a safe trip across the Atlantic, the regiment spent several days in a "rest camp" in Romsey, England. Company D landed in France on August 30. Later that Fall, quite a few soldiers came down with the Spanish flu. Frank entered the spirit world on Oct. 20, 1918. Pvt. Huntsman's body was returned to the US aboard the *Wheaton* which sailed from Cherbourg, France, on May 1, 1921. He is buried in Reliance Cemetery.

Huntsman, Hobart Wesley. Hobart was born on Dec. 7, 1897, on the Lower Brule Reservation to Wesley and Carrie Huntsman. Hobart joined the Army with his brother, Frank. He also was assigned to Co. D, 350th Infantry, 88th Division (ASN 3309956). Pvt. Huntsman sailed for Europe from Brooklyn aboard the *Delta* on Aug. 11, 1918. Most of Company D served in quiet sectors along the Front. The second platoon took part in a night patrol across the German lines. Several German soldiers were captured and Pfc. Emanuel Hauff from Kulm, ND, received a Croix-de-Guerre. After the Armistice, Company D was billeted near Gondrecourt, and later to Naix-aux-Forges. Pvt. Hobart Huntsman sailed from St. Nazaire, France aboard the *Aeolus* on May 19, 1919.

They docked in Newport News, VA. After returning home to Reliance, Hobart married Caroline Hieb on Dec. 11, 1927. Hobart worked as a rural mail carrier. He entered the spirit world in Sacred Heart Hospital in Yankton on Dec. 18, 1969. He is buried in Reliance Cemetery.

I

Iron, Matthew W. Matthew was born on the Sisseton Reservation on April 16, 1895, to Esau Mazahowaste and Hannah Wahorpinawin. In the 1910 Census Roll, he was listed as an orphan. He may have served in the Cavalry before the war, as military records show a discharge date of Dec. 6, 1917. He later served as a Private in a Remount unit during the war. He was discharged on Nov. 10, 1918. He married Frances Gives Water (Ponca) in Oklahoma in August of 1918. In the 1920 U.S. Census, he was still living in Oklahoma. In the 1937 Census Roll, Frances' children listed were Wallace, Levi and Cynthia. Wallace and Levi served with the Army in WWII. In the 1940 U.S. Census, the family was living in Cedar Butte, SD, while Matthew worked in construction. When he registered for the "Old Man's Draft" in 1942, he was living in Ortley, SD. He entered the spirit world on Sept. 21, 1969, and is buried in Ponca City, OK.

Iron Cloud, George L. George was born around Jan. 1, 1901, in Porcupine on the Pine Ridge Reservation. His parents were Iron Cloud and Red Necklace. George enlisted on Dec. 13, 1926, serving as a Private in the Army. He was discharged on Dec. 15, 1927. In the 1930 U.S. Census, George was working for the Pine Ridge agency as a truck driver. He and his wife, Mary, had two children, Cleveland and Lavern. In the early 1930s, he married Pearl Janis. In the 1937 Census Roll, George and Pearl were listed with their children, Robert, Pat and Clara. In the 1940 U.S. Census, George was working as a mail carrier. George later lived at Porcupine. He entered the spirit world at the White River Care Center on April 1, 1995. His sons, Robert, Pat and Cleveland, survived him. He is buried in Christ the King Catholic Cemetery in Porcupine.[1]

Iron Cloud, Jasper. Jasper was born on the Standing Rock Reservation about Feb. 16, 1900. His father was Peter Bulls Eye. His mother, Sarah Wicinyanpi [Trusty], was a daughter of Gall. As a young man, Jasper attended the boarding school at Flandreau. On April 13, 1918, he enlisted in the Army at Jefferson Barracks, MO. He was assigned to Co. L, 48th Infantry, 20th Division. He did not serve overseas. He was discharged as a Private at Camp Jackson, Columbia, SC, on March 18, 1919. Jasper's name was engraved on a plaque honoring veterans from the Flandreau boarding school. In the 1930 U.S. Census, Jasper was living in Wakpala with his wife, Mabel, and their children, Thomas, Peter and Vermond. Jasper entered the spirit world on Oct. 21, 1931, and is buried in St. Elizabeth's Cemetery near Wakpala. Jasper's sons, Thomas and Peter, served in the Army in WWII. In a ceremony held in Wakpala on March 17, 2017, the family of Pvt. Iron Cloud received a Code Talker's Medal in honor of his service.

Iron Cloud, Philip. Philip was born on the Standing Rock Reservation around Nov. 4, 1892, to Peter Bulls Eye and Mary Karpewin Red Bird. In the 1906 Census Roll, he and his brother, Jasper, are listed with Wacinyanpi and step-father, John Redhawk. Jacob Shoots Near is listed as their brother, also. When Philip registered for the draft, he was working as a laborer in Wakpala. When he joined the Army, he was assigned to Co. 41, 163rd Depot Brigade. On July 22, 1918, he was sent to Camp Dodge, IA. Henry White Bird from Standing Rock also served in Co. 41 with Iron Cloud. Philip contracted Tuberculosis while in the Army. He was discharged on Dec. 19, 1919. He entered the spirit world on March 15, 1920. His name is engraved on a monument erected in St. Elizabeth's Cemetery near Wakpala.[2]

Iron Elk, William. He is listed on WWI veteran's memorial at Oglala Lakota College, Kyle, SD. William was born about Feb. 10, 1899, on the Pine Ridge Reservation. His mother was Cora Black Bird. As a youth, William was a student at the boarding school in Flandreau. He enlisted in the Army on May 10, 1918, at Jefferson Barracks, MO, and was assigned to the Medical Department (ASN 485286). Pvt. Iron Elk sailed from New York aboard the *Louisville* on Sept. 14, 1918. He traveled with unit No. 62 Camp Crane. Camp Crane, located in Allentown, PA, was a training site for ambulance drivers. In France, Pvt. Iron Elk served with Evac Hospital #5, Medical Department. He sailed for the States from Brest aboard the *Rotterdam* on Feb. 9, 1919, and was discharged at Camp Dodge, IA, on March 14, 1919. William's name was engraved on a plaque honoring veterans at the Flandreau Boarding School. After returning home, he married Angelic Splintered Horn from Crow Creek. In the 1930 U.S. Census, the family lived in Lyman County with their children, Eva and William Jr. In the 1940 U.S. Census, William was working in the CCC program in Bennett County. William re-enlisted in the Army on March 6, 1942, and served as a Tech Sergeant. In 1944, he married Lena Fast Wolf at Kadoka. William entered the spirit world in Rapid City on Feb. 7, 1969. His widow and daughter, Gladys, as well as six step children, Garfield, William, Leo, Algenia, Joan and Laura, survived him. He is buried in the Black Hills National Cemetery, section E, site 1239. Lena (1902-1976) is buried with him.[3]

Iron Shell, Charles. Charles was born on the Rosebud Reservation on April 5, 1892. In the 1900 U.S. Census, he is listed with his parents, Arnold Swimming Skunk and Nellie, as well as his brother, Isaac, and sisters, Lucy and Emma. In the early 1900s, Arnold served as a Private in the Indian Police. When Charles registered for the draft on June 5, 1917, he was farming near Wososo. He joined the Army on Aug. 26, 1918, and was sent to Camp Funston, KS. Here he was assigned to Battery B, 28th Field Artillery, 10th Division. This division did not go overseas. Pvt. Iron Shell was discharged on Jan. 25, 1919. In the 1920 U.S. Census, Charles was listed as a widower living with his son, Everett. Later that year, he married Cora Rosalie DuBray (1898-1973). In 1921, Charles was a member of the Chauncey Eagle Horn Legion Post in Rosebud. In the 1940 U.S. Census, Charles and Rosalie were farming in Todd County with their children, Viola, Minerva, George, Charles, Eugene, Kenneth, Calvin, Teresa, Marie and Frederick. Several of Charles' sons, including George and Eugene served in the military. Charles later moved to Hastings, NE. He entered the spirit world at the VA Hospital in Grand Island, NE, on Jan. 8, 1971. His widow, four sons, and four daughters survived him. He is buried in St. Charles Cemetery in St. Francis, SD.[4]

Iron Shell, Isaac. Isaac was born on the Rosebud Reservation on April 20, 1897, to Arnold and Nellie Iron Shell. He was a younger brother of Charles. Isaac registered for the draft on June 5, 1918 at Wososo. He joined the Army on Aug. 26, 1918. He was discharged on May 2, 1919. In 1920, he married Susie Standing Bull (1902-1974). In the 1940 U.S. Census, they were farming in Todd County with their children, Mercy, Isaac Jr., Zona, Lucille, Bernadine and Rita Marie. Isaac's father, Arnold was also living with them. Isaac Jr. served in the Army at the end of WWII. His father passed away on Feb. 27, 1972, at a Hot Springs hospital. He is buried in St. Mary's Cemetery at Parmelee.[5]

Iron Shell, Louis Young. Louis was born on the Rosebud Reservation on July 6, 1894. His parents were John Iron Shell and Mary Horned Lightning. When Louis registered for the draft on June 5, 1917, he was farming with his brother, Frank. Louis likely enlisted in a SD National Guard regiment which was sent to Camp Cody, NM, where the 34th Division was training. Louis was assigned to the

Supply Co., 127th Field Artillery, 34th Division (ASN 1434381). Sgt. Iron Shell sailed from New York aboard the *City of York* on Sept. 25, 1918. After the war, Sgt. of Ordnance Iron Shell sailed back to the States from Bordeaux aboard the *Powhatan* on Dec. 25, 1918, arriving on Jan. 7, 1919. He was discharged on Jan. 22, 1919. Louis married Alice Short Bull on July 7, 1925, in Kadoka. They had three children, John, Myrtle and Philomine. In the 1930 U.S. Census, they lived in Todd County. When Louis signed up with the Selective Service in 1942, they were living in St. Francis. In 1945, their son, John, enlisted in the Air Corps. Louis entered the spirit world on Oct. 11, 1949, and is buried in St. Charles Cemetery.

Iron Thunder, Joseph. Joseph was born on the Standing Rock Reservation around June 1889. In the 1892 Hunkpapa Census Roll, he is listed with his parents, Bernard and Agatha, as well as his grandmother, Catch the Eagle. In the 1917 Census Roll, Joseph was listed with his wife, Gertrude Brought Plenty. When he registered for the draft on June 5, 1917, he was farming near Bullhead. He joined the Army at McIntosh on Aug. 15, 1918, and was sent to Camp Dodge, IA. He served with the Convalescent Center. On Sept. 12, 1918, the *Sioux County Pioneer* published a letter that Pvt. Iron Thunder had sent home.

> I am here in the camp for over two weeks leading a soldier's life. It is sure a great life for the boys. It was not so hard for me on the start as I had a little of the training at school, and it sure comes in handy these days. I will ask you to send my paper down here so I will know the doings at home. When you see my wife and baby in town sometime give my best regards and good luck to her. I am anxious to be in France soon, as I am game all around. Will close with my best regards to you.

Pvt. Iron Thunder was discharged at Camp Dodge on Feb. 19, 1919. He became a member of the American Legion in Bullhead. In the 1920 Census Roll, he and Gertrude have two daughters, Margaret and Ethel. After Gertrude passed away, Joseph married Eliza Melbourne in Poplar, MT, on May 26, 1922. In 1935, a worker with the SDERA program interviewed Joseph and Eliza. Joseph was living in a tent near a dam construction project and used the two horses he owned on the work site. He indicated that the dams would not hold water and were located in areas where nobody had livestock. He had a permanent home six miles west and two north from Bullhead. Joseph later married Margaret Archambault in 1945. Margaret had two brothers, Leo and Allan Little Eagle who served in WWI. Joseph entered the spirit world on Sept. 24, 1955, after being struck by a car near McLaughlin. He is buried in a Bullhead cemetery.[6]

Irons, Ben or Bennett. Ben was born about Feb. 13, 1892, in Winfred, SD. In some of the census rolls, his name was written as "Iorns." His parents were Benjamin and Lillian Irons. In the 1910 U.S. Census, his father served as a clergyman in the Congregational Church in Redfield, SD. When Ben registered for the draft on June 5, 1917, he was farming near Morristown in Corson County. He wrote that he had already served three years in the SD National Guard, likely on the Mexican Border. Ben likely enlisted in Co. K, 4th SD Infantry at Lemmon in the summer of 1917. On Oct. 19, 1917, the Morristown newspaper published at letter from Ben in which he said the National Guard companies had been converted to the 148th MG Company after they arrived in North Carolina. Wagoner Irons was assigned to the Headquarters Co., 148th MG Battalion, with whom he sailed from Hoboken, NJ, aboard the *Olympic* on Jan. 11, 1918. After arriving in France, he was assigned to Co. E, 107th Ammo Train, 32nd (Red Arrow) Division (ASN 112409). After the war, Pfc. Irons sailed from Brest, France, aboard the U.S.S. *Louisiana* on May 1, 1919. He was discharged on June 26, 1919. On Oct. 11, 1919, he married Luzetta Ruth Waggoner (1900-1995). In 1927, they were living in

Brainerd, MN. In the 1930 U.S. Census, they were living near Thunder Hawk. In the 1932 Standing Rock Census Roll, Ben is listed but was not enrolled. Their children at that time were June, Ernest William (Billy) and Iris. A few years later they had a son, Allen. In 1935, the family was interviewed by a state worker with the SDERA program. The family was then renting two rooms in a house in Thunder Hawk, while Ben was a patient at the Battle Mountain Hospital near Hot Springs. In the 1940 U.S. Census, the family was farming near Walker, MN. Ben was a member of the VFW and the American Legion. Billy Irons served as a paratrooper in WWII. Allen died in a car accident at Fort Bragg, NC, in 1957. Ben entered the spirit world on Nov. 9, 1964, and is buried in Rest Haven Memorial Gardens in Ft. Collins, CO. Luzetta's mother, Josephine, spent many years working on a history of the Lakota People. Luzetta's son, Billy, was one of the people who worked at helping to get the manuscript ready for publishing. *WITNESS: A Hunkpapa Historian's Strong-Heart Song of the Lakotas* was published in 2013. Ben's brother, Dean, served with the 1st Division in France.[7]

Irving, Amos. Amos was born on the Crow Creek Reservation on June 15, 1896. His parents were Joseph Irving and Eliza Renville. Amos enlisted in the Army on May 1, 1917. He served in Co. H, 159th Infantry, 40th Division (ASN 1420739). The 40th Division arrived in France on Aug. 24, 1918. Many soldiers in the 40th Division were reassigned to other divisions as replacements. Pvt. Irving returned home from Bordeaux aboard the *Edgar F. Luckenbach* on March 22, 1919, and was discharged on April 21, 1919. On April 9, 1920, he married Martha Ellis (1895-1982). In the 1930 U.S. Census, Amos was working as a janitor in a school dorm. He spent his career working as an engineer on several different reservations, until retiring in 1961. In 1963 he moved to Lake Andes, where he entered the spirit world in his home on Jan. 15, 1973. He is buried in Lake View Cemetery in Lake Andes.

Irving, Jerome. Jerome, the younger brother of Amos, was born in Sisseton on March 11, 1899, and moved to Crow Creek as an infant. His parents were Joseph Irving and Eliza Renville. Jerome served in the military from Oct. 9, 1920 to Aug. 27, 1921. In 1925, he married Hulda Petersen (1900-1988). In the 1930 U.S. Census, Jerome was working as a laborer and Hulda worked as a teacher. In the 1937 Crow Creek Census Roll, they have three children, Victor, Katherine and Elizabeth. Victor passed away in 1962, while serving in the Navy. Jerome entered the spirit world in St. Mary's Hospital in Pierre on Feb. 23, 1980, and is buried in Riverside Cemetery in Pierre. His wife, Hulda, and daughters, Kathryn and Elizabeth, survived him.

Iyott, Amos J. Amos was born on the Rosebud Reservation on July 3, 1893. His parents were Henry Iyott and Martha On the Ground. When Amos registered for the draft on June 5, 1917, he was living in St. Francis. He joined the Army on May 25, 1918 at Rosebud. He served in the Headquarters Co. 213th Engineers, 13th Division (ASN 3129718). He was discharged as a Private 1st Class on Feb. 21, 1919, at Camp Lewis, WA. He married Julia Crazy Hawk. In the 1930 U.S. Census, Amos was working as a janitor in the Ashhurst Hospital on the Rosebud Reservation. In the 1940 U.S. Census, Amos was working as a laborer on a CCC landscaping project at the St. Francis Mission. He and Julia had six children, John, Patrick, Frederick, Catherine, Marie and Winifred. John served in the Army during WWII, and Patrick served in the Air Corps. Amos entered the spirit world on March 24, 1950. He is buried in St. Charles Cemetery in St. Francis.

J

Jackson, Arthur. Arthur and his twin brother, Cleveland, were born on the Rosebud Reservation on Nov. 3, 1895. Their parents were Joseph Jackson and Mary Bissonette. Arthur grew up near the mouth of White Thunder Creek on the Big White River. He later attended school in Rapid City. When he registered for the draft on June 5, 1917, he was farming near Wood. He married Laura Claymore. Arthur joined the Army on July 22, 1918. That summer he was photographed in his uniform with other men who had attended school at St. Francis. Pfc. Jackson was discharged on Jan. 26, 1919. The family ranched on his mother's allotment on White Thunder Creek. They had six children, Lavern, Catherine, Melvin, Joseph, Lena and Sylvia. Lavern served in the Army in WWII. Melvin enlisted in the Navy on June 7, 1943, and retired on July 2, 1966, as a Chief Ship Fitter. After retiring, he wrote a book, *War Pipe-Peace Pipe*. Arthur entered the spirit world on April 21, 1980. His wife and six children survived him. He is buried in St. Thomas Catholic Cemetery, Antelope.[1]

Jackson, Cleveland J. Cleveland, the twin brother of Arthur, was born on the Rosebud Reservation on Nov. 3, 1895, to Joseph Jackson and Mary Bissonette. Cleveland was farming when he registered for the draft on June 5, 1917. When he joined the Army, he was assigned to Co. I, 8th Infantry, 8th Division (ASN 507139). Pvt. Jackson sailed from Hoboken, NJ, aboard the *Wilhelmina* on Oct. 28, 1918. After arriving in France, he was reassigned to Co. H, 28th Infantry, 1st Division. Pfc. Jackson sailed from Brest aboard the U.S.S. *Siboney* on Aug. 25, 1919, arriving stateside on Sept. 2. He was discharged on Sept. 24, 1919. After he returned home, he married Phoebe Afraid of Bear (1901-1991). In the 1930 U.S. Census, the family was farming with his parents. They had five children, Floyd, Emma, Adeline, Nick and Lupe. Cleveland entered the spirit world in his home in Wood on Feb. 1, 1968. Military rites were conducted by the McBride Legion Post of Wood and the Otterman Post from White River. He is buried in St. Thomas Catholic Cemetery at Antelope, Todd County.[2]

Jacobs, Donald. Donald is listed on WWI veteran's memorial at Oglala Lakota College, Kyle, SD. Donald was born in Rushville, NE, on May 3, 1895, to William and Caroline Jacobs. When William registered for the draft on June 5, 1917, he was working as a ranch hand near Oglala. He joined the Navy on May 30, 1918. He was discharged as a Ships Cook, 3rd Class. In the 1920 U.S. Census, he was working as a cook in Sheridan County, possibly near White Clay. In 1923, he married Ellen McFarren. In the 1940 U.S. Census, they were farming in Shannon County. They later move to the West Coast. In 1942, Donald was working as a civilian at Mare Island, CA. They later moved to Seattle, where he entered the spirit world on Dec. 27, 1966. He is buried in Williamette National Cemetery, Section K, site 5682.

Jandreau, Daniel. Daniel was born in Avon, SD, on the Yankton Reservation around March 15, 1896, to James and Emma Jandreau. In the 1902 Yanktonai Census Roll, Daniel had a sister, Grace. When Daniel registered for the draft on June 5, 1917, he was farming near Dante, SD. He joined the Army on June 27, 1918, and was assigned to Co. F, 351st Infantry, 88th Division (ASN 3315380). He served with a number of other men from the Yankton Reservation, including Peter Hopkins, Samuel Dion, Jesse Kezena and Roy Cook. The 351st sailed from New York aboard the *Scotian* on Aug. 15, 1918, arriving in France on Sept. 6. The 351st Infantry was billeted in quiet sectors and did not serve at the Front. After the Armistice, Pvt. Jandreau received an evaluation from his commanding officer, stating he was a "well-disciplined soldier. Efficient as a night observer and scout. Is regarded as an unusually good man by whites. Well-liked and mixes readily with whites." Company F of the 351st Regiment was billeted at Liffol-le-Grand, where they did convoy duty on ration trains going to Germany. On May 20, 1919, the 351st boarded the ship *Mercury* in St. Nazaire to return to the States. Pvt. Jandreau was discharged on June 9, 1919. In 1920, he married Maggie World Turner, who had two children, Pansy and Harry, from an earlier marriage. The family farmed in Rouse Township. Daniel entered the spirit world in Dante on Oct. 24, 1972.[3]

Jandreau, Frank H. Frank was born near Geddes, SD, on March 29, 1893, to Mazar and Louise Jandreau. He was living in Geddes when he registered for the draft on June 4, 1917. On Oct. 17, 1917, he married Edith Tuttle (1897-1982). Frank joined the Army on June 27, 1918. He was assigned to Co. F, 313th Ammo Train, 88th Division (ASN 3315318). On Aug. 18, 1918, the 313th Ammo Train sailed for Europe on the ship *Vedic*. He was later transferred to the 7th Corps, Headquarters MP Company. Pfc. Jandreau sailed from Brest aboard the *Mongolia* on July 30, 1919, and was discharged on Aug. 15, 1919. The family farmed in Goose Lake Township. In the 1940 U.S. Census, Frank and Edith were living with their sons, Woodrow and Raymond, as well as Frank's mother, Louise. Raymond served in the Army in WWII. Frank entered the spirit world on Nov. 13, 1966, and is buried in Pleasant Lawn Cemetery in Geddes.

Janis, Bernard. Bernard was born on the Pine Ridge Reservation on Oct. 29, 1899. His parents were Edward and Rose Janis. When Bernard registered for the draft on Sept. 1, 1918, he was working in Conata. He likely enlisted shortly after that. His branch of service is not known. In 1921, he married Cornelia Hunter. He ranched for a number of years before becoming a federal police officer on the reservation. In the 1940 U.S. Census, he was working in road construction. At that time, he and Cornelia had three daughters, Marie, Myrna and Loretta, and a son, Sylvester. Sylvester served in the Army in the 1960s. Cornelia passed away in 1948. In the early 1950s, Bernard started driving a school bus at Kyle. He also served on the Tribal Council. In 1965, he married Jessie Black Bear. Bernard entered the spirit world in the Sioux Sanatorium in Rapid City on Dec. 15, 1970. His widow, son and three daughters survived him. He is buried in St. Stephen's Cemetery, Kyle.[4]

Francis Janis
Oglala Lakota College

Janis, Francis. Francis was born on Aug. 7, 1898, on the Pine Ridge Reservation. His parents were Benjamin Janis and Susanna Richard. Benjamin had served as Sergeant in the Scouts with the U.S. Army. As a young man, Francis went to school at Flandreau. On April 4, 1917, he enlisted in Troop D, 1st SD Cavalry. Without horses and saddles, this regiment drilled as an infantry unit in South Dakota for the summer of 1917. In September, they proceeded to Camp Cody, NM. Pvt. Janis sailed for Europe aboard the S.S. *Tereisias* on June 28, 1918. He was attached to Co. 14, Camp Cody June Automatic Replacement Draft (ASN 1427461). After arriving in France, he was transferred to Battery A, 19th Field Artillery (FA), 5th Division. Three other students from Flandreau served in Battery A with Pvt. Janis. The 19th FA served in the following Sectors: St. Die, Villers-en Haye, St. Mihiel, Limey, and Puvelle. After the Armistice, Pvt. Janis received an evaluation from 1st Lt. William Sumner stating that Janis was "a very good soldier; shows special ability for caring for animals." As part of the Army of Occupation, the 19th FA was stationed near Hasperange, Luxembourg. The 5th Division suffered 8,840 casualties in the war. Pfc. Janis sailed from Brest, France, aboard the *America* on July 13, 1919. He was discharged on July 29, 1919. After the war, Janis' name was engraved on a plaque erected to honor the veterans from the school at Flandreau.

After returning home, Francis married Ida Cora Bird Necklace. In the 1930 U.S. Census, Francis was working as a truck driver with the Indian Service at the Pine Ridge Agency. In the 1937 Census Roll, Francis and Cora are listed with five sons. Clarence and Curtis served in the Army in the WWII era, Guy served in the Navy, and Ival and Pat served in the Air Force. They later had another son, Wendell. Francis entered the spirit world in the Pine Ridge Public Health Hospital on Sept. 20, 1980, and is buried in Red Cloud Cemetery. Cora passed away later that same year.[5]

Janis, Stephen. Stephen was born on June 19, 1898, on the Rosebud Reservation. His parents were Morris and Josephine Janis. Stephen joined the Army on May 6, 1918, and was assigned to Pack Train #327, Quartermaster Corps (ASN 507621). This unit served in France. Pfc. Janis sailed from Brest aboard the *E.L. Doheny III* on June 23, 1919, and was discharged on July 18, 1919. After returning home, he married Rose Whipple, with whom he had a son, Earl. On Sept. 24, 1927, he married Sarah Bordeaux in Mission. They had a daughter, Mildred. In 1935, the family was interviewed by a worker with the SDERA program. They lived with Sarah's brothers, Earnest and Philip, six miles NE of White River. In the winter, they stayed in the house. In the summer, they lived in a tent. Stephen had been working on a reforestation project. Earlier he had worked for a number of years in the mine at Lead, but it was hard work. He stated that he was "thin as a snake" when he left that job. He later was hired by the Indian Service as a police officer. Stephen became sick with Encephalitis and entered the spirit world in the Rosebud Hospital on Aug. 20, 1938. He is buried In Trinity Cemetery in Mission. Stephen's son, Earl, enlisted in the Navy in 1945, and retired after 20 years as a Chief Ship fitter.[6]

George Jensen
Oglala Lakota College

Jensen, George. George is listed on WWI veteran's memorial at Oglala Lakota College, Kyle, SD. He was born on June 18, 1898, on the Pine Ridge Reservation. His parents were John Jensen and Romana Martinez. George attended school at the boarding school in Rapid City. School records show that George would occasionally hop a train to get away from school. George enlisted in the 4th Infantry, South Dakota National Guard in Rapid City on March 28, 1917, which was prior to President Wilson's Declaration of War. When the SD Guardsmen arrived at Camp Greene, NC, they were re-assigned to 41st Division. Pvt. Jensen was assigned to Co. B., 148th Machine Gun (MG) Battalion (ASN 112131). Saddler Jensen sailed with his unit from Hoboken, NJ, aboard the *Olympic* on Jan. 11, 1918. Upon arrival in France, many soldiers were sent as replacements to the 42nd (Rainbow) Division. Pvt. Jensen served in Co. C, 151st MG Battalion. Several other SD soldiers, including Oscar Weasel and Shadrach Ponca, ended up in the same unit. The 42nd Division suffered almost 14,000 casualties in the war. Pvt. Jensen was one of the many men who were gassed. Pvt. Jensen sailed from Brest, France, aboard the *Minnesota* on April 15, 1919, and was discharged at Camp Dodge, IA, on May 12, 1919. George summarized his military service in a statement sent to Joseph Dixon. "Serve in France one year in France and Germany 6 or 7 months. And in trenches 110 days. And on the offences [sic] several months. And lot of experiences. But I won't tell them all." The 151st MG Bn. is credited with service in the following campaigns: Champagne-Marne, Aisne-Marne, St. Mihiel, Meuse-Argonne, Luneville, Baccarat, Esperance-Souain, and Essey-Pannes.

Upon his return home, George worked as a ranch hand and was known as a top cowboy. His picture was displayed in museums in Miles City, MT, and Cheyenne, WY. He worked on ranches in South Dakota, Wyoming, Nebraska and Montana. Around 1930, he married Delilah Peneaux. They had a son, Delbert. In the early 1960s, he was a member of the Oglala Tribal Council from the Medicine Root District. He was a member of American Legion Post No. 265 at Kyle. George entered the spirit world in the Bennett County Nursing Home on Oct. 27, 1988, and is buried in St. Stephen's Cemetery.[7]

George Jewett
JoLavae Gunville

Jewett, George. George was born around Jan. 1, 1889, on the Cheyenne River Reservation. His parents were Louis and Mary Jewett. He was ranching near White Horse when he registered for the draft on June 5, 1917. He joined the Army on Oct. 5, 1917, and was assigned to Troop B, 314th MP Company (ASN 2194453). While stationed at Camp Funston, George and Thomas Hawk Eagle played for the camp's football team. A number of other soldiers from Cheyenne River and Standing Rock Reservations were in that Company. They sailed for France from New York aboard the *Saxon* on June 28, 1918. As part of the 89th Division, they served in the Sectors at Lucey, St. Mihiel, Euvezin and Meuse-Argonne. Two men from their Company, Pvt. Moses Clown and Pvt. Joseph Takes the Shield, were killed in action on Nov. 1, 1918. A group photo of the MP Company was taken in April of 1919. Most of the unit returned to the States in mid-May. About that time, Pfc. Jewett was taken to a hospital in Kyllburg, Germany. He finally sailed for home from Brest, France, aboard the S.S. *Nopatin* on May 30, 1919. He traveled with Brest Casual Co. No. 895. Pfc. Jewett was discharged on June 24, 1919.

In the 1920 U.S. Census, George served as one of the enumerators. On Oct 14, 1920, he married Katherine "Keva" Rousseau. They ranched in Dewey County, except for a number of years in the 1940s when George was a civilian guard at Ellsworth AFB. He served six years on the Cheyenne River Tribal Council, including four years as vice chairman. George was a member of the World War Veterans of Mobridge and the American Legion at Eagle Butte. George and Catherine had 10 children, Corina, Ramona, Iyone, Julie, Juanita, Louis, Keith, Orlin, and the twins, Arthur and Albert, known as Pinkie and Bluie. Both Arthur and Albert served in the Army. Arthur was killed in action in Korea and was MIA until 2009. Louis, Orlin and Keith served in the Navy. George entered the spirit world in the Eagle Butte Hospital on Aug. 13, 1975. Military honors were provided by American Legion Post No. 191 of Eagle Butte. He is buried in St. Theresa's Cemetery, White Horse.[8]

Jewett, Joseph. Joseph was a younger brother of George. He was born about Nov. 22, 1892, on the Cheyenne River Reservation. In the 1896 Census Roll, he is listed with his parents, Louis and Mary, as well as his brothers, Charles and George, and his grandmother, Red Owl. When he registered for the draft on June 5, 1917, he was working for Charles Maupin. Joseph joined the Army on May 24, 1918, and was first assigned to Co. K, 157th Infantry, 40th Division (ASN 2787855). He sailed from Boston aboard the *Berrina* on Aug. 9, 1918. Many of the soldiers from the 40th Division were reassigned shortly before the start of the Meuse-Argonne Offensive. On Sept. 23, 1918, Pfc. Jewett was assigned to Co. K, 305th Infantry (77th Division), along with Pfc. David Drops at a Distance. On Oct. 28, 1918, he went on sick call. He rejoined the regiment on Dec. 23, 1918. The 305th Infantry sailed from Brest, France, aboard the H.M.S. *Aquitania* on April 18, 1919. Pfc.

Jewett was discharged on May 18, 1919. A few years after returning home, he married Agnes Two Lance. In the 1937 Census Roll, the family included two children, Delores and Melvin. Melvin served with the Marine Corps in the Korean War. Joseph and Agnes had several more children, including Carrie, Waldon, Fern, Lillian and Lucille. The family lived near Promise, before moving to Mobridge, after Joseph had a disagreement with the Tribal Cattle Payment Program. Joseph entered the spirit world in the VA Hospital in Hot Springs on Dec. 20, 1962, and is buried near Promise.[9]

Jim, Kiutus. Kiutus was born in Toppenish, WA, on the Yakima Reservation around June 25, 1891. In the 1907 Census Roll, he was listed as an orphan. In the 1910 U.S. Census, he was a student at the Chemawa boarding school, where he excelled as a marathon runner. When he registered for the draft on June 4, 1917, he was working as a laborer at the Cheyenne River Agency. He was one of the young men in the second group of inductees to leave Timber Lake for Camp Funston in September of 1917 to train with the 89th Division. Other local men who were with him on the train were William Bowker, Napoleon Ducheneaux, Armstrong Four Bear and Basil Flanagan. Sgt. Jim was assigned to Co. B, 340 Machine Gun (MG) Battalion (ASN 2193043)). Sgt. Jim sailed for France from New York aboard the *Khyber* on June 4, 1918. The 340th MG Bn. served in the Sectors at Lucey, St. Mihiel, Euvezin and Meuse-Argonne. Sgt. Jim was wounded and later received a Purple Heart. After the Armistice, Sgt. Jim's commanding officer wrote that he was "proven a natural leader in the ranks. Demonstrated fitness for Machine Gun work and scouting." He returned home from Brest, France, aboard the *Leviathan* on May 15, 1919. After the war, Kiutus wrote to Joseph Dixon stating, "my experience of Great War, that American Indian was well thought of by Officers and men."

Kiutus returned to his home near Toppenish, WA, where he married Rose Hadley. As a disabled veteran, Kiutus was active in the American Legion and the DAV. He helped organize a Legion Post at White Swan, which was the first all-native American Legion Post in the Nation. He was also active in tribal government. He was active in supporting athletics for youth. He enjoyed capturing and breaking horses. The Kiutus Jim Memorial Run is still held annually in Yakima. Kiutus entered the spirit world on April 24, 1960, at the VA hospital in Walla Walla, WA. Hs wife, Rose, and nine children, Myrtle, Marie, Maymie, Tillie, Victoria, Robert, Ralph, Russell and Kiutus Jr., survived him. He is buried in Toppenish Creek Cemetery.[10]

Jones, Benjamin H. Ben was born in Flandreau on July 17, 1891. In the 1892 Census Roll, he is listed with his father, William, and his mother, Ellen (Mindutawin), as well as a brother, Hobart. When he registered for the draft on June 5, 1917, he was working as a teamster in Flandreau. Ben served 10 months in the Army and was discharged as a Private on Feb. 1, 1919. He did not serve overseas. He likely served along the Mexican border. After returning home, he worked for 10 years in a packing plant in Sioux Falls. On Feb. 21, 1931, he married Maud Cavander, who had two daughters, Sarah and Hattie, with her first husband. Ben and Maud had a daughter, Evelyn. In the mid-1930s, Ben worked at delivering coal. In the 1940 U.S. Census, he was working as a foreman on a relief project. Ben's mother, Ellen, was living with the family, as was Ben's younger brother, Harry. Ben entered the spirit world in the VA hospital in Sioux Falls on Feb. 13, 1962. He is buried in the 1st Presbyterian Cemetery, Flandreau.[11]

Jones, Harry. Harry, a younger brother of Ben, was born on Sept. 26, 1899, to William and Ellen Jones. Harry was a student at Haskell Institute, where he played football. Harry joined the Army on April 13, 1918. He was assigned as a Bugler to Battery E, 48th Artillery, Coast Artillery Corps (ASN

465358). The 48th Artillery was organized at Camp Eustis, VA, and shipped to France in October of 1918. Bugler Jones sailed with his unit from Newport News, VA, aboard the *Susquehana*. After the Armistice, he sailed from St. Nazaire aboard the *Zeelandia* on Feb. 28, 1919. Bugler Jones was discharged on March 23, 1919. He returned home to Flandreau. His name is engraved on a plaque erected in honor of the students who served in the military during the war. In the 1940 U.S. Census, he was single and living with his brother's family. Sometime after this he moved to Torrance, CA. He entered the spirit world on Dec. 28, 1960, and is buried in Fort Rosecrans National Cemetery, section V, site 206.

Jordan, John. John was born near Mound City, SD, on Nov. 15, 1894. His parents were Arnold and Annie (Tatuye) Jordan. His father had been a soldier in the Army. When John registered for the draft on June 5, 1917, he was working for the Indian Service at Kenel. He joined the Army at McLaughlin on June 23, 1918. He was first sent to Camp Funston, KS. About a month later, he was transferred to Camp Dodge, IA, where the 88th Division was preparing to go to France. He was assigned to Co. D, 352nd Infantry, 88th Division (ASN 2703735). Pvt. Jordan left Brooklyn aboard the *Ascanius* to go overseas on Aug. 15, 1918. On Sept. 23, 1918, he was promoted to Pfc. on Oct. 19, 1918, he was promoted to Corporal. After the Armistice, the 88th Division was assigned to billets around the French city of Gondrecourt. The men of Co. D were billeted in the village of Ribeaucourt, which they regularly policed and swept. After their tour there, the men knew every street corner, every house. They had walked post past its barns and houses, built one to the other, until they knew every window, every iron bar, and every door. Corporal Jordan left St. Nazaire, France, aboard the *Canonicus* on May 21, 1919. John reported that the trip back was a stormy voyage. A floating mine was sighted and sank by sharpshooters on board. His regiment was quartered for a short time at Camp Morrison before traveling by train to Camp Dodge, IA, where he was discharged on June 13, 1919. John brought back a German watch as a souvenir.

After the war, John married Susan Defender, whose brother, Ben, had also served in the Army for a short time. John's brother, Joseph, also served in the Army during the war. The family ranched in Corson County. In the 1930 U.S. Census, John and Susie shared their home with John's mother, Annie, and her husband, Albert Young Eagle. In the 1937 Census Roll, the family had four children, Walter, Delores, Elsie and Irlene. John entered the spirit world in the McLaughlin Community Hospital on Feb. 20, 1976. He is buried in Assumption Catholic Cemetery in Kenel.[12]

K

Keeble, Mark. Mark was born on Aug. 11, 1899, to George Keeble and Walks with Owl. In the 1901 Wahpeton-Sisseton Census Roll, Mark is listed with his father and his sister, Cora. In the early 1900s, the family moved to the Crow Creek Reservation. Mark enlisted in the Army on Aug. 14, 1918, and served as a Private with the 43rd Company, 162nd Depot Brigade at Camp Pike, Arkansas (ASN 3776740). He was discharged on April 19, 1919. Mark married Grace Never Misses (1905-1945). In the 1940 U.S. Census, they lived with their children, Marie, Harriet, Frances and Martha. Mark entered the spirit world in Lake Andes on July 1, 1966, and is buried in St. Joseph's Cemetery, Ft. Thompson, SD.[1]

Keeler, Henry. Henry and his identical twin brother, John, were born about April 15, 1877, on the Rosebud Reservation. Their parents were Alexander and Sarah Keeler. Sarah and her children were enrolled on the Yanktonai Reservation. Henry and his brother attended Haskell Boarding School, and likely played baseball as young men. The roster of the semi-pro team, The Nebraska Indians, included twin brothers who were mentioned as H. Keeler and J. Keeler. They were very good players and liked to confuse the players on opposing teams with deceptive base running. Henry was married several times. His first marriage was to Ellen Howe, with whom he had a son Sylvester. His second marriage was to Millie Yuhapiwin. They had Katherine and Edison. In 1916, Henry married Lillian Birdhead. On Jan. 15, 1918, Henry joined the Army at Jefferson Barracks, MO. He was assigned to Second Wing Concentration Brigade, Air Service at Kelly Field, TX, (ASN 1068993). He was discharged as a Corporal on Jan. 5, 1919. After the war, Henry lived with his family in Wagner. He entered the spirit world in Pinard Hospital in Wagner on Aug. 13, 1922. He is buried in Greenwood Cemetery. Henry's son, Sylvester, served in World War I. His son, Edison, served with the Navy in World War II.[2]

Keeler, John. John was born on the Rosebud Reservation around April 15, 1877, but was enrolled on the Yanktonai Sioux Reservation. He was Henry's identical twin. Many people had trouble telling them apart. John likely played baseball with Henry on some semi-pro teams around the turn of the century. In the 1900 U.S. Census, John lived with his wife, Mary, his son, Vincent, and his brother, Henry. After Mary entered the spirit world, he married Alice Conger. John also enlisted in the Army at Jefferson Barracks, MO, on Jan. 15, 1918. He was assigned to Co. G, 5th Development Battalion at Camp MacArthur, TX, (ASN 1069001). He was discharged as a Sergeant on Nov. 22, 1918. In the 1920 U.S. Census, he was working as a house carpenter in Wahehe Township, Charles Mix County. He and Alice had two daughters, Julia and Rachel. Around 1930, John moved to Minneapolis, where he worked as a carpenter. He passed away in his home there on Dec. 26, 1931. He is buried in Greenwood Cemetery. The Greer Post of the American Legion had charge of the military rites at the grave.[3]

Keeler, Sylvester. Sylvester was born at Wagner on July 21, 1901. His parents were Henry and Ellen (Howe) Keeler. After his mother was divorced from Henry, she lived with Joseph Cooper on the Crow Creek Reservation. Sylvester and his sister were listed with their mother. He enlisted in the Army on April 3, 1918, and was assigned to Co. D, 48th Infantry, 20th Division (ASN 465348). On April 4, 1919, he re-enlisted in the Army and was assigned to Troop A, 13th Cavalry. In the 1920 U.S. Census, he was stationed at Fort Clark, TX, with the Army. He was finally discharged on July 27, 1921, as a Corporal. Sylvester entered the spirit world on Sept. 9, 1923, suffering from tuberculosis in the VA Hospital in Helena, MT. He is buried in the Greenwood Cemetery near his father.[4]

Keith, Hobart. Hobart is listed on WWI veteran's memorial at Oglala Lakota College, Kyle, SD. Hobart was born on the Pine Ridge Reservation on Nov. 25, 1897. His mother, Maggie Goulette, was enrolled with the Yanktonai Sioux. His father, Edgar Keith, was a school teacher at a day school on the Pine Ridge Reservation. His mother worked as a housekeeper at Day School No. 7. In the 1902 Yanktonai Census Roll, Hobart is listed with his mother and sisters, Mary, Jessie, Alice Amanda, Elaine, and Irene. Hobart enlisted in the Navy during the war, and was discharged on July 3, 1919. After his return, he married Louise Ecoffey (1899-1976) on July 31, 1919. They farmed in Bennett County. In the 1930 U.S. Census, they are listed with their children, Verna, Cecil Hobart Jr., Ethel, Joseph and Mary. In the 1940 U.S. Census, Hobart was working on road construction. Later, the family moved out to Poulsbo, WA, where he worked as a carpenter. Hobart may have also served in the Navy during WWII. His son, Cecil, became a tribal judge and was well known as an artist. Cecil served with the Navy in WWII. Hobart entered the spirit world in the Washington

Veterans' Home at Retsil on March 30, 1978, and is buried in Suquamish Memorial Cemetery, Kitsap County.[5]

Kelly, Fred. Fred was born on the Pine Ridge Reservation on April 24, 1894. On Nov. 6, 1917, he enlisted in the Army at Ft. Logan, CO. He was assigned to the 11th Co., 154th Depot Brigade at Camp Meade, Maryland (ASN 1086497). He may also have served with the Air Service. He had some health problems and was discharged at Camp Meade on Oct. 7, 1918. In some records, Fred is also known as Earl Goings. He was married to Gertrude White Bird, whose brother, Henry, served in the Army. Fred entered the spirit world on Jan. 17, 1940 and is buried in Holy Cross Cemetery.

Kemery, Charles E. Charles likely was born on the Crow Creek Reservation around Jan. 5, 1894. His parents were William Kemery and Mattie Oldham. Charles was enrolled with the Yanktonai Sioux at Crow Creek Agency. On May 30, 1917, Charles registered for the draft in Armstrong County. He said he had a .32 caliber bullet in his left knee, but it did not disable him. He was ranching near the Cheyenne Agency. He and his wife, Emma Sheppard, had a daughter, Alive. On July 8, 1918, he registered again. At that time, he was working in the round house for the Rock Island Railroad in Estherville, IA, and did not have any dependents. On Aug. 26, 1918, he joined the Army. He was discharged on Nov. 26, 1918. On July 6, 1936, he married Clela Mullen (1904-1965) in Burke, SD. In the 1940 U.S. Census, he and Clela were living in Vermillion and running plumbing business. When he registered for the Selective Service in 1942, he was working for Melgren Plumbing in Rapid City. Charles later moved to Colorado, where he entered the spirit world on July 3, 1972. He is buried in Crown Hill Cemetery, Wheat Ridge, CO.

Kezena, Jesse. Jesse was born in Greenwood, SD, on Nov. 27, 1894. His parents were Paul (Arrow Beard) Kezena and Eunice Tiyopana [By the Door]. Around 1913, Jesse married Stella Sherman, with whom he had a son, Fred. On April 12, 1915, he married Lema Omaha. When he registered for the draft on June 5, 1917, he was working as a laborer for the Indian Service in Greenwood. When he joined the Army, he was assigned to Co. F, 351st Infantry, 88th Division (ASN 3315291). Pvt. Kezena sailed from New York aboard the *Scotian* on Aug. 15, 1918. He served in Co. F in France with a number of other men from the Yankton Reservation, including Joseph Brother of All, Peter Hopkins, Samuel Dion, Ray Cook and Daniel Jandreau. Pvt. Ulysses Reed also served with them but succumbed to illness while they were still in France. After the Armistice, one of their officers, Lt. J.R. Neely, wrote that these soldiers "are well educated, one being a college man, splendid scouts and good soldiers. The captain would not trade these Indians for an equal number of white men because of their special qualifications." The 351st Infantry returned to the States from St. Nazaire, France, aboard the *Mercury* on May 20, 1919. Pvt. Kezena was discharged on June 7, 1919.

After Jesse returned home, he acquired a life insurance policy. Jesse and Lema had two children, Wilfred and Magdalena. On Armistice Day, Nov. 11, 1920, Jesse was killed while placing his shotgun into his car. After his death, Lema received a payment from the Dakota Life Insurance Co. However, sometime later the insurance company sued to get their money back. They claimed they could only insure Indians who were ¼ Indian blood or less. Jesse was a full blood. In the court case before the South Dakota Supreme Court, Justice Charles Hall Dillon delivered an important dissent, stating,

> The highest function of the court should be to administer justice and not to engage in hairsplitting contests for the purposes of ascertaining the degree of Indian blood that may

be possessed by the insured, especially when investigation, adjustment, and payment of the loss had been made.

Jesse is buried in the Greenwood Cemetery. In March 1921, Lema gave birth to another son, Frank.[6]

Killer, Thomas. Thomas is listed on WWI veteran's memorial at Oglala Lakota College, Kyle, SD. He was born on the Pine Ridge Reservation on March 23, 1898. His parents were Jacob and Emma White Cow Killer. When Thomas registered for the draft on Sept. 12, 1918, he was working as an interpreter for the U.S. Govt. at Pine Ridge. Thomas joined the Army on April 22, 1919 and sailed with his unit from San Francisco for Manila aboard the *Logan* on June 22, 1919. He served with the Coast Artillery Corps in the Philippines (ASN 6411464). He was discharged as a Sergeant on May 2, 1922. Upon returning home, he married Ida Tyon. After his marriage Thomas received a job at the Rapid City Boarding School, earning $720 annually. In 1924, Thomas was earning $1,140. In the 1930 U.S. Census, the family was farming in Shannon County. In the 1937 Census Roll, they had four children, Francis, Robert, Verena and Celeste. In the 1930s, Thomas served as an administrative clerk with the U.S. Indian Service. Thomas developed tuberculosis and entered the spirit world on Feb. 1, 1940. His sons, Francis and Robert, served in the Army during WWII. Francis was killed in action in March 1945 while serving in Europe with the 5th Armored Division. Thomas is buried in Holy Rosary Mission Cemetery.[7]

Kills First, Charles T. Charles was born at Cherry Creek on the Cheyenne River Reservation on Sept. 26, 1895. In the 1899 Census Roll, his mother, Blue Woman, is listed as a widow. When Charles registered for the draft on June 4, 1917, he was ranching at Cherry Creek. He may have first joined the Army in 1917. Records indicate he served eight months overseas. On April 16, 1919, he re-enlisted, serving in Troop E, 13th Cavalry (ASN R4502077). Pvt. Kills First sailed from Hoboken aboard the *Pretoria* on June 13, 1919, traveling with the 28th Co., Camp Meade Replacement Unit #7. In the 1920 U.S. Census, he was stationed at Fort Clark, Kinney, TX. He was discharged as a Corporal on July 29, 1921. In 1925, he married Irene Barrow, with whom he had a son, Frederick. Irene passed away in 1928. Charles lived with his aunt for a while. In 1935, he was interviewed by a worker with the SDERA program. Charles said he had served for four years in the Army and received a small pension. He liked to read and also owned a number of musical instruments. He and several friends, including Charles Fisherman and Thomas Standing Bear played together in an orchestra at white dances, sometimes twice a week. He had previously worked for the Diamond A Ranch. On Jan. 7, 1938, he married Lizzie Carpenter. In 1940, he was working with the C.C.C. program. The family later moved to Rapid City. Charles entered the spirit world on March 15, 1957. He is buried in the Black Hills National Cemetery, Section 5, site 63.[8]

Kills in Sight, George Jake. George was born on the Rosebud Reservation on March 29, 1897. His parents were Charles and Laura (Hollow Horn Bear) Kills in Sight. Charles had served with the 16th Infantry in the early 1890s. George married Emma Medicine. When he registered for the draft on June 5, 1918, he was farming near Wososo. George joined the Army on Sept. 18, 1918. He was discharged as a Private on Dec. 9, 1918. In the 1930 U.S. Census, George was working as a policeman for the Indian Service. He and Emma had two daughters, Mary and Angelline. After Emma passed away in 1938, he married Corrine Flammond (1893-1983). Corrine's first husband, Louis, had served with the Army in France. In the 1940 U.S. Census, George was working as a clerk of court for the Indian Court. His wife, Corrine, was the Postmistress in St. Francis. George also served as chairman of the Rosebud tribal land enterprise. He entered the spirit world in the U.S. P.H.S. Hospital in Rosebud on Sept. 26, 1975, and is buried in St. Charles Cemetery, St. Francis, SD.

Charles Kills in Water
Don Doll, S.J.

Kills in Water, Charles. Charles was born on the Rosebud Reservation on Aug. 19, 1890, to John Kills in Water and Elizabeth Iron Shell. In the 1897 Census Roll, he was listed with his grandparents, Young Iron Shell and Horned Lightning, and a cousin, Louis. When Charles registered for the draft on June 5, 1917, he was living in St. Francis. Charles joined the Army and was assigned to Co. B, 160th Infantry, 40th Division (ASN 3130156). After arriving in France, he was reassigned to 241st Military Police Company. After the Armistice, Cpl. Kills in Water sailed from Brest, France, aboard the *Imperator* on June 12, 1919, arriving on June 20. He was discharged on June 30, 1919. Around 1920, he married Annie White Hollow Horn. In 1921, Charles was a member of the Chauncey Eagle Horn Legion Post at Rosebud. In the 1930 Census, Charles and Annie are listed with their daughter, Adelaide. In the 1940 U.S. Census, the family was farming in Todd County. Charles entered the spirit world on April 16, 1982, and is buried in St. Andrews Cemetery, Spring Creek, SD.

Kills Plenty, Silas. Silas was born on the Rosebud Reservation about Jan. 6, 1894. His parents were James Kills Plenty and Bessie Red Elk. Silas attended the Rapid City Boarding School. In 1911, the school clerk gave him permission to buy a suit of clothes, which cost $15. Silas enlisted in the SD National Guard in May 1917. When he registered for the draft on June 5, 1917, he was working as assistant engineer for the U.S. Government in Rapid City. He told the registration clerk that he had served one month. When he joined the Army, he was first assigned to Co. F, 333rd Infantry, 81st Division (ASN 3955047). He sailed from New York aboard the *Carmania* on Sept. 1, 1918. After arriving in France, he was reassigned to Co. B, 348th Machine Gun (MG) Battalion, 91st Division. He served with Pvt. James Greenwood. The 91st Division, known as the Pine Tree Division, had trained at Camp Lewis, WA. The 348th MG Bn. served in the sectors of Lorraine, Meuse-Argonne and Ypres-Lys. After the Armistice, Pvt. Kills Plenty received an evaluation from his commander, 1st Lt. W.L.H. Osborne, stating that he was "intelligent, good humored, associates readily with whites, good machine gunner, excellent athlete." Pvt. Kills Plenty returned from St. Nazaire, France, aboard the *Orizaba* on March 25, 1919. Pvt. Greenwood was on the ship with him. They arrived in the U.S. on April 2. Pvt. Kills Plenty also served in Casual Detachment 312. He was discharged on April 22, 1919. After returning home, Silas married Lucy Hollow Horn Bear. In the 1937 Census Roll, Silas and Lucy had three children, Phoebe, Theodore and Victor. Silas entered the spirit world in St. Francis on May 14, 1939 and is buried in Spring Creek Cemetery.[9]

Kills Small, James. James was born around 1897 on the Pine Ridge Reservation. In the 1897 Census Roll, James, age 10 mo., is listed with his parents, Henry Ciqala Kte [Kills Small] and Anna. James first enlisted in Co. I, 4th SD Infantry. Pvt. Kills Small served on the Mexican Border from 1916-1917. He then re-enlisted in March or April of 1917. Once these SD National Guardsmen arrived at Camp Greene, NC, many of them were transferred to the 148th Machine Gun (MG) Battalion (ASN 98580). Pvt. Kills Small sailed from Hoboken, NJ, aboard the *Olympic* on Jan. 11, 1918. When the 148th MG Bn. arrived in France, Pvt. Kills Small was reassigned to Co. M, 167th

Infantry, 42nd Division. The 167th Infantry took part in the Sectors at Luneville, Baccarat, Esperance-Souain, Champagne-Marne, Aisne-Marne, St. Mihiel, Essey-Pannes ans Meuse-Argonne. The 42nd Division which suffered 13,919 casualties, was part of the Army of Occupation until April 1919. Pvt. Kills Small sailed for home from Brest, France, aboard the U.S.S. *Minnesota* on April 15, 1919, and was discharged on May 9, 1919. After James arrived home, he married Nellie Good Shield, whose brother, Philip, also served in the Army. In the 1930 U.S. Census, James and Nellie had three children, Jerome, Loran and Sam. James was suffering from tuberculosis, and entered the spirit world on Aug. 13, 1930. He is buried in St. Paul's Cemetery in Porcupine. His son, Loren, served in the Army after WWII.

Kills the Enemy, Charles Joseph. Joseph was born on the Rosebud on April 12, 1899, to Charles and Mary Rosa (Runs Between). As a teenager he was enrolled at Carlisle. He left the school to enlist in the Army on July 22, 1917 (ASN 1020491). He was discharged on July 24, 1919. On Oct. 20, 1920, he enlisted in the Navy. He was discharged on Nov. 4, 1921, as a Seaman 2nd Class. He married Mary Eagle Thunder. Their children were Leroy, Ross, Romeo, Joseph and Vivian. When Joseph registered for the Selective Service in 1942, he lived in Parmelee. In 1945, he lived in St. Francis. His son, Leroy, served with the USMC in Korea. On March 3, 1968, Joseph and his son, Leroy, were killed in a car accident near Upper Cut Meat Community. Joseph is buried in Peyote Cemetery. On his military headstone, his last name is spelled "Kenemy."

Kills Warrior, Allen Ralph. Allen is listed on WWI veteran's memorial at Oglala Lakota College, Kyle, SD. Allen was born about June 12, 1898, on the Pine Ridge Reservation. In the 1907 Census Roll, he is listed as Ralph, the son of Henry Kills Warrior and Elma Crazy Bull. Allen joined the Army on Feb. 1, 1918, and was sent to Camp Funston for training. He was assigned to Bakery Co. #351, Quartermaster Corps (ASN 940252). Pfc. Kills Warrior sailed for France aboard the *Maui* on Sept. 15, 1918. Pfc. Kills Warrior suffered eye and lung damage after a gas attack. He sailed for home from Brest aboard the *Agamemnon* on Sept. 17, 1919, and was discharged on Oct. 3, 1919. After returning home, he married Nellie High Cat. In the 1930 U.S. Census, the family was farming with their children, Louis and Grace. In the 1940 U.S. Census, Allen was working on a C.C.C. dam construction project. He and Nellie had five children, Louis, Grace, Eva, Mildred and Alma. Louis joined the Navy in 1942. In 1947, Allen began working for the Chicago and Northwestern Railway in Chadron. His occupation was firebuilder. He entered the spirit world in Pine Ridge Hospital on June 27, 1951, and is buried in St. John's Cemetery, Oglala.[10]

King, Thomas. Thomas was born near Ft. Sisseton on April 12, 1886. His parents were James (Akicita) and Elizabeth (Rupa) King. James had served as a Scout with the 25th Infantry. In the 1900 U.S. Census, the family was living at Pine Ridge. In the fall of 1906, his parents enrolled Thomas at Carlisle. However, he returned home the following spring due to ill health. Sometime later he entered the Huron Business College, from which he graduated in 1910. When Thomas registered for the draft on Aug. 27, 1917, he was living in Webster. The form that he filled out lists him as a short man of medium build. In December 1917, he wrote to the Superintendent at Carlisle asking if he could re-enroll. He added that he had recently tried to enlist in the Marines, but they said he was too short and too light. He received a reply that he was too old. Thomas enlisted in the Army at Webster on March 13, 1918. He was assigned to Co. M, 59th Infantry, 4th Division (ASN 572607). Pvt. King sailed with the 59th Infantry from New York on May 5, 1918, aboard the *Olympic*. After seven days at sea, the ship's Captain spotted a submarine. He steered the large liner at the sub, and hooked it with the bow, causing the sub to roll. A destroyer following behind picked up some of the crew. By May 18, 1918, the Regiment was in France. As the Regiment was to be supporting

British troops, the soldiers had their Springfield rifles taken and were issued the British Lee-Enfield rifles, which were heavier. The 59th Infantry served in the Sectors at Aisne-Marne, Vesle, Toulon, St. Mihiel and Meuse-Argonne. King was promoted to Sergeant on Sept. 15, 1918. After the Armistice, Capt. David Simpson wrote of Sgt. King, "this man is an excellent soldier and proved himself fearless and brave under fire." Sgt. King sailed from Brest, France, aboard the *Texan* on July 24, 1919, and was discharged on Aug. 11, 1919, at Camp Dodge, IA. After the war, a photo of King was included in a published roster of Day County veterans.

Thomas married Jennie Last Horse at Martin, SD, on June 21, 1930. Thomas lived at Pine Ridge and attended Porcupine Presbyterian Church from 1926 until he returned to Sisseton in 1972. He passed his last years at Tekakwitha Nursing Home in Sisseton. He entered the spirit world on Jan. 8, 1985, at the age of 98, and is buried in the cemetery at Buffalo Lake Presbyterian Church.[11]

Kitto, Howard. Howard was born around Christmas in 1889, at Greenwood, SD. He was enrolled on the Santee Reservation. His parents were Angus Elijah and Bella Kitto (Wauskedan). When he registered for the draft at Porcupine, ND, on June 4, 1917, he was working as a farm hand for a farmer near Flasher, ND. He joined the Army around the first part of 1918, and was discharged on June 20, 1918. In the early 1920s, he was living in Flandreau, where he married Nina Allen. In 1935, the family was interviewed by a worker with the SDERA program. Howard was well known as a musician and had done work as a piano tuner. He also had worked as a janitor at the local Hospital. Nina did part time work at the dress factory at the Flandreau School. The family had a small house near the hospital. In the 1940 U.S. Census, Howard was farming near town. Howard and Nina's family included Samuel, Marcella, William and Gloria. Samuel served in the Army during WWII and Korea. Howard entered the spirit world in the Flandreau Hospital on Nov. 3, 1969, and is buried in the First Presbyterian Cemetery, Flandreau.[12]

Kitto, Reuben. Reuben was born in Mellette County on Feb. 16, 1899. In the 1899 Santee Census Roll, Reuben is listed with his parents, Richard Wacehinakinmani [Eagle Plume that Walks] and Laura Aupetuihduzewin [Dresses Daily Woman], as well as his siblings, Lucy, David, Esther and Silas. Reuben joined the Army and was assigned to the Headquarters Company, 48th Artillery, (CAC) (ASN 505581). He sailed from Newport News, VA, aboard the *Susquehana* in October of 1918. After the Armistice, Pfc. Kitto sailed from St. Nazaire aboard the *Kroonland* on March 12, 1919. Reuben re-enlisted in 1944, serving in WWII. He was discharged as a Tech. 4. In the 1930 U.S. Census, he was living with his parents in Winner, SD, and working as a teamster for a dray line. In the 1930s, he married Alice Skillings (1907-1972). In the 1940 U.S. Census, they were living in Santee, NE, with their children, Reuben Jr. and Laura. Reuben was working as a mechanic with the WPA program. In the 1940s, the family moved to Minneapolis. In the 1950s, Alice was working for the Minneapolis Public Library. Their son, Reuben Jr., served as a warrant officer in the Naval Reserve. Reuben later moved out to California, and entered the spirit world in Los Angeles on April 24, 1966. He is buried in Ft. Snelling National Cemetery, Section K, Site 4587.[13]

Kitto, Silas. Silas, an older brother of Reuben, was born on the Santee Reservation on Aug. 26, 1895, to Richard and Laura Kitto. The family lived in South Dakota from time to time. When Silas registered for the draft on June 5, 1917, he was working as a farm laborer in Santee. When he joined the army, he went to Camp Funston, KS, and trained with the 89th Division. He was assigned to Co. G, 354th Infantry (ASN 2847153). Pvt. Kitto sailed with his unit from Montreal aboard the *Ascanius* on June 4, 1918. Upon arrival in France, the 354th Infantry was billeted near Trampot. The 354th took part in the St. Mihiel Offensive. Pvt. Kitto may have been wounded in that battle.

He entered the spirit world on Sept. 24, 1918, which was two days before the start of the Meuse-Argonne Offensive. Pvt. Kitto's body was shipped from Antwerp, Belgium, aboard the *Cambria* on May 23, 1921. He is buried in the Congregational Cemetery, Santee, NE.

Knight, Wallace. Wallace (Wally) was born in Marshfield, Missouri on June 6, 1897, to Amos and Nancy Knight. Around 1902, his family moved to South Dakota. In 1910, the family had a farm in Stanley County. Wallace joined the Army on Aug. 11, 1917, and was discharged on Feb. 14, 1918. On Aug. 24, 1918, he registered with the Selective Service at Philip, as his brother, Earl, was living near Milesville. In the 1920 U.S. Census, Wallace was working as a ranch hand for Lester Woods in Ziebach County. He was well known as a bronc rider. On Dec. 29, 1922, Wallace married Sarah In Amongst (1899-1989) at Milesville. He and Sarah were living in Cherry Creek. In the 1930 U.S. Census, Wallace and Sarah were farming with their family, which included Lila, Jess, Lucille, Luther and Douglas. In the 1940 U.S. Census, they had a stock ranch, and they now had six children, with the birth of Nadine. They provided riding stock for area rodeos. They also had a number of boarders living with them. Their son, Jess, served in the Army from 1943-1945. Wallace also had a dirt moving business. Wallace entered the spirit world on Nov. 4, 1972, and is buried in Dupree Cemetery.

Knorr, Joseph. Joseph was born on March 9, 1899, on the Fort Peck Reservation. In the 1899 Fort Peck Census Roll, he is listed with his parents, Charles and Josephine. As a youth, he was enrolled as a student at the Flandreau boarding school. In the spring of 1917, he enlisted in Troop D, 1st SD Cavalry. Initially, this National Guard unit was not issued any horses or saddles, so they drilled afoot. In September of 1917, they were transferred to Camp Cody, NM, where Pvt. Knorr trained with the 34th Division. Cpl. Knorr was assigned to Co. D, 136th Infantry, 34th Division (ASN 1427373). He sailed with his unit from New York aboard the *Melita* on Oct. 13, 1918. Upon arriving in France, he was reassigned to Co. L, 49th Infantry. Cpl. Knorr sailed from Brest, France, aboard the *George Washington* on Jan. 12, 1919, and was discharged on April 11, 1919. Joseph's name was engraved on a plaque to honor veterans at the Flandreau boarding school after the war. He returned home to Montana and married Birdie Smith at Wolf Point on April 15, 1922. They had a daughter, Beverly. In late 1929, Joseph was working as a sandhog on the construction of the Wolf Creek Bridge over the Missouri River. This required working in 60 feet of water to excavate for the pilings. After surfacing, he developed caisson disease, or the bends, and became paralyzed. He entered the spirit world at the VA hospital at Fort Harrison, MT, on March 12, 1930. His is buried in the Poplar Cemetery, Poplar, MT.[14]

Ktena, Victor. Victor was born in Greenwood, SD, around 1892. In the 1903 Yanktonai Census Roll, he is listed with his father, Ktena, and mother, Kinyansapewin, and a sister, Anna. Victor married Clara Stricker on Sept. 16, 1914, with who he had a daughter, Eva. When Victor registered for the draft on June 5, 1917, he was farming with his family near Greenwood. Victor joined the Army on May 24, 1918, and was sent to Camp Lewis, WA. He was assigned to 1st Company, Development Battalion #1, 166th Depot Brigade (ASN 3125602). He was discharged as a Private on Feb. 12, 1919. Victor made his home in Ree Township, Charles Mix County. He was later married to Jennie. Victor entered the spirit world in Wagner on Jan. 12, 1959, and is buried in Greenwood, SD.[15]

L

LaBatte, Sidney. Sidney was born on March 10, 1895, on the Sisseton-Wahpeton Reservation. In the 1897 Census Roll, he is listed with is parents, Philip Labatte and Sarah Renville, as well as his older brothers and sisters, Hazen, Mason, Solon, Agnes and Mary. In the 1910 U.S. Census, he is shown as a student at Haskell. When he registered for the draft on June 2, 1917, he was farming near Peever. He joined the Army on Aug. 28, 1918, and was discharged on Dec. 10, 1918. After the war, he married Hannah Hopkins, who had been married to his older brother, Solon. In the 1930 U.S. Census, Sidney and Hannah lived near the Agency with their children, Beulah, Archie, Reuben, Priscilla, Sidney Jr., and Calvin, as well as Sidney's father, Philip. A few years later, Sidney and Hannah were divorced. In 1935, Sidney was interviewed by a worker with the SDERA program. He was living with his mother in her home located about 12 miles SE of Sisseton. The interviewer noted that there were many photos of family members hanging on the walls. Sidney had been doing relief work and had served as the foreman of a gopher eradication crew. In 1937, Sidney married Mae Whipple. In the 1940 U.S. Census, Sidney and Mae were living in St. Paul, MN, with their children, Sidney Jr., Calvin and Marlene. Sidney was working in a lumber yard. His son, Sidney Jr., served in the Navy during WWII. Sidney later returned to South Dakota. He entered the spirit world on March 24, 1984.[1]

LaBatte, Solon. Solon was born on the Sisseton Reservation on Sept. 24, 1884, to Philip LaBatte and Sarah Renville. In the 1900 U.S. Census, he was a student at the School in Chamberlain. He married Hannah Hopkins on July 21, 1907. Their children were Beulah, Archie, Reuben, Agnes and Priscilla. Solon registered for the draft on Sept. 12, 1918. He must have joined the Army shortly after this and was sent to Camp Funston, KS. He died of the flu epidemic at the camp on Dec. 24, 1918. He is buried in St. Mary's Episcopal Cemetery. His brother, Sidney, later married Hannah. Solon's son, Reuben, served on a 16-inch gun crew on the U.S.S. *New Jersey* in WWII.

LaBelle, Benjamin. Benjamin was born around Aug. 17, 1894, near Veblen, SD, on the Sisseton Wahpeton Reservation to Louis LaBelle and Martha Shortfoot. When Ben registered for the draft on June 2, 1917, he was farming near Veblen. He joined the Army on July 22, 1918, and was discharged as a Private on Dec. 1, 1918. On June 19, 1919, he married Ellen Marlow (1896-1965). In the 1920 U.S. Census, he was farming in LaBelle Township, Marshall County. In the 1920s, the family moved to St. Paul, MN. In the 1929 St. Paul City Directory, he was working as a laborer for Rose Bros. CO., a lumber yard. When he registered with the Selective Service in 1942, he was working at the Twin City Ordnance Plant. In 1956, he was working as a construction worker for Foley Bros. He entered the spirit world at Ancker Hospital on Oct. 5, 1964. His widow and a stepdaughter, Evelyn, survived him. He is buried in Ft. Snelling National Cemetery, Section I, site 3492. Ellen is buried next to him.[2]

LaBelle, Daniel. Daniel was born on Oct. 31, 1891, on the Sisseton-Wahpeton Reservation, the son of Louis Labelle and Martha Shortfoot. He married Ellen Renville around 1910. When he registered for the draft on June 1, 1917, he was farming near Veblen, with two young children. He served as a Private in the Army and was discharged on Feb. 8, 1919. In the 1920 Census Roll, he and Ellen are listed with four children, Gerald, Lavina, Lorene and Evelyn. In the 1930 U.S. Census, Daniel was working on a farm near Prior Lake, MN, with William Lacroix, a fellow veteran. In 1932, Daniel married Lucy LaFromboise. In 1935, the family was interviewed by a worker with the SDERA. Their four-room home was located three miles southwest of Veblen. Their livestock included two horses, four milk cows, two heifers, two calves, four hogs and three dozen chickens. They received income from selling cream. Their wheat crop was destroyed by rust and their garden did not survive the drought. In the 1940 U.S. Census, Daniel and Lucy were farming near Veblen with their blended family. Daniel entered the spirit world in the Sisseton hospital on June 13, 1979. He is buried in the Sisseton Cemetery.[3]

LaBelle, Decorah. Decorah was the eldest son of Louis and Martha Shortfoot Labelle. He was born on Nov. 30, 1889, on the Sisseton-Wahpeton Reservation. His father had served as the sheriff on the newly formed reservation. In the 1910 U.S. Census, Decorah was married to Clarissa Decoteau. When Decorah registered for the draft on June 1, 1917, he and his wife were farming and had two children, Everett and Elaine. Decorah joined the Army on June 24, 1918. He was assigned to Co. L, 20th Infantry, 10th Division (ASN 3308372). Pfc. LaBelle was discharged at Camp Funston, KS, on Feb. 14, 1919. In the 1930 U.S. Census, Decorah was a patient in Luther Hospital at Watertown. In the early 1930s, he married Hannah Marks. After she passed away in 1933, he married Emma Renville. In the 1940 U.S. Census, they lived at the Agency and Decorah worked as a teamster on road construction. He earned $10 per week. Decorah entered the spirit world on Sept. 23, 1959, following an automobile accident south of Sisseton. He is buried in St. Mary's Cemetery.[4]

Edward LaBelle
Ed LaBelle, Jr.

LaBelle, Edward. Edward was born at Veblen on the Sisseton Wahpeton Reservation on Nov. 30, 1895. His parents were Baptiste LaBelle and Mary Anne Tunkan. Edward was a student at the United States Industrial Indian Boarding School at Sisseton, SDl, where he learned the carpentry trade. He joined the Army at Britton, SD, on May 25, 1918. He was assigned to Co. B, 144th Machine Gun (MG) Battalion, 40th Division (ASN 2767661) On Aug. 11, 1918, he sailed with his unit from Brooklyn aboard the *Vauban*. On arriving in France, he was assigned as a replacement to Co. A, 341st Machine Gun Battalion, 89th Division. This unit had been in France since June. Pvt. LaBelle took part in the Meuse-Argonne Offensive. After the Armistice, the 341st MG Bn. was billeted in Bleialf, Germany. On May 15, 1919, Pvt. LaBelle's unit sailed from Brest, France, aboard the ship *Leviathan*. They arrived in the U.S. on May 22, 1919. Pvt. LaBelle served briefly with Casual Detachment 606, Demobilization Group, before being discharged at Camp Dodge, IA, on June 2, 1919. He returned home and married Margaret T. Quinn on Dec. 15, 1919. They had seven children. The oldest, Sarah, was born Sept. 8, 1920, Ruby was born June 28, 1925, Eugene was born June 21, 1928, Phoebe was born on Jan. 28, 1931, Edward and Rachel were born on Jan. 10, 1935, and Larry was born April 22, 1941.

The family farmed for a number of years. Edward also did carpentry work. He and his brother, Howard, built a church next to the Mountainhead-LaBelle Cemetery on the reservation. Edward had joined the Dakota Presbytery Mission Society. The family traveled to different reservations, where Edward repaired the church buildings and gave sermons on Sunday. In 1935, the family was interviewed by a social worker for the SDERA. The family was living six miles northwest of Veblen in a one-room, furnished, home which they rented from the church. They hauled water ½ mile from a neighbor's well. They had no livestock. In the 1940 U.S. Census, the family was living in LaBelle Township, while Edward worked as a mechanic on a W.P.A. project. Their children were Ruby, Eugene, Phoebe and Edward Jr. In 1942, the family moved to St. Paul, where Edward found a job at Armour's Meat Packing Plant. The 1954 St. Paul City Directory, Edward is listed as a carpenter. In the late 1960s, Edward and Margaret moved back to South Dakota. Margaret passed away in 1973 and Edward passed away on Oct. 26, 1975. They are buried in Mountainhead-LaBelle Cemetery, Marshall County, where Edward had helped build the church.[5]

Harvey LaBelle
Findagrave

LaBelle, Harvey. Harvey was born at Veblen on the Sisseton-Wahpeton Reservation about Jan. 1, 1887, to Peter and Mary Labelle. In the early 1900s, he was a student at the Carlisle Boarding School, where he met Linda Messawat, a Sac-Fox from Oklahoma. In 1908, Harvey married Linda and moved to Oklahoma for a few years. Their first son was Clifford, who entered the spirit world as a child in South Dakota. They had three other children, Francis, Edith and Arthur. When Harvey registered for the draft, he was farming at Hominy, OK, and supporting his wife and two children. He enlisted in the Army on July 26, 1918, and served as a Private with the Quartermaster Corps. He was assigned to Motor Co. #1 at Camp Greenleaf, Fort Oglethorpe, GA. After his discharge on Jan. 10, 1919, he returned to Oklahoma. He entered the spirit world at the VA Hospital in Oklahoma City on Jan. 29, 1968, and is buried at Ft. Gibson National Cemetery, Section 10, Site 2660. American Legion Post #15 furnished the pallbearers and conducted the flag ceremony.[6]

LaClair, Silas. Silas was born May 2, 1891, on the Yankton Reservation. In the 1895 Ponca Census Roll, he is listed with his parents, William and Eliza, a sister, Susan and brothers, Charles, David and Joseph. On Nov. 28, 1913, he married Lizzie Blue Bird, whose brother, John, served with the Army in France. When Silas registered for the draft on June 5, 1917, he was farming near Herrick. He joined the Army on Sept. 4, 1918, and was discharged on Jan. 29, 1919. Shortly after this, Silas married Mary Loafer from the Rosebud Reservation. In the 1920 U.S. Census, Silas and Mary lived in Ellston Township with her father, Loafer, as well as their daughter, Eleanor. About a year later, they had a son, Everett. In the 1940 U.S. Census, Silas and Mary lived in St. Charles with their daughter, her husband, Thomas Cane, and son, Levi. They farmed near Herrick. The family later moved to Scotland in Bon Homme County. Silas entered the spirit world in the Landmann-Jungman Hospital in Scotland, SD, on Dec. 11, 1979. He is buried in Ponca Creek Congregational Cemetery, St. Charles, SD.

LaCroix, William. William was born on June 6, 1891, on the Sisseton-Wahpeton Reservation. His parents were Louis LaCroix and Madeline LaBelle. When he registered for the draft on June 2, 1917, he was farming near Veblen. He enlisted on July 22, 1918, and was assigned to the 87th Infantry, 19th Division (ASN 3954345). The 19th Division was organized at Camp Dodge, IA, on Sept. 1, 1918, and demobilized in January 1919. Pvt. LaCroix was discharged on Feb. 3, 1919. In 1920, he married Lillian Adney. In 1933, he married Gertrude Wanna. In the 1937 Census Roll, he and Gertie are listed with their son, Morris. William entered the spirit world on March 29, 1938. He was using a pry bar and a team to dig rocks at his home near Veblen. A rock fell on the bar, which then struck him on the head. He is buried in St. Matthew's Cemetery, Veblen.[7]

LaDeaux, Antoine. Antoine is listed on WWI veteran's memorial at Oglala Lakota College, Kyle, SD. He was born on Nov. 3, 1898, on the Pine Ridge Reservation. In the 1899 Census Roll, he is listed with his parents, George and Mary, and his sister, Maggie. Antoine likely attended the Haskell boarding school at Lawrence, KS. Antoine joined the Kansas National Guard on Aug. 11, 1917. He was assigned to Battery B, First Regiment, Kansas Field Artillery at Lawrence. Upon arrival at Camp Doniphan, this National Guard unit was changed to the 130th Field Artillery Regiment. Pvt. LaDeaux served as a Bugler with Battery B, 130th Field Artillery, 35th Division (ASN 1466311). Three other men from Pine Ridge served in Battery B with Bugler LaDeaux. They were Thomas Blackbird, Edward Rooks and Benjamin Pretty Boy. They sailed for France from New York aboard the *Ceramic* on May 19, 1918. The 35th Division played an important role at the opening of the Meuse-Argonne Offensive on Sept. 26, 1918. The artillery regiments from the 35th Division fired more than 40,000 rounds on that day. Bugler LaDeaux suffered lung and eye damage from exposure to German gas attacks. After the Armistice, the 35th Division was billeted near Commercy, along the Meuse River in France. LaDeaux was discharged on June 21, 1919.

In the 1920 U.S. Census, he was living with his mother and working as a salesman in a retail store. He later married Edna McDonald (1903-1977), an Oneida from Oklahoma. In the 1930 U.S. Census, the family was living in Chadron. In the 1940 U.S. Census, Antoine was working as a painter on a building construction project just south of Pine Ridge, in Nebraska. He and Edna had three sons, George, Donald, and Thomas. All three enlisted in the Army in the 1940s. George died in a vehicle accident in Louisiana on August 26, 1941. Donald served in the Army Air Corps. Antoine entered the spirit world in the VA Hospital at Hot Springs on Aug. 31, 1973. He is buried in Evergreen Cemetery in Hot Springs.[8]

Lafferty, Clyde M. Clyde was born about March 28, 1894 near Fort Pierre to Henry Lafferty and Elizabeth Larrabee. He was an enrolled member on the Cheyenne River Reservation. Clyde joined the Army at Timber Lake on April 25, 1918, and trained with the 89th Division at Camp Funston. He served in Co. G, 355th Infantry Regiment, as well as Co. D, 342nd Machine Gun Battalion (ASN 2845277). Pvt. Lafferty sailed from New York aboard the *Baltic* on June 4, 1918. After Armistice, his commanding officer, Captain Ira Barlow, wrote that Pvt. Lafferty was an "average soldier with fitness for automatic rifle." He sailed for home from Breast aboard the *Leviathan* on May 15, 1919. After returning back to the United States, he briefly served with Casual Detachment 646, during the demobilization process. He was discharged as a Private on June 6, 1919. After returning home, he was married on Sept. 12, 1920, in Pierre to Daisy Melven, with whom he had three children, Clyde, Eleanor and Harold. In the 1920s, the family moved to Illinois. Clyde last worked as a painter for Standard Oil. In 1927, he was admitted as a patient to the Soldier's Home in Milwaukee. Clyde suffered from Tuberculosis and entered the spirit world on May 3, 1928. He is buried in Oakland Cemetery in Freeport, IL.[9]

Lafferty, Gilbert D. Gilbert was a younger brother of Clyde. He was born around July 14, 1896, in Fort Pierre. Gilbert was a student at Carlisle in 1914-15. When Gilbert registered for the draft on June 5, 1917, he was living in Oklahoma and also attending school in Chillicothe, Missouri. He was taking book keeping and short hand at Chillicothe Business College. He and another former Carlisle student were planning on taking the civil service exam. Gilbert enlisted in the Missouri National Guard in Kansas City on Aug. 22, 1917. He initially served in Second Regiment Field Artillery, and was assigned to Battery E, 129th Field Artillery, 35th Division (ASN 1465004), which trained at Camp Doniphan, OK. In October 1917, while stationed at Fort Sill, OK, he wrote a letter to the Superintendent at Carlisle, asking a recommendation so he could attend officer's training school. However, the Superintendent turned him down because he had run away from the school several times. Pvt. Lafferty sailed from New York to France aboard the *Saxon* on May 19, 1918. The 35th Division suffered 7,283 casualties in the war. As part of the Army of Occupation, the 35th Division was billeted at Commercy, along the Meuse River. On March 26, 1919, Pvt. Lafferty was admitted to Base Hospital 52 with a sore knee. Pvt. Lafferty sailed for home from St. Nazaire aboard the *Matsonia* on April 13, 1919, traveling with soldiers labeled as "Sick and Wounded." His next of kin was his wife, Lucille Lafferty. He had married Lucille Chambers in Commanche, OK, on May 10, 1918, which was about a week before he sailed for Europe. He was discharged on June 3, 1919, at Camp Funston, KS. After his discharge, he moved to Kansas City with his wife.

After later returning to South Dakota, he married Mary Ora Richard, whose brother, Louis, had served in the Navy during the war. Gilbert lived with Mary on the Pine Ridge Reservation near Tuthill. They had five children, Gilmore, Arthur, William Babe and Luta and Ramona. Gilbert and Mary were later divorced. In the 1930s, his brother thought Gilbert was living in Wyoming. In the 1940 U.S. Census, now using the name, Joe, he was living with his wife, Verna (1909-1969), in Fort Washakie on the Wind River Reservation. Verna, a Shoshone, was an enrolled member on that reservation. They later ranched near Lander. Gilbert served in the military during WWII. His son, Arthur, served in the Navy during the war. His sons, Charles and William, also served in the military. Gilbert entered the spirit world on Feb. 14, 1970, at Bishop Randall Hospital in Lander, WY. His sons, Charles, Arthur and William, survived him. Military graveside rites were conducted by Don Stough American Legion Post 33 and Post 954 of the VFW. He is buried in Mount Hope Cemetery, Lander.[10]

Lafferty, Walter. Walter was an older brother of Clyde and Gilbert. He was born on May 16, 1886, at Pierre. When he registered for the draft on June 5, 1917, he was farming near Dupree. He joined the Army and served nine months in Minneapolis. He was discharged on Jan. 13, 1919. On Dec. 29, 1919, he married Alice Aspdin in Dupree. Alice's mother, Mary, had been at Little Big Horn with her parents. Alice's grandfather was Black Moon. After the battle, Black Moon went to Canada, where Mary married Thomas Aspdin, who served with the Royal Canadian Mounted Police. Walter and Alice had a daughter, Eleanor. Walter worked as a truck driver for the government. In 1930, they lived in Faith, where Walter worked for Potter Lumber Company. Walter had been a member of the American Legion. In 1935, the family was interviewed by a social worker with the SDERA program. In the mid-1930s, they moved to Eagle Butte, and lived in a three-room frame house that was a block west of the school, where their daughter, Eleanor, went to school. Her mother said that her classmates teased her because she did not speak Lakota well. The family purchased drinking water at 25 cents per barrel. Walter mentioned that the last he had heard from his brother, Gilbert, was two years before when he was living in Wyoming. In 1940, Walter was working on a building project in Eagle Butte. Walter entered the spirit world at the Cheyenne River Indian Hospital on April 30, 1957.[11]

LaFramboise, Edward. Edward was born at Wakpala on the Standing Rock Reservation on April 20, 1897. His parents were Frank and Sallie LaFramboise. As a student, he was enrolled at the boarding school at Flandreau. On April 7, 1917, he enlisted in Troop D, 1st South Dakota Cavalry. He was a sophomore in high school at the time. This cavalry troop was not issued horses or saddles, so they performed cavalry drill afoot. On Sept. 15, 1917, the unit traveled to Camp Cody, NM, where they were assigned to the 59th Depot Brigade. Pvt. Laframboise was re-assigned to several different units. He served in Co. D, 136th Infantry Regiment (ASN 1426371); Supply Co., 136th Infantry, 34th Division; and Ordnance Dept. N.A., Rock Island Arsenal. Pvt. LaFramboise sailed from

New York aboard the *Melita* on Oct. 13, 1918, with Supply Co., 136th Infantry, Attached Ordnance Personnel. After the Armistice, he sailed for home from Brest, France, aboard the *Northern Pacific* on July 11, 1919. Traveling with Mehun Ordnance Casual Co. No. 74, he arrived in New York on July 17, and was discharged on July 26, 1919, at Camp Dodge, IA. Edward's name was engraved on a plaque honoring the veterans from the Flandreau Boarding School. On Feb. 2, 1927, Edward married Regina Yellow. They had two sons, John and Protius. In 1935, the family was interviewed by a worker with the SDERA program. They were living in Wakpala in one room of a house they shared with the John Distribute family. Water was carried two blocks from the village well. Edward owned a 1927 Oldsmobile and worked for the State Highway Commission. He received 30 cents per hour and worked a nine-hour day, six days a week, repairing guard rails. Regina was a member of the American Legion Auxiliary. In the 1940 U.S. Census, Edward drove a truck on a C.C.C. project near Wakpala. He and Regina had two more children, Alma and Douglas. Edward entered the spirit world on June 30, 1950, while in the Tacoma Indian Hospital, Tacoma, WA. He is buried in St. Bede's Cemetery in Wakpala. On March 17, 2017, the family of Pvt. LaFramboise received a Code Talker's Medal in a special program at Wakpala, honoring his service.[12]

Lambert, Guy W. Guy was born at Lake Andes on Nov. 23, 1896. In the 1898 Yanktonai Census Roll, he was listed with his parents, Baptist and Annie Lambert. His father was a missionary. As a student, Guy was enrolled at the Flandreau boarding school. Guy enlisted in Troop D, 1st SD Cavalry in the spring of 1917 at Flandreau. When he registered for the draft on June 5, 1917, he stated he had served three months in the SDNG Cavalry and had been promoted to Sergeant. The 1st Cavalry was transferred to Camp Cody, NM, in September 1917, and trained with the 34th Division. Cpl. Lambert was assigned to Co. D, 136th Infantry, 34th Division (ASN 1427351). He sailed with his unit from New York aboard the *Melita* on Oct. 13, 1918. On arriving in France, he was reassigned to Co. L, 49th Infantry. Cpl. Lambert sailed for the States from Brest, France, aboard the *George Washington* on Jan. 12, 1919. He was discharged on Feb. 15, 1919. His name is engraved on a plaque erected at Flandreau honoring veterans from the school. Guy had married Emma Wright on June 7, 1917. In 1921, he was a member of the Chauncey Eagle Horn Legion Post at Rosebud. In 1922, he married Nancy Prue (1891-1966). The ceremony was performed by Guy's father, Baptist Lambert. In the 1930 U.S. Census, the family was living in Okreek, where Guy was working as a police officer for the Indian Service. Living with Guy and Nancy were their children, Velma, Chester, Amos, Gladys, Elinor, the twins, Tracy and Charlotte, and Martha, as well as Guy's mother, Annie. Their sons, Chester and Amos, served in the Army during the WWII era. After World War II, Guy was living in Wakpala and working as a minister. He entered the spirit world on August 6, 1947, in the Mobridge hospital. He is buried in Calvary Cemetery in Okreek.[13]

Lamont, Jasper. Jasper was born on the Yankton Reservation around June 15, 1897. In the 1900 U.S. Census, he was living in White Swan Township with his parents, Duncan and Kate Lamont, as well as a brother, John, and his sisters, Eva and Lillian. In the 1910 U.S. Census, he was a student at the Haskell Institute, Lawrence, KS. In 1913, he enrolled as a student at Carlisle and went on several outings to neighboring land owners. One of these landowners offered Jasper a full-time job as a chauffeur in 1917. He worked in Pennsylvania until enlisting. Jasper joined the Army on Dec. 5, 1917, and was assigned to 444th Aero Construction Squadron. He was stationed at Vancouver Barracks, Vancouver, WA. Pvt. Lamont suffered from broncho-pneumonia and entered the spirit world in the Post Hospital on Feb. 22, 1918. He is buried in Lake View Cemetery in Lake Andes.[14]

Lamoreaux, Paul. Paul was born in Spring View on the Rosebud Reservation around July 4, 1898. In the 1900 Census, he is listed with his parents, Oliver and Alma. His father had started the town of Lamro, later named Winner. Paul was a graduate of Chemawa Boarding School in Salem, OR. Paul joined the SD National Guard on April 2, 1917. When the 4th SD Infantry arrived at Camp Greene, NC, the unit was designated as the 148th Machine Gun (MG) Battalion (ASN 99001). They sailed from Hoboken for France aboard the *Olympic* on Jan. 11, 1918. Upon arrival, Pvt. Lamoreaux was reassigned to the Machine Gun Company, 167th Infantry, 42nd Division. He served with Corp. Harvey Langdeau. They sailed from Brest, France, aboard the U.S.S. *Montana* on April 15, 1919. He was discharged as a Private on May 24, 1919. After the war, Paul married Roy Lessert's widow, Frances (Fannie). After the war, Paul's mother, Alma, married James A. Brown, a fellow veteran. In the 1920 U.S. Census, Paul was living in Gordon, NE, with Frances and her daughter, Royaldine. Paul was working as a salesman in a grocery store. In the early 1920s, the family moved to Portland, OR. Royaldine entered the spirit world in Portland in 1924. In the 1930 U.S. Census, Paul was working as a musician for a radio station. Paul organized his own orchestra, known as "Paul Lamoreaux and the Sweetest Music in Town." Paul and Frances were divorced in the 30s. In the late 30s, Paul married Martha Lang, who was known as Mardi. In the 1940 U.S. Census, Paul is listed as a musician at a radio station (KOIN), while Mardi is listed as an entertainer in a night club in Portland. Paul was the music director for the local radio station and was a member of the Musicians Local 99. He retired in 1971. At that time, he was awarded a gold lifetime membership to Musician's Union, Local 99. Paul entered the spirit world on Sept. 3, 1977. His widow and a daughter, Paulette, survived him. He is buried in the Williamette National Cemetery, Section N, site 3556. Mardi (1916-1981) is buried with Paul.[15]

Langdeau, Harvey. Harvey was born on the Lower Brule Reservation around Feb. 9, 1898. In the 1902 Census Roll, he was listed with his parents, Maurice and Emma. Harvey was enrolled at the Rapid City boarding school. Harvey ran away from school and enlisted in Co. I, Fourth SD Infantry on March 28, 1917. This was before President Wilson had declared war on Germany. The Rapid City soldiers left for Camp Greene, NC, on Sept. 28, 1917. Many became part of Co. B, 148th Machine Gun Battalion, 41st Division. Pvt. Langdeau sailed from Hoboken, NJ, aboard the *Olympic* on Jan. 11, 1918. Once the 41st Division arrived in France, many of the SD soldiers were reassigned to the 42nd, Rainbow, Division. Cpl. Langdeau and Pvt. Lamoreaux were assigned to the Machine Gun Company, 167th Infantry, 42nd Division (ASN 99002). After the Armistice, they sailed from Brest, France aboard the U.S.S. Montana on April 15, 1919. Cpl. Langdeau was discharged on May 9, 1919. Harvey reported that he had lost 10 head of cattle and five horses while he was overseas. On Sept. 21, 1923, Harvey married Aldena Thompkins. In 1935, the family was interviewed by a worker with the SDERA program. They were living in a three-room house in the Iron Nation District. They hauled their drinking water from the river three miles away. Harvey had been a farmer before the drought. Then he worked at herding cattle for a local rancher. After that man lost his cattle, Harvey looked for relief work. In the 1937 Census Roll, Harvey and Aldena had five children, Marlow, Ellsworth, Velda, Marilyn and Gail. Marlow served in the Army in WWII, and Ellsworth served during the 50s. Harvey entered the spirit world on Nov. 8, 1961. He is buried in Holy Comforter Episcopal Cemetery, Lower Brule.[16]

Langdeau, James P. James was born about Dec. 29, 1887, on the Lower Brule Reservation. His parents were Henry Langdeau and Mary Fallis. His father died shortly after he was born. In the 1889 Census Roll, James is listed with his mother and older brother, Joe. When James registered for the draft on June 5, 1917, he was ranching at Lower Brule. He joined the Army on May 25, 1918, at Oacoma. He was assigned to Co. A, 158th Infantry, 40th Division (ASN 3131344), which trained at Camp Kearny, California. The 158th Infantry sailed for France aboard the *Laomedon* on Aug.

11, 1918. Upon arrival, Pvt. Langdeau was reassigned to Co. F, 60th Infantry, 5th Division. Antoine Arpan from Cheyenne River also served in the 60th Infantry. A number of other men from nearby reservations served with the 19th Field Artillery, 5th Division. Most of the 5th Division had sailed for France in the early spring, and took part in the Offensives at St. Mihiel and Meuse Argonne. Pvt. Langdeau received a gunshot wound in his left forearm. He likely spent quite a while in hospitals. He was discharged at Camp Grant, IL, on April 1, 1919. The 5th Division did not return from France until July of 1919. Pvt. Langdeau received a Purple Heart. After returning home, he married Lucy Blackbird. They settled in Tripp County, on the Rosebud Reservation. In the 1940 U.S. Census, they lived with their children, Lawrence, Marie, Clarence, Howard, Earl, Francis and Melvin. James entered the spirit world on June 8, 1956, at the VA hospital in Hot Springs. He is buried in St. Augustine Catholic Cemetery, Dallas, Gregory County.[17]

LaPlant, Alexander George. Alex was born on the Cheyenne River Reservation about Oct. 27, 1898. His parents were Alex LaPlant and Johannah Madsen, who was born in Denmark. In the 1900 U.S. Census, he was listed with his parents and two brothers, Louis and Edward. Alex enlisted in Nebraska to serve in the U.S. Navy on May 23, 1918. He served in the 9th Naval District at Great Lakes and was discharged as a Seaman 2nd Class (NSN 1800427) on Sept. 30, 1921. On Nov. 12, 1921, he married Margaret Austin. They had two children, Donald and Virginia. Alex was run over by a loaded wagon and entered the spirit world on Dec. 13, 1928. He is buried in Timber Lake. His son, Donald, served in the Army during World War II.[18]

Louis W. LaPlant military funeral
JoLavae Gunville

LaPlant, Louis W. Louis was born on the Cheyenne River Reservation about Sept. 14, 1895. His parents were Alex and Johannah LaPlant. When Louis registered for the draft on June 5, 1917, he listed his occupation as cowboy. On June 24, 1917, he married Lucy Arpan, whose older brother, Antoine, served in the Army. Louis joined the Army on July 22, 1918, and was assigned to serve as a cook with the Headquarters Company, 29th Field Artillery, 10th Division. He also served in Battery A, 29th F.A. He was discharged on Feb. 4, 1919. Louis and Lucy had three children, Irene, Louis Jr., and Marjorie. Louis entered the spirit world in Mobridge on Aug. 4, 1921. He is buried in Timber Lake. His son, Louis Jr., served in the Army in WWII. His widow, Lucy, married Stephen Guerue.[19]

James L. LaPointe
Ancestry.com

LaPointe, James, L. He is listed on WWI veteran's memorial at Oglala Lakota College, Kyle, SD. James was born on the Pine Ridge Reservation on April 6, 1893. In the 1893 Census Roll, he is listed with his parents, Jack and Jennie, as well as two sisters, Annie and Eva, and a brother, Oliver. James attended the boarding school in Rapid City, and in 1911, was a member of the first class to graduate from the school. James enlisted in the military on April 2, 1917. This likely was with Co. I, 4th SD Infantry. This National Guard unit likely trained at Camp Meade until they were sent to Camp Greene, NC, in September 1917. Upon arrival, most of the SD soldiers were reassigned to units in the 41st Division. Sgt. LaPointe served with Co. B, 148th Machine Gun Battalion. He sailed with this unit from Hoboken, NJ, aboard the *Olympic* on Jan. 11, 1918. When that unit arrived in France, many of the men were reassigned to the 42nd Division, which suffered a lot of casualties. Sgt. LaPointe was discharged on July 1, 1919.

James was first married to Stella Twiss, with whom he had a daughter, Georgene. In the 1920s, James married Myrle Morrison (1903-1983). In the 1930 U.S. Census, he was working for the Highway Department. In the 1940 U.S. Census, he was working as a draftsman on road construction projects on the Pine Ridge Agency. He and Myrle had five children, James Jr., Yvonne, Richard, Jacqueline, and Adrienne. Their son, James Jr., served with the U.S. Navy on the U.S.S. Laffey in WWII. He was killed in Action in April, 1945 when his ship was hit by kamikaze pilots, killing 32 and wounding 71 other American sailors. From 1955 to 1965, the family lived in Rapid City. James was a member of the American Legion and the VFW. The family moved to Mira Loma, CA, in 1965, and to Fontana in 1974. In 1976, his book, *Legends of the Lakota*, was published. The illustrations were done by Louis Amiotte. James entered the spirit world in a local hospital on Aug. 7, 1979. His wife, Myrle, and daughters, Yvonne, Adrienne, Jacqueline, and Beryl, as well as a son, Richard, survived him. He is buried in Riverside National Cemetery, Section 7, site 5A. Myrle is buried with him.[20]

Samuel LaPointe
Tammy Valdez

LaPointe, Samuel. Samuel was born on Sept. 16, 1875, at the Greenwood Agency. In the 1886 Census Roll, Samuel is listed with his parents, John and Helen Mary (Pacquette), as well as his brothers, Jessie and John. Samuel attended school at the Santee Normal school, and taught school on the reservation. In 1909, he married Susan Dupris, with whom he had three children, Samuel Jr., Corrine and Irene. Susan entered the spirit world in 1915. Before the war, Samuel was working as farmer for the Indian Service at Wakpala. He enlisted in the Army on July 5, 1918, at Winner. He served as a Sergeant with the Headquarters Company, 339th Service Battalion (ASN 3084953). While still stationed in France, he wrote a letter to the *Word Carrier*, noting that "time seems to drag and pass along so slow these days. It seems that way since the 11th of November. Everybody is waiting to be sent home and that's what makes times travel too slow." Sgt. LaPointe sailed with his unit from Brest, France, aboard the *Troy* on Aug. 10, 1919. He also served in Casual Detachment #1348, Demobilization Group. He was discharged on Aug. 31, 1919, at Camp Dodge, IA. After the war, he married Clara Courtis McCloskey. Samuel helped organize the Chauncey Eagle Horn American Legion Post on the Rosebud Reservation. The family moved to Hardin, MT. Samuel and Clara had a daughter, Dorothy. In the early 30s, Samuel began to have some health problems, and became a patient at Battle Mountain Sanitarium, at Hot Springs. He entered the spirit world there on Feb. 1, 1936. He is buried at Bull Creek Mniska Cemetery near Hamill. His son, Samuel, served in the military during WWII.[21]

La Roche, John. John was born about Dec. 26, 1893, on the Lower Brule Reservation, to Norbert and Josephine (Fallis) La Roche. John married Pearl Bartholomew (1884-1979) in 1916. Pearl had attended Haskell Institute and had worked at the Tomah boarding school before coming to Lower Brule to work as a laundress. When John registered for the draft on June 5, 1917, he was working at the Lower Brule Agency. John served as a Private with the 163rd Depot Brigade at Camp Dodge, IA. John and Pearl had three children, Aurelia, Helen and Francis. In 1935, the family was interviewed by a social worker with the SDERA program. The family was living in a six-room house located 14 miles northwest of Lower Brule. This was on John's allotment. Pearl told the interviewer that she was interested in extension type work, but the local people were not interested in having the native people be a part of the program. Pearl's mother and father were living with them. John entered the spirit world in Lower Brule on Dec. 6, 1967. He is buried in St. Mary's Cemetery, Lower Brule.[22]

Larrabee, David. David was born on the Cheyenne River Reservation about Sept. 22, 1892. His parents were William Larrabee and Mary Crow Feather. The family name was sometimes spelled as Larvie. David was a student at the Carlisle boarding school from 1912 to 1914. On Oct. 3, 1914, David married Nancy Elk Head in Dupree. They had two children, Joseph and Mary. When David registered for the draft on June 5, 1917, he lived at Eagle Butte and raised cattle. When he joined the Army, he served in the 37th Co., 164th Depot Brigade, which was stationed at Camp Funston, KS. Sgt. Larrabee came down with pneumonia and entered the spirit world on Oct. 28, 1918. He is buried in St. Thomas Cemetery, Isabel, SD.

Larvie, Peter. Peter was born on the Rosebud Reservation on Sept. 9, 1896. His parents were Alex Larvie and Mollie Gerry. Peter registered for the draft on June 5, 1918. On Sept. 27, 1918, he joined the Army and was sent to Camp Funston. He was assigned to 37th Co. 164th Depot Brigade (ASN 4925103). He was discharged on Dec. 4, 1918, as a Private. After returning home, he married Lucy Eagle Bear. In the 1930 U.S. Census, he was farming at Rocky Ford. In the 1937 Census Roll, he and Lucy are listed with their children, Lloyd, Alvin, Georgiline, Leone, Vera, Peter and Irving. Peter entered the spirit world on Jan. 24, 1937, and is buried in Sacred Heart Cemetery, Norris. His son, Lloyd, served in the Army and his son, Alvin, served in the Navy.

Lawrence, Allen. Allen was born in Peever on the Sisseton-Wahpeton Reservation around Feb. 2, 1893. His parents were Levi and Mary Lawrence. As a child, he was listed as Aaron on the Sisseton Census Rolls. In 1910, Allen became a student at Flandreau, and in 1912, enrolled at Carlisle. The application that his mother filled out indicated that they lived 10 miles from the nearest public school. His father had died a few years before. After Allen returned home, he wrote back to Carlisle asking the school to sell him one of the Carlisle red and gold sweaters. He was living in Peever when he registered for the draft on June 1, 1917. Allen joined the Army and was assigned to the 362nd Ambulance Company, 316th Sanitary Train, 91st Division (ASN 2787730). Pvt. Lawrence sailed from New York aboard the *Olympic* on July 12, 1918. The 316th Sanitary Train served in the Sectors at Aubreville, Meuse-Argonne and Ypres-Lys. The 362nd was designated as an "Animal Drawn" unit. After the war, Pvt. Lawrence sailed from St. Nazaire aboard the U.S.S. *Virginian* on April 7, 1919, and arrived in Hoboken on April 20, 1919. He was discharged on May 7, 1919. In the 1920 U.S. Census, he was living with his mother and step father, John Tasinta. Allen was caught outside in cold weather and entered the spirit world on April 2, 1935.

Lawrence, Henry. Henry was born in Bullhead on the Standing Rock Reservation on May 18, 1894. His family belonged to the Holy Medicine Band of the Hunkpapa. In the 1910 U.S. Census, Henry is listed with his parents, Peter and Hattie, as well as his brother, Joseph. His mother is listed as a bead worker and his father a rancher. Peter, who was a cousin of Rain in the Face, served five years in the U.S. Army. Henry married Lillian Newman, with whom he had a daughter, Angela Viola. When he registered for the draft on June 5, 1917, they were ranching near Little Eagle.

Henry Lawrence (seated)
ND State Historical Society

Henry enlisted in the Army on May 24, 1918. He was sent to Camp Lewis, WA, and was assigned to Co. L, 362nd Infantry, 91st Division (ASN 2787137). Pvt. Lawrence sailed from New York aboard the *Empress of Russia* on July 6, 1918. Upon arrival in France, Co. L was billeted in Avrecourt. The 91st Division took part in the Meuse-Argonne Offensive, which began Sept. 26, 1918. On Sept. 28, the 362nd Regiment was fighting near Epinonville. On that day, Pvt. Lawrence received a bayonet wound in his calf, but taped that up himself. The next day, Sept. 29, he was hit in the ankle by two machine gun rounds while the 362nd was attacking Gesnes. According to a regimental history, the 362nd attacked the Germans in mid-afternoon, shouting "Powder River," the battle cry of the 91st. They successfully drove off the German Army, but over 100 men from the 362nd were left dead on the battlefield. Pvt. Lawrence was hospitalized and spent seven months in a military hospital in New York. He returned home to Little Eagle in May 1919.

After the war, Henry married Amy Gayton, with whom he had a son, Henry Jr. In 1935, the family was interviewed by a worker with the SDERA program. They lived in a two-room house along Spring Creek about seven miles from Little Eagle. One room of the house was constructed of logs while the second room was framed with sawn lumber. They had a good spring nearby. They had raised cattle before Henry went in the Army. They still put up some hay and had harvested a small crop of millet, in spite of the drought. Henry received a disability payment of $25.28, which was enough to buy groceries. Henry's father, Peter, was still living with them. In some Standing Rock Census Rolls in the 1930s, he is listed as Henry Hokakte. Henry later lived in Parshall, ND. Henry came down with pneumonia and entered the spirit world in the home of Gideon Hayes of Little Eagle on Feb. 23, 1972. Henry is buried in St. Paul's Episcopal Cemetery, in Little Eagle.[23]

Lawrence, Thomas H. Thomas was born in Santee, NE, on Sept. 7, 1895. His father was George Lawrence. In the 1910 federal census, he was a student at the boarding school in Genoa, NE. He joined the Army on March 6, 1918, and was assigned to Ambulance Co. 38, 6th Sanitary Train (ASN 938056). He served with Moses Trudell. They sailed from New York aboard the *Darro* on July 7, 1918. The 6th Sanitary Train served in the campaigns of Gerardmer and Meuse-Argonne. This unit sailed for home from Brest aboard the *Kaiserine Auguste Victoria* on June 10, 1919. Pvt. Lawrence was discharged on June 25, 1919. He returned home and lived with his father. In the 1920s Census Rolls, he was listed with the Yankton Agency. He last lived in Yankton, SD, before entering the spirit world on Feb. 15, 1972. He is buried in Grand Island, NE.

Leader Charge, Paul. Paul was born on the Rosebud Reservation on Oct. 19, 1894. In the 1900 U.S. Census, he is listed with his parents, Joseph and Minnie, as well as a brother and sister, Levi and Emma. When Paul registered with the draft on June 5, 1917, he was farming with his father near Wososo. Paul joined the Army on July 22, 1918, and was assigned to Field Remount Squadron (FMS) No. 343, QMC (ASN 3955058). Pvt. Leader Charge sailed from New York aboard the *Orca* on Oct. 27, 1918. FMS No. 343 was stationed at Carbon Blanc. After the Armistice, Pfc. Leader Charge sailed for home from Bordeaux aboard the *Otsega* on June 17, 1919. He was discharged on July 17, 1919, as a Pfc. After the war, he married Winnie Iyott, whose brother, Amos, had served in the

Army. The family farmed in Todd County. In the 1940 U.S. Census, Paul and Winnie are listed with their four children, Garfield, Zona, Wilma and Dana. Paul entered the spirit world on Oct. 11, 1995, and is buried in O Holy Innocents Cemetery, Parmelee.

Leaf, Joseph. Joseph was born in Bullhead on the Standing Rock Reservation about April 27, 1890. In the 1894 Census Roll, he is listed with his parents, Bede and Mary, and two sisters, Emily and Betsy. Around 1908, he married Elizabeth Black Hawk. When he registered for the draft on June 5, 1917, the family was farming and had three children. When Joseph joined the Army, he was assigned as a Wagoner with the Headquarters Detachment, 30th Machine Gun Battalion. This was part of the 10th Division, which trained at Camp Funston after the 89th Division was deployed to Europe. The 10th Division was demobilized in January 1919. Joseph was discharged on Jan. 30, 1919. Joseph and Elizabeth had four children. After she passed away, he married Mary Brought (1890-1967), who had been married to Benedict Short Baldhead, a fellow veteran. Mary's brother, Barney, had died during the war. In 1935, the family was interviewed by a worker with the SDERA program. Mary's son, Barney was living with them, as was Velma, the daughter of Joseph and Mary. Their home was a one log building four miles west of Bullhead. Joseph had been working on conservation relief projects which gave them enough income to live on. Joe used his team of horses on the relief projects, for which he was compensated. In 1934, Joseph had planted a quarter of wheat, but it did not come up. He was a member of the American Legion and Mary belonged to the Auxiliary. He also indicated that he regularly danced at Indian dances. Joseph entered the spirit world in his home in Bullhead on April 23, 1956. He is buried in St. Aloysius Cemetery in Bullhead.[24]

LeBeau, Patrick. Patrick was born on the Cheyenne River Reservation on Oct. 22, 1895. In the 1900 U.S. Census, he is listed with his parents, John Baptiste and Julia, as well as a sister, Amy, and brothers, Edward, Albert and Paul. When Patrick registered for the draft on June 5, 1917, he was ranching on his father's ranch near Promise. Patrick joined the Army on April 25, 1918, and was sent to train at Camp Funston, KS, with the men forming the 89th Division. Patrick was assigned to Co. G, 355th Regiment (ASN 2845243). A number of other SD soldiers served in Co. G, including Clyde Lafferty, Benjamin Comes out Bear, Titus Wilson and Roy Lessert, who was killed in action in France. The ships transporting the 89th Division steamed out of New York on June 4, 1918. Pvt. LeBeau sailed on the *Baltic*. The 355th Regiment took part in the theaters at Lucey, Euvezin, St. Mihiel and Meuse-Argonne. After the Armistice, Corporal LeBeau received an evaluation from Captain Barlow, stating the he was "good at night work, runner, and observer. Has excellent sense of direction." The 89th Division suffered 7,291 casualties in the war. Cpl. LeBeau sailed from Brest aboard the *Leviathan* on May 15, 1919, and was discharged on May 31, 1919.

After he returned home, Patrick married Ida Swift Bird on Nov. 25, 1923. In the 1930 U.S. Census, they were farming in Dewey County with three children, Herbert, Wilma and Emaline. In 1935, the family was interviewed by a worker with the SDERA program. At that time, Patrick was camping at the emergency conservation work site where a dam was being built. His wife and family were at their home, which was a four-room frame house built on his mother's allotment, about 18 miles from the Agency. At the home water was obtained in barrels hauled from the Missouri River about a half mile. Patrick was a member of the American Legion. Ida showed the state worker a book they had about the history of Patrick's regiment, as well as his discharge papers and war relics he had brought back. Patrick's mother and Ida's mother were living with them. In the 1940 U.S. Census, Patrick was working as a night watchman on a road construction site. They had several more children, including Inez, Eric, Harold and Maurice, Emaline, Vetal and Seymour. Their oldest son, Herbert, served in the Army during WWII, while Eric served during the Vietnam era. Seymour also served in the military. Patrick entered the spirit world in the Mobridge Care Center on May 6, 1983, and is buried in St. Mary's Cemetery, north of LaPlant.[25]

Casper LeCompte
JoLavae Gunville

LeCompte, Casper. Casper was born on March 6, 1891, at Fort Pierre. His parents were Louis LeCompte and Julia Narcelle. His mother died shortly after he was born. His father then married Christine Overseth. In the 1900 U.S. Census, they are listed as Sans Arc, but were enrolled at Standing Rock. Casper was a student at the Carlisle Boarding School. When he registered for the draft on June 5, 1917, he was ranching near Wakpala. He joined the Army on June 24, 1918, and was trained at Camp Funston, KS. He was assigned to the 690th Motor Transport Company (ASN 3309353). Pvt. LeCompte sailed for Europe from Newport News, VA, aboard the *Duca Daosta* on Aug. 30, 1918. He was traveling with the "July Detachment Chauffeurs, QMC." After the Armistice, Pfc. LeCompte sailed from Bordeaux aboard the U.S.S. *Santa Malta* on July 3, 1919. He arrived in Brooklyn on July 15, 1919, and was discharged on July 26, 1919. He became a member of the American Legion. While he was in the Army, he lost 20% of his stock, as well as had ruined hayfields and fences broke down. He could not find a renter.

Casper married Virginia LaPlante (1902-1993) in White Horse on Jan. 16, 1921. In 1935, the family was interviewed by a worker with the SDERA program. They were living in a 24' x 28' frame house with four rooms. On their farmstead they had a barn large enough for six teams and a chicken house. They owned 20 horses, 40 head of cattle and 37 hogs. Their farm was located on a trail about four miles from a main market road. The river was about ¼ mile away. Casper moved to Timber Lake in 1949. He entered the spirit world at the VA hospital in Hot Springs on July 10, 1956. His widow and nine sons, Louis, Ivan, Casper, Vetal Stephen, David, Paul, Edward and Morris, as well as his daughters, Memoree and Vivian, survived him. He is buried in Timber Lake.[26]

LeCompte, Cyril. Cyril, a brother to Casper, was born at Fort Pierre on Jan. 7, 1889. His parents were Louis LeCompte and Julia Narcelle. Cyril was also ranching near Wakpala when he registered for the draft. Cyril joined the Army on Oct. 5, 1917, and underwent training at Camp Funston, KS. He was assigned to B. Troop, Military Police (ASN 2194464). In the spring he received a furlough to return home. When it came time to return to camp, the Grand River was flooding. His brother, Casper, described what he did to help Cyril.

> While still under the draft call and three months before I entered the army at Funston, my brother come home on furlough, and he couldn't get back to any railroad as the rivers where all flooded with ice and water and his furlough was up. And to get him back to railroad, I forded the Grand River amidst ice to get a boat for him to cross over to meet his train to Camp Funston before his furlough expired. It was a dangerous under taken [sic] but as he did not swim very well and I did, I under took it knowing I was ready for the Army and just as well be doing something in that respect for my country then, as later. This did not happen over there but all the same during the war. It may not seem much but I never no off [know of] anybody crossing a river in that condition and that river was the highest for 20 yrs. Or more bridges where all washed out. I never mentioned it to an Officier but

have to YMCA man; he thought I ought to mentioned it to my Leutennent [sic]. But I did not think it much so I did not mentioned it. I have got good straight prove for this.

After returning to Camp Funston, Corporal LeCompte was assigned to Troop B, 314th MP Battalion, which sailed from New York aboard the *Saxon* on June 28, 1918. Corp. LeCompte was later reassigned to Co. I, 356th Regiment, 89th Division. The 356th Regiment took part in the Offensives at St. Mihiel and Meuse-Argonne. As part of the Army of Occupation, the 3rd Battalion, 356th Regiment was billeted at Schweich, Germany. They left to return to the States from Brest aboard the U.S.S. *Huntington* on May 16, 1919. Corporal LeCompte was discharged at Camp Dodge, IA, on June 9, 1919. He had lost 14 head of cattle and two horses while overseas.

After returning home, he married Catherine Claymore (1900-1982). For a while they ranched on the Standing Rock Reservation. In the 1930s, they moved on to the Cheyenne River Reservation. Cyril was a member of the American Legion. In 1935, the family was interviewed by a state worker with the SDERA program. They lived near a school south of Mobridge along Claymore Creek. The family owned 19 head of cattle, 8 horses, and 26 chickens. They milked five of their cows, so there was plenty of milk for the family. In the 1940 U.S. Census, Cyril and Catherine had nine children, Cyril Jr., Cleone, Quentin, Marian, June, Claymore, Narcisse, Gordon and Rita. Quentin and Claymore served in the military during the Korean War. Marian served as a nurse in the Army National Guard. Cyril entered the spirit world on Oct. 6, 1975.[27]

Left Heron, Oliver. (see Heron, Oliver) Oliver was born on the Pine Ridge Reservation on March 29, 1898. In the 1904 Census Roll, he is listed with his parents, Pehan Catka and Lottie. When Oliver registered for the draft on June 5, 1917, he was farming near Allen in Bennett County. He joined the Army on April 10, 1918, and was sent to Camp Funston, KS, for training. He was assigned as a Wagoner to the Supply Co., 355th Infantry, 89th Division (ASN 2195583). Pvt. Left Heron sailed with his unit from New York aboard the *Baltic* on June 4, 1918. The 355th Regiment was in the Offensives at St. Mihiel and Meuse Argonne. After the Armistice, 1st Lt. W.F. Whalen wrote an evaluation for Wag. Left Heron, saying he was a soldier of "quiet disposition but associates very readily with white men of Co. Good in care of animals. Excellent courage under fire." Wagoner Left Heron sailed with the 355th Infantry from France aboard the liner *Leviathan* on May 15, 1919. While at Camp Dodge, Corp. Left Heron served briefly with Casual Detachment 585, Demobilization Group. Left Heron was discharged at Camp Dodge, IA, on May 31, 1919. Upon returning home, he married Sallie Short Bear. After she passed away, Oliver married Susie Richard. They had a son, Louis, who served in the Army in the 1960s. In the 1940 U.S. Census, Oliver and Susie lived with their son, Louis and step daughters, Anna and Gladys, as well as a step son, Delbert. Oliver entered the spirit world on Nov. 13, 1956, and is buried in the Inestimable Gift Cemetery, Allen.[28]

LeRoy, Logan. Logan was born in Niobrara, NE, to Henry LeRoy and Tesoua Birdhead on Sept. 22, 1895. He was listed with the Census Rolls for the Yankton Agency. When he registered for the draft on June 5, 1917, he was living in Greenwood, SD, and working for Joe Iron Bear. He joined the Army on Aug. 29, 1918, and was sent to Camp Funston, KS. He served as a Private with the 44th Co., 164th Depot Brigade (ASN 4501784). He was discharged on July 31, 1919. In the 1920 U.S. Census, he was living in Ree Township with his wife, Lillian, a daughter, Susette, and his father-in-law, Joe Iron Bear. Lillian entered the spirit world in 1922. Logan moved his family to Blackbird, NE, on the Winnebago-Omaha Reservation. He entered the spirit world on April 30, 1952, and is buried in the Ponca Indian Cemetery, Ponca City, OK.

Edward Lessert
Ancestry.com

Lessert, Edward. Edward was born on the Pine Ridge Reservation on Jan. 3, 1890, to Samuel Lessert and Mary Valandry. In the 1904 Census Roll, Edward is listed with his father and his brothers, Joseph, Benjamin, Roy and Samuel Jr., and his sister, Olive. In 1913, Edward married his first wife, Minnie Robertson. Minnie's brother, William, also served with the Army. When Edward registered for the draft on June 5, 1917, he was running a garage in Martin. He joined the Army on June 26, 1918 and was sent to Camp Funston. He was transferred to Camp Fremont, CA, where he was assigned to Battery E, 83rd Field Artillery, 8th Division (ASN 3315753). On Oct. 30, 1918, the 83rd Field Artillery embarked from Hoboken, NJ, for France. They arrived shortly before the Armistice. Not all of the 8th Division made it over to France. After the Armistice, the division was demobilized through various camps. The 83rd Field Artillery sailed for the U.S. from Brest, France, aboard the *President Grant* on Jan. 4, 1919, and arrived in Hoboken on Jan. 18, 1919. Pvt. Lessert was discharged on Feb. 18, 1919. Edward's brother, Roy, also served, and his sister, Olive, married another vet, Henry Flood. After the war, Edward worked for the BIA. He worked for many years in Fort Hall, ID, until retiring in February 1953. In 1936, he married his second wife, Addy. Edward entered the spirit world in Portland, OR, on Feb. 15, 1963. His widow and daughter, Marian, survived him. Edward and Addy are buried in Willamette National Cemetery, Section G, site 3342.

Lessert, Roy. Roy was a brother to Edward. He was born on the Pine Ridge Reservation on July 12, 1893. Roy married Fannie Moor in 1915. They had a daughter, Royaldine. When Roy registered for the draft on June 5, 1917, he was working in Martin as an auto driver and laborer. He may have worked with his brother, Edward. Roy joined the Army and trained with the 89th Division at Camp Funston. Roy was assigned to Co. G. (2nd Battalion), 355th Infantry (ASN 2846799). He sailed with his unit from New York aboard the *Baltic* on June 4, 1918. The 355th Infantry served in the Sectors at Lucey, St. Mihiel, Euvezin and Meuse-Argonne. In the Meuse-Argonne Offensive, the 355th Infantry, 2nd Battalion, was attacking German positions in the Bois de Bantheville in late October. Pfc. Roy Lessert was killed there on Oct. 23, 1918. He is buried in the Meuse-Argonne American Cemetery at Romagne-sous-Montfaucon, Plot H, Row 6, Grave 3. After the war, his widow, Fannie, married Paul Lamoreaux, a fellow veteran. In the early 1920s, Paul and Fannie and her daughter, Royaldine, moved to Portland, OR.

John Little
Ancestry.com

Little, John. John was born about February 1896 on the Rosebud Reservation. In the 1900 U.S. Census, he is listed with his parents, Eugene Little and Annie Ledoux, as well as a brother, Henry. Eugene had served with the 6th U.S. Cavalry from 1891-93. John married Helen King at Winner on May 17, 1917. When John registered for the draft on June 5, 1917, he was farming near Winner in Tripp County. He was described as a short man of medium build. When John joined the Army, he was assigned to Co. B, 342nd Machine Gun Battalion, 89th Division (ASN 2185831). Pvt. Little sailed from New

York aboard the *Caronia* on June 4, 1918. He served in the Sectors at Lucey, St. Mihiel, Euvezin and Meuse-Argonne. On Nov. 1, 1918, the 89th Division began an assault on the German Army dug in on the Heights of Barricourt. Sgt. Little was killed in action on that day. Several other SD soldiers in the 89th Division's MP unit were also killed on that day. They were Moses Clown and Joseph Takes the Shield. On Feb. 4, 1919, 1st Sgt. F.O. Rains of Co. B, 342nd MG Bn. wrote a letter to the widow of Sgt. Little, describing his last battle. See Appendix C. Sgt. Little's body was brought back to the U.S. aboard the *Wheaton*, which sailed from Antwerp, Belgium, on Aug. 6, 1921. He was buried in Bull Creek Miniska Cemetery in Tripp County.[29]

Little Bird, Eli. Eli was born in on the Crow Creek Reservation around 1898, to Little Bird and Julia. In the 1912 Crow Creek Census Roll, he was listed with his mother and his step-father, Tiona. Eli joined the Army and was assigned to Co. G, 2nd Infantry, 19th Division. This division was organized at Camp Dodge, IA, in September 1918, but did not go overseas. The men were demobilized in January 1919. He was discharged as a Pfc. On Dec. 11, 1923, Eli married Evelyn Ross at Ft. Thompson. Eli became ill with tuberculosis and entered the spirit world in Wakpala on June 15, 1929. He is buried at St. Elizabeth's Mission, Wakpala. His widow later married William Sazue, a fellow veteran. In a ceremony held in Wakpala on March 17, 2017, Pfc. Little Bird was honored for his service as a Code Talker.[30]

Little Crow, Isaac. Isaac was born in Oak Creek on the Rosebud Reservation on March 18, 1895. His parents were William Cleveland Little Crow and Nellie Red Dog. When Isaac registered for the draft on June 5, 1917, he was working as a night watchman at the Rosebud Boarding School. Isaac joined the Army on April 26, 1918, and was sent to Camp Funston for training. He was assigned to Co. G, 355th Infantry, 89th Division (ASN 2846689). His unit sailed from New York aboard the *Baltic* on June 4, 1918. He served with Pfc. Roy Lessert, from Pine Ridge. They fought together in the Offensives at St. Mihiel and Meuse-Argonne. On Oct. 21, 1918, the 2nd Battalion, 355th Infantry met severe resistance from the Germans in the middle of the Bois de Bantheville. Pvt. Little Crow was severely wounded on that day. Pfc. Lessert was killed in action two days later. Pvt. Little Crow returned home from Brest, France, aboard the *Maui* on March 8, 1919. He was traveling with Detachment #31, labeled as "walking cases requiring no dressing." He was discharged on April 19, 1919. The rest of the 89th Division did not return home till late in May 1919. After his return, his father gave a feast in his son's honor. Elders gave Isaac the name, Sleeping Bear. Isaac married Delphine Roubideaux, with whom he had a daughter, Marjorie. In March 1937, Isaac was awarded a Purple Heart in a special program held in the White Thunder Community Hall. Isaac entered the spirit world on April 30, 1938. The Legion Posts from Rosebud and Winner had charge of his funeral. He is buried in Mosher.

Little Dog, Martin. Martin was born in Bullhead on the Standing Rock Reservation on March 18, 1891. His family were members of the CrossBear band of Hunkpapa. In the 1905 Census Roll, Martin is listed with his father, Sunkaciqala [Little Dog], and mother, Winyankatuya [High woman], and a brother, John. When Martin registered for the draft on June 5, 1917, he was farming at Bullhead. He joined the Army on July 22, 1918, and served as a Private in Company 365, Bakery Battalion, Quartermaster Corps (ASN 3954597). Pvt. Little Dog sailed for France from Hoboken, NJ, aboard the *Northern Pacific* on Nov. 12, 1918. He was traveling with the Camp Johnston October Automatic Replacement Draft, Co. #2, QMC. He spent eight months overseas. Bakery Company 365 sailed from Brest, France, aboard the *Nansemond* on June 28, 1919. He was discharged on July 16, 1919. After returning home, he married Sarah Kills Crow. In 1935, the family was interviewed by a worker with the SDERA program. At that time, the family was living in a tent at a Public

Works site. At this project, they used their own team of horses for road work. The family owned a permanent home on Sarah's allotment, along the Grand River. They had four sons, Ross, Norman, Dale and Miles. While working on the site, somebody had broken into their home and stolen their table. They had managed to put up seven loads of hay for their horses over the winter. Martin was a member of the American Legion and the VFW. Their sons, Ross and Dale served in the Army during the WWII era. Sarah entered the spirit world in 1963. Martin entered the spirit world in the McLaughlin Hospital on Nov. 4, 1967. He is buried in Messiah Congregational Cemetery in Little Eagle.[31]

Little Eagle, Allen. Edward Allen was born on the Standing Rock Reservation about Oct. 1, 1899. In the 1902 Census Roll, he is listed with his parents, George Little Eagle and Her Medicine (Tapejutawastewin). Allan enlisted in the Navy on April 22, 1918. He served as a Seaman 2nd Class with a construction company (NSN 1816147). He was discharged on Sept. 30, 1921. He re-enlisted in the Navy during WWII, serving from 1942-1945. He received his honorable discharge with the rank of Chief Carpenter's Mate. When he returned home from WWI, he married Margaret DeRockbraine, whose brother, Thomas, has served in the Army. Allen's brother, Leo, had also served in the Army. Allen's sister, Jessie, married James Shoestring, also a veteran. In 1935, the Little Eagle family was interviewed by a worker with the SDERA program. Allan was living in a tent on various construction sites while his family lived in a permanent home on the Government Reserve in Bullhead. Allen moved from site to site on various dam construction projects. He did not approve of these projects. He thought they were a waste of money because 75% of them would not hold water and they were not made right. He thought road construction would have been a better use of the money. In the 1940 U.S. Census, Allen and Margaret were living in Fort Yates with their children, Harry, Mary Ellen, and Clement. Allen was working as an assistant surveyor. Allen entered the spirit world on April 2, 1950, and is buried in Bullhead.[32]

Little Eagle, Lee. Lee was born on the Crow Creek Reservation about Aug. 17, 1899. His parents were Henry and Lucy Little Eagle. When Lee registered for the draft on Sept. 11, 1918, he was living in Grosse, SD, and ranching. In August 1919, he married Cordelia Eagle. In 1921, he married Winnie Hawk. Lee entered the spirit world on April 14, 1923, and is buried in St. John the Baptist Cemetery, Buffalo County, which lists him as a veteran.

Little Eagle, Leo. Leo was born on the Standing Rock Reservation on Aug. 11, 1895. His parents were George Wanbliciqala [Little Eagle] and Her Medicine (Tapejutawastewin). His younger brother was Allen. When Leo registered for the draft on June 5, 1917, he lived at Bullhead and was farming. He joined the Army on July 21, 1918, and served in the Quartermaster Corps (ASN 3954586). He had trained at Camp Dodge, IA. Pvt. Little Eagle sailed for France from Hoboken, NJ, aboard the *Northern Pacific* on Nov. 12, 1918. He and Pvt. Martin Little Dog were traveling with the Camp Johnston October Automatic Replacement Draft, Co. #2, QMC. When Pvt. Little Eagle returned home, he sailed from Brest, France, aboard the U.S.S. *Kaiserin Auguste Victoria* on July 9, 1919. He had served with the Graves Registration Service, Headquarters Detachment. He was discharged on July 26, 1919. He joined the American Legion and the VFW. On April 15, 1923, he married Angeline Eagle from Sisseton at Bullhead. Angeline's brother, Joseph, also served in the military. In 1935, the family was interviewed by a worker with the SDERA program. Their home was a one room log house, 24' x 14', located nine- and one-half miles from Bullhead. Leo worked the emergency conservation projects, using his own team of horses. He also owned a mower, plow, drill, disc, a wagon and a set of harness. In the 1940 U.S. Census, he was still working on conservation projects. The family later ranched. He and Angeline had four children, Evelyn, Ruth,

Olay, and Nancy. Leo entered the spirit world in McLaughlin Community Hospital on Jan. 15, 1973. He is buried in St. John's Episcopal Cemetery in Bullhead.[33]

Rolland Little Elk (right)
Mathers Museum

Little Elk, Rolland. Rolland was born on Jan. 4, 1895, in Fort Thompson. In the 1900 U.S. Census, he is listed with his parents, Little Elk and Noisy Cane. Rolland was also known as Red Eagle Feather. In the early 1900s, Rolland was a student at the Crow Creek Agency School. His teacher, Estelle Aubrey Brown, wrote a book, *Stubborn Fool*, which is about her teaching experience at the school. She mentions Rolland as one of her students. Rolland later attended the Haskell Institute, in Kansas. He joined the Army in Kimball, SD, on May 2, 1917. He likely enlisted in Troop L, 1st SD Cavalry, a SD National Guard unit that was sent to Camp Cody, NM. On June 28, 1918, he sailed from New York aboard the *Honorata*. He was part of Co. 18, Camp Cody June Automatic Replacement Draft. Upon arrival in France, he was assigned to Co. A, 308th Infantry, 77th Division (ASN 1429234). The 308th Infantry participated in the fighting in the sectors of Baccarat, Vesle, Oise-Aisne, Forêt d'Argonne and Meuse-Argonne. Eighteen soldiers from Company A, 308th Inf., were part of the "Lost Battalion" which became cut off and surrounded by the German Army in the Argonne Forest in early October of 1918. Pvt. Little Elk likely helped to free the trapped soldiers. After the Armistice, Pvt. Little Elk received an evaluation from his commanding officer, stating that he "was able to orient himself without difficulty, having sense of direction, both at the day and night. Well educated, writes a good hand, a splendid rifleman and very intelligent." Lieutenant Hess added that Pvt. Little Elk did most of the patrol work in the vicinity of Ville Savoye, along the Vesle River, in late August and early September. The soldiers sailed for home from Brest, France, on April 19, 1919, aboard the S.S. *America*. Upon arrival in the U.S., Pvt. Little Elk and a fellow soldier, Pvt. Sam Morris, were photographed on May 2, 1919, by Joseph Dixon. Pvt. Little Elk was discharged at Camp Dodge, IA, on May 18, 1919. After returning home, he married Emma Shepherd on Dec. 11, 1919. Emma was a sister to Peter Shepherd, who also served in France. Rolland became ill with tuberculosis and was admitted to the Battle Mountain Sanatorium on July 22, 1927. He entered the spirit world at Battle Mountain Sanatorium on Aug. 2, 1927, and his body was sent back to Chamberlain. He is buried in Christ Church Cemetery, Ft. Thompson, SD. Emma entered the spirit world on March 4, 1931.[34]

Little Hawk, Robert. Robert (Bert) was born in Spring Creek on the Rosebud Reservation around Sept. 13, 1896. In the 1900 U.S. Census, he is listed as "Burt" and his parents were Samuel Cetan Ciqala [Little Hawk] and Irene. He also had a sister, Agnes. His father, Samuel, had served with the Army in the 16th Infantry in the early 1890s. In 1911, Bert became a student at Carlisle, but had some disciplinary problems and did not do well. After his parents entered the spirit world, Bert reapplied to attend Carlisle, and was admitted. When he registered for the draft on June 12, 1917, as a student, he was on an outing and working for a farmer near Langhorne, PA. He entered the Army with the draft of Aug. 27, 1918, and was sent to Camp Funston, KS. He was assigned to the 390th Bakery Co. In March 1919, he was allowed a few days of furlough to visit his home in Rosebud. After his discharge on May 26, 1919, , he married Winifred Thunder Hawk. In the 1937

Census Roll, they are listed with their daughters, Christine and Lillian. Robert entered the spirit world on July 6, 1968, and is buried in St. Charles Cemetery, St. Francis.

Little Money, Charles. Charles was born on March 16, 1896, on the Rosebud Reservation. His parents were Smith and Rosalie Little Money. His sister, Nancy, married Guy Lambert, a fellow veteran. His sister, Ada, married Bernard Flood. Charles married Lucy Eagle Dog. They were living in Okreek when Charles registered for the draft on June 5, 1917. Charles joined the Army on July 22, 1918. He was assigned to Co. L, 88th Infantry, 19th Division, which trained at Camp Dodge, IA. He was discharged as a Private at Camp Dodge, IA, on Jan. 24, 1919. In 1921, he was a member of the Chauncey Eagle Horn Legion Post at Rosebud. In 1929, he was admitted as a patient to the Battle Mountain Sanatorium, suffering from Trachoma. In the 1940 U.S. Census, he and Lucy were living with her sister, Susie Menard. Charles was working in a CCC project near Okreek. He entered the spirit world on Oct. 21, 1967, and is buried in Calvary Cemetery, Okreek.

Little Owl, Charley. Charley was born around 1898 near Greenwood, in Charles Mix County. His Yanktonai parents were John and Sarah Little Owl. On July 24, 1917, Charley enlisted to serve in the Army. He likely joined Co. M, 4th Infantry, SD National Guard, whose headquarters was at Yankton. When the 4th Infantry arrived at Camp Greene, NC, an officer met Company M as they left the train. The officer said, "You think you're Captain of Company M, 4th South Dakota Infantry. Well, you're not. This is the 147th Field Artillery and you're Captain-Adjutant of the Second Battalion." Many of the Native soldiers who had enlisted in the 4th SD Infantry ended up serving with Battery C, 147th Field Artillery. Pvt. Little Owl (ASN 139512) was one of those soldiers. Pvt. Little Owl sailed from New York aboard the *Olympic* on Jan. 11, 1918. Throughout most of the war, the 147th F.A. was attached to the 32nd (Red Arrow) Division. Pvt. Little Owl received an evaluation from 1st Lt. A. M. Knudtson stating he was an "excellent driver. One of the six Indian drivers in a section that can put their carriages over ground it would seem impossible to pass over. Good judgement and initiative." The 32nd Division suffered 13,392 casualties in the war. Pvt. Little Owl sailed from Brest, France, aboard the *Kansas* on May 1, 1919, arriving in Philadelphia on May 13. Pvt. Little Owl was discharged on May 23, 1919. In the 1920 U.S. Census, Charley was living with his parents in Charles Mix County. Charley later lived with his wife, Cora, in Pukwana. Charley caught pneumonia and entered the spirit world in the Crow Creek Hospital on January 10, 1934, and is buried in St John the Baptist Cemetery, Fort Thompson.

Little Soldier, Philip. Philip was born on the Rosebud Reservation on April 5, 1894. His mother was Shoots at Her. In the 1910 U.S. Census, Philip was living with his step father, Iron Nest, and his mother. Philip married Frances Goodahl. After Philip entered the spirit world on Nov. 1, 1918, *The Indian Sentinel* published an article about veterans and listed him as a casualty. He is buried in St. Charles Cemetery, St Francis.[35]

Livermont, Henry. Henry was born on the Cheyenne River Reservation on Oct. 19, 1893. His parents were Henry Livermont and Amelia Arpan. When Henry registered for the draft on June 5, 1917, he was farming near Timber Lake. He joined the Army on May 31, 1918, and was assigned to Veterinary Hospital #8, 3rd Battalion, Veterinary Corps (ASN 3175919). Pvt. Livermont sailed from Newport News, VA, aboard the *Susquehana* on June 26, 1918. This hospital was in Claye-Souilly, northeast of Paris. After the Armistice, Pvt. Livermont sailed for home from Brest, France, aboard the U.S.S. *Frederick* on May 23, 1919. Pvt. Livermont was later assigned to Casual Detachment #726, Demobilization Group, after returning to the U.S. He was discharged on June 12, 1919. On August 6, 1919, he married Christine Traversie. In the 1920 U.S. Census, they lived in Firesteel. In

Henry Livermont
Philip & Luree Livermont

the 1940 U.S. Census, they family was ranching in Dewey County with their children, Catherine, Imelda, Ramona, Francis, Joseph, Donald, Arlene and Philip. Francis served in the Army during the Korean War, while Joseph and Donald served with the Marines. Henry entered the spirit world near his home on Aug. 25, 1944, and is buried in St. Joseph's Cemetery, Timber Lake.[36]

Lodge, Joseph Grover. Joseph was born about 1884 on the Crow Creek Reservation to William and Eva Lodge. In the 1903 Lower Yanktonai Census Roll, he is listed with his wife Helen Burnt Prairie. In the 1918 Census Roll, he and Helen have two daughters, Elma and Myrtle. Joseph joined the Army on Aug. 14, 1918, and was assigned to Co. C, Development Battalion #1 (ASN 3776757). He was discharged as a Private on Dec. 1, 1918. His wife, Helen, entered the spirit world in 1927. In 1930, he married Helen Hawk. In 1940, he married Sophie Bold. Joseph suffered from Tuberculosis and entered the spirit world in his home in Fort Thompson on Aug. 16, 1943. He is buried in the Episcopal Cemetery in Ft. Thompson.

Long, Alfred William. Alfred Long Pumpkin was born on the Rosebud Reservation on Feb. 21, 1899. His parents were Alexander Long Pumpkin and Talking. Alfred enlisted in the Navy during the war, serving from June 4, 1917 to Sept. 10, 1917. He was discharged as an Apprentice Seaman. Around 1922, he married Frances Siers (1899-1966), who had two brothers who served during the war. In the 1940 U.S. Census, Alfred was working as Assistant Painter in a building construction project. He and Frances had eight children, William, Julia, Arthur, Alexander, Robert, Albert Jr., Marion and Jesse. Alfred entered the spirit world in the Public Health Service Hospital in Rosebud on June 4, 1977. He is buried in Spring Creek Cemetery, Todd County.

Long Bull, Baptiste. Baptiste was born on the Standing Rock Reservation around March 21, 1896. In the 1900 Census Roll, he is listed with his parents, Dominick and Sadie, and two sisters, Christine and Ella. When Baptiste registered for the draft, he was farming near Wakpala. He joined the Army on June 24, 1918. He served in the 20th Machine Gun Battalion, 10th Division, which did not go overseas. He was discharged on June 16, 1919. After returning home, he married Emma Black Tongue. In the 1940 U.S. Census, He and Emma are listed with their two children, Frank and Louella. Baptiste was working in the C.C.C. program at Ft. Yates. Baptiste entered the spirit world in a Bismarck hospital on Oct. 30, 1977. He is buried in St. Peter's Cemetery, Ft. Yates, ND.[37]

Long Elk, Julian. Julian was born on March 4, 1891, at Ft. Yates on the Standing Rock Reservation. His parents were Thomas and Hannah (Walutaokiyewin) Long Elk. They were members of the Grindstone Band of Hunkpapa. Around 1911, he married Margaret Job, who was from the Sisseton Reservation. When Julian registered for the draft on June 5, 1917, he and Maggie were farming near Little Eagle with their two oldest children, Angus and Mary. Julian joined the Army in late September of 1917. He was sent to Camp Funston, KS, where he was assigned to Co. C, 340th Machine Gun Battalion. After 4 and ½ months of training, he was given a medical discharge on Jan. 23, 1919, due to signs of tuberculosis symptoms. Julian received a pension of $50 per month. In the 1930 U.S. Census, the Long Elk family was living on the Pine Ridge Reservation. In 1935, the family was interviewed by a worker with the SDERA program. At that time, they were renting two rooms from Mrs. Paul Long Bull, in the Little Eagle District. This location was convenient for their children to attend school. Julian told the worker that the government construction projects provided work, but resulted in many families not being able to do upkeep on their permanent homes. The Long Elk family had a permanent home located 7 and ½ miles south of McLaughlin. In 1940, they were back in Corson County, where Julian served as a clergyman. His son, Chauncey, served in the Army in World War II. In the late 1940s, Julian was serving as a clergyman in Cherry Creek. He entered the spirit world there on Nov. 26, 1949.[38]

Isaac Looking Back
Findagrave

Looking Back, Isaac. Isaac was born on the Standing Rock Reservation around October 1896. His parents were George Looking Back and Sally Elk Nation. They were members of the Cross Bear Band of Hunkpapa. George had served 16 years as a policeman in the Little Eagle district. When Isaac registered for the draft on June 5, 1917, he was farming with his father. He joined the Army on April 26, 1918, and was sent to Camp Funston, KS. He was assigned to Co. L, 355th Infantry, 89th Division (ASN 2845254). The 355th Infantry sailed for France aboard the *Baltic* on June 4, 1918. In mid-September, the Division took part in the St. Mihiel Offensive. Pvt. Looking Back was killed in action north of Flirey, France, on September 12, 1918. The casket of Pvt. Looking Back was brought back aboard the *Cambria,* which sailed from Antwerp, Belgium, on May 23, 1921. He was buried in Messiah Cemetery in Little Eagle. After the war, the veterans from Little Eagle organized an American Legion Post which was named in honor of Isaac Looking Back. Isaac's father, George, was named an honorary member of the Post. In 1935, Isaac's parents were interviewed by a SD State worker with the SDERA program. Their home was nine miles from Little Eagle on Little Oak Creek. They had a photo on their living room wall of Private Looking Back in uniform. Above the photo, they had a gold star. In a ceremony in Wakpala on March 17, 2017, the family of Pvt. Looking Back received a Code Talker's Medal honoring his service.[39]

Loves The War, George. George was born around July 1894 at Cherry Creek. In the 1900 U.S. Census, he lived on the Cheyenne River Reservation with his parents, Loves the War and White Cow, as well as two brothers, Ernest and Wounded with many Arrows. His mother was sometimes known as Susan Loves the War. In the early census rolls, he is listed as Narcisse. After the 1912 Census Roll, he is listed as George. At that time, his mother was married to William Looking Back on the Standing Rock Reservation. When George registered for the draft on June 5, 1917, he was farming with Looking Back near Wakpala. George joined the Army on July 21, 1918, and was sent to Camp Dodge, IA, for training. Pvt. Loves the War likely volunteered for the Signal Corps (ASN 3954583), which had a training school at Fort Leavenworth. Pvt. Loves the War was sent to Hoboken, NJ, with Fort Leavenworth September Automatic Replacement Draft Co. #2, Signal Corps. His unit was scheduled to sail for France aboard the *Princess Matoika*. He became ill and entered the spirit world in Hoboken on Oct. 5, 1918. He is buried in St. Elizabeth's Cemetery at Wakpala. After the war, his name was engraved on a large monument that was erected in the cemetery. In a ceremony held in Wakpala on March 17, 2017, the family of Pvt. Loves the War received a Code Talker's Medal honoring his service.

Loves War, Harry. When Harry was born around July of 1891, his mother gave him the name, Wounded with many Arrows, by which he was known until he joined the Army. His parents were Yanktonai who had gone to Canada with Sitting Bull's family after 1876. Harry was born in Canada. He was a brother to George Loves the War. Their father died around 1900. The family moved to Wakpala around 1903. When Wounded with Many Arrows registered for the draft on June 5, 1917, he was farming near Wakpala. He joined the Army on June 24, 1918 and was sent to Camp Funston for training. He served in Casual Detachment 318, 164th Depot Brigade. He became known as Harry Loves War. On Aug. 8, 1918, he sent his cousin a letter which was published in the *Sioux County Pioneer*.

> Dear cousin,
>
> It is lucky for me to get in this Headquarters Company for the officers are gentlemen and I am well treated. There are two of us original Americans in this company, myself and Francis Bullhead. It seems this company is permanently stationed here, for they are working at receiving stations. There are soldiers everywhere you look. The camp is like a great city and very clean. We are assigned to training horses and we surely like it pretty well. Most of the Indian boys in this camp have gone to Camp Dodge to fill up two divisions to go across the "pond," and they won't come back until it is all over. Hoping to hear from you, I remain your cousin, Harry Loves War.

Private Loves War was discharged on April 22, 1919. While he was at Camp Funston, he came down with tuberculosis. After his discharge, he began receiving a pension, which in the 1930s was $50 per month. After returning home, he married his wife, Jessie Waters. In the 1930 U.S. Census, they had a son, Norman. Harry's mother, Susan, also lived with them. Susan received a government payment of $57.50 per month after her son, George, died while serving in the Army. In 1935, the family was interviewed by a social worker with the SDERA program. They were living in a two-room log house in Wakpala. Harry was a Legion member and Jessie was a member of the Legion Auxiliary. Harry had been working on some relief projects, driving a dump wagon. Harry indicated that while in the Army, he was known as Harry M. Arrows. In the 1940 U.S. Census, they were still living in Wakpala, with three daughters, Romaine, Bertha and Maxine. Harry's mother, at age 85, was still living with them. Harry entered the spirit world in his home on May 5, 1981. He is buried in St. Bede's Catholic Cemetery in Wakpala. In a ceremony held in Wakpala on March 17, 2017, the family of Pvt. Loves War received a Code Talker's Medal honoring his service.[40]

Lowe, Leland Jerome. Leland was born on Sept. 6, 1902, in Minneapolis to Phoebe Brown and Jerome Lowe. They enrolled members of the Sisseton-Wahpeton Reservation. Leland served in the military but dates of service are not known. In 1926, he married Ebba Wahlquist. In the 1930 U.S. Census, he was working as a roofer in Detroit. When he registered with the Selective Service in 1942, he worked at the Sunset Bowling Center in White Bear Lake, MN. He entered the spirit world in West Branch, MI, on April 3, 1975.

Lufkins, Henry. Henry was born on the White Earth Reservation in Minnesota on April 1, 1895, to George and Margaret Lufkins. He married his first wife, Mary, in May 1917. When he registered for the draft on June 5, 1917, he was working as a painter on the White Earth Reservation. He joined the Army at Walker, MN, on July 22, 1918, and was sent for training at Camp Wadsworth, NY. He was assigned to Casual Detachment # 1161 (ASN 4061642). He later served in Co. H, 3rd Pioneer Infantry. He sailed aboard the *America* from the U.S. on Aug. 30, 1918, and took part in the Meuse-Argonne Campaign. He returned to the U.S. from St. Nazaire aboard the *Mexican* on July 23, 1919, and was discharged on July 30, 1919, at Camp Dodge, IA. He returned home to the White Earth Reservation. In the 1930s, he moved to South Dakota and married Susie LeBlanc (1901-1983). In the 1940 U.S. Census, they were living in Long Hollow with their children, Veronica, Sophoronia, Ramona, Iona and Carl. Henry entered the spirit world on Oct. 31, 1977, and is buried in the Sisseton Cemetery.[41]

Lunderman, Benjamin. Benjamin was born on the Rosebud Reservation on Dec. 8, 1886, to Sanford Lunderman and Julia Tackett. He enlisted in the Army at Bonesteel on May 1, 1918. He served as a Private with Co. E, 8th Ammo Train, and was discharged on Feb. 18, 1919, at Camp Dodge, IA. He did not serve overseas. He married Christina Pfaff, and lived in Hot Springs in 1930. He entered the spirit world on Nov. 18, 1971, and is buried in the Black Hills National Cemetery, Sect. C, Site 1123.

Lunderman, Sanford H. Sanford was born on the Rosebud Reservation on Feb. 24, 1897, to Alfred Lunderman and Nellie Heck. In the 1910 U.S. Census, he was a student at Flandreau. He joined the Army and served as a Private in Co. E, 2nd Infantry, at Ft. Shafter, Hawaii. On Aug. 20, 1918, he married Mabel Knudson, with who he had two children, Berlin and Starling. Sanford developed tuberculosis, and entered the spirit world on Jan. 25, 1920. He is buried in the Indian Congregational Cemetery in Herrick. His son, Starling served in the Army in WWII.

Lytle, John Walter. John was born in Eldora, Iowa, on Nov. 19, 1884. His parents were William and Julia Lytle. The family moved to Dawson, ND, in the early 1900s. John enlisted with his brother, Sam, in Company I, 2nd Infantry, ND National Guard, at Dawson on July 15, 1917. He served with Sidney McLaughlin and a number of other men from the Standing Rock Reservation. Captain A.B. Welch was their commanding officer. John was assigned to the 161st Ambulance Company, 116th Sanitary Train (ASN 2460) in Camp Greene, NC. On Dec. 12, 1917, his unit sailed from the U.S. for France, where he was reassigned to Ambulance Company 3, 1st Sanitary Train. This was part of the 1st Division. On Feb. 14, 1918, he was promoted to Private 1st Class. He took part in the Aisne Offensive which began near Cantigny on May 27, 1918. He was wounded slightly on that day. He later served with the 1st Division at St. Mihiel, Meuse-Argonne, Aisne-Marne, Ansauville and Saizerais. On Nov. 28, 1918, he was promoted to Wagoner. He sailed from Brest, France, aboard the *Von Steuben* on Aug. 24, 1919, and arrived in Hoboken Sept. 1, 1919. While at Camp Dodge, he served with Casual Detachment 1458, Demobilization Group. He was discharged on Sept. 24, 1919. His brother, Sam, received a Silver Star for his service with the Ambulance Company.

John returned to Dawson, ND, before moving to Corson County on the Standing Rock Reservation in the 1920s. In the 1930 U.S. Census, he was running a filling station in McIntosh. On March 13, 1932, he married Verna Sylvia Flying Horse. In the 1934 Standing Rock Census Roll, John is listed with Verna, but was not enrolled. In 1935, they were interviewed by a worker with the SDERA program. At that time, they were living in a 10' x 24' mobile trailer near Sylvia's father, Jim Flying Horse. They were raising livestock, though at that time they only had 14 cows and 4 horses and colts. A few years before they had owned 125 cows, but the government had bought part of their herd. In the 1940 U.S. Census, John and Sylvia were living in Oakland, CA, with their son, Charles. John was working as an Electrician. When John registered for the draft during WWII, he was working in a cannery near Lodi, CA. John entered the spirit world on Jan. 19, 1954, and is buried in Oak Hill Cemetery, Red Bluff, CA. Sylvia survived him till 1994.[42]

M

Makes Life, Ernest C. Ernest was born on the Cheyenne River Reservation around Dec. 7, 1899. In the 1902 Census Roll, he is listed with his father, John, and his mother, Mable Veo. Ernest may have served in the military during the First World War. In the 1930 U.S. Census, Ernest is listed with his wife, Roslind White Bull. They had a son, John. Ernest later married Mary Bear, who had been married to Wallace Cross Bear. In 1935, Ernest and Mary were interviewed by a social worker with the SDERA program. They were living near Bullhead where Ernest worked on emergency construction jobs. Ernest indicated that he had enlisted in the Army on Dec. 6, 1926, and served at Fort Meade until Dec. 10, 1929. His mother's brother, Louis Veo (1903-1983), enlisted the day after Ernest's enlistment. Ernest's cousin, Schuyler Phillips (1908-1991) also enlisted on that day. Schuyler served again in WWII. In the 1940 U.S. Census, Ernest was living with Peter Mound on the Cheyenne River Reservation. Ernest re-enlisted in the Army on Aug. 7, 1942, and was discharged on Nov. 2, 1943. He later moved to Little Eagle, SD, where he married Louisa Eagle Shield on May 29, 1954. Ernest entered the spirit world in Mobridge on Jan. 28, 1975. He is buried in the Black Hills National Cemetery, Plot C, site 850. His headstone shows he served in both WWI and WWII.[1]

Makes Trouble, James. James was born near Bullhead on the Standing Rock Reservation on Feb. 1, 1895. His parents were August Makes Trouble and Annie Canupa [Pipe]. He attended school in Little Eagle and the Santee Indian School. When James registered for the draft on June 5, 1917, he was working with his father. James joined the Army on April 26, 1918, and was sent to Camp Funston. He was discharged after a short time, most likely for medical reasons. In 1921, he married Lillie Clown and moved to the Cheyenne River Reservation. Lillie's brother, Moses, was killed in action in France. Her brother, James, also served in the Army. They lived north of Fire Steel. In 1928, they moved near Thunder Butte. In the 1930 U.S. Census, James lived with his family near Lillie's father, Amos Clown. In 1935, the family was interviewed by a worker with the SDERA program. They were living near Thunder Butte so their daughter could go to school. Their permanent home was a 22' by 13' log home located eight miles north of Thunder Butte. They had planted some corn and a garden, but the hoppers destroyed everything. James also leased some land to the Mossman Cattle Co. He worked as a sheep herder and livestock handler on different ranches. They later moved to Dupree. James entered the spirit world on Sept. 7, 1990, at the Mobridge Care Center. He is buried in the Holy Spirit Episcopal Cemetery near Firesteel. His three daughters, Lorraine, Lois and Esther, survived him.[2]

Many Cartridges, William. William is listed on WWI veteran's memorial at Oglala Lakota, Kyle, SD. He was born on July 18, 1919. In the 1940 U.S. Census, he was stationed at Fort McDowell, Marin County, California.

Many Deeds, Edmund. Edmund was born on the Standing Rock Reservation on July 17, 1896. In the 1896 Census Roll, he is listed with his parents, Stanton Many Deeds and Nora Brave Crow. He belonged to the Gray Eagle band of the Hunkpapa. When he registered for the draft, he was farming near Bullhead. Edmund joined the Army on July 22, 1918, and was assigned to the 61st Balloon Company, Air Service (ASN 3954613). He served at Ft. Omaha, Nebraska, and was discharged as a Private on Jan. 15, 1919. Edmund's sister, Ethel, married a fellow veteran, Henry Ankle. Edmund married Mary J. High Eagle in 1920. Edmund joined the American Legion, and also played semi-pro baseball for 18 seasons. In the 1937 Census Roll, he and Mary are listed with their four children, Lloyd, Edmund Jr., Lenore and Robert. Lloyd and Edmund Jr. served in the Army during WWII. In the 1930s, Edmund was sent to New Mexico to receive training to be a leader in the Indian Emergency Conservation Work program, which was similar to the C.C.C. Program. Edmund's family lived near Little Eagle and owned a 1933 Chevrolet. He was assigned to the position of Foreman for the projects at Shields and Cannon Ball, and received $140 per month. Edmund entered the spirit world on July 17, 1953, and is buried in Messiah Congregational Cemetery in Little Eagle. In a ceremony held in Wakpala on March 17, 2017, the family of Pvt. Many Deeds received a Code Talker's Medal honoring his service.[3]

Many Horses, Francis. Francis was born on the Standing Rock Reservation on March 20, 1891, to Francis Many Horses Sr., and Annie Striped Face. When he registered for the draft on June 5, 1917, he was farming near Wakpala. He joined the Army and was sent to Fort Riley, KS, on March 5, 1918. After his discharge on July 1, 1919, he returned home to Wakpala. He married Louisa Catch the Bear. They had four children, Virgil, Sarafina, Martha and Lucille. Francis entered the spirit world at the Fort Yates hospital on April 6, 1935, and is buried at Wakpala. In the fall of 1935, Louisa was interviewed by a worker with the SDERA program. John Tiger acted as an interpreter in the Many Horses home in the southeast part of Wakpala. Louisa said she had no income and had only received rations once a month, which made it hard to feed her children. John Tiger determined that though Francis had served honorably in the Army, he had never drawn any of his bonus payment. So, the family was entitled to $1600. John said the local officers of the American Legion were looking into the matter. Louisa was a member of the Legion Auxiliary.[4]

Marks, Alex. Alex was born near Buffalo Lake on the Sisseton-Wahpeton Reservation on June 26, 1890. His parents were Thomas and Sarah Marks. In the census rolls for the early 1900s, Alex's name is listed as Ricahowicya. Around 1915, he married Julia Dumars. They had a son, Leon. When Alex registered for the draft, he was living with his family near Eden, Marshall County. Alex joined the Army on June 24, 1918, and was assigned to Co. A, 350th Infantry, 88th Division (ASN 3308518). Private Marks sailed with his unit on Aug. 11, 1918, aboard the H.M.S. *Delta*. The 88th Division saw limited action in the fighting. Private Marks served as a Scout in the Intelligence Platoon for the 1st Battalion of the 350th Infantry. After the Armistice, his commanding officer, Capt. Marion Fonville, wrote that Marks was "regarded by the whites as unusually good man." On Nov. 30, 1918, Co. A, 350th Infantry, marched 70 kilometers to St. Joire. After a few days, they hiked to Naix-aux-Forges, where they remained billeted until they left on May 7, 1919, in preparing to return to the U.S. Pvt. Marks sailed from St. Nazaire aboard the *Aeolus* on May 19, 1919, and was discharged on June 5, 1919. In the 1940 U.S. Census, Alex was living with his son's family near Buffalo Lake. Alex and his son were working on a road construction project. Leon served in the Navy aboard the U.S.S. *Tigney* during WWII. Alex later lived in Sisseton. Alex (Omani Tanka) entered the spirit world on Oct. 13, 1977. He is buried in the Veterans Section of the Sisseton Cemetery. Military rites were conducted by the Native American Veterans Association.[5]

Marsh, Joseph. Joseph was born on March 9, 1893, in Vanderbilt, a settlement founded in Campbell County by his father in 1864. His parents were Andrew Marsh and Spotted Elk Woman. Andrew had served in the Civil War. In the 1896 Standing Rock Census Roll, Joseph is listed with his brothers and sisters, Mollie, Emma, Andrew, Claude and Josephine. Around 1915, Joseph married his first wife, Florence, who was an Ojibwe from Wisconsin. When he registered for the draft on June 5, 1917, he was living in McLaughlin and working as a car driver for George Jewett, a car dealer in McLaughlin. Joseph joined the Army on September 9, 1917. He was sent to Camp Funston, KS, and assigned to the 164th Depot Brigade, before transferring to Co. D, 109th Engineering Regiment at Camp Cody (ASN 1437702). Corporal Marsh was later transferred to Co. D, 37th Battalion, U.S. Guards. He was discharged on Jan. 9, 1919. After the war, he returned to McLaughlin. In the 1930

U.S. Census, he was working as a mechanic in Rochester, MN. In the 1940 U.S. Census, he was living with his wife, Ida, and his step daughter in Dayton, OH, and working as a mechanic. Joseph entered the spirit world on Aug. 29, 1940, and is buried in Dayton National Cemetery, Section R, row 13, site 25.[6]

Marshall, Charles J. Charles was born on the Pine Ridge Reservation on Nov. 14, 1889. His parents were Joseph and Elizabeth Marshall. In the 1899 Pine Ridge Census Roll, the family was living in the Medicine Root District. In 1915, Charles married Martha Roubideaux (1897-1982), whose younger brother, Louis, served in the Army. Charles was living on the Rosebud Reservation when he registered for the draft on June 4, 1917. He joined the Army on July 22, 1918, and was discharged as a Private on Jan. 28, 1919. After the war he continued to farm in Todd County. In the 1940 U.S. Census, he and Martha had six children, Adelia, Joseph, Melvin, Opal, Laveria and Magaretta. Their sons, Joseph and Melvin, served in the Army during WWII. Charles entered the spirit world on Dec. 27, 1974, and is buried in Spotted Tail Cemetery.

Marshall, Elisha. Elisha is listed on WWI veteran's memorial at Oglala Lakota College, Kyle, SD. Elisha was born on Aug. 22, 1896, in Nebraska to George and Sarah Marshall. When he registered for the draft on June 5, 1917, he was farming in Bennett County. He was discharged from the military on Feb. 5, 1919. When he registered for the Selective Service in 1942, he was living in Blythe, CA. Elisha passed away at Dutch Harbor, Alaska on Nov. 25, 1942, and is buried in Sitka National Cemetery. He is listed as a civilian casualty.

Marshall, Luther Adam. Adam was born at Fort Niobrara, NE, on Feb. 12, 1898. His parents were John Marshall and Josephine Black Horse. His father served 30 years in the Army. Adam was an enrolled member of the Rosebud (Sicangu) Nation. Adam enlisted in the 4th Nebraska National Guard on March 28, 1917. When this National Guard unit was transferred to Camp Cody, NM, it was converted into the 127th Field Artillery, 34th Division (ASN 1434386). Pvt. Marshall sailed with his brother, Matthew, from New York aboard the *City of York* on Sept. 25, 1918. After the Armistice, Pvt. Marshall sailed from Bordeaux to the U.S. aboard the U.S.S. *Powhatan* on Dec. 25, 1918. Adam was known as an excellent horseman. He was discharged as a Wagoner with the Supply Company on Jan. 22, 1919. After returning home he was successful as a champion bronco buster. He married Minnie Cooper on July 10, 1920. He entered the spirit world on April 8, 1922, after an accident along the railroad tracks near Valentine, NE. Funeral Services were held under the auspices of the American Legion. He is buried in Mount Hope Cemetery, Valentine.[7]

Marshall, Matthew Elmer. Matthew was born in Nebraska on Aug. 15, 1891, to John and Josephine Marshall. In the 1900 U.S. Census, John was serving as a Scout at Ft. Niobrara. When Matthew registered for the draft on June 5, 1917, he was working for the government on the Rosebud Reservation in Todd County. Matthew enlisted in the Army at Ft. Robinson, NE, on Aug. 13, 1917. He likely was sent to Camp Cody, NM. He was assigned to the Supply Company, 127th Field Artillery, 34th Division (ASN 1434388), which sailed from New York to France aboard the *City of York* on Sept. 25, 1918. Pvt. Marshall sailed for home from Bordeaux aboard the U.S.S. *Powhatan* on Dec. 25, 1918. He later served as a Private in Casual Detachment #45, 163rd Depot Brigade at Camp Dodge, IA, and was discharged on Jan. 22, 1919, because of a disability. He suffered from tuberculosis. On Dec. 2, 1919, he was admitted to the Battle Mountain Sanatorium at Hot Springs. He entered the spirit world there on Dec. 26, 1919. His wife survived him. W.B. Haley, representing American Legion Post No. 90, went to Hot Springs and accompanied the body back to Valentine. Funeral services were conducted under the auspices of the American Legion Post No. 90 and were well attended. Matthew is buried in Mount Hope Cemetery, Valentine, NE. His headstone bears the inscription, "'It is Sweet and Honorable to Die for One's Country."[8]

Marshall, Moses John. Moses was born on May 4, 1895, in Nebraska. His parents were John and Josephine Marshall, who may have been a daughter of Spotted Tail. In the 1900 U.S. Census, the Marshall family lived at Ft. Niobrara, where John had served as a Scout. Moses joined the Army and was assigned to Battery A, 347th Field Artillery (FA), 91st Division (ASN 3129642). Pvt. Marshall sailed from New York aboard the *Adriatic* on July 14, 1918. Other soldiers in Battery A were Elbridge Gerry, Frank Apple and Peter Rouillard. The *Adriatic* first docked at Liverpool, England. After the 347th FA arrived in Cherbourg, France, they were sent to the artillery training area at Camp de Souge near Bordeaux. They were trained with ten-ton tractors and 4.7-inch guns. Shortly before the end of the war, they were stationed in Bois de Brocourt. The 347th FA did not serve at the Front. On Christmas Day of 1918, they were billeted in private homes in several small German towns along the Moselle River. On March 13, 1919, the 347th FA had the distinction of serving as guard of honor for President Woodrow Wilson, who was in France for the Paris Peace Conference. Pvt. Marshall returned from Brest aboard the *Aquitania* on March 23, 1919. Traveling with Camp Dodge Detachment #1, they arrived in the U.S. on April 30. Pvt. Marshall was discharged on April 17, 1919. Moses' brothers, Matthew and Adam, also served in the Army. On May 9, 1918, Moses had married Annie Grant. In the 1930 U.S. Census, Moses was farming in Todd County. He and Annie had five children then, Seth, DeWane, Marie, Catherine, and William. Moses entered the spirit world at his home on Nov. 26, 1969. Annie and their children, Seth, DeWane, Katherine, Cornelia, Joseph, Dorothy, Anita, Patrick, and Harry, survived him. DeWane served in the Navy during WWII and was wounded. Harry served in the Army during the Vietnam War. Moses is buried in St. Charles Cemetery, Saint Francis.

Marshall, William Albert. William was born at Kenel on April 8, 1897, on the Standing Rock Reservation. His parents were Charles (Nogcan) and Bertha (Bearsface) Marshall. They were Hunkpapa. When William registered for the draft on June 3, 1918, he was living in Kenel. William joined the Army on Aug. 5, 1918, at McIntosh. He was assigned to Co. D, 62nd Infantry, 8th Division, which trained at Camp Fremont, CA. Ben Red Legs and Wallace Cross Bear were also in the same regiment. In late October of 1918, some units from the 8th Division did sail from Hoboken, NJ, for France, but the 62nd Infantry never left New Jersey. Pvt. Marshall was discharged on May 13, 1919. On May 28, 1919, the *Sioux County Pioneer* published a notice that William Marshall, recently discharged from Camp Lee, VA, returned to the Farm School. William married Louise Walking Elk in January of 1926. They ranched in Corson County. In 1928, Marshall was Vice Commander of the Martin Yellow Fat American Legion Post. In the 1930 U.S. Census, William and Louise had two children, Bertha and Joseph. In his later years, William lived in Fort Yates. William entered the spirit world in a Bismarck hospital on Jan. 16, 1968. He is buried in Assumption Cemetery, Kenel, SD.[9]

Martinez, Francis A. See **Short Tree, Antoine**.

Max, James Leo. James was born on the Sisseton-Wahpeton Reservation on May 10, 1898, to Daniel Max and May Hakiktawin. James joined the military, and was discharged on March 27, 1919. In the 1920 U.S. Census, he was living with his parents. In 1925, he married Elizabeth Driver, whose brother, Moses, had served in the Army. In 1934, he married Rebecca Shepherd, with who he had two children, Daniel and Verdella. In the 1940 U.S. Census, the family lived in Waubay and

James worked for the W.P.A. He entered the spirit world on Dec. 16, 1946, and is buried in the St. James Cemetery.

McBride, Jerry. When Jerry is first listed on Crow Creek Census Rolls, his first name is Mark. In later rolls, he is listed as Luke. He was born about March 1, 1890, on the Crow Creek Reservation. His parents were Robert McBride and Jennie Dog Back. In October 1909, 'Jeremiah' McBride married Lizzie Randall. They had a son, James. Lizzie entered the spirit world in January of 1917. On May 1, 1917, Jerry enlisted in Troop L, 1st SD Cavalry at Kimball, SD, and was sent to Camp Cody, NM, for training in September 1917. These South Dakota National Guard soldiers became part of the 34th Division. Sgt. McBride was sent to Grenade School, where he became certified as an assistant instructor. He was also sent to Gas School, where he became an instructor. He later was assigned to Co. F, 135th Infantry (ASN 1423874). Cpl. McBride sailed from New York aboard the *Ortega* on Oct. 12, 1918. After the Armistice, Sgt. McBride was assigned to a Prisoner of War Escort Company #205. He helped guard Prisoners of War, and was one of the last men to return home to the reservation. Sgt. McBride sailed from Brest, France, aboard the *Princess Matoika* on Oct. 5, 1919. He arrived in Hoboken on Oct. 15, 1919, and was discharged at Camp Dodge, IA, on Oct. 22, 1919. His left eye was damaged while in the Army. He joined the American Legion. After returning home, he married Dora Whipper, with whom he had a son, Milton, and a daughter, Pauline. When Dora passed away around 1930, he married Mary Bad Moccasin. They lived near Pukwana. In 1935, the family was interviewed by a worker with the SDERA program. They had a one-room house, three miles southeast of Grace Mission. Jerry had been working on a relief dam, but was interested in getting a job as a guard at the state penitentiary. He later farmed near Pukwana. Jerry entered the spirit world near Pukwana on March 21, 1960. He is buried in St. John the Baptist Cemetery in Pukwana.[10]

McBride, Jesse. Jesse was born in Chamberlain on the Crow Creek Reservation on July 15, 1894. His parents were Charley McBride and Susan Carpenter. When he registered for the draft on June 5, 1917, he lived at Grosse, SD, and worked for Peter Picotte. Jesse joined the Army on Oct. 4, 1917, and was assigned to Co. B, 342nd Machine Gun (MG) Battalion, 89th Division (ASN 2185894). On June 4, 1918, Pfc. McBride sailed from New York for Europe aboard the *Caronia*. The 342nd MG Bn. took part in the Offensives at St. Mihiel and Meuse-Argonne. After the Armistice, Pfc. McBride received an evaluation from his commanding officer, stating that McBride was a "fair leader. Associates readily with men. Well respected. Good machine gunner. Good Scout and night worker." Pfc. McBride suffered a severe loss of hearing as a result of his service. Pfc. McBride sailed from Brest, France, aboard the *Prinz Friedrich Wilhelm* on May 18, 1919. He was discharged on June 16, 1919. After returning home, he married Susie Rattle Tail. After they divorced, Jesse married Rose Wounded Knee. In 1935, they were interviewed by a worker with the SDERA program. They owned a two-room frame home that was 10 miles northwest of Ft. Thompson. They hauled their drinking water two miles, from the river. Their children were Ethelbert, Gladys, Ambrose and Robert. Jesse was an American Legion member. Ethelbert served in the Army during WWII, while Ambrose served during the Korean War. Jesse entered the spirit world on Oct. 9, 1967, in Memorial Hospital in Wessington Springs, SD. He is buried in Mission Cemetery, Stephan, SD.[11]

McBride, Walter. Walter was a Yanktonai born in Charles Mix County on April 11, 1890. His parents were John McBride and Irene Wamdnikatawin. He married Mary Bates. When he registered for the draft on June 5, 1917, he was farming near Dante. He joined the Army on Sept. 19, 1917. He was assigned to the Machine Gun (MG) Company, 38th Infantry, 3rd Division (ASN 2193019). Pvt. McBride sailed for Europe from Halifax, Nova Scotia, aboard the *Corsican* on March 25, 1918. The

Corsican first docked at Glasgow, Scotland. The unit then traveled by the Caledonian Railroad to Camp Woodsley in southern England. After hiking 12 miles to Southhampton, the unit sailed in a cattle boat, the *Austrilind,* to Le Havre, France. The 38th Infantry served in the Sectors at Aisne, Chateau-Thierry, Champagne-Marne, Aisne-Marne, Vesle, St. Mihiel, and Meuse-Argonne. After the severe fighting along the Marne River in July 1918, the 38th Infantry became known as "the Rock of the Marne." Pfc. McBride was wounded, most likely in this battle. Pvt. McBride sailed from Brest, France, aboard the U.S.S. *Mount Vernon* on March 3, 1919. He was traveling with Saint Aignan Casual Co. No. 1413. He was later assigned to Casual Detachment #129, 163rd Depot Brigade, Camp Dodge, IA. He was discharged on March 21, 1919. Most of the 3rd Division did not return to the U.S. until late summer of 1919. In the 1930 U.S. Census, Walter was farming with his family in Rouse Township. Their children included Lawrence, Robert, Wallace and James. In the 1937 Census Roll, Walter and Mary are listed with their sons, Robert and Wallace. In the 1940 U.S. Census, Walter was a farm manager in Hancock Township, Bon Homme County. Walter entered the spirit world in the VA Hospital in Sioux Falls on Dec. 4, 1961 and is buried in New Holy Name Cemetery in Dante.

McCloskey, Clement. Clement was born at Okreek on April 26, 1896, on the Rosebud Reservation. His parents were Frank McCloskey and Mary Anna Prue. When he registered for the draft on June 5, 1917, he was a stockman and lived at Carter. Clement served in the Army with the 164th Depot Brigade at Camp Funston, KS, and was discharged on Jan. 20, 1919, as a Private. His brother, Ernest, also served in the Army. After returning home, he married Caroline (1897-1979). In the 1940 U.S. Census, Clement and Lena lived with their daughter, Marcelline, and Clement worked at the Rosebud boarding school. He entered the spirit world on Feb. 27, 1963, and is buried in the Black Hills National Cemetery, Section E, Site 663.

McCloskey, Ernest. Ernest was born in Okreek on the Rosebud Reservation on Oct. 26, 1891. His parents were Frank McCloskey and Mary Prue. Clement was his brother. When Ernest registered for the draft on June 5, 1917, he was working as a mechanic in Carter. He joined the Army on June 24, 1918, and was assigned to Co. D, 69th Infantry, 10th Division (ASN 3315510). The 10th Division was organized at Camp Funston but did not serve overseas. Private McCloskey was discharged on Dec. 23, 1918. Returning home, he married Victoria Lambert, whose brother, Guy, had also served in the Army. In 1921, Ernest was a member of the Chauncey Eagle Horn Legion Post in Rosebud with Guy. Ernest and Victoria moved to Rapid City. In the 1930 U.S. Census, Ernest was working for Warren-Lamb Lumber Co., who operated a saw mill. In the 1937 Rosebud Census Roll, Ernest and Victoria are listed with their children, Victoria and Richard. In the 1940 U.S. Census, Ernest was working on a WPA project in Rapid City. They later moved to Mission. Their son, Richard, served with the Navy in WWII. Ernest entered the spirit world at the VA Center in Hot Springs on Jan. 5, 1954, and is buried in Calvary Cemetery, Okreek.[12]

McCloskey, Hubert P. Hubert Was born in Okreek on Feb. 12, 1893, to Frank and Mary McCloskey. In 1916, he married Clara Courtis. They had a son, Hubert Jr. When Hubert registered for the draft on June 5, 1917, he was working as a Farmer at the Indian School in Mission. He joined the Army and served as a Private with the 7th Aero Squadron at Fort Wayne, MI. He caught the flu in camp and entered the spirit world there on Oct 12, 1918. He is buried in the Winner Cemetery.

McGaa, George Leroy. George was born at Porcupine on the Pine Ridge Reservation Oct. 30, 1893. In the 1894 Census Roll, he is listed with his parents, William and Louise, as well as his brothers and sisters, William Jr., Etta, Charlotte, Albert, Agnes, and Jessie. When he registered for the draft on June 5, 1917, he was ranching near Scenic. George joined the Army on Oct. 15, 1918, and was assigned to the Student Army Training Corps (SATC). He served with Co. N, at the University of Iowa at Iowa City (ASN 5293612). He was discharged as a Private on Dec. 15, 1918. On Jan. 31, 1921, he married Helen Hamm at Hot Springs. They had a son, Harold. In the 1937 Census Roll, they were living in Rapid City. Sometime later, they moved to California. George entered the spirit world on March 25, 1962, and is buried in San Fernando Cemetery, San Fernando, CA.

McGhee, William Taylor. William was born on the Rosebud Reservation on April 23, 1895. His parents were Frank McGhee and Millie Drapeau. In the 1900 U.S. Census, they were living in Castaglia, Charles Mix County. In the 1910 U.S. Census, he was a student at the boarding school in Genoa, NE. Sometime before the war, William moved with his family to Washington State. When he registered for the draft on June 5, 1917, he was farming near CleElum, WA. William joined the Army on April 26, 1918, and was assigned to Co. L, 361st Infantry, 91st Division (ASN 2292016). Pvt. McGhee sailed from New York aboard the *Scotian* on July 6, 1918. He served with Cpl. Alfred Richard, who was killed in the battle of Meuse-Argonne. Pvt. McGhee sailed from St. Nazaire aboard the *Mexican* on April 2, 1919. He arrived at Hoboken on April 15, and was discharged on May 1, 1919, as a Private First Class. On July 9, 1922, he married his wife, Catherine. They had two children, Mary and Richard. In the 1930 U.S. Census, William was managing a gas station on the Skokomish Reservation, west of Tacoma. In the 1940 U.S. Census, he was working as a cook in Port Angeles. In 1948, he was working as a millman at the Puget Sound Naval Shipyard. William entered the spirit world on May 23, 1967, at Bremerton, WA. He is buried in Evergreen Memorial Gardens, Vancouver, WA.

McKenzie, Narcisse. Narcisse was born on Feb. 14, 1890, on the Rosebud Reservation. In the 1895 Census Roll, he is listed with his parents, Baptiste McKenzie and Esther Milk, as well as his brothers and sisters, Eliza, Maggie, Jacob and Frank. When Narcisse registered for the draft on June 5, 1917, he was working for the Indian Police at Saint Charles, SD. He married Virginia Barker on July 16, 1917. He joined the Army at Bonesteel on May 26, 1918, and was first assigned to Co. B, 160th Infantry, 40th Division (ASN 3129660). Pvt. McKenzie sailed from Brooklyn aboard the *Mentor* on Aug. 8, 1918. After arriving in France, he was reassigned to Co. H, 306th Infantry, 77th Division. He served in Co. H with Pvt. James Crowe and Pvt. Frank Comes from War. The 306th Infantry served in the Sectors at Baccarat, Vesle, Oise-Aisne, Forêt-d Argonne, and the Meuse Argonne. After the Armistice, Pvt. McKenzie received an evaluation from his commanding officer, Capt. E.A. Page, stating that he "proved to be an excellent soldier, especially in the wood in the Argonne. He never seemed to tire and always is in good humor. Has been reliable as an observer." Pvt. McKenzie sailed from Brest, France aboard the ship *Mt. Vernon,* on April 17, 1919. Many of the soldiers of the 77th Division were from New York, so the Division marched in a parade in New York City. The unit insignia for the 77th Division was the Statue of Liberty. Pvt. McKenzie was discharged from Camp Dodge, IA, on May 19, 1919.

After he returned home Narcisse continued to work with the Indian Police. He and Virginia had two children, Belva and Narcisse Jr. Narcisse became ill with tuberculosis and was admitted to the Battle Mountain Sanatorium on July 30, 1924. He entered the spirit world at the Sanatorium on May 26, 1925. A flag was provided for his casket. He is buried in Milk's Camp Episcopal Cemetery, Saint Charles, SD.[13]

McLaughlin, James Sidney. Sidney was born on the Standing Rock Reservation at Fort Yates on March 18, 1894. He was the son of Harry and Annie McLaughlin. His grandfather was James

McLaughlin. In the 1894 Standing Rock Census Roll, he is listed with his parents and an older sister. At Christmas of 1904, Frank Fiske took a photo of Sidney serving as an altar boy at the Catholic Church in Fort Yates. Around 1915, he married Zelda LeCompte. When Sidney registered for the draft on June 5, 1917, he was farming near McLaughlin, SD, and providing support for his wife and son, Melvin. On July 24, 1917, he traveled to Bismarck with his brother, Henry, and cousin, Ray Lyon, to enlist in the ND National Guard regiment that Captain A.B. Welch was recruiting for. Henry failed the physical exam, while Sidney and Ray were accepted. Before the 2nd ND Infantry Regiment had left for initial training at Camp Greene, NC, Sidney had been promoted to Corporal. The 2nd Regiment was known as the "Smashed Second" because so many men were transferred to other units. In October of 1917, he had written to the *Sioux County Pioneer,* "we had quite a trip down here and enjoyed much fine scenery along the way. I have been transferred to the 161st Ambulance Co., 116th Sanitary Train, 41st Division. We have auto ambulances and the work is fine. We hope to be the first detachment to leave Camp Green for France. This stunt beats foot soldiering all to hell, and we are considered the highest branch in the service." Cpl. McLaughlin sailed with his unit from Hoboken, NJ, aboard the *Antigone* on Dec. 12, 1917. By the end of the war, Sidney was promoted to Sergeant. He was discharged at Camp Dodge, IA, on July 12, 1919.

After the war, he returned home on July 15. Sidney and Zelda had seven children, Melvin, Roletta, Geraldine, James, Willis, Harry, Michael and Maurine, as listed in the 1927 Census Roll. Around 1930, they became divorced, and Sidney moved to California. In 1931, Sidney was admitted to a VA hospital in Los Angeles. He was still living in Los Angeles when he registered with the Selective Service in 1942. His son, Michael, served in the Army during WWII. Sidney later moved to Grants Pass, OR, and entered the spirit world in Roseburg, OR, on Jan. 22, 1977. He is buried in Willamette National Cemetery (Section L, site 2586) in Portland, OR.[14]

McLean, James. James was born around 1890 near Pollock, SD, to John McLean and Mary Winyanwaste. He was enrolled on the Standing Rock Reservation. When he registered for the draft on June 5, 1917, he lived in Wakpala and worked as a laborer for Paul Hansen. James joined the Army on May 25, 1918, and was sent to Camp Lewis, WA. He was discharged on Aug. 5, 1918. James did not marry. His sister, Elizabeth, did marry a fellow veteran, Leo Eckman. In the 1920 U.S. Census, James was living with his sister, Mary, and her husband, Joseph Claymore. In the 1930 U.S. Census, James was working as a carpenter on a railroad bridge crew near Roundup, MT. In the 1940 U.S. Census, he was working on a CCC project near Wakpala. He retired as an employee of the Milwaukee Road. He entered the spirit world at the Mobridge Hospital on July 31, 1981 and is buried in St. Bede's Cemetery in Wakpala.[15]

Means, David M. David was born around 1898 and lived on the Standing Rock Reservation. He joined the Army and served in the 44th Company, 164th Depot Brigade at Camp Funston, KS. After the war, he lived in McIntosh, SD. In 1921, he married Dora Cook in Wagner. He later married Rosa Gabe at Gettysburg on July 10, 1930. In the 1935 SD Census, he was living in Pierre.[16]

Means, Wesley William. Wesley was born on the Pine Ridge Reservation on Nov. 11, 1899, to Eugene and Nellie Means. His father, Eugene, worked as a financial clerk for the Indian Service in Fort Yates. Wesley enlisted in the Navy at Minneapolis on May 3, 1918 (NSN 1422329). He served his basic training at the Great Lakes Naval Station until June 12, 1918. Then he was stationed at the Naval Air Station, Pauillac, France, until Nov. 11, 1918. After the Armistice, Seaman Means was in the transport service with the Navy. He served as a member of USN Nucleus Crew #2. Subsequently, he served on the USS *Imperator,* and the USS *Eten.* Both of these ships were former

German passenger liners that were commissioned by the Navy for transporting servicemen back to the United States. Seaman Means was discharged at Minneapolis on Aug. 18, 1919.

In the 1920 U.S. Census, collected 1-17-1920, Wesley was working as a laborer in a Detroit auto factory. In May 1920, he returned to Fort Yates after enrolling in the Sweeney Auto School in Kansas City, MO. Wesley played baseball for the Fort Yates team. He also was one of the charter members of the Albert Grass American Legion Post. On July 6, 1922, he married Alma Short in Fort Yates. In the 1930 U.S. Census, Wesley and Alma lived in Fort Yates with their children, Lavinia, Wesley Jr., and Mary. Wesley was working as a laborer doing cement work. In the mid-1930s, he married Louisa Agard, a sister to the veteran, James Agard. In the 1940 U.S. Census, Wesley was working as a steam-fitting mechanic in Fort Yates. Sometime after this, the family moved to California. There was a huge shipyard in Vallejo, CA, so he likely went there for a job during WWII. In 1954, he became a resident of the Veterans Home in nearby Yountville. His son, Wesley Jr. ("Tody"), served with the Army in WWII. Wesley entered the spirit world on June 13, 1978. His daughter, Mrs. Richard Carter, survived him. He is buried in Monument Hill Park, Woodland, CA. Wesley's brother, Walter, was the father of Russell Means.[17]

Medicine, Martin. Martin was born at Kenel on the Standing Rock Reservation on Sept. 7, 1891. In the 1892 Sihasapa Census Roll, Martin is listed with his parents, Martin Medicine and Martina White Deer. Martin was a saddle bronc winner at Fort Yates in 1912. Around 1915, he married Annie Gabe. Annie had two brothers, Ambrose and Charles who served in the military. When Martin registered for the draft on June 5, 1917, he was farming near Wakpala. He enlisted at McIntosh on Sept. 18, 1917, and was sent to Camp Funston, KS. He was first assigned to Co. C, 340th Machine Gun Battalion, 89th Division (ASN 2193020). He was reassigned to the Machine Gun (MG) Co, 38th Infantry, 3rd Division. Pvt. Medicine sailed with the 38th Infantry for Europe from Halifax, Nova Scotia, aboard the *Corsican* on March 25, 1918. Other local men in his unit were Charles Howard, Thomas DeRockbraine and James Eagle Horn. The *Corsican* docked at Glasgow, Scotland. The unit then traveled on the Caledonian Railroad to Camp Woodsley in southern England. After a 12-mile hike to Southhampton, the unit took an old cattle boat, the *Austrilind*, to Le Havre, France. The 38th Infantry served in the sectors at Aisne, Chateau-Thierry, Champagne-Marne, Aisne-Marne, Vesle, St. Mihiel and Meuse-Argonne. Pvt. Medicine suffered a dislocated shoulder while in the service. As part of the Army of Occupation, the MG Co., 38th Infantry was billeted in Obermendig, Germany, in February of 1919. Pvt. Medicine returned home from Brest, France, aboard the *Agamemnon* on Aug. 10, 1919, and arrived at Hoboken on Aug. 18. He was discharged on Aug. 30, 1919, at Camp Dodge. In 1935, the family was interviewed by a worker with the SDERA program. Martin received a veteran's compensation payment of $10 per month, and was an American Legion member, while his wife was a member of the Legion Auxiliary. His two oldest daughters were members of the Junior Auxiliary. The family was living in a two-room frame house in Wakpala, and obtained their water from the Wakpala well. A few years back they had had over 50 head of cattle. At the present, they had 19 horses, one heifer, 16 hens and two guineas. In the 1937 Census Roll, Martin and Annie are listed with their children, Crecensia, Martina, Beatrice, Grace, Lela and Earl. Martin served as the Standing Rock tribal chairman from 1944-45. His son, Earl, served in the Air Force in the 1950s. Martin entered the spirit world in Mobridge on Aug. 13, 1971, and is buried in St. Bede's Cemetery in Wakpala.[18]

Medicine Blanket, Henry Joseph. Henry was born at Norris on the Rosebud Reservation on April 17, 1896. His mother was Sarah Medicine Blanket. When he registered for the draft on June 5, 1917, he was living in Norris. He joined the Army on May 24, 1918, and was assigned to Co. E, 362nd

Infantry, 91st Division (ASN 3127622). The 362nd Infantry trained at Camp Lewis, WA, and sailed from New York for Europe on July 6, 1918, aboard the RMS *Empress of Russia*. The 362nd Infantry served in the Sectors at Aubreville, Meuse-Argonne and finally, at Ypres-Lys in Belgium. After the Armistice, Pfc. Medicine Blanket received an evaluation from his commanding officer stating that he was an "average soldier, demonstrating fitness for automatic rifle." After the 91st Division left Belgium, they were billeted near La Ferté-Bernard, France. Pvt. Medicine Blanket sailed from St. Nazaire, France, aboard the U.S.S. *Lancaster* on April 2, 1919. Pfc. Medicine Blanket was discharged on April 28, 1919, at Camp Dodge, IA. After returning home, he married Lucy Looking White. In the 1940 U.S. Census, they were farming in Mellette County with their children, Madeline, Jennie, Joseph, Luther, and Lenora. Henry entered the spirit world on Dec. 25, 1967, and is buried in Cedar Butte Congregational Cemetery.[19]

Medicine Eagle, William M. William was born on the Rosebud Reservation on May 24, 1897, to Herbert and Sarah Medicine Eagle. Herbert had served in the U.S. Army as a Scout. When William registered for the draft on July 29, 1918, he was living in Carter. He likely joined the Army shortly after this. He was discharged as a Private on Feb. 4, 1919. After returning home, he married Ida Kills Two. In the 1940 U.S. Census, they were farming in Mellette County with their children, George, Richard, Sarah and William Jr. William entered the spirit world on March 6, 1973, and is buried in Holy Spirit Cemetery, Tripp County.

Meeter, James. James was born near Promise around October 1889 on the Cheyenne River Reservation. In the 1891 Census Roll, he is listed with his parents, James and Belle Meeter. They both entered the spirit world when he was young. In the 1902 Census Roll, he was living with Louis and Mary Benoit. In 1912, he married Fannie Hates Him. Their children died as infants. When James registered for the draft on June 5, 1917, he was working near Promise, but made his home in Wakpala. After he joined the Army, he was assigned to Field Hospital No. 37, 6th Division Sanitary Train (ASN 938262). Pfc. Meeter sailed with his unit from New York aboard the *Darro* on July 7, 1918. The 6th Sanitary Train served in the Sectors at Gerardmer and Meuse-Argonne. He was later assigned to the Medical Dept., 53rd Infantry, 6th Division. During the Meuse-Argonne Offensive, the Sanitary Train occupied the site of a former German Hospital near Apremont. After the Armistice, Pfc. Meeter sailed from Brest, France, aboard the U.S.S. *Leviathan* on June 5, 1919, and arriving in the U.S. on June 12. He was discharged on Jne 21, 1919. Shortly after he returned home, his wife passed away. He later married Jennie Red Crow. In 1935, they were interviewed by a worker with the SDERA program. They were living in a one-room log home about two miles from the Moreau River. Their drinking water was hauled from the river. He had raised cattle before the war, but had sold them because he thought he would not return. In the 1940 U.S. Census, James was working as a Missionary with the Episcopal Church. James entered the spirit world in the PHS Indian Hospital in Rapid City on June 27, 1966. He is buried in Eagle Butte Cemetery.[20]

Mern, William. William was born in Mandan, ND, on May 3, 1890, to Ed and Anna Mern. He grew up on a ranch near Sturgis, where his father disappeared around 1900. In 1911, William bought a claim near Isabel with his brother, Dewey. In 1917, they moved to a farm near the mouth of the Moreau River, on the Cheyenne River Reservation. William joined the Army on May 24, 1918. Cpl. Mern was assigned to Co. K, 157th Infantry, 40th Division (ASN 2786560). He sailed with his unit aboard the *Berrina* on Aug. 9, 1918. Joseph Jewett and David Drops at a Distance were in Co. K with Mern. Mern suffered an injury while in the Army. He returned home from Brest aboard the U.S.S. *Mount Vernon* on March 3, 1919. He was traveling with St. Aignan Casual Co. No. 1413. Cpl. Mern was discharged on March 21, 1919. William received a disability payment of $25 per month.

On January 29, 1921, he married Elsie Benoist (1895-1965). William's brother, Dewey, married Elsie's sister, Fidelia. In the 1931 Cheyenne River Census Roll, William is listed with Elsie, but he was non-enrolled. In 1935, they were interviewed by a worker with the SDERA program. They were farming with his brother's family. In the 1940 U.S. Census, William and Elsie were ranching near Piedmont. Dewey lived with them, as well as Dewey's children, Benjamin and Carlyle. Dewey's wife, Fidelia, had passed away in January of that year. Melvin Ducharme, Elsie's brother, also lived with them. In 1957, William and Elsie lived in Rapid City where William worked as a janitor at the Gate Way Motel. William entered the spirit world on April 12, 1966. He and Elsie are buried in the Black Hills National Cemetery.[21]

Middle Tent, Allen. Allen was born about July 23, 1900, on the Crow Creek Reservation to John and Annie Middle Tent. In the 1905 Census Roll, Allen is listed as Coyote, with a sister, Irene. Allen joined the Army at Jefferson Barracks, MO, on Aug. 4, 1918, and served in the Machine Gun Troop, 8th Cavalry. He was discharged as a Private on Oct. 15, 1919, at Fort Bliss, TX. After the war, he farmed near Fort Thompson. He became ill with tuberculosis and was admitted to Battle Mountain Sanatorium on July 22, 1927 and discharged on Sept. 22, 1927. He entered the spirit world on Dec. 18, 1927. He is buried at Joe Creek Cemetery, Hughes County.[22]

Minesinger, James. James was born about Jan. 19, 1888, possibly in Canada. He was enrolled on the Flathead Reservation in Montana. His father was Henry Minesinger. In the 1910 U.S. Census, he was working as a hired man in Grass Valley, OR. He joined the Army on Aug. 17, 1917 and was first assigned to the 11th Aero Service Squadron (ASN 19199). Pvt. Minesinger sailed with his unit from New York aboard the *Orduna* on Dec. 18, 1917. After arriving in Europe, he served with the 1099th Aero Squadron. Some of the enlisted personnel had left the U.S. on Oct. 13, 1917, for training in England. They were the first trained U.S. Air Squadron to report for duty in France. Many of the men were mechanics who worked on the construction and repair of aircraft. Sgt. Minesinger was discharged on March 22, 1919. After the war, James moved to South Dakota. In 1922, he married Lillian Hamilton (1884-1954) in Rosebud. In the 1930 U.S. Census, James was working as a blacksmith at the Rosebud Agency. Around 1940, they moved to Hardin, MT, where he worked at an Indian boarding school. James entered the spirit world on Oct. 3, 1961, in Inyo County, California. He was survived by a daughter, Ernestine Merlin. He is buried in Cortez Cemetery, Cortez, Colorado.

Mitchell, Charles C. Charles was born on Dec. 24, 1889, to Charles and Lillie Lacroix in Santee, Nebraska. In 1911, he married Mabel Chapman, with whom he had a son, Lawrence. Lawrence was killed in Italy in 1944, during WWII. When Charles registered for the draft on June 5, 1917, he was divorced and working in Niobrara as a farm laborer. Charles joined the Army and was assigned to Battery D, 338th Field Artillery (FA), 88th Division (ASN 3228590). He served with Charles Arcoren. The 338th FA served in France, but not on the Front. The unit was sent home in December of 1918, and Pfc Mitchell was discharged on March 20, 1919. On Feb. 17, 1920, he married Annie Half Day in Chamberlain. In the 1920 U.S. Census, he was living in Fort Thompson. He and Annie had two daughters, Winona and Norma. Annie entered the spirit world in 1926. In 1930, their daughters were living at the St. Paul's Boarding School. In the 1937 Census Roll, Charles was living in Sioux Falls with his son. Charles entered the spirit world on Jan. 28, 1972, and is buried in Santee, NE.

Moccasin Top, Job. Job was born on the Pine Ridge Reservation around December of 1894. His parents were Moccasin Top and Nell. When he registered for the draft on June 5, 1917, he was farming with his father. He joined the Army at Allen on July 25, 1918, and served in the 7th Company,

163rd Depot Brigade. He was discharged as a Private from Camp Dodge, IA, on Dec. 11, 1918. After he returned home, he married Louisa Iron Bull. Job entered the spirit world in Nov. 19, 1934, due to complications from a broken leg. He is buried in the Inestimable Gift Cemetery, Allen, SD.

Monroe, Aloysius John. Aloysius was born on July 18, 1894, on the Pine Ridge Reservation, to John Monroe and Sophie Mousseau. When he registered for the draft on June 5, 1917, he was living in Vetal, SD. He enlisted in the Navy. He came down with the flu and was admitted to Pelham Bay Naval Hospital on Dec. 21, 1918. He was discharged from the hospital on Jan. 3, 1919. In the 1920 U.S. Census, he was stationed on the USS *Renshaw*, in San Diego. In the 1930 U.S. Census, he was serving as a Private with the 7th Cavalry at Fort Bliss, TX. The 7th Cavalry was part of the 1st Cavalry Division. In the 1940 U.S. Census, he was living with his wife, Jessie, and children, Elsie and Clara, in Bennett County, SD. He later moved to Porcupine. He entered the spirit world at his home on May 1, 1970. He is buried in Holy Rosary Mission Cemetery, at Pine Ridge.[23]

Monroe, William D. William was a younger brother of Aloysius. He was born on the Pine Ridge Reservation on April 20, 1900. In the 1900 U.S. Census, he was listed with his parents, John and Sophie. He enlisted in the U.S. Navy on July 25, 1918 and was discharged as a Seaman 2nd Class on Sept. 29, 1919. He married Minnie Howard on Sept. 1, 1923. In the 1930 U.S. Census, they were farming in Bennett County. In the 1940 U.S. Census, William was working as a laborer on a water conservation project. He was living in Wood with his family of four children, Aloysius, Mark, William Jr., and Lillian. Aloysius served in the Army at the end of WWII. The family later moved to Alliance, NE, where William entered the spirit world on March 7, 1981. He is buried in Calvary Cemetery in Alliance.

Montreal, Martin. Martin was born on Sept. 14, 1897, in Belcourt, ND, on the Turtle Mountain Reservation. His parents were Francis and Adele Montriel. His father worked with the Indian Police. In the 1910 U.S. Census, Martin was a student at the Fort Totten boarding school. He enlisted in Company D, 2nd Infantry, North Dakota National Guard (ASN 54254) at Devils Lake, ND, on June 30, 1917. On Oct. 13, 1917, he was reassigned to Co. L, 164th Infantry. On Dec. 15, 1917, he sailed from Hoboken, NJ, aboard the *Leviathan*. On arriving in France, he was reassigned to Co. H, 26th Infantry (1st Division) on Jan. 12, 1918. The soldiers being reassigned were loaded into unheated French cattle cars. On Aug. 28, 1918, he was reassigned to Co. L, 26th Infantry. Pvt. Montreal served in the campaigns at Montdidier-Noyon, Aisne-Marne, St. Mihiel, Meuse-Argonne, Ansauville, Saizerais, and Cantigny. He returned to the U.S. on Sept. 2, 1919, and was discharged at Camp Dodge, IA, on Sept. 24, 1919.

Upon returning home, he moved to South Dakota in 1921, and started working for the Fred LaPlante Ranch in LaPlant. In Aug. 1932, he married Isabelle J. Traversie at St. Theresa Church in White Horse. For a few years, they lived with Isabelle's parents. They later lived at the Cheyenne Agency, where Martin started working for the B.I.A. In 1935, they were interviewed by a worker with the SDERA program. They had a two-room house, one of which was used as a kitchen. They prepared meals for the eight inmates in the agency jail. Martin also hauled supplies for the agency. They received $45 per month. He worked for 22 years until retiring in 1960, after moving to Eagle Butte. He later worked at the Sioux SuperValu. He entered the spirit world in a Rapid City hospital on Feb. 18, 1974. His wife and two daughters, Joan and Rosalee, as well as his sons, Nino, Terry, and Gary, survived him. He is buried in the Black Hills National Cemetery, Section C, site 1054.[24]

Moore, Charles. Charles was born around 1890 on the Rosebud Reservation. Some Census Roll information lists his birth as December of 1888. In the 1895 Census Roll, he is listed with his mother, Jessie New, and her other children, Thomas and Mary New. When Charles registered for the draft on June 5, 1917, he was working as a carpenter for the Indian Service at Rosebud. He joined the Army on July 29, 1918, and was assigned to Co. F, 214th Engineers, 14th Division (ASN 3009375). The 214th Engineers was organized in August 1918, at Camp Forest, GA. In October of 1918, the unit was transferred to Camp Custer, MI. Pvt. Moore was discharged on Feb. 7, 1919. In 1921, he was a member of the Chauncey Eagle Horn Legion Post in Rosebud. In the 1920s, he married Laura Darkling Face. In the 1930 U.S. Census, he was working as a policeman for the Indian Service. In the 1937 Census Roll, he was listed with his sons, Robert and George. Charles entered the spirit world on June 3, 1958, and is buried in Grace Chapel Cemetery, Soldier Creek.

Moore, Vance Antoine. Vance was born on the Rosebud Reservation on May 15, 1894, to Charles and Amelia Moore. Vance enlisted in the Navy on Dec. 20, 1915 (NSN 1436413). His rating was Engineman 1st Class. He was discharged on Jan. 5, 1920. In 1921, he was a member of the Chauncey Eagle Horn Legion Post in Rosebud. He later moved to Nebraska and married Aldena Woolhiser. He worked for the railway postal service in Omaha. In the 1940 U.S. Census, he and Aldena had two daughters, Florence and Joyce, and a stepson, Haviland. Vance entered the spirit world in Omaha on Oct. 10, 1953, and is buried in Calvary Cemetery, Okreek, SD.[25]

Morrin, Alvis M. Alvis was born on the Red Cliff Ojibway Reservation in northern Wisconsin on May 22, 1894. His parents were Mike Morrin and Hildur Larson. Alvis was a student at Carlisle boarding school from 1911-1914. When he registered for the draft on June 5, 1917, he was working as an assistant clerk at the Flandreau boarding school. On Nov. 15, 1917, he was stationed with Headquarters Company, 3rd Regiment, Camp Dewey, Great Lakes Naval Training Station. By the summer of 1918, he was stationed in France. He was discharged on July 15, 1919. After the war, Alvis' name was engraved on a plaque honoring veterans at the Flandreau boarding school. Alvis returned to Wisconsin. In the 1920 U.S. Census, he was working in a sawmill at Lapointe on the Bad River Reservation. Around 1924, he married Clara Tucker, a Menominee. In the 1930 U.S. Census, Alvis was working as a property clerk at the Keshena Agency office. In the 1940 U.S. Census, the family was living in Tomah, where Alvis worked as a clerk for the Indian Service at the boarding school. He and Clara had four children, Patricia, Dorothy, Barbara, and Robert. The family was still living in Ashland, WI, in 1950. Sometime after this, the family moved to California. Alvis entered the spirit world in California on Jan. 18, 1967. He is buried in Woodlawn Cemetery, Shawano, WI.

Albert Robert Morrison
Eric LaPointe

Morrison, Albert Robert. Robert, also known as Robert Holy Dance, was born on the Pine Ridge Reservation on March 8, 1888, to Peter Morrison and Buffalo Comes Out. He married Anna Randall on Sept. 24, 1912, with whom he had a daughter, Elvira. Anna entered the spirit world on Dec. 20, 1916. When Robert registered for the draft on June 5, 1917, he was ranching near Wanblee, where his allotment was located. On June 19, 1917, he married Annie Lucy Two Horse/Quigley. When Robert joined the Army, he was assigned to the 420th Bakery Co., Quartermaster

Corps. He was discharged as a Private on Dec. 14, 1918. Robert lived with his family in Todd County. Robert and Annie had a daughter, Ruby, and two sons, William and Frank, who died in their youth. In the 1930 U.S. Census, he was working as a policeman with the Mission school. He also worked in the C.C.C. program. Robert demonstrated how to make stone tomahawks, pipes and flutes to the guests at the dude ranch near Porcupine. He sold his craft items to tourists both on and off the reservations. He was knowledgeable in the use of herbs, roots and plants to heal people with health problems. In *The Medicine Men*, Thomas H. Lewis describes Robert Holy Dance as one of the last Oglala medicine men who was a true herbalist. Robert entered the spirit world in his home at Rosebud on Dec. 9, 1971. He is buried in Spring Creek Cemetery, St, Francis, SD.[26]

Morsea, Charles Ray. Charles was born about Nov. 20, 1897, in Missoula, MT, but was enrolled at Lower Brule. His father, Henry Morsea, was a black soldier and his mother was Elizabeth Desheuquette. Around 1900, his father was stationed in the Philippines. In the 1910 U.S. Census, the family lived in Seattle, where his father was stationed in Fort Lawton. Around 1915, Charles was enrolled at the Hampton boarding school. School records list him as leaving the school in 1918, to enlist in the Marines. In the 1920 U.S. Census, Charles was living in Pierre with his wife, Claudia and working as a fireman in the local power plant. In 1922, he married Grace Dewitt, whose brother, Ben, had served in the military. They had a daughter, Violet. In the 1930 U.S. Census, he was living with his mother and sister in Sioux City, IA. Shortly after this he married Julia Keeler. In 1935, they were interviewed by a social worker with the SDERA program. They were living in a four-room house in the Iron Nation District on the Lower Brule. They hauled their water from the Missouri, two miles away. Charles was the foreman on a dam construction project. In the 1940 U.S. Census, they were living at the Fort Totten boarding school, where Julia was a piano instructor. In 1949, Charles married Bernice Capitan in Navaho County, AZ. He worked as an engineer for the Indian Service at Fort Defiance. Charles entered the spirit world at the Navaho Medical Center on Oct. 11, 1951, at Fort Defiance, AZ. American Legion Post 52 at Window Rock handled the burial in the Navaho Memorial Cemetery.

Mortenson, Hans. Hans was born in Lead, SD, on Jan. 6, 1891, to Christian and Maria Mortenson. When Hans registered for the draft on June 5, 1917, he lived in Eagle Butte and worked for the Diamond A Cattle Co. He served in the military during the war. He was discharged on Jan. 21, 1919. In the 1920s, he married Margaret Claymore, the twin sister of John Claymore, who also served in the military. Hans continued to work for the Diamond A. In the 1931 Census Roll, Hans is listed with Margaret and their children, but he was non-enrolled. In 1935, the family was interviewed by a social worker with the SDERA program. They lived in a five room home a block east of the post office in Eagle Butte. Hans and Margaret had two children, Clarence and Audrey Jean. Hans was a member of the American Legion and Margaret was a member of the Legion Auxiliary. Hans had worked for the Diamond A for many years, and had been foreman for six years. A few years later Hans became ill with cancer and entered the spirit world on March 21, 1940, in a hospital in Rochester, MN. He is buried in Eagle Butte. Margaret later married Ben Young, who had served with her brother, John, in Co. K, 355th Infantry. They managed the Mortenson Ranch.[27]

Mound, Peter. Peter was born on the Cheyenne River Reservation around Oct. 22, 1892. His parents were Philip and Lucy Mound. When Peter registered for the draft on June 5, 1917, he was living at White Horse. He enlisted in the Army on June 23, 1918, and was assigned to Co. A, 350th Infantry, 88th Division (ASN 3304087). The 350th Regiment sailed from New York on Aug. 11, 1918, aboard the H.M.S. *Delta*. Pvt. Mound was assigned as a Scout with the 1st Battalion, Intelligence Platoon. The 88th Division remained in France until May of 1919. Pvt. Mound sailed for home from St. Nazaire aboard the *Aeolus* on May 19, 1919, and was discharged on June 5, 1919. After returning home, he married Blanche Bowker. In the 1930s, he married Stella Swan. In 1935, they were interviewed by a worker with the SDERA program. They were living in a 16' by 20' home located eight miles west of White Horse, on the brakes of the Moreau. Peter had sold his livestock and purchased a new Chevrolet. In the 1940 U.S. Census, he was living with Ernest Makes Life and working on a nursery project. In 1941, he became ill with encephalitis and entered the spirit world on Aug. 17, 1941. He is buried with other veterans in a corner of the Episcopal Cemetery near White Horse.[28]

Mountain, Willis. Willis was born on the Standing Rock Reservation around Nov. 11, 1897. In some census records, his name is White Mountain. In the 1900 U.S. Census, he is listed with his parents, Ralph and Bertha (Murphy), as well as a sister, Susan. Willis enlisted on June 17, 1917, while he was a student at the Flandreau boarding school. He likely first served with the 1st SD Cavalry Regiment, which was sent to Camp Cody, NM, in September of 1917. Pvt. Mountain sailed for France from New York aboard the S.S. *Tereisias* on June 28, 1918. He was traveling with Co. 14, Camp Cody June Automatic Replacement Draft (ASN 1427483). After arriving in in France, he was assigned to Battery A, 19th Field Artillery (FA), 5th Division. Pvt. Mountain served with Pvt. Louis Dog and Pvt. Francis Janis. The 19th FA served in the Sectors at St. Die, Villers-en-Haye, St. Mihiel, Limey, and Puvenelle. After the Armistice, Pvt. Mountain received an evaluation from his commanding officer, 1st Lt. William Sumner, which stated that he was "a very dependable soldier and in caring for animals and harness has shown considerable aptitude." Pvt. Mountain had been gassed twice while in France. He also drove trucks and acted as a chauffeur. The Army had sent him to a vocational course to learn to be a mechanic. Most of his FA unit left France on July 13, 1919, but Pvt. Mountain was transferred to another unit and was not discharged until Dec. 10, 1920. In the 1920s, a monument honoring students who had served in the war was erected at the Flandreau School. The name of Louis [sic] Mountain is engraved on the plaque. After returning home, he married Lucy Crazy Hawk. In 1935, the family was interviewed by a social worker with the SDERA program. Willis was a member of the American Legion and the VFW, while Lucy was a member of the Legion Auxiliary. In the 1940 U.S. Census, they were living with their children, Mildred, Josephine, Joseph, Anthony and Francis. Willis was serving as a judge in the Indian Court System. Willis re-enlisted in the Army on June 8, 1942, and was discharged on March 5, 1943. He later served as a Lay Minister. He entered the spirit world in Little Eagle on Jan. 27, 1968. He is buried in Messiah Cemetery, Little Eagle.[29]

Munnell, David. David was born on the Leech Lake Ojibwe Reservation about Nov. 1, 1900. In the 1909 Leech Lake Pillager Census Roll, he is listed with his parents, Kotamaush and Kahgegaybequay, as well as his brothers, Joseph, Louis, James and William. Around 1913, David came to the Flandreau boarding school. On April 7, 1917, he enlisted in Troop D, 1st SD Cavalry. This unit drilled in South Dakota as an infantry unit, because they were not issued horses or saddles. In September of 1917, they were transferred to Camp Cody, NM, where they trained with the 34th Division. Cpl. Munnell was assigned to Co. D, 136th Infantry (ASN 1427484). He sailed with his unit from New York aboard the *Melita* on Oct. 13, 1918. Eventually, Cpl. Munnell was assigned to P.W.E. (Prisoner of War Escort) Co. 255. Cpl. Munnell was killed by a prisoner on Sept. 17, 1919, in Gievres, France. His body was brought back to the U.S. by the *St. Mihiel*, which sailed from Antwerp, Belgium on Dec. 4, 1921. The ship arrived in New York on Dec. 16. He is buried in Leech Lake Reservation Cemetery, Onigum, MN. His brother, James, enlisted in the North Dakota National Guard while attending the

Wahpeton boarding school. Sergeant James Munnell served in the 1st Infantry Division and was awarded the Silver Star.

Murray, Wallace Aaron. Aaron was born on Nov. 10, 1897, to Stephan Murray and Rosalie Decoteau. In the 1899 Sisseton-Wahpeton Census Roll, Aaron is listed with his mother, who entered the spirit world around 1906. Aaron grew up on the Rosebud Reservation. He attended school in Rapid City, until 1917, when he transferred to the boarding school at Carlisle, PA. On May 16, 1918, he was hired as a waiter at Kamp Kohut in Oxford, ME. He enlisted in the U. S. Marine Corps on Jan. 8, 1919, and served at Parris Island. In the 1920 U.S. Census, he was serving as a Private in Cuba. He was discharged in 1922. Aaron's sister, Laura, married Dwight Heminger, who had served in the Army. Aaron also served with the Marine Corps during WWII, from 1942-1944. He later worked for a time with B.I.A. in Ashland, MT. Aaron married Laura Potton on April 24, 1925. In the early 1930s, he put together a draft of a constitution and bylaws for the Rosebud Tribe. In the 1937 Rosebud Census Roll, Aaron and Laura are listed with their children, Aaron and Shirley. In the 1940 U.S. Census, Aaron was married to Josephine Dorian (1902-1987), and working as an area supervisor with National Youth Administration in Mission. Aaron later worked for International Harvester in Richmond, CA, until retiring in 1962. He was a member of American Legion Post No. 295 in Parmelee, as well as the Westerners International Corral in Rapid City. Aaron entered the spirit world at the VA Hospital in Hot Springs on Aug. 11, 1975. His widow, a daughter, Shirley and a son, Aaron, survived him. He is buried in the Black Hills National Cemetery, Section C, site 681.[30]

N

New, Thomas. Thomas was born about Sept. 24, 1891 on the Rosebud Reservation. In the 1900 Census Roll, he is listed with his mother, Jennie, as well as a brother, Charles Moore, and a sister, Mary New. He married Josephine Desersa (1891-1963). When Thomas registered for the draft on June 5, 1917, he and Josephine had one child. Thomas was working as a laborer for the Indian Service at Rosebud. He entered the Army with the draft of Aug. 27, 1918, at the Rosebud Agency. He was sent to Camp Funston, KS, and was assigned to Co. G, 69th Infantry, 10th Division. He remained there until discharged on Jan. 28, 1919. Josephine's brother, Alex, enlisted in the Army in the 1920s. In the 1930 Census Roll, the family was living in Rapid City. In the 1937 Census Roll, Thomas and Josephine are listed with their children, Clara, Peter, Tom Jr., Mary, Pearl and Albert. Their son, Tom Jr., served in the Navy during WWII. The family later moved to Nebraska. Thomas Sr. entered the spirit world at the Soldier's and Sailor's Home in Sidney, NE, on Oct. 18, 1964. Military graveside services were conducted by the Bayard veteran's organization. Thomas and Josephine are buried in Bayard Cemetery, Bayard, NE.[1]

Nickaboine, William. William (Mah mah we gah bow) was born on the White Earth Reservation on March 6, 1896, to George Nickaboine and Ke toh cumig o quay. Around 1910, he became a student at the Flandreau boarding school. On April 4, 1917, he enlisted in Troop D, 1st South Dakota Cavalry. This National Guard unit drilled in South Dakota, but was never issued any horses or saddles. In September of 1917, the unit traveled to Camp Cody, NM, where Pvt. Nickaboine was transferred to Co. D, 136th Infantry (ASN 1427415). On June 28, 1918, he sailed from Hoboken, NJ, aboard the ship S.S. *Tereisias*. He was traveling with Co. 14, Camp Cody June Automatic Replacement Draft. Pvt. Nickaboine was reassigned to Evac. Hospital 49. He took part in the offensives at St. Mihiel and Meuse Argonne. He also took part in the Army of Occupation, until Aug. 14, 1919. Pfc.

Nickaboine sailed from Breast, France aboard the *Panaman* on Aug. 19, 1919. He arrived back in the U.S. at Brooklyn Navy Yard on Aug. 29, 1919. Private 1st Class Nickaboine was discharged at Camp Dodge, IA, on Sept. 4, 1919. In the early 1920s, Nickaboine's name was engraved on a plaque honoring veterans from the Flandreau boarding school. After returning to Minnesota, he lived in Kathio Township, near Mille Lacs Lake. In the 1930s, he married Susan Kegg (1914-1955). William entered the spirit world in Kathio on Dec. 10, 1963. His sons, Lawrence and William, as well as his daughter, Leona, survived him. He is buried in the Veteran's Cemetery in Onamia, MN.[2]

No Moccasin, Edward. Edward was born about March 7, 1895, on the Lower Brule Reservation. Shortly after this, his parents, Samuel Han Pa Nica [No Moccasin] and Mary Mato Ota Win [Many Bears Woman] took him to the Rosebud Reservation. Edward joined the military on April 25, 1918, and was discharged on April 1, 1919. After returning home, he married Nettie Good Elk. In the 1940 U.S. Census, he and Nettie are listed with their children, George, Helen, Margaret, Alden and Cara. Edward was working as a farm Laborer in Todd County. In the 1940s, he worked for the C & NW RR. Later he moved to Oacoma, SD. In 1962, he married Eunice Scott. Edward entered the spirit world in Chamberlain on May 27, 1972. He is buried in the Presbyterian Cemetery in Crow Creek.[3]

No Water, George. George was born on the Pine Ridge Reservation about Oct. 18, 1889, to Thomas and Louisa No Water. He registered for the draft in Oglala on Sept. 11, 1918. His dates of military service are not known. Given his age, he may have served during the war. He later enlisted in the Army in 1926. In the 1930 U.S. Census, he was living with his wife, Bertha and working as a laborer on a cattle ranch near Buffalo Gap. He entered the spirit world on March 27, 1974, and is buried in the Black Hills National Cemetery, Sect. E, site 914.

O

Obago, Joseph. Joseph was born about Feb. 20, 1893, in Greenwood, SD, on the Yankton Reservation. In the 1896 Yanktonai Census Roll, Joseph Campawaste [Good Chokecherries] is listed with his mother, Mahpiyawakanwin [Sacred Sky Woman]. His father, Obago, had entered the spirit world earlier that year. Joseph married his first wife, Winnie Fassar, with whom he had two children. When Joseph registered for the draft on June 5, 1917, he was farming with Winnie near Greenwood. Joseph joined the Army on April 26, 1918, and was assigned to Co. K, 355th Infantry, 89th Division (ASN 2186643) at Camp Funston, KS. Pvt. Obago sailed with the 89th Division aboard the *Baltic* on June 4, 1918. Upon arrival in France, the 355th Regiment was headquartered in Grand. The 355th served in the Sectors at Lucey, St. Mihiel, Euvezin, and Meuse-Argonne. Pvt. Obago returned from France aboard the *Leviathan* on May 15, 1919. Pvt. Obago was discharged on May 31, 1919. His wife, Winnie, had entered the spirit world while he was overseas. On Nov. 30, 1921, he married Annie Brother of All (1877-1949). Annie had a son, Joseph, who served in the war. They moved to the Crow Creek Reservation. In 1935, the family was interviewed by a worker with the SDERA program. Joe and Annie were living in a tent next to the home of Eugene Brother of All. Joe was working on a relief project, digging ditches. Earlier he had worked on a dam construction project. Joseph entered the spirit world in Buffalo County on May 17, 1943, and is buried near Joseph Brother of All in Christ Episcopal Church, Fort Thompson.[1]

Obashaw, Frank. Frank was born on the Yankton Reservation about Dec. 8, 1892. In the 1893 Yanktonai Census Roll, he is listed with his parents, Robert and Julia, a brother, James, and a sister, Lizzie. Frank enlisted in the SD National Guard on June 2, 1917. This likely was Co. M, of the 4th SD Infantry. On Sept. 28, 1917, the unit traveled to Camp Greene, North Carolina. Upon arrival, their commanding officer was told he now was in command of the 147th Field Artillery Regiment, 41st Division. Pfc. Obashaw served in Battery C, 147th F.A. (ASN 139458). His unit sailed to Europe aboard the *Olympic* on Jan. 11, 1918. On March 25, 1918, they were attached to the 32nd (Red Arrow) Division, which they supported until the Armistice. Around this time, Pfc. Obashaw was diagnosed with Tuberculosis. He returned to the U.S. from Base Section #1 aboard the Pocahontas on March 30, 1918. Pfc. Obashaw entered the spirit world on July 11, 1919, at General Hospital #16, New Haven, CT. He is buried in Holy Fellowship Cemetery, Greenwood, SD.[2]

Oka, Mathew. Mathew was born on the Standing Rock Reservation in 1896, to Louie and Agnes Oka. He was a member of the Mad Bear Band. When Mathew registered for the draft on June 5, 1917, he was farming with his father at Wakpala. He joined the Army on June 24, 1918, and was assigned to Co. D, Development Battalion #1, 163rd Depot Brigade (ASN 3309365). Pvt. Oka was discharged on Nov. 6, 1918, at Camp Dodge, IA. He married Laura Plays with Iron (1901-1971). In 1935, the family was interviewed by a worker with the SDERA program. The family was living at Kenel, so their children could attend school. Their children were, Bernard, Madeline, Charles, Gladys, and Lavina. Mathew's mother was also living with them. Mathew was a member of the American Legion, while Laura was in the Legion Auxiliary. Mathew had received a disability payment. He was in poor health and relatives provided them with food. They had a team of horses and some farm equipment. Mathew entered the spirit world on Nov. 13, 1945, and is buried in Mad Bear Church Cemetery. In a ceremony held in Wakpala on March 17, 2017, the family of Pvt. Oka received a Code Talker's Medal in honor of his service.[3]

Old Crow, John J. John was born on the Standing Rock Reservation on Oct. 18, 1889. His father, Jumping Bull, was a ghost dancer who died when Sitting Bull was killed. John's mother, Karnegewin, married Old Crow. John married Annie Medicine on Aug. 14, 1913. He was living in Bullhead when he registered for the draft on June 5, 1917. John joined the Army on Oct. 5, 1917, and served with Co. D, 136th Infantry, 34th Division (ASN 1427488). The 34th Division underwent extensive training at Camp Cody, NM, before sailing for France in September of 1918. Pvt. Old Crow was discharged on April 14, 1919. In 1920, John and Annie were living in Pleasant Ridge Township. In 1935, John was interviewed by a worker with the SDERA program. He was providing support for his mother. John was a Legion member. He owned three horses, a wagon and a set of harness. He was working on emergency conservation projects. John entered the spirit world on Dec. 27, 1955, following a car accident near Edgemont, SD. He is buried in the Black Hills National Cemetery, Section B, Site 143.[4]

Old Shield, Joseph E. Joseph was born on the Pine Ridge Reservation about Aug. 23, 1897. His parents were Alfred Old Shield and Julia Many Cartridges. Joseph attended the Carlisle boarding school. He enlisted in the Marine Corps on July 9, 1916. On Oct. 13, 1918, he was promoted to Corporal, and then to Sergeant on April 29, 1919. In October 1919, he was stationed on the U.S.S. *Tennessee*. He re-enlisted on July 22, 1920. In the early 1920s, he married Florence Logan who was a member of the Turtle Clan of the Seneca Nation. In the 1925 NY State Census, Joseph and Florence were living with their son on the Alleghany Reservation in western New York. Joseph worked as an auto mechanic. Their sons were Ernest Joseph, and Robert, who both served in the military in WWII. On Oct. 20, 1929, Joseph entered the spirit world after being hit by a tram in

Raleigh, NC. He had been working there with the Barnum and Bailey Circus. He is buried in Chapel Hill, NC.

Omaha Boy, Herbert. Herbert was born on the Rosebud Reservation in November 1897. In the 1900 U.S. Census, he is listed with his parents, Joe and Rose, a brother, George and a sister, Louisa. Herbert enlisted in Co. I, 4th SD Infantry (ASN 98583) at Rapid City on March 28, 1917, while a student at the Indian Training School. When the SD National Guard soldiers arrived at Camp Greene, NC, they were transferred to other units in the 41st Division. Pvt. Omaha Boy was assigned to Co. B, 148th Machine Gun Battalion. He sailed from Hoboken for Europe aboard the *Olympic* on Jan. 11, 1918. Finally, many South Dakota men were assigned to Co. M, 167th Infantry, 42nd Division. In March of 1918, they served in the trenches in the Luneville Sector. In June they were transferred to the Champagne Front, and in July fought in the Battle at Chateau-Thierry. Pvt. Omaha Boy served with Pfc. Chauncey Eagle Horn. Pvt. Omaha Boy was severely wounded on July 26, 1918, in the Ourcq River valley on the same day as Pfc. Eagle Horn was killed. Pvt. Omaha Boy received gunshot wounds in his right hand, forearm, thigh and ankle. He was taken to Base Hospital 36. Two days later he was taken to Base Hospital No. 119, and finally to Base Hospital No. 8. He sailed for the United States aboard the U.S.S. *Finland* on Nov. 18, 1918, arriving on Nov. 29 in Newport News, VA. From Newport News, he was taken to Base Hospital No. 22 in Richmond, and finally transferred to Fort Snelling, MN. On Jan. 13, 1919, he was sent to Camp Dodge, IA, where he was discharged on Jan. 28, 1919. In the 1930 U.S. Census, Herbert was living with his wife, Fannie, as well as her parents, Andrew and Mary Knife. Herbert became ill with Tuberculosis, and entered the spirit world at Battle Mountain Sanatorium on April 11, 1934. He is buried in St. Charles Cemetery, St. Francis.

One Feather, Henry. Henry was born on the Standing Rock Reservation on June 3, 1896, to Antoine Wiyakawanjila [One Feather] and Annie Iron Dog. He was a member of the Bear Ribs Band of the Hunkpapa. His father had served with the Indian Police, and received a pension. In the 1910 Census, Henry was living with his family in Corson County, SD. When he registered for the draft on June 20, 1917, he was living in Fort Yates and working for the government school. He enlisted in the Army on June 22, 1918, and served with the Headquarters Troop, 19th Division at Camp Dodge, IA (ASN 3954611). On Aug. 6, 1918, he wrote a letter from Camp Dodge to the editor of *The Sioux County Pioneer:*

> Dear Chris,
>
> Will write you a few lines to let you know that I am getting along fine in army life so far, and hope that I will make good.
>
> Will you send my *Sioux County Pioneer* here to Camp Dodge? Will close here and send you my best regards. Give my best regards to my folks and friends at home.

Henry was discharged on Jan. 28, 1919. The 19th Division was demobilized at Camp Dodge, IA, in February 1919. In 1918, Henry had married Clara Lucy Swift Cloud in McIntosh, SD. In the 1930 U.S. Census, Henry and Lucy were living in Fort Yates, where Henry was working as a night watchman for the government school. He later ranched near Bullhead, SD. He married Ruby Gayton in Sioux Falls, SD, on July 29, 1935. In the Standing Rock Census Roll for 1940, Henry and Ruby were listed with two daughters, Corrine and Beverly. Henry entered the spirit world in Bullhead on Feb. 7, 1956. He is buried in St. Aloysius Cemetery, Bullhead.[5]

Oneroad, Amos. Amos was born on the Sisseton-Wahpeton Reservation near Drywood Lake on Jan. 15, 1884. His parents were Peter Oneroad and Nancy Shepherd. Amos attended school at Sisseton and Haskell, where he finished around 1909. His father wanted him to study further, so Amos enrolled in the Bible Teachers Training School and the School of Divinity at Columbia University in New York City. While visiting the American Museum of Natural History, he met some anthropologists. He began working with them to translate information on the customs of the Dakota people. He worked with Alanson Skinner, George Bird Grinnell and Melvin Gilmore. He also became a staff member of the Museum of the American Indian. When Amos registered for the draft, he was working as an archeologist with George Heye. On June 10, 1918, he enlisted in the 20th Company, 9th Coast Defense Command, New York National Guard. He was discharged on Sept. 18, 1919. In 1919, he married Etta Ortley. That same year, he was ordained as a minister. In the 1920 U.S. Census, he was serving as a missionary at Fort Peck. In 1926, he married Emma Wantawa. In the 1930 U.S. Census, he was serving as a minister at Greenwood. In the 1937 Census Roll, he and Emma had four children, William, Arlene, Dorothy and Amos Jr. Amos entered the spirit world at the Yankton Indian Hospital in Wagner. He is buried in the Greenwood Cemetery. Amos Oneroad was a co-author with Alanson Skinner of *Being Dakota*.[6]

O'Rourke, John. John is listed on WWI veteran's memorial at Oglala Lakota College, Kyle, SD. He was born on the Pine Ridge Reservation on Aug. 29, 1893. His father, Jack, was born in Louisiana. In the 1894 Census Roll, John is listed with his mother, Georgianna, his brothers, Thomas, Charles and Samuel, and his sisters, Anna and Emma. John attended school in Rapid City and married Nellie Cottier on Nov. 26, 1917. He joined the Army on Aug. 27, 1918, and was assigned to the 22nd Co., 164th Depot Brigade at Camp Funston, KS, (ASN 4499146). He was discharged as a Private on Dec. 5, 1918. Nellie entered the spirit world in 1929. In the 1930 U.S. Census, John was living in Rapid City with his mother, who was now married to William Helm. John was working as a teamster. In 1935, he married Rose Ellston, who was enrolled on the Rosebud Reservation. The family was interviewed by a worker with the SDERA program in 1935. They were living in a one room house in Pennington County. John was doing relief work. In the 1937 Census Roll, John is listed with his children, Anna, Kenneth, Kermit, Laverne, and William. The family lived in Rapid City for a number of years. John was a member of the American Legion. John had an accident with a lit cigarette and entered the spirit world in Rapid City on Aug. 6, 1956. He is buried in the Black Hills National Cemetery, Section A, site 634. Military grave side rites were performed by American Legion Post 22.[7]

Ortley, Wallace G. Wallace was born near Veblen on the Sisseton-Wahpeton Reservation on April 14, 1889. His parents were Henry Ortley and Margaret LaBelle. His father, Henry, had served with the Indian Scouts in 1863. In 1909, Wallace married Alice DeMarrais (1887-1959). When he registered for the draft on June 1, 1917, their family, including three children, was living near Veblen. Wallace entered the Army on July 22, 1918, and served as a Private with Base Hospital 144, Medical Dept. (ASN 3954262). He was discharged on May 1, 1919. In 1935, the family was interviewed by a worker with the SDERA program. They were camping in a 10' by 12' tent near a road construction project. At that time, they had two surviving children, Hilda and Gladys. They liked attending Indian dances. Alice made quilts which she sold to supplement their income. In the 1940 U.S. Census, Wallace was farming in McKinley Township, Marshall County. In his later years he moved into the Tekakawitha Nursing Home in Sisseton. He entered the spirit world at the home on April 7, 1970. His daughter, Gladys, survived him. He is buried in the Soldier's Circle in the Sisseton Cemetery.[8]

Ortley, Wesley. Records from the Flandreau boarding school show that Wesley Ortley enlisted in the military during the war but was given an early discharge for medical reasons. A man named Wesley Ortley was born to John and Minnie Ortley on the Sisseton Wahpeton Reservation around 1901. In the 1906 Census Roll, Wesley is listed with his parents, John and Minnie, as well as his brother, Clarence and sister, Rosa. In 1911, Minnie married Simon Kirk. Wesley, who was suffering from Tuberculosis, entered the spirit world on April 24, 1919, in Wolf Point, MT. He is buried in Peever, SD. His brother, Clarence, served in WWII.[9]

Otterman, Allen. Allen was born on the Rosebud Reservation on May 14, 1893. His parents were Otter Man and Pretty Woman. When Allen registered for the draft on June 5, 1917, he was working as a laborer for the Indian Service at Rosebud. On Aug. 18, 1917, he married Lizzie One Feather. Allen likely joined the Army in the summer of 1918. While he was at Camp Dodge, IA, he became ill with the Spanish Influenza, and entered the spirit world on Oct. 8, 1918. He is buried in St. Mark's Cemetery in Parmelee. A Valentine, NE, newspaper described his funeral in a story written by Wilma Rhodes of Rosebud.

> Several days ago, a young Sioux Indian, by the name of Allen Otterman died at Camp Dodge, IA, of Spanish Influenza. Yesterday he was buried in a little quiet Indian cemetery far out on the Dakota prairie. It was my privilege to attend his funeral, which in some respect was one of the most remarkable demonstrations of patriotism I have ever witnessed.
>
> A short service was conducted in the yard of the father's home, with the casket resting in the shadow of the open summer house so typical of all Indian living, and this service was conducted by an Indian missionary whose education enables him so to minister to his people. The home is situated on a very high hill, so that long before we reached it we could see the large crowd of Indians who had gathered to pay their last tribute to the young hero. Long before we reached the home we could see Old Glory floating from a tall flagpole that had been set up since the news of his death had reached the reservation.
>
> After the brief service at the house the procession started for the church and cemetery. Each of the five young men who were pallbearers has qualified for military service, though some have been rejected on account of physical unfitness and others have not yet been examined. Each one of them had pinned to the lapel of his coat streamers of red, white, and blue. At the front of the procession rode a young Indian brave on an Indian pony and carrying the dear old flag. Behind him moved the automobile carrying the remains of the young soldier and over him floated another large flag. Behind the body rode the pallbearers on swift Indian ponies. Several Indian families were in cars, but many more were in wagons, the old women and men chanting their lamentations for the dead. Surely here was the mingling of the old primitive life with the new regime, and over all a spirit of patriotism that was unspeakably touching and sincere. I cannot think that any more impressive military funeral cortege ever passed along a highway that moved that day over the far Dakota prairies.[10]

Otterman, Joseph. Joseph was the younger brother of Allen. He was born around July of 1895, to Otter Man and Pretty Woman. When Joseph registered for the draft on June 5, 1917, he was working as a stock raiser near Cut Meat, SD. He likely joined the Army in the spring of 1918, and was assigned to Co. E, 351st Infantry, 88th Division (ASN 3309963). Some of these soldiers from South Dakota had first trained at Camp Funston before being transferred to Camp Dodge, IA. Pvt.

Joseph Otterman
Swansong/eBay

Otterman sailed from New York on Aug. 15, 1918, aboard the *Scotian*. By the fall of 1918, they were stationed in eastern France around Hericourt. About this time, the 351st Infantry was hit hard by the Spanish Influenza, with as much as half the men falling sick. Private 1st Class Otterman became ill and entered the spirit world on Oct. 2, 1918. He is buried in the Meuse-Argonne American Cemetery, Romagne-sous-Montfaucon, Lorraine, France. The Otterman American Legion Post No. 94 in White River is named in honor of Joseph and Allen. They had an older brother named Thomas, who also entered the spirit world in 1918. There is no record that Thomas had served in the military.

Owens, Vernie. Vernie was born on the Sisseton-Wahpeton Reservation on Aug. 20, 1899. He was a student at the Flandreau boarding school when he joined the Army. He may have served in the 48th Infantry. After the war, his name was included on a plaque to honor veterans from the school. In the 1920 U.S. Census, he was living with the David Seaboy family at the Sisseton Agency. He entered the spirit world on March 6, 1921. His headstone in St. James Cemetery at Enemy Swim Lake indicates he served as a Bugler.

P

Pacer, Joseph. Joseph was born about August of 1899 on the Pine Ridge Reservation. His parents were Pacer and White Cow. He registered for the draft at Pine Ridge on Sept. 12, 1918. Oglala records indicate he served in the military. He married Mary Fast Thunder. In the 1940 U.S. Census, they lived with their daughter, Vida, while Joseph worked in road construction. In 1947, he started working for the C & NW RR in Hay Springs, NE. Joseph entered the spirit world at the Pine Ridge Hospital on May 9, 1950.[1]

Packard, Ernest. Ernest was born at Greenwood, SD on Aug. 17, 1894. In the 1897 Yanktonai Census Roll, Ernest is listed his parents, Samuel and Mary, and two brothers, George and Orson. After Samuel entered the spirit world, his mother married Baptiste Archambeau. Ernest married Clara Rencountre (1897-1927). When Ernest registered for the draft on June 5, 1917, he was farming with Gilbert St. Pierre near Wagner. He joined the Army on June 27, 1918, and was assigned to Co. A, U.S. Guards (ASN 3315353). While he was serving as a military policeman, his wife's father took care of his corn crop. Private Packard was discharged on Dec. 30, 1918. After he returned home, he sent Joseph Dixon a list of names of 47 veterans from the Yankton Reservation. After his wife entered the spirit world in 1927, Ernest lived with his brother, Orson, who also was a veteran. Ernest became ill with pneumonia and entered the spirit world on Jan. 3, 1933, and was buried in White Swan Cemetery, Lake Andes.[2]

Packard, Orson. Orson, an older brother to Ernest, was born on April 17, 1892, to Samuel Packard and Mary Lyman. Orson first married Mabel Heart in 1912. When he registered for the draft on June 5, 1917, he was farming with Ed Lyman near Faith. He and his wife had two children. Orson joined the Army on Dec. 8, 1917, and was sent to Camp Greenleaf, GA, which was a medical officers training camp. Pvt. Packard left for France from New York aboard the *Aquitania* on June 8, 1918. He was traveling with Camp Greenleaf Replacement Draft Co. No. 9 (Medical Dept.) (ASN 752108). After arriving in France, he was assigned to the 140th Ambulance Co., 110th Sanitary Train, 35th Division. The 35th Division suffered heavy casualties in the opening days of the Meuse-Argonne Offensive. They served five days in the active front and received 7,283 casualties. Many of the soldiers were inexperienced. After the Armistice, Pvt. Packard was cited for "effective service." Pvt. Packard sailed back to the U.S. aboard the S.S. *Antigone* on April 14, 1919. Pvt. Packard also served for a short time with the 421st Casual Detachment, 163rd Depot Brigade, Camp Dodge, IA. He was discharged on May 12, 1919. In 1921, he married Jeanette Crazy Eyes (1896-1977). In the 1937 Census Roll, they were listed with their sons, Homer and Horace. Orson entered the spirit world on Feb. 22, 1958, and is buried in St. Phillip's Cemetery, Lake Andes.³

Patton, Lawrence F. Lawrence was born on the Yankton Reservation on July 21, 1889. In the 1900 U.S. Census, he was living with his parents, Frank Patton and Lucy Shunk, in Lawrence Township, Charles Mix County. In the 1916 Yankton Census Roll, Lawrence is listed with his son, Roland. Lawrence enlisted in the Army on April 21, 1916. He served with the 4th Service Company, Signal Corps (ASN 705696), in Ft. Wood, NY. Sgt. Patton, serving with Co. D, 55th Telegraph Battalion, sailed from Hoboken, NJ, aboard the *Agamemnon* on April 7, 1918. After the Armistice, he sailed from Marseilles aboard the *Guiseppi Verdi* on June 22, 1919. Sgt. Patton was traveling with St. Aignan Casual Co. No. 5957. He was discharged on June 4, 1920, as a Sergeant 1st Class. In the 1930 U.S. Census, he lived with his wife, Madeline, in Denver, CO, where he was working as an electrician with the Public Service Co. In the 1940 U.S. Census, he was living with his mother in Wagner, SD. His mother was the librarian in the city library. When Lawrence registered for the Selective Service in 1942, he was at the VA Hospital in Hot Springs. He entered the spirit world on Oct. 11, 1942 and is buried in the ZCBJ Cemetery in Wagner.

Peneaux, George. George was born on the Rosebud Reservation around Oct. 16, 1889. In the 1892 Census Roll, he is listed with his mother, Mary, a widow, and his brothers, William and Harry, and his sisters, Annie and Lucy. George married Millie War Bonnet (1891-1963) around 1913. When he registered for the draft on June 5, 1917, he and Millie had three children. George joined the Army with his brother, Harry, on Oct. 27, 1917. Upon arriving at Camp Funston, KS, he was assigned to Co. F, 314th Ammunition Train, 89th Division (ASN 2195305). He served with Pvt. Robert Blue Coat and Pvt. Louis Brings Three White Horses. Pvt. Peneaux sailed for Europe from New York aboard the *Honorata* on June 4, 1918. After the Armistice, Pvt. Peneaux was evaluated by his commanding officer, 1st Lt. Frank Brannigan, who stated that he "preferred cavalry. Associated readily with men and was considered a good man." The soldiers returned from Brest, France, aboard the *Agamemnon* on May 16, 1919. Pvt. Peneaux was discharged on June 4, 1919. In the 1940 U.S. Census, George and Millie were listed with their children, Jasper, Verle, Marjorie, Jayne and George Jr. They were living in Mellette County. George entered the spirit world on May 17, 1949, and is buried in Bad Nation Cemetery, near Wood, SD.⁴

Peneaux, Henry Harry. Harry was born on the Rosebud Reservation on Jan. 2, 1888. He was an older brother of George. When Harry registered for the draft on June 5, 1917, he and Mabel had two children and lived near Wood. Harry entered the Army with his brother, George. He also was assigned to Co. F, 314th Ammo Train, but was discharged on Jan. 15, 1918, most likely for medical reasons. His wife, Mable, entered the spirit world in 1936. In the 1937 Census Roll, Harry and his wife, Bessie, lived with their children, Rena, Thomas, Earl, Richard, Orline and Dora. Richard served in the military during the Korean Conflict. Harry entered the spirit world on Dec. 25, 1957, and is buried in Holy Innocents Cemetery, Parmelee.

Pheasant, Thomas. Thomas was a Hunkpapa born on the Standing Rock Reservation about July 1, 1891. In the 1900 U.S. Census, he was listed with the name, Pte Awan Yanka [Watches the Buffalo]. In the 1903 Census Roll, he was listed with his mother, Noise, and step-father, Swift Eagle. Around 1915, Thomas owned 65 head of cattle and 12 horses but was forced to sell them because of some government policies. When Thomas registered for the draft on June 5, 1917, he was farming near Bullhead. He joined the Army on Oct. 1, 1918, and was stationed at Camp Grant, IL. He also served in the Medical Dept. at Base Hospital #128 (ASN 3780745). Pvt. Pheasant was discharged on Jan. 2, 1919. Upon returning home, he married Rosie Fire Cloud on April 22, 1919. In the 1930 U.S. Census, he was farming in Corson County. Thomas and Rosie had two children, Michael and Catherine. In 1935, the family was interviewed by a social worked with the SDERA program. They lived near Kenel in a two-room house with Rosie's brother, Joseph Fire Cloud. They hauled their water for two miles from the Missouri River. Thomas was a member of the American Legion in Kenel. In the 1940 U.S. Census, Thomas was working as a laborer in a C.C.C. Camp, as was his son, Michael. Michael served with the U.S. Army Medical Dept. during WWII. Thomas entered the spirit world at the Standing Rock Hospital in Fort Yates on Feb. 28, 1950. He is buried in the Kenel Cemetery.[5]

Philbrick, Robert Ernest. Robert was born on the Crow Creek Reservation about Feb. 21, 1892, to Robert and Rebecca Philbrick. In 1911, he married Sophie Fearless Hawk, with whom he had two children, Rebecca and Edith. When Robert registered for the draft on June 1, 1917, he was farming near Fort Thompson. Shortly after this, Robert married Annie Irving. Military records show that Robert enlisted in the Army on May 8, 1917. He likely enlisted in Kimball in Troop L, 1st South Dakota Cavalry, which was sent to Camp Cody, NM, in September of 1917, for training with the 34th Division. He was assigned to Co. L, 136th Infantry (ASN 1429260). Pvt. Philbrick sailed with Co. 18, Camp Cody June Automatic Replacement Draft from New York aboard the *Honorata* on June 28, 1918. He later was transferred to Co. M, 163rd Infantry, 41st Division. He was finally transferred to the Machine Gun Company, 308th Infantry, 77th Division. The 308th Infantry served in the Sectors at Baccarat, Vesle, Oise-Aisne, Forêt d'Argonne, and Meuse-Argonne. The 77th Division suffered 10,497 casualties in the war. Pvt. Philbrick sailed from Brest, France, for home aboard the *Orizaba* on Jan. 13, 1919. He was traveling with patients labeled as "Tubercular Cases." Pvt. Philbrick was not discharged until Aug. 11, 1919. He likely spent some time in a military hospital. He received a government pension after having been gassed. Robert entered the spirit world on Dec. 22, 1934, following a fire in his home in Buffalo County. He is buried in St. John's Cemetery in Pukwana, SD. His widow moved in with her sister, Mrs. Alex Sazue.[6]

Phillips, Schuyler. See **Makes Life, Ernest**.

Picotte, Charles. Charles was born on the Yankton Reservation in Greenwood on March 27, 1890. His parents were Charles Picotte and Emily LeDeaux. When Charles registered for the draft on June 5, 1917, he was farming near Ravinia, SD. He joined the Army on June 27, 1918, and was assigned to Battery E, 30th Field Artillery, 10th Division (ASN 3315337). The 10th Division did not serve overseas. Pvt. Picotte was discharged on Jan. 28, 1919. He married Grace LaPointe. In the 1940 U.S. Census, Charles and Grace were listed with five children, Norbert, Benedict, Harald, Vivian and Evelyn. Their home was 14 miles SW of Wagner. Charles entered the spirit world on Feb. 5, 1949 and is buried in the Greenwood Presbyterian Cemetery.[7]

Picotte, George Andrew. George was born in Greenwood on the Yankton Reservation around Jan. 24, 1892. His parents were John Picotte and Julia Drips. George joined the Army on June 27, 1918, and served with the Motor Transport Train, spending his time in the U.S. He was discharged on Feb. 8, 1919. In the 1930 U.S. Census, he was farming in Howard Township, Charles Mix County. In 1935, George was interviewed by a worker with the SDERA program. He was living with his sister-in-law in a two-room frame house in Highland Township. He had planted 55 acres of corn. His livestock consisted of an old horse owned by his grandmother. On Aug. 4, 1936, he married Eva Archambeau Picotte. Eva (1893-1959) had been married to George's brother, Herbert, who entered the spirit world in 1934. In the 1940 U.S. Census, George was working as a fireman at the Indian Hospital in Wagner. They moved to Nevada around 1950. George later married Susan Kephart. George entered the spirit world in Henderson, Nevada in March 29, 1979, and is buried with Eva in Woodlawn Cemetery, Las Vegas.[8]

Picotte, Jesse G. Jesse was born at Greenwood on the Yankton Reservation around Aug. 5, 1888, to Charles Picotte and Louise Benoist. Jesse was a student at the Carlisle Boarding School from 1907 to 1910. He married Viola Lyman (1892-1966) in 1910. When he registered for the draft on June 5, 1917, he and Viola had three children. He joined the Army on Sept. 20, 1917, and was assigned to the Machine Gun Company, 30th Infantry, 3rd Division (ASN 2193023). He served with Jasper Blaine and Oscar Bernie. Pvt. Picotte sailed with his unit from New York aboard the *Aquitania* on April 2, 1918. His commanding officer evaluated Corporal Picotte, saying that he had "participated in five campaigns. Regarded by white men as a good soldier." He was wounded and later received a Purple Heart medal. Pvt. Picotte sailed from Brest, France, aboard the U.S.S. *America* on Aug. 12, 1919. He was discharged on Aug. 26, 1919. Upon returning home, he farmed for a few years before starting work with the Indian Service. In the 1930 U.S. Census, Jesse was working at the school in Bannock, ID. Their children were Noel, Leslie, Jesse Jr., and Mathilda. In the 1940 U.S. Census, the family was living in Ignacio, CO, where Jesse was a boys' advisor. When Jessie registered with the Selective Service in 1942, he was living in Towaoc, CO. His son, Jesse Jr. served with the Navy in WWII and Leslie served with the Marine Corps. Jesse entered the spirit world on Oct. 4, 1954, and is buried in the Black Hills National Cemetery, Section A, Lot 532.[9]

Pine, Straight. Straight was born on the Standing Rock Reservation on April 13, 1896, to Robert and Nancy Pine. In the 1896 Census Roll, he is listed with the name, Owotonla. He attended the boarding school at Bismarck. When he registered for the draft on June 5, 1917, he was farming near Bullhead. He joined the Army on June 24, 1918, and was assigned to Co. B, 351st Infantry, 88th Division (ASN 3309412). Pfc. Pine sailed for Europe from New York with his unit on Aug. 15, 1918, aboard the ship *Saxon*. While serving in France, Pfc. Pine contracted spinal meningitis. He sailed from Brest, France, aboard the S.S. *Harrisburg* on May 15, 1919, with Detachment #247. Pfc. Pine was discharged on June 4, 1919. In the 1920s, he married Susan One Elk. They had a son, Ambrose. In the 1930 U.S. Census, Susan's father, Andrew, lived with them. In 1935, they were interviewed by a worker with the SDERA program. They owned nine head of cattle and two teams, along with a set of harness. Straight was a member of the American Legion and the VFW. In 1928, he was the Finance Officer for the Post. Susan was a member of the Legion Auxiliary. Straight was working on conservation projects. He entered the spirit world on May 1, 1970, at the VA hospital at Hot Springs, and is buried in St. Aloysius Cemetery, Bullhead.[10]

Ploog, William Hugo. William was born in Dennison, IA, on Aug. 29, 1892, to Henry and Christina Ploog. When William registered for the draft on June 5, 1917, he was farming near Thunder Hawk, SD. He joined the Army on June 24, 1918, and traveled to Camp Funston, KS, where he served in the 48th Co., 164th Depot Brigade. Cpl. Ploog was discharged on Dec. 3, 1918. William's brother, John, served with the MPs in France. On Sept. 29, 1924, William married Esther Kempton (1897-1956) in McIntosh. William was listed with Esther in the Standing Rock Census Rolls but was non-enrolled. They had two children, Hugh and Sylvia. They farmed near Thunder Hawk. William entered the spirit world at the VA Hospital in Miles City, MT, on Aug. 18, 1964. He and Esther are buried in Lemmon, SD.[11]

Pocantico, Joe. Joe was born around Aug. 23, 1898, possibly in Lead, SD. Some records list him as enrolled on Pine Ridge. He enlisted in the Army on April 6, 1916, and served as a Wagoner with the Supply Co., 104th Infantry, 26th Division. He was discharged on Aug. 25, 1917. When he registered for the draft on Sept. 26, 1918, he lived in Washington D.C., and worked for the Indian Service. In the 1920 U.S. Census, he was listed as Joseph Turconi, living in Atlantic City, NJ. He may have been with one of the Wild West shows. When he registered with the Draft in 1942, he was listed as an Indian, working for Savage Fire Arms Co., in Hampden, Mass. His wife's name was Anne. Joseph Turconi entered the spirit world on Oct. 7, 1962, and is buried in St. Rose Cemetery, South Hadley Falls, Mass.

Pomani, Buckley G. Buckley was born on the Crow Creek Reservation on Dec. 1, 1897, to Frank Pomani and Celeste Hintowin [Blue Hair Woman]. In the summer of 1917, Buckley married Anna Thick Hair. Buckley enlisted in the 4th South Dakota Infantry on April 29, 1917, (ASN 2314297). When this National Guard unit arrived at Camp Greene, NC, in the fall of 1917, they were told they now were the 147th Field Artillery. Most of the soldiers in the 147th FA sailed from New York on Jan. 11, 1918, aboard the White Star Liner *Olympic*. It is likely that Pvt. Pomani had been sick at that time. He sailed with Overseas Casual Company #90 aboard the *George Washington* on March 30, 1918. The 147th Field Artillery served in support of a total of eight divisions, but the greatest time was spent with the 32nd (Red Arrow) Division. His commanding officer, 1st Lt. A.M. Knudtson, wrote of Pvt. Pomani, "excellent horseman, fearless and extremely courageous. Good judgement and initiative. Good night worker." On May 1, 1919, he sailed home with his unit from Brest, France, aboard the U.S.S. *Kansas*. Pvt. Pomani was discharged on May 23, 1919. In 1932, he married Helen Plays with Iron. In 1935 they were interviewed by a worker with the SDERA program. They were living in a tent that was two miles north of Fort Thompson. Helen indicated they had been moving around quite often. Buckley had been digging ditches for about $16 per month but was interested in doing mechanical work. In 1943, Buckley worked for the CNW Railroad as a freight trucker in Huron. He later ranched. Buckley entered the spirit world in Chamberlain on Feb. 8, 1978. He is buried in Lakeview Cemetery, Fort Thompson.[12]

Ponca, Shadrick. Shadrick was born on Jan. 7, 1898, on the Rosebud Reservation to Damas and Mary (Wing) Ponca. Shadrick's parents had moved from the Lower Brule Agency. Shadrick enlisted in the 4th South Dakota Infantry on March 28, 1917. In late September of 1917, this National Guard unit traveled to Camp Greene, NC. Pfc. Ponca was first transferred to the 148th Machine Gun (MG) Battalion (41st Division) (ASN 112155). Pvt. Ponca sailed with this unit from Hoboken, NJ, aboard the *Olympic* on Jan. 11, 1918. After arriving in France, he was reassigned to the 151st MG Bn., 42nd (Rainbow) Division. He served with George Jensen and Oscar Weasel. In an evaluation of Pfc. Ponca, his commanding officer, Capt. E.F. Travis, wrote, "regarded both by officer and men as an exceptional good man. Uses good judgement at all times." Ponca told his commander that he "hates to have to carry machine gun," and suggested that the dog-cart used by the Germans be used in the American Army for carrying heavy parts of Machine guns and ammunition. Pfc. Ponca sailed from Brest, France, aboard the *Minnesota* on April 15, 1919, and was discharged on

May 13, 1919. In 1921, he married Alvina Walker. They had a son, Jerry, who served in the Army in WWII. Shadrick later married Virginia Gunhammer (1901-1967), who had two brothers, Harry and Abraham, who served in the Army. In the 1937 Census Roll, Shadrick and Virginia were listed with two children, Dorothy and Lloyd. Shadrick entered the spirit world in the VA Hospital on June 13, 1967. He is buried in Evergreen Cemetery, Hot Springs.[13]

Powell, John Henry. John was born on July 9, 1893, on a ranch on the Bad River. His parents were Dan Powell and Fannie Mary Charging Eagle. In the 1902 Cheyenne River Census Roll, John is listed with his mother and his brothers and sisters, Dan, Willis, Maud, Alex, Charles, Mabel and Josephine. John joined the Army on June 27, 1918, and was assigned to the Machine Gun Company, 352nd Infantry, 88th Division (ASN 3313982). The Machine Gun Co. left Camp Dodge, IA, on Aug. 8, 1918. On Aug. 15, the unit boarded the S. S. *Ascanius,* which spotted a submarine on the voyage to England. Upon arrival in France, the unit served in quiet sectors. After the Armistice, Pfc. Powell received an evaluation stating that he was an "excellent horseman. Has demonstrated fitness for cavalry and artillery." The 88th Division was billeted in Gondrecourt until May of 1919. Pfc. Powell sailed from St. Nazaire, France, aboard the ship *Canonicus* on May 21, 1919, and was discharged on June 13, 1919, at Camp Dodge, IA.

After returning home, he married Lola Payne, with whom he had two children, John Jr. and Dorothy. John worked with cattle and horses. In his youth he broke horses and rode bucking horses in Philip and Fort Pierre. From 1939 to 1942, he managed the beef herd for the Cheyenne River Tribe. He later moved to Mission where he was in charge of the beef and horse program for a few years. He trained students in beef and horse handling techniques. After John became divorced from Lola, she enlisted in the WACs during WWII. John entered the spirit world at the Veteran's Home in Hot Springs on Dec. 21, 1994. His son, John, and daughter, Dorothy, survived him. John is buried in the Masonic Cemetery, Philip, SD.[14]

Presho, Joseph. Joseph was born on the Pine Ridge Reservation Oct. 10, 1897. His parents were Luther Standing Bear and Nellie DeCory. In the 1899 Pine Ridge Census Roll, Joseph is listed with Luther and Nellie, as well as his brothers and sisters, Lillie, Arthur, Paul, Emilie, Julie and Annie. Around 1902, Nellie married Harry Presho. Joseph joined the Army on June 2, 1918, and was assigned to Battery E, 46th Artillery, Coast Artillery Corps (ASN 513733). He may have first enlisted in the Air Service. Pvt. Presho sailed for France aboard the *Huron* on Oct. 14, 1918. In France, he was reassigned to Battery E, 59th Artillery. After the Armistice, he sailed from Brest, France, aboard the *New Hampshire* on Jan. 8, 1919. He arrived in Hoboken on Jan. 24, 1919, and was discharged on Feb. 8, 1919. In 1921, he was a member of the Chauncey Eagle Horn Legion Post in Rosebud. He farmed in the Rosebud area before moving to Crookston, NE. In the 1930 U.S. Census, he was working as a laborer in a slaughter house and living with his sister, Julia, and her husband Roy Giroux, a fellow veteran. In March, 1931, he married Edna Emery (1908-1970) in Valentine. In the 1940 U.S. Census, Joe was working as a machine man on a rock crusher. Shortly after this, the family moved to Rapid City, where Joe worked for Warren Lamb Lumber Co. He was a member of American Legion Post No. 71 in Hot Springs. In 1966, he moved into State Veteran's Home in Hot Springs. He entered the spirit world there on Sept. 7, 1980. His son, William, and stepson, Joseph Kennedy, survived him. Joe and Edna are buried together in the Black Hills National Cemetery, Section E, site 1215.[18]

Pretty Bonnet, John. John was a Lower Yanktonai born on the Crow Creek Reservation around July of 1900. His parents were His Pretty Bonnet and Wisica. John registered for the draft on Sept.

12, 1918. He likely served in the Army shortly after. In 1927, he attended the military funeral for Jacob Douglas in Fort Yates. John was listed as a member of the Legion Post at Kenel. He was married to Annie Arrow, with whom he had a son, Clifford. John suffered from Tuberculosis and entered the spirit world on Feb. 9, 1928, and is buried in St. Joseph's Cemetery, Fort Thompson.[16]

Pretty Boy, Benjamin He is listed on WWI veteran's memorial at Oglala Lakota College, Kyle, SD. Benjamin was born on the Pine Ridge Reservation around March of 1897. In the 1900 U.S. Census, he is listed with his parents, Joe and Millie Pretty Boy, as well as a brother, Samuel, and a sister, Mary. Benjamin likely was a student at the Haskell Indian School. He enlisted in Battery B, First Regiment, Kansas Field Artillery at Lawrence, KS, on March 1, 1917. Upon arrival at Camp Doniphan, Pvt. Pretty Boy was assigned to the Headquarters Company, 130th Field Artillery (FA), 35th Division (ASN 1466341). He also served with Battery B. Other soldiers in Battery B were Pvt. Edward Rooks, and Buglers Antoine Ladeaux and Thomas Blackbird. They sailed from New York aboard the *Ceramic* on May 19, 1918. When the 130th F. A. first arrived in France in June of 1918, they were stationed near Angers, before moving to the artillery training site, Camp de Coetquidan. The 35th Division played a leading role in the Meuse-Argonne Offensive. In late September, the 130th F. A. was in position in Varennes, on the east bank of the Aire River. Musician 3rd Class Pretty Boy was wounded in his side. The 35th Division suffered 7,283 casualties in the war. After the Armistice, Mus. 3rd Class Pretty Boy received an evaluation from his commanding officer, Capt. Ralph Spatt, stating that he "has had good training in semaphore and wig-wag signaling. Demonstrated fitness for work with a band." Musician 3rd Class Pretty Boy sailed from Brest, France, to the U. S. aboard the *Mobile* on April 13, 1919. Mus. 3rd Cl. Pretty Boy was discharged on May 10, 1919, at Camp Funston. After returning home, he sent a report of his experience to Joseph Dixon, saying "the very one interest in my experience I had in mind, and biggest one in on Sept. 27, 1918, when we started to open fire on the Hind bur gain [Hindenburg] line in the Argonne Forest. They gave us Hell but we give them double Hell, and capture 563 P.G. in 3th hours. We the artillery men's were catching hell during that drive."

Benjamin married Mattie White Belly. In the 1933 Census Roll, they were living with a nephew, Levi, and a niece, Edith. Benjamin became ill with pneumonia and entered the spirit world on Dec. 26, 1933. He is buried in Porcupine.[17]

Pretty Weasel, Sullivan. Sullivan was also known as Soloman. He was born on the Cheyenne River Reservation on April 5, 1895. In the 1897 Census Roll, he is listed with his parents, Hall and Hattie Pretty Weasel, and his sister, Lucy. When he registered for the draft on June 5, 1917, he was farming near LaPlant. When Sullivan joined the Army on May 24, 1918, he was assigned to Co. K, 157th Infantry, 40th Division (ASN 2787692), which trained at Camp Kearny, CA. Several other men from the Cheyenne River Reservation were also in Co. K, including Joseph Jewett and David Drops at a Distance. However, Pvt. Pretty Weasel may have been transfered, as his name was not included in the Army Transport Records which listed the soldiers of Co. K who left for Europe in August of 1918. He was discharged on April 15, 1919. On Feb. 27, 1924, he married Jennie Two Bulls (1900-1987). In the 1937 Census Roll, Solomon and Jennie are listed with their children, Madric, Catherine, Ira, Wesley and Mary. Wesley served with the Marine Corps in the 1950s. Sullivan entered the spirit world near his home in LaPlant on May 25, 1964 and is buried Virgin Creek Congregational Cemetery in LaPlant.[18]

Provost, George. George is listed on WWI veteran's memorial at Oglala Lakota College, Kyle, SD. He was born on the Pine Ridge Reservation on Jan. 16, 1900. In the 1904 Census Roll, he is listed with his parents, Louis and Alma, as well as a brother, Jack, and his sisters, Emma and Mamie. George likely served in the Navy, as did his brother, Jack. George was discharged on Oct. 23, 1919. On March 26, 1928, George married Capatolia Brooks in Council Bluffs. They were living in Omaha, where George worked as a marble setter. Sometime after this, they moved to California. They had a daughter, Alma Jean. In the 1956 Torrance City Directory, George was working as a rigger in the Navy Shipyard. He entered the spirit world in Torrance on Sept. 29, 1969.

Provost, Jesse Thomas. Jesse was born at Greenwood, SD, on Oct 16, 1893. In the 1895 Census Roll, he is listed with his parents, William and Ida, as well as a brother, Thomas, and a sister, Eva. When he registered for the draft, he was farming near Greenwood. He enlisted on May 24, 1918, and served in 1st Co., 3rd. Batt., 164th Depot Brigade at Camp Funston (ASN 3125610). Pvt. Provost was discharged on March 20, 1919. After the war, he married Cordelia Rouse, with whom he had two children, Ernest and Magda. When Jesse registered with the Selective Service in 1942, he lived in Wagner, SD. He entered the spirit world in the VA Hospital in Sioux Falls on April 12, 1965, and is buried in Wagner Cemetery.

Provost, John B. John, also known as Jack, was born on the Pine Ridge Reservation on June 3, 1898, to Louis and Alma Provost. Jack joined the Navy on Nov. 30, 1917, and served as a Water Tender (NSN 1539548). He served on both battleships and transports. He was stationed on the U.S.S. *Hancock,* and the U.S.S. *Illinois*, as well as the U.S.S. *Carola #4*. He was among the last people to leave France. He was discharged on Oct. 1, 1919. He wrote to Joseph Dixon that he never was down on report or up before the mast. He also bought $400 of Liberty Bonds. In the 1920 U.S. Census, he was living with his father and brother, George, in Gordon, NE. He married Ethel Brandon and worked as a police officer in Omaha. He and Ethel had a son, John William. He later married Thelma. Jack entered the spirit world at the VA Hospital in Lincoln on Dec. 18, 1947, and is buried in Sacred Heart Cemetery in Martin, SD. His wife, Thelma, and children, Lewis, Jack Jr., Judith Ann and Carrine Sue, survived him.[19]

Prue, Frank F. Frank was born on the Rosebud Reservation on June 23, 1890. His parents were Oliver and Millie Prue. Frank was first married to Florence Raymond, but she entered the spirit world in 1916. Frank joined the Army on July 22, 1918, and was assigned to the 434th Casual Detachment at Camp Dodge, IA (ASN 3955049). Pfc. Prue was discharged on May 13, 1919. After the war, he married Mary Sophia Elk, with whom he had a son, Robert. When Sophia entered the spirit world in 1926, Frank moved into the State Soldiers Home. In the 1930 U.S. Census, Frank was working as a pantryman at the home. His son, Robert, was living with his grandparents. Robert served in the Army in WWII and the Korean War. In December of 1950, SFC. Robert Prue was listed as MIA in North Korea. Frank entered the spirit world at the State Veterans Home on Nov. 28, 1952. He is buried in the Veterans Cemetery in Hot Springs.[20]

Prue, Levi. Levi was born on the Rosebud Reservation on Jan. 17, 1896, to Oliver and Millie Prue. Frank was his brother. When Levi registered for the draft on May 31, 1917, he was working as a stenographer at the Haskell Indian School. He joined the Army on April 26, 1918, and was assigned to Co. A, 340th Machine Gun (MG) Battalion, 89th Division (ASN 2846782). Pvt. Prue sailed from New York for Europe aboard the *Khyber* on June 4, 1918. The 340th MG Bn. was first stationed at St. Blin. They took part in campaigns at St. Mihiel, Meuse-Argonne, Lucey and Euvezin. After the Armistice, Captain D. Runkle wrote: "Pvt. Prue proved to be a most reliable man under all circumstances. At present is acting as Co. clerk and is showing ability to learn clerical work very readily." Pvt. Prue sailed from Brest, France, aboard the *Leviathan* on May 15, 1919. Prue was briefly assigned to Casual

Detachment No. 603, Demobilization Group and was discharged on June 2, 1919. After returning home, he married Corinne Cordier (1898-1943). In 1921, Levi was a member of the Chauncey Eagle Horn Legion Post in Rosebud. In the 1937 Census Roll, Levi and Corinne had six children, Margaret, Clarence, Verna, Leona, Harvey and Teresa. Around 1940, the family moved to Omaha. When Levi registered for the Selective Service in 1942, he was working in the WPA program in Omaha. He entered the spirit world in Omaha on Nov. 29, 1955. He is buried in St. Charles Cemetery, St. Francis, SD.[21]

Q

Quick Bear, Richard. Richard was born on the Rosebud Reservation on Dec. 14, 1896, to Reuben and Mary Quick Bear. He joined the Army on Aug. 3, 1917, and likely trained at Camp Cody, NM. He was assigned to Truck Co. No. 6, 109th Supply Train, 34th Division. He was discharged on Nov. 15, 1917, likely for medical reasons. He registered for the draft after returning home, when he worked with his father. In 1921, he was a member of the Chauncey Eagle Horn Legion Post No. 125. In 1928, he and his wife, Ellen, were living in Sioux Falls, where he worked as a truck driver for John Morrell & Co. In the 1940 U.S. Census, he and Ellen had three children, Doris, Walter, and Guy. Walter served in the Army and Guy served with the Navy. In 1959, the family lived in Rapid City. Richard entered the spirit world at Fort Meade, SD, on Sept. 16, 1960. He is buried in the Black Hills National Cemetery, section C, site 250.

Quinn, Charles. Charles was born on the Sisseton-Wahpeton Reservation on March 29, 1890, the son of Thomas and Jennie (Skyman) Quinn. In 1912, he married Rebecca Williams. When he registered for the draft on June 5, 1917, they were farming near Granite Falls, MN. Charles enlisted in the Army on April 26, 1918, and served as a Private in the 355th Infantry, 89th Division (ASN 2845139). Charles was discharged on May 22, 1918. The rest of his regiment sailed for France on June 4, 1918. In 1923, Charles married Emma Starlight. In the 1937 Census Roll, Charles and Emma were listed with their children, Thomas, Willis, Soloman, Clifford and Evelyn. Charles entered the spirit world in the Public Health Service Hospital in Sisseton on April 21, 1957, and is buried in Long Hollow Cemetery.[1]

Quinn, George Lewis. George was born on the Sisseton-Wahpeton Reservation on Feb. 22, 1887, the son of Henry Quinn and Susan Renville. After his mother died, he was enrolled as a student at Carlisle, PA, in 1896. He remained there until 1901. When George registered for the draft on June 5, 1917, he was a plasterer in Peever, SD, working for Fred Lawrence. On June 22, 1917, he married Maggie Oneroad. They had a daughter, Dorothy. George enlisted in the Army on May 2, 1918 and was sent to Camp Fremont, CA, where he was assigned to Co. D, 24th Machine Gun Battalion, 8th Division (ASN 507223). His unit did not serve overseas. Private Quinn was discharged on March 15, 1919. Sometime in the 1920s, George moved to St. Paul, MN, where he worked as a plasterer. He married Irene Scherbonda (1897-1984). In the 1930 U.S. Census, George and Irene lived in St. Paul with their family. Their children were Dorothy, George, Jr., Maynard, Donald and Ruth (twins) and Joyce. Their son, Donald was the State Heavy Weight Boxing Champion in 1961. George entered the spirit world at the VA Hospital on Oct. 7, 1956, after being struck by a car at a St. Paul intersection. George and Irene are buried at Fort Snelling National Cemetery.[2]

R

Raymond, James Garfield. James was born in Tripp County on July 15, 1881, to William and Julia Raymond. He was enrolled on the Rosebud Reservation. He married Eugenia Red Leaf on Dec. 10, 1903. They had a daughter, Sarah. James joined the Army on Aug. 14, 1918. He served as a Private in Battery A, 6th DMB, Coast Artillery Corps (ASN 3776780). He was discharged on Jan. 30, 1919. His daughter entered the spirit world in 1920, and Eugenia later married Samson Crooked Foot, a fellow veteran. In 1924, James married Lucy Campbell in Winner. In 1940, he was farming om Willow Creek in Tripp County. He entered the spirit world on Aug. 6, 1961, and is buried in Ascension Chapel Cemetery in Millboro.

Red Bear, Benjamin. Benjamin, also known as Bernard, is listed on WWI veteran's memorial at Oglala Lakota College, Kyle, SD. Benjamin was born on the Pine Ridge Reservation around 1896. His father, John Red Bear entered the spirit world when Benjamin was a child. In some Census Rolls, he is listed as Bernard. His mother, Susie, later married No Neck. In November of 1912, Benjamin was enrolled at the Carlisle Boarding School. He ran away from there about a year later. On July, 7, 1917, he enlisted in the Nebraska National Guard at Chadron, NE. On March 21, 1918, he wrote to the Superintendent at Carlisle that he was stationed at Camp Cody, NM, with Auxiliary Remount Depot No. 326 (ASN 1444247). He later served as a Sergeant with the 4th Co., 1st Battalion, 164th Depot Brigade at Camp Funston. He was discharged at Camp Funston on Jan. 15, 1919. He married Julia Walking Elk. He developed Tuberculosis and entered the spirit world on March 29, 1926, and is buried in Holy Rosary Mission Cemetery, Pine Ridge.[1]

Red Bear, Charles. Charles was born at Kenel on the Standing Rock Reservation on Nov. 16, 1889. In the 1900 U.S. Census, he is listed with his parents, Gregory and Mary Red Bear. When Charles registered for the draft on June 5, 1917, he and his wife, Elizabeth, were living in Wakpala. He joined the Army on July 21, 1918, at McIntosh, SD, and was sent to Camp Dodge, IA. Pvt. Red Bear was assigned to the Veterinary Evacuation Section #1, Veterinary Corps (ASN 3954595). He sailed from Newport News, VA, aboard the *Argone* on Nov. 15, 1918. He traveled with Detachment #2, Army Mobile Veterinary Clinic Hospital 2. On Jan. 31, 1919, while serving with the 3rd Army, he sent a letter home to the *Sioux County Pioneer*.

> Hello to the Sioux County Pioneer from Charles R. Bear, Coblenz, Germany. I am still alive and sound as a dollar here in Germany. I have not seen any of the boys from Wakpala and Fort Yates yet. I hope I meet some of the fellows. We will be home someday so the folks at home need not worry about us.

Pfc. Red Bear sailed home from Bordeaux aboard the *Kentuckian* on Aug. 18, 1919. He had served with the Veterinary Quarantine Station, and with Casual Detachment #1395, Demob. Group, at Camp Dodge. He was discharged on Sept. 8, 1919. In the 1920 U.S. Census, he was living with Elizabeth and his mother-in-law, Rose Eagle Boy. Charles suffered from Tuberculosis and entered the spirit world on May 28, 1929, and is buried in St. Elizabeth's Mission, at Wakpala. On March 17, 2017, in a ceremony in Wakpala, the family of Pfc. Red Bear received a Code Talker's Medal to honor his service.[2]

Red Bear, Ralph. Ralph is listed on WWI veteran's memorial at Oglala Lakota College, Kyle, SD. He was born on the Pine Ridge Reservation around October 1900. In the 1902 Census Roll, he is listed with his father, George Red Bear, and his mother, Mary Crow Likes Water. Ralph enlisted in the

Nebraska National Guard at Chadron on June 24, 1917. He departed for service on Aug. 9, 1917, likely to Camp Cody, NM. He was assigned to Co. F, 109th Engineers, 34th Division (ASN 1438262). Pvt. Red Bear sailed from New York for France aboard the *Cretic* on Sept. 17, 1918. He served in France with Pvt. Charles White Wolf, Pvt. Lawrence Cross and Cpl. George Red Boy. Pvt. Red Bear was discharged on Sept. 13, 1919. After returning home, Ralph married Josie Takes the Shield. In the 1930 U.S. Census, Ralph was working as a showman with the 101 Ranch Wild West Show. In 1943, he began working as a section laborer for the CNW Railroad, at Chadron. Ralph entered the spirit world on Dec. 19, 1948, and is buried in St. Matthew Cemetery, Pine Ridge.

Red Boy, Charles. Charles was born on the Fort Peck Reservation around 1899. He was the son of Agnes and Philip Redboy. He attended the boarding school at Flandreau, SD. He enlisted in the Army at Jefferson Barracks, MO, on April 13, 1918. He served with the 3rd Co., Coast Artillery Corps (CAC) at Ft. Hamilton, NY until June 20, 1918. Pvt. Red Boy sailed from Hoboken for France aboard the *Northern Pacific* on July 15, 1918. On Aug. 2, 1918, he was assigned to the 54th Artillery, CAC (ASN 464335). On Aug. 26, 1918, he was assigned to Battery A, 42nd Artillery CAC. He was promoted to Pfc. on Nov. 11, 1918. Pfc. Red Boy sailed from St. Nazaire aboard the *Kroonland* on Feb. 5, 1919, and arrived in Newport News on Feb. 18. He was discharged on March 11, 1919. His name is engraved on a plaque honoring veterans that was erected at the Flandreau School. After the war, he returned to the Montana, and lived with his family northwest of Brocton. Charles entered the spirit world on Jan. 4, 1929, following a vehicle accident near Poplar. His widow and two children survived him. He is buried at Riverside, MT.[3]

Red Boy, George. George is listed on WWI veteran's memorial at Oglala Lakota College, Kyle, SD. He was born on April 10, 1895. In the 1898 Pine Ridge Census Roll, he is listed with his parents, Bob and Selina Red Boy. When he registered for the draft on June 5, 1917, he was living in Oglala. On July 7, 1917, he enlisted in the 6th Nebraska Infantry at Chadron, NE. He trained at Camp Cody, NM, and was transferred to Co. F, 109th Engineers, 34th Division (ASN 1438112). Cpl. Red Boy sailed for France from New York aboard the *Cretic* on Sept. 17, 1918. He served with Lawrence Cross, Ralph Red Bear and Charles White Wolf. After the Armistice, Cpl. Red Boy sailed from St. Nazaire for the U.S. aboard the U.S.S. *Pastores* on June 17, 1919, and was discharged at Camp Dodge, IA, on July 2, 1919. George married Angelique Fire Thunder. In 1937, he was working for the CNW Railroad as a boiler maker helper. In 1942, he lived in Chadron, NE, and worked in the roundhouse. He entered the spirit world on July 8, 1961.

Red Buffalo, John. John was born around 1897 at Cherry Creek on the Cheyenne River Reservation. His parents were Adam Red Buffalo and Mary Long Woman. John likely enlisted in the 4th SD Infantry in the spring of 1917. This South Dakota National Guard unit was sent to Camp Greene, NC, in September of 1917. At Camp Greene, Pvt. Red Buffalo was reassigned to Co. B, 148th Machine Gun Battalion, 41st Division (ASN 98593). This unit sailed from Hoboken, NJ, aboard the *Olympic* on Jan. 11, 1918. After arriving in France, he was transferred to Co. M, 167th Infantry, 42nd Division. The 42nd Division saw a lot of combat and suffered 13,919 casualties. Pvt. Red Buffalo headed for home from Brest aboard the U.S.S. *Minnesota* on April 15, 1919. He was discharged on May 9, 1919. After returning home, John married Nellie Dog with Horns. In 1935, they were interviewed by a worker with the SDERA program at their home in the Bridger Precinct. He lived in a two-room log house and hauled their drinking water from the river or from a spring that was four miles away. John worked as a policeman for the district. They had two children, Emanuel and Orville. John entered the spirit world in Faith, SD, on May 25, 1959. He is buried in Bridger Cemetery.[4]

Redday, Joseph. Joseph was born on Aug. 15, 1889, in the Sisseton Reservation to David and Anna Redday. In the 1910 U.S. Census, he was living in McKinley, Marshall County. When he registered for the draft on June 5, 1917, he was farming near Granite Falls, MN. He married Emma Skyman. When he joined the Army on July 25, 1918, he was assigned to Co. M, 54th Pioneer Infantry Regiment (ASN 4065793). He served with Willian Cavender, also of Granite Falls. They trained at Camp Wadsworth, S.C. Pvt. Redday sailed from Newport News, VA, aboard the *Caserta* on Aug. 30, 1918. The ship arrived in Brest, France, on Sept. 12. At the beginning of the Argonne Offensive, Co. M was ordered to Aubreville to assist the 14th and 21st U.S. Engineers in extending light railway lines to the advanced zone. Later they moved to Neivilly to help operate a quarry for the supply of the rail line. In December, after the Armistice, the regiment traveled to Germany, where they occupied several towns along the Rhine River. Pvt. Redday left LeHavre, France, aboard the S.S. *Lorrain* on April 19, 1919. He likely had been sick, as he traveled with St. Aignan Casual Co. No. 3433. He was discharged on May 2, 1919. He likely was suffering from Tuberculosis. He entered the spirit world in Granite Falls on March 27, 1925. He is buried in Doncaster Cemetery.

Red Feather, Edward E. Edward was born on the Rosebud Reservation around March of 1902. In the 1910 U.S. Census, he was listed with his mother, Annie Holy Bear and his step-father, Henry Iron Star. Frank Goings, a tribal police officer, wrote that Edward may have served in the Canadian Army during the war. In the 1920 U.S. Census, he was stationed with the U.S. Army at Camp Jackson, SC. He was discharged on April 24. 1920. In the 1930 U.S. Census, he was stationed at Fort Meade, SD. In the 1937 Census Roll, he is listed with his wife, Alice White Hat, and their children, Eunice, Ernest, Rossiter, Emery, May and Jessie. He entered the spirit world at the VA Hospital in Hot Springs on Sept. 25, 1967. He is buried in the Black Hills National Cemetery.

Red Fox, George. George was born at Selfridge, ND, on the Standing Rock Reservation on March 24, 1888. In the Census Rolls, he is listed with his father Fred Sungila Luta [Red Fox], and his mother, Runs the Horses Off. George was living in Shields when he registered for the draft on June 5, 1917. He joined the Army at Fort Yates with George Santee on March 13, 1918, and was sent to Fort Logan, CO (ASN 503331). He was assigned to the 21st Company, Coast Artillery Corps (CAC), at Fort Strong, MA, until May 12, 1918. He was reassigned to Battery B, 71st Artillery, CAC, and sent overseas on July 31, 1918. Pvt. Red Fox sailed from Boston for England aboard the HMS *Marghu*. Upon arrival in France, the unit was billeted near Angers and trained to use 8-inch howitzers. However, the war ended before they had a chance to fire them at the enemy. On Feb. 5, 1919, the Regiment received orders to move to St. Nazaire. Upon arriving at the port of embarkation, the soldiers were put in an isolation camp where each soldier was deloused and given a physical examination. Next, they received clean uniforms. The unit sailed for the U.S. on Feb. 12, 1919, at 2 a.m., aboard the U.S. Transport *Manchuria*. Private Red Fox remained in the Army after returning home. In 1920, he was with the Supply Co., 3rd Field Artillery at Camp Grant, IL. The 3rd Field Artillery was one of the few military units that actively recruited Native men.

After his discharge he returned to ranch on the Standing Rock Reservation. On Nov. 28, 1922, he married Alice Half in McIntosh, SD. In the 1927 Census Roll, George and Alice were listed with their daughters, Octavia and Mary Seraphine. In the early 1930s, George married May Nationshield. In the 1937 Census Roll, they are listed with their children, Mary, Rosaline and George Jr. The family later lived in Bullhead, SD. George entered the spirit world in the Fort Yates Hospital on Oct. 14, 1964, and is buried in St. Aloysius Cemetery, Bullhead.[5]

Red Hawk, Daniel. Daniel was born in Wakpala on the Standing Rock Reservation on Dec. 16, 1896. In the 1896 Census Roll, he is listed with his parents, Howard and Alice Red Hawk. He was sent to the boarding school at Flandreau. On May 1, 1918, he joined the Army at Jefferson Barracks, MO, and was assigned to Co. D, 44th Infantry Regiment, 13th Division (ASN 476412). He served at Camp Lewis, WA, and was discharged as a Private on Nov. 15, 1918. His name is engraved on a plaque to honor war veterans at the Flandreau boarding school. On May 2, 1924, he married Laura Kiskis at Ft. Thompson. He later married Bessie Hudson. In the 1930 U.S. Census, he was a patient at the VA Hospital in Cheyenne, WY. He later moved to Lake Andes. He had a daughter, Faith. He developed Tuberculosis and entered the spirit world in Lincoln, NE, on March 14, 1938, and was buried in the Episcopal Cemetery in White Swan.

Red Horn, John George. George was born on the Standing Rock Reservation on April 11, 1901, to Hesa [Red Horn] and Wastewin. He grew up in Cannon Ball, until his mother, Wastewin, remarried and moved to Kenel. George was too young to serve in the Army during the war, but he did enlist in Cannon Ball in March 1920. Two Army recruiters came to town to recruit men for the 3rd Field Artillery at Camp Grant, IL. After George returned from Service, he married Grace Bobtail Bear and lived in Kenel. In the 1933 Census Roll, George and Grace are listed with their two oldest children, Nelson and Dewey. George came down with Tuberculosis and entered the spirit world on Aug. 19, 1935. The *Sioux County Pioneer* wrote that "he was easy going and friendly and never was known to have trouble with anyone, his demise cast a shroud of sadness over our community that will not be lifted for many a day." He is buried in Kenel. His wife and three children survived him. In 1936, his widow married August Brought Plenty, a fellow veteran. George's youngest son, William, was killed in action in Korea at the age of 17, and is buried in Arlington National Cemetery, VA.[6]

Red Horse, Charles. Charles was born at Cherry Creek on the Cheyenne River Reservation on June 21, 1892, to George and Nellie Red Horse. When he registered for the draft on May 31, 1917, he was farming at Cherry Creek. He joined the 4th Infantry, SD National Guard on June 20, 1917. When the National Guard arrived at Camp Greene, NC, they were converted to the 147th Field Artillery (F.A.) (ASN 139532). Private Red Horse served with Battery C. As part of the 41st Division, they sailed to Europe on the ship *Olympic* on Jan. 11, 1918. On March 25, 1918, the 147th F.A. was attached to the 32nd (Red Arrow) Division. They supported the 32nd Division until the Armistice. The 147th F.A. served in the Sectors at Toul-Boucq, Center, Aisne-Marne, Fismes, Oise-Aisne, Avocourt, and Meuse-Argonne. The 32nd Division suffered 13,392 casualties. Red Horse's commanding officer wrote that Pvt. Red Horse "demonstrated fitness for mounted service. Good humor and judgement. Natural leader in ranks." Following the Armistice, the 147th F.A. was attached to the 40th Division temporarily, before joining the 88th Division near Gondrecourt, France. On Feb. 26, 1919, the men of the 88th Division took part in a Divisional Horse Show. According to the Divisional Newspaper, *Camp Dodger,* Pvt. Charley Red Horse was applauded by his fellow soldiers for riding a "wild" bronc! Pvt. Red Horse sailed from Brest for the U.S. aboard the *Kansas* on May 1, 1919, and was discharged on May 23, 1919.

After returning home he married Sadie Brown Wolf. He later married Sarah Two Tails of Pine Ridge, with whom he had a daughter, Orpha. In the 1930 U.S. Census, they were living in Washabaugh County on the Pine Ridge Reservation. In the 1940 U.S. Census, Charley was working as a laborer in a tree nursery near Bridger. He later moved to Interior, SD. He entered the spirit world in the V.A Hospital in Hot Springs on March 11, 1975, and is buried in the Black Hills National Cemetery, section E, site 901.[7]

Benedict Red Legs
Patricia Red Legs-Dedman

Red Legs, Benedict. Benedict was born in Bullhead on the Standing Rock Reservation on Oct. 3, 1896. His parents were Francis Husa [Red Leg] and Edith Running Hawk. Benedict was a member of the Running Horse Band of the Hunkpapa. Around 1917, he married Ida Looking Horse. When he registered for the draft on June 8, 1918, he was working for Joe Good Eagle. He enlisted in the Army in McIntosh on Aug. 5, 1918, and served in Co. D, 62nd Infantry, 8th Division (ASN 4267773). Pfc. Red Legs was discharged on Feb. 18, 1919. In 1935, the family was interviewed by a worker with the SDERA program. They were living in a one-room log house and obtained drinking water from a spring located three miles away. The family owned three horses and two cows. Benedict was driving a caterpillar tractor on a PWA project. Judge Robert High Eagle, who served as an interpreter, noted that Benedict was "a natural leader of the people, he was extremely well-liked." At that time, Benedict was serving as the Commander of the American Legion Post. In the 1937 Census Roll, their children were Gabriel, Henry, Medina, Sherman and Bernice. Ida entered the spirit world in May of 1938. In November of 1938, Benedict married Mabel Shoots Enemy. Benedict entered the spirit world in his home on Aug. 9, 1953. He is buried in Good Shepherd Cemetery, Little Eagle. On March 17, 2017, in a ceremony in Wakpala, SD, his family received a Code Talker's Medal honoring his service during the war.[8]

Red Water, Albert. Albert was born in Oacoma on the Lower Brule Reservation around July 3, 1894. His father was Mini Sa [Red Water] and his mother was Rattling Track. Around 1896, the family moved to the Rosebud Reservation. When Albert registered for the draft on June 5, 1917, he was farming near Hamill. Albert joined the Army on April 26, 1918, and was assigned to Co. G, 355th Infantry, 89th Division (ASN 2846900). Other men who served in Co. G were Clyde Lafferty, Titus Wilson, Benjamin Comes Out Bear, and Patrick LeBeau. The 355th Regiment sailed from New York aboard the *Baltic* on June 4, 1918. Upon arriving in France, the regiment was billeted in the towns of Grand, Brechainville and Allainville. The 355th took part in the campaigns at St. Mihiel, Meuse-Argonne, Lucey and Euvezin. While in France, Pvt. Red Water was reassigned to Co. A, 338th Infantry, 85th Division. Pvt. Red Water sailed with this unit from Brest, France, aboard the *Leviathan* on March 26, 1919, and was discharged on April 11, 1919. In 1924, he married Lottie Primeau. In the 1930 U.S. Census, they were farming in Tripp County. Lottie entered the spirit world in 1939. Albert entered the spirit world in the Rosebud Indian Hospital on June 21, 1943. He is buried in Holy Spirit Cemetery, Ideal, SD.[9]

Redwing, Enos T. Enos was born on Nov. 1, 1904, to Obed Redwing and Susan Westerman on the Flandreau Reservation. He was a brother to Jesse. Enos likely enlisted in the Army in the mid-1920s, and was assigned to the Coast Artillery Corps (ASN 6790932). He served with the Artillery in the Philippines. In the 1930 U.S. Census, he was stationed at Fort Snelling with Co. K, 3rd U.S Infantry. He later lived with his wife, Alvina, in Flandreau, SD, and worked as a carpenter. Enos entered the spirit world near Georgeville, MN, on July 31, 1955. He is buried in Buffalo Lake Cemetery near Eden, SD.[10]

Redwing, Hazen. Hazen likely was born in Santee, NE, about Nov. 14, 1884. His parents were Samuel Redwing and Rebecca Spaniard. In 1896, he was listed on the Birch Coulee Medawakanton Census Roll. In the 1898 Census Roll, he was adopted by John and Julia Smith. In the 1910 Census, he was living in Flandreau, and on May 2, 1910, married Cora Cavender. Cora's brother, William, served in the Army during the war. In 1917, Hazen was working as a shoemaker for C. H. Camper in Sioux Falls. Hazen enlisted in the Army on April 2, 1917, and was assigned to Co. B, 127th Machine Gun Battalion, 34th Division (ASN 1420885). He was discharged as a Saddler on Dec. 21, 1918. In the 1920 U.S. Census, he was working as a cobbler in Sioux Falls. In 1925, the Lincoln, NE, City Directory lists him as a shoemaker. By 1930, he was working as a clerk in the shoe factory in Redwing, MN. In the 1940 U.S. Census, he and his wife, Irene (1896-1993), were in Redwing, while Hazen was working on a WPA project. Hazen entered the spirit world in the VA Hospital in Minneapolis on May 22, 1950. Hazen and Irene are buried beside each other at Fort Snelling National Cemetery in Section C-9, sites 9197/9198.[11]

Redwing, Jesse. Jesse was born on Oct. 8, 1899, at Flandreau, SD. His parents were Obed Redwing and Susan Westerman. In the 1905 Flandreau Census Roll, Jesse is listed with his mother and his younger brother, Enos. He attended school in Flandreau, and enlisted in the Army on April 13, 1918. Pvt. Redwing sailed with Pvt. Charles Redboy from Hoboken, NJ, aboard the *Northern Pacific* on July 18, 1918. He served with Battery C, 53rd R.R. Artillery, Coast Artillery Corps (ASN 465362). The 53rd Artillery (Railroad) served in France and supported the Army at St. Mihiel. They returned from St. Nazaire to the U.S. on Feb. 25, 1919, aboard the USS *Nansemond*. Private Redwing was discharged on March 29, 1919, and returned to Flandreau. In the 1930 Sioux Falls City Directory, he and his wife, Alma, lived in Sioux Falls, where Jesse worked as a butcher for John Morrell & Co. In 1940, he started working for C & NW Railroad. He later moved to Spokane, WA, and worked as a painter. In 1965, he moved into the Washington Soldiers Home in Orting. He entered the spirit world in Spokane on July 7, 1965, and is buried in the cemetery at the home in Orting.[12]

Ree, Edward. Edward was born on the Rosebud Reservation about April 17, 1895. In the 1900 U.S. Census, he was listed with his parents, Charles and Nellie, as well as his brother, Hugh, and a sister, Carrie. Edward enlisted at Ft. Meade on May 24, 1917, serving in Co. I, 4th SD Infantry. In September of 1917, he arrived in Camp Greene, NC, where he was transferred to the 148th Machine Gun Battalion, 41st Division (ASN 98576). On Jan. 11, 1918, his unit sailed aboard the *Olympic* from Hoboken, NJ, for Europe. Upon arriving in England, they were transported to Le Havre, France. He was transferred to Co. M, 167th Infantry, of the 42nd (Rainbow) Division. In March of 1918, they were assigned to trenches in the Luneville Sector. He remained in trenches until he was wounded on April 3, while on a night patrol in "no man's Land." He was in a French hospital in Mixte, as well as American Hospital Base, No. 36. On July 14, 1918, he returned to the Front. He took part in the fighting on the Champagne Front, where the 42nd Division captured 500 Germans. On July 27, he took part in a big drive in Chateau-Thierry. He was wounded again on that day, and was taken to Hospital No. 4. He also spent a week in an American Hospital in Paris. On Sept. 1, he was taken to Camp Hospital No. 15 in St. Nazaire, where he was a patient for three months. In December he was transferred to the St. Nazaire embarkation port. On Jan. 11, 1919, he sailed from St. Nazaire aboard the *Manchuria* for the United States, arriving back in Hoboken on Jan. 22, 1919. He traveled with St. Nazaire Casual Co. #127. Pvt. Ree was discharged at Camp Grant, IL, on Feb. 7, 1919. After the war, he married Mary Jones of the Sisseton-Wahpeton Reservation. They lived in Long Hollow Township, where Edward entered the spirit world on Jan. 2, 1929. He is buried in Long Hollow Cemetery. His widow married Louis Titus, who also was a veteran.[13]

Ree, Hosea. Hosea was born in Greenwood, SD, about March 20, 1890. In the 1892 Yanktonai Census Roll, Hosea is listed with his parents, Philip Hinhan Waste [Pretty Owl] and Florence. On Sept. 7, 1916, he married Winnie Whipple. When Hosea registered for the draft on June 5, 1917, he lived at Dante. He joined the Army on Sept. 4, 1918, and was assigned to the 163rd Depot Brigade, Casual Detachment #31 at Camp Dodge, IA, (ASN 4415728). He was discharged as a Private on Jan. 9, 1919. He married Eunice Day (1899-1969) on July 2, 1920. They moved to Ft. Thompson. In the 1940 U.S. Census, Hosea and Eunice had five children, Hosea Jr., Winifred, Glorietta, Doris and Morris. Winifred served with the Army during WWII. Hosea entered the spirit world at his home on Nov. 4, 1946. He is buried in the Episcopal Cemetery in Ft. Thompson.[14]

Ree, Hugh. Hugh was born on the Rosebud Reservation on April 24, 1896. His parents were Charles and Nellie Ree. Edward Ree was his brother. When Hugh registered for the draft on June 7, 1917, he was farming with his father near Mission. He joined the Army and was assigned to Co. C, 309th Engineers, 84th Division (ASN 3315828). He sailed for England from New York aboard the *Scandinavian* on Sept. 9, 1918. He returned with his unit from Brest, France, aboard the *Cap Finisterre* on June 1, 1919. He was discharged on June 21, 1919. In the 1930 U.S. Census, he was living with his brother, Arthur, in Todd County. In the 1937 Census Roll, he was listed with his wife, Eva Kills in Water, and their children, Lavina, Clifford, Victoria and Adeline. Eva entered the spirit world in the fall of 1937. When Hugh registered with the Selective Service in 1942, he was living in St. Francis. In 1945, Hugh married Dora No Leaf. Hugh entered the spirit world on Feb. 14, 1973, in the Indian Health Service Hospital in Rosebud. He is buried in St. Charles Cemetery, St. Francis.[15]

Reed, Ulysses Berry. Ulysses was born around 1894 on the Yankton Reservation to James and Frances Reed. In the 1910 U.S. Census, he lived near Rouse with his parents and brothers and sisters, Morgia, Stephen, John and Grace. Ulysses joined the Army and was assigned to Co. F, 351st Infantry, 88th Division (ASN 3315271). Pvt. Reed sailed to France from New York aboard the *Scotian* with his unit on Aug. 15, 1918. About a month later, many soldiers in the regiment were hit by the Spanish Influenza. Pvt. Reed entered the spirit world in France on Oct. 17, 1918. His body was brought back aboard the *Cantigny* which sailed from Antwerp, Belgium, on Oct. 14, 1921. He was buried in New Holy Name Cemetery in Dante. The American Legion Post in Greenwood was named in his honor.

Rencontre, Albert. Albert was born at Ft. Hale, SD, on Jan. 21, 1897, to Zedo Rencontre and Susie Gillan. In the 1899 Lower Brule Census Roll, he was listed with his father, Zedo. He joined the Army on July 15, 1917, and was assigned to Co. B, 327th Battalion, Tank Corps (ASN 1420982). Sgt. Rencontre sailed with his unit from New York aboard the *Orontes* on Sept. 25, 1918. The 327th Tank Battalion was part of the 304th Tank Brigade, commanded by Capt. George S. Patton. After the Armistice, Sgt. Rencontre sailed for home from Bordeaux aboard the *Susquehana* on April 20, 1919, and docked at Newport News, VA. He was discharged as a Sergeant on May 17, 1919. Albert's sister, Mary Louise, married Eugene Rouillard, a fellow veteran. On Feb. 28, 1920, Albert married Harriet Peckove at Kansas City, MO. They had a daughter, Luachet. Albert later moved to Nebraska, where he married Irene Ingalsbe. In 1934, Albert was working as a mechanic for Johnson Motor Co. in Norfolk, NE. In the 1940 U.S. Census, Albert worked as a mechanic in Weiser, ID. He and Irene had a son, James. In 1947, he was working at the Naval Station in Coeur d'Alene, ID. Irene entered the spirit world in 1952. Albert entered the spirit world in Portland, OR, on Sept. 12, 1963. He is buried in Willamette National Cemetery, Section F, site 4410.

Renville, Felix. Felix was born on the Sisseton-Wahpeton Reservation on Dec. 17, 1895, to Moses and Mary Renville. When Felix registered for the draft on June 5, 1917, he was working with his father. Felix joined the Army on Sept. 22, 1917. He was assigned to Co. D, Squad #13, 341st Machine Gun Battalion, 89th Division (ASN 2192905). Pvt. Renville sailed with his unit from Brooklyn aboard the *Tennyson* on June 4, 1918. Pvt. Renville was severely wounded by five pieces of shrapnel on Nov. 2, 1918. He was hit in the right temple, upper lip, neck, right shoulder and left arm. Their unit was advancing north of Barricourt Heights. After the battle, it was first thought that Renville was dead. Another soldier sent a telegram to Renville's father saying that Felix had been killed. A burying squad later realized that Pvt. Renville was still alive. He regained consciousness about 10 days later. Pvt. Renville left Brest, France, aboard the S.S. *Mt. Vernon* with Detachment #95 on March 3, 1919. The manifest for this voyage read "Walking Patients Requiring No Dressing." On March 11, 1919, he arrived at Greenhut Debarkation Hospital in New York City. While Pvt. Renville was in the hospital, he was photographed and interviewed by Joseph Dixon. Renville stated, "the Nation ought now to recognize our valor as fighters and make us one of the people. It was alright for me to fight for my country and I did not regret my wound." Felix also recalled that his transport for France zigzagged across the Atlantic to avoid German submarines. By the time that he arrived back home in South Dakota, his father had entered the spirit world, on May 11, 1919, and did not get to see Felix. Pvt. Renville was discharged on June 19, 1919. Felix married Christine Blue Dog in 1921. They had a daughter, Pearl. On Jan. 9, 1933, Felix and Christine traveled to New York to appear with Robert Ripley on his radio program, "Believe It or Not." He described his experience of returning to life. Christine entered the spirit world in November of 1933. In 1936, Felix married Lillian White. When Felix registered for the Selective Service System in 1942, he and Lillian were living in Washington, D.C., where Felix was working. Felix has a son, Felix Jr., who said he has a photo of his father holding his own death certificate, which had been issued after his death was reported on the battlefield. Felix survived many years after that experience. He later married Caroline LaBelle. He entered the spirit world at Coteau des Prairies Hospital in Sisseton on May 4, 1986, and is buried in the Sisseton Cemetery.[16]

Renville, Lucas. Lucas, or Luke, was born about Aug. 2, 1889, on the Sisseton-Wahpeton Reservation. In the 1901 Census Roll, he was listed with his parents, Victor and Mary, as well as his brother, David, and sisters, Ellen, Louisa, Etta and Sarah. When Lucas registered for the draft on June 2, 1917, he was farming near Peever. He joined the Army on Aug. 28, 1918, and served at Camp Funston. Pvt. Renville served in the 2nd Battalion, 164th Depot Brigade (ASN 4500045. After his discharge on Dec. 10, 1918, he joined the American Legion. He became ill with tuberculosis, and stayed at the hospital in Hot Springs. He later moved in with his brother, David, who had a large house about 10 miles SW of Sisseton. When David's family was interviewed in 1935 by a social worker with the SDERA program, Lucas was living in a tent next to David's home. Lucas took his meals with the family. In the 1937 Census Roll, Lucas is listed as single. Lucas entered the spirit world at David's home on Jan. 14, 1941, and is buried at St. Mary's Cemetery. The Legion Post took part in the grave ceremony.[17]

Renville, Robert. Robert was born on the Sisseton-Wahpeton Reservation on April 12, 1895. In the 1898 Census Roll, he is listed with his parents, Peter and Sarah Renville. When he registered for the draft on June 1, 1917, he was married and living in Peever. He joined the Army on May 25, 1918, and was assigned to Machine Gun Company, 158th Infantry, 40th Division (ASN 2788064). Pvt. Renville sailed from Brooklyn with his unit aboard the *Vauban* on Aug. 11, 1918. He was re-assigned to Co. C, 121st Machine Gun Battalion, 32nd Division. His commanding officer rated him as "a good soldier." The 32nd Division suffered 13,392 casualties. Pvt. Renville sailed from Brest, France, aboard the T.S.S. *Toloa* on May 5, 1919, and was discharged on May 22, 1919. In the 1927 Census Roll, Robert is listed with his wife, Irene Brown and a son, Kenneth. In the 1930 U.S. Census, He was working as a farm laborer in Stutsman County, North Dakota. He later married Blossom

Keoke. He entered the spirit world on May 26, 1980, in the home of his daughter in Peever. He was survived by his sons, Kenneth, Mandus and Byron, and daughters, Mrs. Roberts Trevino, Mrs. Adrienne Owen, Mrs. Naomi Lufkins, Mrs. Florestine German and Mrs. Chyrel DeCoteau. He is buried in the Veterans Section of the Sisseton Cemetery.[18]

Renville, Thomas H. Thomas was born on the Sisseton-Wahpeton Reservation on Sept. 8, 1895, to Eli and Belle Renville. In the 1907 Census Roll, he is listed with his mother and sisters, Marie, Etta, Stella and Jennie. When he registered for the draft on June 4, 1917, he was working as a teamster for the U.S Government at the Sisseton Indian School. He joined the Army on Aug. 28, 1918. He was discharged as a Private on Dec. 10, 1918. In the 1920 U.S. Census, he was living with the Herman Renville family. In the 1934 Census Roll, he was listed as single. Thomas worked as a carpenter and lived in Peever. He entered the spirit world in the VA Hospital in Fargo on Dec. 13, 1980 and is buried in the Sisseton Cemetery.

Alfred Richard
Eric LaPointe

Richard, Alfred – listed on WWI veterans memorial at Oglala Lakota College, Kyle, SD. Alfred was born on the Pine Ridge Reservation on June 10, 1890. His parents were Peter and Louise (Red Cloud). When Alfred registered for the draft on June 5, 1917, he was working for Richard Littlelight at Hardin, MT. Alfred served in Company L (3rd Battalion), 361st Infantry, 91st Division (ASN 2258419). The regiment underwent basic training at Camp Lewis, WA. On June 22, 1918, the regiment, now part of the 91st, or Wild West Division, traveled by train to the East Coast. On July 6, 1918, the 3rd Battalion sailed for Europe aboard the S.S. *Scotian*. Upon arrival in France, the unit received further training. The first battle that the 361st Regiment took part in was St. Mihiel in early September. When the Meuse-Argonne Offensive began on Sept. 26, 1918, the 361st was stationed near Avocourt. From there they fought northward. On Oct. 10, 1918, the 3rd Battalion of the 361st Regiment received the assignment to capture Hill 255 near Gesnes. Corp. Richard was killed in that attack. The regimental history mentions that "the 3rd Battalion was recalled from its flanking movement just as its front line was again about to come under the guns of the enemy... Intermittent machine gun and shell fire was kept up by the enemy, but in spite of frequent scattered casualties, the losses on that day were small in this regiment in comparison with its previous engagements."

After the war ended, Corporal Richard's commanding officer wrote "excellent soldier, efficient, energetic, and trustworthy. Demonstrated fitness as a scout. Unexcelled as runner, night worker, observer and verbal reporter." Corporal Richard's body was brought back to the U.S. by the *Cantigny*, which sailed from Antwerp, Belgium, on Sept. 1, 1921. He is buried in Red Cloud Cemetery, Pine Ridge Reservation.[19]

Richards, Louis. He is listed on WWI veteran's memorial at Oglala Lakota College, Kyle, SD. Louis was born in LaCreek on the Pine Ridge Reservation on Feb. 19, 1897. In the 1897 Census Roll, he is listed with his parents Charles and Louise Richard, as well as a cousin, Theresha Flesher. When Louis registered for the draft on June 5, 1918, he was working for A.A. Brown in Cody, NE. He enlisted in the Navy on July 12, 1918. He served as a Fireman 3rd Class (NSN 183-30-65) and was discharged on Sept. 10, 1919. Louis' sister, Mary, married Gilbert Lafferty, a fellow veteran. On Oct.

16, 1920, Louis married Anna Grinden. In 1935, the family was interviewed by a worker with the SDERA program. They were living in a three-room home located 15 miles SE of Martin, SD. They owned some farm machinery, five work horses, two saddle horses, a wagon and 10 milk cows. They sold four gallons of cream per week. A few years earlier, some of their cows had starved due to a lack of feed. In the 1940 U.S. Census, Louis and Anna were listed with their children, Denzel, LaVerne, Rosella and Luella. Denzel served as a Corporal in the Army Air Corps during WWII. Louis entered the spirit world in Tuthill, SD, on Sept. 16, 1947, and is buried in Our Lady of the Sacred Heart Cemetery, Martin, SD.[20]

Rivers, Ernest. Ernest was born on the Cheyenne River Reservation on Dec. 8, 1891. His parents were Joseph A. Rivers and Felicia Traversie. In the 1900 U.S. Census, he was a student at the Indian School in Fort Yates. When Ernest registered for the draft, he was ranching near Promise. He joined the Army on June 23, 1918, and was assigned to Co. G, 352nd Infantry, 88th Division (ASN 3309091). The Second Battalion of the 352nd Infantry sailed from Brooklyn for Europe aboard the U.S.S. *Ulysses* on Aug. 15, 1918. They did not take part in the active fighting at the Front. After the war, they were billeted at Ribeaucourt. Pvt. Rivers returned to the U.S. on May 18, 1919, aboard the *Rijndam*. Pvt. Rivers was traveling with a group of sick and wounded soldiers who left from St. Nazaire. He was discharged at Camp Dodge, IA, on July 13, 1919. In the 1930 U.S. Census, Ernest was living with his uncle, Barney Traversie. In 1940, he was working for the WPA program. He never married. Ernest entered the spirit world in his home in Mobridge on Nov. 6, 1957, and is buried in St. Mary's Catholic Cemetery, LaPlant.[21]

Roberts, Robert. Robert was Shoshoni and was born about 1883 in Nevada. In the 1910 U.S. Census, he was living with Louis Benoist. Around 1916, he married Phoebe Nichols (1898-1980) on the Cheyenne River Reservation. Robert joined the Army on Aug. 15, 1918 and served as a Sergeant with Field Remount Squadron #332, Quartermaster Corps (ASN 3777666). Pvt. Roberts sailed for France from Newport News aboard the *Mercury* on Oct. 14, 1918. After the Armistice, Sgt. Roberts left Marseilles aboard the *Dante Alligheri* on May 29, 1919, traveling with Saint Aignan Casual Co. No. 4932. He arrived on June 17, 1919 and was discharged on June 25. He received a disability payment. In the 1920 U.S. Census, he was operating a blacksmith shop at the Cheyenne River Agency. He became ill with pneumonia and entered the spirit world on Jan. 11, 1928, at St. Mary's Hospital in Pierre. His occupation was listed as garage owner. His wife and four children, Stanley, Kenneth, Roberta and Eugenia survived him. He is buried in St. Paul's Episcopal Cemetery, LaPlant, SD. His son, Stanley, served in the military during WWII. His widow, Phoebe, married John Distribute of Standing Rock.[22]

Robertson, Edward. Edward was born about Jan. 1, 1892, west of Veblen, SD, on the Sisseton-Wahpeton Reservation. His parents were Angus Robertson and Nancy Shortfoot. Edward joined the Army and was sent to Camp Lewis, WA, on May 28, 1918, and then to Camp Kearny, CA, where he was assigned to Co. D, 160th Infantry, 40th Division (ASN 2788354). From there he went to Camp Mills, NY. He sailed with the 160th Infantry from New York aboard the *Laomedon* on Aug. 11, 1918. After arriving in France, he was assigned to Co. A, 128th Infantry, 32nd Division. The 128th Infantry took part in the following campaigns: Oise-Aisne, Meuse-Argonne. On November 10, 1918, the 128th Infantry had crossed the Meuse River. The History of the 32nd Division describes the action on that day, as follows.

> A heavy fog hid the advance. The leading elements of the First Battalion of the 128th, which was at the head of the column, made rapid progress. The troops had been in the sector

long enough to have some knowledge of the terrain, and wasted no time in getting off. They encountered enemy troops almost at once, but fought their way through the Bois Pommepre and part way up a hill called Cote de Mont. A combat liaison group on the right, which was there for the purpose of maintaining contact with the French Colonials, advanced even further.

At about this time the fog lifted and the 128th discovered that instead of pursuing a fleeing foe they had fought their way right into the middle of a strong German position which the enemy apparently had no intention of abandoning. The fog had prevented the Germans from effectively defending their works, and the only clashes of the early morning had occurred when our advancing doughboys happened on groups of the enemy.

As the mist cleared the advance guard found itself in a position similar to that of the famous *Gallant Six Hundred* in the charge of Balaklava....

Our men were almost completely surrounded, unable to go ahead against an opposition that was showing increasing strength, subjected to galling flanking fire by machine guns where they were, and confronted with the alternative of filtering through a barrage that they feared was thickened by both their own and the enemy artillery. But in a pinch they proved themselves veterans, and in good order made their way back to a position on a line with the units on the right and left.

Pfc. Robertson was killed in action on that day. He is buried in the Meuse-Argonne American Cemetery, Romagne, France, Plot B, Row 21, Grave 7. American Legion Post No. 76 in Veblen, SD is named in his honor. An Honor Song was written for him.

> Mahpiyahotanka nisnana winica yedo
>
> Tehan inunke do
>
> Loud Voiced Cloud you are the only man
>
> You lie far away[23]

Robertson, Walter C. Walter was the younger brother of Edward. He was born on the Sisseton-Wahpeton Reservation on July 16, 1893, to Angus Robertson and Nancy Marpiyahotanka. In the 1895 Census Roll, Walter is listed with his parents, Angus and Nancy, and his brother, Edward. In 1910, Walter was a student at the Carlisle boarding school. When Walter registered for the draft on June 5, 1917, he was farming near Veblen. He joined the Army on July 22, 1918. He was discharged as a Private on Feb. 13, 1919. In the 1920 U.S. Census, he was living near Veblen with his wife, Jane Adams, and children, Thomas, Melvin and Florence. In the 1940 U.S. Census, Walter was working as a carpenter on a government housing project in McKinley Township, Marshall County. He later married Mitsu Alice Bird. They moved to Oregon. Walter entered the spirit world in Oregon on Sept. 23, 1968, and is buried in Willamette National Cemetery, Section S, site 3596.

Robertson, William Marshall. William was born in Porcupine, SD, on Aug. 23, 1896. His parents were William M. Robertson and Augusta Brown, the daughter of Joseph Renshaw Brown. In the 1897 Sisseton-Wahpeton Census Roll, William is listed with his parents and his brother, Hastings, and his sisters, Martha, Minnie and Emily. When William registered for the draft on June 5, 1918, he was living in Martin. He worked in the newspaper business, including the *Martin Messenger* and the *Bennett County News.* He joined the Army on Sept. 17, 1918, and served in the Intelligence Corps, Communication. He was discharged on Dec. 10, 1918. William's sister, Minnie, married Edward Lessert, a fellow veteran. At one time, William ran a trading post in Allen. He married Agnes Payer, with whom he had three children, Emily, Esther and William. Their daughter, Emily, served in the Army during the Vietnam War. William entered the spirit world in the VA Hospital in Hot Springs on Oct. 12, 1984 and is buried in the Martin Community Cemetery.[24]

Rogers, Gilbert Charles. Gilbert was born on the Rosebud Reservation on Feb. 21, 1895, to George and Louise Clairmont Rogers. George had served in the Army at Fort Niobrara in the early 1890s. In the 1910 U.S. Census, Gilbert was a student at Carlisle. When Gilbert registered for the draft on June 5, 1917, he was farming near Mission. He joined the Army on June 23, 1917, and served as a Sergeant with Co. L, 42nd Infantry, 12th Division (ASN 2524660). The 12th Division trained at Camp Devens, Massachusetts. Sgt. Rogers was discharged on Jan. 25, 1919. After the war, Gilbert's sister, Winnie, married Grover Burnette, a fellow veteran. In the 1920 U.S. Census, Gilbert was living with his wife, Laura, and her father, John Sullivan, in Baltimore. In 1930, Gilbert was working in Baltimore as a cementer for a gas company. He and Laura had three children, Mary, Laura and Clara. When Gilbert registered for the Selective Service in 1942, he was working for Bethlehem Steel at the Baltimore Dry Dock. He entered the spirit world on April 3, 1956, and is buried in Baltimore National Cemetery.

Romero, Edward Manuel. Edward was born on the Pine Ridge Reservation around Jan. 20, 1893. In the 1904 Census Roll, he is listed with his parents, Philip and Katie, as well as two sisters, Maggie and Stella, and two brothers, James and Edward. Corporal Romero served in the Supply Office of the Quartermaster Corps ASN 1508098). In the 1924 Census Roll, he was listed with his wife, Jessie. Edward entered the spirit world on July 10, 1925 and is buried in Holy Rosary Cemetery in Pine Ridge.

Rooks, Edward F. Edward is listed on WWI veteran's memorial at Oglala Lakota College, Kyle, SD. Edward was born about June 10, 1899, on the Pine Ridge Reservation. In the 1904 Census Roll, he was listed with his parents, Joseph and Mollie Rooks. He likely attended the Haskell Boarding School. On June 17, 1917, he enlisted in the Kansas National Guard and served in Battery B, First Regiment, Kansas Field Artillery. When this unit arrived at Camp Doniphan, it was renumbered as the 130th Field Artillery, 35th Division (ASN 1466347). Pvt. Rooks sailed for France from New York aboard the *Ceramic* on May 19, 1918. They served in Alsace-Lorraine and the Meuse-Argonne Offensive. The 35th Division suffered 7,283 casualties. After the Armistice, the headquarters for the 35th Division was at Commercy, France. Pfc. Rooks was later assigned to the 252nd MP Company. He sailed from St. Nazaire aboard the U.S.S. *Santa Paula* on June 16, 1919 and arrived in Hoboken on June 28. Pfc. Rooks served with a Demobilization Group at Camp Funston before his discharge. In 1921, he married Alice Red Bear. He later married Lucy Standing Soldier. In the 1940 U.S. Census, the Rooks family was living in Washabaugh County. Edward later moved to Denver where he worked as a garageman. He entered the spirit world in the VA Hospital in Hot Springs on June 8, 1966, and is buried in Ft. Logan National Cemetery, Section R, site 262.

Ross, Amos. Amos was born on the Pine Ridge Reservation on Oct. 22, 1895. In the 1900 U.S. Census, he was listed with his parents, Amos and Lucy, as well as two brothers, Joseph and Hobart, and a sister, Angelic. When Amos registered for the draft on May 31, 1917, he was working as a student chauffeur at the Haskell Institute in Lawrence, KS. He enlisted in the Army on May 1, 1918, and was discharged on Feb. 12, 1919. He may have served with the 8th Ammo Train. On June 13,

1922, he married Winnie Sackett (1902-1953). In the 1930 U.S. Census, Amos was working as a truck driver for the Indian Service. He and Winnie had two children, Jean and Glenn. In the 1940 U.S. Census, he was working as a foreman on a road construction project. His son, Glenn, served in the Navy during WWII. Amos moved his family to Pomona, CA. In 1945, he was working as a defense worker for Douglas. In 1948, he was a dealer for General Petroleum Corporation. Amos entered the spirit world in Los Angeles on March 10, 1980.

Roubideaux, Louis. Louis was born on the Rosebud Reservation on March 3, 1899. His parents were Louis Roubideaux and Adelia Blunt Arrow. Louis enlisted on June 26, 1920, to serve in the Coast Artillery Corps (ASN 6415125). He was stationed with the 11th Company, and was discharged as a Private on Sept. 3, 1921. He suffered from Tuberculosis and entered the spirit world at the Sioux Sanatorium in Rapid City on Oct. 14, 1946. He is buried in St. James' Cemetery at Ring Thunder.[25]

Rouillard, Cyril. Cyril was born on the Santee Reservation on Oct. 22, 1892, to Louis and Emma (Thornton) Rouillard. In the 1898 Census Roll, he was living with his grandparents, Antoine and Susan Rouillard. When Cyril registered for the draft on June 5, 1917, he was farming near Niobrara, NE. He joined the Army on May 26, 1918, and was assigned to Battery C, 338th Field Artillery, 88th Division (ASN 3228591). In August of 1918, the 338th F.A. sailed for Europe on the Portuguese ship *Traz os Montes.* Upon arrival in France, they were billeted at Camp de Souge near Bordeaux. They did not take part in the fighting. Not long after the war ended, the Field Artillery units began to turn in their equipment. The 338th sailed from France on Dec. 23, 1918. Pvt. Rouillard was discharged at Camp Dodge, IA, on Jan. 17, 1919. After the war, Cyril married his wife, Mathilda Estes, who was from Lower Brule. In the 1930 U.S. Census, Cyril and Mathilda were living in Day County, where he served as a minister. They had two daughters, Margaret and Dorothy. In 1935, the family was interviewed by a worker with the SDERA program. They were living in Little Eagle in a house belonging to Paul Long Bull, while the parsonage was being built. The Episcopal Church provided him with a car. The state worker noted that Cyril had a German officer's helmet hanging on the wall. Cyril was an American Legion member and Mathilda was a member of the Auxiliary. In the 1940 U.S. Census, the family was living at Okreek. They had three more children, Doris, Theodore and Wilma. A fellow clergyman described him as a distinguished-looking man who wore a beautiful beaded stole made of white chamois skin over his regular clerical garb. He also wore a cross around his neck. The family later moved to Charles Mix County. Cyril entered the spirit world at his home in Wagner on Feb. 15, 1954, and is buried in Howe Creek Cemetery, Knox County, NE.[26]

Rouillard, Eugene. Eugene was born on the Santee Reservation on Oct. 9, 1895, to Joseph and Lucy Rouillard. Eugene likely joined the Army in the spring of 1918, and was assigned to Co. H, 355th Infantry, 89th Division (ASN 2847152). Bugler Rouillard left the U.S. on June 4, 1918. On Oct. 19, 1918, the 89th Division was ordered to relieve the 32nd Division in the front line near the Bois de Batheville. On Oct. 20, the 2nd Battalion of the 355th Infantry was one of the assault units. Pvt. Rouillard was wounded on that day. After the Armistice, Pvt. Rouillard received an evaluation from his commanding officer, Capt. Oscar Abel, who wrote that Rouillard was "considered a good man and associated readily with white men. He did very good work as a runner both day and night." Pvt. Rouillard sailed from Brest, France aboard the Leviathan, returning to the U.S. on May 22, 1919.

On Dec. 20, 1923, Eugene married Mary Louise Rencontre (1899-1988) in Kennebec, SD. Mary Louise, who was from Lower Brule, was a sister to Albert Rencontre, who also served in the war.

In the Lower Brule Census Rolls, Eugene was included with the family but listed as non-enrolled. In the 1940 U.S. Census, the family was living in Knox County, NE. They had three children, Orville, Barbara, and Harold. Eugene entered the spirit world on Jan. 18, 1978, and is buried the Congregational Cemetery in Santee.[27]

Rouillard, Jesse. Jesse was born March 4, 1900, to Samuel Rouillard and Nettie Sully. He is listed with his parents in the 1905 Flandreau Census Roll. When he registered for the draft on Sept. 7, 1918, he was working as a laborer in Oglala, SD. He likely enlisted shortly after this. His name is included with a list of WWI veterans engraved on a memorial in the 1st Presbyterian Cemetery in Flandreau, SD. In 1922, he started working as a truck driver for the Indian Service at Rapid City. A few years later, he took a position at the boarding school in Fort Wingate, NM, but did not like it there. He married Ruth Kadel. In the 1930 U.S. Census, he was working as a truck driver at the Indian School in Rapid City. In the 1940 U.S. Census, he was working as a clerk at the Rosebud Indian School. He and Ruth had three children, John, Benjamin and Mary. Their son, John, served in the Army during WWII, and Benjamin served during the Korean War. The family later moved to Falls Church, VA. Jesse worked as a letter carrier. He entered the spirit world in Fairfax Hospital on March 15, 1976, and is buried with Ruth in Lewinsville Presbyterian Cemetery, McLean, VA.

Rouillard, Peter A. Peter is listed on the WWI veteran's memorial at Oglala Lakota College, Kyle, SD. He was born in Santee, NE, on Oct. 7, 1893. In the 1900 Santee Census Roll, Peter was listed with his parents, Oliver and Nancy, as well as his siblings, Mabel, George, Samuel and Josephine. When Peter registered for the draft on June 5, 1917, he was farming near Martin, SD. He enlisted at Martin on May 28, 1918, and was assigned to Battery A, 347th Field Artillery (FA), 91st Division (ASN 3129674). He served with Frank Apple, Elbridge Gerry, and Moses Marshall. Pvt. Rouillard sailed from New York to France aboard the *Adriatic* on July 14, 1918. However, the three field artillery regiments in the 91st Division were sent to the artillery training area at Camp de Souge near Bordeaux, and did not serve on the front line with the rest of the Division. They were trained with ten-ton tractors and 4.7-inch guns. On Christmas Day, 1918, the 347th FA was billeted in private homes in several small German towns along the Moselle River. On March 13, 1919, the 34th FA was assigned to act as guard of honor for President Woodrow Wilson, who was in France for the Paris Peace Conference. The unit returned to the U.S. from Brest aboard the *Aquitania* on March 23, 1919. Pvt. Rouillard was discharged at Camp Dodge, IA, on April 17, 1919. He had also served a short time with Casual Detachment #281. Around 1928, Peter married Sophia Dismounts Thrice. In the 1940 U.S. Census, Peter and Sophia were living in Bennett County with their children, Seymour, Marie, Benjamin, James and Rhoda. Peter was employed as a laborer in a C.C.C. camp. Peter entered the spirit world on Feb. 22, 1966, and is buried in Inestimable Gift Cemetery.

Rouse, Jesse. Jesse was born on March 4, 1896, in Greenwood, SD, on the Yankton Reservation. His parents were George Rouse and Lucy Traversie. When Jesse registered for the draft on June 5, 1917, he was living in Greenwood and had worked as a farm laborer. Jesse joined the Army on Dec. 8, 1917, and was assigned to the Medical Department (ASN 752109). He sailed from New York aboard the *Aquitania* on June 8, 1918, traveling with the Camp Greenleaf Replacement Draft. Pfc. Rouse served in Camp Hospital #8, which was in Montigny-le-Roi, Department Haute Marne. Detachment #8 sailed from Brest, France, aboard the *Agamemnon* on June 10, 1919. Pfc. Rouse was discharged on June 27, 1919. He had also served in Casual Detachment #886. Jesse's sister, Alice, married Martin DuCharme of Cheyenne River, who had served in the Navy. After returning home, Jesse married Minnie Bear (1901-1968). They lived in a number of locations in Charles Mix County. In the 1930s, this area was called the Greenwood Reservation. In 1935, the family was interviewed by a worker with the SDERA program. They were living in two rooms of a four-room house. Their water was hauled one mile from a tubular well. The family owned two horses. Jesse had planted 50 acres of corn, and was looking for jobs as a hired man. In the 1940 U.S. Census, the family included four children, Duwayne, Richard, Ernest and Barbara. Duwayne served in the Army from 1948-1955, while his brother, Richard served in Korea. Jesse came down with Tuberculosis, and entered the spirit world in Lake Andes on Feb. 27, 1946. He is buried in Greenwood Cemetery.[28]

Rousseau, Louis A. Louis was born at Ft Bennett on the Cheyenne River Reservation on July 14, 1894. His parents were Romaldo Rousseau and Esther Narcelle. When Louis registered for the draft on June 5, 1917, he was ranching near Eagle Butte. On Sept. 4, 1917, he married Bessie Dupris. Shortly after this, he enlisted in the 4th SD Infantry. When that unit arrived at Camp Greene, NC, the soldiers were told they were now the 147th Field Artillery (F.A.). Pvt. Rousseau was assigned to Battery C (ASN 139537). They sailed to Europe aboard the ship *Olympic* on Jan. 11, 1918. The 147th F. A. was attached to the 32nd Division for most of the war. They took part in the Campaigns at Toul-Boucq, Center Sector, Aisne-Marne, Fismes Sector, Oise-Aisne, Avocourt, and Meuse-Argonne. In early October of 1918, the 147th F.A., as part of the 57th Field Artillery Brigade, was supporting the 3rd Infantry Division northwest of Verdun. Pvt. Rousseau was seriously wounded on Oct. 5, 1918, near Nantillois. After the Armistice, his commanding officer, 1st Lt. A. M. Knudtson, wrote that Pvt. Rousseau was "daring, intelligent and athletic. Excellent as horseman and driver." Pvt. Rousseau sailed for home with his regiment from Brest, France, aboard the U.S.S. *Kansas* on May 1, 1919. Pvt. Rousseau served 18 months overseas, and was discharged on May 24, 1919. After the war, he wrote to Joseph Dixon describing his experience. "We saw steady service after we were sent to the front. Our Div. 32nd was on and in every front and battles except one. The St. Mihiel sector. We were about the first Art. On the last front (Argonne) went in on the nite of Sept. 23, 1918, to back up the 79th." He was awarded a Purple Heart medal.

After arriving home, he joined the American Legion. In 1923, he married Agnes Oakes, who joined the Legion Auxiliary. In 1935, the family was interviewed by a worker with the SDERA program. Louis and Agnes, with their children, Myrna, Hazel, Monte, William and Robert, were living in a four-room house near the Ford Garage in Eagle Butte. They bought water at one cent per gallon. They said that they did attend some white dances, but felt a racial prejudice from the whites. Louis had worked at a number of jobs, including carpentry work on the Cherry Creek School, and a government well drilling project. Louis likely was suffering from his wartime experience. In the 1940 U.S. Census, he had a job as a time keeper on a road construction project. Louis entered the spirit world in the Indian Hospital in Eagle Butte on Jan. 23, 1964. He is buried in All Saints Cemetery in Eagle Butte.[29]

Rowland, Benton. Benton was born around 1897 on the Northern Cheyenne Reservation near Lame Deer, MT. His parents were Zach and Julia Rowland. He attended a local school for several years. In February 1907, he went to the Carlisle Boarding School, where he stayed until June 1912. A few years later he moved to South Dakota. On March 28, 1917, he enlisted in the Army and was sent to Fort Meade, SD. He was assigned initially to Co. I, 4th SD Infantry. When the 4th SD Infantry reached Camp Greene, NC, in the fall of 1917, the soldiers were transferred to units in the 41st Division. He sailed to Europe on the *Olympic*, on January 11, 1918, with Co. B, 148th Machine Gun Battalion (ASN 98577). Once in France, Pvt. Rowland was assigned to Co. M, 167th Infantry, 42nd Division on Feb. 8, 1918. He fought at Chateau Thierry and the Meuse-Argonne Offensive. He was wounded twice and was consigned to Base Hospitals 1 and 34. One of the times he was wounded was on July 28, 1918. According to a divisional history, the 167th Regiment was in position near the Ourcq River. "On our first morning on the Ourcq our batteries located machine gun nests in the wheat fields. After we got a pretty good line on them the artillery started on the guns we had located. Before nightfall of the 29th machine gun nests in the wheat fields in my immediate front had been cleared. All during our fight my regiment suffered most from artillery fire, especially whiz bangs."

After the Armistice, Pvt. Rowland's commanding officer wrote the following statement about his service.

> Came over with the 41st Div., Co. B, 148th MG Bn. Been on observation posts. Lt. Driver of Co. M, 167th selected Rowland for this work. Made reports every evening, 7 days at a time for 110 days, out every twelve days for two weeks in reserve trenches. About 250 yards from German front lines. Could see Germans working in trenches and see their trucks come up. Was gas guard at night. Lt. Driver would also detail Rowland to find the way and lead troops from reserve up to front line positions by platoons. The woods were thick and dark and Rowland knew the way, and had nerve enough to lead in the dark into proper positions. Ben Rowland say [sic] that four German girls were captured by his platoon and found chained to machine guns. Were out of ammunition going back, one girl seemed to be about 11 years. Boys turned them loose. 2nd Platoon, M Co., 167th, Sgt. Ackenberger was in charge of this platoon when found. When we got back we only had eight men in the platoon. We lost our men going over a hill in the open and group of German machine guns opened up on us from a position in the valley at the base of the hill. We had nothing to eat for three days and no smoking.

Pvt. Rowland returned to the U.S. from Brest, France, aboard the U.S.S. *New Jersey* on Feb. 26, 1919. He was traveling with St. Aignan Casual Co. No. 949. He was discharged at Camp Dodge, IA, on March 24, 1919. He was awarded a Purple Heart medal. After returning to South Dakota, he married Anna Breaks In. The family lived in South Dakota until the late 1930s, when they moved to Montana, In the 1940 U.S. Census, Ben was working on a range development (CCC) project near Kirby, MT. Their children included Marie, Eugene, Rose, Clarence, Benton and Veronica. Benton entered the spirit world on Nov. 8, 1964, following a car accident north of Pine Ridge. He is buried in Red Cloud Cemetery.[30]

Running, Frank Isadore. Frank was born on the Rosebud Reservation on the Rosebud Reservation around 1898. His parents were Runs With and Fourth Ghost. Frank enlisted in the SD National Guard on March 28, 1917. When the 4th SD Infantry arrived at Camp Greene, NC, it was converted to other units composing the 41st Division. Pvt. Running was transferred to Battery B, 148th Field Artillery (F.A.), 41st Division (ASN 246230). The 148th F.A. sailed for Europe on January 11, 1918 aboard the ship *Olympic*. Pvt. likely was sick at that time, as he did not sail until Feb. 27, 1918, traveling with Overseas Casual Co. No. 55 on the *Agamemnon*. The 148th F.A., using 155 mm. guns, served in the Campaigns at Chateau-Thierry, Champagne-Marne, Aisne-Marne, Vesle Sector, St. Mihiel, and Meuse-Argonne. Pfc. Running sailed from St. Nazaire aboard the U.S.S. *Peerless* on June 3, 1919, arriving in Brooklyn on June 15. Pfc. Running was discharged on June 23, 1919. After returning home, he married Alice Janis. In the 1930 U.S. Census, Frank and Alice were living in Todd County with their children, Norbert and Seymour, a sister Nellie, as well as Frank's mother, Fourth Ghost. Frank was in an accident and suffered a broken skull. He entered the spirit world, possibly in Colorado, on March 23, 1937, and is buried in Spring Creek Cemetery.

Joseph Running Bear (right)
Marquette University Archives

Running Bear, Joseph. Joseph was born on the Rosebud Reservation on March 6, 1897, to Running Bear and Comes in Front. When Joseph registered for the draft on June 5, 1918, he was working for the St. Francis Mission. He enlisted on July 29, 1918, and served as a bugler with the 211th Engineer Regiment (ASN 3009400), designated as a "Sapper Regiment." The 211th was part of the 11th Division stationed at Camp Meade, Maryland. Corporal Running Bear did not serve overseas. He was discharged on Feb. 6, 1919. After returning home, he married Francis Natalie Flood (1902-1992). In the 1930 U.S. Census, he was working as a carpenter for the Indian Service. He and Francis had three children, Clara, Margaret and Joseph Jr. In the 1937 Rosebud Census Roll, two younger children, Inez and Lloyd are listed. Joseph Jr. served with the 11th Airborne in WWII, and Lloyd served in the Marine Corps. Joseph entered the spirit world in Denver on April 7, 1966, and is buried in St. Charles' Cemetery, St. Francis, SD.

James Running Hawk
Mathers Museum

Running Hawk, James. (see James Hawk.) James was born about 1896 on the Pine Ridge Reservation, to Harry Running Hawk and Ida Stinking Bear. In the 1905 Pine Ridge Census Roll, he is listed with his grandparents, Psica [Jumper] and Mary Jumper, as well as another grandson of Jumper, Harry Jumping Bull. As a youth, James attended school at the Holy Rosary Mission. In 1912, he was enrolled at the Carlisle Boarding School. He did not like that, and ran away in 1914. When the war started, James joined the Army and was assigned to Headquarters Company, 13th Infantry, 8th Division. The 8th Division was organized at Camp Fremont, CA, and began to head towards the east coast in October of 1918. The 13th Infantry was at sea when the Armistice was signed. Pvt. Running Hawk returned with his unit to Camp Merritt, NJ. On April 2, 1919, he was photographed with two fellow soldiers by Joseph Dixon at Camp Merritt. In an interview with Dixon, he said he "wanted to see the old thing through. My grandfather was a chief and was in the Custer battle and at the battle of Wounded Knee, but I wanted to be in any battle that would wound the Germans." After his discharge, he married Cecelia Black Elk on May 26, 1919. While working as a telegraph operator, he injured his back. He entered the spirit world in Oglala on Nov. 8, 1921. On April 14, 1922, his widow, Cecelia (1902-1986), had a daughter, Ida. Cecelia then married Harry Jumping Bull. James is buried in St. Peters Episcopal Cemetery, Oglala, SD.[31]

Running Rattle, Henry. Henry was born at the Cheyenne River Agency around December of 1888. In the 1896 Census Roll. He was listed with his parents, Robert Running Rattle and Clara Walks, as well as three sisters, Sarah, Nellie Fool Bear and Maggie Fool Bear. When Henry registered for the draft on June 5, 1917, he was working as a day laborer in White Horse. He joined the Army in 1917, but died of the Flu at Camp Funston in 1917. His name is engraved on a monument that honors veterans in Eagle Butte. His parents, who lived in the On the Trees District, received regular insurance payments from the government.

George Runs After
JoLavae Gunville

Runs After, George. George was born at Cherry Creek on the Cheyenne River Reservation on March 11, 1899. In the 1909 Census Roll, he is listed with his parents, Napoleon Runs After, Elsie Red Mane, his brother, Olney, and sisters, Susie, Mary and Rebecca. George joined the Army and served with the 142nd Infantry, 36th Division. The 36th Division trained at Camp Bowie, TX, and sailed for Europe on July 18, 1918. On Sept. 18, 1918, George registered for the draft. At that time, he was working as a laborer in Cherry Creek. He likely had received a medical discharge from the military before the 36th Division left the training camp. Many soldiers from the Choctaw Nation were assigned to the 142nd Infantry. These soldiers used their language to send messages on the battle front. Many of them have been honored as code talkers.

George married Eugenie West, with whom he had three sons, Clarence, Delmar and Jerome. George suffered from Tuberculosis and entered the spirit world at Eagle Butte on Aug. 8, 1927. He is buried in the Episcopal cemetery in Cherry Creek. His sons, Clarence and Delmar, served in the Navy during WWII. Around the era of George's passing, many people thought the American Indians would be assimilated into American culture. Many years later, George's brother, Olney, noted that "we can talk and work like white people, but we're still Indians."[32]

Runs Close to Village, Benjamin. Ben was born on the Rosebud Reservation on April 4, 1895, to Amos and Hannah Runs Close to Village. When he registered for the draft on June 5, 1917, he was farming in Mellette County. Ben joined the Army on July 22, 1918, and was assigned to Co. F, 342nd Remount Squadron, Quartermaster Corps (ASN 3955926). He sailed from New York aboard the *Orca* on Oct. 27, 1918. After the war, Pvt. Runs Close to Village sailed from St. Nazaire, France, aboard the *Calamares* on June 27, 1919, and arrived in Hoboken on July 6, 1919. He was discharged on July 13, 1919. In the 1924 Census Roll, he was listed with Anna Leah Thompson. In 1926, he married Lizzie White Shield. Ben entered the spirit world on July 31, 1927, and is buried in St. John's Episcopal Cemetery, White River.

Russell, Joseph A. Joseph was born on the Pine Ridge Reservation on May 8, 1900, to Andrew and Sophia Russell. When Joseph registered for the draft on Sept. 11, 1918, he was working as a laborer in Wanblee. Sometime later, he joined the Army and was assigned to Co. A, 5th Infantry (ASN 6418397). In 1919, the 5th Infantry sailed to Europe for occupational duty in Germany. In the 1920 U.S. Census, Corporal Russell was serving with the Army in Bendorf, Germany. He and Pvt. John Face were together in the 13th Co., Provisional Guard Battalion, Army Service Corps. After his discharge on April 24, 1924, he returned home. On May 18, 1930, he married Marald Lulu Garner in Martin. Joseph entered the spirit world on Feb. 19, 1932, and is buried in Wanblee Cemetery.[33]

Russell, Oliver W. Oliver was born in Ekalaka, MT, on Oct. 1, 1898, to David Russell and Mary Eagle Man, of Pine Ridge. Around 1902, he moved to South Dakota. In the 1909 Cheyenne River Census Roll, Oliver is listed with his brothers and sisters. Oliver attended the boarding school at

Pierre. Oliver enlisted in the 4th Infantry, SD National Guard on July 16, 1917. When this unit arrived at Camp Greene, NC, it was converted over to a Field Artillery regiment. Corporal Russell served with Battery C, 147th F.A. (ASN 139395). Louis Rousseau also served with him. For much of the war, the 147th F.A. was attached to the 32nd (Red Arrow) Division. After the Armistice, Corporal Russell received an evaluation from his commanding officer, 1st Lt. A.M. Knudtson, stating he was "a good all-around man, excellent mechanic. Took great deal interest in operating machine gun against enemy planes at gun position. Can be used as a cannoneer or driver, mechanic, bugler, visual signaler or scout." Later, a reviewing officer added, "and yet they kept him a corporal." Cpl. Russell was also listed as the Chief Mechanic for the Battery. He sailed for home with his unit from Brest aboard the U.S.S. *Kansas* on May 1, 1919, and was discharged on May 23, 1919. In the 1920 U.S. Census, Oliver was working as the head farmer at the Pierre Boarding School. A fellow Veteran, Ben Dewitt, was living with him. On Oct. 25, 1920, he married Regina May Gilland (1901-1971) from Lower Brule. They had a son, John William. In the 1930 U.S. Census, Oliver was working as a mechanic in Pierre. In the 1940 U.S. Census, he was working as an electrician and plumber for the Indian Service at Rosebud. Sometime later the family moved to Thoreau, NM. Oliver entered the spirit world on April 22, 1972.[34]

Rustemeyer, John Lewis. John was born in Pilger, NE, on March 11, 1897. He served in the Army from Aug. 6, 1918, to March 19, 1919. After the war, he married Julia Lunderman, a sister to Benjamin Lunderman, a fellow veteran. In the 1930 Rosebud Census Roll, his children listed were Noah and Ramona. They were living in St. Charles, SD. John entered the spirit world on Jan. 3, 1976, in the V.A. Hospital in Sioux Falls. He was survived by Ramona and John. He is buried in the Black Hills National Cemetery.

S

Salvis, George H. George was born on April 6, 1893, on the Pine Ridge Reservation to Frank and Lizzie Salvis. When he registered for the draft on June 10, 1917, he was ranching near Martin. He joined the Army on May 25, 1918. Pvt. Salvis sailed from New York aboard the *Ortega* on Aug. 31, 1918 with Mixed Overseas Casual Co. #362 (ASN 3130152). In France, he was assigned to Co. A, 357th Infantry, 90th Division. The 357th Infantry served in the Sectors at Villers-en-Haye, St. Mihiel, Puvenelle, and Meuse-Argonne. Pvt. Salvis sailed from St. Nazaire aboard the *Huron* on May 26, 1919, and was discharged on June 16, 1919. George had two brothers, Levi and Charles, who also served in the Army during the war. After returning home, he married Mary Diane Shabram. George and Mary had a son, George True. In the 1920 U.S. Census, George was running a general store in Washabaugh County with his brother, William. In the late 1920s, George married Rose Anderson on the Crow Reservation in Montana. In the 1930 U.S. Census, George was working as a mechanic in a garage at the Crow Agency. George later moved to California. He entered the spirit world in Alameda County, CA, on Feb. 18, 1965. He is buried in Golden Gate National Cemetery, Section P, site 106. His son, George True, served in the Air Force during WWII.

Salway, Charles Enoch. Charles is listed on WWI veteran's memorial at Oglala Lakota College, Kyle, SD. He was born at Allen on the Pine Ridge Reservation on June 17, 1898, to Frank and Lizzie Salvis. He was a younger brother to George. Charles enlisted in the Army at Jefferson Barracks, MO, on July 2, 1918. He served with Headquarters, #2 Detachment, D.G. He was discharged as a Pfc. at Camp Dodge, IA, on June 5, 1919. He married Mamie Bordeaux in 1924, and worked as a carpenter at St. Francis. In the 1937 Census Roll, He and Mamie are listed with two children, Eileen and Lamoyne. On July 20, 1942, Charles re-enlisted in the Army. He was discharged as a Staff Sergeant. His son, Lamoyne served in the Air Force during the Korean War. The family moved to California, where Charles entered the spirit world on Nov. 28, 1966. He is buried in Golden Gate National Cemetery, Section I, site 4854-A.

Salway, Levi John. Levi is listed on WWI veteran's memorial at Oglala Lakota College, Kyle, SD. He was born on the Pine Ridge Reservation on Dec. 6, 1889, to Frank and Lizzie Salvis. George and Charles were his brothers. Levi joined the Army at Martin on July 8, 1918, and was assigned to Battery C, 29th Field Artillery, 10th Division (ASN 3316988). He served as a saddler. The 10th Division trained at Camp Funston. He was discharged on Jan. 28, 1919. In the late 1920s, he married Nancy Left Hand Bull. In 1935 he was interviewed by a worker with the SDERA program. The family was living in a one room log home located three miles north of St. Francis. They hauled water from a spring three miles away. Levi supported himself by selling wood and was working as a carpenter on the He Dog School. They owned a Chevrolet. In the 1940 U.S. Census, Levi was working as a carpenter in Todd County. When he registered for the Selective Service in 1942, he was still living in St. Francis, SD. Levi later moved to Piedmont, CA. He entered the spirit world on March 8, 1960, and is buried in Golden Gate National Cemetery, Section 2B, grave 438.[1]

Salway, Stacey. Stacy was born on the Pine Ridge Reservation around June 15, 1889, to Alexander and Millie Salvis. When Stacey registered for the draft on June 5, 1917, he was working as a stockman near Allen. After Stacey joined the Army, he sailed for France with the Mixed Overseas Casual Co. #362 from New York aboard the *Ortega* on Aug. 31, 1918. Pvt. Salway was assigned to Co. K, 164th Infantry, 41st Division (ASN 3130160). The 164th Infantry performed provost duty and other non-combat assignments behind the front line. Corporal Salway returned home from Brest, France, aboard the *President Grant* on Feb. 8, 1919. He married Emma Richard. In the 1930 U.S. Census, Stacey and Emma were farming in Bennett County with their son, Marvin. Stacey entered the spirit world in Wanblee on Oct. 22, 1932, and is buried in the Salway Cemetery in Wanblee.[2]

Saves Them, Benedict. Benedict was also known as Benedict Wind. He was born on the Crow Creek Reservation on March 5, 1890. His parents were Wind Saves Them and Mary White Day Woman. Benedict joined the Army on May 24, 1918, and was assigned to Battery E, 39th Field Artillery, 13th Division. He trained at Camp Lewis, WA. Private Saves Them was discharged on Feb. 20, 1919. After returning home, he filled out a questionnaire for Joseph Dixon. Noting that 20 men had enlisted from the Crow Creek Reservation, he described his service.

> I been in the Army 10 mo. And done my very bit in all my work and duty so that I got along fine and dandy. Our Division, the 13th we're well trained. Of course we felt bad as we didn't get to go for over sea duty. But any way I done my part, I went as far as I was told. We were just about to go. Just than the Armistice was sign. I want to say that I learn a great deal in the Army more than if I were to a College. Two or three years. I felt better, stronger, when I was in the Army, than before. I'm still feeling fine as ever up to this present day.

Benedict married Susan Half Day on Aug. 23, 1923, at Highmore. In 1935, the family was interviewed by a worker with the SDERA program. They were living nine miles north of Fort Thompson. Benedict said he had been receiving a small disability pension which ended when Roosevelt was elected president. In the 1940 U.S. Census, Benedict and Susan had four children, Clarence, Laurence,

Madalene and Elias. Benedict entered the spirit world in the hospital in Chamberlain on Nov. 15, 1972, and is buried in the Immaculate Conception Cemetery in Stephan, SD.[3]

Sazue, William. William was born on the Crow Creek Reservation around Dec. 1, 1897. In the 1903 Census Roll, he was listed with his parents, John and Lucy, as well as a brother and sister, Alex and Mable. William served as a Private First Class in the Army during WWI. He also served during WWII from Sept. 22, 1942 to Dec. 5, 1944. In the 1937 Census Roll, he is listed with his wife, Evelyn Ross. William worked as a Carpenter. In the 1945 Rapid City Directory, he was working for Dakota Lime and Rock Co. He entered the spirit world in Fort Thompson on June 24, 1980 and is buried in Christ Episcopal Cemetery in Fort Thompson.

Schmidt, Fred Benjamin. Fred was born on the Rosebud Reservation on March 6, 1897, to George Schmidt and Lizzie One Feather. When Fred registered for the draft on June 5, 1918, he was working with his father at White River. Fred enlisted on Aug. 27, 1918, and was discharged as a Private on Dec. 4, 1918. On June 9, 1919, he married Evelyn Arconge (1897-1987) in Rapid City. Evelyn's sister, Mabel, married Ray Blacksmith, who also was a veteran. In the 1930 U.S. Census, Fred was working as an advisor at the Rosebud boarding school. He and Evelyn had three children, Elinor, Vernon and Lorene. Fred continued to work at the Rosebud school. Fred entered the spirit world in the Rosebud Indian Hospital on June 12, 1969, and is buried in the Black Hills National Cemetery, Section C, site 876. His son, Vernon, served with the Navy during the Korean Conflict.[4]

Scissons, Clarence. Clarence was born at Bonesteel, SD, on July 4, 1898. As an enrolled member on the Rosebud Reservation, his parents were William Scissons and Bertha Fazel. When he registered for the draft on Sept. 12, 1918, he was farming with his father. In the 1920 U.S. Census, he was living at home with his parents. He likely enlisted shortly after that. In the 1930 U.S. Census, he was stationed with Co. H, 23rd Infantry at Fort Sam Houston, San Antonio, TX. In the 1937 Rosebud Census Roll, he is listed as living in Houston, TX. After his discharge, he returned home. In 1945, he was living in Winner. He entered the spirit world on Jan. 13, 1962, and is buried at Winner.

Scissons, Grover Cleveland. Grover was born at Bonesteel on Oct. 22, 1892. As an enrolled member of the Rosebud Reservation, his parents were Jeffrey Scissons and Mary Archambeau. He enlisted in the Army on Aug. 27, 1918, and was discharged as a Private on Jan. 27, 1919. He married Martha Fowlkes, with whom he had a son, Marvin. On Sept. 10, 1929, he married Margaret Scheafer. In the 1930 U.S. Census, he was working in a Logging Camp in the Black Hills. In the 1940 U.S. Census, he was farming in Lincoln Township of Tripp County. He and Margaret had four children at that time, Grover Jr. Mona, Warren and Sylvia. Their son, Grover Jr., served with the Marine Corps during the Korean Conflict. The family later moved to Deadwood, where he retired in 1957. He was a member of the World War I Veterans at Sturgis. Grover entered the spirit world at his home in Deadwood on Dec. 31, 1975. His widow and five children, Mona, Sylvia, Mary Jo, Sally and Grover Jr., survived him. He is buried in the Black Hills National Cemetery, Section E, site 865.[5]

Scissons, Howard H. Howard was born in Bonesteel on Nov. 30, 1894, to Jeffrey Scissions and Mary Archambeau. He was an enrolled member of the Rosebud Reservation. When Howard registered for the draft on June 5, 1917, he was working as a mechanic in Bonesteel. He joined the Army on Dec. 14, 1917, and served with the Fifth Company, 3rd Regiment, Air Service Mechanic (ASN 2402271). Pfc. Scissions sailed from Brest aboard the *Charleston* on June 19, 1919 and was discharged on July 12, 1919. On June 26, 1921, he married Ella Burnham. In the 1940 U.S. Census, he was still working as a mechanic in Bonesteel. He and Ella had three children, Willis, Florine and Eddy. Willis served in the Army during WWII. The family later moved to Oregon. Howard entered the spirit world in Central Point, OR, on Sept. 20, 1988. He is buried in Eagle Point National Cemetery, Eagle Point, OR.

Scissons, John. John was born about Sept. 5, 1893, at Bonesteel to Jeffrey Scissons and Mary Archambeau. He was an enrolled member of the Rosebud Reservation. When John registered for the draft in June of 1917, he was farming in Colorado. Sometime after this, he joined the Army. He was assigned to the Machine Gun (MG) Company, 38th Infantry, 3rd Division (ASN 2193316). He sailed from Halifax, Nova Scotia, aboard the *Corsican* on March 25, 1918. The *Corsican* docked at Glasgow, Scotland. The unit then traveled on the Caledonian Railroad to southern England. After a 12-mile hike to Southhampton, the men boarded an old cattle boat, the *Austrilind,* and sailed to Le Havre, France. The 38th Infantry (Rock of the Marne) served in the Sectors at Aisne, Chateau-Thierry, Champagne-Marne, Aisne-Marne, Vesle, St. Mihiel, and Meuse-Argonne. The 38th Infantry suffered 2,917 casualties in the war. Pvt. Scissons sailed from Brest aboard the *Agamemnon* on Aug. 10, 1919. In the 1920 U.S. Census, he was serving as a mechanic with the Army at Camp Pike, Arkansas. After his discharge he returned home, and married Emma Spotted Eagle (1901-1996) on Nov. 5, 1927. John developed Tuberculosis and entered the spirit world at Battle Mountain Sanitarium on Nov. 14, 1928. He is buried in St. Mary's Cemetery in Bonesteel. His headstone has an American Legion marker near it.[6]

Scissons, William C. William was born in Bonesteel on Feb. 14, 1896, to Jeffrey Scissons and Mary Archambeau. He was an enrolled member of the Rosebud Reservation. When he registered for the draft on June 5, 1917, he also was working as a mechanic in Bonesteel. He joined the Army in Omaha on Dec. 14, 1917 and was assigned to the 266th Aero Squadron (ASN 968408). This Service unit arrived in France around August of 1918. Corporal Scissions sailed from Pauillac, France, aboard the *Huron* on April 25, 1919, and was discharged at Camp Funston, KS, on May 22, 1919. In 1925, he married Olive Nelson (1898-1991). When he registered for the Selective Service in 1942, he was working for Indian Affairs at Rosebud. He entered the spirit world on Sept. 23, 1969, and is buried in Geddes, SD.

Scott, Daniel. Daniel was born on the Lower Brule Reservation to George Scott and Lucy Charging Thunder. When he was a child, his family moved to the Rosebud Reservation. When he registered for the draft on June 5, 1917, he was farming near Hamill. He joined the Army and was stationed at Camp Kearny, CA (ASN 3130107). While at Camp Kearny, he accidentally fell from a wagon and entered the spirit world on Jan. 17, 1919. He is buried in Red Hill Cemetery, Hamill, SD. His sister, Tena, married a fellow veteran, Lott Butte.[7]

Sears, Lee. Lee, also known as Leander, is listed on the WWI veteran's memorial at the Oglala Lakota College in Kyle, SD. He was born possibly in Oklahoma about Aug. 31, 1890, to William Sears and Susan Rouleau. In the 1893 Pine Ridge Census Roll, he is listed with his mother and brothers and sisters, Vincent, Clarence, Maud, Lulu and William Jr. When he registered for the draft on June 5, 1917, he was working as a janitor for the government at Pawhuska, OK. He enlisted in the Army on Feb. 25, 1918, and served as a Corporal with a Demobilization Detachment at Camp Travis (ASN 2251056). He was discharged on April 13, 1919. In the 1930s, he married Myrtle Green. When he registered with the Selective Service in 1942, he was living in Gordon, NE. He entered the spirit world on July 23, 1942, and is buried in Sheridan, WY.

Sharpfish, Leo. Leo was born at Wososo on the Rosebud Reservation about October of 1893. When he registered for the draft on June 5, 1917, he was living in Wososo and doing odd jobs. He joined the Army on July 22, 1918 and was assigned to Co. L, 333rd Infantry, 84th Division (ASN 3955053). He sailed with his unit from New York aboard the *Aquitania* on Sept. 2, 1918. Upon arrival in France, he was reassigned to Co. E, 118th Infantry, 30th Division. The 118th Infantry served in the following Sectors, Canal, Ypres-Lys, and the Somme Offensive. Pvt. Sharpfish was described by his commander as "a good fellow." He sailed home from St. Nazaire aboard the U.S.S. *Mercury* on March 15, 1919. He was traveling with the First Camp Dodge Detachment, 118th Infantry. He was discharged on April 10, 1919. After returning home, he married Louise Iyott. In the 1930 U.S. Census, Leo and Louise were farming in Todd County with their children, Allen, Coolidge and Gertie. Leo entered the spirit world on Sept. 9, 1934 and is buried in Parmelee. His oldest son, Allen, served in the Navy during WWII. Calvin served in the Army during the Korean Conflict.[8]

Shaving, William. William was born along the Moreau River on the Cheyenne River Reservation on Nov. 30, 1890. His parents were Charles Shaving and Isabelle The Pine. William's grandfather was a white man who came to the reservation as a scout. Because he worked as a carpenter, he was given the name Shaving and adopted by the tribe. William had attended school at Flandreau. In 1913, he married Annie Swift Eagle. When William registered for the draft on July 2, 1918, he and Annie had three children and were ranching. William likely joined the Army shortly after this. In 1935, the family was interviewed by a worker with the SDERA program. William told the interviewer that he had served in the Army for a short time but had not joined the American Legion. In 1935, they were building a log home located eight miles north of LaPlant, where they ranched. After Annie passed away, William moved to LaPlant and worked as a jailer at the Agency. He later moved to Eagle Butte and worked as a janitor for the school and the tribe. He entered the spirit world at the Mobridge Care Center on Dec. 1, 1984. His daughter, Lillian LeBeau survived him. He is buried in St. Mary's Cemetery in LaPlant.[9]

Shepherd, Peter S. Peter was born on the Sisseton-Wahpeton Reservation on Jan. 8, 1893, to Joshua and Nancy Shepherd. In the 1899 Census Roll, he is listed with his mother, Gikiyewin, and his sisters, Sarah, Emma and Mary. After his father entered the spirit world in the early 1900s, his mother married William Blue Dog. In the 1912 Census Roll, Peter is listed as Simon Pahamani [Walking Hill]. When he registered for the draft on June 1, 1917, he was working as a farm laborer near Waubay. He joined the Army on March 30, 1918, and was assigned to Co. B, 355th Infantry, 89th Division (ASN 2203336). Pvt. Shepherd sailed from New York for Europe on the ship *Adriatic* on June 4, 1918. Upon arrival in France, the unit was billeted in the towns of Grand, Brechainville, and Aillainville. The 355th Infantry took part in the Offensives at St. Mihiel and Meuse-Argonne. After the Armistice, Pfc. Shepherd received and evaluation from his commanding officer, Capt. John Moorer, which stated he as a "good scout, excellent on patrols. Excellent in keenness of senses and dexterity. Associates well with white men and is regarded as an unusually good man." The 355th Infantry was billeted near Saarburg, Germany. The unit returned to the States from Brest aboard the *Leviathan* on May 15, 1919. Pfc. Shepherd was discharged on May 31, 1919. After he returned home, he married Elizabeth Good Elk. They had a daughter, Dorothy. Peter's sister, Emma, married Rolland Little Elk, who also served in the U.S. Army. When Peter registered with the Selective Service in 1942, he was living in Waubay. He entered the spirit world in his home in Grenville on Jan. 29, 1975 and is buried with Elizabeth in St. James Episcopal Cemetery on the west side of Enemy Swim Lake.[10]

Shield, Amos. Amos was born on April 20, 1890, in White Swan, Charles Mix County. In the 1895 Yanktonai Census Roll, he is listed with his parents, Ezekiel and Louisa Shield, as well as his other brothers and sisters. Amos was first married to Rebecca Hero in 1909. Rebecca's brother, Jasper, served in the Army. When Amos registered for the draft on June 5, 1917, he was farming near Lake Andes. He joined the Army on June 27, 1918, and was assigned to the 407th Bakery Co, Quartermaster Corps (ASN 3815280). He was discharged on April 19, 1919. In 1928, he married Annie Oka, whose brother, Matthew, also served in the Army. In the 1930 U.S. Census, Amos and Annie were living in Wakpala next to Matthew's family. Amos and Annie later moved back to Charles Mix County. In the 1937 Census Roll, they had two children, Rose and Viola. Amos entered the spirit world in Wagner on Feb. 12, 1948 and is buried in the Native American Church Cemetery in Greenwood.[11]

Shoestring, James. James was born on the Standing Rock Reservation about Jan. 1, 1897. In the 1898 Census Roll, he was listed with his parents, Edgar (Wizihankpanyan) and Annie, and a sister, Isabella. James joined the Army on Aug. 29, 1918 and was discharged on Dec. 8, 1918. He became a member of the Barney Brought American Legion Post. On Nov. 4, 1925, he married Jessie Little Eagle, whose brothers, Leo and Allen, also served in the military. James' sister was married to James Agard, a fellow veteran. In 1935, the Shoestring family was interviewed by a worker with the SDERA program. They were living in a 12' x 15' log home in the Bullhead District. Their well had alkali water, so they hauled drinking water from a spring. Their nearest store was in Lightcap, about 10 miles away. They owned three horses, a mower, wagon and a set of harness. They had put up 10 loads of hay. James had been working on a nearby emergency conservation project. He felt that it would be better to build more roads instead of dams. They had two children, Genevieve and Norman. Norman served in the Air Force during the Korean Conflict. James entered the spirit world in the Mobridge Care Center on Jan. 7, 1991 and is buried in St. Aloysius Cemetery in Bullhead.[12]

Shooter, Leo. Leo was born on the Standing Rock Reservation about April 2, 1890, to Edward Shooter and Appears Standing. When he registered for the draft on June 5, 1917, he was farming with his father near Grand Valley. Leo joined the Army in McIntosh, SD, on July 21, 1918, and was assigned to Co. 41, 163rd Depot Brigade in Camp Dodge, IA. He was transferred to Co. L, 333rd Infantry, 84th Division (ASN 3954593). He sailed from New York aboard the *Aquitania* on Sept. 2, 1918. Upon arriving in France, he was reassigned to Co. D, 363rd Infantry, 91st Division. This unit served in the Sectors of Aubreville, Meuse-Argonne and Ypres-Lys. Pvt. Shooter sailed home from St. Nazaire aboard the S.S. *Kentuckian* on March 20, 1919. They arrived in Brooklyn on April 1, 1919. When interviewed later in his life, he said, "by golly there's I don't know how many miles of water, that ocean, quite a while to get there…I don't know…ship must be stuck someplace." Pvt. Shooter was discharged on April 22, 1919, at Camp Dodge, IA. After returning home he lived with his parents. In 1935, he married Mary White Coat. They ranched near Bullhead. He entered the spirit world in the Mobridge Community Hospital on April 3, 1980, and is buried in St. Aloysius Cemetery, Bullhead, SD.[13]

Shooter, William Thomas. Tom was born in Wood on the Rosebud Reservation about April of 1892. In the 1900 Census Roll, he is listed with his parents, John Shooter and Red Mouth, and a sister, Nellie. When he registered for the draft on June 5, 1917, he was farming near Wood. He joined the Army on June 23, 1918, and was assigned to Co. E, 351st Infantry, 88th Division (ASN 3309980). Pvt. Shooter sailed for Europe from New York aboard the *Scotian* on Aug. 15, 1918 and arrived in Liverpool on Aug. 28. Most of the 88th Division did not serve in the front line. After the war, they had occupational duty near Houdelainecourt, France. On May 20, 1919, Pfc. Shooter sailed from St. Nazaire aboard the *Mercury*. Pfc. Shooter was discharged on June 6, 1919. After returning home, he married Hermine Fallis in 1927. Hermine's brother, Antoine, had also served in the Army. In the 1930 U.S. Census, Tom and Hermine lived in Rosebud Township with their daughters, Wilma and Lillie, as well as Tom's mother. Tom entered the spirit world on June 18, 1932. He was survived by his daughters. His wife had entered the spirit world earlier that spring. Tom was buried with full military honors in St. Catherine's Cemetery, Wood, SD.[14]

Shoots Near, Jacob.   Jacob was born on the Standing Rock Reservation on Oct. 16, 1891. His parents were Shoots Near and Sarah Gall. When Jacob registered for the draft on June 5, 1917, he was farming near Wakpala. Jacob was sent to Camp Dodge, IA, on July 22, 1918, and served Field Remount Squadron No. 340 (ASN 3954594). Pvt. Shoots Near sailed with his unit from New York aboard the *Orca* on Oct. 27, 1918. He served with Pfc. Alphonse Thief. Remount Squadron No. 340 spent a day of rest in England before traveling to France. They were billeted at a rest camp in Bassens, before moving first to DeSouge and then Merignac. After the war, Pfc. Shoots Near and Pfc. Thief sailed from Brest, France aboard the U.S.S. *Pueblo* on July 3, 1919. After returning home in 1919, Jacob traveled over to the Cheyenne River Reservation, where he met Rebecca Banged in the Eye. They were married in Timber Lake in October of 1919. In 1935, the family was interviewed by a worker with the SDERA program. They were living in a 10' x 12' tent near the Bear Creek Day School. They hauled their water from a well about 1.5 miles away. They had three children, Edith, Rosie and Ellen. Rebecca's grandfather, James Brave, was also living with them. The family owned five horses, a wagon, mower, and a hay rack. Jacob had worked on emergency conservation projects. Jacob later moved back to Kenel, on the Standing Rock Reservation. After Rebecca entered the spirit world in 1954, Jacob married Esther Demery in 1957. Jacob entered the spirit world at his home on Nov. 4, 1968. He is buried in St. Thomas Episcopal Cemetery, Kenel.[15]

Shoots Walking, Noah.   Noah was born on the Standing Rock Reservation on Nov. 15, 1894. In the 1903 Census Roll, he is listed with his parents, Walcott and Emma, and a sister, Eunice. The family belonged to the Grindstone Band of the Hunkpapa. When he registered for the draft on June 5, 1917, he was farming near Little Eagle. He joined the Army on June 24, 1918, and was sent to Camp Funston, KS. He was discharged after a short time due to Tuberculosis symptoms. After returning home, he sold his allotment and married Sophia Two Arrows. After she passed away, he married Fannie Taken Alive. In 1935, the family was interviewed by a worker with the SDERA program. They were living in a one room home near Little Eagle, so their children could attend school in town. They hauled their water from an earthen dam about a mile away. They did not own any livestock at the time, and had only harvested a few potatoes from their garden, due to dry conditions. Noah had been working on emergency conservation projects. Children living with them were Sophia, Alvina, Anselm and Arlene. When Noah registered with the Selective Service in 1942, he was working on C.C.C projects. After Fannie entered the spirit world in 1948, Noah married Pearl Grindstone. He entered the spirit world on July 1, 1969, in the Mobridge Community Hospital. Noah is buried in the Elk Horn Church cemetery in Little Eagle.[16]

Short Baldhead, Benedict.   Benedict was born around 1888 in Fort Yates on the Standing Rock Reservation. In the 1905 Census Roll, he is listed with his parents, Short Baldhead (Peslaptecela) and Short Woman (Winyanptecela). In the 1910 U.S. Census, Benedict lived with his mother in Wakpala and worked at odd jobs. When he registered for the draft on June 5, 1917, he was a bronc buster at Fort Yates. He was inducted on July 26, 1918, and sent to Camp Custer, MI. Several weeks later, the *Sioux County Pioneer* reported that he was given a medical discharge. Around this time, he married Mary Brought. Mary's brother, Barney, died while serving in the Army. In the 1922 Census Roll, Ben and Mary are listed with their son, Barney, in Bullhead. Ben entered the spirit world while sleeping on Aug. 16, 1924. He is buried in Black Horse Catholic Cemetery. Mary (1889-1967) later married Joseph Leaf, who also was a veteran.[17]

Short Horn, Frank. Frank was born on the Pine Ridge Reservation on Oct. 24, 1896. In the 1897 Census Roll, Frank He Ptecela [Short Horn] is listed with his mother, Pretty Woman, as well as Hail and Shot his Horses. In the 1905 Census Roll, he is listed with his step father, John Wood. When Frank registered for the draft on June 5, 1918, he was living in Porcupine. Frank enlisted in the Navy on Oct. 18, 1920, and was discharged on Oct. 16, 1922. He married Sadie Janis. In the 1940 U.S. Census, Frank and Sadie had seven children, Gladys, Frances, William, Eugene, Albert and Barbara. Two children born later were Edna and Levi. Frank entered the spirit world on Sept. 2, 1974, and is buried in St. Boniface Cemetery, Kyle.

Short Tree, Antoine. Antoine was born in Deadwood about Dec. 15, 1898. Sometime later he was adopted by Frank and Mary Martinez, and was listed in the Pine Ridge Census Rolls as Francis Martinez. He enlisted in the Army at Fort Logan, CO, on Aug. 17, 1917, and first served with 106th Aero Service Squadron (ASN 30943). He sailed for France from St. John, New Brunswick, aboard the *Tunisian* on Dec. 10, 1917. He was assigned to the 351st Aero Squadron, which was an observation unit stationed in France. Pvt. Martinez sailed from St. Nazaire aboard the *Walter A. Luckenbach* on April 9, 1919, and was discharged at Camp Funston on May 3, 1919. Francis worked as a painter. He developed Tuberculosis and entered the spirit world on Feb. 23, 1929, at Battle Mountain Sanatorium, Hot Springs. The Sanatorium provided a flag for his funeral. In the Census Roll, he was listed as Francis Short Tree.

Siers, James. James was born on the Pine Ridge Reservation about Oct. 28, 1893, to William Siers and Jennie Elk Boy. Their name was sometimes spelled Sears. James enlisted in the Army at Ft. Logan, CO, and was first assigned to the 199th Aero Squadron, Signal Corps. Pvt. Siers sailed from New York aboard Ship #508 on Feb. 16, 1918. Upon arriving in Europe, he was reassigned to the 638th Aero Squadron. This unit trained in England and France as a fighter/pursuit squadron. Pvt. Siers likely was a mechanic. He was stationed near Toul in Colombey-les-Belles. He served 18 months in France. After returning home, he married Lucinda Bettelyoun at Martin, SD. Around 1940, the family moved to Scottsbluff, NE. James was in the gravel hauling business for many years. Lucinda entered the spirit world in Scottsbluff on March 28, 1970. James joined her about two weeks later, on April 9, 1970. They are buried in Fairview Cemetery in Scottsbluff, NE. They were survived by their children, Albert, Robert, Roger, James Jr., Emily, Iola and Clara.[18]

Siers, John. John is listed on the WWI veteran's memorial at Oglala Lakota College, Kyle, SD. He is a brother to James Siers. His last name is usually spelled as Sears. He was born on the Pine Ridge Reservation near LaCreek on June 16, 1892, to William Siers and Jennie Elk Boy. When John registered for the draft on June 5, 1917, he was working in Chadron, NE, as a section crew laborer for the C & NW Railroad. He joined the U.S. Navy on May 29, 1918, and was discharged on Aug. 30, 1919. In the 1937 Census Roll, he is listed with his wife, Rosa Fast Horse, and children, John Jr., Fannie and Leo. In 1950, John worked again on a section crew for the C & NW Railroad. The family later moved to Rapid City. John entered the spirit world at the Hot Springs VA Hospital on June 26, 1973. His children, John Jr., Leo, William, Al, Fran, and Annie, survived him. He is buried in the Black Hills National Cemetery.[19]

Sintena, Philip. Philip was born around April 3, 1900, on the Sisseton Wahpeton Reservation. In the 1906 Census Roll, he is listed with his parents, William and Mary Ida, as well as a sister, Mary Dora. In the 1911 Census Roll, Philip and his sister are listed as orphans. Philip was a student at the Flandreau boarding school. He joined the Army on April 13, 1918, and was discharged on March 19, 1919. His name was engraved on a plaque erected to honor veterans at the Flandreau boarding school after the war. After returning home he married Eva Lair and moved to Oklahoma. In the 1937 Census Roll, they were living in Vinita, OK. He worked for U.S. Metal Container Co. for many years, before retiring in 1962. He later moved to Miami, OK, where he entered the spirit world in his home on Jan. 5, 1976. Eva and his step children, Trevis Lee and Wilma, survived him. He is buried in the GAR Cemetery in Miami, OK.[20]

Sitting Dog, Andrew Robert. Robert was born on the Standing Rock Reservation around Aug. 31, 1900. His parents, Richard and Susan Sitting Dog, were members of the Flying By band of the Hunkpapa. Robert enlisted on May 1, 1918, and served with Co. C, 44th Infantry (13th Division) (ASN 476383). He was discharged as a Private First Class on June 27, 1919, but was not overseas. He lived at Little Eagle and married in the early 1920s. In 1921, he participated in the Standing Rock Indian Fair and took 2nd place in barrel roping. After his first wife died, he married Martha Firecloud. Martha's brother, Silas, was a WWI veteran. In the 1930 U.S. Census, Robert and Martha were living with Martha's parents. In 1935, the family was living in a tent while working on a conservation project 11 miles south of Little Eagle. They had a log home in Little Eagle. That home was broken into while they were camping at the work site. Robert owned a team of horses that he used on the project. They had tried to plant a garden that year, but it failed due to the dry weather. Robert was a member of the American Legion. In the 1937 Census Roll for Standing Rock, Robert and Martha were listed with their children, Minerva, Elaine, Cora, Keva and Joel. Robert entered the spirit world in the VA Hospital in Hot Springs on Jan. 22, 1961. He is buried in Messiah Cemetery in Little Eagle.[21]

Skates, Walter. Walter was born in Henton, IL, on March 2, 1895, to John and Ina Skates. Around 1906, the family moved to Haakon County, SD. When he registered for the draft on June 5, 1917, he was working as a farmer and stockman in Haakon County, SD. He joined the Army on Sept. 20, 1917, and was assigned to Co. A, 164th Infantry (ASN 1427722), and trained at Camp Cody, NM. Pvt. Skates sailed for France aboard the S.S. *Tereisias* on June 28, 1918. He was traveling with Co. 15, Camp Cody June Automatic Replacement Draft. After arriving in France, he was assigned to the Headquarters Co. 124th Field Artillery, which served in the Sectors at Lucey, St. Mihiel and Meuse-Argonne. Pvt. Skates was wounded in his left leg and was a patient in Base Hospital #208 at Autun, France. He was transferred to the hospital in Bordeaux. Pvt. Skates sailed from Bordeaux aboard the *Wilhelmina* on March 25, 1919. He was traveling with Convalescent Detachment #237. He was discharged on April 25, 1919. He received a disability payment for a number of years. After returning home, he married Ruth Carlin (1902-1979) and farmed along the Cheyenne River until 1933 in Carlin, SD. During that period, he had four years of crop failure. In the 1930 U.S. Census, they are listed with their children, Ruth, Walter, Doris, Wanda, Jack, and William. Walter was listed with the family on the Cheyenne River Census Rolls, but was not enrolled. Around 1935, they were living in Eagle Butte, where they were interviewed by a worker with the SDERA program. Their home was a block east of the IGA in Eagle Butte. Walter said he had been gassed in the war, and had had a cough since his discharge. He had joined the American Legion. Since moving to town, he worked for the State Highway Department. In the late 1930s, the family moved to Billings, MT. In the 1940 U.S. Census, Walter was working in a sugar factory near Billings. In 1959, he was working as a janitor for Ryan Grocery. He entered the spirit world on Feb. 15, 1970, and is buried in Sunset Memorial Gardens, Billings.[22]

Skinaway, Edward. Edward was born near Mille Lacs Lake on April 10, 1900, as a member of the Mille Lacs Band of Ojibway. His parents were Thomas Skinaway and Lucy Squirrel He was enrolled in the Flandreau Boarding School in 1911. He enlisted in the Army at Flandreau and was sent to Sioux Falls for examinations. He was inducted at Jefferson Barracks, MO, on April 13, 1918. He served as a Private in the Medical Department, General Hospital No. 29 in London, England, (ASN 465345). He was discharged at Fort Snelling on July 31, 1919. His name is engraved on a plaque erected at the Flandreau School to honor the WWI veterans. Upon returning home, he married Clara Peters from Nett Lake. Edward worked in the woods. In 1924, he developed some eye problems due to Trachoma, and applied for his Soldiers Bonus, which amounted to $240. In the 1940 U.S. Census, the family lived in Macville Township, Aitkin County, where Edward worked on a WPA road project. He and Clara had five children, Edward Jr., David Shirley, Myron and Roger. Following a car accident near Aitkin, Edward entered the spirit world in the VA Hospital at Ft. Snelling on Dec. 2, 1943. He is buried in Aitkin, MN.[23]

Skogen, Hendrick S. Hendrick was born on Feb. 9, 1893, in Hjelmeland, Norway, along the coast north of Stavanger. His parents were Samuel and Johren Skogen. Hendrick, also known as "Hank," came to the U.S. around 1903. When he registered for the draft on June 5, 1917, he was farming near Ekalaka, MT. He joined the Army at Ekalaka on Feb. 18, 1918. He first served in 2nd Provisional Regiment, Spruce Production until March 12, 1918, when he was transferred to the 3rd Provisional Squadron, 23rd Spruce Squadron (ASN 866277). He was stationed in the Barracks at Vancouver, WA, where airplanes were built. Private Skogen was discharged on Dec. 21, 1918. In 1924, he married Ramona Waggoner. Ramona had been first married to Alfred Braine, with whom she had two children, Carl and Josephine. In the 1930 U.S. Census, Hendrick and Ramona were farming with their children near Thunder Hawk. In the Standing Rock Census Rolls, Hendrick was listed with the family but was non-enrolled. In the 1940 U.S. Census, Ramona and Hendrick were living in Fort Yates, where Hendrick was working on the government farm. When he registered for the Selective Service in 1942, they were living in Lucerne, WA. Their son, Carl, served in the Army during WWII. The family later moved to Montana. Ramona entered the spirit world in 1966, while Hendrick entered the spirit world on Aug. 6, 1970, in Miles City. He is buried in Custer National Cemetery, Crow Agency, MT. Many years later, their children, Carl and Josephine, helped in the publishing of their grandmother's book, *WITNESS: A Hunkpapha Historian's Strong-heart Song of the Lakotas*.

Skunk, Isaac. Isaac was born on the Standing Rock Reservation on Feb. 10, 1896. His parents were David Skunk and Sarah Big Nest. His father was often listed as David Halfe in Census Rolls. As a youth, Isaac was enrolled at the Flandreau Boarding School, using the name, Isaac Half. When he registered for the draft on June 5, 1917, he was working on the Buckley Ranch near Little Eagle. He was called up for military training at Camp Lewis, WA, on May 25, 1918. After the war, his name (Isaac Half) was engraved on a plaque erected at the Flandreau School to honor the WWI veterans. After returning home, he married Anna One Hawk. In the 1930 U.S. Census, they were living in Wakpala with their children, Frances, Alma, David and Aron. He was later married to Martha. Isaac entered the spirit world in Fort Yates on Jan. 19, 1967, and is buried in Reed Cemetery.[24]

Slow, Asa W. Asa was born about July 13, 1884 on the Crow Creek Reservation at Fort Thompson. He was adopted by his grandfather. On Sept. 21, 1909, he married Lois Belle Tewksbury in Buffalo.

In the 1910 Census Roll, he was listed as Garfield Old Thunder. At that time, he was working as a house carpenter on the Standing Rock Reservation. He was not required to register for the draft because of his age. He joined the Army and was sent to Camp Dodge, IA. He served as a Private First Class in Co. G, 2nd Infantry, 19th Division. This unit did not go overseas. After the war he returned home. On Feb. 4, 1922, he married Narcissa Smith (1897-1968), a Cherokee from Miami, OK. In 1927, Asa accepted a job with the Boy Scouts. He served as a camp counselor and instructor of archery and native ways to scouts in a camp near Springfield. Ohio. He and Narcissa had three daughters, Irene, Fran and Cornelia. In 1940, they were living in Mitchell, SD. When Asa registered for the Selective Service in 1942, he was working at the Umatilla Ordnance Depot in Hermiston, OR. Asa entered the spirit world in Hood River on Sept. 4, 1962. He is buried in Hood River.

Slow, John. John was born at Cherry Creek on the Cheyenne River Reservation around November of 1893. His parents were James and Mercy Two Bulls Slow. He had a brother, Thomas. When John registered for the draft on June 1, 1917, he was farming near Cherry Creek. He joined the Army on Oct. 2, 1917, and was assigned to B Troop, 314th Military Police at Camp Funston, KS. He was discharged as a Private on Nov. 24, 1917. He was not issued a service number. On April 22, 1919, he married Mollie Four Moon at Dupree. They had a daughter, Hattie. In 1927, he married Winnie Bear Eagle. In the 1940 U.S. Census, they were living with their daughter, Susie. John suffered from Tuberculosis and entered the spirit world in Cherry Creek on Feb. 1, 1942. He is buried in the Episcopal Cemetery in Cherry Creek.

Slow, Thomas L. Thomas was a younger brother to John. He was born on April 26, 1899, at Cherry Creek. His parents were James and Mercy Two Bulls Slow. Thomas joined the Army on May 24, 1918, and was assigned to Co. B, Military Police, 13th Train Headquarters Command (ASN 2787174). He was discharged as a Pfc. on Jan. 24, 1919. He reenlisted in April 1919, hoping to learn something from the vocational training classes offered by the Army. He later wrote to Commissioner Cato Sells, asking to be transferred to an all-Indian unit if the War Department created one. On April 14, 1920, he re-enlisted in the Army and served with Co. D, 21st Infantry. For a while, he was stationed at Fort George Wright in Spokane, WA. Pfc. Slow was discharged on July 20, 1921. On May 21, 1924, he married Christine Patterson (1906-2007). She and Thomas had a son, Gaylord. Thomas developed appendicitis and entered the spirit world in the Cheyenne River Hospital on May 9, 1933. He was buried in the Episcopal Cemetery in Cherry Creek. His body was later moved to the Black Hills National Cemetery, Section G, site 5600.[25]

Smith, Alfred Clement. Alfred was born in Dante, SD, on the Yankton Reservation on Jan. 12, 1890. His parents were Alfred Smith and Julia Benoist. He attended school at Carlisle. He married Dorothy Cote in 1914. When Alfred registered for the draft, he lived in Wagner with his wife and child. After the war, Alfred became a charter member of the Arthur Wissman American Legion Post at Avon. Alfred was the first elected Yankton tribal leader. The Smith family moved to California around 1941. When Alfred registered for the Selective Service in 1942, he was working for the Bureau of Reclamation in Parker, AZ. Alfred's son, Leonard, was killed in Action in the Pacific during WWII. Alfred "Washo-Shay" entered the spirit world in Los Angeles, CA, on May 28, 1969. He is buried in Yankton, SD. His children, Clementine, Amy, Emerson, Milan, Ethel, Dorothy, Bonnie, Enda and Martha survived him.

Smith, Elijah. Elijah was born on the Rosebud Reservation on March 3, 1900, to Todd Smith and Zenette Shaw. He had been a student at the Rapid City boarding school. Elijah enlisted in the 4th SD Infantry on March 31, 1917, (ASN 98578). When he arrived at Camp Greene, NC, he was assigned to Co. B, 148th Machine Gun Battalion, 41st Division. He sailed with his unit from Hoboken aboard the *Olympic* on Jan. 11, 1918. Upon arrival in France, he was reassigned to Co. M, 167th Infantry, 42nd Division. Pvt. Smith was wounded in France. The 42nd Division suffered 13,919 casualties. Pvt. Smith sailed for home from Bordeaux aboard the *Walter A. Luckenbach* on March 6, 1919. Smith traveled with Camp Dodge Detachment #4, 160th Infantry, and was discharged on April 8, 1919. The rest of the 42nd Division was discharged about a month later. He later received a Purple Heart medal. After returning home, Elijah married Viola Whipple. In 1935, the family was interviewed by a worker with the SDERA program. Elijah and Viola had two children, Norma and Alvin. Elijah had been doing some painting and had managed to sell some art work. He told the social worker that he would like the chance to attend an art school. The family lived in St. Francis. Elijah entered the spirit world at the VA Hospital in Hot Springs on April 28, 1960. He is buried in St. Charles Cemetery in St, Francis. His son, Alvin, served in the Army in the 1950s.[26]

Smith, Todd Harden. Todd was an older brother of Elijah. He was born on the Rosebud Reservation on Dec. 13, 1897. When he registered for the draft on June 5, 1917, he was working in St Francis as a laborer on construction work for Bro. Andrew Hartman. Todd enlisted in the Army and was assigned to Co. H, 336th Infantry, 84th Division (ASN 3955089). He sailed from New York on the *Grampian* on Aug. 26, 1918. He was reassigned to Co. B, 320th Infantry, 80th Division. The 320th Infantry served in the Sectors at St. Mihiel, Bethincourt, and Meuse-Argonne. Pvt. Smith sailed from Brest aboard the U.S.S. *Mobile* on May 20, 1919. During WWII, he re-enlisted on Oct. 24, 1942. He was discharged on April 24, 1943. Todd married Eliza Four Feathers. He worked as a music teacher at the boarding school in St. Francis. In the 1937 Census Roll, he and Eliza had five children, Delmer, Clarence, Loretta, Letha and Jerome. Todd entered the spirit world in Colorado on May 30, 1975. He is buried in Ft. Logan National Cemetery, Section Q, site 3110.

Snell, George W. George was born on Feb. 22, 1897, at Lodgepole, MT, on the Fort Belknap Reservation. His parents were James Snell and Fannie Black Digger. George attended school at the Flandreau Boarding School, where he was known for his athletic ability in basketball, football and track. He enlisted in Troop D, 1st SD Cavalry on April 4, 1917. He served as a Corporal. The 1st SD Cavalry was sent to Camp Cody, NM. Corp. Snell was reassigned to Co. D, 136th Infantry, 34th Division (ASN 1427355). He sailed with that unit from New York aboard the *Melita* on Oct. 13, 1918. He was reassigned to the 49th Infantry. After the war, Cpl. Snell sailed from Brest, France, aboard the *George Washington* on Jan. 12, 1919, and was discharged on Feb. 15, 1919. Traveling with him were five other men who had also been students at Flandreau. Cpl. Snell had served his platoon as a grenade instructor and was rated as excellent in horsemanship. His name was engraved on a monument erected at Flandreau to honor the WWI veterans. After returning home to Montana, he married Lena Buck in 1922. They ranched in the Milk River Valley. He and Lena had four children, Curtis, Billy, Verna and Charlotte. George worked as a WPA supervisor for the building of the Havre Airport. He also worked for a while for the Bureau of Reclamation. He was a member of the Veterans of World War I of the USA, VFW, and the American Legion. He entered the spirit world in Fort Belknap Hospital on Dec. 19, 1976. He is buried in Hi-way Cemetery, Harlem, MT.[27]

Snow Fly, Moses. Moses was born on the Rosebud Reservation on July 25, 1898. His parents were Joseph Snow Fly and Minnie Fast Hawk. Moses likely enlisted in the 4th SD Infantry on April 6, 1917. This National Guard Unit was sent to Camp Greene, NC, where Pvt. Snow Fly was assigned to Co. B, 148th Machine Gun Battalion. He sailed with his unit from Hoboken aboard the *Olympic* on Jan. 11, 1918. Upon arrival in France, he was reassigned to Co. M, 167th Infantry, 42nd Division. The

42nd Division suffered 13,919 casualties. Pvt. Snow Fly was likely wounded or severely gassed. He returned to the States aboard the U.S.S. *Harrisburg* and arrived on Oct. 2, 1918. He was discharged as a Pvt. on March 10, 1919. He married Mary Red Blanket, with whom he had two sons, Nick and Moses Jr. Mary entered the spirit world in 1924. Moses then married Sophia Pretty Bull. In 1929, Moses married Bertha Horn (1907-1975). In the 1930 U.S. Census, the family was farming in Todd County. In the 1940 U.S. Census, Moses and Bertha are listed with their children, Nick, Moses Jr., Clifford and Mable. In 1945, Moses was living in Rosebud. He entered the spirit world at Soldier Creek on March 10, 1978. He and Bertha are buried in Grace Chapel Cemetery in Soldier Creek.[28]

Speaks Walking, Luke. Luke was born at Fort Yates on March 20, 1900, to Louis Iyamani [Speaks Walking] and Hairy Moccasin. Luke was also known as John. He attended the boarding school at Flandreau. On April 6, 1918, he sent his parents a letter, which was published by the *Sioux County Pioneer*.

> Dearest Father and mother,
>
> I am going to ask or let my brothers and you both know that I plan to enlist in the army tonight. I am a man and want to show my love to our country and then to show my name to the country. We are going to leave here on Wednesday, April 10, for Sioux Falls to be examined. I have the name of my grandfather and which you gave me.
>
> You don't have to worry about me or cry for me. I am well off. We are going to join till the war is over, and if we should win the war we will (reach) the city of Berlin. If you are going to answer me, address it to Chas. Pierce, here and he will send them to us. I don't know if I will pass or not yet. There are lots of boys who enlisted already. I wish to enlist too. After we are examined I will let you know if I pass or not. We are going to come home after six months training to see you folks. Let some who can explain all this to you and read good to you so you will not be mistaken.
>
> I am getting along pretty good for this present writing and hope it will reach you as sure as it leaves me here. I wish you all and relations my best of wishes and regards and kiss every one of you, and close with love to you all, father, mother, and brothers.

Luke did pass his physical exam, and was inducted at Jefferson Barracks, MO. He was assigned to the 31st New York Coast Artillery Corps at Fort Wadsworth, NY, (ASN 465354). On June 17, 1918, he was transferred to Battery B, 74th Artillery, Coast Artillery Corps. He was promoted to Pfc. on that same date. On Sept. 23, 1918, the 74th Artillery sailed for Europe aboard the transport USS *President Grant*. On the trip across the pond, 137 men on the ship died of the flu. Upon arrival in France, they were assigned to a camp at Mailly and Haussimont. They were a Railway Artillery unit that was to be trained in the firing of either the 400-mm or the 340-mm guns. Their training was not completed before the Armistice. They returned home from Brest aboard the USS *Mongolia* on Dec. 22, 1918. Pfc. Speaks Walking was discharged at Camp Dodge, IA, on Jan. 9, 1919.

After the war, Luke married Lucy Tiger. In the 1924 Census Roll, Luke and Lucy were listed with their daughter, Julia. Lucy entered the spirit world on May 20, 1926. On Jan. 18, 1927, Luke married Josephine DeRockbraine in McIntosh. Josephine's brother, Thomas, had served in the Army. In the 1928 Census Roll, Luke and Josephine were listed with their children, Charlotte and Oscar. Oscar only lived a few years. In March of 1928, Luke was admitted to Battle Mountain Sanitarium near Hot Springs with some health problems, including partial deafness. His deafness was probably due to having served in the artillery. His application to the hospital indicates he was receiving a small pension, most likely for the deafness caused by firing the big guns without adequate ear protection. He was discharged about a month later. In the 1936 Census Roll, Luke and Josephine were listed with Charlotte. Luke raised a large garden north of Bullhead. When it was ready to harvest, he made the produce available to widows and elderly. He also used his income to provide for widows and orphans. Josephine came down with tuberculosis and entered the spirit world on Aug. 24, 1945. Luke entered the spirit world in his home on Nov. 23, 1962, and is buried in St. Mary's Cemetery in Bullhead, SD.[29]

Spindler, C.A. He is listed on WWI veteran's memorial at Oglala Lakota College, Kyle, SD. Chester was born in O'Neill, NE, on Feb. 1, 1897, to George and Margaret Spindler. He married Ivy Morrison on Feb. 20, 1918. When Chester registered for the draft on June 5, 1918, he was living in Winner. He joined the Army on Aug. 29, 1918, and was assigned to Salvage Company, Quartermaster Corps at Camp Dodge, IA, (ASN 4821555). He was discharged on Feb. 18, 1919. He and Ivy had two sons, Charles and Joseph. In 1930, Ivy entered the spirit world. Chester later married Shirley Simmons. Chester operated a grocery store in Potato Creek and Shirley worked as the Postmistress. Their son, Joseph, served in the Navy during WWII. Chester entered the spirit world on Dec. 31, 1960, and is buried in Gordon, NE.

Spotted Tail, Stephen. Stephen was the grandson of Chief Spotted Tail. He was born in Valentine, NE, on Oct. 10, 1896. His parents were William and Mary Spotted Tail. He attended the boarding school in Rapid City. He likely enlisted in the 4th SD Infantry in April of 1917. When these South Dakota soldiers arrived in Camp Greene, NC, many of them were reassigned to Co. B, 148th Machine Gun Battalion, 41st Division (ASN 98594). Upon arriving in France, he was transferred to Co. M, 167th Infantry, 42nd Division. Pvt. Spotted Tail served with Herbert Omaha Boy and Chauncey Eagle Horn. Pvt. Spotted Tail sailed for America from Brest aboard the U.S.S. *Minnesota* on April 15, 1919. After returning home, he married Minnie Star Boy, with whom he had three children, William, Sylvan and Neola. He married Emma Iron Shell in 1924. They had seven children, Cornelia, Esther, Dennis, Calvin, Isabel, Norval and Mary Jane. They ranched near Parmelee. Emma entered the spirit world on Sept. 15, 1945. In 1957, he married Nellie Red Fish. Stephen served on the tribal council for over 20 years. He was the first Commander of the Chauncey Eagle Horn Post at Rosebud. Stephen entered the spirit world in Rosebud on Jan. 11, 1971. He was buried in Holy Innocents Cemetery, Parmelee. Full military honors were conducted by the Legion Post.

Sam Spotted War Bonnet
Marquette University Archives

Spotted War Bonnet, Sam. Sam was born on the Rosebud Reservation around 1889. In the 1900 Census Roll, his is listed with his mother, Medicine Owl, and his brothers, Charles, Thomas, and Francis. When Sam registered for the draft on June 5, 1917, he was living in Wososo and working on the Albert Whipple Ranch. He joined the Army on July 22, 1918, and was assigned to Veterinary Hospital #17, Veterinary Corps (ASN 3955065). Pvt. Spotted War Bonnet sailed for Europe from Newport News aboard the *Antigone* on Oct. 28, 1918, and was stationed at Triconville, France. After the war, Pvt. Spotted War Bonnet sailed from Brest,

France, aboard the *Huntington* on June 24, 1919. He arrived in Boston on July 5, 1919, and was discharged on July 11, 1919. After returning home, he married Minnie Attack Him. Sam worked as an interpreter for the U.S. Indian Service. In the 1930 U.S. Census, Sam and Minnie had three children, Howard, Birdie and Sam Jr. Howard served in the Army during WWII. Sam entered the spirit world in Parmelee on Jan. 17, 1936, and is buried in Parmelee. Minnie entered the spirit world two years later. In the 1940 U.S. Census, their children were living with their grandfather.[30]

Standing Bear, Henry. Henry, also known as Henry Flood, was born in Allen, SD, on the Pine Ridge Reservation on Sept 3, 1894. In the 1896 Census Roll, he is listed with his parents, Henry and Elizabeth Standing Bear. He attended school at Haskell Institute and Conway College in Pennsylvania. Henry joined the Army on May 25, 1918, and was assigned to Co. D, 145th Machine Gun (MG) Battalion, 40th Division, which served as a replacement division in France (ASN 3129658). Pvt. Flood sailed with the Headquarters Detachment, 145th MG Battalion from New York aboard the *Metagama* on Aug. 7, 1918. After the Armistice, Cpl. Flood sailed from Pauillac, France, aboard the *Sierra* on April 6, 1919. He was traveling with the Camp Dodge Detachment, 143rd MG Battalion, which arrived in Hoboken on April 17, 1919. Cpl. Flood was discharged on April 28, 1919. After returning home, Henry married Ollie Lessert, who had two brothers who served in the Army. Henry worked at Haskell for several years. In the 1930 U.S. Census, Henry was teaching school in Martin, SD. He later moved to the Flandreau boarding school, where he served as a clerk for many years. Henry came down with Tuberculosis and entered the spirit world on Feb. 2, 1941, at the VA Hospital in Minneapolis. His funeral was held on the 20th anniversary of his wedding to Ollie. Ollie and their two children, Roy and Carmel survived him. He is buried in the Flandreau Cemetery. His son, Roy, served with the USMC during WWII.[31]

Richard Standing Bear
Herman Standing Bear

Standing Bear, Richard – listed on WWI veteran's memorial at Oglala Lakota College, Kyle, SD. Richard was born on the Pine Ridge Reservation on Sept. 3, 1897. His parents were Willard and Lizzie Standing Bear. His father had served as a Sergeant with the Army in the early 1890s. Richard attended the boarding school at Rapid City around 1910. He ran home from there. He may still have been a student when he enlisted in the South Dakota National Guard in September 1917. He and a friend of his, John Thode, were assigned to Troop L, First South Dakota Cavalry. They were sent to Camp Cody, NM, where they were ordered to help break horses and donkeys. Richard sent a postcard to his sister showing him and John in uniform. On the back of the card he wrote, " it is just like home here now after I got used to it. There are 6000 of us soldier boys here in camp now 240 more yet to come yet. There sure is a big crowd of them when they get out to drill." While stationed there, Richard hurt both of his legs. According to his son, Herman, Richard was discharged and never received any compensation. Richard returned home and ranched with his father. In 1927, he married Martha Neck Shield. In the 1940 U.S. Census, they were ranching and had six children, Richard Jr., Delores, Severt, Robert, Andrew, and James. He entered the spirit world on Jan. 2, 1977, at the VA facility in Hot Springs. He is buried at Norris. His son, Severt, served in the Marine Corps during the Korean Conflict.[32]

Stars, Joseph. Joseph was born on Jan. 14, 1892 on the Rosebud Reservation. When he registered for the draft on June 5, 1917, he was living in Herrick. He joined the Army on Sept. 22, 1917, and was sent to Camp Funston, KS. He was assigned to Camp Funston Detachment, Headquarters Battalion, General Headquarters, AEF (ASN 2310846). Pfc. Stars sailed with his unit from Hoboken, NJ, on Ship No. 55 on March 6, 1918. He may also have served with the 89th Division. Cpl. Stars sailed with Co. A, Headquarters Battalion, from Brest, France, aboard the *Leviathan* on Sept. 1, 1919, and was discharged on Sept. 26, 1919. In the 1921 Census Roll, Joseph was also listed as Joseph Stands Along Time. After returning home, he married Belle Peniska (1894-1981), with whom he had a son, Joseph Vance. In the 1940 U.S. Census, the family was farming in Ellston Township, Gregory County. Joseph entered the spirit world on Aug. 25, 1962, and is buried in Ellston Cemetery, Herrick.

St. Clair, Henry Butler. Henry was born in Minnesota, on March 5, 1899, to Henry Whipple St. Clair and his wife, Amelia. They were listed in the Flandreau Census Rolls. Henry enlisted in the 2nd Minnesota Infantry on May 2, 1917, at Redwood Falls. He likely was sent to Camp Cody, NM, for training. He sailed with the 136th Infantry Regiment, 34th Division (ASN 1429127) from Brooklyn aboard the *Lyacon* on Oct. 13, 1918. After arriving in France, he was transferred to Co. H, 58th Infantry, 4th Division. Bugler St.Clair sailed with his unit from Brest, France, aboard the *Mount Vernon* on July 24, 1919. In the 1920 U.S. Census, he was living with his parents at the Sisseton Agency, where his father was an Episcopal Minister. In the 1930 U.S. Census, Henry was living in Sisseton. Around this time, he married Rose Redearth, with whom he had a son, Eugene. He entered the spirit world on Sept. 8, 1931, in Marshall County, SD. He is buried at the Indian Mission Cemetery in Redwood Falls, MN.

St. Clair, Stephen H. Stephen was born on the Santee Reservation in Nebraska on April 25, 1893. In the 1896 Census Roll, he is listed with his parents, Charles and Mary St. Claire, and a brother, Joseph. In the 1900 U.S. Census, he was living with his family in Greenwood, SD. When he registered for the draft on June 5, 1917, he listed his occupation as musician. He joined the Army on March 6, 1918. Cpl. St. Claire was discharged on Aug. 27, 1919. After returning home, he married Florence Brave from the Crow Creek Reservation. They had a daughter, Doris. In the 1930 U.S. Census, Stephen was working as a laborer at the Indian School in Rosebud. After Florence entered the spirit world in 1932, He married Mary Salazar and moved to the Ute Reservation in Ignacio, CO. In the 1940 U.S. Census, he was working for the Indian Service as an assistant farmer in Ignacio. The family later moved to Utah. Stephen was a member of American Legion Post No. 137, East Carbon, Utah. He entered the spirit world in a Price, UT, hospital on Sept. 6, 1972. His widow, Mary (1906-1984), and children, James, Andy, Ted, Joann and Doris, survived him. He is buried in Redwood Memorial Cemetery, West Jordan, UT.

Stifftail, James. See **White Feather, James.**

Stone, Paul. Paul was born on the Rosebud Reservation about April 7, 1895. His parents were Cyrus Stone and Good Robe. When Paul registered for the draft on June 5, 1917, he was farming near Wososo with his father. He joined the Army on May 25, 1918, and likely first served in the 160th Infantry, 40th Division (ASN 3130069). Pvt. Stone sailed from New York aboard the *Ortega* on Aug. 31, 1918, traveling with Mixed Overseas Casual Co. No. 362. After arriving in France, he was assigned to Co. E, 357th Infantry, 90th Division. The 357th Infantry served in campaigns in Villers-en-Haye, St. Mihiel, Puvenelle, and Meuse-Argonne. The 90th Division suffered 9,400 casualties. Pvt. Stone sailed from St. Nazaire aboard the U.S.S. *Huron* on May 26, 1919, and was discharged on

June 16, 1919. After returning home, he married Louise Running Horse. In the 1940 U.S. Census, they were living with their children, Ophilia, Cyrus and Roy. Paul was working as a laborer with the CCC program. Paul entered the spirit world on Jan. 26, 1974, at the VA hospital in Hot Springs. His widow and son, Roy, survived him. He is buried in Epiphany Episcopal Cemetery in Rosebud.[33]

George Stover, Jr.
Ancestry.com

Stover, George, Jr. George is listed on WWI veteran's memorial at Oglala Lakota College, Kyle, SD. He was born about Nov. 29, 1892, on the Pine Ridge Reservation, to George and Jennie Stover. George's father had served in the 7th West Virginia Cavalry in the Civil War. George's sister, Laura, married Edward Desersa, a fellow veteran. When George registered for the draft on June 5, 1917, he was living in Martin. His registration form indicates that he was a baseball player. When George joined the Army, he was assigned to Battery F, 337th Field Artillery (FA), 88th Division (ASN 3315752). Pvt. Stover sailed for Europe from New York aboard the H.M.T. *Bohemian* on Aug. 17, 1918. The ship first landed in Liverpool, England on Aug. 31, 1918. On Sept. 8, 1918, the 337th FA arrived at Clermont-Ferrand, France, for further training with 155 mm guns. While in this camp, many soldiers became ill with the Spanish Flu. Pvt. Stover entered the spirit world on Oct. 29, 1918. His body was brought back to the U.S. by the U.S.A.T *Wheaton*, which sailed from Cherbourg, France, on May 1, 1921. He is buried in the Inestimable Gift Cemetery. The following lines are engraved on his headstone:

> HE LEFT HIS HOME IN PERFECT HEALTH
>
> HE LOOKED SO YOUNG AND BRAVE
>
> WE LITTLE THOUGHT HOW SOON THAT HE
>
> WOULD BE LAID IN A SOLDIER'S GRAVE

Stover, John. John is listed on WWI veteran's memorial at Oglala Lakota College, Kyle, SD. He was born June 30, 1898, on the Pine Ridge Reservation to Edward Stover and Sarah Standing Bear. His father was a brother to George Stover. John joined the Navy on May 10, 1918, and served as a Seaman 1st Class (NSN 1944567). He was discharged on Sept. 30, 1921. A few years later he married Grace Schultz (1907-2009). They had three children, who died as youngsters. In the 1930 U.S. Census, John was working as a laborer in Martin. John entered the spirit world on Aug. 4, 1947, and is buried in St. Mary's Cemetery near Martin.

St. Pierre, Edward Earl. Edward, a Yanktonai, was born in Armour on Sept. 24, 1888, to Gilbert and Carrie St. Pierre. When he registered for the draft on June 5, 1917, he was farming. He joined the Army on May 24, 1918, and was discharged as a Private on Jan. 14, 1919. Around 1921, he married Bessie Sybil McBride. In the 1930 U.S. Census, he and Bessie farmed with their two children, Blanch and Benedict. Edward entered the spirit world on June 2, 1968, in Wagner, SD. He is buried in Greenwood.

St. Pierre, Henry Lee. Henry, a Yanktonai, was born around Dec. 27, 1888, to Henry and Ida St. Pierre. He married Arabella Jandreau around 1908. When he registered for the draft on June 5, 1917, he was working for F.A. Flanigan in Gregory, SD. Henry enlisted on Sept. 22, 1917 and was assigned to Co. A, 340th Machine Gun (MG) Battalion, 89th Division (ASN 2193191). Cpl. St. Pierre sailed from New York for Europe aboard the *Khyber* on June 4, 1918. Upon arrival in France, the 340th MG Battalion was billeted in St. Blin. They served in the Campaigns at Lucey, St. Mihiel, Euvezin, and Meuse Argonne. After the Armistice, Sgt. St. Pierre's commanding officer, Capt. Runkle, wrote of him, "has proved to be one of the most reliable men in the company. In action he was cool and level-headed." The 340th MG Battalion was billeted in Erdorf, Germany. Sgt. St. Pierre sailed for home from Brest aboard the *Leviathan* on May 15, 1919, and was discharged on June 2, 1919. He was awarded the Silver Star medal. In the 1934 Census Roll, Henry and Arabella are listed with their children, Vere, Lee and Ronald. Their son, Lee, served in the Army during WWII. When Henry registered for the Selective Service in 1942, he was living in Dixon. He entered the spirit world on Oct. 27, 1963, and is buried in St. Joseph'd Catholic Cemetery, Gregory, SD.[34]

St. Pierre, Jesse P. Jesse, a Yanktonai, was born around Feb. 25, 1895 to Peter and Julia St. Pierre. He joined the Army on June 2, 1917. He likely enlisted in Co. M, 4th SD Infantry, at Yankton. When the 4th Infantry arrived at Camp Greene, NC, in early October of 1917, the commanding officer of Co. M received a surprising message. A Colonel at the Camp said, "You think you're Captain of Company M, 4th South Dakota Infantry. Well, you're not. This is the 147th Field Artillery and you're Captain-Adjutant of the Second Battalion." So, foot soldiers were trained to use guns and work with horses. Pfc. St Pierre was assigned to Battery C, 147th Field Artillery (ASN 139543). As part of the 41st Division, they sailed to Europe aboard the ship *Olympic* on Jan. 11, 1918. On March 25, 1918, the 147th Field Artillery was attached to the 32nd Division. The 147th FA supported the 32nd Division until the Armistice. After the Armistice, Pfc. St. Pierre's commanding officer wrote his evaluation, stating St. Pierre was "a willing and conscientious worker. Good Driver or cannoneer. Excellent scout on night work." The 32nd Division suffered almost 14,000 casualties. Following the Armistice, the 147th FA served occupational duty with the 88th Division. Most of the 147th FA returned from France in early May. Pvt. St. Pierre was likely in a hospital, as he did not sail for home from Marseilles aboard the *Guiseppe Verdi* until June 22, 1919. He was traveling with St. Aignan Casual Company # 5979, which arrived in New York on July 7, 1919. Pfc. St. Pierre was discharged on July 15, 1919. In 1920, he married Edna Rondell. He and Edna had four children, Susanna, Katherine, Vine and Velma. Jesse entered the spirit world on Jan. 7, 1934, and is buried in the Greenwood Presbyterian Cemetery. His son, Vine, was wounded while serving with the Army in North Korea.[35]

Strampher, Carl H. Carl was born in Nebraska on Nov. 6, 1896, to Carl and Annie Strampher. When Carl registered for the draft on June 5, 1918, he was living in Meckling, SD, in the SE corner of the state. He was drafted shortly before the Armistice and served only a short time. On Feb. 12, 1919, he married Imelda Duncan (1900-1981) in Morristown, SD. Imelda's brother, Jefferson, had served with the Army in France. Carl was listed with Imelda on the Standing Rock Census Rolls as non-enrolled. In the 1930 U.S Census, they were farming near Thunder Hawk. Imelda's brother, Robert was living with the family. In 1935, the family was interviewed by a government worker with the SDERA program. Their farm was four miles west of Keldron. Carl rented 1700 acres, of which 500 acres was cropland and the rest was pasture. Their children were Alberta, Phyllis, George and Doris. A few years later they moved out of South Dakota. When Carl registered for the Selective Service in 1942, he was working for Klies Mining Co. in Niehart, MT. In 1945, Carl was working at the Mt. Rainier Ordnance Depot at Fort Lewis, WA, when he was electrocuted while loading equipment with a crane. He entered the spirit world on Oct. 3, 1945. He is buried in Woodbine Cemetery in Puyallup, WA. His son, George, had served with the Army during WWII.[36]

Stricker, Thomas. Thomas, a Yanktonai, was born on the Lower Brule Reservation on June 25, 1896 to George and Susan Stricker. When he registered for the draft, he was living in Ravinia. He joined the Army and was sent to Camp Funston for training. He sailed from Hoboken aboard the *Agamemnon* on Feb. 27, 1918. He was assigned to the Camp Funston Replacement Draft (February) and was traveling with Casual Co. No. 54 (ASN 246144). Upon arrival in France, he was reassigned to Co. A, 120th Machine Gun Battalion, 32nd Division. The 120th MG Battalion served in the Sectors at Center, Aisne-Marne, Oise-Aisne, Meuse-Argonne. After the Armistice, his commanding officer wrote that Pvt. Stricker was a "good responsible man." The 32nd Division marched into Germany and took up occupational duty near Coblenz. Pvt. Stricker sailed home from Brest aboard the *Von Steuben* on May 5, 1919. He was discharged on May 24, 1919. On Sept. 16, 1929, Thomas married Adelia Pretty Sounding Flute, who entered the spirit world in 1932. In the 1937 Census Roll, he was listed with two children, Navold and Mary Louise. When he registered for the Selective Service in 1942, he was living with his wife, Nancy Hayface near Marty, SD. His son, Navold, served in the Army during the Korean Conflict. Thomas entered the spirit world at his home in Lake Andes on Jan. 12, 1968, and is buried in Cedar Presbyterian Cemetery, across from the Fort Randall Casino.[37]

Strongheart, Walter. Walter was born in Wakpala on the Standing Rock Reservation around April 17, 1890. In the 1894 Census Roll, he is listed as Jasper Horse Thief, along with his parents, Horse Thief (Sungamanon) and Tipiluta [Red Lodge], and a brother, Bad Hail. His father was Hunkpati. In the 1910 U.S. Census, he is listed as Walter Horsethief. A few years later he married Emma LaMont. When Walter registered for the draft on June 4, 1917, he and Emma had a child. He is described as being a tall man of medium build. Walter enlisted in the Army at McIntosh on Sept. 17, 1917. The Army may have suggested that he change his name. He was sent to Camp Funston, KS, to train with the 89th Division. He was assigned to Co. B, 340th Machine Gun (MG) Battalion (ASN 2193080). Pfc. Horsethief sailed from New York for Europe aboard the *Khyber* on June 4, 1918. Upon arriving in France, the 340th MG Battalion was billeted in St. Blin. The battalion served in the campaigns at Lucey, St. Mihiel, Euvezin and Meuse-Argonne. Cpl. Strongheart was wounded in the left knee. After the Armistice, his commanding officer wrote that Cpl. Strongheart was a "good night worker, runner and observer." He also showed "good judgement." Cpl. Strongheart wrote to Joseph Dixon that, "in the last eleven day drive I was still in the front line when the armistice was signed." Cpl. Strongheart served in the Army of Occupation with the 340th MG Bn. in Erdorf, Germany. He returned to the United States from France aboard the *Leviathan* on May 15, 1919, and was discharged on June 21, 1919. Walter's wife entered the spirit world in 1933. About a year later he married Eva Gabe, the widow of Ambrose Gabe, who had also served in the 89th Division. In 1935, the family was interviewed by a worker with the SDERA program. Walter and Eva lived in a three room, two-story house in Wakpala with their children, Carl, Rita, Gertrude, Mary, Ulysses, and Clifford. Walter said he was receiving a disability payment of $25 per month for his war wound. He had also worked on some emergency conservation projects but felt that these jobs interfered with his needing to put up hay for livestock. When Walter registered for the Selective Service in 1942, he was working for L.C. Lippert, the agency superintendent. The family later ranched near Wakpala. After the dam was built on the Missouri River, the ranch was moved to higher ground. Walter entered the spirit world in the Bismarck Hospital on Nov. 21, 1961 and is buried in Wakpala.[38]

Stuart, James Austin. James was born in Mexico, Missouri, on Feb. 3, 1895, to Robert and Susan Stuart. In the 1910 U.S. Census, he lived with his family in Clearwater, NE. He served in the Army during the war. In 1920, he married Elizabeth Red Thunder (1893-1939) from the Sisseton-

Wahpeton Reservation. In the early 1920's, they lived at Fort Totten, ND, where their oldest children were born. In the 1930 U.S. Census, they lived in Wahpeton, where James was working as a clerk for the Indian Service. A short time later, they moved to Browns Valley. In the 1930 Census Rolls, James is listed (non-enrolled) with Elizabeth and their children, Earl, Thomas, Phyllis, Kenneth, Noel and Neal, who were twins. Elizabeth entered the spirit world in 1939. Her sons, Earl and Thomas, served in the Navy during WWII. When James registered for the Selective Service in 1942, he was living in Troutdale, OR. He later moved to Southern California, where he worked for Douglas Aircraft Corp. He entered the spirit world in Anaheim on Aug. 24, 1979, and is buried in Forest Lawn Memorial Park, Cypress, CA.

Sully, Frank. Frank was born at Bonesteel, SD, on March 1, 1889. His parents were John (Jack) Sully and Mary Louisa Goulette. Frank is listed with his mother on the Lower Brule Census Rolls for the 1890s. His father had served with a Minnesota Regiment during the Civil War. Jack was suspected of being a cattle rustler and was killed by a posse in May of 1904. In the 1900 U.S. Census, Frank was attending the boarding school at Chamberlain. Later Frank was listed on the Rosebud Census Rolls. When he registered for the draft on June 5, 1917, he was raising cattle. He joined the Army on July 31, 1918, and was assigned to Co. A, 210th Engineers, 10th Division (ASN 4258918). The 10th Division did not go overseas. He was discharged as a Private on Feb. 6, 1919. In 1922, he married Olga Paulsen (1902-1996) in Martin, SD. They had two daughters, Dorothy and Marjorie. In the 1930 U.S. Census, Frank was the manager of a cream station, while Olga worked as a book keeper for an implement store. In the 1940 U.S. Census, Frank operated a produce station in Wood. They later moved to Rapid City. In 1945, he was an assistant at the State Trout Hatchery. Frank entered the spirit world at the Fort Meade VA Hospital on Aug. 26, 1958, and is buried in the Black Hills National Cemetery, Section E, site 356.

Sully, George. George, a younger brother to Frank, was born on Sept 27, 1890, to John (Jack) and Mary Louisa Sully. George was listed with his mother on the Lower Brule Census Rolls when they were young. In the 1900 U.S. Census, George was a student at the boarding school in Chamberlain. When George registered for the draft, he was raising cattle. He joined the Army on May 4, 1918, and was discharged as a Corporal on Dec. 18, 1918. After returning home, he married Ellen Cadwell (1897-1984). In the 1930 U.S. Census, George was working in the livestock business in Grand Island, NE. He and Ellen had three children, George Jr., Mary and Wilbur. When George registered for the Selective Service in 1942, he was working for the Great Falls Meat Co. in Great Falls, MT. The family later moved to Idaho Falls, where George worked as a livestock buyer. He entered the spirit world in Idaho Falls, ID, on March 2, 1973, and is buried in Idaho Falls. His son, George Jr., served in the Army during WWII.

Sully, Gilbert. Gilbert, a Santee, was born in Bloomfield, NE, on Dec. 17, 1894, to Samuel and Lucy Sully. When Gilbert registered for the draft on June 5, 1917, he was living in Greenwood, SD, and working for Thomas Gullickson. Gilbert joined the Army on June 27, 1918, and was assigned to Butchery Co. #343, Quartermaster Corps (ASN 3315338). Pvt. Sully sailed with his unit for Europe aboard the *Regina de Italia* on Sept. 8, 1918. After he returned to the United States, he served with Demobilization Group # 1485, Casual Detachment at Camp Dodge, IA. He was discharged as a Private on Sept. 27, 1919. After returning home, he married Evelyn St. Pierre in Dante. Her brother, Edward, had also served in the Army. They lived near Greenwood. In 1935, the family was interviewed by a worker with the SDERA program. They were living in a three-room home in Ree Township. They had no trees on their land, so Gilbert had to find odd jobs to have money to buy firewood. He usually found work during harvest time, working on threshing crews. In the 1940

U.S. Census, they were farming in Ree Township with their children, Doyle, Gilbert Jr. Lois, Curtis, Ramona, and Mabel. Doyle served in the Army in WWII, Gilbert Jr. served with the Marines, and Curtis enlisted in the Army in 1945. Gilbert entered the spirit world on April 20, 1961, and is buried in the Episcopal Cemetery near Greenwood.[39]

Sully, John C. John, the older brother of Gilbert, was born in Nebraska on April 25, 1893, to John B. Chapman and Lucy Saul. In 1900, he was attending the Santee boarding school. When he registered for the draft on June 5, 1917, he was living in Bloomfield, NE. He married Cora May Quinn on April 12, 1918, in Lake Andes. He joined the Army on Sept. 10, 1918, and served with Co. I, 2nd Infantry (ASN 4822155). He was discharged on Jan. 15, 1919. In 1933, he married Rebecca Selwyn. In 1935, his family was interviewed by a worker with the SDERA program. At that time, they were living in a two-room frame house with their seven children, Edith, Daniel, Jerry, Caroline, Merle, Thelma and Nathan. John was a member of the American Legion and had been receiving disability compensation of around $35 per month. He was still trying to get permanent compensation. His sons, Jerry and Merle, served with the Army in WWII. In 1951, John married Ida Eagle. John entered the spirit world on Aug. 28, 1965, and is buried in the Episcopal Cemetery near Greenwood, SD.[40]

Summers, Julius. Julius was born on the Oneida Reservation near Green Bay, WI, around May 4, 1900, to Nicholas and Sarah Summers. Julius was enrolled in the boarding school at Flandreau. Julius enlisted on April 4, 1917, with Troop D, 1st SD Cavalry. This cavalry unit trained at Flandreau, but was not issued a saddle or a horse. On Sept. 15, 1917, the 1st SD Cavalry was shipped out to Camp Cody at Deming, NM, where Julius trained with the 34th Division. Cpl. Summers was assigned to Co. D, 136th Infantry (ASN 1427511). He sailed with his unit from New York aboard the *Melita* on Oct. 13, 1918. After arriving in France, he was reassigned to Co. L, 49th Infantry. Cpl. Summers sailed for the States from Brest, France, aboard the *George Washington* on Jan. 12, 1919. He was discharged on May 27, 1919. His name was engraved on a plaque erected at Flandreau to honor the WWI veterans. After returning home to Wisconsin, Julius married Susan Metoxen (1897-1973). They had two daughters, Ethel and Aldonna. In the 1934 Oneida Census Roll, the family was living in Milwaukee. The 1937 Milwaukee City Directory, Julius was working as a buffer. Julius later worked as a laborer for a leather manufacturer. He entered the spirit world at Milwaukee's Good Samaritan Medical Center on May 12, 1981. He is buried in Holy Apostles Episcopal Cemetery in Oneida, WI.[41]

Supangi, Joseph Jonah. Joseph was born on the Sisseton-Wahpeton Reservation around April 12, 1896, to Thomas and Louisa Supangi. In the 1902 Census Roll, he is listed with his parents, a brother, Smiley, and a sister, Nancy. When he registered for the draft on June 1, 1917, he was working as a farm laborer. After he joined the Army, he was assigned to Co. D, 24th Machine Gun Battalion, 8th Division (ASN 507216). Bugler Supangi sailed with his unit from Hoboken, NJ, aboard the *Siboney* on Oct. 28, 1918. His unit likely arrived in France shortly before the Armistice. They may have returned home in January. In the 1920 U.S. Census, he was living with his brother, Samuel, in Bossko Township. In the 1925 North Dakota Census, he was living in Ramsey County, ND, with his wife, Seraphine, and a daughter, Angeline. Joseph contracted Tuberculosis and entered the spirit world on Aug. 7, 1926. In the 1927 Devils Lake Census Roll, they had another daughter, Laura. In the 1930 Devils Lake Census Roll, Seraphina is listed as a widow.

Benjamin Wayland Swallow
Ancestry.com

Swallow, Benjamin Wayland. Benjamin was born in Oelrichs, SD, on Feb. 7, 1894, to Eli Swallow and Julia Guerrier. His father's name was spelled 'Soileau." Ben was enrolled at Pine Ridge. In the 1910 U.S. Census, he was a student at Carlisle. He developed skill as a mechanic. When he joined the Army, he was assigned to the Sanitary Detachment, 109th Ammunition Train, 34th Division (ASN 1441165). Pvt Swallow sailed with his unit in September 1918 from Hoboken aboard the *Olympic*. He married Louise Brown around 1921. She had four brothers who served during the war. In the 1930 U.S. Census, Ben was working as a pipefitter in the railroad shops in Chadron. In the 1940 U.S. Census, he was still working for the C & NW RR in Chadron. He and Louise had four children, Wilma, Wildene, Royaldine and Melba. Ben entered the spirit world on Jan. 22, 1992, in Fort Payne, AL. He is buried in Calvary Cemetery in Chadron.

Swallow, Ernest. Ernest was born in Porcupine, SD, around 1890, to John Thunder Bear and Martha Elk Feather. In the 1900 U.S. Census, he was a student at a boarding school in Reno, OK. He became enrolled with the Cheyenne Arapaho. When he registered for the draft on June 5, 1917, he was living in Calumet, OK. On May 17, 1918, he married Mary Spotted Calf in Canadian OK. When he joined the Army, he was assigned to Co. K, 133rd Infantry, 34th Division (ASN 3654391). After training at Camp Cody, NM, most of the 34th Division sailed to Europe in the fall of 1918. Corp. Swallow sailed with his unit aboard the S.S. *Talthybius* from Hoboken. Upon arriving in France, he was inserted as a replacement into Co. H, 308th Infantry, 77th Division. He returned home, sailing from Brest, France, aboard the *America* on April 19, 1919. In an interview with Joseph Dixon, he said, "as a replacement, I was four days too late. After I saw what the men went through, I ached to get into it and take vengeance on the Boche." In the 1920 U.S. Census, he was farming near Calumet, OK. In the 1940 Census, he was working as a carpenter, and his family included his children, George, Victoria, Orie, Elsie and James. He was starting to lose his eyesight. His son, George, served four years in the Army during WWII. James served in the Navy in the late 1950s. Ernest entered the spirit world on Dec. 13, 1967, in California. He is buried in Roosevelt Memorial Park, Gardena, CA.

Swift Hawk, Paul. Paul was born on the Rosebud Reservation on Feb. 24, 1896. In the 1900 U.S. Census, he is listed with his parents, Joseph and Edna, and a brother, Stanislaw. Paul likely enlisted in the South Dakota 4th Infantry in the summer of 1917. When the 4th Infantry was sent to Camp Greene, NC, in the fall of 1917, Pvt. Swift Hawk was reassigned to Co. B, 148th Machine Gun Battalion, 41st Division (ASN 98574). He sailed with his unit from Hoboken, NJ, aboard the *Olympic* on Jan. 11, 1918. After arriving in France, he was reassigned to Co. D, 361st Infantry, 91st Division. The 361st Infantry served in the Campaigns at Aubreville, Meuse-Argonne, and Ypres-Lys, which was in Belgium. After the Armistice, Pvt. Swift Hawk was described as an "excellent soldier" by his commanding officer. In inspections held during the Occupation, Co. D of the 361st was one of the leading rifle companies. Pvt. Swift Hawk returned to the United States from St. Nazaire aboard the U.S.S. *Mexican* on April 15, 1919. He was discharged on April 28, 1919. After returning home, Paul married Susie Lays on his Belly. They farmed in Todd County. In the 1940 U.S. Census, the family of Paul and Susie included Susie's father, Lays on his Belly, as well as their children, Earl, Benjamin,

Jacob, Sarah, Leroy and Beatrice. Paul entered the spirit world on April 18, 1983, and is buried in Spring Creek.[42]

T

Tail, Charles. Charles was born on the Pine Ridge Reservation on Feb. 26, 1900, to Richard Sinte [Tail] and Ruth Long Soldier. In the 1904 Census Roll, he was listed with his parents and siblings, Daniel, Joachim and Minnie. In the 1920 U.S. Census, he was listed as living with his parents, In the 1930 U.S. Census, he was listed as a veteran of the World War. His years of service are not known. Around that time, he married Rosa Ghost Bear. In the 1937 Census Roll, they are shown with three children, Cleveland, Donald and Theodore. Cleveland served in the military during the Korean War. Charles entered the spirit world in the hospital in Pine Ridge on May 10, 1971. He is buried in St. Julia's Episcopal Cemetery in Porcupine.

Taken Alive, Charles. Charles was born on Dec. 12, 1891, near Little Eagle, SD. In the 1898 Census Roll for Standing Rock, he is listed with his parents, Niyakeyuza [Taken Alive] and Wipiwanica [Eats but is Never Full], as well as his brothers and sisters. In the 1900 U.S. Census, his father is listed as a policeman. Charles entered the military with his brother on June 24, 1918, and was stationed at Camp Funston, KS. He served with the 38th Company, 164th Depot Brigade (ASN 3309361). Private Taken Alive received an honorable discharge on August 20, 1918. In the late 1920s, he was living with his wife, Fannie, when he was admitted to the veteran's hospital at Hot Springs. In the 1940 U.S. Census, he was divorced and was working as a laborer in the CCC camp. Charles entered the spirit world on July 7, 1946 and is buried in Little Eagle.

Taken Alive, Jesse. Jesse, a younger brother of Charles, was born November 21, 1895, near Little Eagle. Jesse entered the military on June 24, 1918 and was sent to Camp Funston. After several weeks of training, he was transferred to Camp Dodge, IA. Private Jesse Taken Alive was assigned to Company L, 351st Infantry Regiment (ASN 3309447), as part of the 88th Division. Once training was completed at Camp Dodge, the unit traveled to Philadelphia, PA. Pvt. Taken Alive sailed from Brooklyn aboard the USS *Ulysses* on August 16, 1918, and debarked at Cherbourg, France, on September 6, 1918. After more training, Co. L, with the rest of the 3rd Battalion, was marching to the Front when the Armistice was declared. After the Armistice, the regiment was stationed near Houdelaincourt, France. Pfc. Taken Alive's commanding officer noted that Taken Alive had special fitness for sniping and scouting. Other men from South Dakota who served with Taken Alive were Pvt. Paul Three Stars, Pvt. David Thief and Pfc. Harry Gunhammer. On May 20, 1919, they embarked on the *Mercury* in St. Nazaire, France, and arrived in the U.S. on June 1, 1919. Pfc. Taken Alive was discharged on June 7, 1919. Jesse returned to Little Eagle and married Madeline Brings Horses. In the 1937 Census Roll, they are listed with their children, Jesse Jr., William, Faith, Peter, Milton and Vera. Around 1938, another son, Ralph, was born. Jesse entered the spirit world in the Mobridge Community Hospital on Aug. 10, 1980. He is buried in Elkhorn Congregational Cemetery in Little Eagle. On March 17, 2017, in a ceremony in Wakpala, the family of Pfc. Taken Alive received a Code Talker's Medal to honor his service.[1]

Takes the Shield, Joseph. Joseph was born about Nov. 16, 1889, in Cannon Ball, ND, on the Standing Rock Reservation. In the 1890 Yanktonai Census, he was listed with his parents, Joseph and Angela, and a brother, Albert. When Joseph registered for the draft on June 5, 1917, he lived in Wakpala and was a rancher. Joseph joined the Army on Sept. 27, 1917, and was sent to Camp Funston, KS, for training as part of the 89th Division. He was assigned to Co. B, 314th Battalion, Military Police (ASN 2194489). Pvt. Takes the Shield sailed from New York to Europe aboard the *Saxon* on June 28, 1918. Upon arrival in France, the 314th MP Battalion was billeted in Rimaucourt. They took part in the offensives at St. Mihiel and Meuse-Argonne. Pvt. Takes the Shield was killed in action during the Meuse-Argonne battle on Nov. 1, 1918. He was initially buried in Grave 180, Plot 4, Section 7, #1232, in the Argonne American Cemetery, Romagne-sous-Montfaucon. In January of 1921, his father wrote to Washington to request that his son be buried in a military cemetery in the U.S. His coffin was brought back aboard the transport ship *Cantigny* from Antwerp, Belgium, on July 21, 1921. As a result of his father's request, Pvt. Takes the Shield was buried on Aug. 15, 1921, at Arlington National Cemetery (Section EUR, Site 2789). In a special ceremony on Memorial Day in 1924, President Calvin Coolidge placed flowers on his grave in the presence of his parents. After they returned to Wakpala, they arranged for a feast in honor of their son.[2]

Tall Mandan, Paul. Paul was born at Rosebud on June 7, 1891. In the 1900 U.S. Census, he is listed with his parents, Tall Mandan and Sugar. When Paul registered for the draft on June 5, 1917, he was ranching at White River. He joined the Army on Oct. 22, 1917. He trained with the 89th Division at Camp Funston, KS. He was assigned to Co. E, 314th Ammo Train (ASN 2195161). Pvt. Tall Mandan sailed to Europe from New York aboard the *Cretic* on June 28, 1918. The 314th Ammo Train was stationed at Euvezin. After the Armistice, Pvt. Tall Mandan received an evaluation from his commanding officer, Capt. Theo. White, who wrote that Pvt. Tall Mandan was "a good horseman and prefers artillery. Very good courage, endurance, and good humor. Associates well with men of organization." As part of the Army of Occupation, the 314th Ammo Train was billeted at Zemmer, Germany. Pvt. Tall Mandan sailed from Brest, France, aboard the *Agamemnon* on May 16, 1919, and was discharged on June 4, 1919. After returning home, he married Agnes Pauline Thompson. In the 1937 Census Roll, they were listed with their children, Mary, Lincoln, and Dorothy. In October of 1951, Paul started working for the C & NW Railroad. He entered the spirit world in the VA Hospital in Hot Springs on Dec. 26, 1959, and is buried in St. Ignatius Cemetery, White River.[3]

Tatankamani, George. George was born in Tokio, ND, on the Spirit Lake Reservation on Sept. 1, 1893. The Devils Lake Sioux Census Roll lists him with his father, Tatankamani [Walking Bull], and his wife, Louisa. George is also listed as Itewanbdi [Face of an Eagle]. In 1916, George married Lucy Meade, whose brother, Gabriel, served in the Army. When George registered for the draft on June 4, 1917, he lived in Tokio and worked as a day laborer. He joined the Army on Aug. 18, 1918, at Minnewaukon. He was sent to Camp Custer, MI, and served in the 160th Depot Brigade (ASN 4046253). Private Tatankamani was discharged at Camp Custer on Jan. 11, 1919. In 1920, his wife, Lucy, entered the spirit world. George later married Mabel Keeble from the Sisseton-Wahpeton Reservation. In the later 1920s, George moved to South Dakota. In the Sisseton-Wahpeton Census Rolls, his name is listed as Walking Bull. In the 1940 U.S. Census, George was living in Benson County, ND. He later moved back to South Dakota, living near Browns Valley. George entered the spirit world in rural Sisseton on July 2, 1975, and is buried in St. Peter's Cemetery, Sisseton, SD.[4]

Taylor, Clarence E. Clarence was born in Kearney, NE, on March 20, 1889, to Herbert and Sarah Taylor. When he registered for the draft, he was farming near Carroll, NE. He joined the Army on May 27, 1918, and was assigned to Battery A, 338th Field Artillery, 88th Division (ASN 3228073). He sailed from Brooklyn aboard the *Tras-os-Montes* on Aug. 18, 1918. The artillery units from the 88th Division were sent to Camp de Souge, near Bordeaux, for further training. They did not serve on the front line. They returned to the U.S. in early January 1919. He served briefly with

Casual Detachment No. 40, 163rd Depot Brigade at Camp Dodge, IA. Pfc. Taylor was discharged on Jan. 16, 1919. In the 1920 U.S. Census, he was working in a lumber yard in Gordon. On March 2, 1927, he married Julia Thompson, an Oglala. They farmed near Batesland. In the 1937 Pine Ridge Census Roll, Clarence was listed with his wife and children, but he was not enrolled. They had three children, Sarah, Alta and Merlin. Clarence entered the spirit world on March 15, 1959, and is buried in the Gordon Cemetery.

Tells His Name, George. George was born on the Pine Ridge Reservation on Aug. 4, 1901, to Peter Tells His Name and Nancy Medicine Leaf. He sometimes used the last name of Gap. In the 1907 Census Roll, he was living with his mother and step-father, Kills in Lodge. George joined the Navy during the war. The 1930 U.S. Census, lists him as a veteran of the World War. At that time, he was living with his wife Rosie. He later married Eva Hawkins, and served as a spiritual leader for the Native American Church. He lived in Scottsbluff, NE, when he entered the spirit world in September of 1975. Eva, a son and two daughters survived him.

Thief, Alphonse T. Alphonse was born on the Standing Rock Reservation on Oct. 20, 1887. His parents were Robert Thief and Julia Yellow Fat. In the early census rolls, he was listed as Thomas. When Alphonse registered for the draft on June 5, 1917, he was working as a laborer for the Department of Interior, Martin Kenel School, in Kenel, SD. He joined the Army on July 21, 1918, and was assigned to Field Remount Squadron No. 340, Quartermaster Corps (ASN 3954590). Pvt. Thief sailed from New York aboard the *Orca* on Oct. 27, 1918. He served with Pvt. Jacob Shoots Near. The 340th Remount Squadron was stationed in Merignac, France. Pfc. Thief sailed from Brest, France, for the U.S. aboard the *Pueblo* on July 3, 1919. Pfc. Thief also served with Casual Detachment, 1073 Demobilization Group. He was discharged on July 21, 1919. His brother, Louis, also served in the Army. Alphonse married Agnes White Horse. In 1928, he served as the Child Welfare Officer for the American Legion Post at Kenel. Alphonse entered the spirit world in the Standing Rock Indian Hospital in Fort Yates on Feb. 4, 1951. He is buried in St. Benedict's Cemetery in Kenel.[5]

Thief, David. David was born on the Standing Rock Reservation on May 27, 1896, to Martin Thief and Ida Her Road. In 1912, David was sent to the Carlisle Boarding School. About a year later, his father wrote to the school, saying that neither he nor his wife had given anybody permission to send David to Pennsylvania. While he was at the school, they changed his last name to "Steel." When David registered for the draft on June 5, 1917, he was farming with his father near Bullhead. David joined the Army on June 26, 1918, and was assigned to Co. L, 351st Infantry, 88th Division ASN 3309356). He served with Pfc. Jesse Taken Alive. Pvt. Thief sailed from Brooklyn aboard the *Ulysses* on Aug. 16, 1918. The 351st Infantry served in quiet sectors. After the Armistice, Pfc. Thief's commanding officer wrote that he had "special fitness for sniping and scouting. The 351st served occupational duty in Houdelaincourt, France, until May of 1919. Pfc. Thief sailed for the U.S. from St. Nazaire, France, aboard the *Mercury* on May 20, 1919. Pfc. Thief was discharged on June 7, 1919. After returning home, he married Emma Little Owl, whose brother, Charley, had also served with the Army in France. In the early 1930s, they lived on the Yankton Reservation. In 1935, David married Lucy One Feather. Later that year the family was interviewed by a SD State worker with the SDERA program at their home in Bullhead. They had a one room log house. They obtained their water from a well at Hatch's store. David worked on emergency conservation projects. He played baseball and enjoyed taking part in Indian dances. In the 1937 Census Roll, the family included their children, Clifford, Theresa, Genevieve and Frank. David entered the spirit world at the Standing Rock Indian Hospital in Fort Yates on April 8, 1959. He is buried in the Episcopal Cemetery in Bullhead.[6]

Thief, Louis. Louis was born in Fort Yates on the Standing Rock Reservation on Dec. 12, 1890. His parents were Robert Thief and Julia Yellow Fat. Alphonse was his older brother. As a child, he was often listed as Henry on the Census Rolls. When Louis registered for the draft on June 5, 1917, he was working as a stock farmer for the Dept. of Interior at Kenel. His hand had been injured. He did serve in the Army. In 1928, he was Commander of the Martin Yellow Fat American Legion Post at Kenel. He farmed near Kenel. On April 4, 1954, he married Elizabeth DeCouteau. Louis later moved into the Mobridge Care Center. He entered the spirit world there on April 4, 1984. He is buried in Assumption Catholic Cemetery in Kenel .[7]

Thin Elk, Francis. Francis was born on the Rosebud Reservation around November of 1899. His parents were Henry and Sophia Thin Elk. Francis joined the Army on May 31, 1918, and was assigned to Battery C, 50th Artillery, Coast Artillery Corps (ASN 3072010). Private Thin Elk was sent to Camp Eustis, VA, for training. On Oct. 7, 1918, the 50th Artillery sailed from Newport News. VA, aboard the ship *America.* They trained in Angers, France at the Operation and Training Center. They used British 9.2" Howitzers, but were still in training when the Armistice was signed. The 50th Artillery sailed from Brest, France, aboard the *Seattle* on Feb. 1, 1919, and arrived on Feb. 13. Pvt. Thin Elk was discharged on Feb. 25, 1919. On June 14, 1924, he married Nellie Hungry. He later developed Tuberculosis and entered the spirit world on May 16, 1938. He is buried in Holy Family Cemetery, White River, SD.

Thomson, James. James was born near Wood Mountain, Saskatchewan, on Dec. 23, 1886. His mother was Mary Iha Wastewin Ceta, whose Lakota family moved to Canada after the defeat of the U.S. Cavalry in Montana in June of 1876. Mary was related to Iron Star, a Hunkpapa chief who was one of the last people to return to the United States. James's father was James Harkin Thomson, a local horse rancher who later joined the Royal Canadian Mounted Police. When James registered for the draft on June 5, 1917, he was working as a laborer near Wolf Point, MT. He likely was still in Montana when he joined the Army on Sept. 18, 1917. He listed his wife, Minnie Thomson, as his next of kin. He was assigned to Battery E, 348th Field Artillery, 91st Division (ASN 2272191). Pvt. Thomson trained at Fort Lewis, WA, and sailed with his unit from New York aboard the *Caronia* on May 14, 1918. The 348th F.A. did not serve on the Front. After the Armistice, Pvt. Thomson sailed from Brest aboard the *Aquitania* on March 23, 1919, and was discharged on April 20, 1919. Shortly after this, he moved to the Standing Rock Reservation in Corson County. In the 1930 U.S. Census, he was living with his son, Willie. In 1931, he married Louisa Standing Bear. They ranched near Little Eagle. In 1935 they were interviewed by a worker with the SDERA program. Their home was along the Grand River, about 13 miles west of Little Eagle. They owned 15 horses and four milk cows. Their equipment included two wagons, three sets of harness, a walking plow and a sulky plow, a harrow, a mower, and a rake. They had put up 20 loads of hay and James had been working on public works projects. James came down with pneumonia and entered the spirit world at the VA Hospital in Hot Springs on Nov. 30, 1958. He is buried in Good Shepherd Cemetery in Little Eagle.[8]

Thomson, John Harkin. John was the older brother of James. He was also born near Wood Mountain, around June 24, 1884, to James and Mary Thomson. In 1906, he married Ethel Olivia Howson. They had three children, John Jr., Ida and Fred. When John joined the Canadian Army on April 17, 1916, he had been working as a telegraph operator. Pte. Thomson (Reg. No. 925692) was discharged on Feb. 20, 1918. This likely was a medical discharge. In 1919, John came to South Dakota and lived on the Standing Rock Reservation. On Jan. 31, 1928, he married Jennie Crow Ghost in McIntosh, SD. In the 1936 Standing Rock Census Roll, John and Jennie had three children, Mary Jane, Gerald and Herman. Jennie entered the spirit world in 1938. In the 1945 SD Census, John was living in Bullhead, SD. Sometime after this he moved back to Canada. He last lived in Turner Valley, Alberta. He entered the spirit world on Aug. 20, 1973. He was survived by his children, Ida, John Jr. and Fred. He is buried in Okotoks Cemetery, south of Calgary, Alberta.[9]

Three Stars, Clarence. Clarence is the younger brother of Paul. His parents were Clarence Three Stars Sr. and Jenny DuBray. He was born on the Pine Ridge Reservation on Feb. 7, 1898. Clarence joined the U.S. Navy on Oct. 20, 1920 and was discharged on Oct. 19, 1922. He married Esther Neibaur (1908-1992) on Aug. 14, 1926. In the 1930 U.S. Census, Clarence was working as a laborer in Bennett County. In the 1940 U.S. Census, he was a foreman working on road construction at Pine Ridge. He and Esther had two daughters, Bette and Jennie. Clarence entered the spirit world at Hot Springs on Feb. 21, 1976 and is buried in Hay Springs Cemetery, NE.

Three Stars, Paul. He is listed on WWI veteran's memorial at Oglala Lakota College, Kyle, SD. Paul was born in Allen, SD, on the Pine Ridge Reservation on Oct. 5, 1894. In the 1897 Census Roll, Paul is listed with his father, Clarence Wicarpi Yamni [Three Stars], his mother, Jennie (Dubray), and two sisters, Sophie and Louise. Around 1916, he married Sarah Red Horse (1893-1988). Paul joined the Army on June 26, 1918, and was assigned to Co. L, 351st Infantry, 88th Division (ASN 3315541). The 351st Infantry sailed for Europe on Aug. 16, 1918. The 3rd Battalion of the 351st sailed on the ship *Ulysses*. Pvt. Three Stars served with Jesse Taken Alive, David Thief and Harry Gun Hammer. They were stationed in quiet areas, the Center Sector, in the Alsace Region. After the Armistice, Pvt. Three Stars received an evaluation from his commanding officer, stating that he "demonstrated special fitness for sniping and scouting." On May 20, 1919, the 351st Infantry sailed from St. Nazaire, France aboard the U. S. S. *Mercury*. Pvt. Three Stars also served in Casual Detachment, #658 Demobilization Group. He was discharged on June 7, 1919. Frank Goings, a tribal official, noted that Pvt. Three Stars brought a scalp back home. In the 1940 U.S. Census, Paul was working as an assistant farmer for the Indian Bureau. He and Sarah had four children listed, Louise, Peter, Harry and Alonzo. Paul entered the spirit world on the Hallie Merrill Ranch on Feb. 22, 1960 and is buried in the Inestimable Gift Cemetery in Allen.[10]

Thunder Hawk, Joseph. Joseph was born at Porcupine, SD, on May 17, 1895 on the Pine Ridge Reservation, to Martin Thunder Hawk and Fannie Twiss. In 1910, Joseph was enrolled at the Carlisle boarding school. When he registered for the draft on June 5, 1917, he was working with his father. After Joseph enlisted in the Army, he was assigned to Co. A, 350th Infantry, 88th Division (ASN 3315795). On Aug. 11, 1918, Private Thunder Hawk boarded the H.M.S. *Delta* and sailed to Europe. The 350th Infantry was stationed in eastern France, in the Center Sector. Pvt. Thunder Hawk was designated as a Scout for the 1st Battalion, Intelligence Platoon. After the Armistice, his commanding officer, Capt. Marion Fonville, wrote an evaluation stating that he was "regarded as an unusually good man." Pfc. Thunder Hawk left St. Nazaire, France, aboard the U. S. S. *Aeolus* on May 19, 1919, and docked in Newport News, VA. Thunder Hawk, like most of the American soldiers who served in France, had been exposed to gas during the war. This affected his health after he returned home. He entered the spirit world on Jan. 21, 1921. He is buried in St. Paul's Catholic Cemetery in Porcupine.[11]

Titus, Louis Jugg. Louis was born near Webster, SD, on July 3, 1893, to Susan and Jugg Titus (Ica Dusmani). When Louis registered for the draft on June 4, 1917, he was farming with his father near Eden. Louis enlisted in the Army on July 22, 1918, and was assigned to 74th Balloon Company, Air Service (ASN 3954256), which trained at Camp Crook, NE. He was discharged on May 28, 1919, as a Private 1st Class. On May 11, 1933, he married Mary Ree (1897-1964) at Sisseton. She was the widow of Edward Ree, a fellow veteran. In the 1940 U.S. Census, Louis was working as a laborer for the U.S. Indian Service at Sisseton. When he registered for the Selective Service in 1942, he was working on a WPA project in Sisseton. Louis entered the spirit world as the Indian Hospital in Sisseton on Aug. 5, 1966, and is buried at Buffalo Lake Presbyterian Cemetery.[12]

Touche, Paul Martin. Paul was born on the Crow Creek Reservation on Dec. 28, 1892, to Joseph Touched and Lizzie Willow Bark. When he registered for the draft on June 1, 1917, he was working for the government at Ft. Thompson as an assistant blacksmith. Paul likely joined the SD National Guard in 1917, and was sent to Camp Cody, NM, where he was assigned to Co. 18, Camp Cody June Automatic Replacement Draft (ASN 1429287). Pvt. Touche sailed with this unit from New York aboard the *Honorata* on June 28, 1918. Upon arrival in France, he was assigned as a Wagoner with the Supply Company, 308th Infantry, 77th Division. The 308th Infantry served in the Sectors at Baccarat, Vesle, Oise-Aisne, Forêt-d'Argonne, Meuse-Argonne. After the Armistice, the Supply Co. was billeted at Orges, France. Pvt. Touche sailed from Brest, France, aboard the *America* on April 19, 1919, and arrived on April 28, 1919. On May 29, 1919, he married Clara Grey Cloud. In the 1930 U.S. Census, they were farming near Stephen, SD, with their children, Florence, Francis and Anthony. When Paul registered for the Selective Service in 1942, he was helping build a dam near Ft. Thompson. Sometime in the late 1940s, Paul moved to Ogden, Utah. He entered the spirit world on Oct. 19, 1967, in Salt Lake City, UT. He is buried in Chamberlain, SD.

Trouble in Front, Albert. Albert is listed on WWI veteran's memorial at Oglala Lakota College, Kyle, SD. He was born on the Pine Ridge Reservation about October of 1890. In the 1900 Census Roll, he is listed with his father, Trouble in Front (Tokali Wosica), his mother, Black Owl (Hin Hanspe Win), and a sister, Lucy. When Albert registered for the draft on June 5, 1917, he was living in Allen. He joined the Army on June 16, 1918, and was assigned to Co. A, 309th Ammo Train, 84th Division (ASN 3315811). The 84th Division trained in Camp Taylor, Kentucky, until August of 1918. Pvt. Trouble in Front sailed for England from Quebec aboard the *Takada* on Oct. 14, 1918. The 84th Division was billeted in LeMans upon arrival in France. The soldiers were used as replacements for combat divisions. Pvt. Trouble in Front sailed home from Bordeaux, France, aboard the *Siboney* on Jan. 23, 1919, and was discharged on Feb. 12, 1919. In the late 1920s, he married Emma Horn Chips, who had previously been married to Dallas Fire Place. In the 1932 Census Roll, Albert and Emma were listed with their children, Pansy, Thomas and Rose. Albert became ill with pneumonia and entered the spirit world on Feb. 16, 1936. He is buried in Trinity Chapel, Allen, SD.

Trudell, John B. John, a Santee, was born in Niobrara, NE, on Dec. 10, 1895, to Peter and Lizzie Trudell. Around 1915, he married Nellie Eastman. They had a daughter, Opal. John joined the Army and was assigned to Co. M, 333rd Infantry, 84th Division (ASN 3955177). He sailed with this unit from New York aboard the *Aquitania* on Sept. 2, 1918. After arriving in France, many soldiers from the 84th Division were reassigned to units who had suffered casualties. Pvt. Trudell was reassigned to Co. G, 363rd Infantry, 91st Division. The 363rd Infantry served in the Sectors at Aubreville, Meuse-Argonne and Ypres-Lys. Pvt. Trudell sailed for home from St. Nazaire, France, aboard the *Siboney* on March 22, 1919. In the 1921 Santee Census Roll, John and Nellie are listed with the Yankton Agency. In 1927, he married Lucy Selwyn at Lake Andes, SD. They were both living in Greenwood.

In 1935, they lived in Wagner, SD. John entered the spirit world on May 23, 1969, and is buried at Santee, NE.

Trudell, Levi Henry. Levi, a Santee, was born in Knox County, NE, on Aug. 28, 1891. His parents were Henry and Nancy (Susceatowin) Trudell. Around 1912, Levi married his first wife, Elizabeth, with whom he had a daughter, Ellen. When Levi registered for the draft on June 5, 1917, he was widowed. Levi joined the Army and was assigned to Battery F, 338th Field Artillery (FA) Regiment, 88th Division (ASN 3228587). Pfc. Trudell sailed from Brooklyn aboard the *Tras Os Montes* on Aug. 18, 1918. The 338th FA was stationed in an artillery training post near Bordeaux, and did not serve at the Front. Shortly after the Armistice, they prepared for their return to the States. Pfc. Trudell sailed from France aboard the *Pocohontas* on Dec. 24, 1918, and arrived on Jan. 5, 1919. He was discharged shortly after this. On Dec. 18, 1919, he married Nancy St. Pierre in Bon Homme County. In the 1920 U.S. Census, they were living in Ree Township, near Greenwood. In 1930, the family was living in Wahehe Township, where Levi was working as a farm laborer. In the 1940 U.S. Census, they were farming near Greenwood with their children, Lucy, Mercedes, Raymond, Beulah, Wilmer and Larry. Also living with them was Nancy's daughter by a previous marriage, Lucinda. Lucinda was married to Abraham Gunhammer, who also was a veteran. When Levi registered for the Selective Service in 1942, he was working for Jesse Dubray in Greenwood. Levi entered the spirit world on Sept. 8, 1968, and is buried in Greenwood Episcopal Cemetery.

Trudell, Moses. Moses was born in Santee, NE, on March 12, 1895. His parents were Frank and Maggie Trudell. Moses joined the Army on March 6, 1918, and was assigned to Ambulance Co. 38, 6th Sanitary Train (ASN 976250). Pvt. Trudell sailed from New York aboard the *Darro* on July 7, 1918. He served with Thomas H. Lawrence, who also was from Santee, NE. The 6th Sanitary Train served in the campaigns at Gerardmer and Meuse-Argonne. This unit left Brest, France, aboard the *Kaiserine Auguste Victoria* on June 10, 1919. Pvt. Trudell was discharged on June 25, 1919. In the 1920s, Moses was listed with the Yankton Agency. He married Julia Mato, who was enrolled on the Sisseton-Wahpeton Reservation. Her brother, Samson, had served in the Army. In the 1930 federal census, they lived in Santee, NE. Moses entered the spirit world on Jan. 21, 1976, and is buried in the Congregational Cemetery in Santee.

Turning Bear, David. David was born on the Rosebud Reservation on Jan. 11, 1896, to John and Rose Turning Bear. In the 1912 Census Roll, David was listed with his mother and a sister, Lizzie. When David registered for the draft on June 5, 1917, he was working as a farm laborer at St. Francis. When he joined the Army, he was assigned to Co. E, 351st Infantry, 88th Division (ASN 3315770). Pfc. Joseph Otterman also served in Co. E with Turning Bear. Pvt. Turning Bear sailed with his unit to France aboard the *Scotian* on Aug. 15, 1918. In October of 1918, many men in the 351st Infantry came down with the Spanish Influenza while the unit was stationed near Hericourt. Pvt. Turning Bear entered the spirit world on Oct. 10, 1918. His body was brought back to the U.S. by the *Cantigny*, which sailed from Antwerp, Belgium, Oct. 14, 1921. He was buried in St. Charles Cemetery, St. Francis.

Turning Holy, Frank. Frank was born at Manderson on the Pine Ridge Reservation on April 15, 1889. His parents were Henry Turning Holy and Yellow Bug. Frank married Louisa Hand Soldier in 1907. In the 1915 Census Roll, Frank was living with his wife and their three children, Angelique, Joshua, and Scott. When he registered for the draft on June 5, 1917, he was working as a carpenter in Allen. After he joined the Army, Pvt. Turning Holy was assigned to Co. H, 2nd Infantry, 19th Division, where he served with Pfc. James Two Dog Snow. The 19th Division was formed at Camp

Dodge, IA, after the 88th Division left for service overseas. The unit was demobilized in January of 1919. Frank and Louisa also had a son, Moses. After Louisa entered the spirit world in 1934, Frank married Jennie Little Hoop (1894-1970). When Frank registered with the Selective Service in 1942, he was working with the C.C.C. program. Frank entered the spirit world on April 10, 1969, and is buried in Inestimable Gift Cemetery in Allen.

Twiss, Charles. Charles is listed on WWI veteran's memorial at Oglala Lakota College, Kyle, SD. Charles was born at Manderson on the Pine Ridge Reservation on Jan. 24, 1899. In the 1904 Census Roll, Charles is listed with his parents, William and Lizzie, as well as a sister, Stella, and two brothers, William and Isaac. Charles joined the Army at Jefferson Barracks, MO, on Jan. 28, 1918 (ASN 1335470). Recruit Twiss sailed from Hoboken, NJ, aboard the *Manchuria* on April 30, 1918. He traveled with the Camp Sevier April Replacement Draft Detachment F, Signal Corps, Air Service. He was assigned to the 33rd Aero Squadron, which was a training unit stationed at Issodun Aerodrome in France. After the war, Pvt. Twiss sailed from Pauillac, France, aboard the *Arizonian* on March 18, 1919. Twiss was discharged on April 15, 1919, at Camp Dodge. After the war, he farmed at Buffalo Gap with his wife, Dorothy. He later married Pearl Jones (1902-1982). In the 1940 U.S. Census, Charles and Pearl were farming with their children, Charles Jr, and a stepson Edward Jones. They later ranched near Interior. Charles entered the spirit world on April 18, 1979. He is buried in the Black Hills National Cemetery, Section E, Site 2242. Pearl is buried with him.

James Two Dog Snow
A.B. Welch

Two Dog Snow, James. James was born in North Dakota about March 10, 1878, on the Standing Rock Reservation. In the 1895 Standing Rock Census Roll, he is listed with his parents, White With Snow (Awaska), Chaffer (Baza), as well as his siblings, Quick and Good Woman. James was a student at the Carlisle boarding school from 1902-1906. He learned the carpentry trade and was known as one of the best two-mile runners ever at the school. James married his wife, Elizabeth Walker (1888-1970), in 1908. She was from Crow Creek. In 1910, James was hired as assistant carpenter at the Crow Creek Agency. He joined the Army on Aug. 14, 1918, and was assigned to Co. H, 2nd Infantry, 19th Division (ASN 3776751). He served with Frank Turning Holy. The 19th Division was formed at Camp Dodge, IA, after the 88th Division left for Europe. Pfc. Snow was discharged on Feb. 26, 1919. While he was in the Service, he lost a mare and a colt, and ten acres of corn. After his discharge, he returned to his home on the Crow Creek Reservation. In 1935, the family was interviewed by a worker with the SDERA program. They lived in "Big Ben." Their home was a one-story frame building located about six miles SW of the Agency. They hauled their water from the Ness home about two miles away. Their children living with them were John, Mable and Augusta. They owned a Model T Ford and had a productive garden which furnished much of their food. James has been doing common labor work but would have preferred carpentry work. He was a member of the American Legion. He entered the spirit world in the VA Hospital at Fort Meade on Nov. 19, 1950 and was buried in Fleury Cemetery in Pukwana.[13]

Two Eagle, George. George was born on the Rosebud Reservation on Sept. 15, 1896. His parents were Two Eagle and Good Voice Hawk. When George registered for the draft on June 5, 1918, he was working for the Dixon Cattle Co. near White River. He likely joined shortly after registering. He was discharged as a Private. He married Lillian Leader Charge (1897-1953), whose brother, Paul, had served in the Army. In the 1930 U.S. Census, the family was farming in Todd County. George's parents were living with the family, which included their children, Mable, Colbert and Angeline. Colbert served with the Army during the Korean Conflict. George entered the spirit world on May 3, 1968 and is buried in Sacred Heart Catholic Cemetery in Parmelee.

Two Eagles, John. John is listed on WWI veteran's memorial at Oglala Lakota College, Kyle, SD. John was born on the Pine Ridge Reservation around January 1897. His parents were Two Eagles and Susie Kills in Timber. He had an older brother, Joseph. When John registered for the draft on June 1, 1917, he listed his occupation as showman with Deveaux Shows. John joined the Army on March 2, 1918, and was first assigned to Battery B, 110th Field Artillery, 29th Division (ASN 466359). While serving in the Army, he used the name, John T. Fels. He sailed for Europe from Baltimore aboard the *Keemun* on June 22, 1918. In the spring of 1919, He was temporarily transferred to the Motor Transport Corps. He finally sailed from Brest for the States aboard the U.S.S. *Siboney* on June 27, 1919, arriving on July 5 at Newport News. Musician 3rd Class Fels was discharged on July 13, 1919. His commanding officer wrote that "soldier has a good military record. Has a good character." In the 1920 U.S. Census, John was living in Chadron. In 1929, John was married to Lizzie Whitt, a Cheyenne from Oklahoma. In the 1930s, John traveled as an entertainer with different shows. In the 1937 Pine Ridge Census Roll, he and his wife, Lily, an Aztec, were "somewhere in Japan." In the 1940 U.S. Census, John and his wife, Mary, were listed as entertainers in St. Louis. John entered the spirit world on July 19, 1966, and is buried in the Black Hills National Cemetery, Section E, Site 1484. Mary (1909-1984) is buried with him.[14]

Two Eagles, Joseph. Joseph is listed on WWI veteran's memorial at Oglala Lakota College, Kyle, SD. Joseph was born on the Pine Ridge Reservation around 1894. His parents were Two Eagles and Susie Kills in Timber. John was his younger brother. Joseph was enrolled at the Flandreau boarding school. While a student there, he enlisted in Troop D, SD 1st Cavalry on April 4, 1917. This National Guard unit trained in South Dakota, but never was issued any horses or saddles. When they were sent to Camp Cody, NM, most of the men were reassigned to units in the 34th Division. Pvt. Two Eagles sailed from Brooklyn aboard the S.S. *Tereisias* on June 28, 1918. He was assigned to Co. 15, Camp Cody June Automatic Replacement Draft (ASN 1427521). After arriving in France, he was reassigned to the Headquarters Co., 123rd Field Artillery, 33rd Division. He served as a Musician 3rd Class with the Regiment. The 123rd FA served in the Sectors at Lucey, St. Mihiel, and Meuse-Argonne. In mid-October of 1918, the 123rd FA was sent to the rear to be motorized. Mus. 3rd Cl. Two Eagles sailed from Brest, France, aboard the *America* on May 16, 1919. He was discharged at Camp Grant, IL, on June 8, 1919. After the war, his name was engraved on a plaque honoring the war veterans at the Flandreau boarding school. After returning home, Joseph married a woman from the Yankton Reservation. They had a daughter, Lucille. In the 1930 U.S. Census, Joseph and his daughter were living with his mother. He was employed as a catechist for the local church. Joseph developed pneumonia and entered the spirit world at the Pine Ridge Hospital on March 25, 1938. He was buried in the Presbyterian Cemetery in Pine Ridge.[15]

Two Teeth, Cecil. Cecil was born on the Rosebud Reservation on Nov. 5, 1894. In the 1900 U.S. Census, he was listed with his parents, Two Teeth and Flying, as well as a sister, Susie. When Cecil registered for the draft on June 7, 1917, he lived in Wososo and helped his father on his allotment. He joined the Army on Aug. 26, 1918, and was sent to Camp Funston, KS. He served with Battery E, 29th Field Artillery, 10th Division (ASN 4265925). This Division was formed at Camp Funston after the 89th Division had left to serve in France. Cecil was discharged as a Private on Jan. 24,

1919. The 10th Division was demobilized in February of 1919. Upon returning home, Cecil married Mary White Thunder, with whom he had a daughter, Charlotte. They farmed in Todd County. Cecil suffered from Tuberculosis and entered the spirit world in the PHS Indian Hospital in Rosebud on Oct. 10, 1966, and is buried in Ironwood Cemetery in Todd County.[16]

U

Useful Heart, Peter. Peter was born at On the Tree camp on the Cheyenne River Reservation around Dec. 31, 1889. His parents were Rufus Useful Heart and Olive Sits Down. Peter married Lucy Horn in 1915. They had a daughter, Melda. Peter served six months in the Army, most likely at Camp Funston. He possibly was in the 20th Infantry. While at Camp, he contracted Trachoma and spent some time in the base hospital. He was discharged on Feb. 8, 1919. His first wife, Lucy, entered the spirit world in March 1919. In 1921, he married Lucy Egna. She entered the spirit world in 1932. In 1935, the family was interviewed by a worker with the SDERA program. Peter was living with his children, Melda, Levi, Rufus and Grace Marie in the Sans Arc Precinct. They had a one room log cabin that was 16' x 23.' Their water was hauled from a dam two miles away. Peter was working on relief projects, as well as for Sam Charger. He later worked for the V-E Ranch east of LaPlant. Around 1972, he moved into the Veteran's Home in Hot Springs, where he entered the spirit world on Jan. 9, 1976. His daughters, Melda and Grace, survived him. He is buried in LaPlant Cemetery.[1]

V

Vandall, Forrest M. Forrest was born in Greenwwod, SD, to Edward Vandall and Mary White Crow on April 15, 1894. His mother was Seneca. In the 1895 Yankton Census Roll, he was listed with his father and mother, who was from Oklahoma. In the 1910 U.S. Census, Forrest lived at White Swan. When he registered for the draft, he was working as a clerk in Sioux City. He enlisted in Sioux City on July 28, 1918, and was assigned to Co. B, 212th Engineers, 12th Division (ASN 3010216). Pfc. Vandall was discharged at Camp Dodge on Feb. 8, 1919. On Oct. 11, 1923, he married Felice Smith in Sioux City. She was a sister to Alfred Smith, a fellow veteran. In the 1930 U.S. Census, Forrest was living in Milwaukee. He entered the spirit world on June 16, 1935, and is buried in Wood National Cemetery, Milwaukee.

Veo, Louis. See **Makes Life, Ernest**.

Vermillion, Arthur. Arthur was born in Pollock, SD, near the Standing Rock Reservation on Aug. 6, 1889. His parents were Winfield and Mary Vermillion. When Arthur registered for the draft on June 5, 1917, he was living in McLaughlin. He joined the Army on June 24, 1918, and was sent to Camp Funston, KS. He was assigned to Co. H, 69th Infantry, 10th Division (ASN 3309427). The 10th Division did not serve in Europe. Pvt. Vermilion was discharged on Jan. 29, 1919. Arthur's sister, Annie, married George Molash, a fellow veteran. In the 1930 U.S Census, Arthur was working as a laborer for the City of McLaughlin. Arthur entered the spirit world on March 22, 1937, and is buried in St. Benedict's Cemetery, Kenel.[1]

Village Center, Joseph. Joseph was born near the mouth of Oak Creek on the Standing Rock Reservation on July 12, 1889. He belonged to the Bullhead Band of Hunkpapa. His parents were Village Center and Hawk Eagle (Cetanwanbliwin). Joseph joined the Army on June 24, 1918, and was sent to Camp Funston. He was discharged on March 1, 1919. On Jan. 18, 1921, he married Agnes Looking Elk. In 1935, the family was interviewed by a worker with the SDERA program. Their permanent home was a log cabin along the Grand River, in the Bullhead District. Their water was obtained by digging a hole in the river bed of the Grand. For the summer, they had been living in a tent in the Little Eagle Precinct, where Joseph was the foreman of a crew on a public works project. Their children living with them were Dorothy, Vincent, Alec, Floyd, Michael, and Mary. Floyd served in the Army during WWII, while Michael served during the Korean Conflict. Joseph entered the spirit world at the Hospital in Fort Yates on May 14, 1976. He is buried in St. Aloysius Cemetery in Bullhead.[2]

W

Wabashaw, William H. William, known as "Boots," was born on the Santee Reservation in Nebraska on May 11, 1893. His parents were Joseph White and Elizabeth Isabella Wakanna. About a month after his birth, his mother married William Wabashaw Sr. He was adopted by his step father, but in some records, he was still listed as William White. His occupation was listed as painter and decorator. He joined the Army and was assigned to Co. F, 355th Infantry, 89th Division (ASN 2194513). Bugler Wabashaw sailed from New York aboard the *Baltic* on June 4, 1918. Upon arrival in France, the 355th Infantry was billeted in the towns of Grand, Brechainville, and Allianville. The regiment served in the Sectors at Lucey, St. Mihiel, Euvezin and Meuse-Argonne. After the Armistice, Bugler Wabashaw received an evaluation from his commanding officer, Capt. Neville Fisher. He said Wabashaw showed "good courage, endurance, humor, keenness of senses and dexterity, good judgement and initiative, good ability to utilize mechanical methods and is very good as night worker, runner, observer and verbal reporter." As part of the Army of Occupation, the 355th Regiment was billeted in Saarburg, Germany. They returned from France aboard the ship *Leviathan* on May 15, 1919, docking in Hoboken, NJ, on May 22. In the 1920 U.S Census, William was working as a house painter in Pine Ridge. He was living with his wife, Dora, and step daughters, Katherine and Victoria Picotte. In 1921, William was listed as a member of the Chauncey Eagle Horn American Legion Post in Rosebud. A few years later he married Eugenia Abraham (1899-1984). They had two daughters, Frances and Irene. When William registered with the Selective Service Program in 1942, he was working for the C.C.C. in Niobrara, NE. He entered the spirit world on April 7, 1966, and is buried in Santee Catholic Cemetery.[1]

Alexander Wakeman
Mona Miyasato

Wakeman, Alexander. Alexander was born at Flandreau on May 11, 1895, to Peter Thompson (Hepidan) and Judith Wakeman (Tatiyohnakemazawin). He was raised by his grandmother, Mary St.

Cloud. In 1915, he enrolled himself at the Carlisle boarding school. While a student, he purchased a baritone saxophone to take on an outing. While a student, he enlisted in the USMC on July 5, 1918. He served as a Corporal in the 13th Regiment Band (Serv. # 133048). While overseas, he played with the band at the Inter-allied games in Pershing Stadium in Paris. Cpl. Wakeman sailed from Brest, France, aboard the U.S.S. *Siboney* on July 31, 1919, and was discharged on Aug. 13, 1919. After returning home, he married Carrie Allen in 1922. They had a son, Keith. In 1929, Alexander married Elsie Heldt (1901-1986). They lived in Sioux Falls for a number of years, where Alex worked as a tailor for Louis Bogdon. Alex was a member of the Sioux Falls municipal band. In 1940, Alex and Elsie moved back to Flandreau, where they had a truck garden and raised chickens. They also formed an orchestra named Al's Aces. Alex was a member of the Moody VFW Post 3351, and served as president of District 2. His son, Keith, served with the U.S.M.C. during WWII and the Korean Conflict. Alex entered the spirit world on May 21, 1962, and is buried in Rosehill Cemetery in Wentworth, SD.[2]

Wakin, Henry George. George was born on the Sisseton-Wahpeton Reservation on July 16, 1894. His parents were Peter and Melvina Wasin. In most of the Census Rolls, he was listed as George Wanna or George Wasin. He joined the Army on May 25, 1918, and was assigned to the 89th Spruce Squadron, Air Service (ASN 2787461). This unit was formed at Vancouver Barracks, and then transferred to Waldport, OR, where they worked on railroad construction and dams to control and divert local creeks. The 89th Spruce Squadron was demobilized at Vancouver Barracks.

Charles Walking Bull
A. B. Welch

Pvt. Wakin was discharged on Jan. 10, 1919. In the 1927 Census Roll, Henry George Wakin was listed with his wife, Anna Roberts Two Bears, and a stepson, Henry Two Bears. When George registered for the Selective Service in 1942, he was living in Veblen. In the early 1950s, he moved to Minneapolis, MN. He entered the spirit world in his home in Minneapolis on July 27, 1953, and is buried in St. Matthews Cemetery, Veblen, SD.[3]

Walking Bull, Charles. Charles was born on the Rosebud Reservation about March 5, 1892. His parents were Walking Bull and Bear Killed Her. In the 1917 Census Roll, Charles and his wife, Maggie, had three children, Florence, Louis and Wallace. When he registered for the draft on June 5, 1917, he and Maggie had three children. Charles joined the Army on Sept. 21, 1917, and trained at Camp Funston, KS, with Co. A, 340th Machine Gun (MG) Battalion, 89th Division (ASN 2192804). On April 30, 1918, Pvt. Walking Bull sailed from Hoboken, NJ, on the *Kroonland*. He was attached to Casual Detachment 3rd Division. A document prepared on May 10, 1918, while the ship was still at sea, listed Pvt. Walking Bull with the 9th MG Battalion. On May 30, 1918, the Battalion was rushed to the Chateau-Thierry Sector. They also served in Sectors at Aisne-Marne, Vesle, St. Mihiel and Meuse-Argonne. Pvt. Walking Bull likely was wounded or gassed. He sailed home aboard the *Princess Motoika* from St. Nazaire on Jan. 30, 1919. He was traveling with St. Aignan Casual Company No. 378, GSD, A.P.O. 712. The Army had a large hospital in St. Aignan. The rest of the 9th MG Battalion did not return home until the summer of 1919. Walking Bull also served in Casual Co. 72, 163rd Depot Brigade, at Camp Dodge. Pvt. Walking Bull was discharged on

Feb. 22, 1919. Charles later married Edna Weasel. In the 1937 Census Roll, they had three children, Florence, Allen and Gilbert, living with them. When Charles registered for the Selective Service in 1942, he was working in Rapid City. In 1943, he was working as a sectional laborer for the C & NW RR. As Charles got older, he needed crutches to get around on. On March 15, 1963, he started hitchhiking to Wanblee from Kadoka. On March 16, a snowstorm hit that part of South Dakota. Rapid City received over 14 inches of snow. Charles was believed to have died of exposure. His body was found east of Wanblee on March 17. He is buried in the Episcopal Cemetery in Wanblee. His son, Gilbert, was the author of several books about Lakota culture.

Walking Crow, Otto. Otto was born at St. Francis on the Rosebud Reservation on Jan. 2, 1893. In the 1900 U.S. Census, Otto was listed with his parents, Walking Crow and Holy Hand. He married Josephine Mary Stone. When he registered for the draft On June 5, 1917, he and his wife had two children. Otto served in the military during the Great War. In the 1930 U.S. Census, Otto was working at odd jobs in Todd County. Living with him and Jennie were their children, Bernard, Esther, Virginia, Stanley, Agnes, and his mother, Holy Hand. In the 1940 U.S. Census, Otto was the proprietor of a saw mill in Todd County. He entered the spirit world in the home of Alex One Star on March 30, 1970 and is buried in Soldier Creek Cemetery.[4]

Walking Eagle, James. James was born at St. Francis on the Rosebud Reservation on Aug. 26, 1896. In the 1900 U.S Census, he is listed with his parents, Thomas and Mary (On the Ground), and a sister, Julia. When James registered for the draft on June 5, 1917, he was working as a barber. He joined the Army and was assigned to the 20th Infantry, 10th Division at Camp Funston, KS. He was discharged as a Private. In the 1920 U.S. Census, James was a patient in U.S. Army General Hospital No. 21, near Denver. James married Susie Bear. James suffered from Tuberculosis and entered the spirit world in Todd County on March 26, 1923 and is buried in Spring Creek. His daughter, Viola, was born after his death.[5]

Walking Shield, Eugene. Eugene was born at Wakpala on the Standing Rock Reservation on July 13, 1896. His parents were William (Wahacankamani) and Lizzie Walking Shield. When he registered for the draft on June 5, 1917, he was working with his father. On April 26, 1918, he was sent to Camp Funston, KS. He served in Co. G, 355th Infantry, 89th Division (ASN 2845221), which left for Europe aboard the *Baltic* on June 4, 1918. Pvt. Walking Shield became ill and entered the spirit world in France on Nov. 29, 1918. His body was returned to the United States aboard the *Wheaton,* which sailed from Cherbourg, France, on May 1, 1921. After the war, Eugene's name was engraved on a tall monument erected in the St. Elizabeth Mission Cemetery at Wakpala. On March 17, 2017, in a ceremony in Wakpala, the family of Pvt. Walking Shield received a Code Talker's Medal to honor his service.

Walking Shield, George. George was the younger brother to Eugene. He was born around 1901. As a young man, he attended the boarding school in Flandreau. George joined the Army during the war. After the war, his name was engraved on a monument honoring the war veterans at the Flandreau boarding school. In the 1930 U.S. Census, George was serving with Co. G, 3rd Infantry at Fort Snelling. In the 1937 Census Roll, George was single. He entered the spirit world at the Standing Rock Hospital in Fort Yates on July 30, 1945 and is buried in Wakpala.[6]

Waloka, Frank. See **Bear Looks Running, Frank**.

Wanna, George. See **Wakin, Henry George**.

Warren, James Benjamin. James was born on Aug. 9, 1895, on the White Earth Reservation to Alfred and Saddie Warren. He received an allotment in the E1/2, NW ¼, Sec. 24, T.143, R. 41, in Lake Grove Township. Mahnomen County. When his father entered the spirit world in 1900, his mother moved to Huron, SD. She married Delbert Root, who owned a photo studio. When James registered for the draft on June 5, 1917, his home was in Huron, but he had already enrolled in ROTC at Fort Snelling. His enlistment dates from Aug. 15, 1917. He was sent to Camp Dodge, IA, as a newly trained 2nd Lieutenant, assigned to Co. C, 350th Infantry, 88th Division. 2nd Lt. Warren sailed with his regiment from Brooklyn aboard the *Delta* on Aug. 11, 1918. Upon arriving in France, the 350th Infantry underwent further training and marched to a number of locations. In early November, they were scheduled to move to the Front to support the 28th Division. However, the signing of the Armistice came suddenly, on Nov. 11. The regiment then became part of the Occupational Army. 1st Lt. Warren sailed with his unit from St. Nazaire aboard the *Aeolus* on May 19, 1919. He was discharged on June 23, 1919. In the 1920 U.S. Census, he lived with his mother and step-father in Huron. Sometime after this he moved to Minneapolis, where he married Luella Gruetzmacher. In 1930, James was working in Minneapolis as a salesman for Remington Cash Register Co. When he registered for the "Old-man's Draft" in 1942, he was working for Dayton's. After he retired, he moved to California. He entered the spirit world on July 27, 1982, and is buried in Greenwood Memorial Park, San Diego.

Warrior, James. James was born on the Cheyenne River Reservation in May of 1895. In the 1897 Census Roll, he is listed with his parents, Joseph Warrior and Nellie Many Horses, and a sister, Alice. When James registered for the draft on June 5, 1917, he was living in White Horse. James Warrior's name was included in a list of veterans prepared by Henry Fielder after the war. On Sept. 21, 1920, James married Esther Kills at Night. James was a known for his artwork. A number of his drawings are on display at the museum in Timber Lake. He also was a fancy trick rider with the 101 Circus. James entered the spirit world following a vehicle accident in White Horse on May 9, 1941. He is buried in the Episcopal Cemetery in White Horse.[7]

Weasel, Oscar J. Oscar, also known as Oscar White Weasel, was born at Cherry Creek on the Cheyenne River Reservation on Feb. 22, 1898, to Charles and Louise Weasel. He attended school in Cherry Creek and Rapid City. While in Rapid City, he enlisted in Co. I, 4th SD Infantry on March 28, 1917. On Sept. 28, 1917, this National Guard unit took the train to Camp Greene, NC. Many of the soldiers of Co. I, including Pvt. Weasel (ASN 112167), were transferred to the 148th Machine Gun Battalion, 41st Division. They sailed to Europe aboard the *Olympic* on Jan. 11, 1918. Upon arriving in France, Pvt. Weasel was once again transferred, this time, to Co. C, 151st Machine Gun Battalion, 42nd Division. The 151st MG Battalion served in the Sectors at Luneville, Baccarat, Esperance-Souain, Champagne-Marne, Aisne-Marne, St. Mihiel, Essey-Pannes, Meuse-Argonne. The 42nd Division suffered 13,919 casualties. After the Armistice, Pfc. Weasel's commanding officer, Capt. E.F. Travis, wrote of Weasel, "this Indian is a good soldier." Pvt. Weasel sailed from Brest aboard the *Minnesota* on April 15, 1919 and was discharged on May 12, 1919. On Nov. 4, 1920, Oscar reenlisted in the Army, and was discharged on Feb. 29, 1924. On Oct. 18, 1924, he married Esther Ward (1903-1967) at Cherry Creek. He worked as a foreman in road building between Cherry Creek and Red Scaffold and on Rattlesnake Dam. In 1935, the family was interviewed by a worker with the SDERA program. They were living in a one room house in Cherry Creek so their children could go to school. Their children were Marjorie, Beatrice and Lewis. Oscar was a member of the VFW and the American Legion. He mentioned that he had had some health problems while in the Army, and had been in a hospital in Panama Canal and Walter Reed in Washington, D.C. He had learned motor mechanics while in the Army and felt proficient in that line of work. Oscar later moved to Sturgis and worked in nursing service at Fort Meade for 11 years. After his wife entered the spirit world, Oscar moved to a retirement home in Dupree. He was a member of World War I Barracks No. 3028, in Sturgis. He entered the spirit world at Fort Meade Medical Center on Feb. 12, 1979. His children, Beatrice, Corrine, Margie, Lewis and Timothy, survived him. Lewis served in the Army in the 1950s, while Timothy served in Vietnam. Oscar is buried in the Black Hills National Cemetery, Section C, plot 455.[8]

James Weasel Bear
Ancestry.com

Weasel Bear, James. James was born in September 1890 near Bullhead, SD, on the Standing Rock Reservation. He was the son of Leo and Apollonia Weasel Bear. Leo was known as a warrior in his younger days, and in the 1870s, was chosen to cut the Sun Dance poles. He was also proud of his vegetable gardens, and often won prizes at the Standing Rock Fairs. As a youth, James played baseball for the Fort Yates team. When he registered for the draft on June 5, 1917, he was working with his father. He married Josephine Bullhead on Dec. 20, 1917. James traveled to Camp Funston, Kansas, on June 24, 1918. James and Josephine had three daughters, but two of them did not survive childhood. In the 1930 U.S. Census, James was a patient at the Veterans Hospital in St Cloud, MN. In 1935, the family was interviewed by a worker with the SDERA program. They lived near Bullhead in a one room home that was 16 feet X 20 feet. They had a well about 350' from their home. In the winter they used to water their livestock from the well if the river was frozen. However, they had to sell their livestock recently to pay the medical bills of the sick daughters. Their daughter, Maxine, lived with them. James was receiving a disability payment of $45 per month and had also been a patient in the VA Hospital in Fort Harrison, Montana. Josephine was a 4-H leader and had won blue ribbons for her canning exhibits at local fairs. James entered the spirit world in Bullhead on March 27, 1944. He is buried in Blackhorse, SD. His widow, Josephine (1899-1952), later married Johnson Bagola, a fellow veteran.[9]

Wells, Alfred H. Alfred was born at Fort Thompson on the Crow Creek Reservation on Nov. 14, 1895. His parents were William Wallace Wells and Emma Johnson. In the 1899 Crow Creek Census Roll, Alfred is listed with his father and his brothers, Willie, George, and Louis. Their father (Yanktonai) had served as a scout with the Army under General Crook. When Alfred registered for the draft on June 5, 1917, he was working as a farm hand near Vega. He joined the Army on June 24, 1918, and was assigned to the 275th Military Police Company (ASN 3309997). The 275th MP Co. did serve in France. Pfc Wells sailed from St. Nazaire aboard the *Koningin Der Nederlanden* on May 21, 1919, docking in Newport News, VA. He was discharged on June 15, 1919. He married Lenora Piskule. In the 1940 U.S. Census, Alfred and Lenora lived at Fort Thompson with their son, James. Alfred was working as an auto mechanic. Alfred entered the spirit world on Oct. 24, 1949, and is buried in Pukwana.[10]

Wells, Mark Aaron. Mark was born on the Pine Ridge Reservation on June 20, 1894, to Philip and Mary Wells. When he registered for the draft on June 5, 1917, he was farming with hid dad near Kadoka. He enlisted in the Army on Nov. 9, 1917, and was discharged on March 26, 1919. In the 1930 Federal Census, he was ranching with his dad. When he registered for the Selective Service in 1942, he was living in Lewiston, MT. Sometime later he moved to the Coos Bay, OR, where he worked for ranchers. He entered the spirit world on Feb. 27, 1981, and is buried in Coos Bay.

Westman, George. George was born on the Flandreau Reservation on July 4, 1900, to Benjamin Westman and Josephine Jones. He enlisted in the Nebraska National Guard on July 7, 1917, and was sent to Camp Cody, NM, where he trained with the 34th Division. Pfc. Westman sailed with Pvt. John Flood aboard the *Olympic* on Sept. 2, 1918. After arriving in France, he was reassigned to Co. D, 49th Infantry (ASN 1441629). Pvt. Westman was discharged on May 28, 1919. In the 1930 U.S. Census, he was living with John and Betty Redwing in Sioux Falls and working as a knife man for John Morrell & Co. In the 1930s, he married Nellie Trygstad (1905-1958). He was still working for John Morrell. He entered the spirit world in McKennan Hospital in Sioux Falls on Feb. 23, 1956, and is buried in 1st Presbyterian Cemetery, Flandreau.[11]

Whalen, Richard. Richard was born on the Pine Ridge Reservation on June 15, 1891. His parents were John Whalen and Jennie McCloskey. In the 1893 Census Roll, Richard was listed with his mother and his brother, James, and his sisters, Rosa, Julia, Nellie, Jennie and Mary. Around 1911, he married his first wife, Sophie. When Richard registered for the draft on June 5, 1917, he and Sophie had three children, Thelma, Richard Jr., and Lavina. Richard was working for C & NW Railroad as a round house laborer in Chadron, NE. He served in the military during the war. On Jan. 19, 1927, Richard married Emma Rae Henry (HO-Chunk). Emma had a brother, Sam Thundercloud, who had served in the 32nd Division during the war. In the 1940 U.S. Census, Richard had been working as the postmaster in Pine Ridge. He later owned a café. He entered the spirit world in the VA Hospital in Hot Springs on March 3, 1966. He is buried in Holy Cross Cemetery in Pine Ridge.[12]

John Whirlwind Horse
Mathers Museum

Whirlwind Horse, John. John is listed on the WWI veteran's memorial at Oglala Lakota College, Kyle, SD. John was born on the Pine Ridge Reservation on Nov. 15, 1892, to Whirlwind Horse and his wife, Ada. In the 1898 Census Roll, John was living with his grandparents, American Bear and Isabel. When John registered for the draft on June 5, 1917, he was farming with his father near Allen. John joined the Army and was assigned to the 160th Infantry, 40th Division, which was used for replacements (ASN 3129689). Pvt. Whirlwind Horse sailed from New York aboard the *Ortega* on Aug. 31, 1918, traveling with "mixed casuals Co. #362." Other soldiers traveling with him were Paul Stone, George Salvis, Stacy Salvis and Steven Foote. Many of these soldiers from the 40th Division were assigned to fighting units a few days before the start of the Meuse-Argonne Offensive. Pvt. Whirlwind Horse was transferred to Co. C, 357th Infantry, 90th Division. The 357th Infantry served in the Sectors at Villers-en-Haye, St. Mihiel, Puvenelle and Meuse-Argonne. Pvt. Whirlwind Horse was wounded in the right shoulder during the Meuse-Argonne Battle. He sailed from Bordeaux aboard the U.S.S. *Mercy* on Feb. 27, 1919. His fellow soldiers were identified as "sick and wounded in hospital." Convalescent Casual Detachment #158, from Base Hospital No. 208, Bordeaux, arrived in the U.S. on March 12. Pvt. Whirlwind Horse was photographed by Joseph Dixon in the Debarkation Hospital in New York on March 21, 1919. On March 30, Dixon interviewed Pvt. Whirlwind Horse, who related, "I was on the front line. I was then in Co. C, 357th Inf., 90th Div. I was fighting as hard as I could fight. I knew they would get me unless I got them, and so I was shooting away as I could all the time. The Germans kept shooting until we got up and then again gave up and ran. They feared the bayonet." After the war, John wrote about his experiences.

> I met Dr. J. K. Dixon in New York and told him of what little experience I had in the war.

> For what short time I was on the front, I figured that I have done enough damage to the Germans for two ordinary men, as I have handled all kinds of small fire-arms ever since I was strong enough to lift them.

> I can only say that I have done the best I could until I got wounded, as that was what I was called for.

After returning home, John married Mollie Six Feathers. In the 1930 U.S. Census, John was working as a salesman in a general store. In the 1940 U.S. Census, John and Mollie had three children, Raymond, Verna and Russell. John also ranched. The family lived east of Allen. John entered the spirit world in St. Anthony's Hospital in Martin on Sept. 7, 1969, and is buried in St. John's Cemetery, Allen, SD.[13]

Whistler, Charles N. Charles was born on the Pine Ridge Reservation on May 12, 1895. In the 1897 Census Roll, he is listed with his parents, Julian Whistler (Yasle) and Her Door (Tatiyopa), as well as a brother, Newman, and a sister, Sarah. Charles had attended school at Haskell. When he registered for the draft on June 5, 1917, he was living in Bullhead, SD. He joined the Army at Camp Dodge, IA, on July 22, 1918. Pvt. Whistler was discharged on April 7, 1919. On Aug. 16, 1919, he married Mary Little Chief at Kadoka. She was from the Rosebud Reservation. In 1935, the family was interviewed by a worker with the SDERA program. Charles and Mary were living in a log cabin located northwest of Norris. They owned a team of horses and a wagon. They hauled their water about 1.5 miles from a nearby creek. They had four children, Lena, Minnie, William Jr. and Elta. Charles had worked on some relief projects building roads and dams. After Mary passed away in 1945, Charles married Eunice Crazy Bear on Jan. 16, 1946. He was a member of the Wanblee American Legion Post. Charles entered the spirit world on Sept. 12, 1977. His widow and three daughters, Lena, Minnie and Lana, a son, Charles, and two step daughters, Bernice and Florence, survived him. He is buried in the Black Hills National Cemetery, Section E, site 2025. Military rites were performed by the Legion Post No. 240 from Martin and Post No. 289 from Wanblee. Eunice, who passed away about three months later, is buried with him.[14]

White, Abel. Abel was born on the Standing Rock Reservation on Feb. 18, 1897. In the 1900 U.S. Census, his parents are listed as Benedict Skala [White] and Rose Wanbliipiwin [Full Eagle Woman]. In the 1905 Census Roll, Abel and his younger brother, George, are listed with their mother, who later married Pius Shoots First. Abel attended school in Flandreau. Abel likely enlisted in Troop D, 1st SD cavalry at Flandreau in the spring of 1917. This National Guard unit was never issued horses or saddles before going to Camp Cody, NM, in September of 1917. Upon arrival in Deming, NM, the soldiers were reassigned to other units, many to the 34th Division. Records from the Flandreau School note that he was given a medical discharge due to eye trouble on Oct. 16, 1917. He became a member of the Martin Yellow Fat Legion Post at Kenel. Abel was a good athlete, and enjoyed taking part in foot races and playing baseball for the Kenel team. At the Standing Rock Fair in 1921, he took 1st place in the ½ mile run, and 2nd place in the 220-yard dash. On Dec. 2, 1930, he married

Elizabeth Red Bear, the widow of fellow veteran, Charles Red Bear. Abel entered the spirit world at the McLaughlin Hospital on March 13, 1968. He is buried in St Thomas Cemetery in Kenel.[15]

White, George. George was the younger brother of Abel. He was born on the Standing Rock Reservation around January of 1900 to Benedict and Rose White. George enlisted in the Army on April 13, 1918, at Jefferson Barracks. He was attached to the 23rd Recruit Company, General Infantry (ASN 465344). He was discharged at Jefferson Barracks on June 16, 1918, with 100% disability. The Army felt he was too ill to travel home by himself, so they assigned Pvt. L.P. Boyd to accompany Pvt. White back to Fort Yates. George had developed pneumonia, which turned into tuberculosis. George entered the spirit world on April 9, 1919, and is buried in St. Benedict's Cemetery in Kenel, SD.[16]

White, Jonah. Jonah was born on the Sisseton-Wahpeton Reservation on June 8, 1899. His mother was Hannah White. Jonah joined the Army while attending school at the Flandreau boarding school. He was first assigned to the 18th Company, 163rd Depot Brigade in Camp Dodge, IA. He was transferred to Jefferson Barracks, MO. While there, he came down with pneumonia. Pvt. White entered the spirit world in the base hospital on April 25, 1918. He is buried in St. James' Cemetery next to Enemy Swim Lake. His name is engraved on a plaque honoring war veterans that was erected at the Flandreau School after the war.[17]

White Bear, Samuel. Samuel is listed on WWI veteran's memorial at Oglala Lakota College, Kyle, SD. He was born in Oglala on the Pine Ridge Reservation on Nov. 15, 1891. In the 1898 Census Roll, he is listed with his parents, White Bear and Day, as well as a brother, Frank. Samuel likely enlisted in a SD National Guard unit in 1917. The 1st SD Cavalry was sent to Camp Cody, NM, in September of 1917. Samuel entered the spirit world at Camp Cody in Deming, NM, on March 28, 1918. He is buried in St. Peter's Episcopal Cemetery, Oglala, SD. The Sam White Bear Legion Post No. 251 in Pine Ridge was named in his honor.

White Bird, Henry. Henry was born in Bullhead on the Standing Rock Reservation around May 13, 1896. His parents were Joseph and Augusta White Bird. Henry joined the Army on July 21, 1918, and was assigned to the 41st Company, 163rd Depot Brigade, at Camp Dodge, IA. Pvt. White Bird was discharged at Camp Cody, NM, on Dec. 10, 1918. On Feb. 1, 1928, he married Bessie Brave Thunder in McIntosh, SD. They did not have any children. He married Helen Highcat in 1933. In 1935, they were interviewed by a worker with the SDERA program. At that time, Henry and Helen and their daughter, Margaret, lived with Henry's mother. Henry indicated he was a member of the American Legion. He and Helen liked to attend and take part in Indian dances. Henry had been working on emergency relief projects near Bullhead. They did not own any livestock but did have a wagon and a set of harness. Henry entered the spirit world in Bullhead on Dec. 5, 1970 and is buried in St. Aloysius Cemetery in Bullhead.[18]

White Boy, Louis. Louis was born around 1882 on the Crow Creek Reservation. Around 1905, he married Lulu How. In the 1909 Census Roll, Louis and Lulu had two children, Amy and Johnson. Louis joined the Army on Aug. 14, 1918, and was assigned to Co. G, 88th Regiment, 19th Division (ASN 3776768). The 19th Division trained at Camp Dodge, IA, after the 88th Division left for Europe. Pvt. White Boy was discharged on Dec. 12, 1918. In the 1920 U.S. Census, Louis and Lulu had three children, Percy, Hermine and Laura. When Louis registered for the Selective Service in 1942, he was living in Pukwana. Louis entered the spirit world in Rapid City on June 23, 1944. He is buried at Grace Mission in Buffalo County.

White Bull, George. George is listed on WWI veteran's memorial at Oglala Lakota College, Kyle, SD. He was born near Porcupine on the Pine Ridge Reservation around May 5, 1896. His parents are listed as White Bull #1 and Deer. As a young man, he was sent to school at the Flandreau boarding school. While there, he enlisted in Troop D, 1st SD Cavalry, which trained as infantry before being sent to Camp Cody, NM, in September of 1917. He was assigned to Company 15, Camp Cody June Automatic Draft Replacement (ASN 1427528). This Company sailed for Europe aboard the S.S. *Tereisias* on June 28, 1918. He later served with infantry and Ammo Train units. He was wounded in October of 1918 during the Meuse-Argonne Offensive. Pvt. White Bull sailed home from Brest aboard the *Mongolia* on Dec. 13, 1918. He had been serving with Co. B, 4th Ammo Train, 4th Division. This unit served in the Sectors at Aisne-Marne, Vesle, Sommedieue, St. Mihiel, and Meuse-Argonne. The manifest for the ship *Mongolia* read: "Walking Cases requiring dressing Class C." After returning home, he wrote about his experience to Joseph Dixon.

> Very many items of interest is connected with my experience overseas. But the only one that has caused me more interest then and now is this.
>
> Why is it that all persons in every walk of life Rich and poor, From a hobo to a college or University Graduate who has went thro the war has prayed sometimes while there. Fellows who never pray before have prayed at those trying times.
>
> From this I know each and every one will pray when they know the time of death is near.

After the war, George's name was engraved on a plaque honoring veterans that was erected at the Flandreau School. In the 1930 U.S. Census, George was living with his wife, Ella, and a son, Isaac, in Wanblee, and working as a Presbyterian minister. In 1940, he was living in Pine Ridge. George entered the spirit world in Porcupine on April 5, 1970 and is buried in the Presbyterian Cemetery in Porcupine.[19]

White Bull, Jacob. Jacob was born at Kenel on the Standing Rock Reservation on Oct. 25, 1895, to Jake Cetanpahaakayanka [Rides a Hawk on a Hill] and Genevieve White Bull. Jacob attended school at Haskell. He joined the Army on June 24, 1918, and was sent to Camp Funston, KS. Later he was transferred to Camp Dodge, IA, and was assigned to Co. A, 351st Regiment, 88th Division (ASN 3309360). Pfc. White Bull sailed with his unit for France on Aug. 16, 1918. Most of the 88th Division did not fight on the Front Line. Pfc. White Bull's commanding officer stated that he "had a splendid physique, character excellent. Shown special excellence in the Browning Automatic." The 88th Division served occupational duty near Gondrecourt, France until May of 1919. The 351st Regiment left St. Nazaire, France, aboard the U.S.S. *Mercury* on May 20, 1919. Pfc. White Bull was discharged on June 7, 1919. He married Julia Red Fish in Selby on July 11, 1925. Jacob served as post historian for his Legion Post. In the 1937 Census Roll, Jacob and Julia are listed with their children, Cecil, Melvin, Cynthia, Frank, Patricia, Wilbert and Albert. Sometime after 1950, Jacob lived in Fort Yates, until returning to Kenel. He entered the spirit world in the Fort Yates hospital on July 13, 1973. He was buried in Assumption Catholic Cemetery in Kenel.[20]

White Eyes, John Emerson. John was born on the Pine Ridge Reservation on Feb. 8, 1898, to Joseph Broken Rope and Susie White Eyes. When John registered for the draft on Sept. 10, 1918, he was ranching near Pine Ridge. He enlisted in the Army on Oct. 14, 1920, and served in the band with Co. A, 56th Infantry. Pvt. White Eyes was discharged on July 19, 1921. In 1923, John married Helena Brown (1903-1972), who had four brothers who served in the military. In the 1930 U.S.

Census, John and Helena lived in Crawford, NE, where he worked as a construction laborer. In the 1940 U.S. Census, John was the foreman on a CCC dam project. Their children included Joseph, Juanita, Melvin Lawrence, Phyllis, Carl, Theodore and Blaine. Hi son, Melvin, served in the Navy during WWII. John entered the spirit world in the VA Hospital in Hot Springs on July 10, 1953. He is buried in Edgemont Cemetery, Edgemont, SD.[21]

White Face Woman, Fred. Fred was born on the Rosebud Reservation on Aug. 29, 1897. In the 1910 U.S. Census, Fred is listed with his father, White Face Woman, and his sisters, Nellie and Bessie. Fred enlisted in Co. I, 4th SD Infantry at Rapid City on March 28, 1917. In August of 1917, Fred married Margaret Clifford. On Sept. 28, 1917, the 4th SD Infantry took the train to Camp Greene, NC. Many of these South Dakota soldiers were assigned to Co. B, 148th Machine Gun Battalion, 41st Division (ASN 98581). Pvt. White Face sailed from Hoboken, NJ, aboard the *Olympic* on Jan. 11, 1918. Upon arrival in France, Pvt. White Face Woman was transferred as a replacement to Co. M, 167th Infantry, 42nd Division (ASN 98581). The 167th Infantry took part in the campaigns at Luneville, Baccarat, Esperance-Souain, Champagne-Marne, Aisne-Marne, St. Mihiel, Essey-Pannes, Meuse-Argonne. The 42nd Division suffered 13,919 casualties. Pvt. White Face returned to the United States from Brest, France, aboard the U.S.S. *Minnesota* on April 15, 1919, and was discharged on May 9, 1919. In the 1920s, he married Rose Whipple. In the 1937 Census Roll, they had five children living with them, a stepson, Steven Janis, Winnie, Phillip, Clifford and Doris. In the 1940 U.S. Census, Fred was working on road construction in Todd County. Fred entered the spirit world in his home in Rosebud on May 26, 1957 and is buried in Parmelee.[22]

White Feather, James. James was born about May 2, 1900, near Cherry Creek on the Cheyenne River Reservation. His father was Thomas Stifftail. As a small boy, he was legally adopted by George White Feather. As a youth, he attended the boarding school in Rapid City. James enlisted in Co. I, 4th SD Infantry in Rapid City on March 27, 1917. On Sept. 28, 1917, this unit was sent to Camp Greene, NC, where Pvt. Stifftail was assigned to Co. B, 148th Machine Gun Battalion, 41st Division (ASN 98592). Pvt. Stifftail sailed with his unit from Hoboken aboard the *Olympic* on Jan. 11, 1918. Upon arriving in France, many of the soldiers were transferred to units in the 42nd Division. Pvt. Stifftail was reassigned to Co. M, 167th Infantry. He was wounded by shrapnel in battle, and may have been listed as missing in action, as a Rapid City Newspaper reported that he had been killed. This was near Fere-en-Tardinois, along the Ourcq River in July of 1918. He recovered from his wounds and sailed home with his unit aboard the U.S.S. *Minnesota* on April 15, 1919. Pvt. Stifftail was discharged on May 9, 1919. After returning home, he married Louise Fisherman. In 1935, the family was interviewed by a worker with the SDERA program. They were living near the Cherry Creek Station in a one room log house. They hauled their water from the Cheyenne River, about ¼ mile away. James supported his family by selling hay and working on emergency conservation projects. He had put up 88 tons of hay, most of which he sold to the government at $8 per ton. He and Louise had three children, Flora, Burley and Maida. Earlier he had been a member of the American Legion and the VFW, but had dropped his membership because he didn't have enough money to pay his dues. He said he liked going to Indian dances and was known as a good singer. In the 1940 U.S. Census, James was working on a reservoir construction project. He later started using the name, White Feather. In 1952 he married Ida Cain. James entered the spirit world at the hospital in Eagle Butte on Nov. 22, 1977. He was survived by Ida and his children, Cornelius, Evan, Lamont, Flora, Ernestine and Maida. He is buried in the Episcopal Cemetery in Cherry Creek. His son, Burley, served in the Army during the Korean Conflict.[23]

White Feather, Jesse. Jesse was born around March 4, 1900, on the Rosebud Reservation. Also known as Jesse Running Horse, his parents were Benjamin and Susie Running Horse. His sister, Louise, married Paul Stone, a fellow veteran. When Jesse registered for the draft on Sept. 12, 1918, he was farming near Wososo. He likely enlisted shortly after that. He served with the 4th Cavalry, which was stationed at Fort Meade. The 1930 U.S. Census lists him as a veteran of the World War. He was then living in Todd County. He re-enlisted in the Army during WWII. Jesse later worked in building construction. He married Lucy Good Shield in 1958. He entered the spirit world at the VA Hospital in Hot Springs on Nov. 23, 1974. He is buried in a Rosebud Cemetery.

White Hand Bear, Joseph. Joseph was born in March of 1896, possibly on the Pine Ridge Reservation. His parents were Pius White Hand Bear and Mary Yellow Fat. In the 1910 U.S. Census, Joseph was living with his parents and brother, Francis, in Bullhead on the Standing Rock Reservation. Joseph joined the Army and was sent to Camp Funston, KS. After serving about seven months, he was discharged on account of his eyes, on June 3, 1918. He was married to Louise Kills the Enemy by J.P. Deloria, an Episcopal Minister on Dec. 29, 1918, at Wakpala. Joseph suffered from tuberculosis and entered the spirit world at his home in Bullhead on March 2, 1919. He was buried at Bullhead. According to the *Sioux County Pioneer*, "Rev. Charles Long delivered a sermon and burial was made according to military fashion, taps being sounded as the casket was lowered in the grave and a firing squad fired three volleys. The casket was draped in a large American flag and a number of Indians who had returned from the Army dressed in their uniforms and stood at attention. The funeral was one of the largest ever held in the Bullhead vicinity and friends and relatives came from all parts of the reservation to pay their last sad tribute." A year later, Mrs. White Hand Bear gave a feast to honor her son. Many former service men attended.[24]

White Horse, John. John was born on the Rosebud Reservation on June 22, 1893, to George and Mary White Horse. In the 1903 Census Roll, John was living with his step father, Joseph Claymore. When John registered for the draft on June 5, 1917, he was working as a farm laborer near Kyle. He joined the Army on Aug. 2, 1918, and was assigned to Battery C, 30th Field Artillery (ASN 4262314). The 30th Field Artillery was part of the 10th Division, serving at Camp Funston, KS. Pfc. White Horse was discharged on Jan. 27, 1919. After the war, he wrote to Joseph Dixon about his experiences. "I've been with the field artillery in U.S. for 6 month. And it is nothing like being a soldier. I am intended to try every thing. But we were not having chance to do it, only what we were assign to. We were well taken care off and we were directed by the captain and Lieutenant to go through a physical exercised, which provide us with a perfect and sound health. I am learning to talk the English language correctly and fluently." In 1928, he married Fannie Bird in Sioux City, IA. In the 1930 U.S. Census, John and Fannie lived in Winnebago, NE, with their children, John, Florence, Ruth, Charlie George, Julia, Vienna and Daniel. John was later married to Eva. When registered with the Selective Service in 1942, he was working for Edward Wilson in Alliance, NE. John entered the spirit world in the VA Hospital in Hot Springs on May 8, 1945, and is buried in Mediator Cemetery in Wood, SD.[25]

White Horse, Louis. See **Brings Three White Horses, Louis**.

White Lance, John. John was born on the Rosebud Reservation on Aug. 11, 1899, to Jesse and Cecilia White Lance. His father worked for the Indian Police. John likely enlisted in the 4th SD Infantry in the spring of 1917. Many of those early enlistees were transferred to the 147th Field Artillery when they arrived at Camp Greene, NC. Pvt. White Lance served in Battery C, 147th F.A. (ASN 139561). As part of the 41st Division, these soldiers sailed aboard the ship *Olympic* for Europe on

Jan. 11, 1918. On March 25, 1918, the 147th F.A. was attached to the 32nd Division. They supported the Red Arrow Division until the Armistice. After the Armistice, the 147th F.A. was attached to the 88th Division, until the 32nd Division was ready to return to America. Pvt. White Lance sailed for home from Brest, France, aboard the U.S.S. *Kansas* on May 1, 1919. He was discharged on May 23, 1919. In the 1920 U.S. Census, John was living with his parents. In the 1920s, he married Clara Eagle Deer. In the 1928 Census Roll, they had three children, Martha, Titus and Christopher. John later married Loraine Bear Heels. John lived at Parmelee. He entered the spirit world near Rosebud on Aug. 4, 1969, and is buried in St. Charles Cemetery in Saint Francis.

White Turtle, Paul. Paul was born at Norris on the Rosebud Reservation on April 16, 1895, to Jacob and Louisa White Turtle. In the 1902 Census Roll, Paul is listed with his father, Keya Ska [White Turtle], his mother, and an older brother, James. When Paul registered for the draft on June 5, 1917, he was farming with his brother. He joined the Army on June 23, 1918, and trained with the 88th Division at Camp Dodge, IA, and was assigned to Co. M, 350th Infantry Regiment (ASN 3310020). Pvt. White Turtle sailed from New York aboard the *Kashmir* on Aug. 15, 1918. He was assigned to the Intelligence Platoon, serving as a Scout for the 3rd Battalion. The 350th Infantry served in quiet sectors during the war. After the Armistice, the 350th served as part of the Army of Occupation near Gondrecourt, France. Pvt. White Turtle was photographed with the rest of his unit. This photo was published in the unit history. Pvt. White Turtle sailed from St. Nazaire aboard the *Aeolus* on May 19, 1919, and was discharged on June 12, 1919. In the 1930 U.S. Census, Paul was living in Cedar Butte Township. He was single. Paul entered the spirit world on March 10, 1952, and was buried in St. Paul's Episcopal Cemetery in Norris.[26]

Whitewash, Lyman. Lyman was born on the Rosebud Reservation on June 9, 1898, to George and Alice White Wash. He attended the boarding school at Flandreau. He joined the Army on April 13, 1918, and was discharged on March 18, 1919. After the war his name was engraved on a plaque to honor the war veterans that was erected at the Flandreau boarding school. On June 20, 1923, Lyman married Dallas Little Warrior (Oglala) in Gregory. They had a son, Chauncey. In the 1940 U.S. Census, Lyman was farming in Washington County. His family name was listed as White Wing. Lyman entered the spirit world on Aug. 2, 1972, and is buried in Alliance Cemetery, Alliance, NE.

White Wolf, Charles. Charles is listed on WWI veteran's memorial at Oglala Lakota College, Kyle, SD. He was born on the Pine Ridge Reservation on Aug. 15, 1896, to John White Wolf and Alice Horn Cloud. In the 1904 Census Roll, Charles is listed with his parents and his sisters, Rose and Susie. Charles attended school at the Holy Rosary Mission before being enrolled at Carlisle in 1912. He learned to play the clarinet. Charles enlisted in the 6th Nebraska Infantry in Chadron on Aug. 16, 1917. After this National Guard unit was transferred to Camp Cody, NM, Charles was assigned to Co. F, 109th Engineers, 34th Division (ASN 1438185). Pvt. White Wolf served with Pvt. Lawrence Cross, Pvt. Ralph Red Bear and Corp. George Redboy. These soldiers remained at Camp Cody for almost a year before shipping over to France. They sailed from New York aboard the *Cretic* on Sept. 17, 1918. Company F worked at constructing barracks for wounded soldiers near the Mesves Hospital Center, south of Paris. Pvt. White Wolf was transferred to 1st Replacement Depot on June 15, 1919. He sailed from Brest, France, aboard the *Imperator* on July 7, 1919, traveling with Brest Casual Co. #2230. He was discharged at Camp Mills, NY, on July 22, 1919. After he returned home, he married Winnie Big Eagle. In the early 1930s, he was working as a tribal policeman. In the 1940 U.S. Census, Charles was working as a farm aid for the U.S. Indian Service. He and Winnie had five sons, Robert, Vincent, Louis, Edward, and Charles Jr. Louis served with the USMC in Korea. Edward also served during the Korean Conflict. Charles entered the spirit world in the VA Hospital in Hot Springs on March 21, 1961, and was buried in the cemetery at Holy Rosary Mission.[27]

Widow, Paul. Paul was born on the Cheyenne River Reservation on March 20, 1891. His parents were Jacob Widow and White Blanket. In 1910, he married Eliza Medicine Bird. After divorcing her he married Agnes Talks in 1914. They had seven children, of which three survived childhood. In the 1916 Census Roll for Cheyenne River, Paul is listed as Came at the Camp. Paul registered for the draft on July 20, 1918. He was a tall man of medium build. On July 22, 1918, he joined the Army. After being assigned to Co. M, 333rd Regiment, 84th Division (ASN 3954556), he traveled to France aboard the ship *Aquitania,* which sailed from New York on Sept. 2, 1918. He was reassigned to Company D, 363rd Infantry Regiment, which was part of the 91st Division. He spent nine months overseas. The 91st Division suffered heavy casualties in the fighting at St. Mihiel and Meuse-Argonne. In October 1918, the Division was moved to Belgium, where they took part in the Ypres-Lys Offensive. The total casualties for the 91st Division were 5,778 killed and wounded. After the Armistice, the 91st Division was billeted near La Ferté-Bernard, France, after leaving Belgium. Pvt. Widow sailed from St. Nazaire aboard the S.S. *Kentuckian* on March, 20, 1919. After arriving in Brooklyn on April 1, Pvt. Widow was discharged on April 22, 1919.

In 1935, Paul's family was living in a 14' x 20' log home 13 miles west of Thunder Butte, where Agnes' allotment was located. Their meals were cooked outside over a camp fire. Their water source was a spring that was 2.5 miles away. The family had planted a large garden that year, bugs and yellow beetles destroyed their crop. The family owned five horses, a set of harness, wagon, mower and harrow. Paul also owned a Model-A Ford which he used to haul people for a fee around the district. He likely used it to haul water for some of his neighbors. Paul was a member of the VFW. A number of years before, Paul had been accused of taking some horses. In the old time, capturing another man's horses was considered honorable, but in 1935, the SD law looked at it differently. Paul was also having trouble with Trachoma, which affected his ability to work on relief projects. Paul entered the spirit world on May 30, 1978, at the Fort Meade Veterans Hospital. His son, Edward, and daughter, Mary Buffalo, survived him. Agnes had entered the spirit world in 1943. Paul is buried in the Black Hills National Cemetery, Section E, Site 2297.[28]

Williams, Chauncey Depew. Chauncey was born at Fort Pierre on July 26, 1895, to John Williams and Helen Aungie. In the 1900 Cheyenne River Census Roll, Chauncey is listed with his mother and his brothers, Forrest and Luther, and his sisters, Lillie, Maud, and Olive. Chauncey attended the Carlisle Boarding School from 1914-1916. Chauncey joined the Army on May 18, 1918, and was sent to Camp Taylor, Kentucky, where the Army had a Field Artillery (F.A.) Training School. Pvt. Williams sailed from Brooklyn aboard the *Kursk* on Oct. 20, 1918. He was traveling with Camp Taylor October Automatic Replacement Draft, Battery #9, F.A. After arriving in France, he was reassigned to the 160th Infantry, 40th Division (ASN 3437786). After the Armistice, he sailed from Bordeaux aboard the *Walter A. Luckenbach* on March 19, 1919. He was traveling with Camp Dodge Detachment No. 4. Pvt. Williams was discharged on April 8, 1919. On Dec. 9, 1924, he married Lorena Archambeau, whose brother, David, had served with the Coast Guard during the war. In the 1930 U.S. Census, Chauncey was working as a plumber at Pine Ridge. In the 1940 U.S. Census, the family was living in Gettysburg, where Chauncey worked as a plumber and steam fitter. He and Lorena had three children, Forest, Chauncey Jr., and Sandra. When Chauncey registered for the Selective Service in 1942, he was living in Seattle and working in the Tacoma Shipyard. His son, Forest, served in the Navy during WWII. Chauncey entered the spirit world in southern California on Nov. 17, 1979. He is buried in Desert Lawn Memorial Park in Yuma, AZ.

Williams, Gideon. Gideon was born around 1886 on the Sisseton-Wahpeton Reservation to John and Jennie Williams. In the 1900 U.S. Census, he was listed with his parents and his brother, Asa. When Gideon registered for the draft on June 2, 1917, he was living in Sisseton. He joined the Army on May 25, 1918, and was assigned to Battery D, 347th Field Artillery (FA), 91st Division (ASN 2788126). Pvt. Williams sailed with his unit from New York aboard the *Adriatic* on July 14, 1918. The ship first docked at Liverpool, England. After the 347th FA arrived in Cherbourg, France, they traveled to the artillery training facility at Camp de Souge near Bordeaux. They were trained to use ten-ton tractors to pull the 4.7-inch guns. Near the end of the war, the unit arrived in Bois de Brocourt. On Christmas day, the 347th FA was billeted in private homes in several small German towns along the Moselle River. On March 13, 1919, they acted as guard of honor to President Woodrow Wilson, who was in France for the Paris Peace Conference. Pvt. Williams sailed from Brest, France, aboard the *Aquitania* on March 23, 1919, and was discharged on April 17, 1919. Other soldiers returning with him were Dwight Heminger, Elbridge Gerry, Moses Marshall and Peter Rouillard. After returning home, Gideon married Elizabeth Tawicu. They separated around 1924. A few years later, Gideon moved to the Spirit Lake Reservation. In the 1930 U.S. Census, he was living with his wife, Clara. He later married Nancy Walking Cloud. He entered the spirit world on Jan. 5, 1966, in his home in St Michael, ND. He is buried in St Michael's Cemetery. Military rites were performed by the Neathery-Simonson VFW Post No. 756 of Devils Lake.[29]

Williams, Johnson Fred. Johnson was born around July 4, 1902, on the Yankton Reservation to James and May Williams. In the 1903 Yankton Census Roll, his listed with his father and a brother and a sister, James Jr, and Jennie. Johnson joined the Army on May 11, 1920, and was discharged on May 10, 1921. In the 1920 Census Roll, he was listed with his daughter, Pearl. In the 1937 Census, he had two daughters, Pearl and Thelma. In the 1940 U.S. Census, he was working as a farm laborer in Strike Axe Township, Oklahoma. He later moved back to Lake Andes. He entered the spirit world in the Wagner Community Hospital on Jan. 18, 1982, and is buried in Cedar Presbyterian Cemetery.

Williams, Luther A. Luther was an older brother to Chauncey. He was born on the Cheyenne River Reservation on March 15, 1894. When Luther registered for the draft on May 31, 1917, he was living in Wichita and working as a clerk/stenographer. He joined the Army and served in the Medical Department (ASN 978739). Sgt. Williams sailed from Hoboken aboard the *Leviathan* on Aug. 31, 1918. He was traveling with staff for the Army Base Hospital No. 81, located in Bazoilles-sur-Meuse. After the Armistice, Sgt. 1st Class Williams, now at Base Hospital 100, sailed from St. Nazaire aboard the U.S.S. *South Bend* on July 5, 1919. He also served in the military in WWII. He stayed single. In the 1920 U.S. Census, he was working as a stenographer in a Minneapolis bank. In 1930, he was a clerk at the Colorado River Indian School in Yuma, AZ. In 1940, he was working as a senior clerk for the U.S. Indian Service in Billings. In the 1950s, he was working as a clerk on the Seminole Reservation in Dania, FL. He entered the spirit world in Jackson Memorial Hospital in Miami on Jan. 1, 1955. He is buried in Riverside Cemetery in Pierre, SD. An American Legion marker is next to his headstone.[30]

Williams, Maurice. Maurice was born around 1896 at LaCreek on the Pine Ridge Reservation, to Alexander Williams and Mary Conroy. In the 1910 U.S. Census, he was a student at the Haskell boarding school. When Maurice registered for the draft on June 5, 1917, he was farming with his parents at LaCreek. He wrote on his registration form that he was a "ward of Federal Gov. and my rights of American citizenship deprived." He joined the Army on July 22, 1918, and was sent to Camp Dodge, IA, where he was assigned to Co. K, 2nd Infantry, 19th Division (ASN 3955628).

The 19th Division trained at Camp Dodge after the 88th Division had left for Europe. Pvt. Williams was discharged on April 15, 1919. On Sept. 2, 1919, Maurice married Margaret Flute in Sisseton. Maurice moved back home with his mother and brother, George, after separating from Margaret. In 1935, he was interviewed by a social worker with the SDERA program. The family lived in a four-room frame house located 15 miles SE of Martin. Maurice was partially disabled. The family owned seven milk cows and three turkeys. They felt that "their home was located in the best part of South Dakota." About that time, much of that land was taken for a wildlife refuge. Maurice entered the spirit world on May 18, 1940, after a car accident near Sweet Grass, MT. He was buried in Grace Church Cemetery at LaCreek.[31]

Williams, Samuel Tohocoka. Samuel was born on the Sisseton-Wahpeton Reservation on Aug. 4, 1893, to Daniel Tohocoka and Nancy Longie. When he registered for the draft on June 1, 1917, he lived in Sisseton and listed his occupation as stationary engineer. He joined the Army on May 25, 1918, and was assigned to Battery D, 347th Field Artillery Regiment (FA), 91st Division (ASN 2787816). Pvt. Tohocoka sailed with his unit from New York aboard the *Adriatic* on July 14, 1918. Other soldiers from Sisseton in his unit were Gideon Williams and Dwight Heminger. The 347th FA did not serve at the Front. Pvt. Tohocoka became sick and was admitted to Base Hospital No. 5. He sailed for home from Bordeaux aboard the U.S.S. *Mallory* on Dec. 8, 1918, with passengers labeled as "sick and wounded." The rest of his unit returned home in March of 1919. He was discharged on Jan. 26, 1919. In 1926, he married Estella Marks (1903-1984). In 1935, the family was interviewed by a worker with the SDERA program. They were living in a house on church property located 16 miles SW of Sisseton. Samuel was the janitor there, and had trouble finding more work to support his family, which included four children, Percy, Lois, Geraldine and Merle. They hauled water from a neighbor's well. Earlier Samuel had been treated for Trachoma at the Veteran's Bureau in Sioux Falls. When he registered for the Selective Service in 1942, he was working in the C.C.C. program. His son, Percy, served in the Air Force during the Korean Conflict. His wife, Stella, entered the spirit world on Feb. 4, 1984, and Samuel followed her on Sept. 19 of that same year. He is buried in Goodwill Presbyterian Cemetery.[32]

Williams, Smiley Shepherd. Smiley was born on the Sisseton-Wahpeton Reservation on Feb. 2, 1894, to Louis Williams and Jessie Shepherd. In the 1899 Census Roll, he is listed with his mother and a brother, Edward. He married Luvelva Quarton (1899-1989) on April 5, 1917. When he registered for the draft on June 4, 1917, they lived in Peever. Smiley joined the Army on Aug. 26, 1918, and was discharged on Dec. 10, 1918, as a Private. In the 1930 U.S. Census, Smiley and Luvelva were living in Marysville, CA, where he worked as a farm hand in an olive grove. They later moved back to Roberts County. In the 1940 U.S. Census, he was working as a policeman with the Indian Service. He and Luvelva had four children, Darrell, Margery, Calvin and Perry. Smiley entered the spirit world on May 3, 1975 and is buried in Goodwill Presbyterian Cemetery.

Williams, Titus. Titus was born in Morton, MN, on the Lower Sioux Reservation on March 23, 1886. In the 1892 Flandreau Census Roll, he was listed with his parents, Johnson and Jane (Wakeman) Williamson, and a sister, Rebekka. In the 1905 SD Census, the family was living in South Dakota. When Titus registered for the draft on June 5, 1917, he was living in Granite Falls, MN. He was working as a painter before he entered the service. He enlisted at Granite Falls on Feb. 26, 1918, and was sent to Camp Dodge, IA. He was initially assigned to Co. D, 352nd Infantry, 88th Division (ASN 2161085). At the end of March of 1918, he was transferred to Company B of the 43rd Engineers, who were training at Washington, D.C. Pvt. Williams sailed with his unit from New York aboard the ship *Leviathan* on May 22, 1918. They arrived in Brest, France, and traveled to eastern France. The 43rd Engineers were re-designated as the 47th Engineers. This unit conducted extensive lumbering operation near St. Julien, which was north of Dijon. They remained there until May 3, 1919. Pvt. Williams sailed from St. Nazaire, France aboard the *Antigone* on May 17, 1919, with St. Aignan Casual Co. #4498. He arrived in Newport News, VA, on May 29, 1919, and was discharged at Camp Lee, VA, on June 2, 1919. Titus' sister, Rebekka, was married to Charles Quinn, a fellow veteran. In the 1920 U.S. Census, Titus lived with Charles and Rebekka in Minnesota Falls. He later moved to Peever, SD, where he married Haggie Johnson on Aug. 9, 1927. They had a son, Johnson Thomas. A few years later, they moved to St. Paul, where Titus worked as a laborer. In the 1940 U.S. Census, they were living in Granite Falls. They later moved to South Dakota. Their son served in the Army during the Korean Conflict. Titus entered the spirit world in his home in Spring Grove, Roberts County, on Jan. 4, 1966, and is buried in Pijihutazizi Presbyterian Cemetery in Granite Falls, MN.[33]

Wilson, Charles W. Charles was born on the west edge of the Pine Ridge Reservation on Nov. 15, 1900. His parents were Thomas and Zona Wilson. Charles grew up around Hot Springs. He enlisted in the Navy on May 24, 1918, in Omaha. He was discharged in Miami on Jan. 4, 1919, after injuring his arm. He received a disability payment of $32/mo. In the early 1920s, he married Julia Knuepple. In the 1925 Census Roll for the Oglala Nation, Charles is listed with his oldest daughter, Arlene. In the 1930 U.S. Census, Charles was working as a truck driver. In 1935, Charles and Julia had four children, Arlene, Alice, Nadine and Zona. In the 1940 U.S. Census, Charles was divorced and living in Sioux Falls. Charles also served in the military during WWII. He later ranched at Buffalo Gap. He entered the spirit world in Lutheran Hospital in Hot Springs on March 23, 1958 and is buried in Buffalo Gap Cemetery.[34]

Wilson, Titus. Titus was born on the Sisseton-Wahpeton Reservation on Dec. 22, 1893. In the 1895 Census Roll, he is listed with his parents, David (Tunwanmaza) and Mary, his sister, Dolly, and an older brother, Hazen. Titus joined the Army on April 26, 1918, and was assigned to Co. G, 355th Infantry Regiment, 89th Division (ASN 2845068). Pvt. Wilson left New York aboard the *Baltic* on June 4, 1918. When the 355th Infantry finally arrived in France, they were billeted in the villages of Grand, Brechainville and Aillainville. They later served in the sectors at Lucey, St. Mihiel, Euvezin and Meuse-Argonne. After the Armistice, Pfc. Wilson received an evaluation from his commanding officer, Capt. I. J. Barbour, who wrote that he was "proud of his service with AEF. Good man especially with automatic rifle." After taking part in occupational duty, Pfc. Wilson sailed with the 355th Infantry from Brest, France, aboard the ship *Leviathan* on May 15, 1919. Pfc. Wilson was discharged on May 31, 1919. After returning home, Titus lived with his brother, Hazen, and his family. In 1935, the family was interviewed by a worker with the SDERA program. They lived in a five-room frame house located five miles north of Sisseton. Their water was drawn from a well with a bucket. They owned a team of horses, plus Titus owned an older car. Before the drought they had had dairy cattle. In the 1940 U.S. Census, Titus was living in Long Hollow, and in 1941, he married Eunice Redday. Titus entered the spirit world in the Tekakwitha Nursing Home in Sisseton on June 12, 1991 and is buried in Sisseton Cemetery.[35]

Wing, John. John was born on the Sisseton-Wahpeton Reservation on May 6, 1893, to Daniel and Esther Wing. John enlisted in the Army at Britton on May 5, 1918. He was assigned to Co. D, 158th Infantry, 40th Division at Camp Kearny, California. After the 40th Division left for Europe, he served with the 32nd Infantry, 16th Division which was organized at Camp Kearny in August of 1918. Pvt. Wing was discharged at Camp Dodge, IA, on March 1, 1919. In the 1926 Census Roll, he was married to Anna Max. Their children were Elijah, Lucy and Clarence. In the 1930 U.S. Census, he was living with his parents. John entered the spirit world on Nov. 13, 1932, and is buried in Sisseton Cemetery.[36]

Winter Chaser, Thomas James. James was born near Oacoma on the Lower Brule Reservation around June 28, 1887. His parents were Waniyetu Wakuwa [Winter Chaser] and Wears Eagle (Wanbli Kayake). Around 1896, they moved to the Rosebud Reservation, where they were enrolled. Around 1910, James married his wife, Martha King (1877-1941). When he registered for the draft on June 5, 1917, they had two children. James joined the Army and was assigned to the 335th Field Artillery, 87th Division, which was organized at Camp Pike, Ark. The division arrived in France on Sept. 13, 1918, and was assigned to work with the Service of Supply. The 87th Division returned home in December of 1918. In the 1930 U.S. Census, James and Martha were farming with their son, Loyd, in Tripp County. Martha entered the spirit world in 1941. When James registered for the Selective Service in 1942, he lived with his son near Ideal. He entered the spirit world in Winner on June 16, 1945, and is buried in Holy Spirit Cemetery in Ideal.[37]

Witt, Charles. Charles was born in Oklahoma around June 3, 1895, to John Witt and Rebecca White Bear, who was Cherokee. In 1901, Rebecca was working as a baker at the Seger Boarding School in Colony, OK. The family was still living there during the 1910 U.S. Census. Sometime after this, the family moved to Norris, SD. When Charles registered for the draft on June 5, 1917, he was farming near Norris. On June 26, 1917, he married Belle Arcoren. They had two children, Lulu and Walace. Charles joined the Army on Sept. 21, 1917, and was assigned to Co. M, 7th Infantry Regiment, 3rd Division (ASN 2192808). Pvt. Witt sailed for France from Hoboken, NJ, aboard the *Agamemnon* on April 7, 1918. They arrived off the shores of Brittany on April 15, 1918. As they arrived in Brest, the regimental band played "Goodbye Broadway; Hello France." The 3rd Battalion marched to a rest camp outside the city. The 7th Infantry served in the Sectors at Aisne, Chateau-Thierry, Champagne-Marne, Aisne-Marne, St. Mihiel and Meuse-Argonne. Pvt. Witt was wounded during the war. He may have lost an arm. He returned home early from France and was discharged on Dec. 23, 1918. Most of the 3rd Division remained in France until the summer of 1919. Charles married Julie Quiver at White River on Jan. 5, 1921. She was from Pine Ridge. In the 1940 U.S. Census, Charles and Julie lived with their children, John, Mary, Lillian, Milford, Chas. Jr. and Edna. When Charles registered for the Selective Service in 1942, the family was living in Wanamaker, a small town west of Norris. The town was named for John Wanamaker, who owned a large department store in Philadelphia, and was Postmaster General. After Julie entered the spirit world in 1956, Charles married Lucy Quick Bear in 1959. Charles later moved to Rapid City. He entered the spirit world in Bennett-Clarkson Hospital in Rapid City on July 10, 1973 and is buried in the Episcopal Cemetery in Wanblee. He was survived by his children, Mary Woodknife, Lillian Larvie, Edna Brown, Milford and Charles.

Witt, James. James was born on Nov. 9, 1894, in Indian Territory in what is now Oklahoma. His parents were John W. Witt and Rebecca White Bear. In 1901, Rebecca was working as a baker at the Seger Boarding School in Colony, OK. In 1909, James became a member of the Dutch Reformed Church in Colony. In 1917, Rebecca was living in Norris on the Rosebud Reservation. James likely joined the Army around this time and was sent to Camp Funston, KS. Pvt. Witt sailed for France from Hoboken, NJ, aboard the *Susquehana* on Feb. 17, 1918. He was traveling with the Camp Funston Replacement Draft. He was assigned to the Co. L, 104th Infantry, 26th Division. On April 23, 1918, the 104th Infantry became the first American Regiment to be decorated by the French with the Croix de Guerre for Bravery under Fire. In mid-July of 1918, the 104th Infantry was stationed in Bois de Belleau, when the 3rd Battalion was ordered to attack the German Army in the towns of

Belleau and Givry. Pvt. Witt was killed in action on July 19, 1918. He is buried in the Aisne-Marne Cemetery in Belleau (Plot A, Row 1, Grave 62).

Wolf, Michael V. Michael was born on the Lac Courte Oreilles Reservation in Wisconsin on Sept. 21, 1891, to Peter Wolf and Angeline Rousseau. Around 1914 he married Mary Emma Sherer (1893-1983). Mary was from the White Earth Reservation. When Michael registered for the draft on June 5, 1917, he and Mary had two children. They lived in Reserve, WI. Shortly after this they moved to South Dakota. Michael joined the Army on Oct. 20, 1918 and served in the Student Army Training Corps at Huron College (ASN 5287975). He was discharged on Dec. 11, 1918. In the 1920 U.S. Census, Michael was working in the Cherry Creek District on the Cheyenne River Reservation as the boss farmer. In the 1930 U.S. Census, he was working on the Rosebud Reservation. By 1940, the family was living at Fort Peck, where Michael was a farm agent. They had seven children, Vincent, Burton, Raymond, James, Richard, Donald and Darlene. The four oldest boys served in the Army during WWII. Michael entered the spirit world in Minot, ND, on March 27, 1953, and is buried at Fort Snelling National Cemetery. Mary is buried next to him.

Woodlock, Lawrence A. Lawrence is listed on the Oglala Tribe veterans list. He was born in Michigan on May 21, 1873. In 1899, he married Mary Olive Dumont in Michigan. Lawrence was a physician. He and Mary had two children, Wallace and Esther. He enlisted in the Army on June 25, 1917, and was assigned to Ambulance Company No. 128, 107th Sanitary Train, 32nd Division, as a 1st Lieutenant. His unit sailed from Hoboken, NJ, on Feb. 17, 1918. The 32nd Division suffered 13, 392 casualties. Capt. Woodlock sailed for home from Brest, France, on July 30, 1919. He was discharged on Aug. 30, 1919. In the 1930 U.S. Census, Dr. Woodlock was working on the Lac du Flambeau Reservation in Wisconsin. In 1935, the Woodlock family was living in Wanblee, SD. Mary Woodlock passed away in 1938. On May 3, 1939, he married Laura Whirlwind Soldier. In the 1940 U.S. Census, they were living in Brownsville, TX. Dr. Woodlock entered the spirit world at Hot Springs on June 29, 1948. He is buried in Hot Springs National Cemetery.

Y

Yellow Earrings, Daniel. Daniel, a Hunkpapa, was born about May 5, 1886, on the Standing Rock Reservation. In the 1903 Census Roll, Daniel was listed with his parents, Ziowin [Yellow Earring] and Iyuskinpiwin [Happy Woman], and a brother, Martin, and a sister, Harriet. Daniel attended the Carlisle boarding school from 1902-07. He was listed as a harness maker. Daniel took part in athletics at the school. After returning home, he did some interpreting with the allotting crew on Standing Rock. He first married Rose Fly around 1910. When Daniel registered for the draft on June 5, 1917, he and his wife had three children. They were ranching near Bullhead. Daniel joined the Army on Aug. 16, 1918, and was assigned to Veterinary Hospital No. 15 (ASN 3685042). This unit was trained at Camp Lee, VA, before sailing from Newport News, VA, for France aboard the U.S.S. *Antigone* on Oct. 28, 1918. Veterinary Hospital No. 15 was stationed at Gievres, France. Cpl. Yellow Earrings sailed from Brest, France, aboard the U.S.S. *Pueblo* on July 3, 1919, arriving on July 13. After Cpl. Yellow Earrings returned to the U.S., he served with Casual Detachment No. 1090, Demobilization Group at Camp Dodge, IA. He was discharged on July 22, 1919. On Oct. 31, 1933, he married Nellie Pass Beyond. In 1935, the family was interviewed by a worker with the SDERA program. They were living in a one room log home, 18' x 30', in the Bullhead District. Their family included four children, James, Melda, Andrew and Annie. Daniel was a member of the American

Legion and the VFW. The family liked to attend Indian dances. They owned 75 sheep, 32 cattle, 25 horses and 25 chickens. Daniel owned a 1929 Buick and his son, James, owned a 1930 Roosevelt Eight. Daniel said that before the drought, he had farmed 3000 acres with a tractor, and had owned 200-300 head of horses and cattle. Daniel told the worker, "we have all the dam building we want." He felt that funds would be better spent on truck trails and highways in the community and home improvement. He also thought the government should install telephone service across the reservation. With an opportunity offered them for developing a livestock industry, Daniel felt that people could be self-supporting in a short time. Daniel entered the spirit world in the Standing Rock Hospital in Fort Yates on Oct. 20, 1948. He is buried in St. Aloysius Cemetery in Bullhead. His son, Andrew, served in the Army during the Korean Conflict.[1]

Yellow Eyes, Edward. Edward was born at White River on the Rosebud Reservation on April 7, 1897, to Amos and Julia Yellow Eyes. In the 1910 U.S. Census, he was listed with his parents, a sister, Sallie, and brothers, Thomas and James. He registered for the draft on June 5, 1918. He joined the Army shortly after this. He was assigned to Co. A, 1st Battalion, Replacement and Training, at Camp MacArthur, TX. He also served in Casual Detachment No. 87, 163rd Depot Brigade at Camp Dodge, IA. He was discharged as a Private on March 4, 1919. In the 1921 Census Roll, he was listed with his wife, Belle Moves Camp, and their daughter, Edna. Edward entered the spirit world on Aug. 8, 1922 and is buried in the Episcopal Cemetery in White River. His younger brother, **Thomas Yellow Eyes**, may have served in the Army in the 1920s. The 1930 U.S. Census lists Thomas (1900-1977) as a veteran.[2]

Yellow Fat, James. James was born on the Standing Rock Reservation on Feb. 24, 1894, to Joseph Yellow Fat and Margaret Thunder Hawk. When he registered for the draft on June 5, 1917, he was ranching near Kenel. Shortly after this he married Mary Edgar. When he joined the Army, he was sent to Fort Logan on May 1, 1918, and discharged on May 4, 1918. His younger brother, Martin, also joined the Army. After Martin entered the spirit world in 1919, the American Legion Post in Kenel was named in his honor. James was a member of the Legion Post. In 1928, James served as the Americanization Officer for the Post. In the 1930 U.S. Census, James was farming. In the 1940 U.S. Census, James was working on a WPA project near Kenel. He and Mary had four children, Martin, Raymond, Robert and Theresa. James later worked in Fort Yates for the Bureau of Indian Affairs doing vehicle maintenance and driving a school bus. He entered the spirit world in a Bismarck Hospital on May 15, 1977 and is buried in Assumption Cemetery in Kenel.[3]

Yellow Fat, Martin. Martin was born at Kenel on the Standing Rock Reservation on Nov. 23, 1897, to Joseph Yellow Fat and Margaret Thunder Hawk. He was a younger brother to James Yellow Fat. While attending school in Rapid City, Martin enlisted in the 4th Infantry, South Dakota National Guard on March 28, 1917. In September of 1917, this unit was sent to Camp Greene, NC. Pvt. Yellow Fat was reassigned to Co. B, 148th Machine Gun Battalion, 41st Division (ASN 98582). On Jan. 11, 1918, he sailed from Hoboken, NJ, aboard the *Olympic* for France. Upon arrival in France, Pvt Yellow Fat was transferred to Co. M, 167th Infantry, 42nd Division. The 167th Infantry served in the Sectors at Luneville, Baccarat, Esperance-Souain, Champagne-Marne, Aisne Marne, St. Mihiel, Essey-Pannes, and Meuse Argonne. Pvt. Yellow Fat was gassed and wounded slightly in the Meuse Argonne Campaign. Later while serving near Sedan in November, he was shot in the hip while rescuing a Red Cross nurse who had been wounded. After recovering in the hospital, he joined the regiment in occupational duty. Pvt. Yellow Fat sailed with his fellow soldiers from Brest, France, aboard the U.S.S. *Minnesota* on April 15, 1919. During a medical exam, Pvt. Yellow Fat was found to have Tuberculosis. He was sent to Fort Bayard, NM, but he did not recover. He was discharged on Dec. 8, 1919. On his return to South Dakota, Martin became so weak that he was admitted to St. Luke's Hospital in Aberdeen. He entered the spirit world on Dec. 15, 1919. He was buried in Kenel with full military honors. The pallbearers were all service men. A salute was fired over the grave and the national anthem was sung. The American Legion Post in Kenel was named in his honor.[4]

Yellow Head, Joseph. Joseph was born at Timberlake on the Cheyenne River Reservation on Jan. 4, 1896. His parents were Jerome and Sarah Yellow Head. Joseph attended the Carlisle boarding school from 1914-1917. He was still a student at Carlisle when he registered for the draft. He joined the Army on Aug. 28, 1918, and was discharged on June 8, 1919. He may have served in the 20th Infantry. In the late 1920s, Joseph worked for the Miller Brothers 101 Wild West Show. He rode broncs and buffaloes, and did rope spinning. On Oct. 18, 1929, he married Mamie West. In 1935, they were interviewed by a worker with the SDERA program. They lived in a two-room log home located north of the Moreau River bridge and ½ mile from Highway 63. They obtained their water from a spring one mile away, going every other day. In 1934 and 1935, Joseph had been in the VA Hospital at Hot Springs, and was on relief. He owned three horses, a wagon and a set of harness. They had put up three tons of hay. Joseph entered the spirit world at the PHS Hospital in Eagle Butte on May 22, 1974, and is buried in Eagle Butte Cemetery.[5]

Yellow Woman, Silas. Silas was born on the Rosebud Reservation, possibly around 1887. In the 1905 Census Roll, he was listed as 18 years old and living with his mother, Yellow Woman, and a sister, Short Woman. When Silas registered for the draft on June 5, 1917, he was farming about 3 acres at Cedar Butte. When he joined the Army, he was first assigned to the 10th Detachment, Administrative Labor Co., Quartermaster Corps (ASN 3955923). This unit was scheduled to sail for Europe on Oct. 7, 1918. Before the ship left, Pvt. Yellow Woman was transferred to a hospital. He likely had the flu. A few weeks later on Oct. 20, 1918, he sailed from New York with the 332nd Bakery Company (QMC) aboard the *Orsova*. After the war, Pfc. Yellow Woman sailed from Brest, France, aboard the ship *Orizaba* on Sept. 27, 1919. He arrived in Hoboken, NJ, on Oct. 6, 1919, and was discharged on Oct 12, 1919. After returning home, he married Bessie Plenty Bull on Jan. 26, 1922 at Cedar Butte. Silas entered the spirit world on Aug. 19, 1924, and is buried in St. Paul Episcopal Cemetery, Norris.

Young, Benjamin. Ben was born to Warren and Frances Young in Chamberlain, SD, on Aug. 29, 1888. When he registered for the draft on June 5, 1917, he was working as a stockman with the Diamond A Cattle Co. in Eagle Butte. He enlisted in the Army on April 25, 1918, and was assigned to Co. F, 355th Infantry, 89th Division (ASN 2187048). Pvt. Young served with William Wabashaw, who was a Bugler with Co. F. They sailed from New York aboard the *Baltic* on June 4, 1918. Pvt. Young was wounded. He sailed from Brest, France, on April 15, 1919, with Detachment #190. These enlisted men were identified as "walking cases, requiring dressing." Pvt. Young was discharged on Sept. 16, 1919. After returning home, he married Leona Marion in 1922. She passed away in 1935. On Jan. 21, 1942, he married Margaret Claymore, the twin sister to John, who had also served in the 355th Infantry. Margaret was the widow of Hans Mortenson. Ben and Margaret ranched until his health intervened. Margaret's son, Clarence took over management of the ranch. Ben passed away on Jan. 26, 1968. He is buried in Scotty Philip Memorial Cemetery, Ft. Pierre, SD.

Young Bear, Henry. Henry was born on the Pine Ridge Reservation around June 29, 1897, to Martin Young Bear and Rachael Belly Woman. Henry joined the military on Feb. 12, 1918, and was discharged on April 10, 1919. His branch of service is not known. After the war, he married

Sophia Smoke. In the 1940 U.S. Census, the family was farming in Shannon County with their children, Ernest, Severt, and Elizabeth. Sophia's parents, Emma and Melvin were also living with them. Ernest served in the Navy in WWII, while Severt served in Peace Time. In 1944, Henry lived in Porcupine and worked for the C & NW Railroad. He entered the spirit world on Oct. 30, 1962.

Young Hawk, Eugene. Eugene was born on the Standing Rock Reservation about Aug. 15, 1886. His parents were Eli Young Hawk and Mary Wacinyanpiwin. Eli had served as a scout for the Army for five years and later as a policeman for 20 years. Eugene's grandfather was a Kootenai named Bison, who had been captured by the Lakota. Eugene Joined the Army on June 24, 1918, and was sent to Camp Funston. He was assigned to Co. F, 69th Infantry, 10th Division (ASN 3309368), which was formed at Camp Funston after the 89th Division left for Europe. Corporal Young Hawk was discharged on Jan. 29, 1919. In 1928, Eugene was the Commander of the Legion Post at Bullhead. In the 1930 U.S. Census, he was living with his step father, Gabriel Grey Eagle. In 1935, Eugene was interviewed by a worker with the SDERA program. Eugene had been working as an interpreter with that program. He was living in a small frame building on the government reserve in Bullhead. He obtained his water from the well at Hatch's store. He was single. Eugene entered the spirit world at the VA Hospital in Hot Springs on Oct. 29, 1965, and is buried in St. Aloysius Cemetery in Bullhead.[6]

Youngman, Julius. Julius was born in Poplar, MT, on the Fort Peck Reservation about July 9, 1891. In the 1905 Census Roll, Julius was listed with his parents, Youngman and Woodchuck, and his siblings, Dora, Owns the Whip, Chased by Piegan (Louis) and Looks at Her. When he registered for the draft on June 5, 1917, he was living in Wakpala, SD, and working for Noah Flying Earth. Julius joined the Army on Sept. 21, 1917, and was sent to Camp Funston with other soldiers from South Dakota. He was assigned to Co. B, 340th Machine Gun (MG) Battalion, 89th Division (ASN 2193100). Pfc. Youngman sailed from New York aboard the *Khyber* on June 4, 1918. Upon arrival in France, the 340th MG Battalion was billeted in St. Blin. Pvt. Youngman took part in the Sectors at Lucey, St. Mihiel, Euvezin, and Meuse-Argonne. After the Armistice, Pvt. Youngman received an evaluation from his commanding officer, Capt. Daniel Runkle, which read: "Regarded as an average good man. Associates readily with white men of company. Has good endurance and is good humored. Excellent night worker and runner." After completion of occupational duty in Erdorf, Germany, Pfc. Youngman sailed from Brest, France, aboard the *Leviathan* on May 15, 1919, arriving on May 22 at 3:25 PM. He was discharged on June 2, 1919. After returning to Poplar, he married Elizabeth Ida Brown on May 5, 1928. In the 1940 U.S. Census, he was farming with his family. He served as a tribal judge on the Fort Peck Reservation. Julius entered the spirit world in Poplar on July 4, 1971. His son, John, and a daughter, Ida, survived him. He is buried in the Poplar Cemetery.[7]

Youngman, Louis. Louis (Bpikanakuwapi) was born in Poplar on the Fort Peck Reservation around May 22, 1900. His parents were Youngman (Koshka) and Woodchuck (Shkecana). Julius was an older brother of his. When he reached school age, he was sent to the boarding school at Flandreau, SD. At the age of 16, he enlisted in Troop D, 1st SD Cavalry (ASN 1427535) on April 4, 1917. This National Guard unit trained as infantry in South Dakota during the summer of 1917. They were not issued horses or saddles. In September, they traveled to Camp Cody, NM, for advanced training. Pfc. Youngman was assigned to Co. 15, Camp Cody June Automatic Replacement Draft, and sent to Europe on June 28, 1918, aboard the S.S. *Tereisias*. Upon arrival, he was transferred to Headquarters Co, 124th Field Artillery, 33rd Division. The 33rd Division suffered 7,255 casualties in the war. After the Armistice, Pfc. Youngman received an evaluation from his commanding officer, stating that "he is always present for duty and considered one of the best men in the

Company." Pfc. Youngman received the Silver Star medal. He left Brest, France, aboard the ship *America* on May 16, 1919. After returning to the U.S., he served briefly with Casual Detachment 668, Demobilization Group at Camp Dodge, IA. He was discharged on June 8, 1919. His name was engraved on a plaque erected to honor the war veterans at the Flandreau School. On July 2, 1921, he married Grace Horn at Sisseton. He later moved back to Poplar, where he married Mary Eagleman in 1924. He operated a service station in Poplar for a while. He also served as tribal chairman. In 1940, he was driving a school bus. From about 1942 to 1954, he lived with his family in Portland, OR. Louis entered the spirit world in the Agency hospital on his birthday, May 22, 1959. His wife and two sons, Lewis Jr. and Warren, and five daughters, Arlene, Janet, Agnes, Mrs. William Keever and Mrs Henry Sharvoneau, survived him. He is buried in the Poplar Cemetery.[8]

Z

Zephier, Wallace H. Wallace was born about 1887 on the Crow Creek Reservation. In the 1888 Crow Creek Census Roll, he was listed with his parents, David and Mary (Dion), and his older brothers and sisters, Joe, Dave, Melissa and Susie. Wallace married Philomon McBride (1892-1973) in 1908. When Wallace registered for the draft on June 5, 1917, he and Philomom had four children and were living in Dante, SD. Wallace joined the Army on Sept. 20, 1917, and was sent to Camp Funston for training with the 89th Division. He was assigned to Co. C, 340th Machine Gun Battalion. Pfc. Zephier was discharged on Jan. 6, 1918. This was prior to the 89th Division leaving for France. Philomon's brother, Walter McBride, also served in the Army. In the 1930 U.S. Census, Wallace was living with his family at the Crow Creek Agency and working as a clergyman. They had five children, Nephie, Alvin, Guy, Fennette and Harvey. In 1935, they moved to Wanblee. Wallace entered the spirit world in the Yankton Indian Hospital in Wagner on Jan. 17, 1952 and is buried in Holy Name Cemetery in Dante.[1]

APPENDIX A

In the 1930 U.S. Census, people were asked if family members had served in the military. Those who served during the time of the "Great War" are marked "WW." The following men were listed with service in the WW. No other information is known about their service.

Name	Age	County
Roy Bear Nose	31	Washington
Steven Brave Boy	28	Mellette
Robert Clifford	31	Shannon
Levi Elk Looks Back	39	Todd
Charles Ghost Bear	34	Shannon
Garnet Goings	33	Shannon
Henry Hennesey	38	Roberts
Sidney High Rock	35	Charles Mix
Andrew Laplante	34	Charles Mix
Charley Leaf	42	Marshall
David LeClaire	49	Charles Mix
John Little Chief	33	Mellette
James Max	31	Day
David Mills	33	Shannon
Samuel Poorman	40	Charles Mix
Christopher Red Feather	32	Shannon
Thomas Red Hawk	32	Dawes Co., NE
Moses Stranger Horse	39	Todd
William P. Wilson	35	Lyman
Solomon LaPointe	42	Gregory

APPENDIX B

After the war, an article about Arthur Frazier was published November of 1921 in the *Word Carrier*, published in Santee, NE. This article was translated from Dakota and edited by Louis Garcia of Tokio, ND.

ARTHUR FRAZIER OKICIZE EKTA KTEPI OYAKAPI

Arthur Frazier, So. Dakota ehantan Waawanyaka akicita opa April 4, 1917 en. Tunkasidan akicita wicada qon he ehan. Qa Mexico un, qa August 5, 1917 en Waawanyaka akicita he etanhan ayustan. Qa U.S. taakicita en opa qa August 6, 1917 en miniwanca akasampa yapi kta en opa. Demings, New Mexico ekta un July 14, 1918 hehanyan, he hetanhan France ekta iyaya. Qa August ihanke kiya Argonne Forest en okicize kin en opa qa taopi, Qa wayazanka oti at anpetu topa qaiS zaptan cen wanka qa hehan ake okicize etkazi, Qa October 6, 1918 qaiS wahehau Argonne makoce en okicize kin en ktepi. Om icage cin etanhan ehake dena nipi, wica yamni qa winyan yamni qa atkuku, qa hunku. Cinyeku Earlwin, Winner, SD, en ti qa Be, Martin, SD en un. De cinyetu kinkici anpetu wanjidan en akicita opa qaiSeya France makoce ekta okicize en opa. Robert, nakun Martin, SD, en un. Qa winyanpi kin Mrs. Ed Ross, Winner, SD, enti, qa Mrs. E. Raymond, nakun Winner, SD, enti, en ti. Qa Miss Stella, hunkake tipi en un. Atkuku Rev. Charles Frazier, Rosebud makoce en Wotawin WaSte oyaka heca un, KoSka de waniyetu wikcemna nonpa sampa wanji. Flandreau wayawa tipi he en un kin icunhan okicize tanka he icaga. Hecen iye cin on akicita opa. Frazier wicowazi otapi, qa heon takuwoecun owasin en wanji un kta iyecea seca. Heun okicize de en wanji opa, qa ekta ktepi qa woyaonihan heca.

Translation by Louis Garcia.

"Arthur Frazier from South Dakota joined the National Guard on April 4, 1917. He joined at that time because he had a lot of regard for the President. On August 5, 1917 while in New Mexico he was transferred from the National Guard. On August 6, 1917 he joined the Army and will be shipped across the ocean. On July 14, 1918, he left Deming, New Mexico and was shipped to France. At the end of August, he was wounded in the battle at Argonne Forest. He lay in the hospital for 4 or 5 days and was sent back to the battle. On October 6, 1918 or so he was killed in the battle for the Argonne territory. He grew up the last child of the family, leaving 3 brothers and 3 sisters along with his father and mother. Older brother Earlwin of Winner, SD, and Ben of Martin, SD. This older brother, Earlwin, was also in France and in the battle. Robert also lives in Martin, SD. And the women, sisters, Mrs. Ed Ross of Winner, Mrs. E. Raymond also of Winner. Miss Stella lives at home. His father Reverend Charles Frazier is a gospel preacher on the Rosebud Reservation. He was at Rosebud Reservation for 21 years. After the war (1862?) he grew up and went to school in Flandreau. Then he wants to be a soldier. The Frazier family is large and they all received one perhaps (notice of his death?). So, he joined the Army and was killed and became the only one to do so."

APPENDIX C

This letter was sent to Mrs. Helen Little by the Army after her husband was killed in France.

> Co. B 342 M.G. Bn.
> American E. Forces Pfalzel Germany
> Feb. 4th 1919

Mrs. Helen Little,

Winner, S. Dak

How I wish I could write that it was not your husband that made the supreme sacrifice for I know the burden thrust upon you is all the greater, having to acknowledge that it was your husband that was killed Nov. 1st. Sgt. Little had been reduced to private due to fact that he was away from the company. You may rest assured your husband was a good soldier and willing to defend the great country we love. Your husband was on a burial detail two days before the drive. A number of our company made the sacrifice on the way to help dig emplacements for the company. He was happy up to the last minute and felt like the rest of us---if I can pull thru this drive, I am safe. The company took position the night before the drive on Nov. 1st. Our position was on Hill 277, Bantheville Woods, Bantheville, France.

Your husband was with his squad in the belt filling emplacement. We knew that the woods would be difficult to take for the divisions that we relieved had suffered severe losses, but, Uncle Sam had planned an enormous barrage to break the front lines of the Huns and to save his boys. At the zero hour all guns spoke and consequently the Germans opened up on us and unfortunately placed a big shell in the belt filling station where your husband was helping filling belts for our machine guns.

Pvt. Little was killed instantly. A big piece of the shell hit him in the head and after a short time when I visited the station I found him dead but still sitting upright ready to perform his duties.

I shall gladly answer any questions you may want to ask. I expect to be home soon.

Accept my deepest sympathy.

> Yours sympathetically,
> F.O. Rains
> 1st Sgt. Co. "B", 342nd M.G. Bn.

Dear Mrs. Little:

Your letter received requesting information of your husband's death. The matter was referred to Sgt. Rains who was an eye witness and has given you the details as above.

Accept my heartfelt sympathy.

> I am
> Yours very respectfully
> Edwin Lindray
> Captain, 342nd M.G. Bn.

APPENDIX D

More Than Names

Soldiers of the Great War from Dewey and Ziebach Counties, South Dakota

Honoring Lakota Warriors of World War I from Cheyenne River Reservation

By

JoLavae Gunville

October 24, 2011

When I was a little girl growing up on the Cheyenne River Sioux Reservation in the seventies, I never knew the significance of one particular monument. This monument stood all alone on Main Street in Eagle Butte, South Dakota. Many days I would pass by this monument on the way to the grocery store to buy penny candy or Bazooka Joe bubble gum. I would jump over the white, three-planked fence that enclosed it, and then I would sit at the bottom of this stepped-monument and eat my candy. I would gaze up at it and wonder what it was all about. It states the following:

This Memorial is erected by the authority of Congress

of the United States of America Act of April 20, 1030

In honor of deceased Chiefs of the Cheyenne River Sioux Tribe of Indians

And the Valiant men of that tribe who made the supreme sacrifice in the

Service of the United States in the World War

1917-1918

Henry Running Rattle		**Isaac His Horse Is Fast**
Joseph Dupris	**Moses Clown**	**David Larabee**

As I grew older, a bar took the place of the monument. It was moved to the Harry V. Johnson Cultural Center along Highway 212. I would play for countless hours at the cultural center. This monument served as a base when we played tag or hide-n-go-seek. As a kid, I was never interested in history, and as each birthday passed, I slowly forgot about the monument. Until one day, as I was taking an evening walk with my son, we walked to the cultural center, and my little boy ran around and ended up sitting exactly where I sat many times. He climbed to the top step, looked up at me, and said, "What does this say, mom?" I read the monument and explained the significance of this forgotten monument.[1] I vowed one day I would honor those brave men who fought in The Great War. Who were these brave men and what were their stories? By writing this paper, I honor all those men from Dewey and Ziebach counties who fought and gave their lives for the United States of America.

World War I involved many nations. It began in 1914 and initially involved the European powers of Russia, Austria-Hungry, Turkey, Germany, France and Great Britain. There were many factors that led to World War I. Historians agree that the assassination of Austro-Hungarian Arch Duke Franz Ferdinand set the wheels of war into motion.[2] As European powers chose sides, they each called upon other countries to join their fight. According to the PBS documentary *The Great War and the Shaping of the 20th Century*, whatever the reasons for the war, the whole world became involved, which made it the costliest and deadliest war the world had ever witnessed as of that time.[3]

The United States Commander-In-Chief, Woodrow Wilson, looked toward diplomacy to quell the thunderous noise of war. President Wilson took a neutral stance at the onset of the war. However, President Wilson's view changed in 1917 when British intelligence intercepted a telegram from Germany's Foreign Secretary Zimmerman to Mexico. The telegram stated that Germany would see to the return of Mexican territory taken during the Mexican-American War, including the states of Texas, New Mexico, and Arizona, if Mexico would become allies with Germany. Germany at this time was conducting unrestricted submarine warfare.[4] Wilson decided to make the telegram public knowledge, which sparked national opinion on joining the war effort. On April 6, 1917, President Wilson called on Congress to declare war. By the time the United States passed a declaration of war, millions of soldiers from many nations had already lost their lives.

On May 18, 1917, the United States passed the Selective Service Act. This act allowed the United States to draft eligible men into active military service. Men, young and old, from every nationality flocked to register for the draft. Many were new immigrants or sons of immigrants. Some could hardly speak English, and many were not citizens of the United States. Young men, too young to register for the draft, lied about their age in order to go off to war.

One group of this population was Native Americans. Men from all tribes were willing to enlist in the Armed Forces to fight for a country that did not acknowledge them as American citizens. For many Lakota whose fathers or grandfathers fought in the Battle of Greasy Grass (Battle of Little Big Horn) and whose relatives were killed at the Massacre at Wounded Knee, this memory was still in the hearts and minds of the men who went off to war. On the other hand, there were many American Indians who refused to enlist in the draft, as well as many German immigrants.[5]

Enoch Herbert Crowder served as the chief author of the Selected Service Act, and he then became responsible for administrating the draft under the title Provost Marshall General.[6] In this newly created position under the Selective Service Act, Chowder received the task of initiating the draft and planning the logistics of getting the men trained and off to war. On June 5, 1917, the United States mandated that all men between the ages of twenty-one and thirty-one report to their local draft boards for registration. From August 8-10, 1917, Dewey County called for the first round of the draft for the area. Ziebach County also called for the first round draft during the same time. During this time, the men who were selected were given physical examinations and were able to apply for exemptions. According to the *Timber Lake Topic,* ninety men were eligible for the draft. It should be noted, that in this same article, the editor writes, "There are five aliens in the list, which have been rejected and discharged from service under the rules and regulations."[7] The rules and regulations varied from state to state and from draft board to draft board. Many American Indians were not citizens of the United States; therefore, they were called aliens. Those Native Americans who were of mixed blood usually had citizen status. In Thomas A. Britten's book, *American Indians in World War I*, he writes, "Such was the case with the local board at the Cheyenne River Indian

Reservation in South Dakota. Although the local board correctly classified the non-citizen Sioux into Class V, the district board (which had the authority to overrule the decisions of local draft boards) reclassified them into Class I." The district board initiated the change because it reasoned that the Indians were not Alien Enemies nor Resident Aliens, in fact not aliens at all. But after reviewing instructions from the Provost Marshall General's office the district board rescinded its decision.[8] In many, cases Native Americans were classified as white so local draft boards could fill their quota. On the other hand, many Native Americans refused to serve unless they were declared United States citizens. James D. Stewart, editor of the *Dupree Leader,* wrote, "Among the drafted boys who left for Camp Lewis American Lake, Wash., last Saturday, was Thomas Slow of Cherry Creek. Although exempt from service by being a non-citizen Indian, Tom said he wanted to go and fight for his country, considering it is his duty and that he was no better than his white brothers. This act of patriotism is commended and puts him as an example of true Americanism in the eyes of the general public."[9] The Lakota, or "Sioux", came from warrior societies, and military service showed this tradition of their bravery and honor as warriors. This mind set is still strong today as many Lakota men and women are fighting and have lost their lives for the sake of democracy and the United States of America.

On June 2, 1918 the second round of draftees left for training at Camp Funston, Fort Riley, Kansas. The article, *"Dewey* County Boys Given Big Send-Off" from the *Timber Lake Topic,* described the day the new recruits left Timber Lake. Families, relatives and friends gathered around to say farewell to the men. Twenty-six men in all boarded a train amidst the Timber Lake-Isabel band. There were whoops and hollers as the Lakota men gave their war cries. Lakota women cried and gave their tremolos and old warriors stood proud as their sons, brothers and nephews answered the call to fight. The article concluded with, "Five Indians stepped off to war and fighting shoulder to shoulder with their white brothers of the plains they will help drive the blond beast form the soil of France and Belgium.[10]

Sixteen men left Ziebach County for Fort Riley, Kansas in the third installment of the draft, which included Adolph Abraham, Redelm; Frederick Mueller, Isabel; Orville Minning, Redelm; John Slow, Cherry Creek; Oscar L. Herron, Chase; Albert J. Benoit, Faith; Lee Slagel, Isabel; Luke Black Eagle, Dupree; Thomas Irwin Munyon, Coal Springs; James Bear Stops, Zeal; Edward B, Ship, Faith; Anton Hannemann, Redelm; Ellsworh Brush, Duree; Emil Pudwill, Faith; Thomas Hawk Eagle, Dupree; and Ole J. Sundsrud, Redelm. Ziebach County residents also sent their soldiers off with fanfare. According to the article, "Citizens of County Bids Boys Farewell" from the *Dupree Leader,* September 17, 1917, there was a parade led by the local band followed by the Red Cross, veterans of the Civil and Spanish Wars, and the new recruits. Mayor Shelton of Dupree encouraged the people who were at the parade to pass the hat. Amongst cheers and tears the new recruits boarded the train to Fort Riley. James D. Stewart, editor of the *Dupree Leader* wrote, "Ziebach County is proud of her boys, a husky lot, hardened by toil on the farms and ranches making of a military organization whose recorded no doubt will excel all in past history."[11]

Whether in the first or the second round of the draft selection, the new recruits traveled on a special train from Timber Lake to Mobridge and eventually arrived at Camp Funston. Along the way, they traveled to Sioux City, Iowa then onto Omaha, Nebraska, and from there, they went to Lincoln. The trip took two days to get to Funston. Arthur Nelson from Trail City wrote to County Judge P.O. Urban to tell of their safe arrival. Nelson noted that, throughout the trip, people in the towns would greet the men. He wrote, "It seemed as the whole town turned out to bid us goodbye and the women went through our coaches and distributed cigars, tobacco, papers, magazines and all kinds of fruit."[12]

At Camp Funston, like all new recruits, their lives became regimented and regulated. New recruits were given physical and mental examinations. The psychological test determined what positions or jobs the recruits were assigned. The tests were based on the Stanford-Binet tests. The tests, however, were created and geared toward educated white males. Native Americans and men from rural areas did not fare so well on the tests. Consequently, these men were assigned in large numbers to infantry and detail units. According to an essay in the *Kansas Historical Society Journal* written by Sherow and Bruce titled "How Kola From Camp Funston," "Indian recruits, with little exposure to off reservation culture, psychological testing of this kind automatically relegated them to the lowest levels of Army hierarchy." Although they were not formally segregated into units like African Americans, Native Americans found themselves in units with a high number of Native Americans. Nonetheless, the Federal government saw this as an extension of assimilation.[13]

While at Camp Funston, new recruits were trained in all aspects of the military from personal appearance to rifle training. Men were also trained in chemical warfare, which was a new form of weaponry at this time. Besides all the training, recruits were given a series of shots that made many sick. R.W. Kraushaar wrote, "Our Dewey County boys, however, got over all vaccinations and inoculations without any effects," He also wrote, "the heat at Funston doesn't let up very much. We are getting used to the 100 and 110 degrees in the shade."[14] Men from Dewey and Ziebach County saw one another on occasion. In the same letter, Kraushaar wrote how he visited with Whitney Laplante, as they passed one another, and he said how he was happy to see him. After training at Camp Funston, the soldiers were deployed with their units to bases around the country. Private Irving Scranton wrote home from Co. K., 157th Infantry, Camp Kearny, California, "I will give you the names of the boys that are with us now, Harry Nisse, Chas. McAllister, L. Johnson, F. Laurenx, W.M. Merns, Christ Schmidt, Sullivan Pretty Weasel, David Drops At A Distance. We are now what they call First Class Soldiers - ready to fight anything."[15] Maurice P. Cahill wrote home from aboard the U.S.S. Trinidadian. In his letter, he wrote that he is homeward bound from his second trip to Europe. He also wrote, "An American fighting man certainly rates good treatment in the land of our Allies. The spirit of the people is very good, and conditions generally, in a good way."[16] Although the young men showed enthusiasm and bravery, they were amidst terrible conditions and horrible experiences. The young men of The Great War, as in any war, saw their friends killed and shared experiences that they would never forget.

Soldiers from the Dewey and Ziebach Counties fought bravely from the Chateau-Thierry in May of 1918 to the bloodiest and larges battle of World War I, the Meuse Argonne. Chateau-Thierry was fought five miles from the town of the same name. It is the first battle in which the American Expeditionary Forces saw a large number of soldiers killed.[17] The battle at Meuse-Argonne started on September 26, 1918 and became the last battle fought during World War I. Six hundred thousand American soldiers of the First Army American Expeditionary Force led by General John Pershing advanced to the front trenches. This force was made up of young, inexperienced men. Pershing and his men attacked German soldiers who were well-fortified and knew the terrain. This battle took place northwest of the town of Verdun, France. During the Meuse-Argonne, over 25,000 servicemen lost their lives. According to an article, "no other single battle in American military history even approaches the Meuse-Argonne in size and costs, yet few know much about it, even though it constituted the most important U.S. contribution to the allied effort in World

War I."[18] General Pershing broke through German forces protecting major railways. On the other hand, German soldiers protected the railroad junction located near Sedan, France at all costs. General Pershing pushed forward even though the Germans were highly equipped and armored. The American soldiers were no match for the Germans for they had several years experience fighting in the trenches. However, the inexperienced American soldiers overcame the overly tired German Army.[19]

American soldiers, commonly known as "Doughboys," came from every nationality, race, and social class. Britten, in his book *American Indians In World War I*, wrote, "Many were recent immigrants or sons of immigrants and could barely speak English."[20] Many of them were way too young to enlist and lied to get into the military. Valiant stories of Lakota men who served have found their way into history books such as the story of Chester Armstrong Four Bear. He registered for the draft in Dewey County and trained as a sniper. Armstrong, while carrying a message from his company commander on the front line, faced heavy attack. Armstrong Four Bears helmet can be seen at the Timber Lake Historical Museum, and one can see where a bullet grazed it.[21] While Armstrong was running to Regimental headquarters, the enemy shot gas cannons in his direction. Although he had to crawl, he delivered the message safely. His commanding officers ordered him to get medical attention; however, he refused and returned to the front line. On the way, he came across a wounded French soldier, and Armstrong helped him to safety and gave him first aid. The French soldier took off his Croix De Guerre and gave it to Armstrong.[22] Armstrong received his discharge from the Army on May 8, 1919. He returned home to become a successful cowboy, who became known for his trick roping and performed with Buffalo Bill's Wild West Show. He even performed his roping skills in front of Britain's King George V. In 1985, Armstrong became an inducted member into the South Dakota Cowboy and Western Heritage Hall of Fame. Victor Thill of the Timber Lake area served with the 3rd Division and fought in all the major battles in France. Thill was one of five from his company who survived, but he suffered severe shell shock.[23] Oscar White Weasel went with the Army to the Mexican border to search for Poncho Villa, and upon his return, he went to Germany. There are likely many more stories such as these that are out there. I hope that others are listening for the stories of the Lakota Doughboys, or the stories will slowly be lost.

An ironic story from World War I involves a couple of men who fought on opposite sides during The Great War who later became friends. Fred Beer was a soldier for the Imperial German Army who later immigrated to the United States and worked on a farm in Plankinton, South Dakota. Later, Fred then moved near the Glad Valley area of Ziebach County in 1925 and, in 1926, married Mary Boeding. He then moved to a farm north of Isabel and made his home there. Glen R. Buckly of Spearfish was a soldier for the American Expeditionary Force. Corporal Buckley was with Co. B. 340th Machine Gun Battalion with the 89th Division. The two men exchanged bullets across the river near Muese-Argonne in France; however, neither of them knew each other during the war. As time passed, Mr. Beer became County Commissioner for Ziebach County, and Mr. Buckley became Harding County Commissioner. As fate would have it, these two gentlemen began a conversation about the war and learned more about one another. There was no animosity between the two former soldiers, and a friendship was born.[24]

On the home front, civilians were doing their patriotic duty by helping the war effort any way they could. Tony Rivers of the Timber Lake area contributed to the war by supplying the United States with horses. Mr. Rivers owned a large herd of horses that he sold to the United States

Government. The horses all had the J brand on them and were used by the United States Calvary in Germany. A local soldier, Casper LeCompte, Sr. recognized the J brand and stated that he rode one of Mr. River's horses while in Germany.[25]

Local Red Crosses were formed and organized in many of the communities. The Red Cross served many purposes from organizing community events for the soldiers to making care packages to send overseas. These care packages contained items ranging from chewing gum and clothing to cigarettes. In the article titled "Organized a Red Cross Branch At Cherry Creek" in the *Dupree Leader*, it stated that local members of the Ziebach Chapter of the Red Cross traveled to Cherry Creek to help organize a local chapter. Thirty-four members of the community and surrounding area became members. Officers that were elected included: Mrs. John Derby, Chairman; Mrs. Axe, Vice-Chairman; Miss Zola White Feather, Secretary. Executive Board members were as follows: Mrs. Jennette Elk Thunder, Mrs. John Swan, and James Swan. It was also reported that the Reverend Andrew White Face donated his log cabin to hold meetings. In addition, many of the community members donated money for the cause.[26] The Red Cross provided an important service for American soldiers and the patriotism of the American Red Cross continues today.

The United States Army, under the orders of General John Pershing published a military newspaper called *The Stars and Stripes*. *The Stars and Stripes* was published from February 8, 1919 to June 13, 1919. As American soldiers were scattered throughout Europe, *The Stars and Stripes* kept everyone informed on news, major announcements, sports, cartoons and news from home. Many articles featured American Indians. One article titled, "Redskin Tribes in Single Company" reported that the Prussian Army came across a company of American Indians on October 8th on the hills near Champagne, France. American Indians from thirteen tribes put the Prussian Guards on the run. The article included the Sioux among the tribes listed. It is very possible that one of the local men from Dewey or Ziebach County served among them. The same article reported that the American Indian privates would spend their passes riding in automobiles and hanging out with a company championship football team consisting of Carlisle Indian School all-stars. One soldier, by the name of George Jewett from White Horse played on the Carlisle Indian School football team along with Jim Thorpe. Jewett was in the Army and was very athletic, and he later played on a local baseball team upon his return from the war. Thomas Hawk Eagle also played for Carlisle Indian School in 1914 according to Tom Benjey's book, *Wisconsin's Carlisle Indian School Immortals*. Benjey noted that Hawk Eagle played right guard and "was a very good player."[27] Local newspapers, such as the *Timber Lake Topic*, *Dupree Leader* and the *Redelm Reader*, also did their duty by reporting on the war, encouraging patriotism and printing letters from local soldiers. One article, "Advice to Soldier Boys" read as follows:

> "Say, boys at the front, listen: Write to your mothers. Don't be kidded into the notion you're your principal duty lies in writing to the girls. It is well enough to write to the girls, of course-the dear things. They miss you and expect to hear from you, but don't miss you as your mothers do and their hearts are not breaking as your mothers hearts are. Write to your mother first (putting in a little at the bottom for dad, for you can't imagine how he will appreciate it) and when you have discharged that duty and pleasure, then pencil a few to the chickens."[28]

People all across the United States rallied behind the American War effort; each giving selflessly of their time, money or whatever they could.

American Indians also contributed to The Great War by using their native languages. It wasn't until the end of the war that American Indians used their native tongue to relay messages. The Central Powers had no idea how to decipher the messages. As reported in *The Stars and Stripes*, the Sioux were instrumental in initiating use of American Indian languages during the war. The Germans tapped into telephone lines, listened to orders involving attacks, and then used this information against Allied Forces. One company commander, upset by the wire-tapping, enlisted the help of two Sioux soldiers, who would relay messages in Lakota. The article called the men, "intelligent, willing men," who did their job. Choctaw code talkers also played a vital role in confusing the Germans.[29]

The Great War was not great for the millions of soldiers from both the Allied and Central powers who lost their lives. Soldiers from Dewey and Ziebach Counties were included among those who lost their lives for "The War to End All Wars." Many people from Dewey and Ziebach Counties lost husbands, sons, brothers, uncles and friends. From Ziebach County, eleven men were killed in action. For instance Dewey County's Private Moses Clown or Running Eagle, Co. B of the 314th military police, 32nd Division died just days before the Armistice. Moses was a close relative of the great Lakota leader Crazy Horse. Friendly fire by the USS Felix Taussig sunk the USS SC-209 on August 27, 1919 killing Fireman 3rd Class Edwin F. Hodgdon from Ziebach County.[30] The Dupree Legion Post is now named in his honor. Private Emerson Smith from Isabel, who served with the 148th Machine Gun Battalion, died in action in the Battle of Sissian on July 19. Private Philip Wright suffered severe wounds by a German sniper, and a few days later, died on July 20, 1918. He was in the 38th Infantry Machine Gun Company. Isabel's Legion Post, the Smith-Wright Post is named after their local heroes. Gene Gelino of the Timber Lake area also died during his military service. The Timber Lake Legion Post is named after this fallen soldier. Private Isaac His Horse Is Fast, of Co. C., 128th Infantry; Private Jacob Christensen, of Co. C, 126th Infantry and Private 1st Class Joseph Dupris, of Battery C., 147th Field Artillery of the 32nd Division were all killed in action. The 1st Division became the first Americans to set foot on Germany's soil and fought in the battles of Alsace, the Marne, and Aisne, Oise and Argonne offensives.[31]

The men who fought in World War I from Dewey and Ziebach counties are more than names on a monument or wall. They have stories that are long lost and remain only in the documents, newspapers and scrapbooks of their families. World War I, also called The Great War, affected nations throughout the world. This paper includes the stories of just a few of the soldiers of World War I. The stories of the men of Dewey and Ziebach County will remain forever in my heart to share with students, historians and whoever else will listen. Now my son can tell his children about the monument on which he once played and tell the true stories of the men of World War I from Dewey and Ziebach Counties.

Sources and Acknowledgements

We wish to thank the Tribal Veteran's Service Officers for providing lists of tribal veterans from the South Dakota Reservations. Using these lists as a starting point, we found further information on www.Ancestry.com. This website has information on the tribal census rolls from 1890-1940, Application for Headstones for Veterans, as well as WWI Army Transport Rolls. These rolls include the soldier's service number, rank, unit, home town and next of kin. We also want to thank the staff of the South Dakota Vital Records for providing copies of death certificates. The volunteers at the Rapid City Society for Genealogical Research provided many copies of obituaries from the local papers.

Once the fighting was over, the U.S. military officials and some private organizations were interested in finding out how the Native servicemen had performed. Officers and NCOs were asked to identify and evaluate the men who served under them. Joseph K. Dixon, who had traveled around Indian Country as a photographer before the war, was also interested in recording how the war affected the veterans. Working with Rodman Wanamaker, Dixon developed his own questionnaire that he sent to men on the reservations to complete. Dixon had plans for publishing a book on the war experiences of the men from Indian Country, but never was able to finish it. Those unpublished documents and photos are now part of the Wanamaker Documents, William Mathers Museum of World Culture at the University of Indiana, Bloomington, IN. Ellen Sieber helped us find the records and photos which pertained to men from South Dakota. The museum has records on many Dakota and Lakota men who served in the war.

When the depression hit South Dakota in the 1930s, the South Dakota Emergency Relief Administration (SDERA) conducted surveys on the South Dakota reservations. The workers discussed health conditions and employment situations of the residents. The interviews were typed up and kept. We wish to thank Vicky Valenta for providing copies of these reports.

We want to thank the many people who have shared photos and stories about their relatives who served during the WWI era. Pilamaya

ROSTER OF VETERANS

A

1. MT Death Certificate; Wanamaker Documentation, WW-75_26; "Wesley Ackerman Services Held Wednesday," *The Glacier Reporter*, 9/22/1966, p. 1.
2. MN Death Certificate; "John Adams of Ponsford is Dead at 62," *Detroit Lakes Tribune*, 9/19/1962, p. 3; Minnesota Historical Society, WWI Bonus File.
3. SDERA, Rosebud File #8.
4. SD Death Certificate; "Jim Agard, Well Known Bullhead Indian, Killed in a Shooting Scrape," *Sioux County Pioneer-Arrow,* 6/5/1931; Susan A. Krouse, *North American Indians in the Great War,* (Lincoln, NE, 2007), p. 114.
5. SD Death Certificate.
6. Krouse, pp. 197-98; SD Death Certificate; *Sioux County Pioneer*, 1/30/1919, p. 1; "Fatal Crash Kills Bullhead Indian and Injures North Country Rancher," *Sioux County Pioneer,* 8/6/1954, p. 1.
7. Folder 1081, Box 25, MS71, Beecher Family Papers, Yale University Library; District of Columbia Death Certificate; "Illustrious Indian Dies at Capital," *Sioux County Pioneer*, 3/14/1930, 1.
8. *Rapid City Journal*, 10/7/1972, 7.
9. SD Death Certificate.
10. Krouse, 188; MT Death Certificate; "Arthur T. Arrow Rites Set Today," *The Montana Standard*, 4/4/1953.
11. Photo published online (Ancestry.com) in American Soldier of World War I
12. *Rapid City Journal*, 4/12/1979, 5.
13. SD Death Certificate.
14. *Rapid City Journal,* 4/11/1978, 5.
15. SD Death Certificate.
16. ND Death Certificate, *The Dunseith Journal*, 11/9/1950, 1.

B

1. SDERA File #12, (Pine Ridge), South Dakota Death Certificate.
2. SD Death Certificate; Wanamaker Documentation, WW-75_92.
3. SD Death Certificate; Wanamaker Documentation, WW-75_90; SDERA File # 1, Lower Brule.
4. SDERA File #2, (Pine Ridge).
5. SD Death Certificate; SDERA File #12 (Pine Ridge); Wanamaker Documentation, WW-75_92.
6. SD Death Certificate; SDERA File #2, (Crow Creek); *Sioux County Pioneer,* 2/13/1919.
7. WA Death Certificate.
8. "Patricia Man Dies, Blairmore," *Lethbridge Herald,* 1/26/1960, 2; "The Bailly Story," *Spurs and Shovels Along the Royal Line*, 1979, 264-268.
9. SD Death Certificate; SDERA File #18 (Standing Rock).
10. ND Death Certificate; "Funeral at Dunseith for Francis F. Baker," *Bottineau Courant,* 7/8/1970, 4.
11. SD Death Certificate.
12. SD Death Certificate.
13. SD Death Certificate; SDERA File #8 (Sisseton).
14. *History of the 306th Infantry.* New York, 1935, 92.
15. Wanamaker Documentation, WW-75_90.
16. *Sisseton Courier,* 3/5/1964, 5.
17. SD Death Certificate; Wanamaker Documentation, WW-75_54.
18. *Rapid City Journal,* 4/27/1994, C2.
19. SD Death Certificate; SDERA File #18 (Standing Rock); "Bearshield Cook and Baker," *Sioux County Pioneer,* 6/16/1927, 1.
20. SD Death Certificate.

21. SDERA File #59 (Cheyenne River).
22. *Sisseton Courier*, 4/12/1979, 9.
23. Wanamaker Documentation, WW-75_20; Russell Means, *Where White Men Fear to Tread*. New York, 1995,27.
24. Wanamaker Documentation, WW-75_20.
25. SD Death Certificate.
26. SDERA File #22 (Cheyenne River).
27. NY Death Certificate; "Foul Play is Seen in Man's Death," *Niagara Falls Gazette*, 4/30/1957, 1; "Lockport Plant Worker's Hands Tightly Bound,' *Union Sun and Journal*, 4/29/1957, 1.
28. ND Death Certificate; SDERA File #29 (Standing Rock).
29. Wanamaker Documentation, WW-75_90.
30. 1948 *Huron City Directory*, 35.
31. Wanamaker Documentation, WW-75_90; Proctor Fiske, *History of the Three Hundred Fiftieth Regiment of U.S. Infantry.* Cedar Rapids, IA, 1919, 234.
32. SD Death Certificate; SDERA File #66 (Cheyenne River).
33. Wanamaker Documentation, WW-75_90.
34. SD Death Certificate; SDERA File #1 (Yankton); Wanamaker documentation, WW-75_20; *History of the Third Division, United States Army, in THE WORLD WAR, for the period December 1, 1917 to January 1, 1919,* Andernach-On-The- Rhine, 1919, 302.
35. Wanamaker Documentation, WW-75_69.
36. Wanamaker Documentation, WW-75_92; *Rapid City Journal,*9/11/1968, 28.
37. SD Death Certificate; SDERA File #41 (Cheyenne River).
38. SD Death Certificate.
39. Krouse, 126.
40. Zitkala-Sa, *American Indian Stories,* Lincoln, NE, 2003, xvi-xvii.
41. "Jim Thorpe Great Marble Player," *The Montana Standard,* 3/26/1942; *Sacramento Union,* 8/15/1960, 4.
42. *Rapid City Journal,* 7/27/1972, 8.
43. SD Death Certificate; Correspondence with Patty Bordeaux Nelson.
44. SD Death Certificate; SDERA File #31 (Cheyenne River); C.E. Lovejoy, *The Story of the Thirty Eighth,* Coblenz, 1919, 39.
45. Krouse, 123.
46. SDERA File #5 (Standing Rock).
47. SD Death Certificate; SDERA File #5 (Standing Rock).
48. SD Death Certificate; SDERA File #16 (Cheyenne River).
49. Bonnie Lynn-Sherow and Susannah Ural Bruce, "How Cola" From Camp Funston, *Kansas History,* 2001, 93-94; National Archives at Kansas City, Record Group 129, File #32536.
50. SD Death Certificate; Wanamaker Documentation, WW-75_90.
51. SDERA File #5 (Standing Rock).
52. ND Death Certificate; *Minot Daily News,* 12/10/1956, 6; Wanamaker Documentation, WW-32-01.
53. SD Death Certificate; Krouse, 144.
54. SD Death Certificate.
55. Krouse, 99.
56. MT Death Certificate.
57. SD Death Certificate.
58. SDERA File #5 (Standing Rock).
59. Wanamaker Documentation, WW-75_39; SDERA File #12 (Rosebud); SD Death Certificate.

C

1. CA Death Certificate; Krouse, 143; SDERA File #29 (Standing Rock).

2. *Rapid City Journal,* 5/18/1980, 5.
3. "Crow Agency Man Killed at Havre," *The Hardin Tribune-Herald,* 8/6/1942, 1; MT Death Certificate.
4. *Rapid City Journal,* 1/18/1977, 10.
5. SD Death Certificate.
6. SDERA File #31 (Cheyenne River); SD Death Certificate; R. Alton Lee, *A New Deal for South Dakota,* 138.
7. NY Death Certificate; Thomas A. Britten, *American Indians in World War I,* Albuquerque, 1997, 166.
8. MN Death Certificate; State of Minn. Military Service Record.
9. *Rapid City Journal,* 7/6/1976, 24.
10. SD Death Certificate
11. SDERA File #3 (Rosebud).
12. MN Death Certificate.
13. SDERA File #8 (Rosebud); Wanamaker Documentation, WWQ-di42.007.
14. *Aberdeen Daily News,* 12/26/1972; SDERA File #2 (Sisseton).
15. *Rapid City Journal,* 11/13/1968, 8.
16. SDERA File #73 (Cheyenne River); George H. English, *History of the 89th Division, U.S.A.*, Denver, 1920, 440.
17. SD Death Certificate; SDERA File #8 (Sisseton).
18. SDERA File #60 (Cheyenne River); SD Death Certificate.
19. Photo from WWI file on Ancestry.com
20. Wanamaker Documentation, WW-75_66.
21. Wanamaker Documentation, WW-75_92.
22. *Rapid City Journal,* 12/18/1974.
23. Wanamaker Documentation, WW-75_90.
24. SD Death Certificate.
25. WI Death Certificate; Wanamaker Documentation, WW-32-01; *The Daily News* (Green Bay), 4/11/1974.
26. WI Death Certificate; *Green Bay Press Gazette,* 6/18/1984, B-8; Wanamaker Documentation, WW-75_36.
27. Krouse, 88; English, 440.
28. Krouse, 97; *Rapid City Journal,* 7/30/1980, 10.
29. SD Death Certificate.
30. SD Death Certificate.
31. SD Death Certificate; *Rapid City Journal,* 1/28/1975, 7.
32. SDERA File #12 (Rosebud).
33. Krouse, 106.
34. SDERA File #23 (Standing Rock).
35. SD Death Certificate; Wanamaker Documentation, WW-75_90.
36. SDERA File #8 (Rosebud).
37. *Camp Dodger,* 2/3/1919 and 2/10/1919, 4; Wanamaker Documentation, WW-75_90; SD Death Certificate; SDERA File #6 (Standing Rock).
38. Edgar J.D. Larson, *Memoirs of France and the Eighty-Eighth Division,* Minneapolis, 1920, 128; ND Death Certificate; SDERA File #15 (Standing Rock).
39. Krouse, 57; *Rapid City Journal,* 10/25/1972, 29; Wanamaker Documentation, WW-75_66 and WWQ_di77_007; *History of the 306th Infantry,* New York, 1935, 92.
40. SDERA File #66 (Cheyenne River).
41. Krouse, 106-7, 162; *Rapid City Journal,* 7/11/1987, 32.

D

1. MN Death Certificate; State of Minn. Military Service Record.
2. WI Death Certificate.
3. SD Death Certificate.
4. ND Death Certificate.
5. SD Death Certificate.
6. SD Death Certificate; SDERA File #15 (Standing Rock).
7. Krouse, 129, 152.
8. *Sioux County Pioneer,* 11/25/1945, 1.
9. *Green Bay Press-Gazette,* 7/23/1998, B-6.
10. "Four Killed in Badger Ordnance Explosion," *Baraboo News-Republic,* 7/20/1945, 1; Michael J. Goc, *Powder, People and Place,* 169.
11. SD Death Certificate.
12. Wanamaker Documentation: WW-75_54.
13. ND Death Certificate; Britten, 163.
14. SDERA File #6 (Standing Rock): SD Death Certificate.
15. ND Death Certificate; SDERA File #6 (Standing Rock); Lovejoy, 39.
16. SD Death Certificate; SDERA File #24 (Pine Ridge).
17. WA Death Certificate.
18. SD Death Certificate; *Camp Travis,* New York City, 1919, 84.
19. SD Death Certificate; SDERA File #13 (Pine Ridge).
20. SD Death Certificate; Wanamaker Documentation: WW-75_92.
21. Obit: *Los Vegas Review Journal,* 9/26/1990.
22. Wanamaker Documentation: WW-75_90.
23. *Rapid City Journal,* 1/17/1974.
24. SD Death Certificate.
25. Wanamaker Documentation: WW-75_26.
26. WI Death Certificate.
27. *Rapid City Journal,* 2/22/1968, 3.
28. Wanamaker Documentation: WW-75_92; *History of Company E 355th Infantry A.E.F.,* 76
29. SD Death Certificate.
30. CA Death Certificate; Krouse, 123.
31. *Sisseton Courier,* 8/24/1972, 2; English, 430.
32. SD Death Certificate; SDERA File #67 (Cheyenne River); Krouse, 29; Frank B. Tiebout, *A History of the 305th Infantry,* New York, 1919, 399.
33. *Rapid City Journal,* 11/20/1988, B2; SDERA File #13 (Rosebud).
34. Wanamaker Documentation: WW-75_20.
35. SD Death Certificate.
36. *Rapid City Journal,* 8/19/1995, B2; Joe Starita, *The Dull Knifes of Pine Ridge,* Lincoln, NE, 1995, 211.
37. SDERA File #9 (Sisseton).
38. WA Death Certificate.
39. Wanamaker Documentation: WW-75_90; NARA, RG 75, Series 1327, Box 82, Folder 3864.

E

1. MT Death Certificate.
2. Wanamaker Documentation: WW-75_90.
3. Lynn-Sherow and Bruce, 89.
4. SD Death Certificate.
5. SD Death Certificate.

6. Henry J. Reilly, *Americans All, The Rainbow at War*, Columbus, OH, 1936, 360-61; Jennings C. Wise, *The Red Man in the New World Drama*, Washington, D.C., 1931, 528.
7. SD Death Certificate; SDERA File #30 (Standing Rock); Lovejoy, 39.
8. SD Death Certificate.
9. SD Death Certificate; Krouse, 117; *Sioux County Pioneer*, 1/30/1919.
10. SD Death Certificate; SDERA File #4 (Rosebud).
11. SD Death Certificate; SDERA File #31 (Standing Rock.
12. *Rapid City Journal,* 12/14/1971, 6; Scott Riney, *The Rapid City Indian School 1898-1933,* 85.
13. CA Death Certificate; *Red Lake News,* 6/1/1919 and 1/1/1920, 3.
14. *Rapid City Journal,* 8/26/1968, 9.
15. MN Death Certificate; *St. Cloud Telephone Directory*, 1947, 14

F

1. SDERA File #4 (Rosebud); *Rapid City Journal,* 7/12/1971, 18.
2. SD Death Certificate.
3. SD Death Certificate; Krouse, 23.
4. ND Death Certificate.
5. *History of Company E 355th Infantry A.E.F.,* 38.\
6. SD Death Certificate.
7. SD Death Certificate.
8. SD Death Certificate; SDERA File #3 (Pine Ridge).
9. *South Dakota Historical Collections*, Vol. XXII, 35-37.
10. *The Harlem News,* 5/7/1954, 4.
11. SD Death Certificate.
12. FL Death Certificate; Franklin F. Holbrook, *St. Paul and Ramsey County in the War of 1917-1918,* 393.
13. SD Death Certificate.
14. SDERA File #9 (Rosebud); *Rapid City Journal,* 11/30/1994, B2.
15. "Indian Ball Players Cause Stir in East," *Sioux County Pioneer,* 5/17/1923, 1; *Rapid City Journal,* 9/7/1974.
16. SD Death Certificate.
17. Lynn-Sherow and Bruce, 85.
18. SD Death Certificate.
19. SD Death Certificate; Krouse, 193-94. Conversation with Marcella LeBeau.
20. SDERA File #7 (Standing Rock; *Rapid City Journal,* 10/25/1973, 11.
21. "Arthur Frazier Okicize ekta Ktepi Oyakapi," *Word Carrier,* Nov. 1921; correspondence with Virginia Driving Hawk Sneve.
22. SD Death Certificate.
23. Wanamaker Documentation: WW-75_29; SD Historical Collections, Vol. XXII, 37-38.
24. SD Death Certificate.
25. SD Graves Registration Service, 6/11/1941.
26. Wanamaker Documentation: WW-75_90.
27. Krouse, 32.
28. Wanamaker Documentation: WW-75_57; *33rd Division A.E.F.,* Diekirch, Luxembourg, 1919, 9-10.

G

1. SDERA File #31 (Standing Rock); SD Death Certificate; Robert Lee, *Fort Meade and the Black Hills,* U. of Nebraska, 1991, 206.
2. SDERA File #7 (Standing Rock); SD Death Certificate.
3. *Rapid City Journal,* 3/21/1994, B2.

4. *Rapid City Journal,* 1/27/1969, 9.
5. Wanamaker Documentation: WW-75_66; conversation with Frieda Garreau; Douglas R. Eisenstein, *Whispers in the Wind* (Xlibris Corporation, 2000), 219-220.
6. *Rapid City Journal,* 12/23/1973, B2.
7. SD Death Certificate; SDERA File #67 (Cheyenne River)
8. SD Death Certificate; Robert Gilland, *Along the Trail to Thunderhawk,* 2010.
9. SD Death Certificate.
10. Wanamaker Documentation: WW-75_97; SDERA File #13 (Rosebud).
11. *Rapid City Journal,* 12/29/1982.
12. SD Death Certificate.
13. Wanamaker Documentation: WW-75_51.
14. *Sioux City Journal,* 7/20/1961; Krouse, 50.
15. SD Death Certificate; Conversation with Alvina Feather Earring.
16. "World War I Veteran Passes," *Sisseton Courier,* 11/2/1944, 1.
17. SD Death Certificate.
18. NJ Death Certificate.
19. SD Death Certificate.

H

1. SD Death Certificate.
2. SD Death Certificate.
3. Wanamaker Documentation: WW-75_66; SD Death Certificate; Eisenstein, 219-220.
4. SD Death Certificate; Krouse, 32.
5. SD Death Certificate; Krouse, 198.
6. SD Death Certificate.
7. SDERA File #13 (Pine Ridge).
8. SD Death Certificate.
9. SD Death Certificate.
10. MT Death Certificate; Roster of the 347th Field Artillery.
11. *Rapid City Journal,* 6/19/1975, 20.
12. *The Sioux City Journal,* 10/11/1955, 4; Wanamaker Documentation: WW-75_92; Krouse, 36.
13. SD Graves Registration Service.
14. Krouse, 33; SD Death Certificate; SDERA File #62 (Cheyenne River); Wanamaker Documentation: WW-75_20, WWUS_WWQ_di03_030-pdf.
15. Krouse, 144; SDERA File #36 (Cheyenne River); SD Death Certificate.
16. *The 32nd Division in the World War 1917-1919,* Madison, WI, 1920, 62.
17. Wanamaker Documentation: WW-75_51; Krouse, 77; MT Death Certificate; *Billings Gazette,* 2/24/1981, 6; "Peyotism in Montana," *Montana,* Vol. 33, No. 2, Spring 1983, 9.
18. SD Death Certificate; SDERA File #49 (Cheyenne River).
19. Krouse, 185; *Rapid City Journal,* 8/31/1991, 1.
20. SD Death Certificate; SDERA File #11 (Sisseton).
21. Wanamaker Documentation: WW-75_90; SDERA File #2 (Yankton); SD Death Certificate.
22. Krouse, 111; ND Death Certificate.
23. CA Death Certificate.
24. SD Death Certificate; SDERA File #32 (Standing Rock).
25. SD Death Certificate; *Sioux County Pioneer,* 5/29/1919.
26. Wanamaker Documentation: WW-75_26.

I

1. *Rapid City Journal,* 4/4/1995, B2.

2. SD Death Certificate.
3. *Rapid City Journal,* 2/8/1969, C2.
4. *Hastings Tribune,* 1/11/1971.
5. *Rapid City Journal,* 2/28/1972, 5.
6. SD Death Certificate; SDERA File #9 (Standing Rock).
7. SDERA File #8 (Standing Rock); Josephine Wagoner, *Witness,* Lincoln, NE, 2013.

J

1. *Rapid City Journal,* 5/3/1980, 6.
2. *Rapid City Journal,* 2/2/1968, 6.
3. Wanamaker Documentation: WW-75_90.
4. SD Death Certificate.
5. SD Death Certificate; Wanamaker Documentation: WW-75_26.
6. SD Death Certificate; SDERA File #4 (Rosebud).
7. Krouse, 39; *Rapid City Journal,* 10/29/1988, B2.
8. *Rapid City Journal,* 8/15/1975, 8.
9. Tiebout, 401; SD Death Certificate.
10. "Kiutus Jim, Prominent Yakima Indian, 70, Dies," *Yakima Republic,* 4/26/1960, 18; Krouse, 196-97; Wanamaker Documentation: WW-75_92; *The Timber Lake Topic,* 9/28/1917, 3.
11. *Moody County Enterprise,* 2/15/1962, 1.
12. SD Death Certificate.

K

1. SD Death Certificate.
2. SD Death Certificate; Krouse, 188; "Henry Keeler Dead," *Wagner Post,* 8/17/1922, 1.
3. MN Death Certificate; "Prominent Indians Die This Week," *Wagner Post,* 1/7/1932, 5.
4. MT Death Certificate.
5. WA Death Certificate.
6. SD Death Certificate; "Fatal Accident," *Wagner Post,* 11/18/1920, 5; Wanamaker Documentation: WW-75_90; "2010 Dillon Lecture: Rebooting Indian Law in the Supreme Court," *South Dakota Law Review,* Vol. 55, Issue #, 2010, 510.
7. SD Death Certificate.
8. SD Death Certificate; SDERA File #36 (Cheyenne River).
9. SD Death Certificate; Wanamaker Documentation: WW-75_97.
10. Lynn-Sherow and Bruce, 95.
11. Wanamaker Documentation: WW-75_23; *Sisseton Courier,* 1/24/1985, 2.
12. SD Death Certificate; SDERA File #3 (Flandreau).
13. *Minneapolis City Directory,* 1956, 732.
14. MT Death Certificate; "Caisson Disease Victim Expires," *The Helena Independent,* 3/13/1930.
15. SD Death Certificate.

L

1. SDERA File #11 (Sisseton)
2. MN Death Certificate; *St. Paul Pioneer Press*, 10/7/1964, 26.
3. SD Death Certificate; SDERA File #6 (Sisseton).
4. SD Death Certificate; SDERA File #11 (Sisseton).
5. SDERA File #6 (Sisseton); Correspondence with Ed LaBelle Jr.
6. *Muskogee Daily Phoenix,* 1/31/1968.
7. SD Death Certificate.

8. SD Death Certificate; *Rapid City Journal*, 9/4/1973, 9; Lynn-Sherow and Bruce, 95.
9. Wanamaker Documentation: WW-75_92.
10. "Gilbert Lafferty succumbs at 74," *Wyoming State Journal,* 2/16/1970.
11. SD Death Certificate; SDERA File #37 (Cheyenne River).
12. WA Death Certificate; *The Tacoma News Tribune,* 7/2/1950, C9; SDERA File #32 (Standing Rock).
13. SD Death Certificate.
14. WA Death Certificate.
15. *Oregon Journal,* 9/5/1977.
16. Krouse, 144.
17. SD Death Certificate.
18. SD Death Certificate.
19. SD Death Certificate.
20. *Rapid City Journal,* 9/1/1979, 7; Correspondence with Eric LaPointe.
21. Obit in collection of clippings from Timber Lake Historical Society; Britten, 159; Correspondence with Tammy Valdez.
22. SD Death Certificate; SDERA File #2 (Lower Brule).
23. SD Death Certificate; SDERA File #23 (Standing Rock); *History of the 362 Infantry*, Ogden, UT, 1920, 35.
24. SD Death Certificate; SDERA File #9 (Standing Rock).
25. SD Death Certificate; SDERA File #40 (Cheyenne River).
26. SDERA File #69 (Cheyenne River); Krouse, 29-30.
27. SDERA File #32 (Standing Rock); Krouse, 144.
28. Wanamaker Documentation: WW-75_92.
29. Letter, Appendix C.
30. SD Death Certificate.
31. SDERA File #23 (Standing Rock).
32. SDERA File #9 (Standing Rock).
33. SD Death Certificate; SDERA File #9 (Standing Rock).
34. Wanamaker Documentation: WW-75_66; Estelle A. Brown, *Stubborn Fool,* Caldwell, ID, 1952, 41.
35. *Indian Sentinel*, 1916-19, Vol. 01, no. 12, 35.
36. SD Death Certificate.
37. ND Death Certificate; SDERA File #32 (Standing Rock).
38. SD Death Certificate; SDERA File #23 (Standing Rock).
39. SDERA File #23 (Standing Rock).
40. SD Death Certificate; SDERA File #33 (Standing Rock); *Sioux County Pioneer,* 8/8/1918, 1.
41. MNHS Military Bonus File.
42. SDERA File #10 (Standing Rock).

M

1. SD Death Certificate; SDERA File #10 (Standing Rock).
2. *Rapid City Journal*, 9/11/1990, B2; SDERA File #63 (Cheyenne River.
3. SDERA File #24 (Standing Rock).
4. ND Death Certificate; SDERA File #33 (Standing Rock).
5. Proctor M. Fiske, 234; *Sisseton Courier*, 10/20/1977, 2; Wanamaker Documentation: WW-75_90.
6. Ohio Death Certificate.
7. *The Republican*, Valentine, NE, 4/14/1922.
8. *The Republican,* Valentine, NE, 1/2/1920.
9. ND Death Certificate.
10. SD Death Certificate; SDERA File #5 (Crow Creek); Krouse, 102-3.
11. SD Death Certificate; SDERA File #5 (Crow Creek); Wanamaker Documentation: WW-75_92.

12. SD Death Certificate.
13. Wanamaker Documentation: WW-75_66.
14. *News Review,* Roseburg, OR, 1/26/1977, 14; *Sioux County Pioneer,* 10/25/1917, 1.
15. SD Death Certificate.
16. Wanamaker Documentation: WWQ-divD.027.
17. *Napa Register,* 6/15/1978; Wanamaker Documentation: WWQ-alMO.013; Krouse, 109; *Sioux County Pioneer,* 7/13/1922, 1.
18. SD Death Certificate; SDERA File #34 (Standing Rock); Lovejoy, 39.
19. Wanamaker Documentation: WW-75_97.
20. SD Death Certificate; SDERA File #56 (Cheyenne River).
21. SDERA File #57 (Cheyenne River).
22. SD Death Certificate.
23. SD Death Certificate.
24. SDERA File #28 (Cheyenne River); Jerry Cooper and Glenn Smith, *Citizens as Soldiers,* Fargo, 1986, 207; *Eagle Butte News,* 2/28/1974, 1.
25. *Omaha World-Herald,* 10/13/1953, 27.
26. Thomas H. Lewis, *The Medicine Man,* Lincoln, 1990, 166-8; Correspondence from Eric LaPointe.
27. MN Death Certificate; SDERA File #37 (Cheyenne River).
28. Proctor M. Fiske, 234; SDERA File #70 (Cheyenne River).
29. SD Death Certificate; SDERA File #14 (Standing Rock); Wanamaker Documentation: WW-75_26.
30. *Rapid City Journal,* 8/14/1975, 27.

N

1. *Scotts Bluff Star Herald,* 10/22/1964.
2. *Onamia Independent,* 12/12/1963, 1; MN Death Certificate; State of Minn, Military Service Record.
3. SD Death Certificate.

O

1. SD Death Certificate; SDERA File #6 (Crow Creek).
2. CT Death Certificate.
3. SD Death Certificate; SDERA File #16 (Standing Rock).
4. SD Death Certificate; SDERA File #10 (Standing Rock).
5. SD Death Certificate; *Sioux County Pioneer,* 8/15/1918, 4.
6. SD Death Certificate; Amos Oneroad and Alanson Skinner, *Being Dakota,* St. Paul, 2003, 25.
7. SD Death Certificate; SDERA File #24 (Pine Ridge); *Rapid City Journal,* 8/10/1956, 10.
8. SD Death Certificate; SDERA File #7 (Sisseton); *Sisseton Courier,* 4/23/1970.
9. MT Death Certificate.
10. *The Republican,* Valentine, NE, 11/15/1918.

P

1. SD Death Certificate.
2. SD Death Certificate; Krouse, 153.
3. Wanamaker Documentation: WW-75_54.
4. SD Death Certificate; Wanamaker Documentation: WW-75_92.
5. ND Death Certificate.
6. SD Death Certificate; SDERA File #6 (Cheyenne River).
7. SD Death Certificate.
8. Krouse, 116; SDERA File #4 (Yankton).

9. Wanamaker Documentation: WW-75_20.
10. SD Death Certificate; SDERA File #11 (Standing Rock).
11. MT Death Certificate.
12. SD Death Certificate; Wanamaker Documentation: WW-75_90.
13. SD Death Certificate; Wanamaker Documentation: WW-75_62.
14. Wanamaker Documentation: WW-7_90; *Rapid City Journal,* 12/24/1994, B2.
15. *Rapid City Journal,* 9/9/1980, 5.
16. *Sioux County Pioneer,* 10/27/1927, 1; SD Death Certificate.
17. Krouse, 197; Wanamaker Documentation: WW-75_54.
18. SD Death Certificate.
19. Krouse, 109-110; *Omaha World-Herald,* 12/20/1947, 14.
20. SD Death Certificate.
21. Wanamaker Documentation: WW-75_92.

Q

1. SD Death Certificate.
2. MN Death Certificate.

R

1. SD Death Certificate.
2. SD Death Certificate; *Sioux County Pioneer,* 3/6/1919.
3. MT Death Certificate; *The Poplar Standard,* 1/10/1929, 1.
4. SD Death Certificate; SDERA File #21 (Cheyenne River); *The Faith Independent,* 5/27/1959, 1.
5. Krouse, 160; ND Death Certificate; Bowman Elder, *An Illustrated History of the 71st Artillery (CAC),* 1919, 14.
6. "Taps Sound at Kenel for World War Veteran," *Sioux County Pioneer,* 4/23/1935, 1.
7. SD Death Certificate; Wanamaker Documentation: WW-75_90; "352nd Wins First Horse Show Honors," *Camp Dodger,* 3/3/1919, 1.
8. SD Death Certificate; SDERA File #25 (Standing Rock).
9. SD Death Certificate.
10. MN Death Certificate.
11. MN Death Certificate.
12. WA Veterans Home records; *Spokesman Review,* 7/8/1965, 18.
13. Military Service Record Book, 1917-1919, courtesy of Marquette University; SD Death Certificate.
14. SD Death Certificate.
15. SD Death Certificate.
16. SD Death Certificate; Wanamaker Documentation: WW-30-01; Britten, 75.
17. "Lucas Renville of Old Agency Passes," *Sisseton Courier,* 1/16/1941, 1; SDERA File #13 (Sisseton).
18. *Sisseton Courier,* 6/5/1980, 10; Wanamaker Documentation: WW-75_48.
19. Wanamaker Documentation: WW-75_97; Harold Burton, *600 Days Service,* Cleveland, 1919, 90.
20. SD Death Certificate; SDERA File #4 (Pine Ridge).
21. SD Death Certificate.
22. SD Death Certificate.
23. *The 32nd Division in the World War 1917-1919,* Madison, WI, 1920, 123; correspondence from Louis Garcia.
24. SD Death Certificate.
25. SD Death Certificate.
26. SD Death Certificate; SDERA File #25 (Standing Rock); John Iron Eye Dudley, *Choteau Creek,* New York, 1992, 117.
27. Wanamaker Documentation: WW-75_92.

28. SD Death Certificate; SDERA File #4 (Yankton).
29. SD Death Certificate; SDERA File #38 (Cheyenne River; Krouse, 138; Wanamaker Documentation: WW-75_90.
30. SD Death Certificate; Wanamaker Documentation: WW-75_06 and WW-75_62; Henry J. Reilly, *Americans All: The Rainbow at war,* Columbus, OH, 1936.
31. SD Death Certificate; Krouse, 22.
32. SD Death Certificate; Peter Iverson, *We Are Still Here*, Wheeling, IL, 1998, 19.
33. Krouse, 188.
34. Wanamaker Documentation: WW-75_90.

S

1. SDERA File #10 (Rosebud).
2. SD Death Certificate.
3. SD Death Certificate; SDERA File #8 (Crow Creek); Krouse, 125.
4. SD Death Certificate.
5. *Rapid City Journal,* 1/2/1976, 5.
6. SD Death Certificate; Lovejoy, 39.
7. CA Death Certificate.
8. Wanamaker Documentation: WW-75_45.
9. SD Death Certificate: SDERA File #44 (Cheyenne River); *Rapid City Journal,* 12/4/1984, 5.
10. Wanamaker Documentation: WW-75_92; SD Death Certificate.
11. SD Death Certificate.
12. SD Death Certificate.
13. SD Death Certificate.
14. SD Death Certificate; "Tom Shooter Shot Saturday Morning," *The Mellette County News,* 6/24/1932, 1.
15. SD Death Certificate: SDERA File #18 (Cheyenne River).
16. SDERA File #25 (Standing Rock).
17. SD Death Certificate; *Sioux County Pioneer,* 8/15/1918, 8.
18. NE Death Certificate; *Scottsbluff Star Herald,* 4/11/1970.
19. *Rapid City Journal,* 6/30/1973, 2.
20. *Miami Daily News Record,* Jan. 1976.
21. SD Death Certificate; SDERA File #26 (Standing Rock).
22. SDERA File #38 (Cheyenne River).
23. MN Death Certificate; State of Minn, Military Records.
24. ND Death Certificate.
25. SD Death Certificate; Britten, 41 and 164.
26. SD Death Certificate; SDERA File #10 (Rosebud).
27. MT Death Certificate; "George W. Snell funeral is held December 22nd," *The Harlem News,* 12/22/1976, 1.
28. SD Death Certificate.
29. SD Death Certificate; *Sioux County Pioneer,* 5/2/1918.
30. SD Death Certificate.
31. MN Death Certificate: "Flood Funeral On Anniversary Nuptial Event," *Flandreau Herald,* February 1941.
32. *Rapid City Journal,* 1/4/1977, 5.
33. *Rapid City Journal,* 1/28/1974, 8.
34. Wanamaker Documentation: WW-75_92.
35. SD Death Certificate; Wanamaker Documentation: WW-75_90; Joseph Mills Hanson, *South Dakota in the World War 1917-1919,* 1940.

36. WA Death Certificate; SDERA File #12 (Standing Rock).
37. SD Death Certificate; Wanamaker Documentation: WW-75_48.
38. ND Death Certificate; SDERA File #35 (Standing Rock); Wanamaker Documentation: WW-75_92; Krouse, 39.
39. SDERA File #4 (Yankton).
40. SDERA File #4 (Yankton).
41. WI Death Certificate.
42. Wanamaker Documentation: WW-75_97.

T

1. Wanamaker Documentation: WW-75_90; SD Death Certificate.
2. Letter from Supt. Mossman to Joseph Mills Hanson, 3/23/1927, NARA.
3. SD Death Certificate; Wanamaker Documentation: WW-75_92.
4. SD Death Certificate.
5. ND Death Certificate; Joseph Mills Hanson, "The Fourth Comes To The Rosebud," *The American Legion Monthly,* Vol. 5, No. 1, July 1928, 14.
6. ND Death Certificate; SDERA File #12 (Standing Rock); Wanamaker Documentation: WW-75_90.
7. Joseph Mills Hanson, *American Legion Monthly,* 14; SD Death Certificate.
8. SD Death Certificate; SDERA File #26 (Standing Rock).
9. Correspondence with Lethbridge, Alberta Genealogical Society, 2/11/2015.
10. Wanamaker Documentation: WW-04_19; SD Death Certificate.
11. SD Death Certificate; Proctor M. Fiske, 234.
12. SD Death Certificate.
13. SD Death Certificate; SDERA File #8 (Crow Creek); Wanamaker Documentation: WWQ_di19.009.
14. Wanamaker Documentation: WW-75_42.
15. SD Death Certificate.
16. SD Death Certificate.

U

1. SD Death Certificate; SDERA File #55 (Cheyenne River); *Rapid City Journal,* 1/13/1976, 15.

V

1. SD Death Certificate; *Sioux County Pioneer,* 3/26/1937, 1.
2. SD Death Certificate; SDERA File #27 (Standing Rock).

W

1. Wanamaker Documentation: WW-75_92.
2. Correspondence with Mona Miyasato, 12/13/2017.
3. MN Death Certificate.
4. SD Death Certificate.
5. SD Death Certificate.
6. ND Death Certificate.
7. SD Death Certificate.
8. SDERA File #26 (Cheyenne River); *Rapid City Journal,* 2/14/1979, 31; Wanamaker Documentation: WW-75_62.
9. SD Death Certificate; SDERA File #4 (Standing Rock); Josephine Waggoner, 432.
10. SD Death Certificate.
11. SD Death Certificate.
12. SD Death Certificate.

13. SD Death Certificate; Krouse, 59.
14. *Rapid City Journal,* 9/14/1977, 5; SDERA File #7 (Rosebud)'
15. SD Death Certificate.
16. *Sioux County Pioneer,* 7/4/1918, 1.
17. In *The World War, Day County, So. Dakota, 1917-1918-1919,* 78.
18. SD Death Certificate; SDERA File #13 (Standing Rock).
19. SD Death Certificate; Krouse, 65.
20. ND Death Certificate; Wanamaker Documentation: WW-75_90.
21. SD Death Certificate.
22. SD Death Certificate;
23. SD Death Certificate; SDERA File #25 (Cheyenne River); *Hughes County WWI 1916-1919,* scrapbook by Helen Sorenson, Oahe, SD, SD State Archives.
24. SD Death Certificate; "Bullhead Soldier Dead," *Sioux County Pioneer,* March 1919; *Sioux County Pioneer,* 5/20/1920, 5.
25. SD Death Certificate; Krouse, 125.
26. Proctor M. Fiske, 167.
27. Krouse, 106.
28. SD Death Certificate; SDERA File #65 (Cheyenne River).
29. ND Death Certificate; *Devils Lake Daily Journal,* 1/6/1966, 6.
30. FL Death Certificate.
31. MT Death Certificate; SDERA File #6 (Pine Ridge).
32. SD Death Certificate; SDERA File #7 (Sisseton).
33. SD Death Certificate; State of Minn. Service Records.
34. SD Death Certificate; SDERA File #6 (Pine Ridge).
35. SD Death Certificate; SDERA File #15 (Sisseton); Wanamaker Documentation: WW-75_92.
36. SD Death Certificate.
37. SD Death Certificate.
38. *Rapid City Journal,* 7/13/1973, 5; *History of the Third Division, United States Army, The World War from the Period December 1, 1917 to January 1, 1919,* Andernach-on-the-Rhine, 1919, 85.

Y

1. ND Death Certificate; SDERA File #14 (Standing Rock).
2. SD Death Certificate.
3. ND Death Certificate.
4. "Indian Soldier Died on his Way Home," *Sioux County Pioneer,* 12/18/1919, 1; "Character Excellent: Honest and Faithful," *Sioux County Pioneer,* 1/25/1920, 1.
5. SD Death Certificate; SDERA File #55 (Cheyenne River); Richmond Clow, ed., *The Sioux in South Dakota History,* Pierre, 2007, 93.
6. SD Death Certificate; SDERA File #14 (Standing Rock).
7. Wanamaker Documentation: WW-75_92; *Poplar Shopper,* 9/9/1971.
8. Wanamaker Documentation: WW-75_51; "Stroke Takes Life of Tribal Leader on 59th Birthday," *The Herald News,* Wolf Point, MT, 5/28/1959, 1.

Z

1. SD Death Certificate.

BIBLIOGRAPHY

Manuscripts

Beecher Family Papers, MS 71, Box 25, Folder 1081, Yale University Library.

Certain Agreements with Rosebud and Lower Brule Indians for a Cession of Lands and Modification of Existing Treaties, Together with Drafts of Bills Relating Thereto, Secretary, Department of Interior, Washington, D.C., 1898.

Fletcher, Matthew L. M., 2010 Dillon Lecture: Rebooting Indian Law in the Supreme Court, South Dakota Law Review, Vol. 55, Issue 3, 2010.

Indian Sentinel, 1916-1919, Vol. 01, No. 12, p. 35.

Records of the Bureau of Indian Affairs, Record Group 75, National Archives

Records of the Bureau of Prisons, Record Group 125, National Archives.

South Dakota History Collection, Vol. XXII, 1956, pp. 35-38.

State of Minnesota, Application for Soldiers Bonus, MNHS.

State of Minnesota, Military Service Records, MNHS.

Wanamaker Documentation, Mathers Museum of World Cultures, Indiana University, Bloomington, IN.

WWI Campaign and Service Credits, Arlington, VA, Planchet Press, 1996

References

Adler, Julius Ochs, ed. *History of the 306th Infantry.* New York: 306th Infantry Association, 1935.

Brantner, Cecil Frank. *351st Infantry.* St. Paul: Randall Co., 1919.

Britten, Thomas A. *American Indians in World War I: at home and at war.* Albuquerque: U. of New Mexico Press, 1997.

Brown, Estelle Aubrey. *Stubborn Fool.* Caldwell, ID: The Caxton Printers, 1952

Burnette, Robert. *The Tortured Americans.* Edgewood Cliffs, NJ: Prentice-Hall Inc., 1971.

Clow, Richmond L., ed. *The Sioux in South Dakota History.* Pierre: South Dakota Historical Society Press, 2007.

Crosby, Capt. P.L. *Between Shots.* New York: Harper & Brothers Publishers, 1919.

Cooper, Jerry and Glenn Smith. *Citizens as Soldiers: A History of the North Dakota National Guard.* Fargo: North Dakota Institute of Regional Studies, 1986.

Dudley, Joseph Iron Eye. *Choteau Creek.* New York: Warner Books Inc., 1992.

Eisenstein, Douglas R. *Whispers in the Wind.* Xlibris Corporation, 2000.

Elder, Bowman (compiled by). *An Illustrated History of the 71st Artillery (CAC).* Indianapolis: Wm. B. Burford, 1919.

English, George H. *History of the 89th Division, U.S.A.* Denver: The War Society of the 89th Division, 1920.

Fiske, Proctor M. *History of the Three Hundred Fiftieth Regiment of U.S. Infantry.* Cedar Rapids, IA: The Laurance Press Company, 1919.

Gilland, George and Sharon Rasmussen. *Along the Trail to Thunder Hawk.* 2010.

Hanson, Joseph Mills. *South Dakota in the World War: 1917-1919.* Pierre: State Historical Society, 1940.

_____. "The 4th Comes to the Rosebud," *The American Legion Monthly,* Vol. 5, No. 1, July 1928, pp. 13-15, 60-63.

History of Company E, 35th Infantry, A.E.F. Heath & Ross, 1919.

History of the Third Division, United States Army in The World War for the Period: December 1, 1917 to January 1, 1919. Anderbach-on-the-Rhine, 1919.

History of the 362nd Infantry. Ogden, UT: The 362nd Infantry Association, 1920.

Holbrook, Franklin F., ed. *St. Paul and Ramsey County in the War of 1917-1918.* St. Paul: Ramsey County War Records Commission, 1929.

Larson, Edgar J.D. *Memoirs of France and the Eighty-Eighth Division.* Minneapolis: privately printed, 1920.

Lee, R. Alton. *A New Deal for South Dakota.* SD Historical Society, 2016.

Lee, Robert. *Fort Meade and the Black Hills.* Lincoln: U. of Nebraska, 1991.

Lewis, Thomas, H. *The Medicine Man.* Lincoln, NE: University of Nebraska Press, 1990

Lynn-Sherow, Bonnie and Susannah Ural Bruce. "'How Cola' From Camp Funston: American Indians and the Great War, *Kansas History,* 2001.

Means, Russell. *Where White Men Fear to Tread.* New York: St. Martin's Press, 1995.

Oneroad, Amos E. and Alanson B. Skinner. *Being Dakota.* St. Paul: Minnesota Historical Society Press, 2003.

Rainsford, W. Kerr. *From Upton to the Meuse.* New York: D. Appleton and Company, 1920.

Reilley, Henry J. *Americans All: The Rainbows at War.* Columbus, OH: The F.J. Heer Printing Co., 1936.

Riney, Scott. *The Rapid City Indian School 1898-1933.* Norman, OK: The University of Oklahoma Press, 1999.

Roster of the 347th Field Artillery A.E.F. 1918-1919. H.S. Crocker Company, Inc. San Francisco.

Starita, Joe. *The Dull Knifes of Pine Ridge.* Lincoln, NE: University of Nebraska Press, 2002.

The 32nd Division in the World War 1917-1919. Madison, WI: Wisconsin War History Commission, 1920.

Tiebout, Frank B. *A History of the 305th Infantry.* New York: The 305th Infantry Auxiliary, 1919.

33rd Division A.E.F. Diekirch, Luxembourg, 1919.

Waggoner, Josephine. *WITNESS: A Hunkpapha Historian's Strong-Heart Song of the Lakotas.* Lincoln, NE: University of Nebraska Press, 2013.

Endnotes – Gunville Paper

1. *50th Anniversary, Establishment of the Cheyenne River Indian Agency, August 16, 1891 at Cheyenne Agency, S.D., September 12-13-14, 1941*, (Souvenir program commemorating the 50th anniversary of the Cheyenne River Indian Agency, 1941), 22. This monument was dedicated at the Cheyenne Agency in August 1932. It was then moved to Eagle Butte when the Cheyenne Agency was flooded. It was then moved to its present location in the early 1980s.
2. Heir to the Austro-Hungarian throne Archduke Franz Ferdinand and his wife were assassinated in Sarajevo. Public Broadcasting Service (PBS), "The Great War: Prologue," http://www.pbs.org/greatwar/chapters/index.html (accessed November 20, 2011).
3. Over nine million people died total among all forces which involved every industrial nation in the world. Ibid.
4. The Zimmerman Telegraph was intercepted and decoded by British Naval Intelligence. Cryptographers of Room 40. Kennedy Hickman, "Zimmermann Telegram - Zimmermann Telegram 1917." http://militaryhistory.about.com/od/worldwari/p/zimmermann.htm (accessed December 8, 2011).
5. There were many tribes that encouraged their men to enlist for the draft; however, there were just as many who, due to isolation and the interpretation of the law, refused to enlist. German immigrants felt it traitorous to fight against their homeland. Thomas A. Britten, *American Indians In World War I*. (Albuquerque: University of New Mexico Press, 1997). 63.
6. Crowder was promoted Brigadier General and appointed Judge Advocate General of the Army. He was then promoted to Major General in the fall of 1917. Chaplain E. Earl Boyd, "Enoch Herbert Crowder, Major General, United States Army," Arlington National Cemetery Website, http://www.arlingtoncemetery.net/ehcrowder.htm (accessed December 8, 2011).
7. "Dewey County Exemption Board, List of Registrants Who Passed Examination, and Are For Service, Unless Excused by District Board. *Timber Lake Topic*. August 17, 1917.
8. Class I included registrants whose entry into the military would least interfere with the industry, economy and agricultural welfare of the nation, which posed few grounds for exemption. These men were the first to be called into duty. Class II and III classification were men who were married and whose vocation served the war effort. Class IV registrants were married men with children. Class V were clergy, pilots and alien enemies who were non-citizens from nations allied with the Central Powers and resident aliens who were noncitizens from nations other than those allied with the Central Powers. Britten, 55.
9. James D. Stewart, "Thomas Slow is True Blue." *Dupree Leader*, 1918.
10. "Dewey County Boys Given Big Send-Off, *Timber Lake Topic*, June 28, 1918.
11. James D. Stewart, "Citizens of County Bids Boys Farewell," *Dupree Leader*, September 27, 1918.
12. "Safe Arrival At Camp Funston, Kans.," *Timber Lake Topic*, October 5, 1917.
13. Bonnie Lynn-Sherow and Susannah Ural Bruce, "'How Cola' From Camp Funston." *Kansas History*, 24, No. 2. (2001), 84-97.
14. Letter written to Mr. W.E. Prann of Timber Lake, S.D.; R.W. Kraushaar, Co. 37, 164 D.B., "Kraushaar Writes On Life At Funston,"July 25, 1918. *Timber Lake Topic*, 1.
15. Irving Scranton, "Written to Our Friends and the Timber Lake Topic," *Timber Lake Topic*. 1918.
16. Maurice P. Cahill Armed Draft Detail, City Park Barrocks, U.S. Navy Yard, Brooklyn, N.Y. Timber Lake S.D. July 7th, 1918
17. Chateau-Thierry is also called the Battle of Belleau Wood. There was no clear distinction on where the front line was located resulting in confusion and a great loss of life. Michael E. Hanlon, "Chateau-Thierry: The Battle for Belleau Wood." http://www.worldwar1.com/dbc/ct_bw.htm (accessed December 8, 2011)
18. Edward G. Lengel, "America's Bloodiest Battle," *American Heritage*, 60, Issue 2 (Summer 2010), 36-37.
19. Ibid.
20. Britten,
21. Jim Nelson, Armstrong Four Bear's WWI Helmet. Timber Lake Historical Society.
22. Timber Lake Historical Society
23. Timber Lake Historical Society History
24. The original article of the two men from opposite sides came from the Aberdeen American News and was written by Bob Overturf in the 1960's. Bob Overturf, "Freed Beer, Glen Buckley Fought On Opposite Sides," *Timber Lake and Area Historical Society Newsletter*, 15, No. 2 (1997).
25. Ginny Cudmore and Jim Nelson, eds., *Timber Lake and Area 1910-1985*, (Timber Lake, SD: Timber Lake and Area Historical Society, 1984),
26. James D. Stewart, "Organized a Red Cross Branch At Cherry Creek," *Dupree Leader*, April 1918.
27. Tom Benjey, "Tom Benjey's Weblog – October 2009," http://tombenjey.com/2009/10 (accessed November 20, 2011).
28. James Stewart, "Advice To Soldier Boys," *Dupree Leader*, September 27, 1918.
29. Gary Robinson, *The Language of Victory: American Indian Code Talkers of World War I and World War II*, (Bloomington, Ind.: iUniverse, Inc., 2011), 11.
30. "Navy and Naval History.Net." Navy and Naval History.Net. http://naval-history.net/ (accessed   December 8, 2011).
31. *Memoirs of France and the 88th Division*, E.J. D. Larson, p. 43.

Bibliography – Gunville Paper

Benjey, Tom. "Tom Benjey's Weblog – October 2009." http://tombenjey.com/2009/10 (accessed November 20, 2011).

Britten, Thomas A. *American Indians In World War I*. Albuquerque: University of New Mexico Press, 1997.

CEHIP Incorporated. "Native Americans and the U.S. Military." *Naval History and Heritage*. http://www.history.navy.mil/faqs/faq61-1.htm (accessed September 22, 2011).

Cudmore, Ginny and Jim Nelson, eds. *Timber Lake and Area 1910-1985*. Timber Lake, SD: Timber Lake and Area Historical Society, 1984.

E. Earl Boyd, Chaplain. "Enoch Herbert Crowder, Major General, United States Army." *Arlington National Cemetery Website*. http://www.arlingtoncemetery.net/ehcrowder.htm (accessed December 8, 2011).

50th Anniversary, Establishment of the Cheyenne River Indian Agency, August 16, 1891 at Cheyenne Agency, S.D., September 12-13-14, 1941. Souvenir program commemorating the 50th anniversary of the Cheyenne River Indian Agency, 1941.

Golden Jubilee Book Committee. *Golden Jubilee 1910-1960 Timber Lake, South Dakota*. Timber Lake: Timber Lake Historical Society, 1960.

Hanlon, Michael E. "Chateau-Thierry: The Battle for Belleau Wood." http://www.worldwar1.com/dbc/ct_bw.htm (accessed December 8, 2011)

Hickman, Kennedy. "Zimmermann Telegram - Zimmermann Telegram 1917." http://militaryhistory.about.com/od/worldwari/p/zimmermann.htm (accessed December 8, 2011).

Kraushaar, R.W., Co. 37, 164 D.B. "Kraushaar Writes On Life At Funston." *Timber Lake Topic*. July 25, 1917.

Larson, E.J.D. *Memoirs of France and the Eighty-Eighth Division*. Minneapolis: United States Monument, 1920.

Lengel, Edward G. "America's Bloodiest Battle," *American Heritage*, 60, Issue 2 (Summer 2010), 36-37.

Lynn-Sherow, Bonnie, and Susannah Ural Bruce. "'How Cola' From Camp Funston." *Kansas History* 24, No. 2 (2001): 84-97.

"Navy and Naval History.Net." Navy and Naval History.Net. http://naval-history.net/ (accessed December 8, 2011).

Overturf, Bob. "Freed Beer, Glen Buckley Fought On Opposite Sides." *Timber Lake and Area Historical Society Newsletter* 15, No. 2 (1997).

Public Broadcasting Service (PBS). "The Great War: Prologue." http://www.pbs.org/greatwar/chapters/index.html (accessed November 20, 2011).

Public Broadcasting Service (PBS). "The Great War: Timeline – 1914." http://www.pbs.org/greatwar/timeline/time_1914.html (accessed November 20, 2011).

Public Broadcasting Service (PBS). "The Great War: Timeline - 1916." http://www.pbs.org/greatwar/timeline/time_1916.html (accessed November 20, 2011).

Robinson, Gary. *The Language of Victory: American Indian Code Talkers of World War I and World War II.* Bloomington, IN: iUniverse, Inc., 2011.

Scranton, Irving, "Written to Our Friends and the Timber Lake Topic." *Timber Lake Topic.* 1918.

Stewart, James. "Advice To Soldier Boys." *Dupree Leader.* September 27, 1918.

Stewart, James D. "Citizens of County Bids Boys Farewell." *Dupree Leader*, September 27, 1918.

Stewart, James D. "Organized a Red Cross Branch At Cherry Creek." *Dupree Leader*, April ??, 1918.

Stewart James D., "Thomas Slow is True Blue." *Dupree Leader*, 1918.

The Stars and Stripes (Paris, France). "Boche Wire Tappers Run Into New Code Sioux Observer and Receiver Make Things Easy For Gunners." Vol. 1 No. 49, (January 10, 1919). http://memory.loc.gov/service/sgp/sgpsas/1919/191901/19190110/05.pdf (accessed November 10, 2011).

The Stars and Stripes (Paris, France). "13 Redskin Tribes in Single Company," Vol. 1 No. 40, (November 8, 1918). http://memory.loc.gov/service/sgp/sgpsas/1918/191811/19181108/08.pdf (accessed November 10, 2011).

Timber Lake Topic. "Dewey County Exemption Board, List of Registrants Who Passed Examination, and Are Now In Line For Service, Unless Excused by District Board," August 17, 1917.

Timber Lake Topic, "Dewey County Boys Given Big Send-off," June 28, 1918.

Timber Lake Topic, "Safe Arrival At Camp Funston, Kans.," October 5, 1917.

Timber Lake Topic, "The Dewey County Exemption Board," September 17, 1917.

Ziebach County Historical Society. *South Dakota's Ziebach County, History of the Prairie.* Dupree, SD: Ziebach County Historical Society, 1982.

www.ingramcontent.com/pod-product-compliance
Lightning Source LLC
Chambersburg PA
CBHW080239170426
43192CB00014BA/2497